D0083757

# The Civil War and Reconstruction

DAVID HERBERT DONALD

JEAN H. BAKER

MICHAEL F. HOLT

 W • W • NORTON & COMPANY

NEW YORK • LONDON

# THE CIVIL WAR
# AND RECONSTRUCTION

Copyright © 2001 by David Herbert Donald, Jean H. Baker, and Michael F. Holt

All rights reserved
Printed in the United States of America
First Edition

Library of Congress Cataloging-in-Publication Data

Donald, David Herbert, 1920–
The Civil War and Reconstruction / David Herbert Donald, Jean H. Baker, Michael F. Holt.
   p. cm.
Includes bibliographical references and index.
**ISBN 0-393-97427-8 (pbk.)**
   1. United States—History—Civil War, 1861–1865   2. Reconstruction—I. Baker, Jean H. II. Holt, Michael F.   (Michael Fitzgibbon)

E468+.2001
973.7—dc21                                                        00-046034

W. W. Norton & Company, Inc., 500 Fifth Avenue, New York, N.Y. 10110
www.wwnorton.com

W. W. Norton & Company Ltd., 10 Coptic Street, London WC1A 1PU

3 4 5 6 7 8 9 0

# Contents

# Maps

# Preface

This book has its origin in James G. Randall's *The Civil War and Reconstruction*, first published in 1937. That was a remarkable work, notable for its accuracy and comprehensiveness. Incorporating the latest and best scholarship, Professor Randall's book became the standard work in its field, an indispensable guide for generations of graduate and undergraduate students. It was responsible, in considerable measure, for the tremendous outpouring of books, dissertations, and articles on the Civil War and Reconstruction era in the years following its publication.

Inevitably, this new research required revision of Professor Randall's findings, and in 1961, at the request of Ruth Painter Randall and the publisher, I prepared a revised edition of his text. Generally well received, that version also became a guidebook for a generation of students. But the explosion of historical knowledge and methodology during the past four decades has made much of that revision also out of date; an extensively revised edition, reflecting recent scholarship, was called for.

In bringing out this newest version of *The Civil War and Reconstruction* I was fortunate to enlist as collaborators two of my ablest former graduate students, who have since become distinguished authorities in the field: Professor Jean Harvey Baker of Goucher College and Professor Michael F. Holt of the University of Virginia. Professor Baker has been primarily responsible for revising the chapters dealing with the antebellum period and the Civil War years, while Professor Holt has rewritten the chapters on the Reconstruction era. But this edition is truly a joint work. We have all read and criticized each other's drafts of chapters, from time to time squabbling amicably about small matters of fact and usage but agreeing on larger questions of scope and interpretation.

Those who have used previous editions of *The Civil War and Reconstruction* will find many changes, both small and large, in this version. The most obvious of these is the omission of a detailed bibliography. The literature is now so vast that a comprehensive bibliography would run almost to the length of the present text. Most students will be better served by our extensive notes, which serve as a guide to the primary and secondary sources, and by the lists of selected readings for each chapter.

Many of the changes in this edition correct errors or fill omissions that recent scholarship has brought to light. Some problems, once highly controversial, have now been substantially settled and consequently require less space. For instance, it no longer seems worthwhile to debate whether George B. McClellan was the Union's greatest commander; the unanimous verdict of military historians for the past quarter of a century has been adverse to the general. Other issues that were of special interest to Professor Randall—such as the partition of Virginia and the creation of the new state of West Virginia—no longer seem to require such detailed treatment.

In many chapters we have refocused the argument and made revisions that are extensive and significant. For example, in the chapters on the prewar period, Professor Baker has introduced a full discussion of the role of women and the family—a topic almost wholly omitted from previous editions—and has presented a fresh and revealing account of slavery and the African American experience. In dealing with the war years, she has given extended attention to the life of the common soldier and to military operations—subjects in which Professor Randall had little interest.

Professor Holt has substantially rewritten the chapters on the Reconstruction era, in order to incorporate the rich and important scholarship of the past generation. He offers a carefully nuanced picture of what the postwar era meant to both ex-Confederates and the freedmen and traces the painful evolution of a new social order in the South. Viewing Reconstruction as a national, not just a sectional, problem, he has brought out, more successfully than any previous writer, the linkages between southern economic and political developments and simultaneous parallel changes in the North.

Though this is a substantially different book from the previous editions, we trust that it has retained their virtues of objectivity, accuracy, and readability. *The Civil War and Reconstruction* remains one of the few books that offer comprehensive coverage of the antebellum era, of the war years, and of the postwar era. It is our hope that this record will help the next generation to understand the greatest and most devastating war in which the United States has ever been engaged and to appreciate its tangled legacies, which are at the root of so many of our national problems today.

—David Herbert Donald

# THE CIVIL WAR
## AND RECONSTRUCTION

CHAPTER 1 | # A Modernizing Nation, 1840–1860

The American Civil War was not inevitable. There was no necessity for the North and the South to engage in a bloody military conflict from 1861 to 1865, especially since the two sections had peacefully coexisted since the American Revolution. Like civil wars in other countries, this one emerged within a specific set of political, economic, and social changes that increasingly differentiated the North from the South. In the North these transformations, as they eroded traditional attachments to local communities, promoted a sense of national spirit. They also led to a development of the North's commercial capacities, which would make that section the stronger of the two warring sides. To a limited degree, the South participated in these economic and cultural transformations. To understand why it became impossible to negotiate the kinds of sectional compromises that had marked earlier periods of American history, it is necessary to examine the nation in the twenty years from 1840 to 1860.

## EXPANSION IN SIZE AND NUMBERS

In the twenty years before the Civil War, the United States experienced dramatic increases in size, population, industrial and agricultural production, and urbanization. The settling of British claims to the Oregon territory, the annexation of Texas, and the peace treaty ending the Mexican War in 1848 added half a continent to the United States. In 1853 the purchase of thirty thousand additional square miles of Mexican territory in the Southwest completed the boundaries of the continental United States. Justifying expansion on the grounds of natural right, God's will, and—in the case of expansion into Mexico—the need for reform, Americans generally celebrated the nation's growth from 880,000

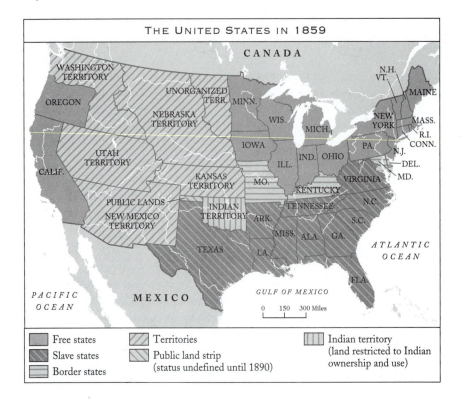

THE UNITED STATES IN 1859

square miles in 1783 to over three million square miles in 1860. Yet for individuals the process of resettlement often dissolved ties to family and community along with traditional political bonds to state governments.

In time these territorial gains entangled the nation in sectional controversies that would lead to the Civil War, but at first optimism reigned. "We go ahead," wrote the historian William Prescott, "like a lusty brat that will work its way into the full size of man. . . ."[1] There were thoughtful critics of expansion, but public opinion generally supported national growth. "No race but our own can either cultivate or rule the Western Hemisphere," concluded the editor of the *Democratic Review*.[2]

The population of the nation also grew impressively, increasing in the 1850s from twenty-three million to thirty-one million at a time when the premier world power, Great Britain, had slightly over twenty-three million inhabitants. Of the European nations only France and Russia had more residents than the United States. Population growth fueled a robust economy whose gross national product grew at an annual average rate of 4.8 percent from 1840 (when the total value of domestic goods produced in a year was only slightly larger than tiny Jamaica's) to 1860.

As a result of 35 percent increases in population every ten years, Americans were filling in the vast spaces between California and Maine in a westward movement believed to be the white man's destiny. The center of population no longer hugged the seaboard. In the 1790s it was twenty-three miles west of Baltimore; in 1850, it was at Chillicothe, Ohio. Seven new states joined the republic in the two decades from 1840 to 1860 as Americans followed the newspaper editor Horace Greeley's famous advice: "Seek the West and rear your children there to larger opportunities than await them on the rugged hillsides or in the crowded streets of the East."[3]

In the process Native Americans, whose numbers continued to shrink, were pushed from their lands. Familiar with the eastern woodlands Indians, pioneers now encountered the Plains Indians on a large-scale basis. The Sioux, Shoshone and Cheyenne, along with the southwestern Comanche, Ute, and Apache tribes were a formidable obstacle to white settlement. Government officials met this challenge by building a chain of forts through the West and by persuading some tribes at the Fort Laramie (Kansas) Council in 1851 to stay in defined areas. Attacked by federal forces and militia bands, shunted aside into reservations, and inadequately provided for, Indians—some of whose tribes would play an important part in the coming war—became casualties of American growth in the 1850s.

White Americans of this generation also experienced the effects of new technology (the word itself coined by an ambitious New Englander) and transportation, as especially the Northeastern and Middle Atlantic states adopted mechanical means for producing goods and applied steam and coal power to locomotives and ships. Traditional methods of making goods were changing. Villages were becoming towns, towns were transformed into cities. Communication with strangers replaced associations with relatives, although in some communities such as the Wilamette Valley in Oregon neighbors and kin often purposely settled on adjacent farms.[4] The young especially cut familiar ties to work out their individual destinies far from former associations.

An Englishman offered a comparative perspective: "Progress crawls in Europe, but gallops in [an] America" marked "by the go-aheadedness of the people."[5] The transformations of the period heralded a process of modernization that, though it brought many material benefits, also unsettled the lives of Americans on the eve of the Civil War.[6]

Jacksonville, Illinois was typical of the impermanence and instability of many new communities. Between 1850 and 1860 this town on the Illinois prairie doubled in population, but many new residents soon moved on, to be replaced by other transients. Those who remained complained, in the words of one, that "the people, gathered from all quarters, had not coalescence enough for mutual helpfulness."[7]

Though all regions of the country were expanding, not all did so with equal rapidity. The sparsely settled Pacific Coast states generally showed the greatest proportionate growth. In San Francisco gold dusters joined merchants in a growing community, while on the fringes of the city the number of farmers doubled in five years. The largest numerical increase came in the Midwest. Minnesota's population grew by an astronomical 2,760 percent in the 1850s; Vermont's barely increased at all.[8] In the 1850s the older states of the South and Northeast were about equal in population, and they grew by less than the national average, that is, by 24 and 23 percent.

Most of this increase came from high birthrates that produced, on the average, households of four children in a society whose median age was nineteen. The abundant land and resources of the United States fueled a confidence about the future that encouraged fertility levels higher than those in Europe. Typically, women of this generation in the United States bore five children, one of whom was likely to die during childhood from a bacterial infection. In 1800 the fertility rate had been higher, but gradually white, native-born, urban women who married later and were better educated than their grandmothers began to rationalize the process of reproduction. In antebellum America, a formerly natural process, like many other aspects of life, could now be managed.

In order to limit their childbearing, women used abortifacients (such as the popular French "periodical pills," guaranteed to induce a miscarriage), diaphragms (called "womb veils" in the nineteenth century), douches, coitus interruptus, and abstinence. But even in decline, American fertility, though accompanied by a slight drop in life expectancy in the 1850s, accounted for three-quarters of the population increase in the decade.[9]

The United States also grew because the nation was an attractive haven for immigrants, principally from Germany, the British Isles, the southern counties of Ireland after the potato famine of 1846, and Scandinavia. But the varied national origins of immigrants—who in 1859 included 106 Poles, 65 Russians and 15 Turks—were as diverse as the geography of the nation to which they came. During the 1850s the number of foreign-born in the United States doubled; by 1860 the number exceeded four million. Between 1845 and 1855 over two million immigrants arrived in the United States, accounting for 15 percent of the population in 1845, the highest proportion in the nineteenth century.[10] All parts of the country were affected by this influx, though the South with its inhospitable institution of slavery received the fewest, proportionally. By 1850 only 14 percent of the foreign-born lived in the slave states. Still, southern cities such as New Orleans, Savannah, and Memphis had pockets of foreign-born as well as second-generation populations.

Far heavier concentrations of the foreign-born settled in the Midwest than in the South. Wisconsin became almost another Germany; areas in Michigan and Minnesota other Scandinavias. The East, too, was disarranged by the arrival of so many immigrants: New York in 1855 was the residence of 469,000 Irish-born and 218,000 Germans who together accounted for one-fifth the state's population. In the Far West increasing numbers of Chinese—some 35,000 by 1860 in a white and Latino population of 360,000—made their home in California.

## REACTIONS TO IMMIGRATION

Native-born Americans were uncertain about these new arrivals. Some Americans, usually those who lived in the coastal cities of the East and in California, greeted the newcomers with hostility and violence. In the 1840s Catholic convents became the targets of mobs incited by Jesuit-baiting Protestant ministers and nativist propagandists. Ten years later, when Catholics accounted for two-thirds of an annual immigration of 370,000, fears of an impending papal conspiracy reinforced anxieties about neighbors who drank, danced on Sundays, and competed for jobs. To some native-born, immigrant churches, associations such as German Turnvereine (gymnastic clubs) and Irish Hibernian Societies, and even efforts to obtain public funding for schools signaled the permanent presence of an unacceptable minority. The stereotype of Paddy as a pugnacious, bibulous fool provided an ethnic counterpart to racial images of Sambo and Uncle Tom, especially in the expanding cities of the Northeast.[11]

On the West Coast, portrayals of rat-eating, opium-smoking, pigtailed Chinamen presented similar stereotypes. In San Francisco, Committees of Vigilance recruited white citizens into militia companies that practiced systematic discrimination against Asians, denying them free access to jobs and neighborhoods. Of all the Far West's immigrants only the Chinese were forced to pay prohibitive fees for mining licenses.

Because the Irish, Germans, and Chinese were generally poor and lived in slums, native-born Americans held them responsible for the increased crime and poverty in their communities. Baltimore's nativists pointed out that from 1849 to 1854, the years of greatest immigration into the city, the jail population rose 40 percent. In Cincinnati, the foreign-born population was believed to be the recipient of disproportionate municipal funds. Competition for jobs also spurred violence, especially in eastern cities, where foreign-born workers held over half of the artisan and semiskilled jobs as well as over three-quarters of those filled by unskilled laborers during the 1850s. In industrializing states such as New York, Ohio, Pennsylvania, and Massachusetts, this large pool of labor depressed wages and employment opportunities.[12]

Yet in another paradox of the decade, immigrants were welcomed in the soil-rich midwestern territories, which needed more citizens to qualify for statehood. Wisconsin became the first of several states to grant immigrants the right to vote before citizenship, and in Milwaukee German immigrants were elected to local offices. Efforts in Congress to extend the naturalization period from five to twenty-one years (supposedly like children, the foreign-born must learn to be Americans) floundered on the conviction that all Americans were immigrants, so there could be no ethnic exceptions to the pledge of equality in the Declaration of Independence.

In response to the sharp increase in foreign-born and second-generation voters in northern cities—immigrants of this period were disproportionally young and male—disagreements over immigration entered the party politics of the 1850s through an important third party—the American party. Nicknamed the Know-Nothings, this organization sought to lengthen the naturalization period and to arouse nationalistic sentiments. Always more popular in the North than the South, the Know-Nothing Party instructed Americans in a patriotism that was transferred during the war to the Union.

The growing strength of the Catholic Church was not the only change that aggravated Protestant Americans of this period. So too did the spread of the Mormons—a religous minority who offended the dominant society because of their polygamous practices. Under attack by mobs east of the Mississippi, the Latter-Day Saints moved westward, settling in arid, unpopulated Utah. Expansion soon brought non-Mormons to the area Mormons called Deseret. As what was later the state of Utah became more linked to the rest of the country, conflict developed between the federal government and the Mormons.[13] In 1857, President James Buchanan sent twenty-five hundred troops to Utah to remove the Mormon leader, Brigham Young, and install a governor more responsive to federal authority.

## CHANGES IN AGRICULTURE

Despite nativist fears that the United States was being overwhelmed by immigrants, parts of the country had an abundance of fertile unoccupied land as well as a labor shortage. Although a majority of free Americans no longer earned their living as farmers, in the 1850s land remained the principal economic opportunity and real estate the major source of wealth.[14] Of the over five million white and free black males whose occupations were listed in the 1850 census (working women were not counted), farming, though making up a declining proportion of workers in a modernizing economy, comprised the largest number of Americans. By 1860, though there were a million new farmers, farm laborers, and planters the percentage had further declined .[15]

Yet the production of basic agricultural crops accelerated, as the fertile fields of the nation produced sufficient food to ensure low prices for consumers. Corn, wheat, and cotton production made impressive gains in the 1850s.[16] The prairie state of Illinois was representative of this expansion in agriculture. In 1849 the state produced nine million bushels of wheat; in 1859 the output increased to nearly twenty-four million, with the price per bushel rising from $1.20 to $1.55.

Increased immigration, improved transportation, an abundance of cheap land, and new machinery enabled, according to a Senate report, "agriculture to more than keep pace with the increase of population"—and in fact to create surpluses for overseas export.[17] Agriculture was principally responsible for the surge of exports from $166 million in 1840 to $438 million in 1860.

As agricultural production increased, a two-tiered system developed. Some farms became specialized enterprises devoted to the production of market crops. In central Illinois, for example, Matthew Scott and his tenant farmers raised wheat and corn, transported them first by railroad to the new industrial hub of Chicago, and then shipped them by steamer through the Great Lakes waterway to either eastern cities or Europe. No longer was it necessary, even on smaller farms, to produce time-consuming essentials such as textiles, butter, soap, and candles, which could now be purchased in retail centers like Bloomington and Peoria. Instead, farmers negotiated the sale of their crops in a national market created by an expanding urban population, overseas trade, and the proliferation of railroads, canals, and telegraph lines. In such a system a family farm generally ensured prosperity. "Ownership of a farm placed one in the upper half of the contemporary wealth distribution."[18]

But not all farmers were part of this evolving arrangement. Many, especially those beyond the reach of trains, boats, and macadamized roads and those working marginal, often marshy land, remained self-sufficient save for occasional purchases from peddlers and trips to town.[19] Others, even after five years of settlement, could not afford the minimum price of twelve and a half cents an acre for forty acres under the terms of the Graduation Act of 1854. Some independent farmers lived to see their sons become tenants earning ten dallors a month. By 1850 in central Illinois the richest 20 percent of the farm population owned nearly one-half of the wealth, compared with the lowest 20 percent's ownership of less than 5 percent.[20]

Notable among the reasons for both the expansion of American agriculture and the economic stratification of farmers were expensive new agricultural implements such as cast-iron harrows, corn planters, seeding machines, and hay rakes. The horse-drawn McCormick reaper, first produced in 1831, led thousands of farmers to abandon harvesting methods in use from time immemorial. With the costly new machinery, average yields increased, though have-not farmers remained mired in less productive, traditional ways of raising crops.

The inventor Cyrus McCormick had developed his new machine in Virginia. Enlisting the help of the railway magnate William Ogden, who had moved from the East to Chicago in 1835, he established several factories in that rapidly growing city. Soon his enterprise was turning out four thousand machines a year, to be shipped to farmers who often shared the purchase price and use. The business methods of the McCormick company were an example of the interlocked process of economic development during the 1850s. McCormick had several

The McCormick reaper, first produced by Cyrus McCormick in 1831 and then patented in 1834, helped transform traditional methods of farming into more modern and efficient means of production.

competitors, and he used high-pressure salesmanship to establish his product. Convincing advertising and easy conditions of payment brought quick profits, which along with capital from Europeans, were reinvested in the company.

McCormick was hailed, in Europe and the United States, as one of the great men of his time, though he was only one of a new breed of American businessmen who understood the importance of improved transportation, technology, and promotion. At the International Exposition of 1855 in Paris his reaper cut an acre of oats in twenty-one minutes. Europeans were astonished: their machines took three times as long. In 1854 the New Yorker William H. Seward concluded that "No General or Consul drawn in a chariot through the streets of Rome ever conferred upon mankind benefits so great as [McCormick,]" who had vindicated "the genius of our country."[21]

Other inventors transformed traditional practices with their ideas, although Americans were not noted for basic scientific research. Their talents lay rather in the applications of knowledge.[22] The pneumatic tire appeared in 1845; the sewing machine and rotary press in 1846; the hydraulic turbine in 1849; the electric locomotive in 1851. In the late 1850s, Cyrus Field was making headway on his Atlantic cable, and by 1860 the United States was crisscrossed by a rapid-communications system of over fifty thousand miles of telegraph wire.

In Washington, clerks in the Patent Office struggled to keep pace with new designs for watches, printing presses, artificial limbs, and steam locomotives. By 1859, "Chicago had acquired the three key institutions that defined its grain trade: the elevator warehouse, the grading system and, linking them, the privately regulated central market governed by the Chicago Board of Trade."[23] To market the huge grain surplus, capitalist methods of financing were soon applied to agriculture, and fortunes were made and lost in speculations on future prices.

## THE MODERNIZATION OF TRANSPORTATION AND COMMUNICATION

In the development of the economy, the railroad played a major part. Not only did railroads require large amounts of iron for rolling stock, rails, and bridges; they also demanded heavy capital investment, which in turn accelerated the change from joint-stock companies to the modern corporation. Some funds came from Europeans who saw opportunities for profitable investment in the United States. The federal government contributed as well, with loans of over $64 million, land grants, and exploration of the West by the Army Corps of Engineers.[24] So too did local communities whose future depended on the proximity of the railroads.

Railroad lines grew rapidly, though their incompatible track gauges symbolized lingering parochialism amid modernization. In 1850 there were only 8,500 miles of railroad in the United States; by 1860 thirty thousand miles of track connected the nation in a network that lowered transportation costs and that in the war years enhanced economic integration among the Union states.

As in other aspects of American development, regional differences prevailed. Construction was especially slow in some southern states that had no north-south connections into the upper Mississippi Valley save for the Mobile-Ohio line. At the same time building was especially rapid in the Midwest and along the east-west lines that joined the nation's granary with its ports and factories. By 1860 Kentucky had only 569 miles of track compared with 3,000 for nearby Ohio; Arkansas only 38 miles compared with Illinois' 2,790.

Despite the accelerating significance of the railroads, water transport on canals, rivers, and oceans remained important. One out of every five workers was still connected with the maritime industry. Shipbuilding reached its peak in 1854–55, when over a million tons of ships were produced, a record unmatched until World War I. More goods in 1860 traveled from the Appalachian West by the northern gateway of the Erie Canal than by railroad.[25] The large, swift clipper ships carried exports across the oceans and around Cape Horn (one sailed 436 miles in a single day during an Atlantic crossing), as the volume of international trade carried on American ships doubled in a decade. But the romantic clippers with their tall masts and canvas sails towering above harbor skylines soon gave way to steam-propelled ships largely independent of the vagaries of nature.

## CHANGES IN INDUSTRY

Industry, like agriculture and transportation, also changed dramatically before the Civil War. Processes accomplished either by one artisan or in the putting-out system, by giving raw materials to individuals to work on in their homes, now

This advertisement for the Empire Sewing Machine Company helped bring sewing machines into the homes and businesses of many Americans. By 1859, northern factories were turning out thirty-seven thousand machines a year.

Mills such as this one in New Jersey reflected the modernization of the North. As industries grew and the number of small firms declined, workers were consolidated into larger factories. Here workers are fashioning railway forgings.

became centralized in one location. The number of firms declined, while the number of employees in each grew. Clothing and shoe manufacturers filled their factories with large sewing machines whose basic design had been patented by Elias Howe of Massachusetts in 1846. As the United States developed a market economy, increases in production came especially rapidly in New England and the Middle Atlantic states and in cotton textiles, glass, paper, machine tools, and woodworking.

In 1860 a U.S. census report described a revolution in the shoe industry, which now displayed "the characteristics of a factory system, being conducted in large establishments of several stories, each floor devoted to a separate part of the work, with the aid of steam-power, and all the labor-saving contrivances known to the trade. It is safe to predict that the change will go on until the little 'work-shop' of the shoemaker, with its 'bench and kit,' shall become a thing of the past"—as, according to the report, had already occurred in the manufacture of clothing.[26]

In Europe, the United States gained fame for its innovations, though many of these, including the system of interchangeable, standardized parts that was demonstrated at a London international exhibit in 1851, were borrowed from the Europeans.[27] Soon Europeans were describing a unique *American* system of manufactures supported by the pillars of specialized machinery, standardized parts, new business practices, applications of steam power, the growth of factories, a large national market, and transportation. Before the Civil War, lake ports such as Milwaukee, Chicago, Toledo, Cleveland, and Buffalo, with their natural advantages of location, increased their exports and became important processing centers for agricultural products. The opening of the Sault Ste. Marie Canal in 1855—a project, like many others, subsidized by the federal government—made iron ore available through the Great Lakes water system.

The finished products of the new factory system, now transported cheaply throughout the United States, were in constant demand. The average per capita income of Americans increased from $109 in 1840 to $144 in 1860, with no inflation and comparatively low food costs, ensuring a market for the new goods. Middle-class Americans now decorated their homes and bodies with household goods unknown to their parents—perhaps a clock, or one of the new Thompson stoves, a paisley shawl, or even a carpet. The 1850s were the decade in which profits from the Irish immigrant Alexander Stewart's dry-goods store permitted him to begin planning a six-story marble department store, promptly dubbed by a fellow New Yorker "one of the wonders of the Western World." New luxuries also became available in less grand stores to an increasingly self-conscious, "refined" public. *Harper's Weekly* described "a shopping mania . . . a dry goods epidemic."[28]

## A CHANGING SOCIAL STRUCTURE

Most Americans of this generation accepted the national ideology of economic mobility. "We are not prepared to allow that wealth is more valued in America than elsewhere, but in other countries the successful pursuit of it is necessarily confined to a few, while here it is open to all," was a common sentiment.[29] In fact most wealthy Americans were born to families of substance. "Evidence on the more likely movement from a lower social position to an adjacent one remains in pitiful supply," although there is evidence of the movement for some Americans from a dependent status of wage earner or tenant farmer to self-employment as the owner of a farm.[30]

Overall, economic development widened the gap between the rich and the poor as the United States changed from a rural society to a more urban, industrialized one on the eve of the Civil War. "Wage rates between the skilled and unskilled spread during the antebellum period, as did the gap between salaried workers, professionals, and employers in the community and wage earners in general."[31] By 1860 the proportion of unskilled workers living on the brink of or in poverty increased to nearly a quarter. The top 10 percent of those owning some form of wealth increased their holdings, controlling, by 1860, 70 percent of all assets. This was the age of the fabulously wealthy Astors; of August Belmont, the agent of the Rothschilds; of Corcoran and Riggs, the Washington bankers; of Moses Grinnell, the shipping magnate; of Amos and Abbott Lawrence, the Boston magnates; and of Commodore Vanderbilt, the owner of several steamboat and railroad lines.[32] It was not, however, the economic discrepancies that were new in America; rather it was the glaring differences between the rich and the poor.

## THE WORKING CLASS

Despite the inclusionary aspects of the rags-to-riches mentality or even the more realistic expectation of advancing to the status of property owner, the modernizing process brought considerable anxiety to the working class. The market revolution increased the scale and intensity of work and in some instances liberated workers from the older arrangements of household production. These changes were especially profound for the first generation of female workers who were recruited to work in textile mills and cigar factories. Visiting the cotton mills in Lowell in 1850, the Scandinavian visitor Frederika Bremer praised factories as "palaces of labor" with glittering lights, the whir of machines and "a procession of operatives . . . All was nice and comfortable."[33]

But inside the mills the monotonous tasks at dangerous machinery, the long hours, and the supervisors' authority dramatically altered the lives of the nearly million and a half who worked in manufacturing by 1860. Unlike the artisans of the 1820s and 1830s, laborers now minded the work bell and the foreman or were replaced by someone who did. In 1857 a worker described his routine: "all employees were to be at their posts in their work clothes at the first bell rung, there to remain until the last bell and to be prevented from leaving work in between." This same worker compared his new circumstances to "a slavery to which I have not been brought up."[34]

By 1860 women, usually single, young, and foreign-born, represented 15 percent of the work force.[35] Although the ten-hour day was standard by the early 1850s, in the Lowell mills admired by Bremer, women toiled thirteen-hour, six-day weeks during the summer. But the largest group of women working outside the home (for nearly all worked inside it) were employed as domestics, laundresses (over forty thousand in 1860), and seamstresses without fixed wages or hours. Throughout the 1850s wage-earning women suffered from the hostility of male workers who viewed them as competitors willing to work for lower wages.

Generally excluded from labor unions (the Cordwainers Society, for example, resolved in 1850 to bar any woman not the wife or daughter of a member), some working women formed their own associations. In Lynn, Massachusetts, they protested labor conditions by striking. Yet the cult of domesticity—the conventional attitude that required women to stay at home and be pious, pure, and domestic—and the traditional notion of a family wage, earned by a male breadwinner with female family members remaining at home, placed female workers beyond the bounds of propriety.[36]

To protect themselves from changes in the business cycle as well as from wage cuts, layoffs, and speedups, male workers formed labor associations. There were no national labor unions in 1850, only loosely affiliated federations of, among others, printers, hat finishers, stonecutters, iron molders, cigar finishers, and cotton spinners. Many workers in larger communities formed local craft associations, and these organized into citywide coalitions of industrial organizations. In this novel world of employment, workers occasionally formed cooperatives designed to improve conditions and to remove bosses who interfered, according to one worker, with the "inalienable rights of men to receive material resources sufficient for their subsistence and comfort."[37] Originally intended for the limited purpose of securing discounts on consumer goods, these early workingmen's protective unions offered members few of the social and educational benefits of later cooperatives.

## THE GROWTH OF CITIES

During these antebellum decades the expansion of industry and transportation accompanied, and in turn spurred, the growth of cities. Compared with rural areas and small towns, cities experienced disproportionate increases in population.[38] Cities such as New York and Philadelphia nearly doubled in size in ten years to become metropolitan centers with diverse populations; smaller cities also expanded. Chicago's population numbered 4,470 in 1840; twenty years later it was 109,260. That same year there were 156 more urban places with populations over 2,500 than there had been in 1850. By 1860, 20 percent of Americans lived in communities with 2,500 or more residents, a redistribution of population especially pronounced outside the South.

The nation's first cities had developed because their coastal locations and deep harbors encouraged trade. The fast-growing cities of mid-century were often enlarged towns where farm products such as pigs in Cincinnati or wheat in Pittsburgh were put in portable form and shipped by railroad or river to another city. By 1850 workers in cities were as likely to work in commerce, transportation, and services as in manufacturing. And they were more likely to be victims of epidemics that festered in poor, crowded living conditions.[39] A mobile group, a third of whom moved every decade, city residents followed transportation lines to the next job. Thus the location of railroads set the course for the future of both individuals and communities. Losers like Lexington, Kentucky, Arcadia, Colorado, and Hudson, Illinois stagnated.

The growth of cities exposed a growing number of Americans to modern ways where work was specialized, neighbors diverse, and social relations neces-

Horse-drawn carriages and people line the streets in this prewar picture of Broadway in New York City. The population of cities such as New York grew rapidly in the decades before the Civil War.

sarily more impersonal and less devoted to local institutions. Many Americans found the changes chaotic, especially in the second half of the 1850s, when a downturn in the economy brought paralysis to industry and misery to thousands in the North.

The depression of 1857 was both financial and industrial. President James Buchanan attributed the economic slowdown to "the vicious system of paper currency and bank credits exciting the people to wild speculations and gambling in stocks."[40] But a better explanation appeared in the interrelated forces of excessive railroad building, real estate and mining booms, the withdrawal of European capital, enormous loans, and rampant greed in the scramble for quick fortunes. In 1857 liabilities from business failures mostly in the North and West (the South was unaffected by the depression) amounted to nearly $300 million.

The human aspects of the panic appeared in the bankruptcies of those struggling with lowered wages, debt, and foreclosure; in the suffering of the unemployed (forty thousand were thrown out of work in New York City alone); in the shivering crowds of city beggars in a period before even primitive municipal social services; in decreased immigration; and in labor unrest. A new underclass expanded in the larger cities; in New York's Bowery district, scenes of streetwalkers, homeless mothers and children, and panhandling orphans scavenging the streets provided a counterpoint to the optimism of the middle classes. The British consul in New York, familiar with social unrest in Europe, noted "bands of men parading in a menacing manner through the streets demanding work or bread."[41] In time the economy recovered, but class differences, labor activism, and concern about life changes made both the victims and the beneficiaries of the new economy uncertain about the future.

## CHANGES IN EDUCATION

Accompanying these economic changes was the manifest growth of formal schooling, as both public schools and private academies expanded in numbers, length of the school year, and percentage of students enrolled. Although there was resentment on the part of taxpayers unaccustomed to supporting institutions used by a special group of citizens, most Americans accepted Horace Mann's conviction that the common school was essential in a democracy. Mann and other educational leaders argued that besides providing young Americans with the tools necessary to get ahead in the world, schooling could dilute class and ethnic divisions. Through the Massachusetts state board of education, of which he was president, Mann introduced revolutionary changes in the state's public school system that placed Massachusetts in the forefront of educational development. Schooling, for Mann and for increasing numbers of Americans, had a market value. Businessmen throughout the United States came to value employees who had been to school, believing that they made industrious, disciplined workers in a society whose future no longer rested with self-directed, uninstructed farmers.

The acceptance of the public school brought dramatic changes in enrollments for whites between five and nineteen, whose attendance increased from 38 percent in 1840 to 57 percent in 1860, at the same time that the length of the school year nearly doubled.[42] Throughout the nation girls were less likely than boys to attend school, although in the northeast a number of private academies such as Emma Willard's Troy Female Seminary trained women teachers through a curriculum similar to that in male seminaries.

The South, a region with poor roads and a scattered population, lagged behind the Northeast and West. In 1840 fewer than 20 percent of southern white children were in school, though there was some progress in the 1850s. Under the prodding of Calvin Wiley, its first superintendent of education, North Carolina spent $279,000 a year on its nearly three thousand schools; Alabama's $474,000 tax dollars paid for the education of ninety thousand students.[43]

Other educational advances paralleled the extension of public education. City high schools, emphasizing Latin and mathematics and conceived as preparatory schools for college admission, grew in numbers until in 1860 Massachusetts had seventy-eight, New York forty-one, and Ohio forty-eight. In most regions of the United States, private, tuition-charging institutions offered a similar curriculum to males. In 1850 there were three thousand academies in the South, and even a state as undeveloped as Arkansas had ninety.

Everywhere institutions of higher learning for the training of teachers improved, as did colleges, which multiplied in a society that needed more trained engineers, bookkeepers, and managers. When Americans moved to town, they worked in occupations that required book learning, and as a result of this shift, by 1861 the United States boasted 182 colleges of varying merit. Most were affiliated with a religious denomination, usually the Presbyterians, Methodists, or Baptists. But even in church-connected institutions students rebelled over issues of curriculum and college management. The latter have been interpreted as student efforts to achieve the more systematic vocational training needed in a modernizing economy.[44]

Nonsectarian public state universities also proliferated in numbers and size. Prior to the Civil War, twenty states (of thirty-four) boasted colleges of higher learning subsidized by land grants from the federal government. The curriculum of these institutions was similar to those offered in private colleges. At Brown University between 1855 and 1858, John Hay, who later became President Lincoln's secretary, studied chemistry, mathematics, rhetoric, physics, Latin, Greek, German, moral philosophy, history, declamation, and political economy.[45]

Because colleges (except for Oberlin, Antioch, and the University of Michigan) and public and private high schools were closed to women, an alternative, separate-but-similar system of women's education developed. Leaders such as Emma Willard, Catharine Beecher, Mary Lyons, and Almira Phelps encouraged schoolteaching as a profession that could benefit from the nurturing qualities of females. To this end they organized seminaries for women, offering chemistry, physics, and philosophy, though with less emphasis on the classical languages that became the standard for admission to male universities.

By the 1850s more women than men were entering low-paid, low-status schoolteaching jobs. Communities had discovered that the schoolmarm, as Beecher had predicted, was "the cheapest guardian and teacher of childhood."[46] "Soon in all parts of our country, in each neglected village, or new settlement, the Christian female teacher will quietly take her station, collecting the ignorant children around her, teaching them habits of neatness, order, and thrift, opening the book of knowledge, inspiring the principles of morality, awakening the hope of immortality."[47] Besides creating respectable jobs for even married women, the education of more women was one reason for the declining birthrates of this generation.

Initially nineteenth-century female schooling was not intended for individual satisfaction. Rather it emerged from a national understanding that the so-called daughters of Columbia could fulfill their domestic duties and the training of their families more competently with some education. In time academic training encouraged a public consciousness, especially among northern women, who obtained more schooling than their southern counterparts.

## THE SPIRIT OF THE AGE

Although some Americans shared a romantic optimism about their present and future, others feared the materialism they saw as undermining their culture. Later, Ralph Waldo Emerson described a new American at a time in which "the individual is the world and [there are] young men born with knives in their brains, and a tendency to introversion, self-dissection and the anatomizing of motives."[48] The most famous expression of this sentiment was Emerson's aphorism that "things are in the saddle and ride mankind."

Like Emerson, others were unhappy with what they considered a commercial assault on the essential nature of the American republic—the latter based on civic virtue and a community spirit endangered in the modernizing United States. What the popular journal the *American-Whig* derided as the "bank-note age" was softening the national character and promoting greed, according to these critics, at the same time that the growth of trade, cities, and geographic mobility encouraged the selfish passions of individualism.[49]

Some Americans took their dissatisfactions into the reform movement of the period, seeking, among other changes, to improve the status of women, to prohibit alcohol, and to end slavery. The impulse to reform emerged in part from evangelical Protestantism. An important value system at mid-century, the latter was a religious expression that encouraged its practitioners to think they must strike against the imperfections of their time and produce in America the near-perfect society ordained, especially for *this* nation, by God.

But the reform mentality also developed because of economic dislocations and the shaping of modern, self-conscious personalities in an environment that highlighted the differences among Americans. Improved communication and heightened interest in issues among a more educated public living in cities promoted national crusades for improvement. Social ideals melded with idealistic intentions of Christian morality to produce collective efforts at social change. The proliferation of reform movements in the 1840s and 1850s earned for this period a historical reputation as the Age of Reform.

There was no more popular crusade than that of temperance. Local temperance societies conducted an assault on "demon rum," using lectures and pamphlets and lobbying state legislatures for prohibitory or licensing laws. In 1851 Maine became the first state to prohibit liquor sales, and during the 1850s temperance forces succeeded in obtaining restrictions on liquor in twelve other states. But in some cases such as Illinois and Indiana, the experiment was no sooner begun than overturned by opponents and by the courts. Still, as a result of temperance propaganda promoted in songs, novels, and lectures given by Neal Dow, "the father of the Maine law," as well as by a crusading group of reformed drunkards known as the Washingtonians, Americans of the 1850s drank less than ever before.[50]

Among the most important reform movements of the period was that to obtain women's rights, with the decade before the Civil War marking the beginning of American feminism. In 1848 Lucretia Mott and Elizabeth Cady Stanton

Elizabeth Cady Stanton, Susan B. Anthony, and Lucretia Mott led the movement for women's rights. At the 1848 Seneca Falls Convention in New York, Mott and Stanton drafted the "Declaration of Sentiments," in which they called for measures such as equality before the law, the right to appear on public platforms, and women's "sacred right to the elective franchise."

Lucretia Mott

organized a convention in Seneca Falls, New York. Surprised by the turnout—the roads were thronged with wagons that hot July day—the convention based its Declaration of Sentiments on the Declaration of Independence itself. The leaders of the movement included among their specific charges the denial of human rights, disenfranchisement, the doctrine of couverture (which rendered married women unable to control property and wages), and the monopoly of men over "all profitable employments." Throughout the 1850s women who had never before spoken in public lectured, amid heckling and abuse, against the "injuries and usurpations" of their status. The political success of women's rights was limited, although some states passed married women's property acts. Others such as Kentucky permitted widows the right to vote in local elections for the school board, and a few states liberalized divorce statutes.

The most pertinent reform movement for any understanding of the coming of the war was the antislavery movement. Unlike some of the period's other humanitarian movements, organized efforts to end slavery were confined to the North and West. It had not always been so, especially in the early days of the Republic, when many national leaders such as Thomas Jefferson proclaimed a theoretical opposition to black slavery. In fact antislavery activities had at first known no sectional lines. The American Colonization Society, which sought to expatriate free Negroes to Africa, had supporters throughout the South. But by the 1830s most white southerners had come to believe that slavery was the necessary basis of their section's way of life, and the only way in which an allegedly inferior race could be kept subordinate.[51]

At the same time, an important transformation occurred in northern antislavery opinion. Abolitionism (the demand for the immediate, uncompensated emancipation of all slaves) is usually dated from 1831, when William Lloyd Garrison founded his newspaper the *Liberator*. Actually Garrison, who offended many reformers because of his insistence on immediate emancipation, his boycott of politics, and his renunciation of the U.S. Constitution, was only part of a new, increasingly strident northern attack on the South's "peculiar institution" as a sinful, barbaric relic of the past. Yet even among the most vociferous critics it was possible to be profoundly opposed to slavery as immoral and still not believe in racial equality.[52]

Among the important influences on the antislavery movement were the evangelistic labors of the Reverend Charles Finney, the organizing efforts of the philanthropists Arthur and Lewis Tappan, the petition drives and antislavery fairs of thousands of northern women, the reverberating effects of an important debate among students at Lane Seminary in Cincinnati in 1834, and the antislavery agitation of Theodore Weld. The subject of slavery increasingly insinuated itself into the official meetings of churches, leading in the 1840s to division in two important American denominations—the Methodists and Baptists, who separated into northern and southern factions over the issue of slaveholding.

This increasing opposition to slavery occurred at a time of growing anxiety

In 1833, William Lloyd Garrison helped establish the American Anti-Slavery Society. At this 1840 convention, members of an antislavery society denounce the injustices of the institution.

about changes in labor practices as a result of unregulated industrialization. Because they pictured slave plantations as places of unremitting physical torture, abolitionists indirectly sanctioned the less barbarous modes of social discipline in the North. Thus the factories of New England and the Middle Atlantic states—no matter what their hours and conditions of work—appeared mild when compared with slave labor in the South at a time when depressed wages afflicted many native-born workers.[53]

Much of the actual work of organizing and financing the antislavery crusade was done by Finney, the Tappans, Weld, and their New York allies; this regional identification has obscured the importance of the New England wing of the abolition movement. Yet Garrison was for twenty-two years the president of the American Anti-Slavery Society and was always its most eloquent voice. If few approved of his rejection of political action as the way to end slavery, still the ideological agreements among abolitionists should not be lost among their differences over tactics. All abolitionists accepted the position that a moral commitment to end slavery must begin immediately; all believed that they must educate other Americans in the justice of their cause through petitions, speeches, and pamphlets; all came to hold southerners guilty for an institution that violated the basic values of the Republic, and all feared the growing influence of the "slave power's conspiracy."[54]

Yet within this northern reform movement, differences remained not only about tactics but also in emphasis. Many antislavery men and women—including politicians such as Joshua Giddings of Ohio, John Hale of New Hampshire, and George Julian of Indiana—transferred their condemnation of slavery into antisouthern sentiments. To them, slavery seemed to have transformed the South into a repressive society that had no place in a civilized republic.[55]

African Americans were the most zealous abolitionists of the period. With a restricted freedom that slaves did not enjoy, some northern blacks such as Frederick Douglass and Charles Remond joined antislavery societies where they campaigned with a special passion. Other African Americans served the antislavery cause by working in the Negro Convention Movement, which flourished in Ohio, New York, and Massachusetts in the 1850s. In these assemblies black leaders such as Martin Delaney and Frances Watkins moved beyond opposing slavery to urge emigration and in some instances resistance to a government that sanctioned slavery. According to the Cleveland Platform of 1854, "If we desire liberty, it can only be obtained at the price others paid for it."[56]

Both black and white abolitionists suffered persecution from organized vigilante groups. In 1835 a Boston mob treated Garrison so brutally that he was put in jail for his own protection. The Alabama-born abolitionist James Birney was threatened so often that he moved north to Cincinnati, where he founded an antislavery newspaper, the *Philanthropist*, in 1836.

Another case of exile from the South was that of the Grimké sisters, Angelina and Sarah. Having moved from her Episcopalian roots in her native Charleston,

South Carolina to Philadelphia and Quakerism, Angelina published an antislavery pamphlet in 1836, which led to threats of her imprisonment should she return to Charleston.[57] Meanwhile Sarah followed her sister into exile and onto the antislavery podiums of the North, where both the Grimkés spoke out against slavery to northerners, some of whom were increasingly anxious about the survival of the Union.[58]

In Alton, Illinois, in 1837 the abolitionist Elijah Lovejoy had been murdered while trying to protect his printing shop from men who believed that his views endangered the peace of the community. Across the Ohio River, in Lexington, Kentucky, when Cassius Clay argued the heretical position that slavery retarded the southern economy, a committee of citizens delivered an ultimatum that he stop printing his aptly named *True American*. Defiantly refusing, Clay placed two cannons in front of his shop, armed a small band of friends with shotguns, and prepared for battle. Eventually a committee of Lexingtonians dismantled his press and sent it out of the state in another example of what many northerners believed the natural repressiveness of a slave society.

Although some white abolitionists were the victims of mobs, all blacks suffered from the harsh Jim Crow system and the threat of being kidnapped into slavery. In 1860 free Negroes numbered approximately 240,000 in the states north of the Mason-Dixon line. The discriminations practiced against them varied from state to state. In Illinois fines were levied against African Americans entering the state; black men who tried to buy land were often forcibly returned to the South. Only five northern states with less than 6 percent of the northern black population allowed blacks to vote.[59]

A few opportunities were open for free blacks as barbers, waiters, and servants; a few communities organized segregated schools and colleges such as Wilberforce University in Xenia, Ohio and Avery College in Pittsburgh, along with the schools organized and funded by state manumission societies. Generally the caste system with its neglect of public education for blacks was the rule, though Massachusetts was an exception. In 1855, a school desegregation law was passed in Boston, the result of agitation by black Bostonians and effective leadership by William Nell and Benjamin Roberts, along with an influential white champion of human rights, Charles Sumner, who served as their counsel. Overall, however, most northerners treated blacks as inferiors; even antislavery advocates never promoted racial equality, and for most northerners anxiety about the Union held a higher priority than opposition to slavery.

## ANTEBELLUM CULTURE

Not surprisingly, antebellum culture reflected contemporary society and its transformations. "Nearly everyone in America from city merchants to country housewives must have been aware of the immense social changes that came with aggressive market expansion."[60] This awareness was the result of better transportation, more schooling, a more efficient postal system based on prepaid mail, and adult lyceums and lecture programs where Americans listened to speakers such as Ralph Waldo Emerson and the British-born Fanny Kemble discuss the issues of the day. Public libraries remained exceptions—only sixty-five librarians were listed in the 1860 census—but the Astor library in New York illustrated the use of private fortunes for the endowment of institutions designed to raise the general level of information.

One critical factor in a better-informed, politically active population involved the expansion in numbers and size of cheap newspapers and periodicals. As a result of faster printing methods that relied on rotary cylinder presses, the number of American newspapers, most of which were tightly tied to local political parties, increased from 1,200 in 1835 to 2,526 in 1850.[61] Circulation, aided by changes in the postal service that enabled publishers to pay for the cost of mailing papers, surged to over five million. Magazines grew in number and quality, as the religious press claimed a large share of readers.

The editor-proprietors of the period emerged as influential figures. By 1859 William Cullen Bryant had completed thirty years as editor of the New York *Evening Post*. Under his leadership and that of Parke Godwin, the *Post* grew steadily as a daily newspaper with high standards of reporting, which now included international news. Of a different breed was James Gordon Bennett who lashed out against reformers and their crusades and who, in turn, was once assailed as "an impudent disturber of the public peace."[62] But Bennett spared nothing in his search for news. Despite not being affiliated with any particular party in this very partisan age, the *New York Herald* became one of the most widely read cheap dailies.

By 1860 Bennett's chief rival, Horace Greeley, had made the New York *Tribune* into a national institution whose columns were often reprinted in other newspapers. A hard-working eccentric, Greeley had risen from poverty to a position of authority. As a member of the Whig and later the Republican party, he demonstrated the power of the press. His influence was paralleled throughout the United States by that of prominent editors such as Joseph Medill of the Chicago *Tribune*, Murat Halstead of the Cincinnati *Commercial*, and Robert Barnwell Rhett of the Charleston *Mercury*. To these must be added the editors of county newspapers whose partisanship often determined local elections and whose international news moved mid-century readers beyond local affairs.

Along with newspapers came a remarkable flowering of literary talents in a period later characterized as the American Renaissance. Some writers, such as the poets Henry Wadsworth Longfellow and Walt Whitman, mirrored the exuberant expansiveness and romantic emotionalism of the times; others such as Herman Melville spoke more pessimistically about their society. Whatever else Melville meant to convey by his vast work on whaling, *Moby-Dick*, published in 1851, the book expressed contemporary concerns about the consequences of the nation's new entrepreneurial spirit. The boundlessness and excitement of the ocean stood as a fictional counterpoint to "men tied to counters, nailed to benches, clinched to desks . . ."[63]

Most original of a group of New England writers whose urban environment nourished their intellectual community was Henry David Thoreau, who sought the meaning of life in nature. The train's whistle connoted for Thoreau the despised march of civilization; the lives of quiet desperation that men led were likely to be in cities. Thoreau's friend Ralph Waldo Emerson earned his living by lecturing throughout the United States, and his social commentary included criticism of an American society he believed shallow—"a wild democracy, the riot of mediocrities and dishonesties and a fudge . . ."[64]

Among the most popular authors of the 1850s were a group of women whom Nathaniel Hawthorne dismissed as mere scribblers and whose writing has long been undervalued. Like those of their male counterparts, the works of women reflected the times—the realities of social change embedded in the growth of cities, the disruptions of families by mobility, and the anxieties of a new economic culture along with the universal troubles of women. Writing in what Walt Whitman called "the age transformed," women created imaginative texts often based on themes celebrating female autonomy in a time of rapid social change.[65]

Harriet Beecher Stowe was the most famous of these writers. In 1852 she published *Uncle Tom's Cabin*, a novel that portrayed an African American slave as a Christian martyr and presented harrowing pictures of slavery's destruction of family life, one of the great themes of this group of authors. The factual basis on which Stowe chiefly relied was the abolitionist tract *Slavery as It Is, The Testimony of a Thousand Witnesses*, which was compiled by Theodore Weld and widely circulated by the American Anti-Slavery Society. Stowe kept the pamphlet in her work basket by day and under her pillow at night while she raised her children and ran her household. Of her fifteen completed novels, *Uncle Tom's Cabin* was the most popular, selling one hundred thousand copies within two months and three hundred thousand within the year.

*Uncle Tom's Cabin* dramatized and made personal the intensifying sectional conflict and the cruelty of slavery, which had become a principal target of northern reformers.[66] Southerners, of course, regarded the book as abolitionist slander, believing that the public would forget those passages in which the gentler side of slavery was revealed and would take as representative the murderous brutality of Simon Legree.

Although Stowe was later hailed by President Lincoln as "the little lady who made the war," others contributed novels that addressed the oppression of women. Susan Bass Warner, whose *Wide Wide World* appeared in 1850, and Maria Cummins, whose *Lamplighter* became a bestseller in 1854, provided a vast audience with tales of domesticity and female fortitude. Sarah Josepha Hale's *Godey's Lady Book* offered similar plots in short stories so admired that with one hundred and fifty thousand subscribers in 1850, *Godey's* had the largest circulation of any American magazine.[67]

Even Americans who never read Stowe or Emerson participated in a culture that seemed crass, materialistic, and chaotic to European travelers. Mid-century Americans appeared to outsiders to worship the dollar. Europeans noted that in earlier children's games points were awarded for moral virtue and religious faith, but by 1860 winners of Milton Bradley's board game *The Checkered Game of Life* depended on material success for their victories. The excitability of Americans, their boastfulness, their hospitality, and their love of novelty caused comment. To Frederika Bremer, Americans were a go-ahead species who shrank from nothing and were forever building and starting afresh and trying something new. To another visitor it seemed that every day was moving day for restless Americans.[68]

Behind the contradictory notions of confidence and uncertainty rested convictions widely shared by intellectuals and the common people that God ruled their lives, not the railroad or the marketplace. In his 1860 essay "Fate," Emerson wrote that Americans believed themselves in the hands of God. But, concluded Emerson, "in an epidemic, in war, they believe a malignant energy rules."[69] By mid-century this belief in Providence coexisted with the secular conviction that individual Americans—those men Emerson described as having knives in their brains—could fulfill their private ambitions.[70] Through the giant steps taken toward modernization in this dynamic, destabilizing age, the United States had become a nation of tensions and discrepancies—between traditional providential thinking and the ideology of success, between types of agriculture, between cities and farms, between those embedded in the new economic system and those still practicing traditional ways of earning a living, between haves and have-nots, and most critically for the coming decade, between the North and the South.

| # The Antebellum South

One of the most controversial issues confronting students of the Civil War is the degree of difference between the antebellum North and South and the role any such differences played in the coming of the conflict. Clearly the two sections shared a common history and a reverence for the Constitution, as well as a devotion to democracy among white males. But alongside these similarities were growing differences in economic systems, political philosophies, and mutual perceptions that came to undermine the commonalities earlier binding the North and South together in a federal republic. By the 1850s southerners insisted that it was the modernizing North that had changed and was intent on modifying the contract that had led to the formation of the United States of America in the 1780s. Having examined the ways in which the North was changing in this period, let us now focus on the South.

## SECTIONAL SIMILARITIES

On the eve of the Civil War, the South shared certain characteristics with the rest of the United States, among them its diversity. In the region of over seven hundred thousand square miles that would make up the Confederacy, the climate ranged from semitropical areas of perpetual summer to mountainous regions where snow fell at Easter. Low coastal plains, deltas, piedmont stretches, sea islands, rice swamps, cattle ranges, cotton fields, and pine barrens offered a physical setting varied in weather, topography, and soil. The South's people—blacks and native and foreign-born whites as well as a declining number of Native Americans—and its dwellings were likewise diverse. To pass from the spacious grandeur of the plantation to the world of the self-sufficient yeoman or the isolation of the mountaineer was to enter new worlds—worlds whose outlooks were as different as their dialects were strange.

On the fringe of what became the Confederacy was a layer of so-called border states sharing some of the characteristics of the South, such as slavery and staple-crop production. These four states—Delaware, Maryland, Kentucky, and Missouri—had larger proportions of free blacks and lower percentages of slave owners than was the case in the lower South. Slaves comprised less than 20 percent of their population; free blacks 21 percent, compared with 2 percent in the states of Georgia, South Carolina, Florida, Alabama, Mississippi, and Texas. And slaves were held by fewer than a quarter of all families.[1]

Besides variety, white southerners shared their Protestant religion, Western European traditions, and English language, law, and governmental structure with the rest of the nation. They supported mainstream American ideas about democracy and capitalism and were committed to individual rights, viewing the ownership of slaves not as a contradiction to liberty but as an example of private property. Southerners also looked back on the same past, praised the same Constitution, and engaged in the same electoral process as other Americans.

Like other regions, the South had undergone successive waves of settlement—what W. J. Cash called "the history of the roll of frontier upon frontier—and on to the frontier beyond."[2] Migration stripped the older seaboard states of the youngest, most energetic members of their population, white and black. "Most young men who considered migration were in their twenties, and most wanted to be planters. . . . [T]hey believed that soil exhaustion prevented them from becoming successful planters in their native states and [that] there was no future there. . . ."[3] As a result of these attitudes, from 1840 to 1860 only 20 percent of all southerners lived in the same place for twenty years.[4] By 1860, only 59 percent of those born in South Carolina continued to live there. The rest had moved west, chiefly to Georgia, Alabama, Mississippi, Tennessee, and Texas.

So many residents of Virginia and Kentucky migrated to the adjacent free states of Ohio, Indiana, and Illinois that by 1860 "some 800,000 more white Southerners lived outside the Southern states than Northerners lived in the South."[5] Consequently the southern seaboard states, like parts of New England, were in a transient condition. Houses fell into disrepair because, as a contemporary noted, "Nobody knows how long he will live where he is. . . ."[6]

If the southern states along the Atlantic seaboard were declining in wealth, rate of population growth, and soil fertility, the newer Gulf states were booming. During the 1850s, when the population of South Carolina grew by only 5 percent, that of Texas leaped by 184 percent. The combination of fertile land, slave labor, and harvests of 175 pounds of cotton per acre spurred a continuing westward migration. An Arkansas paper reported in 1845 that "the ferry at Little Rock has been crowded, for several days, with movers, going South, some to Texas, but principally to settle in the fertile lands of the Red River district."[7]

In this rural society individualism and democracy for white males flour-ished—just as they did in other frontier areas in the United States. The effect of these attitudes was to bring more democracy to the South, in the same process that was occurring in the North. Even the governments of the older southern states underwent a process of constitutional reform. Though South Carolina continued to resist most forms of democratization, by the 1850s other southern states had installed white male suffrage, increased the number of elected officials, and abolished property qualifications for holding office. The representatives of yeomen farmers endorsed plans to equalize school funds for white children, to tax slaves, and to expropriate Indian lands, at the same time that they contested legislative apportionment based on the total population (black and white), an arrangement that favored the planters' interest. Cash notes that "of the eight governors of Virginia from 1841 to 1861, only one was born a gentleman, two began their careers by hiring out as plowhands, and another (the son of a village butcher) as a tailor."[8] Elected to the Alabama legislature, the illiterate Jacinth Jackson of Pike County joined his children in school so that he could learn to read the legislation on which he voted.[9]

As in the North, the plebeian origins of many southern politicians should not obscure their wealth—and slaveholding. By the 1850s a disproportionate 44 per-cent of the Alabama legislature consisted of planters who owned more than twenty slaves, whereas the "large farmer middle class which had been half the legislature in 1830 fell to a third and then to a quarter of the members."[10] In the decade before the Civil War, every southern governor for whom information is available was a slaveholder.

The period's reform efforts also reached the antebellum South, with the ex-ceptions of women's rights and abolition. Most southern states supported insti-tutions for the training of the deaf and dumb with tax funds, and somewhat fewer made special provisions for the blind. Before 1848 Louisiana, South Car-olina, Tennessee, and Georgia endowed state hospitals for the care of the insane. The penalties on debtors were reduced in southwestern states; some prohibited imprisonment for debt. Similarly, efforts were made to better the conditions in jails. A popular movement to improve public education was a part of these gen-eral democratic reforms, although the South lagged behind the rest of the nation, except for the newest settlements in the West.

The antebellum South also exhibited the characteristics of the frontier in other parts of the United States. As in many rapidly changing societies, violence became a way of life. In the newly settled areas of Alabama, Mississippi, Texas, and Arkansas, "many planters now adopted more aggressive, self-absorbed forms of behavior. . . . Sex roles became extreme versions, almost caricatures, of the ideals of male independence and female dependence that seaboard men articu-lated in the 1830s." Husbands embraced a "manly independence manifested in a kind of daredevil masculinity, with an emphasis on prodigious drinking, gambling, skill with a gun and perhaps less clandestine sexual activity with slave women, while [their] obligations to family became more tenuous."[11]

## SECTIONAL DIFFERENCES

Despite many similarities to the rest of the Union, the antebellum South was, in ways critical for its future, different from the rest of the United States to such a degree as to create a distinct, increasingly self-conscious section. If we apply national measures of the modernizing 1850s, the region can best be described by what it was not.

First of all, the South was not urban, though there were a few cities. English travelers were impressed with the brilliance of Charleston, the urbane quality of Richmond, and the charm of New Orleans, the most cosmopolitan of all American cities.[12]

The antebellum South's real cities were on the periphery of the region; in the border states of Maryland, Kentucky, and Missouri, Baltimore, Louisville, and St. Louis faced north; the coastal cities of Norfolk, Wilmington, Charleston, Savannah, Mobile, New Orleans, and Galveston looked outward toward Europe. The section had no urban focus, nor any city of the size and importance in its regional life that New York, Philadelphia, and Boston played in the Northeast. A New Yorker drifting down a quiet river perceptively inquired of his southern host, "Where's your towns?"[13]

The characteristic southern city was a town of fewer than four thousand. Although the rate of urbanization in the South during the 1850s was higher than that in the North because of its lower starting point, southern cities retained their rural flavor. They survived as processing and commercial adjuncts of agriculture, lacking the industry that attracts workers and that in a ratcheting process leads to further urban services and growth. Instead the Old South, a term usually applied to the Confederate South, underwent "urbanization without cities," that is, its cities retained a country atmosphere. Southern cities were "distinctly horizontal, low in density and in profile and closer to nature." Essentially they were agrarian centers influenced by planters and lacking in financial systems and metropolitan services.[14]

In all these communities, the ethos of the city was dominated by a planter aristocracy. Many resisted the changes that were transforming northern cities into densely populated, industrial centers. When Charleston businessmen asked planters who kept second homes there to invest in any proposed corporation, wealthy slave owners usually responded that such enterprises would ruin Charleston's charm for its most important residents—the planters.[15] Instead the flowering gateways, secluded gardens, magnolia trees, the stately architecture of St. Michael's and St. Phillip's churches, and the vista onto the bay must remain a gracious setting for families with immense local pride. In Virginia, Alexandria,

Fredericksburg, Richmond, Williamsburg, and Norfolk were well known for their architectural beauty and cultural institutions. But the fact remained that Virginians, like other southerners, believed their region would lose its character if urban centers were to define its way of life.

Not only did the South lack cities, it also remained less densely populated than the North. In the rest of the Union, the median population per county was thirty-two persons per square mile. In the South 95 percent of all counties had fewer than the national median, with Arkansas having only eight, Louisiana fifteen, and North Carolina twenty residents per square mile.[16]

Nor was the antebellum South industrial, remaining in its ideals and attitudes essentially committed to agriculture. To be sure, by international standards the South ranked fifth as a manufacturer of cotton textiles, second in railroad mileage, and eighth in iron production in the world. "Compared with any country in Europe except England," write Stanley Engerman and Robert Fogel in their controversial study of slavery, "the South's economic performance was quite strong."[17] The value of manufactured goods in the South nearly tripled from 1840 to 1860 as factories in Richmond, Petersburg, Augusta, Graniteville, and Columbus, Georgia grew in size and output. Cotton manufacture increased in the same period from $1,500,000 to $4,500,000; the number of spindles grew from fifteen hundred to eight thousand. As for railroads, the mileage in the South increased from four hundred in 1840 to more than nine thousand in 1861. But these measures reflect modernizing influences throughout the nation, rather than the commitment of most southerners.

Compared with the North in the value of goods produced, the amount of capital invested, and the proportional number of industrial workers, the South lagged behind. Indeed, most of the South's economic growth during the decades before the Civil War came from putting new land into production, not from developing new economic structures or ventures. The absorption of capital into slavery and profitable plantations retarded southern industry, and nowhere did manufacturing benefit significantly from the financial resources or even managerial guidance of the most powerful voice in the community—that of the planters. The average southern factory operated on less than one-half the amount of investment capital as did the typical New England plant; only a few heretics argued that the South's future lay with more factories, better communication, and bigger cities.[18]

Furthermore, industrial expansion was hampered by labor shortages. The South did not attract as many immigrants as the North (except for cities on its rim like New Orleans and Louisville). Slaves, some 5 percent of whom worked in factories in the 1850s, were too expensive a form of human capital to provide the necessary work force. The South's wages were too low to attract white farmers into industry, as occurred during the North's process of modernization, and southern attitudes made factory work disreputable for white women. With pater-

After publishing a pamphlet called "Essays on Domestic Industry," in which he advocated the development of manufacturing in the South, William Gregg opened a mill in Graniteville, South Carolina in 1846. Gregg not only constructed eighty-five cottages to house his workers, but also built a school where attendance was compulsory.

nalistic intention but little success, William Gregg tried to make his mills in Graniteville, South Carolina, into "the home of the poor widow and helpless children or of a family brought to ruin by a drunken worthless father. Here they are met with protection, are educated free of charge, are brought up to habits of industry under the care of intelligent men."[19] But compared with those in Lowell and Lynn, Massachusetts, female factory workers remained the exception in the South.

Something in the social philosophy of southerners was antagonistic to industrialism. Amid the transformations of the antebellum period, the South came to defend its way of life against northern charges of its backwardness and to make a virtue of its differences. "We have no mobs, no trade unions, no strikes for higher wages, no armed resistance to the law, but little jealousy of the rich by the poor," boasted George Fitzhugh in 1854.[20] The South also had little business culture to encourage the training of accountants and clerks; rather it was northern bankers, shippers, traders, and insurers who "greased the wheels of the southern economy."[21] The South had fewer colleges and sent many of its young males to the North for their higher education. By 1860 nearly twice as many northern children between the ages of five and nineteen were in school.[22]

Investment in slaves, not industry, brought the highest profits and status. As one Alabamian berated another, "your wealth acquired through manufacturing rather than agriculture made you step above your station."[23] Despising "the filthy, crowded, licentious factories . . . of the North," southerners opposed "the efforts of those who, dazzled by the splendors of Northern civilization, would endeavor to imitate it"—an imitation which, they feared, could be achieved "only by the destruction of the planter."[24] "Unlike northern conservatives, [southerners] increasingly condemned the very social system of the North as rotten to the core, and they doubted it could be reformed adequately."[25]

Unlike the North, which by the 1840s was linked to slavery only indirectly through its dependence on slave-grown cotton for its factories, the South was irrevocably bound to a system of coerced labor. By the early nineteenth century, northern states had ended both slavery and indentured servitude, with New Jersey, where the process of gradual emancipation begun in 1804 ended in 1846, the last to do so. The future Confederacy and the four border states did not follow suit, and by the 1850s African American slavery touched every aspect of life in the region. Above all, the system of slavery was an agricultural labor system used on farms and plantations; it was ill suited to urbanization and industrialism.[26]

Southerners such as Virginia's George Fitzhugh argued in the 1850s that slavery was a more humane system than the wage slavery endured by those who toiled in northern factories. The latter, according to Fitzhugh, were only conditionally free because of their necessary subservience to harsh capitalistic relationships that offered neither security nor living wages and that denied the paternalistic solicitude extended by southern slave owners to their "hirelings." Such a view separated northerners, who came to believe local government and private philanthropy the best protectors of the poor, from southerners, who claimed slaves as dependent laborers within individual households. But the theoretical argument overlooked an essential difference. The 40 percent of the South's population in 1860 that was enslaved was human property, subject in every way, in the words of a Louisiana code, "to the will of [a] master."[27] And most of the latter were dedicated to agriculture, not industry.

The South also differed from the North in its household arrangements. Like most institutions below the Mason-Dixon line, southern families resembled, but in critical ways diverged from, those in the rest of the United States. "In the South," concluded the Alabamian Daniel Hundley in 1860, "the family is a much more powerful institution than in other portions of the Republic. . . . [with] the parental discipline more rigid."[28] Certainly, Hundley argued, the idealized relationship among wife, children, and in one-quarter of all southern families, the slaves that southerners counted as part of their family, was based "on a subordination that was natural and a coercion that was nothing more than the subtle interplay tempered by affection between the patriarch and his dependents."[29] The obvious parallel between slavery and marriage legitimized a version of legal and social authority that gave more power to southern men over

Many southern women, such as these from North Carolina, were confined by the southern patriarchal household: male slaveholders equated slavery with marriage in order to exert dominance over both their slaves and their wives.

the female and black members of their households than was the case in the North.[30]

The position of white women was demonstrably different in the South. James Hammond expressed a generally accepted male view of their purpose: "Women were made to breed and men to do the work of the world. As a toy for recreation . . . or as bringing wealth and position, men are tempted to marry them and the world is kept populated."[31] Unlike their counterparts in the North, southern women did not have a self-conscious, collective identity. This was in part because slavery created a culture that made any reform in their status a potential threat to a social order precariously balanced on black slaveholding and in part because the rural lifestyle of the South made the meetings of women more difficult.

Instead, middle-class women who might have organized conventions or signed petitions were encircled and enclosed by the southern institutions of church and family. Slaveholding women especially understood themselves as wives and mothers. In the North a few women were beginning to see themselves as individuals beyond their family roles and to consider their public rights and responsibilities.[32] Such differences destroyed any chances for an antislavery or emerging feminist movement as developed in the North, at the same time that the lack of organization reinforced the authority of men over their households.

More so than in the North, southern families represented social units in which white southern women married at a younger age than those elsewhere in the United States, a circumstance that indicates the influence of their fathers over their choice of mate. Once married, they were less likely to exercise the authority of naming their offspring. Compared with northern women, they were more likely to die in childbirth. Nor did southern wives control their fertility to the extent that northern women did. In one sample, 7 percent of all southern women had twelve or more children, compared with fewer than 1 percent in the North. "Most antebellum women [in the South] exceeded the national rate [of 5.4 children per family] and often devoted thirty or more years of their lives to bearing, nursing, and raising children."[33]

Nowhere in the United States was the influence of the male patriarch more obvious than in southern domestic law, which was less likely than that of the North to recognize the individual rights of family members. Concentrating on the head of the household, southern laws emphasized the organic unity of a domestic arrangement controlled by its male head. Southerners divorced less frequently than northerners (it was not permitted in South Carolina), and little effort was made before the Civil War to consult the interests of children in custody cases, in which fathers routinely prevailed. "One of the chief purposes of the law in the Old South . . . was to uphold patriarchal authority, providing individual heads of households with the right to police their own spheres."[34]

Southern men were well known for their hot tempers and hair-trigger individualism. Fighting, whether the bloody eye gouging of the frontier, wrestling matches, or the ritualized assassination of the duel touched every aspect of culture. "Even those who sought careers in politics, agriculture, or elsewhere found it difficult to pursue the paths of peace. A fledgling lawyer might, and frequently did, carry a brace of pistols in his portfolio. A planter, however absorbed in his crops and slaves, did not lose his early acquired skills with knives and pistols. A young editor, daily running the risk of offending someone with his pen, was most unwise if he neglected any of the honorable means of self-defense."[35] The penchant for violence and the importance of honor and pride could also be found in the numbers of military schools and local militias, and in enthusiastic volunteering during the 1812, Seminole, and Mexican wars, as well as the sanctioning of local mobs.

## SOUTHERN LIFE AND SOCIETY

Diverging at an accelerating pace from the rest of the Union in its economic and social culture, the South found its common identity in slavery and staple agriculture. Although thousands of southerners made their living by subsistence farming and grazing, the section as a whole depended heavily on the production of five staple crops for the market.

Hemp, used in the manufacture of rope, was widely cultivated in the upper South; tobacco flourished in Virginia and Kentucky, and to a lesser extent in Tennessee, Maryland, North Carolina, and Missouri. Rice was a market staple in South Carolina and Georgia, whereas the production of sugar cane was chiefly confined to Louisiana.[36] Elsewhere the South was a "fabric of cotton." At once more than a plant and a source of livelihood, cotton transformed the South into a section. "If cotton fastened slavery to the South, slavery fastened cotton on the South," writes Kenneth Stampp.[37]

"Cotton is King." As James Henry Hammond proclaimed, cotton was the staple crop of the South. Here blacks carry cotton on their heads after picking it in the fields.

In 1791 cotton production in the entire United States amounted to only four thousand bales. Two years later Eli Whitney invented the cotton gin, a cylinder contraption equipped with teeth and brushes that removed the pesky seeds of short-staple cotton. By 1849 total production had increased to over two million bales, and by the end of another decade this amount had more than doubled.[38]

The importance of cotton to the southern economy and the section's values is suggested by the elaborate care devoted to its cultivation and marketing. Southerners invested considerable resources in bedding up, hoeing, thinning, drainage and the prevention of erosion; to rotation, fertilization, and the eradication of weeds, and to the war against insects. These concerns, as well as the advantages of various grades and the fluctuating price of cotton, were reviewed at length in agricultural journals like the *Southern Planter* and the *Southern Cultivator*. According to one editor, "Since the demand for cotton exceeds the supply, it is no longer a matter of doubt that our readers have a bright future."[39] Indeed, from 1840 until the time of the Civil War, Great Britain imported about four-fifths of its cotton from the South.

Cotton was everywhere in the antebellum South. Walking along Charleston's wharves, the English visitor James Buckingham saw bales "piled up with mountains of Cotton, and all your stores, ships, steam and canal boats, crammed with . . . Cotton." The daily papers and the conversation of travelers focused on cotton, according to Buckingham, who had to dodge from side to side "to steer clear of the cotton wagons." Arriving in Augusta, he found cotton boats crowding the river and cotton warehouses covering whole squares. And in Hamburg, South Carolina, it was hard to tell "which was the largest, the piles of cotton or the houses." Journeying through the back country, the English traveler overtook "hordes of cotton planters from North Carolina, South Carolina, Georgia, with large gangs of negroes, bound to Alabama, Mississippi, and Louisiana 'where the cotton land is not worn out.'" Continuing his travels to Mobile and New Orleans, he attended a play in a cotton-press house; anxious to play pharo (a gambling game), he was told that he could do so "at the Louisiana Coffeehouse, just below the cotton-press, opposite to a cotton ware-house."[40]

Socially as well as economically, the white antebellum South was bound together by the ideal of the slaveholding cotton, rice, and tobacco plantation. Southern society found its focus in a plantation system that determined every facet of life from its dependence on river transportation to the politics of the region. This is not to suggest that great numbers of southerners could consider themselves planters, for most white southerners were yeomen farmers of limited means. In Texas, for example, only 30 percent of the white families owned slaves; 20 percent owned neither land nor slaves, and 50 percent owned land but no slaves.[41] In the South as a whole, according to a recent study, 30 to 50 percent of all white farmers owned no land and made their livelihood as tenants, renters, or day laborers working the fields of others.[42]

Nor did the plantation "aristocracy" entirely control the political destinies of the region. Democratic currents undermined the powers of the gentry until "whatever influence the planters exercised over the political action of the common people was of a personal and local nature."[43] The ability of southern yeomen farmers to be self-sufficient created a class of independent producers who lived outside the planters' market-driven economy. With economic autonomy came some political self-determination. Still, by the 1850s the plantation played a growing role in the economic and social life of the Old South, and large slaveholders came to dominate state legislatures and congressional delegations to a degree that they had not earlier. In the years before the Civil War, the South balanced an equality among white males created by voting and officeholding with an economic, political, and social hierarchy dominated by planters.

There were exceptions, and it would be hard to argue that the mountain areas of Appalachia running from Virginia to Alabama or the wire-grass regions of Tennessee were entirely controlled by the planters of the "big house." And even in the cotton areas of states like Alabama clashes often erupted between planters and poorer whites over such economic issues as access to markets.[44]

Several groups remained beyond the influence of the staple crop–plantation–slave nexus, working on farms that did not depend on growing staple crops or owning slaves or land. Many of these non-slaveholding whites inhabited the

Eppes House in Avoyelles Parish, Louisiana, was home to a yeoman. Yeoman farmers may have owned a few slaves, but they had a much lower social and economic status than plantation owners.

pine woods and barrens as well as the sand hills of the back country; others lived off the main roads or in inaccessible areas of counties where staple crops were grown. In Georgia, "most upcountry whites farmed their own land or resided in households that did so," although as many as 30 percent owned no real estate.[45] In a western North Carolina county where landlessness was common, one yeoman noted in his diary "Land! Land! All want Land."[46] Slavery influenced their fortunes to the extent that it dampened their opportunities to rent land and hire out as day laborers and to the degree to which it became an ambition driving them westward. Slavery also perpetuated their poverty because it limited the development of industrial jobs and therefore the need for white farm labor—the latter one of the important paths to economic mobility pursued by northerners.

Some of these families scratched out a marginal existence on sandy soil where they raised legumes, cowpeas, and corn on small, usually infertile tracts. Disparaged as crackers and sandhillers in Georgia and Alabama and as squatters and rag-tags in Virginia, they were snubbed as poor white trash. Their homes consisted of simple cabins of round logs, and their food was often wild game. Other slaveless farmers had achieved self-sufficiency and produced more than enough grain and meat for their own sustenance in an arrangement that depended on the household production of various items such as soap and clothing. These farmers grew corn, wheat and oats, sweet potatoes, and fruit, and often put in an acre of the ubiquitous cotton.[47]

In their isolation these poor white farmers were sometimes confused with the herdsmen who kept livestock on open ranges and in forests, where the animals foraged, without expense to their owners, on acorns and grass. Sometimes overlooked because of their nomadic lives, herdsmen were in fact largely responsible for the enormous quantity of pork that helped make the South self-sufficient in food. Of Scottish and Irish backgrounds, they were in effect southern cowboys who drove their hogs and cows long distances to market, stopping at "hog hotels" on the way. By 1860, "hogs and other Southern livestock were worth half a billion dollars—more than twice the value of that year's cotton crop."[48]

Another group who had little contact with the rest of southern society were the "highlanders," who lived in inaccessible mountain regions of the Appalachians and Ozarks. In the past an accident such as the breaking of a linchpin or the death of an ox had fixed their residence for generations. In politics these outsiders frequently opposed piedmont and coastal residents over issues such as legislative apportionment, bank charters, taxation of slaves, and land policy. Even with the comparatively slow growth of towns and railroad systems, southern states needed higher taxes in the 1850s. The debates over improvements laid bare the differences within the states, as isolated counties in states such as Alabama faced a foreign world of commerce and contract that in some instances strained class and regional relations by the 1850s.[49]

During the 1850s the non-slaveholding class, which was interspersed in the cotton belt, increased in numbers and yet declined in significance. The black belt—the band of rich black soil stretching across central Alabama into north-central Mississippi—became the domain of large landowners, and the yeomen who lived there inhabited a world dominated by planters and plantations.[50] This yeoman culture has been described as centering on

> a small farm, ranging from a fifty-acre to a five-hundred-acre tract, tilled by the owner, undriven by competition, supplied with corn by his own toil and with meat from his own pen or from the fields and forests. The amusements might be . . . the three-day break-down dances which David Crockett loved or horse races, footraces, cock and dog fights, boxing, wrestling, shooting, fishing, log-rolling, house-raising, or corn-shucking. . . . The houses were homes, where families lived sufficient and complete within themselves, working together and fighting together. And when death came, they were buried in their own lonely peaceful graveyards, to await doomsday together.[51]

High cotton prices led ambitious young southern yeomen to go west to the fertile cotton fields in Georgia, Alabama, Mississippi, and Texas. Studies of those who remained in the same counties of the cotton belt reveal that only one of every four became a slave owner. Those who continued without slaves were restricted to the least fertile, most remote areas, away from roads and rivers.[52] Many were condemned to permanent poverty and had almost no chance to ascend into the ranks of those who owned more than three or four slaves.

Serving as adjuncts to plantations to which they were linked by ties of kinship and economics, small farmers ginned their few cotton bales and milled their flour at the local plantation. They sold their excess pigs to neighbors to feed slaves they aspired to own. And on barbecue night at the "big house," both rich planter and small farmer talked of the weather and soil as comrades in the never-ending struggle against nature. Indeed, dirt farmers often were related to the gentry. Joshua Venable of Hinds County, Mississippi, never ate inside at his cousin Jefferson Venable's mahogany dining-room table, though he was welcome at the latter's barbecue pit.

Besides food, both men—along with yeomen farmers and planters throughout the South—shared what has been called the ruling-race mentality of white, male superiority over the blacks in their community. Enveloped in a system of racial egalitarianism and thereby set apart by the color of their skins and their gender from both disenfranchised, dependent slaves and white and black women who constituted most of the southern population, rich and poor white males considered themselves privileged to be included "in a small elite of enfranchised men."[53]

Like black southern women, the wives and daughters of yeomen farmers worked in the fields, delivering critical labor power to the economic survival of the farm. Frederick Law Olmsted, the northern landscape architect, found "more white native American women at work in the hottest sunshine in a single month, and that near mid-summer in Mississippi and Alabama than in all my life in the Free States, not on account of emergency as in harvesting either, but in the regular cultivation of cotton and corn, chiefly of cotton."[54] So extensive was this work and so contradictory to the image of the fragile southern lady on a pedestal that southerners created an alternative vision of the ideal farm wife as a sensible, hard-working helpmeet.[55]

As was the case in politics, despite this yeoman culture the slave plantation increasingly dominated the South's economy. Plantations with fifty or more slaves in Georgia, Louisiana, Alabama, and Mississippi produced more than a third of the region's 1859 crop on less than a quarter of the improved land.[56] The largest 5 percent of cotton producers grew 42 percent of the South's cotton, and the largest 5 percent of slave owners held 39 percent of the slaves used in agriculture, a disproportion that widened during the 1850s.[57]

In 1860, despite a white population one-third that of the rest of the Union, the South contained two-thirds of all Americans worth $110,000 or more. Every one of the 116 American counties where per capita wealth was over $4,000 was located in the South as well. In terms of income, one thousand southern planter families "had incomes over $50 million a year, while all the remaining 666,000 families received only about $60 million."[58] With only 30 percent of the nation's population, the South contained 60 percent of the nation's wealthiest men. Viewed from another perspective, the free residents of the South Atlantic states who owned slaves had per capita annual incomes in 1860 of $674, compared with $84 for non-slaveholders.[59] In counties where there were rapid increases in the number of slaves held in large units and rising land values, tenant farmers frequently ended up as farm laborers. A student of the southern economy concludes that in the cotton South planters held more and better land and, increasingly in the years before the Civil War, more slaves.[60]

Socially as well as economically and politically, the plantation played a paramount role in southern life. For the entire region the plantation gentry became "the model for social aspiration" in a system that culminated not as in the North with industrialists, but with planters.[61] In contrast to the North, urban and professional classes found the plantation a sure road to the highest social standing, and there was a pattern of professionals and artisans investing in agriculture as fast as they could accumulate capital. James Oakes discovered twenty-one thousand businessmen, merchants, and civil servants who raised, bought, and sold slaves in 1850.[62]

A British trader who toured the South found the "passion for the acquisition of money much stronger in this country than in any other under the sun at least that I have visited." Materialism emerged as one of the cardinal tenets of planters in a rural society preoccupied with affluence. One planter characterized the Mississippi slaveholders as "engrossed in selling cotton in order to buy negroes—to make more cotton to buy more negroes—the [planter's] whole soul is wrapped up in the pursuit."[63]

But although the commercial orientation of planters and their relation to world markets made them superficially resemble northern industrialists, the master-slave relationship and the restricted market for labor power made the southern economy not capitalistic, but rather a hybrid. As two modern historians conclude, "The Old South emerged as a bastard child of merchant capital and developed as a noncapitalist society increasingly antagonistic to, but inseparable from, the bourgeois world that sired it."[64]

The plantation system and the sense of a white master class overall dampened antagonism between whites, though there was always some tension between the classes. Only rarely did small farmers try to disrupt the plantation economy or challenge their wealthier neighbors. There were some exceptions to this equanimity, as large slave owners came to fear close contacts between blacks and poor whites. This was especially true in west-central Mississippi, where fears of a biracial uprising in 1835 led to the hanging of six white men "who lived on the fringes of society."[65] But for the most part dissatisfied southern men drifted westward to begin life anew in the rising cotton states, where they aspired to obtain the two necessary vehicles of southern status—land and slaves.

Thus, although aspects of the South's economic hierarchy and materialism were identical to those of the North, in another sense the South's social arrangements were entirely different because they rested on a common racial identity. Poor whites accepted the argument expressed by many planters that they would suffer the most from emancipation. "What social monstrosities, what desolated fields . . . what civil broils, what robberies, rapes and murders of the poorer whites by the emancipated blacks who would then disfigure the whole fair race," concluded the southerner Daniel Hundley.[66]

## LIFE IN THE "BIG HOUSE"

Despite their common purpose as slave owners and farmers of staple crops, the lives of individual gentlemen planters at the top of this economic pyramid varied in terms of habits, customs, and values, as was the case with yeomen farmers. Especially in Virginia, the tone was, as George Cary Eggleston remembered, "a soft, dreamy, deliciously quiet life, a life of repose, an old life, with all its sharp corners and rough surfaces long ago worn round and smooth."[67] The distinctive southern mansions, usually set on a hill, resting in a park, or facing a river bend, displayed the taste and ease of their owners. Within the mansion the furniture, silver, coats-of-arms, and ancient portraits revealed a dominant characteristic of the planter—his family pride. In Virginia the Carter family had its Nomini Hall in Westmoreland County; the Byrd family lived at Westover near Richmond; William Bolling had three plantations on the James River—Pocahontas, The Island, and Bolling Hall. Farther west in Tennessee the great plantation house was that of William Harding's Belle Meade. In fact, every state had its exemplars of the large mansions that became the stereotype of the Old South.

However, southern plantation life rarely lived up to its idealized conception. If a number of planters thought of themselves as aristocrats and the natural leaders of the free white men in their communities, in fact their high status had sometimes been attained in one generation. For those who were born with land and slaves, like Thomas Chaplin of Tombee Plantation in South Carolina, there was always the possibility of sliding into the tenant class. During bad times

The home of Henry McAlpin near Savannah epitomized the ideal southern plantation house. Spanish moss covered the trees leading to his home.

Chaplin sold land, slaves, and even fish to his neighbors. Rather than a stately mansion, he inhabited a two-story clapboard house with a leaky roof.[68] Other houses of the owners of over twenty slaves (the latter the usual standard for planter status) were no more than "a rude ungainly structure made of logs, rough hewn from the forest . . . with a lazy pack of egg-sucking hounds or noisy sheep-killing curs, half starved."[69]

Yet most of this planter class was an educated elite that placed great emphasis on higher education for its sons. Many planters were diligent readers; some knew the United States Constitution and their own state constitution by heart. They subscribed to their party press: Whigs read the *National Intelligencer*, Democrats the *Globe*. As politicians they aspired to be wise statesmen, who did not seek office but were "called" to lead the people. In many southern communities, such a style of leadership led to a political culture marked by "a Southern devotion to retirement; resignation, dramatic switches of alliance, and a remarkable turnover rate among state office holders."[70] And much of their local power came from the personal admiration smaller farmers held for them.

Attracted to the evangelical Protestantism of the Baptists, Methodists, and Presbyterians, the planter class joined small farmers at the revival meetings that culminated in conversion experiences. Much as did slavery, the church served as a "catholic institution, one of the inextricable elements of the Southern social system"; planters found there an endorsement of their peculiar institution. The conviction held by evangelical Christians that God controlled all earthly events supported "their convenient sin," for as one Baptist clergyman explained, "We who own slaves honor God's law in the exercise of our authority."[71] So believing, the clergy produced many proslavery tracts.

Some planters retained a paternalistic, somewhat feudalistic approach to their plantations at odds with the market commercialism of capitalism.[72] Jefferson Davis, for example, disdained the importance of the much-circulated rules for managing slaves and convened extralegal slave juries that tried slaves for offenses; John McDonogh permitted his slaves to buy their freedom through extra work on his Louisiana sugar plantation. Others stressed the importance of an efficient organization to produce maximum profits. Though discredited in some of its statistical models, the work of Robert Fogel and Stanley Engerman indicates the financial acumen of planters "who priced slaves and their own assets with as much shrewdness as could be expected of any Northern capitalist." Interested in profits, southern planters avidly gathered economic information and promptly shifted their slaves westward to follow the surge in demand for cotton. Their success resulted in what Robert Fogel has termed "a flexible, highly developed form of capitalism."[73]

Most planters worked hard for their profits, as the planter became simultaneously the head of a family, a conscript army, a matrimonial bureau, a nursery, and a divorce court—the latter for slaves.[74] The seasons dictated the rhythm of his activities. In the spring the planter saw to the breaking of the ground and the planting of his crops, though he did not work the land with his own hands; in the summer he supervised the weeding and hoeing and thinning and the ceaseless care necessary to battle insects; in the fall he directed the picking, the ginning, and the marketing of his cotton; in winter he looked after the repair of his houses, fences, and drainage ditches. Even with an overseer, his was the ultimate responsibility for keeping the plantation functioning smoothly. All the while he gave close attention to the financing of his enterprise and struggled with the account books which, depending on his land, his crop, the weather, and world prices, would show whether his annual efforts had been successful.

Nor was the planter's wife the dainty, delicate female of southern fiction, sermon, and literary journal. Supposedly created for less laborious occupations, she was to be "timid and modest, beautiful and graceful . . . the delight of every circle she moves in."[75] In fact, mistresses rose early each day to supervise household activities: cooking, candle making, sewing, weaving, churning, and jelly making. They taught, nursed, and supervised slaves; they oversaw housecleaning; they managed money and organized the entertainments that were an essential feature of southern hospitality.

Quite unlike the contented mistresses of southern myth, many resented a fate that made them serve the same male masters as their slaves. Others despised the double standard that permitted white males in their households to have sexual access to black slaves and to rationalize such liaisons as pardonable offenses. "Like the patriarchs of old our men live all in one house with their wives and their concubines," wrote Mary Chesnut, "and the mulattoes one sees exactly resemble the white children—and every lady tells you who is the father of all the mulatto children in everybody's household but those in her own she seems to think drop from the clouds, or pretends so to think."[76]

## THE DEVELOPMENT OF "SOUTHERNISM"

From these distinctive features of a rural society based on a plantation system and slavery emerged a growing regional self-consciousness. Long before the Civil War southerners referred not to state and nation, but to section, as the cynosure of their allegiances. "The South is my home—my fatherland," exclaimed Georgia's Alexander Stephens, soon to become the vice president of the Confederacy. "There sleep the ashes of my sire and grandsires; there are my hopes and prospects; with her my fortunes are cast; her fate is my fate, and her destiny my destiny." More and more "Southrons" (as they proudly called themselves) held their regionalism to be the highest expression of their loyalty. George Fitzhugh, the proslavery propagandist, hoped that his fellow southerners would become "provincial, and cease to be imitative cosmopolitans."[77] By the mid-1850s, this group consciousness based on southern distinctiveness and defensiveness hardened into a cultural and political nationalism that located in New England and the Republican party the negative influences of what one southerner called "fanatics in religion, fanatics in politics, the ravening demagogue hunting after office and the spoils of office."[78]

It had not always been so. In the early days of the Republic, George Washington, James Madison, and John Marshall had been Americans first and southerners afterward. The South's cosmopolitanism had received expression in Thomas Jefferson, whose interests included music, art, architecture, philosophy, science, law, and literature, and whose friendships were worldwide. At the beginning of the nineteenth century most intelligent southerners expected the eventual extinction of slavery, and many, like the young John C. Calhoun, hoped to diversify the economy of their region by introducing industry similar to that in New England.

But gradually southern sectionalism diverged in intensity and priority from that of northerners and westerners, whose allegiances to nation also included vaguer attachments to their region. Of course some ties to the Union remained and resisted even the Civil War. In the 1850s the South still retained a two-party system, with both Whigs (until their decline) and Democrats sharing its partisan allegiances. In presidential elections from 1836 to 1852 the popular vote in the South for Democrats surpassed that of the Whigs by less than a tenth of a percent. The southern people "divided politically in these years over much the same questions as Northern voters, particularly on questions of banking and financial policy." Small farmers tended to be on the Democratic side; urban commercial and banking interests, supported by a majority of the planters, were Whigs.[79]

The forces that eroded southern attachment to the Union and created a self-aware Confederacy were complex. The divergence involved slowly differentiating "systems of economy, modes of literature, methods of education, practices of religion and the conduct of politics."[80] The change was also spurred by the cotton gin, which made slavery, once considered near extinction, enormously profitable. The transformation also was a reaction to an agricultural depression from 1819 to 1832, which destroyed a long-established farm system. Suspicious southern farmers and planters came to believe that they were being victimized by federal protective tariffs, ship subsidies, and internal improvement bills designed to assist the North. In trade conventions—themselves an example of southern distinctiveness—leaders spoke of their resentment of "the degrading shackles of commercial dependence" on the North.

Meanwhile the new territories gained from Mexico sparked an expansionism undertaken in the name of slavery, the South, and "the mission and destiny allotted to the Anglo-Saxon Race."[81] Such patriotism helped to curb internal criticism as the needs of a slave economy increasingly set northerner and southerner apart. "By 1860 to protect wage labor was to restrict the slaveholders. Capitalism and slavery after coexisting for centuries now came to arms."[82]

It is impossible to date exactly this transformation in southern attitudes, but by the 1830s the process was well under way. Calhoun's shift from nationalism to sectionalism, as exemplified in his "Exposition and Protest" against the tariff of 1828; the suppression of Nat Turner's uprising in Virginia in 1831; the defeat of gradual emancipation programs in the Virginia legislature in 1831–1832; and South Carolina's nullification of the tariff in 1832 are milestones along the road to a self-conscious southernism undergirded by the rising cotton prices of the 1850s.

Thereafter southern history displays the conversion of what had been a regional identity within a federal system into southern nationalism. By the 1850s numbers of southerners believed their concerns were incompatible with those of the rest of the Union. Yet within the South political unanimity was not achieved, even outwardly, until the start of the Civil War, although after 1830 there was agreement over the slavery question. "To prosper in the South a political party had to present itself as a champion of Southern honor and a protector of Southern interests."[83] The division of churches along sectional lines advanced the process, as did the suppression of antislavery sentiment within the South. More and more, southerners came to think of themselves as a people apart, characterized by a unique and superior culture that resisted the crass influences of the transformed North.

Incurably romantic, some southerners fancied themselves descendants of English cavaliers and proudly practiced the cult of chivalry. Others organized jousts and tournaments, where gallant champions styling themselves "Brian de Bois-Guilbert" and "Wilfred of Ivanhoe" vied, with the victor crowning his mistress "the Queen of Love and Beauty." A far larger number experienced their chivalry vicariously, through the romantic novels of Walter Scott, who was unquestionably the favorite southern author.[84]

Despite its internal differences the South had developed "a fairly definite mental pattern associated with a fairly definite social pattern—a complex of established relationships and habits of thoughts, sentiments, prejudices, standards and values, associations of ideals, which, if not common strictly to every group of white people in the South, [was] still common."[85] The most binding value was an attachment to the notion of honor, which served as the desired moral framework for behavior. Perhaps this notion was inherited through their Scots and Irish ancestors, but surely it was encouraged by the traditionalism of those who worked the soil, maintained a system of slavery, and resisted modern tendencies. Southerners now developed an ethical code defined by physical valor, the approval of others (which constituted a reputation), and a concern for a self-defined sense of personal autonomy.[86]

As for slavery, although there had always been Americans, North and South, who had been proponents of a forced labor system, southerners became fervent defenders of what they argued was a beneficent arrangement justified on historical, biblical, scientific, economic, political, and sociological grounds. With slaves an economic status symbol as well as a sign of what the loss of liberty would mean for the South, proslaveryism penetrated the materialistic society of the antebellum years. Its interests became the touchstone of its politics. As Senator Robert Hunter of Virginia argued, "there is not a respectable system of civilization known to history . . . whose foundations were not laid in the institution of domestic slavery."[87] Southern clerics scoured the Bible for justifications, and "by the 1850's the Constitution had been wrenched in every conceivable direction to provide legal guarantees for the maintenance of slavery."[88]

Under the onslaught of abolitionism, southerners responded with a conservative counterattack. Holding themselves to be the orthodox republicans of the nation, they accused the North of substituting for the ideals of the revolution those of a recent, warped society espousing materialism, corruption, free love and atheism. As the North modernized, the differences between the two regions grew, and southerners found more targets for a distaste that helped establish their own uniqueness and superiority. In *Cannibals All! or Slaves Without Masters*, George Fitzhugh tried to demonstrate that in free society there was an antagonism between capital and labor that inevitably culminated in the North's "robber barons" and "pauper slavery." In a slave society, where capital and labor were united in the person of the African American, such antagonisms were avoided.

Using supposedly scientific evidence from brain and skull measurements, Dr. Josiah Nott of Mobile tried to prove that blacks belonged to a different species from whites. This new field of "niggerology" required a rewriting of Genesis to provide for a separate creation for blacks. In turn, the acceptance of black inferiority and an associated view of the proper role of women promoted an organic view of society that held slavery to be a benevolent, necessary institution in a harmonious society based on a hierarchy. Supported by these arguments, Albert Gallatin Brown of Mississippi informed the United States Senate that "slavery is a great moral, social and political blessing—a blessing to the slave, and a blessing to the master."[89]

In rejecting any opposition to slavery, southerners closed their ears to criticisms of their society and employed the proslavery argument to paste together a white southern America of divergent economic interests and political concerns. In many ways, southern convictions were distorted exaggerations of previous American sentiments and behaviors. The southerners' increasingly angry view that they were oppressed by the North—now substituted for England—their use of a forced-labor system, the rural nature of their society, and the primacy of male heads of households were echoes of values held by most earlier Americans.

By the 1850s an important segment of public opinion even encouraged the reopening of the African slave trade in order to give poor men in the South the opportunity to become slaveholders and therefore be, as one young Georgian wrote, "more and more identified with slavery and more ready to defend the institution."[90] "Negro slavery has become a part of our very being. Our natural prosperity, and domestic happiness are inseparable from it," argued antebellum southerners.[91] The linking of southern culture to slavery and the values of the American Republic, which southerners saw themselves as upholding, was made in the title of an essay by Reverend Iveson L. Brookes, published in South Carolina in 1850: *A Defense of the South against the Reproaches and Encroachments of the North; in Which Slavery is Shown to be an Institution of God Intended to Form the Basis of the Best Social State and the Only Safeguard to the Permanence of a Republican Government.* Around this ideal, the antebellum South found its unity in the 1850s.

CHAPTER 3 | # Slavery, 1830–1860

A s both symbol and reality, slavery emerged as the most significant difference between the North and South in the 1850s. What southerners acknowledged as their "peculiar institution" played a crucial role not only in
causing the war, but also in defining the ways in which it was fought, its goals, and
its meaning for postwar Americans. Woven into the pattern of southern life, the
institution was at once a legal structure, a sectional difference after 1810, a labor
system, a social and cultural arrangement affecting both blacks and whites, and a
southern version of a practice that, by the 1850s in the Western Hemisphere, survived only in Brazil and on the Spanish islands of Cuba and Puerto Rico.

## PAST STUDIES OF SLAVERY

Despite the importance of slavery in the history of the United States, the
records available for its study are limited and flawed. Most contemporary accounts were written by whites either to justify or condemn "the peculiar institution." Travelers in the antebellum South saw what they set out to find, and no
matter what their opinion of slavery, their attitudes toward blacks were tainted
by their white supremacist convictions. The numerous business and family
records kept by southern slave owners, which have served as the data for recent
quantitative evaluations of the institution, are not representative because most
relate to the management of large plantations. Also atypical are the autobiogra-
phies and narratives of escaped slaves such as Frederick Douglass, Harriet Jacobs,
and William Wells Brown. Such first-hand experiences have been supplemented
by interviews conducted with ex-slaves, mostly by the publicly financed Works
Project Administration in the 1930s.[1] Yet such recollections were gathered seventy years after the end of slavery, mostly by white interviewers.

As the study of slavery has shifted from masters to slaves and from slaves as individual victims of a brutal system to the society the slaves made, scholars have used spirituals, work songs, and folktales to describe the ethos of this slave community. Also useful are comparative studies on other slave societies, but differences in the historical settings of the institution blunt the validity of generalizations derived from such studies.

Although scholars generally depend on the same sources, differences remain over such issues as the nature and autonomy of the slave community, especially during the hours from sundown to sunup. Nor is there historical agreement over the extent to which the African heritage of the slaves survived, was replaced by a white Southern culture, or was melded into a new African American derivative. Historians also differ in their interpretation of the economic character of slavery as a system, of the living conditions of slaves, and of the significance of the limited legal protections afforded those in bondage. To a great extent these differences among the experts reflect the reality that slavery in the American South varied over time and place. Marked by heterogeniety, the system was never a static arrangement. What did not vary was the timeless element of slavery's deprivation of freedom from birth to death.

## EARLY ATTITUDES TOWARD SLAVERY

Just as the North was not united in its opposition to slavery, so the prewar white South, especially before 1830, was far from unanimous in supporting slavery. In fact both individuals and areas such as eastern Tennessee and northern Alabama remained ambivalent about it. As slave owners, southerners such as Thomas Jefferson, Robert E. Lee, and George Washington deplored the institution. There were fervent southern abolitionists such as James Birney, Cassius Clay, and the Grimké sisters of South Carolina. "The identification of proslavery thought with the South is among the most pernicious errors of proslavery historiography. . . . Even after 1830 a proslavery republic had its adherents in the North."[2]

Illinois, for instance, during most of the period from statehood to the Civil War, possessed some characteristics of a slave state. Because the Northwest Ordinance of 1787, the basic charter for the new states between the Ohio and the Mississippi Rivers, prohibited only the further introduction of slaves, African Americans brought in before that date remained in bondage. Recognition of slavery might have been included in the 1818 Illinois constitution if some state leaders had not feared that such recognition would defeat the admission of the state to the Union. A subsequent movement in 1823 sought to amend the state constitution in order to legalize slavery, and as late as 1840 the United States census reported 331 slaves in Illinois.

In Indiana, where as in Illinois many southerners had settled, somewhat the same situation prevailed. In 1805–1806 the territory of Indiana petitioned Congress, asking for a suspension of that article of the Northwest Ordinance which forbade slavery. A committee of Congress reported in favor of the suspension, thus approving slavery in Indiana. The suspension of the article, they urged, was desired by the people of the territory, because the legalization of slavery would accelerate the settlement of the territory of Indiana. Even the slaves themselves would profit, said the committee, because they would gain the advantages of exposure to the white man's culture. Although Congress did not approve this recommendation, it is significant that such an idea could be made by a congressional committee in 1806.

But gradually throughout the old Northwest, the development of free farming, the emergence of a commercial system that had no place for slavery, and the evolution of liberal humanitarian principles made slavery an anomalous institution. Northern opinion, in both the Midwest and New England, came to oppose slavery, if not to embrace abolitionism, the reform movement dedicated to its eradication. Meanwhile in the South, the existence and even extension of slavery into the West and possibly Cuba and Latin America became an uncontested article of faith.

## THE SLAVE TRADE

The historical context for American slavery emerged from the slave trade among Europe, the west coast of Africa, and the Western Hemisphere. Although forced-labor systems existed in Europe, the earlier Roman and Teutonic forms of slavery gave way to medieval serfdom, which in turn was gradually replaced by the conditions of modern peasantry. But in North Africa and the Iberian peninsula, the persistence of slavery provided a precedent for the New World, especially in the West Indies and Brazil.[3] With the discovery, colonization, and settlement of the New World, the native system of slavery in Western African societies was adapted to new circumstances in the Americas. For four centuries the African slave trade was an integral part of the New World as Arabs, Africans, Italians, Portuguese, Jews, Germans, Dutch, Swedes, French, English, Danes, Americans, and even Native Americans participated in what David Brion Davis calls the "Atlantic slave system."[4]

The inclination of all colonial powers to coerced labor, first on sugar and later on tobacco, rice, and cotton plantations, reflected labor shortages in areas with a low ratio of humans to abundant acres of land. After 1500, once the native peoples in the West Indies and Brazil proved an unsatisfactory labor force, extensive efforts were launched to import black slaves. At first the Spanish and Portuguese controlled the slave trade, but by the end of the sixteenth century, English sea captains began supplying Spanish-American settlements with slaves. Not only did English buccaneers such as John Hawkins make huge profits, but their sea-faring activities challenged the Spanish and Portuguese monopoly of this lucrative trade.

By 1730 "slavers" under the English flag had become so active that for the next century most slaves were carried to the West Indies and South and Central America in English ships.[5] Initially the Royal African Company enjoyed a monopoly on this trade. But in a commercial age rapidly obliterating the monopolistic principles of mercantilism, independent shippers obtained charters from Parliament so that they too might engage in the profitable exchange of manufactured goods for cargoes of blacks. Soon the slave trade had grown into an important vested interest that brought powerful claims on a government appreciative of the capital returned to England in profits. "The trade to Africa," explained an English clergyman in the early eighteenth century, "is so beneficial that the wisdom of each nation can never be too much exercised in cherishing and encouraging it, as the most valuable branch of all their trade."[6]

At first, importations into the future American colonies were few, but stimulated by profits from tobacco plantations, by the 1750s the trade was bringing five thousand Africans a year to British North America. Despite a slowing during the American Revolution, "there were in fact about as many Africans brought into the United States during the thirty years from 1780 to 1810 as during the previous one hundred and sixty years of the slave trade."[7] Even so, the 600,000 Africans brought to North America during the eighteenth century represented fewer than 6 percent of the ten to twelve million humans transported to the Western Hemisphere during the four centuries of the Atlantic slave trade.

A natural increase unknown in the West Indies and South America enabled the black population in the United States to expand to nearly 750,000 by 1790 and 3.9 million by 1860. Given the harsh working conditions on the sugar plantations in Brazil and the Caribbean islands where slave deaths exceeded the number of slave births, only large imports permitted the slave population to grow. But in the United States natural increases led to a creole (American-born) slave population. After the abolition of the slave trade in 1808, "the number of African slaves plunged and by 1865 . . . almost all Southern slaves—over 99 percent—were American-born."[8]

Sanctioned by government, religion, and the white traders' careless fiction that the African blacks to be shipped overseas were already slaves and criminals, the international slave trade was an unspeakably brutal business. Some captives died in the caravans bringing them to the African coast. While awaiting shipment across the Atlantic, others succumbed to diseases in barracoons and fortified enclosures. For the societies these Africans left, the slave trade meant a destabilization of traditional politics, as the strong coastal nations turned against weaker interior communities in their search for the profitable commodity of human beings.[9]

Herded like cattle onto unsanitary slave ships, shackled in pairs with insufficient room, inadequate ventilation, and little food and water, 10 to 15 percent of these forced immigrants perished before reaching America. An eyewitness described the horrors of the "middle passage" as "400 wretched beings . . . crammed into a hold of 12 yards in length and only 3-½ feet in height . . . suffered the suffocating heat of the hold which caused a panic among the Negroes in their efforts to escape to the upper air and next day fifty-four crushed and mangled corpses were lifted up from the slave deck."[10] Desperate captives occasionally mutinied or hurled themselves overboard; others perished in the shipwrecks that made the slave trade a grave for white sailors as well. Although there were some improvements in conditions on these ships by the mid-eighteenth century, the mortality rate continued high, fluctuating not according to government requirements or even the growing economic incentive to keep the cargo alive, but rather according to the length of the trip.[11]

Most of those who survived the journey to British North America eventually found themselves working on the tobacco and rice plantations of the South. Many had first arrived in the West Indies where they were "seasoned," meaning they were hardened to the New World's climate and diseases, before being sold to the mainland colonies. Although slavery existed in the North, neither the soil nor the growing season permitted the production of the labor-intensive staple crops that spawned slavery. For the most part it was slave trading, not owning, that connected the North to this nefarious commerce. Especially in Rhode Island and Massachusetts, influential figures such as John Brown of Providence and Peter Faneuil of Boston made their fortunes from the profits of the middle passage.

In the colonial period some efforts were made, notably in Virginia where some slaveholders wanted to sell their slaves south, to prohibit the traffic, but such attempts were overruled by the king and his Privy Council. In 1776 when the Continental Congress wished to explain to "a candid" world the reasons for its rebellion, Thomas Jefferson included a stirring passage denouncing George III's "cruel war against human nature itself, violating its most sacred rights in the persons of distant people who never offended him, captivating and carrying them into slavery in another hemisphere, or to incur miserable death in their transportation thither." But in deference to South Carolina and Georgia, which had not attempted to suppress the trade, and because as Jefferson explained in his autobiography, "our Northern brethren . . . had been pretty considerable carriers," that passage was deleted from the final Declaration of Independence.[12]

Eleven years later at the Constitutional Convention in Philadelphia, another attempt to outlaw the trade was defeated. Connecticut's Roger Sherman explained that it was better to let the southern states continue to import slaves than give up those states—with the result that the United States Constitution protected the slave trade until 1808. Subsequently, all states except South Carolina prohibited their residents from engaging in the foreign (though not interstate) slave trade. Such laws, along with statutes requiring gradual emancipation in the Middle Atlantic and New England states, seemed to lay the groundwork for the end of slavery. When Congress outlawed the importation of slaves beginning January 1, 1808, the United States became the third nation to do so.

Although ending the slave trade commanded the moral support of most Americans, the illegal importation of slaves continued. The government commissioned revenue cutters and cruisers to patrol the coast and hunt down the slavers. Blacks were recaptured from bootleg slave ships and transported to an area in western Africa later to become known as Liberia. But despite such efforts and despite the eventual prohibition by all the principal nations involved, the terrible traffic in humans, largely financed by Americans, continued. According to a congressional report in 1860, "Almost all the slave expeditions for some time past have been fitted out in the United States, chiefly in New York."[13] Lax American standards that permitted the American flag to be attached to foreign slavers became a scandal; those who wanted to end the trade realized that an international effort buttressed by treaties, vigorous enforcement, and capital punishment offered the only solution. Under the leadership of Great Britain the trade decreased, although fifty-four thousand African slaves entered the United States after 1808, when the slave trade officially ended.

## THE DEVELOPMENT OF SLAVERY IN THE SOUTH

Slavery gradually took root everywhere in colonial America, but especially in the Chesapeake region and in South Carolina. Blacks, against whom there was already prejudice in England, came first; slavery as an institution developed afterward; slave laws came still later.[14] Thus slavery was not introduced in Virginia in 1619 with the arrival of the first blacks. What really happened was that in 1619 a Dutch man of war sold "twenty Negars" to the tiny Jamestown colony. Those first blacks were not immediately treated as slaves bound for life. At the time no precedent existed for establishing the institution of slavery. Instead, for decades blacks lived under conditions similar to the white indentured servants who sold their labor for a period of time, usually five to seven years. After a period of experimentation and uncertain control, during which blacks were usually called "servants," the legal institution of slavery gradually took shape.[15]

According to George Fredrickson, "The evidence strongly suggests that Africans and other Europeans were enslaved not so much because of their physical type, as because of their legal and cultural vulnerability."[16] In the seventeenth and early eighteenth centuries those Africans who were Christians were less likely to be enslaved for life than were non-Christians, but unlike in other slave societies, in the American South conversion to Christianity did not result in freedom.[17] Eventually, in what has been characterized as "an unthinking decision," each of the American colonies, even the Quaker colony of Pennsylvania, developed some form of slave code.[18]

As the number of indentured servants arriving from England declined, labor-hungry tobacco farmers replaced them with Africans who became, both by law and by custom, bound to servitude for life. In 1680 less than 10 percent of the Maryland population was black; by 1750, the figure had grown to over 30 percent, with Virginia undergoing a similar transformation as the percentage of its black population grew from 6 percent to over 40 percent during the same time period.[19]

In the eyes of the law, these slaves who inherited their condition from their mothers were "less a person than a thing." "At the heart of every code was the requirement that slaves submit to their masters and respect all white men." The Louisiana code of 1806 expressed the idea bluntly: "The condition of the slave being merely a passive one, his subordination to his master and to all who represent him is not susceptible of modification or restriction. . . . [H]e owes to his master, and to all his family, a respect without bounds, and an absolute obedience, and he is consequently to execute all the orders which he received from him, his said master, or from them."

Restrictions on leaving the master's premises were always severe. Slaves were forbidden "to beat drums, blow horns, or possess guns; periodically their cabins were to be searched for weapons. They were not to administer drugs to whites or practice medicine. . . . A slave was not to possess liquor, or purchase it without a written order from his owner. He was not to trade without a permit, or gamble with whites or with other slaves."[20] Teaching a slave to read or write was forbidden. And anyone with a "palpable strain of negro blood" was considered a slave unless he or she could prove the contrary.

Certainly "the slaveholders as a socio-economic class shaped these codes and the entire legal system to their interests."[21] For ordinary offenses the master had the power to punish his slaves, although in the seventeenth and eighteenth centuries planters had often used the courts. Writes Ira Berlin, only in the next century did "slaveowners assume they were absolute sovereigns within the confines of their estate." When cases did get into the legal system, slaves were denied standing in court, and any testimony contradicting that of white witnesses was not accepted. As late as 1819, Virginia castrated any slave convicted of an attempt "to ravish a white woman," while other southern states executed slaves accused of rape.[22]

Studies of the southern criminal justice system reveal higher conviction rates, harsher punishments, and more procedural irregularities when slaves were defendants.[23] Also, because the common law was not extended to slaves whose status was defined by property law, they remained unprotected from crimes committed against them by other slaves.[24] For example, the conviction of a slave for the rape of a ten-year-old black girl was overturned by a Mississippi court in 1846 on the grounds that the act was not covered by any statute.[25]

As the social and economic conditions of bondage improved during the nineteenth century, masters came to consider slavery a reciprocal relationship involving duties and obligations on both sides. It was "natural," according to William Harper of South Carolina, that masters would deal "kindly" with dependents they had raised, just as it was natural for slaves to look for protection and direction from those who cared for them.[26] Such a paternalistic understanding was predicated on the master's belief that he was a benevolent patriarch who, as parent with child and husband with wife, looked after his "people," caring for them and when necessary punishing them.

In this arrangement the state intervened only when the male head of a household "neglected his obligations in such a way that he posed a threat to the legitimacy of [the] patriarchy as a social system."[27] These paternalistic relationships raised perplexing legal questions because they assumed that the slave was both property and partner to a contract. Implicitly recognizing the humanity of slaves, southern paternalism established obligations among individuals, thereby eroding solidarity among slaves as a group.

The existence of a slave code, not to mention the belief that slaves were a part of white families, presumed that the slave was not chattel. "The slave," determined Judge Nathan Green of the Tennessee Supreme Court in 1846, "is not in the condition of a horse. He has mental capacities and an immortal principle in his nature that constitute him equal to his owner, but for the accidental position in which fortune has placed him." Yet four years earlier, another Tennessee judge had ruled in the case of *Jacob (A Slave) v. State* that "the right to obedience in all lawful things is perfect in the master."[28]

But the right to enforce that obedience was never complete. "The notion that slave owners could commit virtually any act against slaves with impunity is not borne out by the willingness of courts to convict whites accused of murder."[29] Yet in the isolated settings of plantations the murder of slaves often went uninvestigated; even when indicted and convicted, whites served no more than ten years.

During the nineteenth century, as slave codes and state laws made the emancipation and schooling of slaves nearly impossible, slaves simultaneously benefited from a relaxation of work regulations. Slavery was "domesticated," as slave owners came to think of their slaves as members of the family who should not be overly abused.[30] Limits were placed on the number of hours that slaves might be forced to work; owners were required to give adequate care to those in bondage as they had not had to do in the eighteenth century. Even the number of stripes delivered in a whipping was regulated, as owners were forbidden to mistreat their slaves. But many infractions occurred outside the legal system, and the laws were not always enforced. For example, when a South Carolina committee of citizens investigated reports that a slave owner had murdered some of his slaves, they merely encouraged the offender to leave the county, which he promptly did.[31]

Still, any view of slavery that places many restraints on masters neglects the degree to which this institution was an economic system. Slaves were valued primarily as producers of commodities whose sale brought their masters "wealth, honor and status." From the point of view of masters, the key issue here was how to increase productivity—a goal that might lead to incentives for slaves, but which was always promoted in the name of profit.[32]

### FREE BLACKS

Although some blacks were not slaves, no blacks in the United States were entirely free. Wherever they lived, all suffered sexual, economic, political, and social oppression. In earlier decades the free Negro population had increased rapidly; from 1790 to 1810 it grew by 90 percent. But by the 1840s this rate of growth had slowed to 10 percent a decade, a figure that reflected the increasingly stringent regulations in all southern states about "manumitting" (freeing) slaves.

In the North, where 227,092 blacks lived in 1860, only those in New England could vote. (In New York, after 1821, blacks were entitled to vote only if they held property worth two hundred fifty dollars.)[33] Free blacks were entitled to trial by jury and could hold and convey property except in Oregon. But in Illinois, Ohio, Indiana, Iowa, and California the testimony of African Americans was prohibited in cases where a white man was a party to the proceedings. In many northern communities there was fierce racial competition for jobs, and northern free blacks were often the victims of white mobs.

In 1860, 261,918 of the 488,010 free blacks in the United States resided in slave states, with over half in Virginia and Maryland, where economic factors such as the exhaustion of tobacco fields and an expanding labor market in Baltimore had undermined slavery. On the eve of the Civil War, Maryland's African American population—the majority of whom had been slaves—was evenly split between slaves and free blacks, a marked change from thirty years before, when 70 percent had been enslaved. Further south, clusters of free blacks were concentrated in southern cities such as New Orleans, Memphis, and Charleston. There, according to one southern newspaper, they performed "many menial offices to which the white man of the South is adverse. They are hackmen, draymen, our messengers and barbers, always ready to do many necessary services."[34]

But such a benign view was not universally held, as free blacks and white immigrants came to compete—and sometimes battle—for jobs. White men in the prewar South increasingly petitioned state legislatures to reenslave free blacks, whom they viewed as depressing wages. Also tenuous was the free black population's economic position in the countryside, where two-thirds lived, for they did not own land and generally did day labor and odd jobs for little remuneration.

Barely tolerating the presence of the free blacks, southern states qualified their status. Female free blacks were everywhere barred from economic, political, and social rights by custom and common law, as were white women. In many southern states free blacks, if found to be vagrants, could be sold into temporary slavery. In Kentucky slaves could be emancipated only if they left the state or were hired out to provide sufficient funds for the purpose.[35] Meetings of free blacks without white supervision were illegal, and migration even to another county was prohibited. The limited rights and freedoms permitted were further constrained by public opinion so that "in actual practice free blacks had a good deal less liberty than the law provided."[36]

At all times the free African American was subject to the hazards of kidnapping, or arrest as a suspected fugitive, and of ultimate reenslavement. The New Yorker Solomon Northrup suffered such a fate. While working with a circus in Washington, D.C., in 1841 he was drugged, kidnapped by slave catchers, and forced to spend twelve years as a slave on a Louisiana cotton plantation.[37] In the late 1850s free blacks who had lived for decades in southern communities faced possible reenslavement when states such as Florida passed legislation forcing blacks to select masters and become slaves or risk, on the complaint of a white, being sold at auction. If seized by an official and charged with being a runaway slave, the free black was not permitted to testify on his own behalf and was at the mercy of unscrupulous officials who were rewarded for his "recapture." Marriage between free blacks and whites was forbidden, as was any interracial sexual contact, though brothels remained the most integrated public places in the South.[38]

Despite their deteriorating position in a white South that demanded a two-tiered racial system of white free men and black slaves, a few free blacks prospered. Some owned property; a few held slaves of their own. The majority of these African American slave owners had "some personal interest in their property. Frequently the husband purchased his wife or vice versa...."[39] In some southern cities in the 1850s, free male blacks continued to make up a disproportionate percentage of the skilled workers. Doubly penalized by race and sex, free African American women usually worked at menial domestic jobs that in Petersburg, Virginia included cooking, cleaning, washing, and "stemming," that is, removing the stems of tobacco plants in factories.[40]

One of the most successful southern free blacks was William Ellison of South Carolina, who managed to purchase freedom for himself and other members of his family. By the 1840s Ellison owned a cotton plantation outside of Charleston, thirty slaves, and a gristmill, though his economic success never erased the uncertainty of his position. In 1860, when the South Carolina legislature debated enslaving all blacks, Ellison sent his children north to freedom. In time his neighbors, some of whom had been free for thirty years, lost their property and were forced to wear slave badges.[41]

## THE DISTRIBUTION AND CONCENTRATION OF SLAVES

As was the case with free blacks, the geographical distribution of slaves varied. In slaveholding states, slaves constituted one-third of the population. But in vast areas in the South and border states, slaves constituted less than one-tenth of the population, whereas the ratio ran as high as 80 to 90 percent in other regions. The highlands of the Appalachian Mountains, stretching southwestward from Pennsylvania to Alabama, formed a huge contiguous region in which slaveholding was rare. On the other hand, the Atlantic seaboard from Maryland to Florida remained an equally extensive region where slavery was widespread. In Virginia, slaves were concentrated in the eastern half of the state, that is, in the region east of Lynchburg. In a section near Petersburg the percentage of blacks in the population was 72; near Lexington the proportion was 30 percent; in mountainous regions the slaves numbered usually no more than 5 percent of the population; in the panhandle around Wheeling, the number of slaves was nearly zero.

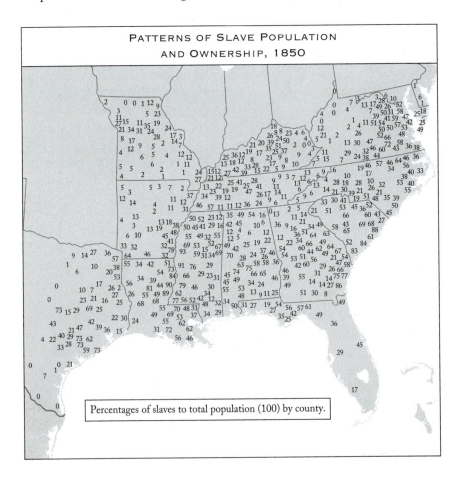

### PATTERNS OF SLAVE POPULATION AND OWNERSHIP, 1850

Percentages of slaves to total population (100) by county.

The concentration of slaves was largely a matter of geography. Where climate, land, and soil features favored the institution by promoting the plantation system, slaves were plentiful. In barren, dry and mountainous regions slaves were not only few, but their proportion to the white population was low. In Charleston the percentage of slaves in the total population was 61 and rose as high as 88 just north of Charleston, but as low as 21 in the back country. Taken as a whole, however, South Carolina had a high concentration of slaves. On the Georgia seacoast, the percentage was over 80, while near Atlanta it was 16, and along the Tennessee line 2 or less. In central Alabama the percentage was about 70 near Selma and 65 near Montgomery, but remained as low as 4 or 6 percent in some of the northern mountainous counties. Records for Mississippi, a state with a large slave population, reveal percentages as high as 93 in some counties, though in the northeastern corner where the soil was sandy, the percentage of slaves was 12 percent.

Beyond the Mississippi River, the state of Louisiana contained areas where the slave ratio ran to over half the total population. But in Arkansas and Missouri such concentrations were almost unknown. In Texas there were wide variations in slave ratios, with the highest concentration along the Colorado River.

Unevenly concentrated in terms of geography, slaves were also unequally distributed among the population. Throughout the history of slavery in the United States, slave owners constituted a minority of the population; those who owned enough African Americans to support sizable plantations numbered only a few thousand families. In 1860 there were only 393,967 slave owners out of a total white population of slightly over eight million individuals in the fifteen slave states. But more meaningful than this is the number of slave-owning households, in which all members had a stake in the system; these numbered a million and a quarter. However, even measuring the number of family units does not adequately convey the degree to which nonowners were directly involved in the institution as overseers, as farmers who hired a slave for a special purpose, and as town dwellers who used slave women as domestic servants.

In a startling display of economic inequality, by 1860 three-quarters of all southern families owned no slaves, and of those who did, half owned fewer than five slaves. Owners of more than fifty slaves numbered fewer than eight thousand—representing only 3 percent of all slave owners. The median slaveholding was from four to six slaves per master in a society in which a third of all whites owned little more than the clothing they wore. Thus the characteristic slaveholding pattern in the South involved a small group of southern slaves living on a modest-size holding with a resident master. On the other hand, because of the size of their holdings, 3 percent of masters owned a slight majority of all the slaves in the antebellum South.[42]

These few slave magnates had an influence far beyond their numbers, and counties in which slaveholding predominated had disproportionate representation in the legislatures. Furthermore, the millions of non-slaveholding whites who were either indifferent to slavery or who aspired to the status of slave ownership were tenacious in defending the institution. At least nine thousand residents of the South and the border states became new slave owners in the 1850s, revealing a degree of economic mobility in this society. But in these years before the war, the proportion of slaveholders among whites was declining.[43] Certainly large slave owners determined public opinion on many regional issues, and the United States may never, before or since, have had such a concentration of wealth and social power in the hands of so few.

### SLAVE MANAGEMENT

On individual plantations the regime of slavery involved a definite system of rules and regimentation. Manuals such as Thomas Affleck's *Cotton Plantation Record and Account Book* provided advice to slave owners not only about agricultural techniques, but also about the management of slaves. On the ordinary small plantation the owner himself saw to the carrying out of these regulations. On larger estates, even when the master resided on the plantation, as was characteristic of the South, the execution of these rules fell to the overseer who, under the authority of the owner, functioned as a manager or steward. Usually either a relative or a member of an itinerant group of overseers and managers, the overseer organized the planting, cultivating, and harvesting of the crops, supervised the care of the livestock, and "oversaw" the welfare and discipline of the slaves.[44] Operating under instructions from the planter, he assigned work groups to the fields, apportioned tasks, supervised slave labor in the fields, and on many plantations was expected to visit the cabins in the slave quarters once a week.

Although only one of every ten southern farms operated with a white overseer, nearly all of those with more than fifteen slaves used slave drivers. "The term driver itself expresses the primary function of keeping the field hands moving," a task that when accomplished effectively made these black drivers invaluable to their masters.[45] On most plantations drivers set the pace for the day's field work, showing each gang of twenty to twenty-five slaves the daily quota of labor and using the masters' instrument of power, the whip, when necessary. Under the task system used in rice cultivation, it was the duty of the slave driver, acting under the overseer, to give out the day's jobs to the slaves in his charge and to be responsible for their completion. Drivers often ran the agricultural operations when the owner was away, and their success depended on their relations with the other slaves, who must respect their commands.[46] Most of these "cotton generals," as they were called in the quarters, were respected leaders in the slave community. One North Carolina driver provided weekly accounts of his performance: "Dear Master," went a dictated report in 1856, "I commenced laying by the corn the 7th of June. . . . The People has been faithful and dutiful."[47]

## S L A V E   L I F E   A N D   C U L T U R E

Most of these "people" were field hands, male and female, whose lives were spent toiling in the master's fields. Nearly 60 percent were under twenty years old. On the eve of the Civil War, three-quarters of all slaves were agricultural workers; of those, 55 percent worked in cotton, 15 percent in tobacco, and the rest raised sugar, rice, and hemp. Typically, their days began at daybreak with a horn or bell signaling what were, in summer and harvesttime, fourteen-hour days, with half-days on Saturday and time off on Sunday and during the Christmas holidays. Sometimes the hours were lengthened by the need to gin the cotton or boil the sugar cane at night. Dressed in jeans, linsey-kersey, and for women, calico and homespun, slaves had a half-hour to get to the fields. In summer, an hour's noontime rest was a necessary respite.

As to the specific tasks of slaves, "Depending upon the season or the crop the laborer would grub and hoe the field, pick worms off the plants, build fences, cut down trees, construct dikes, pull fodder, clear new land, plant rice, sugar, tobacco, cotton and corn, and then harvest the crop." During slack periods the slaves cleared forest land, built fences, repaired slave cabins, killed hogs, and engaged in a multitude of other tasks.[48] Although some plantations had rules protecting their slaves' health, according to Frederick Douglass, "It was never too hot or too cold; it would never rain, snow or hail too hard for us to work."[49]

The 25 percent of plantation slaves who did not work in the fields filled skilled positions as blacksmiths, cooks, nurses, carpenters, and maids, many providing services for their masters' comfort such as grooming horses or driving coaches. On smaller farms, work was not so specialized, and slaves routinely worked alongside their owners in similar endeavors.[50]

Nor, on smaller farms, were the differences between labor in the "big house" (with its reputed advantages) and labor in the field as significant. In fact, some slaves preferred the autonomy of gang labor on plantations to the enforced individual contact with whites that came with the big house assignments. On farms with many bondsmen, "We could talk and do anything we wanted to, just so we picked the cotton," said a relieved cook temporarily recruited into the fields.[51]

The experience of slave women deserves special mention. Slave women worked, as Elizabeth Fox-Genovese has explained, "in the kitchens and smoke houses, prepared and served food, washed and ironed clothes, helped the plantation mistress with her herb and flower garden, and often nursed both her own and her mistress's infants."[52] But the mammy of romantic myth had a counterpart who by the age of ten was chopping cotton, hoeing tobacco, and weeding corn. Most owners gave these field hands a month's leave after the birth of a child, though customarily slaveholders were negligent about released time for the nursing of infants. Separated into female gangs, some slave women worked in the fields all their lives. Frederick Law Olmsted described one Louisiana hoe gang composed of "forty of the largest and strongest women I ever saw together:

Many slave women faced the double burden of working in the fields and tending to their own families in the slave quarters.

they were all in a single uniform dress of a bluish check stuff. The skirts reached little below the knee; their legs and feet were bare; they carried themselves loftily, walking with a free powerful swing, like Zouaves on the march."[53]

Common to all female slaves, whether they worked in the house or the field, was the substitution of the white master's domination for that of their own fathers and husbands. Harriet Jacobs, a slave in North Carolina, remembered her master beginning to whisper "foul words in my ear" as he began his sexual exploitation of her when she was fifteen.[54] The prerogatives of ownership made black women the sexual prey of white males, and the privileges of masculinity made them the target of black males. A modern historian calculates that during a lifetime, every slave woman had a 58 percent chance of being sexually coerced by a white male, with the consequence that 4 to 8 percent of all slaves were fathered by whites.[55] One Missouri slave named Celia killed her abuser and burned his body, for which she was eventually hanged.[56]

In return for their labor, slaves received food, clothing, and housing from their masters. Southern apologists often argued that slavery was a burdensome duty for them, a misleading sentiment that overlooks the profitability of this forced-labor system. Recent studies reveal that the economic value of this return was far less than the value of the slave output, and it was from this differential that the planter's profits came. According to Roger Ransom and Richard Sutch, "slaves received only 21.7 percent of the output produced on large plantations and well over one-half of their potential income was expropriated from them without compensation."[57]

A few plantation owners provided services such as community nurseries and infirmaries presided over by elderly female slaves too old to work in the fields. Others used bonuses of food and the passes necessary to travel off the plantation in order to spur the performance of their slaves. In Louisiana, John McDonogh permitted his slaves to buy themselves by working for pay extra hours on Saturday afternoons and after hours during the summer. At the price of $600 for men and $450 for women, this paternalistic system of self-emancipation usually required fifteen to twenty years, after which slaves began the laborious process of freeing other family members.[58]

Modern historians disagree as to the adequacy of slave living conditions. A few have concluded that the standard slave diet of one peck of cornmeal and three to four pounds of bacon a week was calorically adequate, especially since it was supplemented by game, fish, cowpeas, and the ubiquitous sweet potato.[59] Others find the slave ration monotonous, crude, nutritionally suspect, and certainly deficient in the thiamine necessary to prevent beriberi.[60] Although the typical sixteen-by-eighteen-foot slave log cabin, with its dirt floor and holes for ventilation, was no doubt similar to peasant housing in other countries, slaves were nonetheless housed at the minimal level.

When compared with those of other slave societies in the Western Hemisphere, fertility rates were high. The average female slave gave birth to about seven children, and the typical slave cabin contained four to seven residents. But fertility rates declined after 1830 because of the increased proportion of slaves living on large plantations, where households of wives and husbands living together were less common. In any case conditions fostered by the slave owners' paternalistic capitalism, which made a healthy, well-treated slave into a good business investment, permitted the slave population in the United States to increase by 30 percent each decade after 1810, levels that were not attained among slave populations in Latin and South America or the Caribbean.

However deficient, slave quarters were the origin of an African American culture that survived the middle passage and the emergence of a black population that was overwhelmingly American-born by 1860. In their quarters, beyond the master's constant surveillance, slaves created a sanctuary that nurtured the human instincts so often denied by their masters. The concentration of slaves in

Slave children gather in front of their quarters on this Georgia plantation. While smaller children play, the older children help with household duties such as washing clothes.

large units (over one-half lived in groups of twenty or more) encouraged the continuation of African folklore, crafts, musical instruments, work songs, and especially along the Georgia and South Carolina coasts, language. The most important institutions of the slave community—religion and family—merged with American culture to form a "survival zone" within this brutal system.

Certainly religion provided emotional solace and psychological comfort for slaves, though the increasing paternalism of whites led them to intervene even in the spiritual affairs of their slaves. "There were actually three churches in the community—the Christianity imposed by the master, the independent black church and the invisible church" of surreptitious assemblies convened along hedgerows, in woods, and sometimes on the edge of swamps.[61] Most blacks detested the white preachers who encouraged them to obey their masters, even as they absorbed the Christian message of the equality of all sinners and the captivity of the Hebrews, themes that made their own circumstances more endurable. But Christianity among the half million slaves who were counted as church members never superseded the need for slave control, as masters violated the Protestant tenet that each follower be able to read the Bible. Still, their spiritual lives created for the slaves a semi-autonomous environment in which to manifest their feelings, dreams, and hopes.

Like religion, the slave family incorporated both African and American elements; in this case the primacy of kinship relations between cousins was merged with Europe's (and to some extent West Africa's) preferred arrangement of the family of parents and child.[62] Currently there is controversy over whether most slaves lived in two-parent families. One study of three Virginia counties reveals a predominance of nuclear family households, with 54 to 62 percent composed of husband, wife, and children, whereas a recent investigation concentrating on Loudoun County, Virginia suggests that the more typical familial setting for young antebellum slaves was an extended family.[63] For many slaves a marriage relationship that had no standing in southern law nonetheless provided companionship, love, sexual gratification, sympathetic understanding, and possibilities for self-esteem.

On the other hand, the fragility of the slave family should be recognized. At the whim of the master, a marriage could be broken or a parent-child relationship permanently severed. Slaves had a 70 percent risk of sale in the thirty-year period that was a typical slave lifetime. As a result, from 15 to 30 percent of all slave marriages were broken. William Wells Brown's mother had seven children fathered by seven different men—white and black. The struggles of Harriet Jacobs to keep her children from the auctioneer's block exemplify the pressures exerted on slave families in a society where only the New Orleans markets outlawed the sale of children under ten away from their parents.[64]

Moreover, the slowing of the economy in the older states coincided with an accelerated development in the new cotton states, which encouraged slave exportations. As slavery expanded across the continent, many young adults found themselves separated permanently from their families. After young Laura Clark was shipped from North Carolina to Alabama, she came to appreciate the reason for her mother's anguish: "I knows now and I never seed her mo' in dis life."[65] As slave prices in the 1850s rose to $1,500 for "no. 1 men" and $1,325 for "best grown girls," the master's labor needs and desire for profits eclipsed any paternalistic desire to maintain the slave family.

## SLAVE RESISTANCE

Slaves resisted their enslavement in various ways. There were some notable uprisings, although the dispersal of slaves, their surveillance by well-armed masters, and the high ratio of whites to blacks made organized slave insurrections rare. The three most important collective efforts for freedom were organized by Gabriel in Richmond in 1800, Denmark Vesey in Charleston in 1822, and Nat Turner in Southampton County, Virginia in 1831. The Gabriel and Vesey plots were discovered before they began; the Turner rebellion resulted in the death of nearly sixty whites. There were other organized revolts but, faced with over-whelming power in the hands of their masters, most slaves protested their condi-tion individually by malingering, stealing, committing acts of sabotage, running away, mutilating themselves, and killing their babies.[66]

Typical of slave resistance was "the silent sabotage" of slaves who "mistakenly" pulled up plants rather than weeds, mishandled livestock, and destroyed farm equipment. Slaves were never free agents, but by choosing between resistance and accommodation, they affected their own lives. An especially cruel overseer might find opposition to his regime displayed in an increase of sick slaves or a decrease in the work pace. Individual slaves employed more drastic measures, such as poisoning their owners or committing suicide.

Terrified of uprisings, slave owners did their best to make their property "stand in fear." Plantation records substantiate contemporary charges that slaves were branded and beaten. If the earlier, more barbarous punishments of studded iron collars and muzzles generally disappeared during the nineteenth century, the whip survived. Slave owners occasionally might question its use and consider the larger philosophical issue of whether slavery encouraged the tyrannical behavior of masters, but slaves themselves daily suffered a reality remembered by one as

Although South Carolina, Mississippi, and the Georgia seacoast had a high percentage of slaves, most slaveholders only owned a few. As a result, organized slave insurrections were rare. Here is the work force from a South Carolina plantation.

Shown here is a slave with chains around his ankles and an iron collar around his neck. Although most slaveholders did not want to risk damaging what they considered their property, some inflicted unusually cruel punishment on their slaves.

"such brutish doin's—runnin' niggers with hounds and whippin' them till they was bloody."[67]

Because fugitive slaves stole themselves and thereby provided a bad example for other slaves, runaways were harshly punished.[68] Most of those who tried to escape were young men, some of whom benefitted from support from other members of the slave community who were constrained from running away by age or family obligations. A study of runaways based on newspaper advertisements reveals that, among other motives, blacks sought to renew family ties, to break away from professional traders or new masters, to escape heavy work in the cotton fields, to avoid punishment for misdeeds, and, always, to gain freedom. Ordinarily departing alone, the fugitive usually took nothing with him but the clothes on his back.[69]

The Underground Railroad was a conspicuous part of the process of moving slaves northward.[70] With its "agents" and "forwarding merchants," it zealously promoted the secret work of spiriting African Americans away from southern

Harriet Tubman (far left), who dedicated her life to working on the Underground Railroad, is pictured here with some of the slaves she helped to free. In actuality, the Underground Railroad was neither a railroad nor underground. Railroad terms were used as code words: hiding places were called stations, and people who aided slaves in their efforts to escape were often referred to as conductors.

masters, hiding them in barns and closets, and moving them at night along established routes between "stations." From Maryland's Eastern Shore Harriet Tubman, an escaped slave herself, repeatedly conducted runaways through the forests and fields she knew so well on journeys that often ended in Canada. There former slaves were on free soil; international law did not require their reclamation as in the case of fugitive criminals. Although never the extensive conspiracy of southern legend or abolitionist reminiscence, the liberty line displayed the growing significance of slavery to both sections.

Only some fifteen hundred slaves a year in the 1850s ever reached the North, in part because southern states had drastic laws for their apprehension. Abuses connected to the hunting of runaways limited the chances of success. Southern lawmakers continually made demands for the rigid fulfillment of the federal duty of remanding to servitude those who escaped from one state to another. Under the Fugitive Slave Act of 1850 a slave suspected of escaping bondage got short shrift. Not only federal marshals and their deputies but all citizens were expected to help. When arrested the accused was taken before a federal court or commissioner. In the judicial hearing the statement of the white claiming ownership, even in his absence, was taken as the main evidence, but the testimony of the alleged fugitive was not admitted.

## SLAVERY AS A REGIONAL ECONOMIC SYSTEM

Along with their concentration on the slave community, modern historians have also focused their attention on slavery as a regional economic system. Few scholars dispute the assessment of antebellum white southerners that slave labor permitted the South to contribute disproportionately to U.S. exports. Nor is there disagreement over the per capita wealth of white southerners, which in the west south central states was higher than the national average and for the South as a whole was fourth in the world, at $103 per capita in 1860, compared with $141 in the North.[71] Astute contemporaries such as the Virginia agricultural reformer Edmund Ruffin found the explanation for such prosperity in the level of specialization possible on the plantation, what modern economists refer to as economies of scale.[72] Certainly some of the profitability of the system resulted from a high rate of exploitation, the latter measured by economists as the expropriation of the product of labor without compensation.[73]

Using sophisticated measurements, economists have validated these conclusions, although the prosperity of Maryland's and Virginia's soil-exhausted plantations rested on the breeding of slaves who were sold from the seaboard and border states. "The breeding returns were necessary to make the plantation operations on the poorer lands as profitable as alternative contemporary activities. . . ."[74] In 1857 a legislative committee in South Carolina reported that 234,638 slaves were exported from Maryland, Virginia, Kentucky, and the Carolinas during the decade 1840–1850 at an aggregate profit to the sellers of $184 million.[75] All observers agree that the returns on slave capital—whether slaves were used as saleable commodities, plantation hands, or rented property—were competitive with other opportunities for southern investment.

In recent years Robert Fogel and Stanley Engerman have argued that slavery as a labor system was profitable, productive, and efficient (35 percent *more* efficient than northern family farming), especially on large plantations. Although some southerners insisted after the war that slavery was about to die out because of the overproduction of cotton or the geographic limits of its natural expansion, in fact the institution was flourishing on the eve of the war. Omitted from this economic assessment is the reality that this profitability was the result of a forced-labor system increasingly incompatible with the values of other Americans.

Studies of urban slavery (6 percent of all slaves worked in towns) offer further evidence of the system's pervasiveness.[76] Not only did slaves work in urban homes as well as in sawmills, gristmills, quarries and fisheries, but the largest factories in the South, such as the Tredegar Iron Company in Richmond and the Saluda textile factory in South Carolina, employed slaves.

The skilled tasks accomplished by this urban population suggest to some historians that slavery was not a premodern anachronism that would disappear if the south modernized. Thus even if the natural limits of rural slavery were reached in west Texas and Arkansas by the 1850s, the urban potential for slave labor was unlimited. So too, according to this argument, were its possibilities in the still undeveloped agricultural regions of the Old South, where thousands of acres of unimproved land could sustain an increased slave population.[77] Yet southern economic growth, which at this point was based on the production of staple crops, was sustained only by putting more and more land into cultivation, not as in the North by the evolution of a developed economy.[78]

Clearly slavery did not benefit every economic group in southern society. However profitable for southern cotton planters, slaves, who represented over a third of the region's population, were rewarded with goods and services amounting to only 22 percent of their output on large slave plantations.[79] Nor was the slave economic system profitable for white yeomen farmers, who were unable to afford the inflated prices of slaves, whose cost by the 1850s reached fifteen hundred dollars for males and thirteen hundred dollars for females. Moreover, southern capital was so absorbed in slavery as to preclude regional investment in soil improvements, ships, buildings, and machinery for factories. Frederick Law Olmsted observed in the 1850s that a hundred thousand dollars transferred from Massachusetts to Illinois meant mills and machinery would be built and schools and other progressive institutions would take root. If the same amount were transferred from South Carolina to Louisiana, nine-tenths would go toward the purchase of slaves for the plantation.[80]

Viewed in this context, "although the southern economy was clearly not stagnating, it was growing along lines increasingly different from the northern, failing to undergo the same kind of qualitative transformation. Virtually every major index of modernization except per capita income growth—population growth, absolute level of per capita income, industrialization, mechanization, scientific endeavor, education—indicated what most contemporaries recognized: the South was legging further and further behind the North."[81]

Since the southern chance for economic prosperity depended on fickle world cotton prices, and these were rising in the decade before secession, the system's ability to transfer human capital to other employment was problematical. The proportion of slaves who were hired out in cities did decline slightly in the 1850s, in part because of the profitability of cotton and the hostility of white workers. Slavery and city life were potentially incompatible, for in cities slaves "were allowed to locate their own place of residence and buy their own meals. Slaves socialized both among themselves and with their slave friends"; they signed contracts, received wages, and assumed various responsibilities that challenged the very basis of unfree labor.[82]

"What slavery could not do despite its economies of scale and its financial advantages was to lay the foundations for sustained growth," write Elizabeth Fox-Genovese and Eugene Genovese. "Nowhere did it advance science and technology, generate self-expanding home markets adequate to encourage diversification, accumulate capital within its own sphere for industrial development, or encourage the kind of entrepreneurship without which modern industry would have been unthinkable. It produced spectacular growth in response to the demand of an outside society but simultaneously guaranteed stagnation and decline once that support was withdrawn"[83]—as was the case after the Civil War, when cotton prices plummeted.

Yet no matter what the predictions of scholars about the future of a system that ended with the Civil War, in the final analysis the attitude of the white southerners toward their "peculiar institution" was not determined by economic forces. Slavery had become for them a way of life; they took it as a matter of course. The sense of social stability, based on antagonism toward innovation and pride in the distinctiveness of southern life, operated as a determining force. And the hardening of these attitudes before the war made this anachronistic institution crucial to the growing differences between North and South. No argument was more potent than the question of what would happen if millions of blacks were freed. Fearful southerners, who like most Americans thought that the African American was innately inferior, believed that they had solved the problem of race relations. To southern blacks slavery was an issue of liberty and freedom, but to southern whites slavery was both a matter of social control and their own business.

| # Sectionalism Politicized, 1848–1857

Differences between the South and the rest of the United States over slavery and other issues did not make civil war inevitable. Many societies have tolerated dissimilarities without bloodshed, and sectional disagreements, especially over slavery, had existed since the formation of the Republic. But the reality of a war encourages later generations to find only dissension between the North and South when hostility over issues such as land policy and federal support of internal improvements frequently divided the West and the East.

Still, the war that came in 1861 was fought not across the Appalachians or the Mississippi, but instead across the Ohio and the Potomac. Its timing can be explained by four interrelated factors that, in the fifteen years after the Mexican War, deepened already existing fissures separating the North and the South. These were the increasingly uneven impact of modernization, which sharpened economic sectionalism and transformed differences from unimportant abstractions into concrete, noticeable realities; the intensification of the slavery issue as a result of territorial expansion; the disruption of an established national party system that had earlier contained sectionalism; and the ambiguity of the Constitution on crucial matters relating to slavery and secession. Embedded in the public controversies of the 1850s, these factors form the background of this chapter.

## WEDGES OF SEPARATION

In the 1840s and 1850s the North and the South accused each other of seeking to use the federal government to advance their interests. Southerners were repeatedly reminded by *De Bow's Review* that their region fared less well than the Northeast and the West at the hands of the federal government. They read about such economic injustice in Thomas Kettell's pejoratively titled *Southern Wealth and Northern Profits*.[1] Kettell marshaled an imposing array of data to show that the South was the wealth-producing section, whereas the North, like an economic leech, sucked up the wealth of the South, on which it depended for raw materials. American commerce, according to this view, drew fundamentally from the South, which supplied most exported products in the form of its principal agricultural staple of cotton and bought the bulk of imported goods. Northern manufacturers depended on southern materials. Yet the North enjoyed the lion's share of the profits.

Kettell did acknowledge that this economic inequality resulted from the concentration of manufacturing, shipping, banking, and international trade in the North. But he overlooked the fact that northern brokers assumed risks by extending planters loans in exchange for a future claim; instead, Kettell located in greedy northern speculators and monopolists the source of an intolerable commercial exploitation that operated at the expense of the South.

Like Kettell, many southerners were well aware of the carrying costs paid to Yankee shipping interests by the 1850s. As early as the 1830s, a Georgian, writing in the *Niles Weekly Register*, insisted that southerners "be our own importers and exporters for . . . we furnish nearly all the articles of export in the great staples of cotton, rice, and tobacco. Yet with all this in our favor by nature, we employ the merchants of the Northern agents in this business." In time the tariff became a special, although hardly novel, symbol of southern concern, since southerners remembered South Carolina's refusal to accept what leaders in that state in the early 1830s had called a tariff of abominations. But heightened economic differences intensified the perception of government favoritism. To redress their economic disadvantage southerners organized regional commercial conventions in the 1840s and 1850s that encouraged, with little success, greater reliance on southern commercial facilities.[2]

Northern business leaders held opposing economic views. Eager for liberal immigration policies that would assure a cheap labor supply, for federal subsidies for shipping and improvements in roads, canals, and harbor facilities, a sound monetary system, and high tariffs, northerners complained that the backward, agrarian South dominated the national government. Although the tariff was never an entirely sectional or partisan issue, by 1860 northern businessmen remembered that southern votes had been chiefly responsible for the low Walker Tariff of 1846 and the even lower Tariff of 1857, which reduced rates and expanded the free list.

From the northern perspective, southern votes during the Jackson and Van Buren administrations had helped destroy the Second Bank of the United States, thereby depriving the nation of coordinated financial direction. The votes of southern congressmen had likewise retarded necessary appropriations for internal improvements. Northerners believed that southern jealousy delayed federal assistance for the construction of a transcontinental railroad linking Chicago or St. Louis with the Pacific coast. And southern congressmen repeatedly defeated homestead legislation that would have encouraged free-soil settlement of the national territories. To many irate northern capitalists, the South seemed to require "the federal government . . . do nothing for business enterprise while the planting interest was to be assured the possession of enough political power to guarantee it against reenactment of the Hamilton-Webster program,"[3] the latter a reference to Alexander Hamilton and Daniel Webster's desire for federal support of business.

These opposing economic arguments furnished activists on each side with material for reciprocal denunciation. It was true that the South had an essentially colonial economy, from which profits were drained off by northern middlemen. It was also true that southern political power, disproportionate to the section's economic strength, helped retard measures favored by northern capitalists. Yet southerners refused to admit that the North was making a major contribution to their economy, while northerners sometimes failed to see how much of their profit depended on the southern trade and how their factories depended on turning cotton into textiles.

Besides these disagreements over economic issues, a number of divisive policy questions relating to slavery arose: Should slavery continue to exist on American soil? Was it reasonable for Congress to table antislavery petitions as it did from 1836 to 1844? Should the United States in its international dealings continue to assume the positions of a proslavery power? Should steps be taken toward cooperation with Britain in efforts to stamp out the international slave trade? What possibilities existed for the colonization of blacks outside of the United States, notably in Liberia? To what extent did slave labor provide unfair competition to the labor of free white men in the territories? Would slavery expand across the continent with the South as its political agent? If certain slave states found the institution unprofitable and wished to emancipate their slaves, would they be denied that right by southern majorities? Were southern whites dangerously lashed to a rigid, unalterable social and economic order controlled by planters?

Just as these questions about slavery narrowed into an argument over slavery in the territories, the long-standing two-party system in existence since Andrew Jackson's day went through a process of realignment. For decades men in the North and South had chosen between two national organizations—the Whigs and the Democrats. In turn party leaders took positions on programs not because of their section but because they were Whigs or Democrats. Nowhere was this more apparent than in the votes of congressmen in the Twenty-seventh (1841–1843) through the Thirty-second (1851–1853) Congresses. The party system of this period manifested a high degree of intersectional comity. Yet in the 1850s what one southern newspaper called the "shrine of party"[4] became more and more deserted, as different political organizations and issues attracted support to new partisan temples. "The disappearance of perceived party alternatives on almost all issues by 1852 enormously increased popular resentment of politicians by exacerbating a fear that republican government itself was endangered."[5]

As sectional differences sharpened, they were played out against a constitutional system ill equipped to deal with them. After the American Revolution, the Constitution established an institutional framework that enhanced nationalism. But by mid-century southerners found in the amendment process, earlier considered an opportunity for needed changes, the possibility of slavery's destruction. Governor Andrew Moore of Alabama predicted that northerners would create new states in the West "in hot haste, until they have a majority to alter the constitution. Then slavery will be abolished by law."[6] Because of the Constitution's ambiguity on the status of slavery in the territories, on federal jurisdiction over runaway slaves (which was challenged by state personal liberty laws), and on authority over slavery in the District of Columbia, sectional differences were elevated to irresolvable arguments.

In time these four divisive issues led to misunderstandings that isolated the sections from each other. "[I]nstead of reacting to each other as they were in actuality each reacted to a distorted mental image of the other—the North to an image of a southern world of lascivious and sadistic slavedrivers; the South to the image of a northern world of cunning Yankee traders and of rabid abolitionists plotting slave insurrections." Such stereotypes, which emerged during the bitterly debated public crises of the late 1840s and 1850s, transformed political discourse from a "progress of accommodation to a mode of combat."[7]

## THE IMPACT OF WESTERN EXPANSION

Western expansion and the creation of new territories fueled the sectional controversies of the 1840s and 1850s. More than the names of future states, the words Texas, Oregon, Utah, and California marked great episodes in the epic of western development and encouraged sentiments of American exceptionalism. Exuberant slogans ("Remember the Alamo," "Fifty-four forty or fight") signaled war in Texas and the threat of conflict in Oregon. The repetition of such phrases as the "star of empire" and "Manifest Destiny"—the latter the faith that Americans were destined to expand across the continent—revealed impatient stirrings of a nationalistic spirit. What had been unsettled, arid land crossed by Native Americans and buffalo and known to a few white trappers and traders now beckoned to all Americans.

By 1836 Sam Houston had led American settlers in Texas in their successful battle for independence; nine years later Houston shepherded this huge commonwealth into the Union, thereby humiliating Mexico and setting the stage for war after rumors of a Mexican invasion sparked a show of force by the administration of President James Polk. After six months of conflict with the Mexicans, Americans controlled both California and New Mexico. The Guadalupe Hidalgo Treaty of 1848 transferred to the United States a vast new territory that was to comprise California, Utah, and Nevada, along with large portions of Arizona and New Mexico.

Yet the disposition of this territory heightened tensions between the two sections, a fact earlier anticipated by some northerners who saw the Mexican conflict as a war of conquest and who suspected that the new territory would lead to the expansion of slavery. Even before the war, debates had erupted in Congress over the issue of slavery in the territories, and in 1846 the Pennsylvania Democrat David Wilmot's resolution to prohibit slavery in the Mexican Territory passed the House of Representatives.

Just as territorial expansion made slavery into an issue difficult to contain in what had been nonsectional parties, so the Wilmot Proviso polarized the nation. Southerners believed any congressional prohibition on slavery threatened their rights. Wilmot and other northern Democrats were angry that southern Democrats, who increasingly controlled the party, had themselves violated the traditional party policy of keeping slavery out of national politics. When the Senate refused to act on the Wilmot Proviso, it could not become law. In 1849, the House again voted to apply the Wilmot restriction to New Mexico and California. Once more the Senate prevented the proviso from becoming law, as southerners began to coalesce across party lines to oppose it.[8]

Outraged by the threatened exclusion of slavery in the territories as well as by growing abolitionist criticism, many southerners who supported the ideal of Manifest Destiny now questioned the value of the Union. In 1850, South Carolina, the state with the highest percentage of slaves, was the center of this movement. Through the efforts of John C. Calhoun, a southern convention was held in Nashville. Its purpose, the moderates said, was to consider what action to take if antisouthern measures like the Wilmot Proviso passed a Congress that in sectional terms was increasingly nonsouthern. For extremists, the purpose of the Nashville convention was to move at once for southern independence. Within South Carolina a battle ensued between public leaders such as Robert Barnwell Rhett, who favored unilateral secession, and "cooperationists" such as Langdon Cheves, Andrew Butler, and Robert Barnwell, who favored the coordination of secession initiatives with similar efforts in other southern states. A third, smaller group, led by James Petigru and Joel Poinsett, opposed secession whether by "cooperation" or not.

Thus the vital question in South Carolina in 1850 was not Shall we secede? but Shall we secede independently?[9] Although expressions of southern nationalism were less apparent in other slave states, mass meetings across the South endorsed Calhoun's position that citizens could take their slave property into the federal territories, which southerners insisted belonged equally to all the states.

Through such propaganda the southern ear was becoming accustomed to the language of disunion.

Not the least disturbing factor to southerners in 1850 was the prospect that the numerical balance of free and slave states was about to be upset. In 1812 there had been nine slave and nine free states. As the years passed, the admission of six more states in the North had been balanced, state by state, by six in the South[10] so that in 1850 there were fifteen states on each side of the line. When California was admitted, however, the free states would have a majority. With northerners determined to keep the Southwest for free, not slave labor, southerners saw no prospect of restoring the balance. Their disadvantage would only increase as the North's population and number of states increased.

If, in addition to this disturbing of the "balance," the Wilmot Proviso should apply to all future territory, thus shutting off the hope of admitting any additional slave states, the South would become a distinct minority, the maintenance of its "rights" in the Union hopeless. Disunion offered the only hope of preserving a distinctly southern culture, thought many southerners, but the transition from thought to action was not easy. It awaited the collapse of the party system.

## THE COMPROMISE OF 1850

As southern separatism passed ominously from propaganda to programs, a troubled and divided Thirty-first Congress assembled in December 1849 for one of its stormiest sessions. Such was the intensity of sectional feeling that neither party could mobilize its full vote. For seventeen days the House could not choose a speaker. Not until the sixty-third ballot did the deadlock between Robert Winthrop of Massachusetts, the Whig candidate (who had some southern support), and the Georgia Democrat Howell Cobb end with the choice of Cobb by a plurality.

During this session intemperate language, verbal attacks, fistfights, and calls to the dueling grounds in nearby Maryland replaced debate and discussion. Speaking of a bill objectionable to the South, Georgia's Robert Toombs threatened, "If it should pass, I am for disunion." Then his colleague Alexander Stephens cried, "Every word of my colleague meets with my hearty approval." If slavery should be excluded from the territories, William Colcock of South Carolina asserted, he would offer a resolution declaring that the Union ought to be dissolved.[11]

With such disruptive elements at work, it took statesmanship to prevent an open break in 1850, especially after President Zachary Taylor stunned the South by recommending in his annual message to Congress that New Mexico and California avoid the territorial stage and apply for statehood immediately as nonslaveholding states. Yet Taylor lacked an effective floor leader to marshal support for a program aimed at ending the sectional controversy.[12] So it was Kentucky's Henry Clay who proposed a formula in the Senate to thwart disunion.

Henry Clay is depicted here speaking to the Senate about the Compromise of 1850. Clay spent a significant part of his political life attempting to preserve the Union. A marker by Clay's grave has a quotation from one of his speeches: "I know no North—no South—no East—no West."

Clay's proposal went as follows: Let California come in as a free state; pass a strict fugitive slave law to please the South; organize new territories in the Southwest without the Wilmot Proviso; abolish public slave auctions in the District of Columbia; compensate Texas for surrendering its claims to part of New Mexico. For ten weeks Clay's measures were debated in an atmosphere of apprehension for the future of the nation. In this and other debates on the territorial issue there were four basic positions: the position of Wilmot that slavery should be prohibited from the territories; the position espoused by Calhoun and others that there must be no congressional restrictions on slavery; Stephen Douglas's position of popular sovereignty, that settlers in a community should make the decisions about slavery; and finally that the Missouri Compromise 36° 30′ line should be extended to the Pacific Ocean, with slavery permitted south of the line.

Early in February Clay took the floor in favor of his resolutions. He insisted that there was no need for the Wilmot Proviso because slavery would not survive in the new territories in any case. The North could surrender its insistence on the congressional prohibition of slavery without loss of any substantial interest. To avert southern secession it must make that concession. As the debate proceeded, all the great protagonists of the sectional struggle weighed in—John Bell of Tennessee, Stephen A. Douglas of Illinois, Thomas Hart Benton of Missouri, Lewis Cass of Michigan, Salmon P. Chase of Ohio, William H. Seward of New York, Daniel Webster of Massachusetts, and the mortally ill John C. Calhoun of South Carolina.

None was more impressive than Calhoun. Slumped in his chair, too weak to read his speech in these weeks before his death, he still attended the session of the Senate when it was read. In this final address he lamented the growth of disunion sentiment, citing the divisions in the churches as evidence. Such disruptive tendencies he attributed to the deplorable change in the nature of the government, which had lost its original character as a federal republic and had taken on the nature of a centralized democracy. He spoke of the development of abolitionism as a serious menace to the South and urged that if the Union was to be saved the causes of southern discontent must be removed. California's admission as a free state, he warned, would justify secession.

In fact, both sides in the debate deplored sectionalism, though most speakers intensified the crisis by blaming the opposite section. There were, however, some notable exceptions to this generalization: Douglas and Webster—the latter anxious for southern support for a possible presidential bid—pleaded for an understanding of southern interests and denounced what they believed the excesses of their own sections. Daniel Webster was now sixty-nine years of age, and his speech in this debate was the last great oratorical effort of his life. With the galleries packed and with a crowded Senate chamber breathless as he arose on March 7, 1850, he struck a note of conciliation, speaking "not as a Massachusetts man, nor as a Northern man, but as an American." His emphasis was on the preservation of the Union; his strategy was to restrain the North and offer an olive branch to the South.[13]

Webster did not taunt the South with slavery, but the Massachusetts Senator instead treated it as a problem for both North and South, a problem to be solved not by recrimination and agitation, but by conciliation. Referring sympathetically to southern grievances, he deplored the growth of abolition societies and expressed regret at the extremism of journalists in both sections. As for California and New Mexico, he believed slavery was excluded in both territories by the "law of nature;" he saw no reason to "reenact the law of God." Northerners, he insisted, had an obligation to return fugitive slaves, and he would gladly support a new fugitive slave bill. Peaceable secession he declared unthinkable. "Why, sir," he said, "our ancestors . . . would . . . reproach us; and our children and grandchildren would cry out shame upon us, if we of this generation should dishonor these ensigns of the power of the Government and the harmony of the Union. . . ." Although some northerners praised Webster, many despised his position on the fugitive slave bill. The poet John Greenleaf Whittier characterized the Massachusetts senator in the scathing lines of "Ichabod" as "So fallen! so lost! . . . the glory from his gray hairs gone forever more."[14]

On March 11, Seward responded to Webster by referring to a moral law above the Constitution that one day would destroy slavery—"a higher law than the Constitution." Salmon P. Chase of Ohio also vigorously opposed the compromise under consideration. Then Douglas, whose part in the debate was of primary importance, opposed the Wilmot Proviso and urged the doctrine of "popular sovereignty," adding that the whole controversy over slavery in the territories was academic, because slavery would never find a foothold in the region obtained from Mexico.

Gradually an alignment developed, pitting compromisers against those in each party who did not want any adjustments. Some southerners and some northerners were in each camp. But after six months of debate in Congress, Clay's compromise was defeated. Following his valiant attempt to obtain its passage, the old Whig leader, in failing health, retreated to Newport, Rhode Island, in order to escape the torrid Washington summer. Meanwhile, in Washington Stephen Douglas replaced him as floor leader. Aided by the new president Millard Fillmore's support (Zachary Taylor had died in July), Douglas separated the parts of Clay's compromise and sought different voting coalitions for each bill. His plan was successful, and in September, with more Democrats than Whigs supporting its various parts, the Compromise of 1850 passed both houses. As Jefferson Davis remarked at the conclusion of the protracted congressional contest, "[I]f any man has a right to be proud of the success of these measures, it is the Senator from Illinois."[15]

Although the efforts of Douglas and other compromise leaders deserve praise, outside forces pushed toward an agreement. The holders of depreciated securities issued by the Republic of Texas anticipated immense profits if the compromise passed, because Texas would receive $10 million to pay off their claims. These speculators included highly placed politicians and the influential Washington banking firm of Corcoran and Riggs, which held more than $650,000 in Texas bonds.[16] But even the matter of the Texas border had ramifications beyond its seemingly local considerations, for if the claims of Texas to the Rio Grande were not resolved, then no territory could be organized without settling boundary disputes. Moreover, the issue of Texas territory was of great importance to southerners.[17]

The measures known as the Compromise of 1850 comprised five different parts: California was admitted to the Union as a free state; the territories of Utah and New Mexico were organized on the basis of popular sovereignty, later to be "received into the Union, with or without slavery, as their constitutions . . . [might] prescribe at the time of their admission"[18]; adjustments of the Texas–New Mexico boundary were made with appropriate compensation to

Texas; public slave auctions in the District of Columbia—but not slavery itself—were prohibited, and power was given to the local authorities there to "abate, break up, and abolish any depot or place of confinement of slaves"; and a severe law for the recovery of fugitive slaves was enacted.

As much as any provision in the Compromise of 1850, the Fugitive Slave Act suggested the degree to which the slavery controversy had become sectionalized. Few pieces of legislation could have been designed to irritate northerners more or to remind otherwise apathetic Americans of the differences between the North and the South. Owners pursuing alleged fugitives were permitted to seize or arrest them without due process. Those claiming ownership could submit proof directly or indirectly, orally or in writing, to the federal courts or to special commissioners granted jurisdiction, rather than as in the past to state judges. These authorities received a larger payment if the fugitive was returned to slavery. Moreover, the testimony of the alleged fugitive was not admitted in any trial. There were penalties for helping fugitives or assisting their escape. Federal marshals were made personally liable for damages if responsible for any escapes. Furthermore, "all good citizens" were "commanded to . . . assist in the . . . execution of [the] law," power being given to officials to call bystanders to their aid, or to summon a *posse comitatus* for the purpose.[19]

As part of the Compromise of 1850, a tough fugitive slave law was enacted. Here slave catchers in Maryland attempt to capture runaway slaves and return them to their owners.

When the passage of these bills was announced, in many communities jubilant crowds celebrated in the streets, confident that another threat to the Union had been turned aside.[20] "Newspapers expressed their relief from fear of disunion and civil war, their pride in the perpetuation of the union and their renewed confidence in the nation's future."[21]

But any analysis of the congressional vote shows a sectional pattern among representatives of the deep South and the northern Whigs. "Southern Whigs secured a national settlement based on a new fugitive slave law. . . . Northern Whigs scorned that goal." Meanwhile, support for the fugitive slave law was nearly universal among southern Whigs and Democrats, suggesting the so-called Compromise of 1850 "everywhere failed to defuse explosive questions."[22]

In the meantime the Nashville convention had met, adjourned without taking radical action, and reassembled in November 1850 with fewer delegates. Although convention fire-eaters denounced the Compromise, a majority of southerners accepted the new legislation as at least an armistice, at most a settlement. In Mississippi, for example, the 1851 gubernatorial contest indicated a swing away from disunion sentiment. John Quitman, running on a states' rights platform, was opposed by Henry Foote, who endorsed the Compromise. So strong was the reaction against secession that Quitman withdrew; Jefferson Davis took his place on a platform renouncing secession, and in the end Foote was elected. Pro-Compromise Union coalitions also defeated their southern rights critics in Alabama and Georgia.

In South Carolina, however, the success of the Compromise and the "failure" of the Nashville Convention (which was a failure only on the assumption that its purpose was immediate secession) did not end the secession movement. One faction in the state still worked for unilateral secession. The other, enthusiastic disunionists led by Langdon Cheves, Andrew Butler, and Robert Barnwell, continued to favor secession in cooperation with other states, expecting a "Southern Congress" to make secession a reality. For the time being, the cooperationists won the day, and when the other states of the South did not choose to "cooperate," agitation for separation ended. Yet many southerners agreed in principle with the Georgia Platform, which rejected disunion but warned the North that continued encroachments on states' rights (including a failure to accept the fugitive slave law) would justify secession. Thus the movement remained dormant, ready to reassert itself when another "crisis" should arise.

Many northern Democratic and Whig leaders shared the southern expectation that the Compromise had solved sectional disagreements. With good reason party organizers believed that the slavery question had been buried, and they sought a return to the traditional economic issues that had stoked the fires of party division in earlier decades. Yet "if the compromise was good for the country, it was bad for the Second American Party system," which had helped to contain sectionalism through its national organizations.[23] No longer salient, by the

1850s familiar partisan issues like the tariff and internal improvements had lost their power to mobilize Whigs and Democrats, and both parties failed to address such immediate topics as temperance and nativism.

## PIERCE, DOUGLAS, AND THE KANSAS-NEBRASKA ACT

Franklin Pierce, whose credentials rested in his handsome face, his friendly personality, and a slavery policy acceptable to the South, was president from 1853 to 1857. Representative of the so-called doughfaces, a group of northerners who supported southern interests and who, in these sectionally polarized times, were anointed with a disparaging label, Pierce had emerged as a dark-horse candidate at the Democratic National Convention in the summer of 1852. He finally received his party's nomination on the forty-ninth ballot after better-known leaders had defeated each other. As a spokesman of the New England "Democracy," in the presidential election Pierce won the electoral vote by 254 to 42 and the popular vote by 51 percent, compared with the Whig candidate Winfield Scott's 44 percent and the free-soiler John Hale's 5 percent. (The latter party had consolidated around the failure to enact the Wilmot Proviso in 1848; now in its second national election, it polled fewer votes than in 1848.)

As president, Pierce focused his domestic policy on development of the West and conciliation of the South. Abroad he concentrated on expansion and attracted "Young Americans" and filibusters—the latter term applied to the adventurers who organized armed expeditions to Latin America, intending to gain territory for the expansion of slavery. In a chaotic time of urbanization, European immigration, and industrial growth, this quiet New Englander's belief in democracy as a panacea simply did not fit. The president would have liked to make his contribution, as he said in his inaugural address, by securing "the acquisition of certain possessions not within our jurisdiction," resisting anti-Catholic bigotry, and promoting party unity. Actually his administration is remembered for two things, the Ostend Manifesto and Bleeding Kansas.

The Ostend affair resulted from a set of complex factors involving American diplomacy toward Cuba, a Spanish possession of special concern to southerners as well as to European nations. Britain, working with Spain to suppress the international slave trade, could not overlook slave trading in Cuba. The acquisition of the island, as of other parts of Latin America, seemed an objective of British diplomacy. And visions of British abolitionists creating a free black republic encouraged southerners to consider filibustering expeditions in Cuba.

By the time the Louisianian Pierre Soulé was appointed minister to Spain in 1853, Pierce advocated acquiring Cuba. After Spain rejected an American offer of $130 million for the island, and an internal uprising to be followed by "liberation" under American forces floundered, administration diplomats issued the

Ostend Manifesto in 1854. This memorandum held that the United States could never rest until Cuba was within its boundaries; that an effort should be made to purchase the island; and that, if Spain should refuse to sell it and if Spanish possession seriously endangered American peace and union, "then, by every law, human and divine, we shall be justified in wresting it from Spain if we possess the power."[24]

This saber-rattling doctrine, which had been signed in Ostend, Belgium by James Buchanan, the minister to Great Britain, and John Mason, the minister to France, along with Soulé, was repudiated by Secretary of State William Marcy. A flood of newspaper denunciations descended on both Pierce and Soulé, and the latter's erratic mission ended with his resignation. Still, the failure to annex Cuba as a future slave colony rankled many southerners who, according to one, insisted that the "safety of the South is to be found only in the extension of its peculiar institutions." Thus, the southern dream of a Caribbean empire persisted throughout the 1850s.[25]

Only four years after the Compromise of 1850, the Pierce administration faced a second major controversy. Again it involved the explosive mixture of economic sectionalism, the destruction of the Second Party System (which had been effective in managing national legislation on a nonsectional basis), and the future of slavery in the western territories. Again it was Senator Stephen Douglas who played the critical role in shaping public policies.

Stephen Douglas became a member of the U.S. Senate in 1847. As floor leader in 1850, he played an instrumental role in the passage of the Compromise of 1850. When it came to territorial issues, Douglas was a strong supporter of popular sovereignty.

Few men have risen so quickly to political leadership. Born in Vermont, Douglas struggled as a lawyer in Illinois, became active in promoting the Democratic organization of his state, and served in the state legislature alongside Abraham Lincoln. For two years he was a member of the Supreme Court of Illinois, and he bore the title "Judge Douglas" throughout his life. After serving briefly but impressively in the House of Representatives, he held the office of senator from Illinois during the critical years from 1847 until his death in 1861. His vigor, his force as a debater, his talent as political strategist, and his persistent nationalism brought the "Little Giant" (he was only five feet, four inches in height) distinction in an age when the sectionalism of many national leaders was all too evident.

Western problems and territorial issues had been Douglas's specialty. Since 1847, he had been chairman of the Senate's committee on territories, after having held a similar chairmanship in the House. In 1854 no one was better informed than he about territorial politics. No one understood more thoroughly than he the sectional solutions proposed to end the slavery question—either by the North's preference for a congressional prohibition of slavery in the territories or by the South's desire for federal protection of slavery in the territories. To these Douglas added, though he was not the first to do so, a third option: popular sovereignty, whereby slavery should be neither positively established nor arbitrarily prohibited by the federal government. Rather, the issue should be settled by the American principle of local self-determination: that is, each territory should be left free to deal with slavery as the majority of its citizens decided.

By 1854, the so-called Platte country west of Missouri and Iowa awaited organization, which according to the Missouri Compromise of 1820 must be accomplished without slavery. Speaking for his committee, Douglas reported a bill for the territorial organization of the Platte country on January 4, 1854. Most of the provisions of what came to be called the Kansas-Nebraska bill were familiar, but those concerning slavery attracted attention. Douglas declared that his bill was in tune with "certain great principles" already enacted in 1850. "Your committee," he said, "deem it fortunate . . . that the controversy then resulted in the adoption of the compromise measures, which the two great political parties . . . have affirmed . . . and proclaimed as a final settlement of the controversy and an end of the agitation." Briefly, these principles were that the residents of the territories, through their representatives in the territorial legislature, should decide about slavery in the territories, with the right of appeal on matters of constitutionality to the Supreme Court of the United States.[26]

Historians have argued over Douglas's motives in introducing this measure, which seemed indirectly to repeal the Missouri Compromise ban on slavery in the region and thus to reopen sectional conflict.[27] Some critics have maintained that Douglas had a personal interest in the promotion of slavery, since his first wife had inherited a plantation with one hundred and fifty slaves. Douglas received a fifth of its income as well as reports from the overseer on the behavior of the slaves.[28]

But Douglas was also angling for the Democratic presidential nomination in 1856 and hoped to win southern support. Moreover he wished to assist the powerful proslavery Missouri Senator David Atchison, who despised the Missouri Compromise, in his campaign for reelection, and he desired as well to promote the building of a transcontinental railroad with eastern terminals in Chicago and St. Louis. Furthermore, though this is less certain, Douglas may have seen the Kansas-Nebraska bill as a means of reestablishing the flagging Second American Party System through the introduction of a new issue over which Whigs would oppose Democrats.[29]

Douglas himself declared that his purpose in introducing the Kansas-Nebraska bill was to remove the "barbarian wall" of Indian tribes checking further settlement in the central plains and "to authorize and encourage a continuous line of settlements to the Pacific Ocean."[30] His central idea of continental expansion included railroad development. As he expressed his version of Manifest Destiny:

> The tide of emigration and civilization must be permitted to roll onward until it rushes through the passes of the mountains, and spreads over the plains, and mingles with the waters of the Pacific. Continuous lines of settlements with civil, political and religious institutions all under the protection of law, are imperiously demanded by the highest national considerations. These are essential, but they are not sufficient. . . . We must therefore have Rail Roads and Telegraphs from the Atlantic to the Pacific, through our own territory. Not one line only, but many lines, for the valley of the Mississippi will require as many Rail Roads to the Pacific as to the Atlantic.[31]

Hoping to finesse the slavery question and knowing that he had no chance whatever of getting a territorial bill adopted without southern votes, Douglas presented a deliberately ambiguous measure that did not explicitly exclude slavery from the area, but which almost certainly would have left the Missouri Compromise prohibition in effect during the territorial stage. Personally indifferent to slavery, Douglas did not think the South's "peculiar institution" could ever extend into the arid Great Plains. Consequently he believed that his token concession to the South—that states could be admitted to the Union with or without slavery, thereby violating the Missouri Compromise prohibition—in no sense endangered liberty. Rather, the matter was a moot point. "It is to be hoped," he argued, "that the necessity and importance of the measure are manifest to the whole country, and that so far as the slavery question is concerned, all will be willing to sanction and affirm the principles established by the Compromise measures of 1850."[32]

But once the measure was presented to the Senate, it became the object of intense political pressure. Free Soilers attempted to add amendments reaffirming the Missouri Compromise ban on slavery. Angered by these maneuvers, southerners informed Douglas that slavery must be permitted in the Nebraska country during the territorial phase of its organization. Reluctantly yielding on this point, Douglas added a section to his bill, which, he asserted, had previously been omitted through a "clerical error." It provided "that all questions pertaining to slavery in the Territories, and in the new States to be formed therefrom, are to be left to the people residing therein, through their appropriate representatives."

Though this provision clearly implied the repeal of the Missouri Compromise, proslavery leaders were still not satisfied. After a carriage ride with Senator Archibald Dixon, a Kentucky Whig who argued that the Missouri Compromise must be explicitly repealed, Douglas is reported to have exclaimed, "By God, you are right. I will incorporate it in my bill, though I know it will raise a hell of a storm."[33] Douglas then added an amendment declaring the Missouri Compromise "inoperative and void." At the same time his bill was modified in another way by dividing the area under consideration into the two separate territories of Kansas and Nebraska. Thus, the final version of the bill was not Douglas's alone, although Douglas later claimed, "I passed the Kansas-Nebraska Act myself." It was rather the work of many political strategists. Assisted by relentless pressure from the Pierce administration, the bill, after months of debate, passed and became law on May 30, 1854.

At once, the reaction in the free states that Douglas had predicted took place. Infuriated opponents of slavery and free-soil partisans who wanted to preserve unsettled land for whites took steps to have the action of Congress repudiated. Salmon P. Chase of Ohio was among the first to argue that Congress lacked authority to recognize or create slavery anywhere. "Freedom," Chase told the Senate, "is national; slavery only is local and sectional." The Ohio senator, who had supported the Liberty party in 1840 and the free-soilers in 1848, now headed a movement to create a new antislavery party in the North. In the "Appeal of the Independent Democrats in Congress to the People of the United States," he denounced Douglas's action as a violation of a solemn, pledge, predicted its dire effect on immigration to the West, warned the country that freedom and union were in peril, and encouraged all Christians to rise in protest against this "enormous crime."[34]

At first southerners showed either indifference or resentment toward a law that they believed offered them insufficient protection. But soon they came to endorse the Kansas-Nebraska Act as "a measure . . . just in regards to the rights of the South, and reasonable in its operation and effect."[35]

The passage of the Kansas-Nebraska Act accelerated the process of party decay that had begun with the Whig and Democratic failure to address popular concern over issues of temperance and nativism. In 1854 opposition to slave expansion united former political antagonists who wanted the territories kept free "for a wide variety of reasons: economic self-interest, moral opposition to the institution, a desire to limit the political power of the South, the wish to keep all blacks from the territories, and the need to expand the free labor system and thus preserve a cluster of social values—opportunity, social mobility, and economic development."[36] And by the early 1850s, growing numbers of northerners resented what they considered the aggressiveness of slaveholding southerners in the national parties, "a political influence and arrogance symbolized by the epithet 'Slave Power.'"[37]

### NEW PARTIES

Other forces besides sectionalism were roiling politics in the early 1850s. By the fall of 1854 several new organizations were running candidates, as former Whigs and Democrats in both the North and the South lost faith in the parties that had earlier retained their loyalty. These new groups included the Anti-Nebraska, Fusion, Free Soil, People's, Know-Nothing, and Republican parties.

In many parts of the country, including border states like Maryland and Kentucky as well as urban areas of the North, the Know-Nothings were the fastest growing party in the United States during the early 1850s. The Know-Nothings espoused an Americanism built on hostility to Catholics and the foreign-born, which could expand to include opposition to the corrupting influences of the slaveocracy. Its platform of limiting the naturalization process and ending corrupt politics appealed to many former Democrats. The Know-Nothings were crucial to the final disruption of the Second American Party System and to the creation of a voter realignment. But eventually they split, like churches, over the sectional issue of slavery.

The Republican party became the most enduring of these new parties of the 1850s. From its beginnings it was a northern organization. Later, many communities claimed to be the site of the first Republican meeting, but a Ripon, Wisconsin assembly is usually accorded the credit. There on July 6, 1854, a mass meeting resolved that the repeal of the Missouri Compromise by the Kansas-Nebraska Act required that old parties be discarded and a new party built. Yet the future of the Republicans as the major opposition to the Democrats was not assured. From 1854 to 1858 they struggled for primacy against the weakening Whigs, the New York–based Free-Soil Democrats, and especially the Know-Nothings. "More than a century later, it is difficult to appreciate the Republican party's precarious situation [even] in the spring of 1856."[38] Nor was its early growth the result of commitment by hard-core antislavery proponents. Instead, its success originated in its attraction to former Know-Nothings, free-soil Democrats, and new voters.

Thus, the Kansas-Nebraska Act led to the opposite of what Douglas had intended. Far from easing sectional conflict and uniting his party, he had reopened the strife that he himself called the "fearful struggle of 1850"; he had split the oldest party in the United States; he had supplied the occasion for the entrance of a sectional party onto the scene; and he had driven many northern Democrats into its ranks. In the fall elections of 1854, a piece of legislation that seemed to many northerners to be part of a Slave Power plot to spread slavery throughout the North led to the defeat of over sixty Democratic congressmen from the free states.

## SECTIONALISM IN KANSAS

Events in Kansas soon demonstrated the effect of the repeal of the Missouri Compromise and how popular sovereignty worked in practice, not just theory. Nebraska, settled at the same time as Kansas, hardly entered into the national story until after the Civil War. But Kansas occupied center stage in the fifties. Given the heated passions of the time, the settlement of Kansas was not envisioned by Americans as a typical project of western pioneering. Rather in the South it was viewed as a competitive matter of rescuing Missouri from contamination by abolitionist neighbors and of "saving" the territory from the "destruction" of its "rights." For northerners, Kansas involved creating a free state and thwarting the southern slave owners' conspiracy. Artificially stimulated emigration, outside interference, frontier brawls, violence in Congress, election frauds, and partisan efforts to make political capital out of the situation in Kansas—all marked the turbulent affairs in this territory.

In some ways the settlement of Kansas did not differ greatly from that of other frontier areas. The key to its development was land ownership, and for the thousands of Missourians who poured into the territory as soon as it was opened in May 1854, establishing farms took priority over sectional disagreements.[39] But since the national government had failed to extinguish Indian titles and had neglected to provide for surveys, not an acre of land was available for preemption or purchase.[40] This uncertainty over land titles played a major role in heightening tensions in an already dangerous situation.

The struggle in Kansas can be depicted as a contest between pro and antislavery forces, but there were many other reasons for conflict. These included competition for public offices, such as commissioner of land and official surveyor, and the desire to gain contracts for army procurement and post offices. On the unsettled frontier even the proposed route of a railroad or road was cause for disagreement among residents and communities.[41]

Feeding this instability were the activities of groups organized to promote immigration into Kansas. In April 1854, even before the Kansas-Nebraska Act was passed, Eli Thayer of Worcester, Massachusetts organized the Massachusetts Emigrant Aid Company (later the New England Emigrant Aid Society) in order to "assist" settlement in the West. Thayer wished the project to be a profit-making enterprise, but many investors ignored its financial aspects for its political implications.[42]

Under the stimulus of the Thayer society, over a thousand free-state settlers, mostly from the Midwest and not, as the South insisted, from "abolitionist" New England, migrated to Kansas in 1854 and 1855. Though their numbers were small, their influence on the territory's development was great. The society gave "encouragement, advice and money" to the free-state leaders in Kansas. It published a newspaper, the *Herald of Freedom*, and the society's widely publicized "Plan of Operations" made nearby Missouri slaveholders question how secure slavery was.

Overall the activities of the New England Emigrant Aid Company "furnished the excuse, and in some measure the provocation, for the Missouri invasion" of Kansas by proslavery "border ruffians."[43] The South countered by sending into the territory an expedition of several hundred men from Georgia, Alabama, and South Carolina, led by Jefferson Buford of Alabama. Thereafter, in a ratcheting effect, proslavery and antislavery forces reacted to what each side considered the lawlessness of the other.

The first governor of the territory, Andrew Reeder, arrived in October 1854 to find that the several thousand settlers already in Kansas lacked a government. During his brief tenure, proslavery forces were particularly aggressive. When

FORCING SLAVERY DOWN THE THROAT OF A FREESOILER

In this political cartoon from 1856, supporters of slavery are forcing a free-soiler to accept their institution. Popular sovereignty was used to decide whether Kansas would enter the Union as a free or slave state.

members of the territorial legislature were elected in March 1855, several thousand armed intruders from Missouri marched into the territory and stuffed the ballot boxes with fraudulent votes. Most had been encouraged by former Senator David Atchison, who led seventeen hundred armed Missourians to the Kansas polls, promising "if that ain't enough, we can send five thousand—enough to kill every God-damned abolitionist in the territory."[44] This legislature met at Shawnee Mission and adopted a drastic slave code that limited officeholding to proslavery men. Imprisonment at hard labor was decreed for anyone who claimed that slavery did not legally exist in the territory.

Repudiating the "bogus" Shawnee legislature, the free-state men of Kansas held a constitutional convention in Topeka that barred slavery from the territory but also banned free blacks, in a display of the racist sentiment which wanted to keep all blacks, free or slave, out of Kansas. After an election in which the proslavery supporters took no part, the free-state community ratified this constitution and launched a state government with Charles Robinson as governor. In early 1856, Kansas contained two rival, irregularly created governments. Yet throughout the territorial period the majority of Kansans were antislavery, if only to exclude blacks, and the practice of holding slaves never took root. As Amos Lawrence, one of the chief supporters of the New England Emigrant Aid company, pointed out in March, 1855, "So far not a slave has been taken into the Territory (who stayed more than a night), and I do believe there never will be one."[45] The census of 1860, taken after the territory had been legally open to slavery for six years, revealed only two slaves in Kansas.

Nothing better illustrates the unsettled and partisan nature of the Kansas situation than the "Wakarusa War" in December 1855. When a free-state settler was killed by a proslavery opponent in a private feud, the proslavery sheriff, instead of pursuing the murderer, collected a posse to apprehend a friend of the murdered man on a charge of threatening revenge. Though the citizens of Lawrence, the antislavery stronghold, disavowed any intention to make the cause their own, Governor Wilson Shannon, who replaced Reeder and was a favorite of the proslavery forces, declared the town of Lawrence to be "in rebellion." The town was promptly besieged by an informal militia, many of whom came from Missouri with arms stolen from a federal arsenal. Under the leadership of James Henry Lane and Charles Robinson, the free-state citizens of Lawrence responded by arming themselves with rifles, the latter nicknamed "Beecher's Bibles" after the clergyman Henry Ward Beecher sanctioned them as more necessary than Bibles to protect morality in Kansas. Violence seemed inevitable when the governor brought the conflict to a close by a "treaty" negotiated with the citizens of Lawrence. The "war" had terminated with only a few skirmishes.

Then in May 1856 a force of about eight hundred men, many of them from Missouri, invaded Lawrence, and more violence followed. Led by the local sheriff and the federal marshal, they intended to execute warrants for "treason." Despite the lack of resistance of the Lawrence citizens, this raid degenerated into an attack by proslavery guerrilla forces. During the attack, the hotel housing the Emigrant Aid Company was destroyed, citizens were terrorized, newspaper presses were smashed, and houses were burned. The raid was almost bloodless, but northerners were electrified by lurid descriptions in the press of "the sack of Lawrence." The effect of the incident was heightened by two other acts of violence that occurred almost simultaneously—the Pottawatomie massacre and the Sumner-Brooks affair.

A grim revolutionary now entered the conflict in Kansas. Born in Connecticut in 1800, John Brown had tried tanning, land speculation, sheep raising, and various business ventures without success. He had also suffered family misfortunes, and had moved from Ohio to Pennsylvania, Massachusetts, and New York. In 1856 he settled with his four sons at Osawatomie, Kansas, and became a "captain" in the emergency force recruited by free-state citizens to defend the town of Lawrence. Up to this time, killings in Kansas had been few. Then, on the night of May 24–25, 1856, a small party made up chiefly of Brown and his sons descended on the cabins of proslavery families on Pottawatomie Creek. There they murdered five men and left their mutilated bodies as "a Free State warning to the proslavery forces that it was to be a tooth for a tooth, an eye for an eye."[46]

One student of Brown's Kansas career maintains that Brown's motive for the massacre was political assassination. Certainly all of the murdered men were connected with the proslavery government's nearby district court, and Brown seems to have feared that they might convict him of "treason" because he supported the rival Topeka regime.[47] Other evidence indicates that Brown was retaliating for proslavery atrocities, including the recent murder of six free-state men and the destruction in Lawrence.[48] In response, Brown and his partisans were attacked by several hundred proslavery men in what was called the "battle" of Osawatomie, during which Brown's son Frederick was killed and the small settlement burned. More convinced than ever of the necessity of a violent overthrow of slavery, Brown soon after left Kansas for the East.

Four days before Brown's raid, Charles Sumner of Massachusetts delivered a speech entitled "The Crime against Kansas" in the Senate. With his habitually superior attitude, Sumner inveighed against lawlessness in Kansas, using sexual metaphors of that community's "rape" by the South along with traditional abolitionist rhetoric on the lasciviousness of southern slaveholders. He also denounced the state of South Carolina and its Senator Andrew Butler, who was not in the Senate chamber at the time.

Butler's cousin, the South Carolina congressman Preston Brooks, decided that, according to his code of personal honor, the slander of his relative must not go unpunished. On May 22 Brooks entered the nearly empty chamber after the Senate had adjourned, walked to Sumner's seat, faced him, explained that he had come to punish him for slandering an aged and absent relative, and then struck him repeatedly over the head with a cane. Brooks said that he meant to "whip" Sumner, not to hurt him; but it took over three years for Sumner to recover, during which time the state of Massachusetts reelected him to his seat in the Senate.

Applauded as a "spirited action" by the South, Brooks's caning of Sumner angered the North and came to serve as a notorious illustration of southern barbarism.[49] The simultaneous news of the sack of Lawrence reinforced what had been a minority view of the South as an aggressive Slave Power intent on subverting freedom in the Republic. Soon members of the fledging Republican party linked bleeding Sumner to Bleeding Kansas, and both incidents became resonant symbols for the North's growing antisouthernism. One northerner believed that "the most effective deliverance by any man to advance the Republican party was made by the bludgeon of Preston S. Brooks."[50]

Members of the Kansas Free State battery stand beside a cannon from the Mexican War. Attempting to influence the future status of Kansas, abolitionists and slaveholders frequently engaged in violence in what became known as "Bleeding Kansas."

## THE ELECTION OF 1856

During the controversy over Kansas, the nation faced a presidential election. The venerable Whig party, whose leader Winfield Scott had been defeated for the presidency in 1852, had virtually disappeared. Only a feeble group of its partisans met in Baltimore in September 1856 to ratify the Know-Nothing nominations, avoid the issue of slavery, and pronounce the Union "in peril." The American, or Know-Nothing, party held its national meeting in Philadelphia in February 1856. There its delegates passed a noncommittal resolution concerning the burning question of slavery in the territories (thus offending the delegates of various northern states, who promptly withdrew), and nominated Millard Fillmore for president and Andrew Jackson Donelson for vice president.

Taking a prosouthern stance, the Democratic party, at its nominating convention in Cincinnati, committed itself to the principle of noninterference by Congress with slavery in state and territory. Democrats rejected Pierce, Cass, and Douglas, instead nominating the dignified and "available" James Buchanan of Pennsylvania for president and John C. Breckinridge of Kentucky for vice president. Buchanan had served in Congress as early as 1821 and for thirty years had been an influential force in his state's powerful Democratic organization. Though at first a Federalist, he became a Jackson Democrat in the United States Senate and had been appointed secretary of state by Polk. His prosouthern bias had been demonstrated in 1854, when he had joined John Mason and Pierre Soulé in supporting the Ostend Manifesto. Because he had been out of the country since 1853, however, he escaped the stigma of the Kansas-Nebraska Act and Bleeding Kansas.

Like many Americans, Buchanan believed that the United States was in crisis, with, as he wrote, "Republicanism sweeping over the North like a tornado [and] the Union [is] Tottering." With the possibility of a Republican as president, he concluded that "the dissolution of the Union is [at hand] and this immediately. . . . God save the Union. I do not wish to survive it."[51]

With the Democrats tilting toward the South and the Know-Nothings suspect in the minds of many northerners, the new Republican party offered the only choice, especially to those growing numbers who believed that slavery should not be extended. Playing on Kansas as the principal question before the country, the new party held its first national nominating convention in Philadelphia in June. Though only two years old, the Republican party had acquired power in several state governments in the North, and its members faced the coming contest with confidence.

Yet the party contained many diverse interests, a fact illustrated by its various candidates for the nomination. Those who held opposition to slavery as a priority favored either John Charles Frémont or Salmon P. Chase. Conservatives preferred the aged John McLean of Ohio, who, though a member of the United States Supreme Court for thirty years, had often been drawn into politics. Others regarded William H. Seward of New York as the logical standard bearer. But after Republican managers gained the support of northern Know-Nothings repelled by their party's proslavery adherents, it was considered undesirable to nominate a man who, like Seward, had been hostile to the Know-Nothings.

There was, in fact, no serious contest. Frémont was nominated on the first ballot. With a creditable army record and a dashing reputation for western exploration, the forty-three-year-old "Pathfinder," though lacking in solid qualifications for the presidency, supplied those elements of romance and adventure which appealed to the youthful Republicanism of 1856. Senator William L. Dayton, an old-line Whig of New Jersey, was chosen as the vice-presidential candidate.

In one of the most thoughtful and farthest-reaching party platforms of the nineteenth century, the Republicans took their stand against the repeal of the Missouri Compromise, opposed the extension of slavery, denounced the tyrannical and unconstitutional course of events in Kansas, favored that territory's admission as a free state, denounced southern expansionism as represented in the Ostend Manifesto, and declared it the duty of Congress to stamp out from the territories the twin relics of barbarism—Mormon polygamy and southern slavery.

The party also went on record as favoring national subsidies for a Pacific railroad and congressional appropriations for local improvements. Finally, in an ambiguous plank designed to appeal to both nativists and naturalized citizens, the Republican platform opposed legislation that restricted "liberty of conscience and equality of rights." Nativists interpreted this pledge as a response to Catholic opposition to the use of the Protestant Bible in the public schools. The foreignborn read this resolution, though the sentiment was restricted to the liberties of *citizens*, as protecting them from nativists.[52]

In the campaign that followed, the differences between Douglas's "popular sovereignty" and the Wilmot Proviso doctrine of the Republicans occupied the attention of most newspapers. To a lesser extent there was discussion of Republican opposition to what party members called the southern "Slave Power." To northern Democrats popular sovereignty meant what Douglas meant, namely, that the people of a territory should decide the slavery question for themselves. To southerners, "noninterference" by the federal government was understood to mean protection for slavery during the territorial stage, leaving to the people of the territory the privilege of choosing between slavery and freedom only at the time of making a state constitution and applying for admission to the Union. Buchanan did not clarify the ambivalence that arose from this double interpretation of the platform. Nor did the United States constitution provide any clarification of what the Founding Fathers intended.

The results of the election of 1856 revealed the growing sectionalism in the country. It was a prosouthern Democratic party that gave Buchanan his narrow margin of victory. Though he obtained 174 electoral votes to Frémont's 114 and Fillmore's 8, he was chosen by less than a majority of the popular vote. Thus, if Fillmore's 21 percent of the vote was added to Frémont's 33 percent, Buchanan was the choice of a minority of voters. Yet Buchanan carried the entire South together with the border states, except for Maryland, which cast its vote for Fillmore. In addition, he obtained the votes of Illinois, Indiana, California, New Jersey, and Pennsylvania.

The Republicans received negligible support in the slave states, but their impressive strength in the North made the results seem to them "a victorious defeat." They carried Connecticut, Maine, Iowa, Massachusetts, Michigan, New Hampshire, Ohio, New York, Rhode Island, Vermont, and Wisconsin, besides receiving a large minority vote in Illinois, Indiana, New Jersey, and Pennsylvania. Moreover, there was a surge of political interest in the North as 83 percent of the northern electorate went to the polls, an increase of 7 percent over the 1852 presidential election. Of the three parties, only the vote for Fillmore could be regarded as nonsectional.

Clearly, the Republicans had mass support in the rapidly growing North. Yet so long as the Democratic party remained friendly to slavery and at the same time retained the support of large numbers of northern Democrats, the Union seemed assured. Nevertheless, the notable gains of the Republicans in the North, together with the growing discontent of northern Democrats with the South's intransigence, gave Frémont's followers hope for a victory in 1860. Although the Republicans later made the Union their slogan, in 1856 they were denounced as "disunionists" because their support was regional. Having won the control of state governments in most free states, they redoubled their efforts to win in 1860. Meanwhile, the South, though relieved, anxiously awaited the future.

CHAPTER 5 | # A House Dividing, 1857–1860

S ectional disagreements over economic, social, political, and constitutional issues continued from Buchanan's inauguration in 1857 until southern states began seceding after Lincoln's election in 1860. Controversies over the expansion of slavery into the western territories provided the catalyst for the growing perceptions of northerners and southerners that they held different intentions for the republic's future. Episodes such as the Dred Scott case, turmoil in Kansas, the 1858 Illinois senatorial contest between Abraham Lincoln and Stephen Douglas, John Brown's raid on Harpers Ferry in 1859, and finally the presidential election of 1860 fixed public attention on the critical issues dividing the North and the South.

Both sides believed that if slavery were confined to the fifteen states where it existed in 1850, its failure to spread would inevitably condemn it to extinction. In the South, loyalty to slavery and its required expansion became the hallmark of party politics as the region's politicians—Whig, Know-Nothing, and Democrat—competed to demonstrate their loyalty to southern rights. By the mid-1850s, "a party could survive in the South only within the politics of slavery."[1] Even former Unionists sought to defend their region against northern "aggression" by promoting economic and intellectual sectionalism. Convinced that the Republican party intended the destruction of slavery by opposing its constitutional right to exist throughout the United States, southern leaders began to think that separation was inevitable. They felt they would be forced either to leave the Union or to give up slavery and a way of life they increasingly saw as different from that in the North.

## RADICAL EXPRESSIONS OF SECTIONALISM

Influential southern editors began to argue for cultural and economic autonomy. For example, J. D. B. De Bow, editor of an influential commercial journal, encouraged the section to "build her own ships and conduct her own trade with foreign powers; manufacture at home every bale of cotton; diversify her industry, and build roads and railroads; cease the annual migrations to Northern watering places; educate all children at home and encourage a native literature."[2]

More extreme spokesmen sought to strengthen the South's position by encouraging filibustering expeditions against Cuba and Central America, which were regarded as potential slave states. Others worked to reopen the African slave trade. Virginia's George Fitzhugh carried the position of southern nationalists to the conclusion that the slave society of the South was superior to the free society of the North. The latter was marked by "the despotism of skill and capital" and was a "system of antagonism and war." In the North, free laborers were "slaves to capital," without the rights and protections afforded southern slaves, who were fed and clothed. When "the labors of the day were over, [the slaves] were free in mind as well as body; for the master provides food, raiment, house, fuel, and everything else necessary to the physical well-being of himself and family." Slaves, according to Fitzhugh, were happy and contented and "at peace with all around them." The North should therefore adapt southern slavery to whites or give its "slaves without masters" enough property and capital to live on.[3]

In the North a similar feeling of unity was growing. Angered that the South was not satisfied with the concessions it had gained in the Compromise of 1850 and the Kansas-Nebraska Act, many northerners came to accept the abolitionist charge that the insatiable "slaveocracy" intended further expansion and that the planters of the South would not be satisfied until slavery had been "nationalized" and made legal in every state. Southern hostility to homestead legislation ensuring free land after a period of settlement caused many northern mechanics and small farmers to favor the Republican party, at the same time that large numbers of northern Know-Nothings came to see southerners, along with the foreign-born and Catholics, as conspirators intent on subverting the republic. When southern congressmen, assisted by free-trade northern Democrats, lowered the tariff again in 1857, powerful Eastern business interests began to consider the Republican party as their only hope of capturing the federal government for the cause of protection.

Sectional feeling in both the North and the South intensified during the financial panic of 1857. Northern businessmen believed that the depression was the inevitable consequence of southern, low-tariff, Democratic domination of the nation's economic policies. In the South, where the impact of the panic was slight, distress in the northern manufacturing community was taken as additional proof of the superiority of southern economic institutions.

Growing sectionalism gave activists, many of whom were members of evangelical Protestant congregations, the chance to express their moral outrage. In the South such extremists tried to unite their section and to bring an end to the Union. Slavery, they argued, was a positive good. "That slavery is a blessing to the masters," insisted Albert G. Brown of Mississippi, "is shown by simply contrasting a Southern gentleman with a Northern abolitionist. One is courageous, high-bred, and manly. The other is cowardly, low-flung, and sneaking." Lawrence Keitt of South Carolina warned southerners that "the Black Republican party, an amalgam of isms, a base conglomerate of opposing elements tied together by fanaticism" had pledged "its intention to abolitionize every department of the government and use them to the overthrow of slavery." The remedy, argued William Yancey of Alabama, was to form "Committees of Safety" throughout the states of the Deep South. Through such means, he believed, "we shall fire the Southern heart, instruct the Southern mind, give courage to each other, and at the proper moment, by one organized concerted action, we can precipitate the Cotton States into a revolution."[4] Belatedly, southerners encouraged regional printing presses, magazines, and institutions of higher learning. Some even rewrote arithmetic texts with problems requiring future Confederates to calculate the accident rate on northern railroads, along with the profits earned by greedy Yankee traders who adulterated meat and milk.[5]

The North, too, had its propagandists. Typical was Joshua Giddings, who in 1859 completed twenty years of service in the House of Representatives. In an 1855 speech delivered to the House, the fiery, white-haired Ohio congressman described the South as tyrannical. "When human governments overstep the bounds of their constitutional powers to rob men of life or liberty, their enactments are void. . . . The advocates of freedom are not to be intimidated. They know their power. It is the power of truth."[6]

As committed as Giddings were the abolitionists who met in Worcester, Massachusetts, in January 1857. Such men as William Lloyd Garrison, Wendell Phillips, Thomas Higginson, and Samuel May argued for the dissolution of the nation on the basis that there should be no Union with slaveholders. Later, this convention resolved in effect that the sooner the separation took place, the more peaceful it would be; but that peace or war was a secondary consideration, when compared with the freeing of the slaves. Such extreme views were held by only a few northerners, as most of those even with antislavery principles failed to see how separation would advance the freeing of slaves.

## SLAVERY AND THE SUPREME COURT

Always susceptible to contemporary social passions, the Supreme Court of the United States soon became entangled in the issue of slavery in the celebrated case of a Missouri slave. In 1833 Dred Scott was purchased from the estate of a St.

Louis hotel keeper, Peter Blow, by John Emerson, a St. Louis doctor. When Emerson became a surgeon in the federal army, he was ordered first to Rock Island, Illinois, and then to Fort Snelling, in federal territory north of the line 36°30′. He took his slave with him as a servant. Thus Dred Scott resided in a free state and later in a portion of federal territory in which slavery had been prohibited by the Missouri Compromise of 1820. At Fort Snelling Dred Scott married Harriet Robinson, a slave who belonged to an Indian agent. While the court case that bears his name smoldered on, the couple had four children, two of whom at one point became parties to the suit. In 1838 Emerson returned with Scott to Missouri.

In 1846, after Emerson's death, Scott applied to Mrs. Emerson for his freedom; when she refused, Scott brought suit. Exactly how the case got started is unclear. One authority believes that Scott initiated the idea of going to court, and certainly the lawyers who participated must have encouraged him, for he had a solid case.[7] In the past the Missouri courts had held that a master who took his slave to reside in a state or territory without slavery automatically freed him. Arguing that he was free because of residence in a free state and later in free territory, Scott obtained a judgment in his favor. But on appeal this decision was reversed by the state supreme court, which applied the rule that under Missouri law a slave, on returning voluntarily from residence in a free state, resumed his bondage. The appeals court now applied the argument that the laws of other states had no "intrinsic right to be enforced beyond the limits of the state for which they were enacted."[8]

In November 1853, the case entered a new phase. During the course of the earlier litigation, Mrs. Emerson had married Dr. Calvin Chaffee, a Massachusetts politician of antislavery and Know-Nothing affiliations. Under the doctrine of couverture, whereby married women lost their civil rights and became nonbeings in the eyes of the law, she could no longer act in any capacity in regard to her first husband's estate. Instead her brother, John Sanford,[9] whom Emerson had named an executor of his will, became the administrator of the Emerson property, including the slaves. Since Sanford was a resident of New York, Scott's lawyers claimed that the case should now be heard in the federal courts on the ground of diverse citizenship, and they brought an action for trespass against Sanford, with the object of securing Scott's freedom.

Thus the case of *Dred Scott v. Sanford* was heard in the United States circuit court in Missouri. Sanford tried to quash the suit by arguing that Scott, because of his race, was not a citizen of Missouri, and consequently that the circuit court did not have jurisdiction. Unimpressed by this defense, the court took jurisdiction on the basis that access to the federal courts required nothing more than residence in a state, and African Americans were "enough of citizens" to be covered by the diverse citizenship clause, which afforded citizens of each state the privileges and immunities of citizens in other states. But when it came to instructing the jury, the federal circuit judge, R. W. Wells, decided that the law was with Sanford on the issue of Scott's freedom.

As expected, the case was now appealed to the Supreme Court of the United States, where it was argued in February 1856, then reargued during the December term by some of the best-known lawyers in the country, including Montgomery Blair and Reverdy Johnson of Maryland. In keeping with its custom, the Court deliberated on February 15, 1857 as to how to dispose of the case. In this conference the Court agreed to avoid the question of the constitutionality of the Missouri Compromise and to decide the case against Scott on the grounds that, by the law of Missouri as now interpreted in the state supreme court, Scott remained a slave despite previous residence on free soil. Justice Nelson, directed to prepare the opinion of the Court to this effect, produced a short opinion which, following a previous decision by the Supreme Court, concluded that the brush of freedom by virtue of residence in a free state was wiped off on return to a slave state.

It is not certain why the court failed to accept Nelson's limited opinion, which left untouched the two vexing issues of black citizenship and congressional power over slavery in the territories. Some historians have charged that the northern justices who intended to dissent—John McLean of Ohio and Benjamin Curtis of Massachusetts—compelled the proslavery majority of the court to take a position on all aspects of the case. Yet it was the court's majority—the southern judges and especially James Wayne of Georgia—who proposed that Chief Justice Roger B. Taney of Maryland write a broad opinion to cover even the constitutionality of the Missouri Compromise. In fact this majority had never been willing to let the moderate New Yorker Samuel Nelson speak for them. Such a change of judicial tactics may have reflected a desire by the southern-dominated court to settle an issue that some southerners had long insisted the courts must resolve.

Buchanan supported a broad-ranging judicial decision. In his inaugural address in March 1857 the new president had predicted that the nation's highest tribunal would soon settle the question of slavery in the territories. In an extraordinary act of executive interference, Buchanan had also put pressure on his friend and political ally Justice Robert Grier of Pennsylvania to join with the southern judges.[10] If the president, who had always wanted to be a member of the Supreme Court, had not written to Grier, the latter might not have added a sixth vote, and a northern one at that, to those of the five southern judges. In turn, without the concurrence of a northerner, the southern judges might not have issued such an expansive decision.[11]

On March 6, two days after the inauguration, each of the nine justices issued a separate opinion. This, in itself, was not remarkable, for such diversity of views was characteristic of the Taney court. Two important questions were "decided," or rather announced as decided by the majority of the Court: first, that a Negro "whose ancestors were . . . sold as slaves" could not become a member of the political community created by the Constitution or be entitled to the rights of federal citizenship; second, that the Missouri Compromise, by prohibiting slavery in a part of national territory, was unconstitutional. It is because of these two fundamental points that the decision possesses historical importance.

In developing an argument to support these points, Taney declared that Negroes were not citizens of the several states at the time of the adoption of the Constitution and that the language of the Declaration of Independence did not embrace them as part of the "people" of the United States. He then proceeded:

> [That unfortunate race] had for more than a century before been regarded as beings of an inferior order, and altogether unfit to associate with the white race, either in social or political relations; and so far inferior, that they had no rights which the white man was bound to respect; and that the negro might justly and lawfully be reduced to slavery for his benefit. . . . This opinion was at that time . . . universal in the civilized portion of the white race.[12]

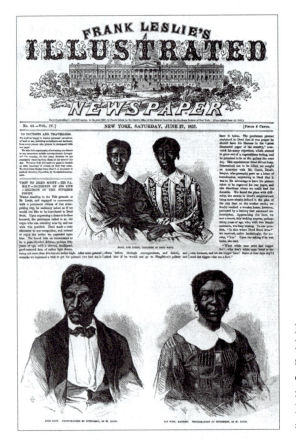

In 1857, Chief Justice Roger B. Taney spoke for the majority in the *Dred Scott* case, ruling that blacks, even free blacks, were not citizens. Depicted here are Dred Scott and his wife, Harriet.

In his argument Taney denied federal citizenship to all African Americans, not just those of slave ancestry. By treating emancipation "as legally meaningless," the chief justice mixed "free blacks with slaves in one legal category based on race."[13]

At this time there was no constitutional definition of federal citizenship, but the Constitution in Article IV, Section 2 provided that the "Citizens of each State shall be entitled to all Privileges and Immunities of Citizens in the several States." Taney, however, drew a distinction between "the citizenship which a State may confer within its own limits, and the rights of citizenship as a member of the Union." A man might be a citizen of a state, he declared, but it did "not by any means follow . . . that he must be a citizen of the United States." Though the general rule was that federal citizenship resulted from state citizenship, there was a limit to this rule, because "no State can . . . introduce a new member into the political community created by the Constitution of the United States. . . . It cannot introduce any person, or description of persons, who were not intended to be embraced in this new political family, which the Constitution brought into existence, but were intended to be excluded from it." He therefore concluded that "Dred Scott was not a citizen of Missouri within the meaning of the Constitution of the United States, and not entitled as such to sue in its courts." Consequently, the circuit court had no jurisdiction in the case.[14]

Taney next addressed the constitutional validity of the Missouri Compromise. Stressing that slaves were property and invoking the Fifth Amendment, which prohibits Congress from taking property without "due process of law," Taney declared that the "only power conferred" on Congress by the Constitution in the matter of slavery in the territories was "the power coupled with the duty of guarding and protecting the owner in his rights."[15] The ban on slavery north of 36°30', he declared, was not "warranted" by the Constitution and was therefore void.

Justices Campbell, Catron, Daniel, Grier, and Wayne concurred, although each arrived at his conclusions by a different reasoning process. Nor did they all agree with the chief justice's argument on every point. The opinion of Justice Nelson has special historical significance because it contains the original opinion of the Court before the case was reconsidered. Nelson avoided both the question of black citizenship and that of congressional power over slavery in the territories. He held that the case was controlled by Missouri law, and that despite previous residence in regions where slavery did not exist, Scott resumed his status as a slave on his return to Missouri.

The two dissenting opinions were those of Justices McLean and Curtis. Curtis's opinion was important because it was widely circulated in the North and was applauded by antislavery men and women. Curtis showed that before the adoption of the Constitution, free Negroes were state citizens in New Hampshire, Massachusetts, New Jersey, New York, and North Carolina. He found "nothing in the constitution which . . . deprives [them] of their citizenship." In view of the reciprocal citizenship clause, he therefore concluded that free Negroes were also citizens of the United States. In his opinion the federal circuit court therefore had jurisdiction.

Avoiding the inconsistency of Taney and the majority, who argued that the court had no jurisdiction because Dred Scott was black and then proceeded to take jurisdiction, Curtis examined the case on its merits. Curtis pointed out that, in the language of the Constitution, Congress is expressly granted the power to "make all needful Rules and Regulations respecting the Territory . . . belonging to the United States"; that the Constitution makes no exception to this power in the matter of slavery; that judicial construction for over fifty years would forbid such an exception; and that "it would . . . violate every sound rule of interpretation to force that exception into the Constitution upon the strength of abstract political reasoning."

In Republican and antislavery circles the Taney decision instantly became a lightning rod for antisouthern sentiment and was denounced as a "new and atrocious doctrine," a "deliberate iniquity," a "willful perversion," "a dictum prescribed by the stump to the Bench," and "the greatest crime in the judicial annals of the Republic." Defiant meetings of northern free blacks whose citizenship had been denied by Taney protested the decision. Frederick Douglass called it the "judicial incarnation of wolfishness." Ironically, the decision had no effect on its original subject: three weeks after the announcement, Dred Scott was freed by his new owner in Missouri.

On the other hand, some influential newspapers in the North defended the decision, while in the South it was everywhere accepted as the correct interpretation. Today it is clear that Taney and his southern colleagues were the radicals. They had invalidated a major piece of federal legislation, at the same time that they denied Congress a power it had long exercised. Whatever they intended, the *Dred Scott* decision strengthened Republican claims that southerners were conspiring to nationalize slavery, even as the decision held that the Republican party's policy to stop slavery expansion was unconstitutional.[16]

Two years later, the Taney court made another controversial ruling. After the passage of the Fugitive Slave Act of 1850, some northern states had continued to deny the use of their jails for the detention of fugitive slaves. A few still extended trial by jury to blacks claimed as slaves and permitted habeas corpus writs to be issued by state authority for their release.[17] In Wisconsin, Sherman Booth, an abolitionist editor who had been convicted in federal court of violating the Fugitive Slave Act by assisting the flight of a slave, was later freed by the state supreme court. On appeal the U.S. Supreme Court, with Taney again writing for the majority, denied the right of state courts to interfere in federal cases. Booth was then imprisoned, but the Wisconsin legislature responded by passing a resolution attempting to nullify the Taney decision.

## KANSAS

Meanwhile the crisis in Kansas continued to divide northerners and southerners. Both sides offered plans to move the territory into the Union as a state, with the proslavery faction supported by the national administration under Pierce and Buchanan. In July 1856 the House of Representatives considered a bill to admit Kansas under a free-state constitution that had been adopted at Topeka in October 1855, and "ratified" in a one-sided antislavery election. This bill passed the House, but it was voted down in the Senate. In the territory, the free-state faction had elected an assembly which functioned as a "provisional" state legislature, choosing U.S. senators and fulfilling other official functions. But the failure of the movement to have Kansas admitted under the Topeka constitution left this antislavery legislature stranded as a spurious government. Lacking a single government considered legitimate by all residents, Kansas was now overrun by marauders and criminals who subjected the inhabitants to repeated acts of violence.

In these circumstances President Pierce, who had attributed the troubles in Kansas to the "spirit of revolutionary attack on the domestic institutions of the South," removed Governor Shannon and appointed John Geary of Pennsylvania. Geary's charge was to establish order with the assistance of federal troops, and the new governor acted impartially to suppress lawlessness. At the same time the president disclaimed any intention of interfering with elections, declaring that the people were "all-sufficient guardians of their own rights" and that he had no power over local elections.

By the end of the year Governor Geary had so successfully restored order that in his annual message of December 2, 1856, Pierce expressed optimism about the prospects for peace in Kansas. Through the "wisdom and energy" of Governor Geary and the "prudence, firmness, and vigilance of the military officers on duty," said the president, "tranquillity [had] been restored without one drop of blood having been shed . . . by the forces of the United States."[18] Meanwhile Republican spokesmen were denouncing Pierce for what they regarded as proslavery interference. In March 1857, Robert J. Walker, a northern-born former Mississippi senator and cabinet officer under Polk, replaced Geary as Kansas governor.

The struggle for Kansas statehood intensified with the controversy over another constitution. After a census that omitted fifteen of the thirty-four counties of the state, a constitutional convention was chosen by less than a fourth of those listed as entitled to vote. Gerrymandered districts had given the proslavery forces such an unfair advantage that free-state supporters refused to participate. Such disagreements were sharpened by inadequate definitions of who the legal voters were.[19]

Meeting at Lecompton, the convention so chosen (or rather a portion of it, for many of the delegates did not attend) adopted a proslavery constitution that

declared that the "right of property is . . . higher than any constitutional sanction, and the right of the owner of a slave . . . is . . . as inviolable as the right of
the owner of any property whatever." After a struggle within the convention, it
was decided not to submit the entire constitution to a popular vote as was customary and as Walker had stipulated must be done before he would accept the
governorship. Instead, male residents were permitted to vote for the "constitution with slavery" or for the "constitution with no slavery." In case of the latter
vote, slavery was to exist "no longer" in the state "except that the right of property in slaves now in this Territory shall in no measure be interfered with."

This provision meant that voters faced a choice between the constitution as
written, which protected slavery, or the constitution with a provision disallowing
more slaves from coming into the territory. Antislavery proponents therefore had
no way of voting against slavery. Nor was it possible to consider other aspects of
the document, such as provisions excluding free Negroes from the state and as-
signing more than sixteen and a half million acres of land, approximately one-
fifth of the territory, for the support of schools and favored railroad projects.[20]

When the vote was taken in December 1857, with the usual irregularities and
frauds characteristic of Kansas elections in the fifties, six thousand voters cast ballots for the "constitution with slavery"; fewer than six hundred for the constitution "with no slavery." In a voting population of sixteen thousand, fewer than
seven thousand had voted and those who abstained included not only free-state
men but also those who opposed the constitution. In a second referendum called
by the territorial legislature in January 1858, which free state men now controlled,
over ten thousand Kansans rejected the entire constitution; only 138 voted for the
constitution with slavery and 24 for the constitution without slavery.

Though the Lecompton constitution was clearly a fraud, President Buchanan
urged Congress to admit the state. He defended the action of this Lecompton
convention on the grounds that had the convention submitted the whole constitution to the people, the free-state men, whom he denounced as adherents of a
rebellious organization, would "doubtless have voted against it . . . not upon a
consideration of [its] merits . . . but simply because they have ever resisted the
authority of the government authorized by Congress . . ." Citing the *Dred Scott*
decision, the president declared that "Kansas is . . . at this moment as much a
slave State as Georgia or South Carolina." Speedy admission of Kansas, he said,
would "restore peace and quiet to the whole country," whereas its rejection would
be "keenly felt" by the residents of those states where slavery was recognized
under the Constitution of the United States.[21]

In the congressional struggle over admitting Kansas, Stephen Douglas, recognizing that this violation of popular sovereignty would wreck the Democratic
party in the North, opposed the administration and broke with proslavery
Buchanan Democrats. There was even talk of his joining the Republicans. Like
other opponents of the referendum, the Illinois Democrat noted that voters had

no means to reject the constitution outright and that the option of voting for the constitution without slavery actually protected slave property in the territory.

Finally, the bill to admit Kansas under the Lecompton constitution passed the Senate by a vote of 33 to 25, with Douglas in the minority with most Republicans. Ominously, southerners in Congress voted in its favor nearly unanimously, as they responded to slogans of "Lecompton or Disunion." But the border slave states were divided.

Since it was known that the bill could not pass the House, a compromise was struck in a measure known as the "English bill," named after William English, an anti-Lecompton Democratic representative from Indiana. English's proposal received the support of both houses and became law on May 4, 1858. Under this act the Lecompton constitution was to be resubmitted as a whole to the people of Kansas, in connection with a federal land grant that would become available if the constitution were adopted. Republicans denounced the measure as a bribe, referring to "the English swindle." Henry Wilson of Massachusetts called it "a conglomeration of bribes, of penalties, and of meditated fraud."[22] It did, however, provide for a popular vote on the constitution, and it did not contain an exceptionally large offer of land but rather a grant identical to that offered to Minnesota the year before and roughly similar to those given to several states. On August 2, 1858, the popular vote was taken as prescribed in the English bill, and the constitution was decisively rejected by a vote of 11,300 to 1,788. Kansas had played its part in the sectionalization of the country. In 1861, with southern representatives no longer in Washington, Congress accepted Kansas as a free state without controversy.

## THE LINCOLN-DOUGLAS DEBATE

Amid this jarring sectionalism a note was struck in Illinois that resonated through the coming years. "A house divided against itself cannot stand. I believe this government cannot endure, permanently half slave and half free. . . . It will become all one thing or all the other."[23] The occasion for these memorable words, which echoed the fears of many northerners about the expansion of slavery, was the meeting of the Republican state convention in Springfield on June 16, 1858. The speaker was Abraham Lincoln, whom the convention chose as its candidate for the United States Senate. The new leader, now entering on a hard-fought campaign with Douglas, was the product of pioneer Kentucky. His ancestors included simple farmers in Virginia, as well as squires and community leaders in Pennsylvania and Massachusetts. Recent generations of Lincolns and Hankses (his mother's birth name) had lived close to the soil in the backwoods without taking root in any community. Still, Abraham Lincoln "belonged to the 7th generation of a family with competent means, a reputation for integrity and a modest record of public service."[24]

To his Illinois neighbors, Lincoln was no genius but a familiar and effective politician. Known as a rail-splitter, flatboatman, storekeeper, country postmaster, surveyor, and captain in the Black Hawk War, he had come up through the ranks as a politician. He had served four terms in the state legislature and one in Congress. As a practicing lawyer, he had traveled from county seat to county seat, mingling with the people on court days, amusing them with homespun stories and exciting them with effective political speeches.

Nor had he moved only among the common people. He had married into the Todds, an important Whig family of the Kentucky aristocracy; he had risen to the top of the legal profession in his state. After emerging as a prominent Illinois Whig, he had now taken his place as an outstanding Republican leader. With his homely, rugged face, his tall, awkward frame, his reputation for honesty, and his mental tenacity combined with his crusading zeal, his Jeffersonian instincts, and his mastery of terse, epigrammatic English, he stood out in 1858 as a vigorous spokesman for the new Republican party and its principle of preventing the spread of slavery.

After several years of little political activity, Lincoln had returned to politics in 1854, attacking what he called "the wrong and injustice of the repeal of the Missouri Compromise and the extension of slavery into free territory."[25] He had become increasingly prominent after his denunciation of Douglas's concept of popular sovereignty. In 1856, the Republicans at their national convention in Philadelphia had given him 110 votes for the vice-presidential nomination. Now, as a candidate for the United States Senate in an era when senators were still chosen by state legislatures, he gained prominence by challenging the well-known Douglas to a series of joint debates at a time when Douglas was damaged by his party's split between his own followers and the powerful Buchanan faction. Actually, Lincoln had been publicly debating Douglas for years, but something in this formal series of encounters seized the imagination of the country.

Beginning in Ottawa on August 21, 1858, the debates continued at Freeport, Jonesboro, Charleston, Galesburg, and Quincy, closing at Alton on October 15. During this period of American history debates between contenders for office were a common form of campaigning throughout the United States. On this occasion the importance of the issues, the prestige of the contestants, and the intellectual power with which they addressed the concerns of the day especially regarding the expansion of slavery focused attention on the Lincoln-Douglas debates.

Douglas taunted Lincoln for his seemingly radical "house divided" declaration, accused him of promoting a war between sections, ridiculed the idea of uniformity in domestic institutions, and sneered at "black Republicans" whom he accused of demanding racial equality. Interspersed with his attack on Lincoln, Douglas expounded his own doctrine of letting the people decide the slavery question. He scored Lincoln and his followers for seeking to abolitionize the country and for defying the Supreme Court after the *Dred Scott* decision.

In 1858, Abraham Lincoln and Stephen A. Douglas, both vying for the Senate, engaged in a series of debates that centered around the extension of slavery into the territories. These debates made Lincoln a national figure and gave the Republican party a new prospect for the presidency.

He bitterly denounced the alliance he suspected between the Republicans and the Buchanan Democrats, and he accused his own party of trying to defeat him with the aid of federal patronage because he had opposed the Lecompton constitution. "What do you Republicans think," Douglas asked, "of a political organization that will try to make an unholy . . . combination with its professed foes to beat a man merely because he has done right? . . . You know that the axe of decapitation is suspended over every man in office in Illinois, and the terror of proscription is threatened every Democrat by the present administration unless he supports the Republican ticket in preference to my Democratic associates and myself."[26] Throughout the debates Douglas emphasized his role as a statesman who, in this moment of crisis, had risen above partisanship. On the other hand Lincoln, according to Douglas, had varied his message to suit the slavery preferences of his audience.[27]

In his response to Douglas's charge that he favored the amalgamation of the races, Lincoln revealed the attitudes toward African Americans that he shared with most white Americans, North and South. Though he denounced the *Dred Scott* decision for its doctrine that a black could not be a citizen, he said, "I am not in favor of negro citizenship."[28] Similarly, he disclaimed the doctrine of social equality for the races; he did not advocate the repeal of the fugitive slave law; and he qualified his "house divided" declaration by explaining that it contained no threat of violence or sectional strife. And he charged the Democrats with a conspiracy to spread slavery.

At the same time the sincerity of his hostility to slavery shone through his rhetoric. Lincoln insisted that the right of self-government did not extend to the enslavement of others. "No man is good enough to govern another without that other's consent. I say this is the leading principle—the sheet anchor of American republicanism." And Lincoln shaped disagreements over slavery into partisan issues. As he said:

> The difference between the Republican and the Democratic parties . . . [in] this contest is, that the former consider slavery a moral, social and political wrong, while the latter do not consider it either a moral, social or political wrong . . . The Republican party . . . hold that this government was instituted to secure the blessings of freedom, and that slavery is an unqualified evil to the negro, to the white man, to the soil, and to the State. Regarding it an evil, they will not molest it in the States where it exists . . . but they will use every constitutional method to prevent the evil from becoming larger. . . . They will, if possible, place it where the public mind shall rest in the belief that it is in the course of ultimate peaceable extinction, in God's own good time.[29]

Although Lincoln dwelled at length on the moral wrong of slavery, his most important political position was his support for the exclusion of slavery from the territories—an issue that had become the central public issue of the late 1850s— and his insistence that the Democrats had conspired to spread it. He favored the emancipation of slaves in the District of Columbia, although in his view freedom should be accomplished gradually and with compensation to slave owners after a referendum. He held that the *Dred Scott* decision, in denying to Congress the power to exclude slavery from the territories, was wrong and would be reversed. For all his moderation and tolerance, Lincoln still managed to inject enough fiery denunciation into his speeches to inspire the antislavery wing of his party.

Lincoln's shrewd question to Douglas at Freeport and Douglas's answer were destined to have important consequences. "Can the people of a United States Territory," asked Lincoln, "in any lawful way . . . exclude slavery from their limits prior to the formation of a state constitution?" If Douglas followed the cue of the Supreme Court and answered *No*, he would disappoint many voters in his own state and in the North. Should he answer *Yes*, he would offend his prosouthern supporters in southern Illinois and would alienate the slaveholding South. The chance that Douglas would lose the presidency in 1860 with an answer that would gain the senatorship in 1858 may not have been in Lincoln's mind. He was merely pursuing his twofold purpose, everywhere evident in the debates, of exposing the inconsistency between the *Dred Scott* doctrine and the principle of "popular sovereignty," and of widening the split between the Douglas and Buchanan wings of the Democratic party.[30]

Douglas replied:

> I answered emphatically . . . that in my opinion the people of a Territory can by lawful means exclude slavery before it comes in as a state . . . Whatever the Supreme Court

may hereafter decide as to the abstract question of whether slavery may go in under the Constitution or not, the people of a Territory have the lawful means to admit it or exclude it as they please, for the reason that slavery cannot exist a day or an hour anywhere unless supported by local police regulations.... Those local and police regulations can only be established by the local legislature. If the people of the Territory are opposed to slavery they will elect members to the legislature who will adopt unfriendly legislation to it. If they are for it, they will adopt the legislative measures friendly to slavery.[31]

The "Little Giant" had voiced this opinion within months of the *Dred Scott* decision, but after his opposition to the Lecompton constitution, its repetition at Freeport made him obnoxious to southern Democrats. Now southerners began to argue that if territories could prevent the extension of slavery simply by declining to adopt a slave code, which was what Douglas's Freeport Doctrine amounted to, then it was the obligation of the federal government to protect the slave property of southerners by enacting a national slave code.

As to the outcome of the election in Illinois, it ended in a paradox not uncommon in American politics: Lincoln's party carried the legislative districts containing a larger population than those carried by the Democrats, but because of an inequitable apportionment Douglas gained a majority of the delegates in the legislature, insuring his election. Two aspects of the debates had national significance: Douglas's position was so advertised and clarified as to intensify the rift in the Democratic party, and the Republicans found a new leader in Abraham Lincoln, who was soon being mentioned for the presidency.

## JOHN BROWN'S RAID

A year after an inflammatory speech by the New York senator William Seward predicting an "irrepressible" conflict between two societies based on opposing systems of free and slave labor, John Brown, still remembered for the Pottawatomie massacre, acted on what he considered the moral necessity of the times. Scorning the "milk-and-water" abolitionists of the parlor variety, John Brown believed that "what is needed is action—action!" Long before he moved to Kansas, he had resolved to combat slavery by any means necessary, for he considered words and even political action against slavery ineffective. Somehow his erratic, compelling personality attracted men of culture and education such as Gerrit Smith, Theodore Parker, Samuel Howe, Thomas Higginson, and other prominent northerners. Tireless in his efforts, Brown obtained money and arms from respectable antislavery sources. He established himself in Canada with a band of twelve whites and thirty-four blacks, held a "Convention," drew up a document labeled a "provisional Constitution and Ordinances for the People of the United States," and concocted a daring plan of emancipation.

His scheme was to capture the federal arsenal at Harpers Ferry and to arm slaves who would, as he told Frederick Douglass, swarm to his forces after the raid. Then he would establish this guerilla band in the mountains and defeat any military force, whether state, militia, or federal troops. He intended to take slaveholders as hostages and to force southern states to adopt emancipation. Later he intended to organize free blacks into a government, offering African Americans vocational and academic instruction. Having assembled his miniature army on a Maryland farm across from Harpers Ferry, he waited and prepared.

It was from this place that, on the night of October 16, 1859, he led his band of eighteen followers, including three of his own sons and five African Americans, in an assault on Harpers Ferry. He succeeded in capturing the federal arsenal and armory and seizing some of the citizens of the town and surrounding countryside as hostages. But there was no response on the part of Virginia slaves, who were unaware of Brown's daring effort to emancipate them. His small band was soon attacked by local citizens, who rallied to defend themselves against what neighbors called "insurrection" and "slaves raping and butchering in the streets."[32] Strengthened by his own impending sense of martyrdom, Brown had not designated an escape route. Refusing to retreat to the mountains while the chance to do so remained, Brown defended himself from the arsenal, where his hopeless little force was routed by United States marines under Colonel Robert E. Lee. Ten of his followers were killed, including two of his sons. Brown himself was wounded and captured.

Reaction throughout the country revealed the deep divisions among Americans. Many northern Democrats condemned the raid. They demanded, and got, a congressional investigation of the Brown affair after documents were found linking Brown to various New England abolitionists such as Thomas Higginson and Theodore Parker. Many Americans in the North agreed with the *New York Herald* that Brown was a criminal and a fanatic. Others in the North compared Brown with Christ and considered him a saint and hero. Contempt for Virginia as an inferior civilization became the theme of antislavery speeches and editorials. Virginia, said Wendell Phillips, "is no government . . . She is a pirate ship, and John Brown sails the sea a Lord High Admiral of the Almighty with his commission to sink every pirate he meets on God's ocean of the nineteenth century."[33]

Amid this excitement, Brown and his conspirators were brought to trial. On October 31, the jury found him guilty of treason against the state of Virginia, inciting slave rebellion, and murder. For these crimes he was hanged at Charles Town on December 2, 1859. Six of his followers suffered a similar fate later. But before he died, Brown impressed those who interviewed him with his courage and zealous commitment to the cause of black freedom. As he informed the court: "If it is deemed necessary that I should forfeit my life for the furtherance of the ends of justice and mingle my blood further with the blood of my children and with the blood of millions in this slave country whose rights are disregarded by wicked, cruel, and unjust enactments, I say let it be done."[34]

John Brown was injured during the raid on Harpers Ferry, but rose from his gurney to testify during his trial. He was convicted and hanged. This inspired Ralph Waldo Emerson to say that Brown would "make the gallows as glorious as the cross." Here, in a contemporary drawing, he insists on standing to argue his case.

Brown's raid heightened secession sentiment in the South. Although his effort presented no realistic threat, rumors magnified the incident, reinforcing the southern fear that northerners intended to free slaves, by force if necessary. Southerners were also reminded of earlier slave rebellions in Santo Domingo. There seemed a fateful reluctance in the South to accept as representative northern opinion which condemned the outrage. Instead, the attack was identified with the abolitionists who praised Brown, and responsibility was laid at the door of the Republicans. Even Stephen Douglas declared that "the Harpers Ferry crime was the . . . logical inevitable result of the doctrines . . . of the Republican party."[35]

"John Brown's body" became a symbol and a shibboleth. In the superficial sense of a northern nation going to war in the spirit of Brown's fanaticism, the slogan has little meaning. If, however, Americans ponder those elements of misunderstanding between North and South that became associated with Brown's strangely inspired crime and they remember Brown's intentions, the slogan becomes a harbinger of conflict to come and an appropriate symbol of a civil war that freed the slaves.

## The Presidential Contest of 1860

By 1860 a struggle loomed not only between but also within the nation's political parties. The disruptive power of sectionalism was proving stronger than the nationalizing force of political attachments recently disturbed by the party realignment of the 1850s. The Republicans, one of the rare sectional parties in American history, had absorbed the Know-Nothings, thereby solidifying their position in the North. Meanwhile the Democrats, the oldest of all American political organizations, were threatened by internal dissension. Yet only a united "Democracy" could command the loyalty of both northerners and southerners.

Remembering the recent turmoil in Kansas and Virginia, many southerners held only a qualified devotion to the Union. Southern Democrats were less interested in conciliation than in a clear-cut statement of party principles protecting slavery. In many cases these southern Democrats were reacting to the growing power of the Republicans. "As secessionists read the political world now unfolding, Republican rule would lead to an unacceptably restrictive society with a dominant, snooping, interfering government forcing conformity to a narrow set of behavioral norms."[36] In this view the party they labeled as "Black" Republicans would soon be doing the unthinkable—interfering with slavery in the states.

In April 1860, a struggle among Democrats erupted in that party's nominating convention, held in Charleston, South Carolina, a city overheated by secessionist passions and the weather. South Carolina, which had lacked a two-party system to dampen its proslavery demagoguery since the nullification crisis of the 1830s, was an especially unfortunate place for the Democrats to meet. At first the internal battle involved the precise phrasing of the party platform. Two platforms—those of Alabama's William Yancey and Illinois' Douglas—were submitted. The former asserted that the federal government must protect slavery in the territories; the latter reaffirmed the Cincinnati platform of 1856, evaded the issue of slavery in the territories, and declared that the party would abide by the decisions of the Supreme Court.

When the convention debated the reports from the divided platform committee, Yancey, who believed that the election of a Republican president merited secession, delivered an impassioned speech in which he attributed the existing discord to the North's invasion of southern rights. Acting on instructions from the Alabama state convention, he now presented an ultimatum: either the platform of the Lower South (approved by the majority of the platform committee) must be accepted or the delegates from the Lower South would withdraw. But Douglas and his followers, who constituted a majority of the delegates, would not accept any platform inconsistent with popular sovereignty. Inspired by Yancey, the Alabama delegation stalked from the hall, followed by most delegates from the cotton states. Now the convention faced the choice of a nominee, even more crucial than that of the platform. According to one delegate, "The struggle over the platform was a mere sham; the real contest was about the candidate. Douglas out of the way, the platform was of no consequence to the central managers who combined for his destruction."[37]

The disrupted convention, unable to choose a candidate in a process that required nomination by two-thirds of the delegates, adjourned to meet in Baltimore. There in June 1860 the secessionists reappeared, whereupon a fierce contest ensued over the seating of rival delegations. When the Douglas supporters won, another secession of southerners occurred, after which the remaining delegates nominated Douglas for the presidency and Senator Benjamin Fitzpatrick of Alabama for the vice presidency. When Fitzpatrick declined, the nomination was conferred upon a Georgia moderate, Herschel Johnson. Subsequently conventions of southern "bolters" were held in Baltimore and in Richmond. In both cities southern Democrats nominated John Breckinridge of Kentucky for president and Joseph Lane of Oregon for vice president. Southerners favoring secession exulted over the party split. According to the Charleston *Mercury*, "the last party pretending to be a national party is broken up . . . and the antagonism of the two sections has nothing to arrest its fierce collisions."[38]

In the weeks between the Charleston and Baltimore conventions, the issues causing the division of the Democratic party led to bitter debate in the United States Senate between Jefferson Davis and Stephen Douglas. The debate focused on resolutions opposing popular sovereignty and supporting a federal slave code and states' rights that Davis had introduced in February 1860. Both senators tried to support their position with logic, history, the "laws of nature," legal citations, and personal attacks. Often joined by colleagues, Douglas and Davis confronted basic legal, constitutional, and party concerns. In so doing, they summarized the sectional differences that would soon lead to the South's secession: Can the people of a territory decide for or against slavery, or do they first become invested with this power only when forming a state constitution? What is the meaning of territorial sovereignty? Of sovereignty in general? Was the Ordinance of 1787 confirmed by the Constitution? What was the meaning and result of the action taken at Charleston? Who caused the division of the Democratic party? Why cannot Mississippi and Alabama, which voted for Buchanan in 1856, support another candidate on the same platform in 1860? Eventually the Senate affirmed the *Dred Scott* decision by voting that neither Congress nor a territorial legislature could prohibit slavery in the territories, the latter considered the "common possession" of all the states.[39]

With high hopes as a result of its strong showing in the North in 1856, the Republican party had a front runner for the nomination in William Seward of New York. The party also had several other contenders, of whom Salmon P. Chase was the best known. But Chase's antislavery zeal placed him at odds with Republican sentiment in 1860. He also lacked astute managers, and even in his home state of Ohio he failed to receive the full support of the state delegation. Edward Bates of Missouri was conservative on the slavery question and enjoyed the support of several powerful party leaders, including Horace Greeley and Maryland's influential Blair family of publishers and politicians. If nominated, Bates would presumably appeal to voters in the border states. Yet he was weakened by his approval of Know-Nothing principles, and in an election in which the German-American vote would be a factor, his nativism was a handicap. Simon Cameron of Pennsylvania commanded little more than first-ballot, favorite-son status. Abraham Lincoln's name was frequently mentioned by midwesterners, though such regional backing did not often lead to winning the nomination. Until the opening of the convention in May Lincoln's managers could not count on more than the Illinois delegation, while at this stage Chase, Bates, and Cameron each had more than twice as many delegates as Lincoln.

Seward's fate presented the familiar spectacle of an outstanding leader whose long career made him controversial—in a political system and at a time when mediocre men without records to attack, such as Frémont and Fillmore, had emerged as necessary solvents in the volatile political climate. A prominent Whig and Republican, Seward had been in public life for over twenty years.[40] He had served as governor of New York and as a United States senator; he had been more the acknowledged leader of the Republican party than its first presidential candidate, Frémont; his antislavery principles were consistent. In addition, he had an able manager in Thurlow Weed, and he was acceptable to some ethnic groups because of his tolerance toward Catholics and his opposition to nativism. Yet fatally for his chances, he was associated with the "higher law" doctrine and the concept of an "irrepressible conflict," the former based on the idea that the morality of abolitionism superseded the evils of even a constitutionally established slavery and the latter the view that a free society was incompatible with a slave one.

Meanwhile, Lincoln's star had been rising. The debate with Douglas had given him a national reputation on which he capitalized by giving speeches in Ohio, Indiana, Illinois, Iowa, Wisconsin, and Kansas. Lincoln took a step toward the presidency by delivering an important speech before a large audience at New York's Cooper Union in February 1860. Defining the terms that the new party should offer to the country, he repudiated John Brown's raid and spoke of sectional conciliation. "It is exceedingly desirable," said he, "that all parts of this great Confederacy shall be at peace. . . . Let us Republicans do our part to have it so. Even though much provoked, let us do nothing through passion and ill temper. Even though the southern people will not so much as listen to us, let us calmly consider their demands, and yield to them if, in our deliberate view of our duty, we possibly can. Judging by all they say and do . . . let us determine . . . what will satisfy them."[41]

In the past, Lincoln's attitude toward the German-Americans had been friendly. To many of them, as to others, he was the second choice if Seward's campaign stalled. He was better able than any other candidate to muster the support of such diverse elements as the old-line Whigs and the crusading abolitionists. The abolitionists recalled Lincoln's comment in 1859 that "the Republican principle [is] the profound central point that slavery is wrong and ought to be dealt with as a wrong."[42] Certainly Lincoln gained from the atmosphere and surroundings of the Chicago convention, where the "wigwam," a huge structure constructed for the convention's use, seemed to pulse with the spirit of the prairie West and where resounding Lincoln "yawps" matched the noise of Seward's boosters.

On the first ballot Seward led with 173½ votes to Lincoln's 102, Chase's 49, Cameron's 50½, and Bates's 48. On the second ballot Lincoln gained when the large delegations from Pennsylvania and Ohio gave him support. Now "the field" against Seward was centering on Lincoln. When on the third ballot the transfer of four Ohio votes gave him the necessary majority for nomination, one delegation after another changed their votes to the Railsplitter.

Although there were differences among the Republicans, they were generally avoided during the convention. Instead the party reaffirmed the doctrine of equality in the Declaration of Independence without defining it in terms of black citizenship. By no means as far reaching as the party's program in 1856, the platform deplored "the threats of disunion" made by Democrats; recognized the power of each state to control its own domestic institutions; denounced Buchanan and the Lecompton constitution; and reaffirmed the Wilmot Proviso, which denied the authority of Congress, territorial legislatures, and any other powers, to legalize slavery in the territories. The delegates opposed efforts to reopen the African slave trade, affirmed the principle of a protective tariff, and pledged support for such measures as a homestead law, internal improvements, a railroad to the Pacific, and "the full and efficient protection of the rights of citizens, whether native or naturalized." This economic program was based on the party's commitment to "the ethic of free labor," that is, a set of ideals affirming the dignity of labor, the importance of a dynamic expanding capitalist society, and the expectation of social mobility within this society.[43] With just enough emphasis on the slavery issue, the Republicans were strongly supported by eastern business interests, which were generally not abolitionist but which were now weaning the Northwest and the Middle Atlantic states away from their southern alliance.

A fourth party also entered the 1860 presidential campaign. Elements of the former American or Know-Nothing party, now revived as the Constitutional Union party, meeting in convention in Baltimore, took an evasive, middle-of-the-road course. Ignoring the slavery issue and spurning the disruptive force of party platforms, it appealed to a distracted country on the sole issue of the Constitution, the Union, and the laws. Led by the conservative candidates John Bell of Tennessee and Edward Everett of Massachusetts, the party hoped to obtain both old-line Whig and Democratic support. Its supposed strength was in

This campaign banner for the election of 1860 shows John
Bell and Edward Everett standing beside the Constitution.
The goal of their party, the Constitutional Union party,
was the preservation of the Union.

the border states where Lincoln's support was negligible and where both Breck-inridge and Douglas were generally rejected as being too partisan.

The subsequent four-way contest evolved into two contests: that between Douglas and Lincoln in the free states and that among Douglas, Bell, and Breck-inridge in the slave states, with Lincoln not even on the ballot in the Lower South. Each candidate proclaimed devotion to the Union. "The Federal Union must be preserved," said Douglas. "The Constitution and the equality of the States . . ." said Breckinridge, "are symbols of everlasting union. Let these be the rallying cries." To Lincoln the "perpetual union" was fundamental; to Bell it was virtually the only issue.[44]

As the campaign proceeded, the factional war between the two wings of the Democratic party grew bitter. Douglas accused southern disunionists of wanting Lincoln's election so that it might be used as a signal for secession. "I do not believe that every Breckinridge man is a disunionist," he declared, "but I do believe that every disunionist in America is a Breckinridge man."[45] As for Lincoln, he avoided speeches during the campaign, allowing his cause to be advanced by a well-filled party chest (the national party raised over sixty thousand dollars), by efficient managers and enthusiastic campaigners, and by vociferous parades and demonstrations reminiscent of the Whig campaign for Harrison in 1840.

Nor was the slavery issue much emphasized by the Republicans. Instead they endorsed the popular causes of free land and American citizenship for the Germans; promised homesteads to farmers; urged protection for American industry in the manufacturing regions of the East; and held out alluring prospects of commercial expansion as the result of Lincoln's election. As one Republican leader explained, "the Republicans stand before the country, not only as the antislavery party, but emphatically as the party of free labor."[46]

Although southerners feared the worst from Lincoln, he made no threats against the region or slavery. But he also made no public effort to reassure them. In confidential letters he explained that his conservative opinions had often been stated, that persons honestly seeking his views would have no trouble in learning them, that "bad men . . . North and South" would misinterpret any new expres-

This political cartoon shows Dred Scott (in the center) and the candidates in the election of 1860. Pictured clockwise from the upper left are John C. Breckinridge with President James Buchanan, Abraham Lincoln with a black woman, John Bell with a "real" Native American, and Stephen A. Douglas dancing with a "squatter sovereign."

sion and that any reiteration of his policies would do no good.[47] Consequently the perception of Lincoln as an abolitionist continued in a region that, given its preference for aristocratic leaders, also disliked his humble origins.

John Breckinridge, the leader of the southern Democrats, though "sound" in his proslavery and states' rights views, was not a radical of the Yancey stripe. Descended from Kentucky aristocrats, he had studied law, had been a major in the Mexican War in 1847, had served in Congress from 1851 to 1855 and, as vice president under Buchanan, had presided over the Senate during many tumultuous sessions. His views on the issue of slavery in the territories hardly jibed with the southern Democratic platform of 1860. In supporting the Kansas-Nebraska bill he had declared that it placed slavery decisions in the hands of the people of the territories, and he denied that the bill legalized slavery in Kansas or Nebraska. "The right to establish involves the right to prohibit," he declared; "and, denying both, I would vote for neither."[48]

In the presidential vote, Lincoln received 180 electoral votes; Breckinridge 72; Bell 39; and Douglas 12. Lincoln had a clear majority in the electoral college, which ensured that the election would not go to the House of Representatives as many had feared, and as some southerners hoped would be the case. As in three

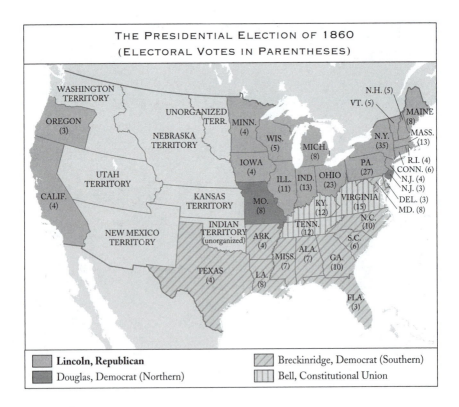

THE PRESIDENTIAL ELECTION OF 1860
(ELECTORAL VOTES IN PARENTHESES)

WASHINGTON TERRITORY
OREGON (3)
UNORGANIZED TERR.
NEBRASKA TERRITORY
MINN. (4)
WIS. (5)
MICH. (8)
IOWA (4)
UTAH TERRITORY
CALIF. (4)
KANSAS TERRITORY
MO. (8)
ILL. (11)
IND. (13)
OHIO (23)
KY. (12)
N.H. (5)
VT. (5)
MAINE (8)
N.Y. (35)
MASS. (13)
PA. (27)
R.I. (4)
CONN. (6)
N.J. (4)
N.J. (3)
VIRGINIA (15)
DEL. (3)
MD. (8)
NEW MEXICO TERRITORY
INDIAN TERRITORY (unorganized)
ARK. (4)
TENN. (12)
N.C. (10)
S.C. (6)
MISS. (7)
ALA. (7)
GA. (10)
TEXAS (4)
LA. (8)
FLA. (3)

Lincoln, Republican
Douglas, Democrat (Northern)
Breckinridge, Democrat (Southern)
Bell, Constitutional Union

of the four preceding presidential elections since 1844, the winner did not carry a majority of the popular vote, with Lincoln drawing only 39 percent of the votes cast.

Under the winner-take-all electoral college system, which encouraged parties to abandon campaigning for electors at the congressional district level in favor of statewide appeals for the popular vote, Lincoln still would have won the electoral college even if all the opposition votes had been combined. He scored heavily over Douglas in the East and won in the western states by narrower margins. As a result he had the electoral votes of every northern free state except New Jersey, receiving 98 percent of the North's electoral vote, but only 54 percent of its popular vote.[49] Breckinridge carried the entire Lower South; in the Upper South and on the border he carried only Delaware, Maryland, and North Carolina. Douglas's twelve electoral votes came from Missouri and New Jersey. Bell carried Tennessee, Kentucky, and Virginia.

The popular vote revealed the sectional complexion of this election. Lincoln ran ahead of his three opponents, polling 1,865,000 votes (39 percent) compared with Douglas's 1,375,157 (29 percent), Breckinridge's 847,953 (18 percent), and Bell's 589,581 (13 percent). In ten southern states Lincoln, who was not even on the ballot, did not receive a single vote, and in the border states he ran last. Among his northern constituents, Lincoln was especially popular among Republicans who had voted for Frémont in 1856, among former Know-Nothings and Whigs who had voted for Fillmore in 1856, among farmers (rather than city dwellers), and among the native-born and the young. More naturalized Germans supported him than supported Frémont, and this increase was important in some states. Still, he did not get disproportional support from ethnic voters.[50]

In contrast, although Breckinridge received a far heavier vote in the North than Lincoln did in the South, the Kentuckian's strength lay in the South and border states—an area that contained 30 percent of all white Americans, but 36 percent of the nation's electoral votes because of the Constitution's three-fifths clause.[51] Yet Breckinridge failed to carry a majority of the popular votes of the fourteen slave states (there was no popular vote in South Carolina, where presidential electors continued to be chosen by the state legislature.) His competitors garnered 108,338 more ballots than he, even though, as Douglas had noted, he was implicitly connected with disunion.

The complexity of voting choices, which especially in the case of the presidency are never single-issue plebiscites, prevents any simple explanation of the meaning of this vote. The popularity of Bell and Douglas over Breckinridge in the South cannot be taken as a southern mandate to maintain the Union by voting for candidates who were conservative on the question of secession. Nor did Americans vote in unusual numbers in 1860. In the North, turnout was high with 82 percent of the eligible voters going to the polls, a rate of participation that was above average for presidential balloting from 1840 to 1860. But in the

South, despite the connection of this election to secession and war, even the usual four-year proportional increase did not occur, as overall voter participation in 1860 remained below average.

When the results were known across the nation, some Republicans celebrated the election of Lincoln as a victory over slaveholders, while in the deep South flags appeared emblazoned with the motto "Death rather than submission to a Black Republican Government."[52] A South Carolinian took note of contemporary sentiment in her diary:

> [Charleston, S.C. Nov. 8, 1860] Yesterday on the train . . . before we reached Fernandina, a woman cried out – "That settles the hash." . . . " – Lincoln's elected." . . . The excitement was very great. Everybody was talking at the same time – One, a little more moved than the others stood up – saying despontly [sic] – "The die is cast – no more vain regrets. – Sad forebodings are useless. The stake is life or death –" . . . And some cried out.– "Now that the black radical Republicans have the power I suppose they will Brown us all." No doubt of it.[53]

CHAPTER 6 | # The Secession Winter

After the presidential election of 1860, southern states began to secede from the Union. Although the election of Lincoln was the precipitating cause, hostility toward the North had been festering for decades. Still, before secessionists could accomplish what some had intended for over a decade, they had to win popular support for the radical action they proposed. That process proved easiest in those Lower South states with the most slaves, more difficult in the Upper South states of Virginia, Tennessee, Arkansas, and North Carolina, and eventually impossible in the slave states of Maryland, Delaware, Kentucky, and Missouri.

Even before the secession of the seven states of the Lower South, which began in late December 1860 and continued through the early winter of 1861, President Buchanan responded to the disruption of the nation by seeking avenues of compromise, while questioning any state's right to leave the Union. Both a congressional committee and a peace conference also sought to bring the South back into the Union. Yet after South Carolina's secession in December and the creation of the Confederate government in February, there remained few realistic possibilities for a return of the South. Most northerners and to a lesser extent residents of the border states denied the legality of a movement that southerners claimed as a constitutional and moral right. Nor did most Americans support any compromise on the central issue of slavery in the territories. The arguments over these issues in both the North and South were hardly new, but in the great secession winter of 1861 they set the stage for war.

## THE SECESSION OF THE LOWER SOUTH

Throughout 1860 many southerners reacted with near hysteria to their perception of national events. Haunted by the fear of slave insurrections, they increased patrols to deal with suspected rebellions that never took place. Fires, during the unusually hot and dry summer, were believed to be arson committed by slaves.[1]

To cope with such fears, many southern states reorganized their military systems. Encouraged by U.S. Senator Jefferson Davis, the Mississippi legislature provided funds for a state armory to manufacture arms and ammunition. Similar legislation to improve militias passed elsewhere in the South, as fire-eaters such as William Yancey of Alabama kept before the public southern demands for a federal guarantee of slavery in Kansas and the legitimacy of secession if the Republicans won the presidency.[2]

Even before the presidential election, Governor William Gist of South Carolina had sent his brother (aptly named States Rights Gist) to the governors of other southern states, informing them that if Lincoln was elected, South Carolina would call a convention, and asking them whether they would cooperate. The answers varied from the Florida governor's response that his state was "ready to wheel into line with the gallant Palmetto State" to the governor of Alabama's reply that if two or more states left the Union, his state would also secede. The governor of North Carolina replied that North Carolinians would not consider Lincoln's election as sufficient cause for disunion.

Consequently even before the presidential voting had begun, a range of possible actions had emerged, with only Florida, Mississippi, and South Carolina having a clear majority of immediate secessionists and with the South as a whole unable to sustain the movement for a regional convention. In most cases southerners were divided between those who would leave the Union immediately and unilaterally and those "cooperationists" who would delay to see if other states joined in their rebellion. A third, much smaller body of Unionists supported the summoning of a convention that would require, in return for staying in the Union, Lincoln's acceptance of various southern demands. Almost no one in the South spoke for staying in the Union and doing nothing.

Certainly no one did in South Carolina, where there was little difference of opinion over the proper course to follow. After Lincoln's election, the legislature of South Carolina, already assembled in Columbia for the choice of presidential electors, immediately called a convention to consider "the dangers incident to the position of the State in the Federal Union." Within weeks the state's citizens, represented by delegates chosen at mass meetings, unanimously passed an "ordinance declaring that the Union now subsisting between South Carolina and other States under the name of United States of America is hereby dissolved."

Comparing themselves with the revolutionaries of 1776, these South Car-

Southern separatists cheer the announcement that South Carolina has officially seceded from the Union. Many of these southerners compared themselves with the revolutionaries of 1776.

olinians believed that their movement reaffirmed traditional principles of "free men." Hence they cloaked their extremism in ancient symbols of the American Revolution, even to the point of writing "a declaration of the immediate causes which induce and justify the secession of South Carolina."[3] They argued that the United States Constitution was created as a compact with the states retaining "reserved powers." And just as Jefferson and his generation had indicted George III and his ministers, so they charged that political corruption in Washington and the North had contaminated the Republic. According to South Carolina's Governor Pickens, "We must start our Government free from the vulgar influences that have debauched and demoralized the Government at Washington."[4]

In the late fall and winter of 1860–1861, other states in the Lower South also began the process of secession. In most instances (Texas was the exception), the process was the same. For example, Governor Joseph Brown of Georgia was an aggressive secessionist who lost no time in moving for immediate action. The day after Lincoln's election, Brown addressed the legislature, recommending the calling of a convention accompanied by vigorous military measures. These even-

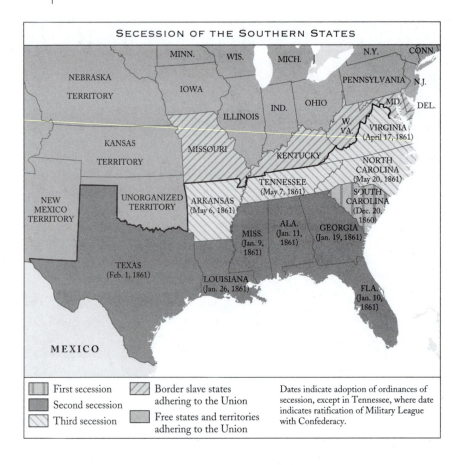

SECESSION OF THE SOUTHERN STATES

| | First secession | | Border slave states adhering to the Union | Dates indicate adoption of ordinances of secession, except in Tennessee, where date indicates ratification of Military League with Confederacy. |
| | Second secession | | Free states and territories adhering to the Union | |
| | Third secession | | | |

tually included the appropriation of $1 million for defense, provisions for a state force of ten thousand troops, and plans for the seizure of federal installations.

The purpose of the convention, in Brown's mind, was to take the state out of the Union. In addition to Brown, the cause of immediate secession was advocated by political leaders such as Robert Toombs, Howell Cobb, and his younger brother Thomas. Other figures in the future Confederacy such as Alexander Stephens, Benjamin Hill, and Herschel Johnson, although admitting the theoretical right to withdraw from the Union, opposed immediate secession. Cautioned by Stephens that revolutions once begun were hard to control and that slavery was safer inside the Union, the legislature rejected the plan for an all-southern convention and issued a call for a state convention to meet in early January. In the vote for delegates to this convention, the balloting was extremely close: 44,152 Georgians chose delegates committed to secession, while 41,632 preferred those who would delay action until the intentions of other southern states were known. The total vote represented less than 80 percent of the state turnout in the 1860 presidential election.[5]

Georgia's secession convention met on January 16. There was sentiment to try further measures before moving to secession as a "last resort." Some have maintained that most delegates favored delay. Herschel Johnson, a former Georgia governor, believed that "a fair and energetic canvass would have shown a large majority of the people against the policy [not the right] of secession." Even the most radical delegates (who gave most of the speeches, according to Johnson) insisted that secession "would be peaceable—that it would not bring war—that if it should the Yankees were cowards and would not fight—and that, at the worst it would be a short war, in which the South would achieve an easy victory."[6]

Some delegates believed that the election of Lincoln was not sufficient cause for secession and that the president neither could nor would interfere with slavery.[7] But gradually even moderates, intent on protecting "southern honor," came to the conclusion summarized by Toombs, who had changed his mind several times: "that all further looking to the North . . . ought to be instantly abandoned . . . Secession by the 4th of March next should be thundered from the ballot box by the unanimous voice of Georgia. Such a voice will be your best guaranty for liberty, security, tranquillity, and glory."[8]

When the crucial vote was taken in the Georgia convention on a motion to substitute "cooperation" for immediate secession, the count stood 133 for to 164 against. A change of 16 votes out of a total of 297 would have denied the immediate secessionists victory. Some delegates considered secession in the interest of non-slaveholders. Under abolitionist control, their reasoning went, the South would become a society of landless tenants in a black society abandoned by white planters; others accepted Thomas Cobb's impassioned plea that the South could make better terms out of the Union rather than in it. Alexander Stephens believed that two-thirds of those voting for the ordinance expected a re-formation of the Union. In a spirit of state solidarity, the Georgia ordinance of secession, passed by 166 to 130 on January 19, 1861, was later signed by nearly all the convention's antisecessionists.[9] "And so the Rubicon was crossed," wrote Herschel Johnson in a comment that could be applied to the other states of the Lower South, "and . . . Georgia was launched upon a dark, uncertain and dangerous sea. Peals of cannon announced the fact, in token of exultation. The secessionists were jubilant. I never felt so sad before. The clustering glories of the past thronged my memory, but they were darkened by the gathering gloom of the lowering future."

In the interval before the assembling of the Georgia convention, Alabama, Mississippi, and Florida completed their secession from the Union. In Alabama a vigorous minority, drawing strength from the northern counties and the commercial and plantation areas of the Tennessee Valley, opposed immediate secession, urging that the action of the state be delayed while awaiting a southern convention. The divisions in the state over secession reflected previous local tensions over economic development and government power, as Alabamians responded to disunion not as a separate issue but in terms of "rival ambitions and ideologies."[10]

At the Alabama convention the prevailing view favored secession, but varying shades of opinion found expression in four days of discussion. Then on January 11 the convention was swayed by Yancey, who asserted that a sectional party was now in control of the national government and that the Republicans would use their power to destroy the rights of the South. The ordinance of secession was then voted on and passed 61 to 39, though earlier the minority report to avoid immediate secession had been defeated by the closer vote of 54 to 45.

Florida and Mississippi had already acted almost simultaneously. The Mississippi convention, meeting at Jackson, passed its ordinance of secession on January 9 by a vote of 84 to 15; the Florida ordinance was passed the following day, 62 to 7.

Commissioners were now sent from those states that had seceded to other slave states to urge secession. Herschel Johnson himself was asked to serve as a commissioner to Virginia. But he declined, having recently spoken in Richmond against secession. "How could I have the face," he said, "with that speech fresh in their memory, to urge Virginia to commit the same mistake which Georgia has done?"[11]

The prompt action of two more states now completed the secession of the Lower South. The Louisiana convention passed its ordinance of secession on January 26. Although this ordinance was accepted by a vote of 113 to 17, the popular vote for delegates to the convention revealed a much smaller proportion of immediate secessionists. On February 1 the Texas convention voted secession by 166 to 8, with Governor Sam Houston unwavering in his opposition. On March 18, 1861, he was removed from office for refusing to take the oath to support the Confederacy. Texas secessionists congratulated themselves that "for far less cause than this, our fathers separated from the Crown of England."[12]

Although rigid generalizations about who the immediate secessionists were falter before the evidence, in the Lower South they were more likely to be from large new cotton lands that normally voted Democratic, with southern-rights Democrats often providing the leaders of the secessionist movement. Immediatists were slightly wealthier and younger, and held more slaves than cooperationists. On the other hand, cooperationists showed strength in the predominantly white, hill counties, in the pine-barren, wire-grass, and upcountry regions of the Lower South, and sometimes in previously Whig areas in the black belt. Urban areas with immigrants were consistently opposed to immediate secession.[13]

More than a month before the inauguration of Lincoln, secession had been accomplished in the seven states of the Lower South. Once the movement started, it gained momentum with each passing week until a vast section, with shared climate, labor system, and economic interests, presented a united front.

The legal formula by which secession was accomplished was classically American in that the movement's leaders legitimized their revolution by appropriating the convenient constitutional device of a state "convention." In constitutional theory, sovereign power rested in such a convention, which was elected by the people with the understanding that it should exercise ultimate and fundamental powers of government.

Popular referendums to ratify the action of state conventions had sometimes been used in the process of state making during and after the Revolution. But southern opinion in 1861 inclined to the belief that the conventions themselves were competent to take final action and that ratification by referendum was unnecessary. In Texas alone (of the states of the Lower South) the secession ordinance was submitted to the male electorate, winning overwhelmingly in a vote that was 10 percent less than the total cast a few months earlier in the 1860 presidential election. In other states sovereignty was considered to derive from the fact that the delegates who voted for secession had been chosen by the people.

Fervent early secessionists were aided by the U.S. Constitution's avoidance of the issue of whether a state had the right to leave the Union. For all its advantages to the growth and development of the nation, federalism was silent on the overriding issue of 1860. In his first inaugural Lincoln later concluded that "perpetuity is implied, if not expressed, in the fundamental law of all national governments. It is safe to assert that no government proper, ever had a provision in its organic law for its own termination."[14] But his was not the final word on an indeterminate matter whose ambiguity fueled southern extremism.

Thus, the "secessionist impulse" was many layered. For over two decades a few southern leaders had warned of northern interference in their economic and racial affairs. With the election of a Republican president, their warning gained force in the Lower South. Slaveholders, the established political leaders of their society, were able to appeal to the majority of the region—that is, non-slaveholding whites—with alluring promises of racial control and the future expansion of an independent South. In some areas the growing difficulty of becoming a slave owner, the drought of 1860, and the fears of a conspiracy led by "Black Republicans" contributed to a mentality prepared to accept any change as improvement. "The ambitious non-slaveholder, already faced with rising prices for slaves and land, was further squeezed in the fall of 1860 by shortages and tight money. He had little to lose by backing secession."[15]

To make their case in the Lower South, the immediatists appealed to states' rights sentiments as well as to the historic republican doctrine that despised the abuse of power and the corruption they now feared. These Lower South states began their brief independence with confidence and exuberance, determined to have home rule, generally unmindful of a future civil war, and insistent on the protection of southern values. Yet southern secession, which looked backward to

1776 as its model, was not a typical revolution undertaken to expand rights and liberties. Instead the movement, with its insistent linkage of black slavery to white freedom, was a counterrevolution undertaken to maintain an anachronistic status quo within a nation dedicated to progress and economic development.[16] What was revolutionary was the severing of an eighty-five-year-old federal Union.

## THE REACTION OF THE BUCHANAN ADMINISTRATION

As secession progressed from state to state, uncertainty characterized efforts to avert a war that neither side sought. Buchanan, who faced a more difficult crisis than any of his predecessors had, was anything but a strong president, and his critics have painted a damaging picture of his administration: unethical meddling in the *Dred Scott* case, blunders in the handling of Kansas, treasonable conspiracy of secession leaders with the southern members of his cabinet; army rifles sent to the South and given to the enemy, and most damaging of all, the disregarding of General Winfield Scott's warning that the federal forts in the South should be garrisoned to prevent their seizure.[17] Certainly his administration was the one of the most graft ridden in American history.[18] Through vacillation, the corruption of certain subordinates, and his own subservience to proslavery southern senators, he forfeited respect. Southerners had always been his partisans, and Jefferson Davis was regarded as his spokesman in the Senate. To advocate southern rights in the North as a way of dampening sectionalism had been his policy for nearly half a century. Tired and querulous, Buchanan spent the secession crisis "nervously hoping that the deluge might not descend until he was out of office."[19]

With conflicting currents swirling about him, the president intended to avoid provoking war by committing any aggressive act. He believed correctly that a conciliatory policy would prevent the Upper South and the border states from joining the Lower South. Then when the leaders of the Lower South realized that they could not command even a majority of the slave states, he mistakenly believed secession schemes would break down.

Buchanan's policy did avert war for a time, and as a lame-duck president he afforded the incoming Republicans an opportunity to work out their own schemes of possible conciliation. Avoiding any recognition of the Confederacy, he made no commitments that would seriously embarrass his successor. Buchanan's do-nothing program must also be considered in the context of constitutional arrangements that required one-third of a year to elapse between the election of Lincoln in November and his inauguration in March.

Buchanan's message to Congress on December 3, 1860—delivered after South Carolina's secession but before that of the next state, Mississippi—

displayed his bias. He began by pointing out the responsibility of the abolitionists for the critical state of the country. "Many a matron throughout the South retires at night in dread of what may befall herself and her children before the morning." All that the South wanted, he continued, was to be left alone to manage its domestic institutions. Still, the recent presidential election did "not of itself afford just cause" for dissolving what he considered to be a perpetual Union, which, like Lincoln, he held to be "great and powerful."[20] Buchanan denied the legitimacy of secession at the same time that he declared the federal government unable to do anything about it. "Seldom," wrote one disgusted northern editor, "have we known so strong an argument come to so lame and impotent a conclusion."[21]

Although Buchanan saw secession as a reversable condition, South Carolinians envisioned their departure from the Union as final. When "commissioners" appeared in Washington from South Carolina to "negotiate" on the assumption that the main issue of their state's independence and status as a foreign nation had already been settled, the conflict between the president's prosouthern tendencies and his unionism was put to a test. Just at this juncture, a crisis arose over the status of the forts in Charleston harbor—Fort Moultrie, Fort Sumter, and Castle Pinckney.

On December 2, 1860, Major Robert Anderson withdrew from Fort Moultrie (shown here) in Charleston Harbor, in order to move to Fort Sumter.

Buchanan refused to hand over these federal properties as South Carolina demanded. Major Robert Anderson, in command at Fort Moultrie, was under instructions to avoid any aggressive act, but to hold the forts and if attacked to defend himself "to the last extremity." Because his entire force numbered fewer than a hundred men and because Fort Moultrie could easily be taken by land (Sumter was on an island), Anderson moved his force from Moultrie to Sumter on December 26, 1860. His reason for the change was the desire to avoid a clash and the belief that the more formidable Sumter would discourage attack.

This action proved one of the most misunderstood incidents of the crisis. South Carolinians interpreted the move as an aggressive act, although the intentions of the president, of the secretary of state, Joseph Holt, and of Anderson himself were the opposite. State forces at once seized Moultrie, demanded through their commissioners that the president evacuate Charleston harbor, and insisted that Anderson be ordered back to Moultrie—orders that were inconsistent with a total evacuation. On the 28th of December the commissioners harangued the president for two hours, but he refused, then and thereafter, to accede to their demands. An ominous clash of authority and hardening of opinion on both sides ensued.

It is impossible to locate the precise moment in the remaining weeks of Buchanan's term when the possibility for compromise ended. Until January 9, only one state had seceded; by the end of January, six states had done so. Yet the formation of the Confederacy of the Lower South did not occur until February. Even as a confrontation loomed in Charleston harbor, moderates continued their efforts to reach a compromise solution.

## CONGRESS AND THE SECESSION CRISIS

During the winter of 1861, not only did some southerners discuss what terms they could obtain by returning to the Union, but in Virginia and other states of the Upper South, the Lower South's haste was criticized. The key to the situation, in the view of moderates, was not in Charleston or even Montgomery Alabama (the capital of the Confederacy after February 1861), but in Washington, where Congress served as a national body capable of discussion and resolution of these sectional conflicts.

The second session of the Thirty-sixth Congress began its lame-duck meeting on December 3, before South Carolina had left the Union. In its halls proposals for reconciliation piled up in such quantity that each house chose a committee to sift through numerous schemes and to report an anticipated solution. In the House of Representatives this function was performed by the "Committee of Thirty-Three," a committee with one representative from each state, created at the suggestion of Representative Alexander Boteler of Virginia. Republicans, in Congress and elsewhere, at first refused to compromise on the issue of protecting slavery in the territories. Then a group of Republicans, under the leadership of the Massachusetts congressman Charles Francis Adams, offered a proposal for the immediate admission of New Mexico, presumably as a slave state. Such a plan was calculated to please the border states.

But secessionist leaders, already committed to disunion, declared any compromise hopeless. As a Virginia senator suggested, Congress could not understand "the dangers with which we are threatened."[22] Many southerners were under pressure from radicals in the Lower South who feared that Congress would accomplish a reconstruction of the Union they detested.

On December 13, before secession had been decided in any state, southern Congressmen issued an address to their constituents:

> The argument is exhausted. All hope of relief in the Union, through the agency of committees, Congressional legislation, or constitutional amendments, is extinguished, and we trust the South will not be deceived by appearances or the pretence of new guarantees. The Republicans are resolute in the purpose to grant nothing that will or ought to satisfy the South. We are satisfied the honor, safety, and independence of the Southern people are to be found only in a Southern Confederacy—a result to be obtained only by separate State secession—and that the sole and primary aim of each slaveholding State ought to be its speedy and absolute separation from an unnatural and hostile Union.[23]

In its final report to the House, the compromise committee advocated the enforcement of the fugitive slave law, the repeal of the personal liberty laws, which prohibited state officials from returning fugitive slaves in some northern states, and the adoption of a constitutional amendment to protect the South against future interference with slavery in the states. The wording of this amendment was:

> No amendment shall be made to the Constitution which will authorize or give to Congress the power to abolish or interfere, within any State, with the domestic institutions thereof, including that of persons held to labor or service by the laws of said State.

This proposed thirteenth amendment to the Constitution presented an anomaly in that by introducing an unamendable amendment it sought for all time to restrain the American people from abolishing slavery by a constitutional provision. Yet it was adopted, with 40 percent of the House Republicans voting in the affirmative, by the requisite two-thirds of both House and Senate.[24] Fast-moving events, however, soon altered the horizon, and the amendment failed to be ratified.

In the Senate, the efforts toward compromise officially centered on a "Committee of Thirteen" composed of leaders such as Crittenden of Kentucky, Seward of New York, Toombs of Georgia, Douglas of Illinois, Davis of Mississippi, and Wade of Ohio. Their plan, presented to the Senate by the respected John Crittenden of Kentucky and called the "Crittenden Compromise," was to prohibit slavery in national territory north of the line 36° 30', but to permit its establishment and protection by the federal government south of that line; to allow future states, north or south of the line, to enter the Union with or without slavery as they chose; to prevent Congress from abolishing slavery in places under national jurisdiction surrounded by slave states; to compensate owners in communities where intimidation prevented federal officials from arresting a fugitive slave; to enforce the fugitive slave law; and to let Congress recommend the repeal of the personal liberty laws, which, though null and void by the provisions of the Constitution, have "contributed much to the discord . . . now prevailing." These compromise articles, when ratified, were to become irrevocable amendments to the Constitution, and no future amendment was ever to be made which would authorize Congress to touch slavery in any of the states.[25]

Southern Democrats on the Senate compromise committee, including Davis, Toombs, and Hunter, had declared that no terms should be accepted by the South unless supported by a majority of Republicans. When Republican support was withheld, these southern leaders considered that compromise had been tried and had failed, and that the failure was to be laid at the door of the Republicans. Meanwhile, Republicans attributed the committee's failure to southern insistence on the Breckinridge platform, which required the federal government to protect slavery in the territories. In fact the most that Lincoln and the Republicans would concede was always considerably less than the southern lawmakers in Washington demanded. Negotiation was possible in some areas, such as the collection of customs off shore to prevent the possibly inflammatory use of federal installations, but the issues separating North and South were beyond the solution of congressional committees.

Throughout the crisis, the cautious president-elect avoided public statements, but he did permit various spokesmen to express his views for him. Lincoln refused to accept any agreement that did not recognize the Wilmot Proviso. The latter expressed his bedrock principle that slavery must not expand into the territories. As he informed William Kellogg, a congressman from Illinois and a member of the Committee of Thirty-Three: "Entertain no proposition for a compromise in regard to the extension of slavery. The instant you do, they have us under again; all our labor is lost, and sooner or later must be done over. . . . Have none of it. The tug has come, & better now than later." On December 17, he wrote to Thurlow Weed: "Should the convocation of Governors . . . seem desirous to know my views on the present aspect of things, tell them you judge from my speeches that I will be inflexible on the territorial question; that I probably think either the Missouri line extended, or [Douglas's] . . . Pop[ular] Sov[ereignty] would lose us everything we gained by the election; that filibustering for all South of us, and making slave states of it, would follow. . . . Also, that I probably think all opposition, real and apparent, to the fugitive slave [clause] of the constitution ought to be withdrawn."[26]

Though Lincoln had little confidence in the Crittenden Compromise (which was thought to give a powerful incentive for slavery's expansion into Cuba and Mexico), and though he stood firm in his refusal to give up slavery restriction in the territories, he was ready to offer concessions on other matters. His administration would in fact urge repeal of personal liberty laws, and four northern states modified these statutes during the secession winter of 1860–1861. Lincoln repeated his belief in the right of the states to maintain slavery and explained that he intended no interference with that right. He favored enforcement of the fugitive slave law. Furthermore, though this was a difficult concession, he was willing to accept a constitutional amendment protecting slavery in the states where it existed. What he would not do was consider any proposals for the extension of slavery into the territories. Few of his convictions were understood in the South, where he was characterized as an abolitionist opposed to any compromise.

Having failed to achieve his objectives through the work of the Committee of Thirteen, Senator Crittenden proposed on January 3 that Americans hold an unprecedented referendum on his compromise, which was designed to satisfy the South on controversial aspects of the slavery question. By one calculation, it was estimated that an overwhelming majority of Americans was "in favor of conciliation, forbearance, and compromise."[27] Northern commercial financial and shipping interests certainly wanted to end the sectional strife, as did residents of border states. The referendum proposal, however, was novel in American constitutional procedure. A majority of Republican senators did not favor it, and the chance for taking an appeal to the people was lost.

## THE WASHINGTON PEACE CONFERENCE

The most ambitious effort to avert war was that of the Peace Convention, a conference of twenty-one states that assembled in Washington on February 4, 1861, at the call of the Virginia legislature. The failure of this peacemaking body, soon nicknamed "the old gentlemen's convention," was not attributable to a lack of distinguished personnel. John Tyler, the former president, presided, and William Fessenden, William Rives, Lot Morrill, David Wilmot, Reverdy Johnson, Salmon Chase, Thomas Ewing, Caleb Smith, and Stephen Logan were among its delegates. Yet from the beginning it was handicapped by the absence of representatives from all the states of the Lower South and Arkansas, as well as three northern states and California and Oregon.

Moreover, the Washington Convention assembled too late to be authoritative, and it was weakened by indifference and opposition from both sides. Southern secessionists, displeased with the confidence which men of the border states placed in prospects for compromise, proceeded with the formation of their Confederacy while the convention was in session. Republicans, on the other hand, made light of the convention and insisted that their partisans adopt an unyielding position.

On February 27, the convention presented to Congress a plan based on seven amendments to the Constitution. In general the proposals resembled the abortive Crittenden Compromise: the Missouri line was to be extended westward to California; slavery was to be protected in territory south of that line; no further territory was to be acquired without the consent of a majority of the senators from the slave states; Congress was never to have power over slavery in the states, not even by a future constitutional amendment; slave owners were to be compensated when prevented by intimidation from recovering fugitives. Despite these concessions to the South, Virginia's leaders repudiated the plan, and it received negligible support when brought to a vote on March 2 in the United States Senate.[28] This was a discouraging omen. If consultation and deliberation among prominent state leaders could not bring peace, the situation was indeed alarming.

Yet some southern delegates continued to display their enduring affection for the Union. The convention was called "in an earnest effort to adjust the present unhappy controversies," declared the general assembly of Virginia. "[What] our godlike fathers created," said John Tyler, "we have to preserve. They built up. You have . . . a task equally grand. . . . You have . . . to preserve the Government and to renew and invigorate the Constitution. If you reach the height of this great occasion, your children's children will rise up and call you blessed." "Virginia steps in," said Rives, "to arrest the progress of the country on its road to ruin. . . . I have seen the pavements of Paris covered with fraternal blood! God forbid that I should see this horrid picture repeated in my own country." "Sir, I love this Union," said another Virginian, George Summers. "The man does not live who entertains a higher respect for this Government than I do. I know its history—I know how it was established. . . . I do not wish to survive its dissolution."[29]

As evidence of the strength of unionism in the upper South and on the border, the Peace Convention is historically important. It did strengthen southern moderates in the elections in border states and helped keep all the border states in the Union until Lincoln's inauguration.[30]

But this significance should not be mistaken for achievement. Extremists on both sides celebrated the failure of the convention. Abolitionists now considered the possibilities for an improved, reformed United States with the sinful slaveholders of the South gone from the Republic. Michigan's Zachariah Chandler wrote that "no Republican State should have sent delegates," and that the "whole thing was gotten up against my judgment and advice, and will end in thin smoke. . . . Without a little blood-letting this Union will not, in my estimation, be worth a rush."[31] Southerners matched his militancy. A Georgian announced that he "would prefer to see the whole South from the Delaware to the Rio Grande, one charnel house of destruction [than] to submit a single day to Lincoln's administration, upon any terms that any body could imagine."[32]

## BUCHANAN STIFFENS

Meanwhile Buchanan's policy on what he considered the illegal act of secession stiffened. In part this reaction was the result of Cabinet changes. Buchanan had always depended on his Cabinet for more than consultation, and the shift of personnel among his closest advisers clearly influenced his policies. After Secretary of Treasury Howell Cobb of Georgia, Secretary of Interior Jacob Thompson of Mississippi, and Secretary of War John Floyd of Virginia were replaced by Unionists, Buchanan addressed himself with increasing firmness to the task of upholding a fragmenting Union.

Floyd and Thompson were guilty of more than prosecessionist views. For years they had allowed the sale of government properties to southern friends and had permitted bribes and graft in their departments. As his last official act Floyd transferred cannon to southern arsenals and gave secret information to secessionists. Angry supporters of the Union linked such malfeasance to southern efforts to "corrupt" the Republic. "Only the other day it was announced that a million dollars had been stolen from Mr. Thompson's department. Now it is proposed to give up Sumter," said the disgusted Edwin Stanton of Pennsylvania, the new attorney general.[33]

The most sensational of these cabinet departures was that of Secretary of State Lewis Cass, who resigned in mid-December when the question of the Charleston forts was under consideration. Representing a northern constituency, Cass believed that he would bring dishonor to it and to himself if he remained in the cabinet with conspirators and traitors.[34] But his high principles evidently dissolved the next day, when he asked for his resignation back. Buchanan refused.[35]

The hardening of the Buchanan administration was evident in the president's message to Congress on January 8, 1861. No state, said Buchanan in his address, "has a right by its own act to secede from the Union or throw off its federal obligations at pleasure." Nor had the president the right to recognize the independence of any seceded state. Furthermore, the president must collect public revenues and protect public property "so far as . . . practicable under existing laws." Though he had no right to "make aggressive war upon any State," he must use military force against those who "resist the Federal officers . . . and . . . assail the property of the Federal Government . . ." Appealing first to patriotism, then to material considerations, Buchanan stressed the rich legacy of the Union, dwelt upon its advantages, and warned of the calamity which its destruction would bring to every part of the country.[36]

This message followed by three days the sending of a ship to reinforce the garrison at Sumter. Buchanan had already worked out a compromise with Floridians whereby the garrison at Fort Pickens, commanding the approach to Pensacola Bay, would be resupplied but not reinforced. At first favoring the warship *Brooklyn* for the Sumter expedition, the president yielded to the suggestion that the substitution of a merchant ship would be less threatening. So it was an unarmed chartered steamer, the *Star of the West*, that sailed from New York Harbor on January 5 with two hundred men, together with arms and ammunition, on a mission to place the government in a stronger defensive position.[37] When it arrived in Charleston harbor on January 10, the vessel was fired on by South Carolina forces on Morris Island and in Fort Moultrie who had been warned by Secretary of War Floyd. Without any specific orders, Major Anderson was about to return fire from Sumter when the *Star of the West* turned back and steamed out of the harbor.

Thus not a shot was fired by the United States, although the flag of the United States had been fired on by South Carolinians. As always in such incidents, each side considered the other the aggressor. Charleston resented the attempt to reinforce and believed the expedition an invasion of an independent state by a foreign power.

On the other hand, Washington stressed the nonaggressive nature of the expedition, pointed out that no attack from Sumter was contemplated, and resented the firing on an unarmed ship. The incident might have started the war, but ensuing negotiations smoothed it over. A similar expedition under Lincoln, an even less threatening one, did bring war three months later.[38]

The incident demonstrated that there was dynamite in the Sumter situation. Northern sentiment applauded the president's determination to hold Sumter and maintain federal authority in the South. Earlier opinion in the North had focused on slavery and antisouthern concerns; now northerners drew together as nationalists intent on maintaining their government against a destructive enemy.

## THE FORMATION OF THE CONFEDERACY

In contrast to the gloomy mood in Washington, southerners meeting in Montgomery, Alabama on February 4, 1861, to launch a new nation were exuberant. Some viewed this new government as an expression of states' rights; others envisioned a centralized nation that would expand from the Mississippi to the Pacific and southward to Cuba and Mexico. With revolution in the air, southern efforts at nation building were nonetheless grounded in the traditional American process of law making and constitution building.

The Montgomery convention had not been called to consider the advisability of secession, but rather to organize a government. With the assembling of that body, leaders had, so far as the Lower South was concerned, accomplished their main purpose of independence. Even so, the Montgomery meeting was incomplete, for at its assembling a month before Lincoln's inauguration it contained representatives from South Carolina, Georgia, Alabama, Mississippi, Florida, and Louisiana—that is, only six of the fifteen slave states. (The Texas delegation did not arrive until March.) These states had chosen their delegates in various ways. Each sent a number equal to that of its delegation in the Congress at Washington; each state had one vote.

The atmosphere in Montgomery was one of excitement and elation, accompanied by the drama of office seeking and the stir of restless men maneuvering for position. As yet there was no war. The United States was quietly permitting this rival government to be organized in a peaceable manner, and the attainment of popular support was easier if talk of war was kept in the background. Not only did southerners hope that war could be avoided; they were led to believe that even if the northerners did fight, the Yankees would not make a determined effort to defeat the South. As a result when war broke out, according to Jefferson Davis, "many of our people could with difficulty be persuaded that it would be long or serious."[39]

When plans might have been proceeding for exporting cotton, negotiating for European gold, and putting the Confederacy on an efficient war footing, the Montgomery convention instead devoted five weeks to writing a constitution. Throughout, the framers of the Confederacy emphasized the peaceful nature of their policies. In their minds, the right to alter their forms of rule and to frame a government of their own choosing was undeniable. The exercise of that right offered no just cause for war. But the stakes were high. Mary Chesnut, whose husband James was a delegate, acknowledged that "this Southern Confederacy must be supported now by calm determination and cool brains. We have risked all, and we must play our best, for the stake is life or death."[40]

The first task in Montgomery was to justify the legal right of secession, which was easily accomplished. The Georgia Unionist Alexander Stephens provided the most famous constitutional defense of secession. Stephens based his argument on the premise that "sovereignty" rested ultimately in the people of the states, as distinguished from their state governments. The supreme law of the federal Constitution, so the argument ran, did not make the national government sovereign over the people of the states. It was the people of the states who had originated the supreme-law clause as part of a federal structure and who could alter a grant that they themselves had made.

In a more parochial, locally oriented understanding of authority than generally prevailed in the North and which highlighted the growing differences between North and South, states, as decreed by the people, could secede, especially if the original structure of government had been abused. In this interpretation the constitution was a compact among people of different states. When violated by some of the confederated parties, the other parties could declare its dissolution.[41]

Besides justifying secession, the Montgomery convention accomplished three main goals: it wrote a constitution for the Confederate states; it chose the provisional president and vice president; and it acted as a provisional legislature for the new government, pending regular congressional elections to be held in

Although Alexander H. Stephens provided the most famous defense of secession at the Montgomery convention, he opposed immediate secession for Georgia. Once Georgia seceded, he supported the state. He was then chosen vice president of the Confederate States of America.

November 1861. Little originality went into framing the new instrument for the southern nation.[42] "Southerners were convinced that their document was a restoration of the original federal order that had gone awry. Operating as if they were anti-Federalists of the 1790s, their modifications of the U.S. Constitution were intended as defenses of an imperiled American federalism."[43]

In its general pattern, the constitution closely resembled that of the United States; indeed, at most points its wording was precisely the same. It offered its leaders an appropriate vehicle, as did the United States version, for creating a strong national government. Hence from the Confederacy's beginnings the tension between states and federal government, so significant in its creation, was reinvented. In time these unresolved differences were to play a part in the Confederacy's defeat.

The main differences between the United States Constitution and the Confederate Constitution appeared in those features which guaranteed states' rights, safeguarded slavery, and instituted minor improvements in governmental machinery. The emphasis on states' rights appeared in the preamble, which held that each state acted "in its sovereign and independent character, in order to form"—not a "more perfect union" but "a permanent federal government." There was no general welfare clause, and the importance of the states was further recognized by a provision that any federal officer, acting solely within the limits of any state, might be impeached by the state legislature.

On the other hand, state officers, as in the United States Constitution, were under oath to support the federal Constitution. In the Confederate States as in the United States, the federal Constitution, laws, and treaties were declared to be the "supreme law of the land," binding on state judges and enforceable against contrary provisions in state constitutions or laws. Moreover, the provision for a supreme court and almost the entire judicial article remained unchanged, although no supreme court was ever created.

Restrictions on the states were established in much the same terms as those of the United States Constitution. No state could enter any alliance or confederation; coin money; pass any bill of attainder, or ex post facto law, or law impairing the obligation of contracts; grant any title of nobility; keep troops or warships in time of peace; form any compact with another state or a foreign power; or engage in war except in case of invasion or imminent danger.

In practical terms a confederacy without limitations on the states would have been impossible, for in various spheres federal authority must of necessity be exclusive. State sovereignty meant not the authority of any government at all, but the sovereignty of the people of each state, considered severally. At some point the sovereign people would limit their state governments, at other points their federal government.[44]

The people had the right to recall the public power they had bestowed. This they might do by the process of amendment—or, if it should come to that, by secession. Consistency required that each of the states of the Confederacy retain the right of secession, though such right was nowhere specifically mentioned in the Confederate Constitution. In the opinion of the southern constitution makers such mention was unnecessary, for their own right of secession had not been vitiated by the lack of explicit statement in the Constitution of the United States.

Slavery was explicitly defended in the southern constitution. No federal law "denying . . . the right of property in negro slaves" could be passed. In territory acquired by the Confederate States, slavery was to be "recognized and protected by Congress and by the territorial government;" inhabitants of the states were guaranteed the right to take their slaves into such territory. Unlike Americans in 1787, the founding fathers of the Confederacy did not hesitate to use the word *slave*. The clause on reciprocal citizenship guaranteed to the citizen of any state the right to travel and live with his slaves in any other state. If any state in the Confederacy abolished slavery, such abolition would not impair the slaveholding rights of other citizens.

Proslavery sentiment, however, did not extend to the point of legalizing the foreign slave trade. On the contrary, the importation of slaves "from any foreign country other than the slaveholding States or Territories of the United States of America" was prohibited in the Constitution. Moreover, the possibility of retaliation against slave states not joining the Confederacy was introduced by empowering Congress to prohibit the importation of slaves from any such state.

The framers of the Confederate Constitution provided some modifications of the U.S. Constitution. They altered the process of amendment so that a convention of states could bypass Congress and gain ratification by vote of two-thirds of the state legislatures. With certain exceptions Congress was not to appropriate money except by two-thirds votes of both houses, and then only when the amount and purpose of each appropriation were precisely specified.

"Riders" on money bills were discouraged by the provision that the president might veto a given item of an appropriation bill without vetoing the entire bill—the so-called line-item veto so attractive to succeeding generations of Americans. Each law was to deal with one subject, to be expressed in the title. A step toward parliamentary government was taken by providing that heads of executive departments might sit in either house of Congress, although in the Confederacy's short life cabinet members did not do so. Expenses of the post office were to be paid out of that department's revenues, and no protective tariff was allowed. The president was restricted to one term of six years.

Without waiting for the Constitution to become final through the slow process of ratification, the Montgomery convention installed a full-fledged government that later transformed itself into the provisional legislature of the Confederate States.

The choice for president fell on a man of considerable ability and public experience. Though lacking the aristocratic background often associated with southern leaders, Jefferson Davis rose to a career of influence and distinguished service. He was born in Kentucky in an unpretentious cabin, the tenth child of a pioneer family. His grandfather, Evan Davis, was a Welsh immigrant who had lived in Philadelphia and had moved later to Georgia. His father, Samuel Davis, had served in the Revolutionary army in Georgia, had lived near Augusta for a time, and had moved with his family to Christian County in western Kentucky, where he was making a modest living as tobacco planter and stock farmer when his son Jefferson was born on June 3, 1808. It was a remarkable coincidence that the birthplace of the Confederate leader was not more than a hundred miles from that of Abraham Lincoln.

Yet the difference in the political histories of the two men owes much to the fact that Samuel Davis, during his son Jefferson's childhood, moved his family to Wilkinson County, Mississippi, whereas the Lincolns moved to Indiana and later to Illinois. After his father's death, Davis was encouraged and supported by an older brother. Educated at Transylvania University in Lexington, Kentucky, and at West Point, Davis saw service in a Wisconsin army post and as an officer in the Black Hawk War. Then he left the army to become a Mississippi planter. In the 1830s on his plantation, Brierfield, overlooking the Mississippi River, he introduced a regime of self-discipline and limited self-government among his slaves. Having first married the daughter of Zachary Taylor, who died after a few months, Davis next married Varina Anne Howell, the daughter of an aristocratic

Jefferson Davis became one of the strongest supporters of states' rights. He was inaugurated president of the Confederacy on February 22, 1861. As the war carried on, Davis's popularity in the Confederate states began to decline.

and wealthy Mississippi planter. Elected to Congress, he resigned his seat to become the colonel of a Mississippi volunteer regiment in the Mexican War. After distinguishing himself at Monterrey and Buena Vista, he took pride in his military reputation.

First appointed and then elected to the Senate from Mississippi in 1850, Davis, who held secessionist views at this point, opposed Clay's Compromise of 1850 and tried hard to defeat the admission of California as a free state. Then his ideas changed. Serving as Pierce's secretary of war, he displayed a strong sense of nationalism along with support of expansionist schemes in Cuba and Nicaragua. His national vision was illustrated by his efforts in behalf of a transcontinental railroad via a southern route. Briefly he dreamed of a united South which would not withdraw from the Union, but would dominate the Union.

As a senator from 1857 to 1861, he opposed Douglas on the Kansas question, and by joining with Rhett and Yancey to prevent the nomination of Douglas at Charleston, he played a part in the breakup of the Democratic party. When, however, the prospect of Lincoln's election loomed during the campaign of 1860, he offered Douglas his personal intervention to get Breckinridge and even Bell to withdraw if Douglas would follow suit.[45] Davis's plan was to run a conservative around whom all opponents of Lincoln could unite to win the election and thereby save the Union.

Committed to cooperation with other states rather than Mississippi's unilateral departure from the Union, he did not favor the secession movement of 1860. On November 10, 1860, he wrote to Rhett that he doubted whether South Carolina ought to withdraw from the Union by itself, and he believed that Mississippi should not follow. He warned Congress of the destructiveness of a sectional war.

Yet when the time came, Davis was a logical choice for president. The other leading candidates were either too extreme like Yancey the fire-eater or too alcoholic like Robert Toombs. The need for unanimity and the desire to attract the other uncommitted slave states pushed delegates toward a centrist like Jefferson Davis, who also gained support because his political and military background reminded delegates of the American superhero George Washington. The convention chose Alexander Stephens of Georgia as provisional vice president, a member, until recently, of the U.S. Congress. Stephens had opposed the secession of Georgia, but like so many other southerners, had no thought other than that of following his state once secession had been determined.

The unanimous choice of such "moderates" by the Montgomery convention revealed the new government's abandonment of the radicalism that had been necessary for its creation. Davis had not sought the presidency; some, including his wife, believed him ill suited to politics. But after his election Yancey announced "that the man and the hour have met." Later, at the inauguration, the sprightly tune "Dixie"—soon to become the Confederacy's anthem—seemed poorly matched to Davis's somber presidential address, which proclaimed a policy of peace and sympathy with the border states so essential to the hopes of the Confederacy.

Because the first Confederate regime was provisional, it was necessary to launch a permanent government. The two inaugurations of President Davis mark the division between the provisional and permanent phases. On February 18, 1861, Davis was inaugurated as provisional president, an office that had been conferred by the Montgomery convention. On February 22, 1862, he was inaugurated as president under the permanent regime. Between these two dates the Montgomery convention completed the permanent constitution, which was adopted unanimously by the Montgomery Congress on March 11, 1861. The seceding states ratified the constitution in state conventions; a decision was made to move the capital to Richmond; and the government held general elections for Congress and for presidential electors in November 1861. In this nonpartisan election (as all Confederate elections were), Davis and Stephens received all 109 electoral votes.

The Confederate government quickly became for the South the successor to the federal government at Washington. A flag, the "Stars and Bars," was adopted for the new republic after study by a committee that concluded that keeping the United States "Stars and Stripes" would be impractical and unpatriotic. Commissioners were sent to Washington to negotiate the surrender of federal forts and arsenals within the Confederacy and to give assurance of the wish to "preserve the most friendly relations." Other commissioners were sent to Europe. A committee was appointed to refit the statutes of the United States for the Confederacy and to keep all laws that were not inconsistent with the Confederate Constitution. The Confederate Congress resolved to employ an "agent at Washington to furnish any documents or information which may be useful to this body" and it also voted to continue existing customs officers in the South.[46] Throughout, the difficulty of creating a new government was simplified by taking over, with adaptations, the Constitution of the federal government, its laws, and even its personnel.

The Confederacy faced important problems in these early weeks of its existence. The tariff, the navigation of the Mississippi River, the post office, the seizure of United States funds, the organization of the courts, appeals to the other slaveholding states to join the Confederacy, the control of Indian affairs, and the deportation of northern "alien enemies" occupied the lawmakers. An army and a navy were organized. In a harbinger of the future, tension emerged between South Carolina authorities, who were intent on taking over Fort

At this early meeting of the Confederate Congress in February 1861, the problems of organizing the Confederacy were already present. Unlike the United States government, which had existed for nearly one hundred years, the Confederate government was newly formed and unprepared to handle the challenges of war.

Sumter, and the Montgomery government, which wished to delay such action, at least until Davis was inaugurated.

By the closing weeks of his administration, Buchanan faced a new nation. Most federal arsenals and forts in the South had been seized. The national government retained possession only of Florida's Fort Pickens off Pensacola, where a truce was in effect, and South Carolina's Fort Sumter. But South Carolina opposed the landing of provisions and demanded federal evacuation. The withdrawal of southern members of the House and Senate in Washington intensified the impression of a crumbling union. Southern oratory was tinged with tragedy and pathos as the seceders delivered "farewell addresses."

On February 11, Lincoln left Springfield and started east. He arrived in Washington on February 23, and his quarters at the Willard Hotel became, for both statesmen and clamoring office seekers, the temporary White House. A month before his seventieth birthday, the harassed and haggard Buchanan left office, not sure whether the challenging movement at Montgomery or the lingering Peace Convention, which continued its sessions until nearly the end of his term, held the story of America's future.

CHAPTER 7 | Lincoln, the Upper South, and the Sumter Crisis

F ew presidents have begun their administrations with as little prestige and as much controversy as Abraham Lincoln did on March 4, 1861. Critics ridiculed his lack of experience, homeliness, and frontier ways. Detractors throughout the nation complained that he had been elected to the presidency by a minority of voters, although that had also been the case in the presidential elections of 1848 and 1856. In the East Lincoln was regarded as inadequate to the crisis that confronted him, while in the Upper South Unionists sought to enlist Lincoln and other Republican leaders in futile compromises intended to defuse the sectional crisis.[1] In the Confederacy Lincoln continued to be held in contempt as a radical intent on destroying slavery.

During his first six weeks in office, the new president made critical choices that influenced not only when the war began, but also where and among whom it was fought. Because his election had failed to draw the entire South into the Confederacy as leaders in South Carolina had thought it would, Unionists in the Upper South explored the possibilities for cooperation with the Republicans. But Lincoln declined to work toward any coalition, telling his friends to oppose compromises as "with a chain of steel," and especially not to negotiate on the issue of extending slavery into the territories, which the new president believed the essential Republican position.[2] In April his policies and those of Jefferson Davis concerning Fort Sumter led to the decision of another four southern states—Virginia, Arkansas, Tennessee, and North Carolina—to secede from the Union and join the Confederacy.

## LINCOLN TAKES OFFICE

The new administration began with a secret night train ride into Washington, to which Lincoln reluctantly agreed under pressure from advisers who feared an assassination attempt. Thereafter opponents abused him for ignominiously creeping into the capital, and cartoonists caricatured his disguise. Even his friends were humiliated. Lincoln's preoccupation with office seekers to the neglect of weightier matters, his social awkwardness, his seeming caution in approaching critical problems, his inexperience in the management of national affairs, all contributed to the unfavorable initial impression. Many thought that Lincoln would be president in name only and that his Cabinet would be the directing force in the new administration.

Nor were Americans impressed with Lincoln's seven-man Cabinet, which brought together a diverse group of Republican rivals. More than half had once been Democrats; the rest were former Whigs. Representing New England, the Midwest and the Middle Atlantic regions, Lincoln's Cabinet fulfilled various campaign pledges.

Its two ablest members were Seward and Chase—Seward chosen as secretary of state because of his commanding influence within the party; Chase an obvious choice for secretary of treasury because of his antislavery leadership, his ability, and his prominence as a presidential rival. Secretary of War Gideon Welles of Connecticut appealed as a former Democrat and a New Englander. Pennsylvania's Simon Cameron was reluctantly appointed to head the War Department in order to comply with a prenomination bargain in which Lincoln personally had no part and which ran counter to his better judgment. Edward Bates of Missouri

When Abraham Lincoln took office as the sixteenth president of the United States in March 1861, he already faced a dividing Union. Many southerners viewed Lincoln's election as a direct threat to slavery and to their political, social, and economic way of life.

Standing in front of the unfinished dome of the Capitol, Lincoln delivered an inaugural address in which he discouraged both sides from going to war.

as attorney general, Caleb Smith of Indiana as secretary of the interior, and Montgomery Blair of Maryland as postmaster general completed a Cabinet whose members often disagreed. Lincoln had intended to include a southerner, but John Gilmer of North Carolina, who wanted Lincoln to shape an intersectional coalition with former Whigs, eventually declined.[3]

In his masterful state papers, Lincoln soon demonstrated his ability to think through complex public controversies and to present his conclusions in a simple, logical style graced with allusions meaningful to all Americans. His inaugural address, delivered on March 4, 1861, in an atmosphere of national apprehension, struck a note of firmness, conciliation, and friendliness to both the Confederacy and to the eight slave states that had not seceded. Yet he made it clear that the government could not consent to its own destruction by recognizing secession and that it must maintain its authority against the challenge of disunion. As for the federal forts and property in the seceded states, he said: "The power confided to me, will be used to hold, occupy, and possess [he did not say "repossess"] the property, and places belonging to the government." He added that "no bloodshed or violence" was involved in this policy. There would be no invasion, he said, "no using of force against, or among the people anywhere."

"Physically speaking," he urged, "we cannot separate." No "impassable wall" could be erected between the sections. They "cannot but remain face to face; and intercourse, either amicable or hostile, must continue between them.... Can aliens make treaties easier than friends can make laws? ... Suppose you go to war, you cannot fight always; and when, after much loss on both sides, and no gain on either, you cease fighting, the identical old questions ... are again upon you."

Regarding slavery, he advised the enforcement of all laws, repeated his former declaration that he had "no purpose, directly or indirectly, to interfere with the institution of slavery in the States where it exists," and affirmed that "the property, peace and security of no section are ... in anywise endangered" by his administration. On the advice of his friend Orville Browning, he omitted the pledge "to reclaim the places which have fallen"; at Seward's urging he softened language that the secretary of state thought would encourage the secession of Virginia. Lincoln closed with a stirring appeal to the southern people:

> In your hands, my dissatisfied fellow countrymen ... is the momentous issue of civil war. The government will not assail you. You can have no conflict without being yourselves the aggressors. You have no oath registered in Heaven to destroy the government, while I shall have the most solemn one to "preserve, protect, and defend" it.
>
> We are not enemies, but friends. We must not be enemies.... The mystic chords of memory, stretching from every ... patriot grave to every living heart and hearthstone, all over this broad land, will yet swell the chorus of the Union, when again touched, as surely they will be, by the better angels of our nature.[4]

### REACTIONS TO LINCOLN'S INAUGURAL

Contemporaries and historians have disagreed as to what Lincoln intended with his inaugural address. What, for example, did the new president mean by his statement that he would hold property now in the hands of the Confederates? How could he deliver the mail and collect customs duties? And what was the effect of leaving vacant federal offices in the South if the local population opposed having such officials? "He would assert the Federal authority vigorously but he would not exercise it. He would enforce the laws—where an enforcement mechanism existed. He would deliver the mails—unless repelled. He would collect the duties—offshore. He would hold the forts—at least those Buchanan had held, and that seemed capable of holding themselves."[5]

Yet southerners who associated Lincoln with Republicanism could not forget that his party included Charles Sumner as well as supporters of John Brown. Nor could they overlook the fact that the Republicans refused to accept the *Dred Scott* decision as final; that they had pushed their antislavery agenda in Kansas; that the "personal liberty laws" of the North were largely their work, and that Lincoln had been silent during the campaign of 1860.

Thus despite the mildness of Lincoln's inaugural message, southerners feared that what they saw as radical tendencies within his party would eventually influence him. Hence most Confederates and many residents of the Upper South refused to take seriously Lincoln's disclaimer of any intention to interfere with slavery in the states. Others, hearing only rumors about the new president, were unaware that he had made any such disavowal. The controlling influence in his administration, southerners feared, would be that of such men as Massachusetts Senator Henry Wilson, who promised to deliver the government from the grasp of the Slave Power. As a Charleston editor put it: "If Mr. Lincoln was to come out and declare he held every sacred right of the South with respect to African slavery, no one should believe him; and if he was believed, his professions should not have the least influence on the course of the South."[6] Meanwhile, Unionists in Virginia and North Carolina, some of whom contacted Lincoln for clarification, accepted the president's vague reassurance that "[his inaugural] meant peace."[7]

The issue was not so much Lincoln's intention as it was southern fears that Lincoln's election signified an attack on slavery in the states. In fact both Lincoln and the Republican party were committed to not interfering with slavery in the South. Republicans were even ready to compromise on the issue of personal liberty laws. And the president himself was by background and intellect a moderate. His Virginia ancestry and Kentucky birth; his many personal contacts with southerners and with Illinoisians of southern antecedents such as John Todd Stuart, his first law partner, and Joshua Fry Speed, his best friend; and his marriage into an aristocratic slaveholding Kentucky family, made him as sympathetic to the southern point of view as to that of northern abolitionists, even as he determined his own position of opposition to slavery in the territories. Moreover, the Republican party during this period tried to draw conservatives into its ranks and to attract old-line Whigs, of whom the new president was a conspicuous example.

Ironically, southerners themselves had given the Republicans their opportunity to control the Union government. By splitting the Democratic party and abandoning their seats, they contributed to the Republican control of Congress. In the second session of the Thirty-sixth Congress (elected in 1858 and in office until March 1861), Republicans held twenty-six seats in the Senate, Democrats thirty-six, and Know-Nothings two; two seats were vacant. In the House, Republicans held a comfortable majority over the Democrats. Yet during this session the entire South Carolina delegation was absent from both houses, accounting for the six vacancies in the House and the two in the Senate.

Nor would Republicans have controlled the Thirty-seventh Congress, elected in November of 1860, if the southern states had stayed in the Union. In this session the Republicans numbered only twenty-nine in the Senate, compared with thirty-seven for the opposition; in the House the opposition could have mustered 129 to the Republican's 108. As Andrew Johnson of Tennessee noted, if the southern states remained in the Union the Democrats would command a majority in the Senate, the opposition could block appointments and refuse appropriations, and the incoming administration would be "hand-cuffed, powerless to do harm . . ."[8]

## RELUCTANT CONFEDERATES

In Virginia, Arkansas, Tennessee, and North Carolina, the interpretations of Lincoln's inaugural address—and the overall intentions of the president and his party—were especially important as these states wavered between secession, staying in the Union, and attempting to create a border-state coalition that might broker a settlement between the sections. Virginia was the largest and by every measure the most important of what later became essential additions to the Confederacy.

After Lincoln's election, the state's governor, John Letcher, had immediately summoned the legislature into special session. On January 7, 1861, Governor Letcher criticized South Carolina's hasty exit from the republic, but a week later a bill providing for a convention to consider the relations of Virginia to the United States passed the legislature. In the election that followed Virginians demonstrated their moderation. They rejected prosecession candidates and mandated that any action taken by this special session must be ratified by a referendum. Assembling in Richmond in February, the convention contained a majority of Unionists, many of whom, like the governor, were optimistic about the chances of a compromise that would restore the Union.

Although moderate Virginians wanted to stay in the Union, they also believed that the North must make concessions. "There will not be one man in [the convention] who is not for a final separation of the states, in double quick time—unless there is reason to hope for a perfectly full final and unqualified surrender of the slavery question [to southerners]," predicted one delegate.[9] As for coercing any southern state, the convention held that the federal government ought not to use force against any state that chose to invoke its right to leave the Union.

Lincoln's inaugural address produced mixed feelings in the state. On March 9, Governor Letcher described Lincoln's address as creating "quite a sensation here. The disunionists were wild with joy, and declared that if the Convention did not pass an ordinance of secession at once, the State would be disgraced. . . . The tendency now is to a conference with the border slaveholding states. . . ."[10]

Though disapproving of Lincoln's policy, which was to keep the forts in federal hands but not use them to attack the Confederacy, most Virginians wanted to stay in the Union. But if the South was "coerced" or if war should come, Virginia must come to the aid of its sister states. "I do not approve of the inaugural of Mr. Lincoln," wrote the future Confederate general Jubal Early on March 5, "but, sir, I ask if it were not for the fact that six or seven states of this Confederacy have seceded from this Union, if the declarations of President Lincoln that he would execute the laws in all the states would not have been hailed throughout the country as a guarantee that he would perform his duty? . . . I ask why is it that we are placed in this perilous condition? And if it is not solely from the action of these states that have seceded from the Union without having consulted our views?"[11]

When commissioners from the Confederacy visited Richmond to encourage that state's secession, the convention resisted their impassioned appeals, recommending instead various constitutional amendments protecting slavery along with support for a convention of border states to meet in Frankfort, Kentucky in May. On April 4, a motion to draw up a secession ordinance was voted down, 88 to 45, and on April 8 the convention made a final effort to avert secession by sending a committee to confer with Lincoln.

Elsewhere in the non-Confederate South in the early months of 1861, there was the same tension between Unionists, supporters of states' rights, proponents of a border state confederacy, and unconditional secessionists. In Arkansas a vigorous Unionist coalition resisted the state's secessionists, who included Governor Henry Rector. With the governor's encouragement, military preparations began in early 1861, and mass meetings kept the theme of secession before the people. Yet when secessionists in the legislature passed a bill calling for a state convention—usually the first step along the road to secession—Unionists gained a small majority of delegates against secession. Assembled at Little Rock on March 4, the convention's sessions were turbulent, lengthy, and subject to pressure from outside prosecessionist agitation.[12]

Still, the Unionists had sufficient power to defeat a resolution condemning Lincoln's inaugural address and also to prevent the passage of a secession ordinance. As was the case in Virginia, expectations for peace rested with the proposed border-state convention that was to meet in Frankfort, Kentucky in May. Before adjourning in March, the Arkansas convention resolved to hold a popular referendum in August on the issue of cooperation with the border states or secession with the Confederacy.

Meanwhile, in Tennessee, the predominant Unionism of the people was frustrated by the legislature in its special session of January 1861. In early January Governor Isham Harris denounced northern assaults on "the rights of the Southern citizen." Harris also recommended the calling of a convention composed of delegates elected by the people to meet in Nashville on February 4, to discover the grounds on which the federal Union and the constitutional rights of the slave states could both be preserved. But ominously for the state's future Unionism, the legislature resolved to urge Lincoln and each of the southern states to maintain the status quo concerning the forts.

The voters of Tennessee were even more Unionist minded than the legislature. The proposition to call a convention to consider secession was rejected by a popular vote of 69,675 to 57,798. On the issue of secession or no secession, the vote, as judged by the delegates' positions on the issue, was even more decisive— 24,749 for and 91,803 against.[13]

Nowhere was the contrast between the Upper and Lower South better demonstrated than in the difference between the two Carolinas. South Carolina was the first state to pass an ordinance of secession, North Carolina was the last. In North Carolina, opposition to secession appeared in several arenas: the states's delegation to the 1860 Democratic National Convention favored cooperation with the northern Democrats and refused to abandon the convention, no matter what the platform; and the presidential campaign of 1860 gave new life to the state's moribund Whig organization because of that party's commitment to the Constitution and the Union. Thus, although Breckinridge carried the state, his majority over the combined vote of Bell and Douglas was fewer than a thousand votes. The existence of a vibrant two-party system was clearly a factor in dampening secessionist impulses.[14]

Accordingly, North Carolina voters did not consider Lincoln's election a sufficient cause for secession. When the legislature, at the prodding of Governor John Ellis, submitted to the electorate a proposition calling for a convention to consider secession, it was defeated on February 28 by a vote of 47,323 to 46,672, "with the strongest Whig counties tending to be the strongest Unionist counties [and] the strongest Democratic counties usually the strongest secessionist counties."[15]

As was the case in Arkansas, Tennessee, and Virginia, Unionist sentiment in North Carolina was conditional, gradually weakening as prospects for a peaceful settlement diminished. "I am a union man," asserted one of Zebulon Vance's correspondents, "but when the [Lincoln administration] sends men south it will change my notions. I can do nothing against my own people."[16] This conviction was shared by many in the Upper South.

## CONTROVERSY OVER THE FORTS

Against the backdrop of conditional support for the Union in these four important states, Lincoln confronted the problem of conciliating the Upper South so as to halt the secession movement, at the same time that he considered the closely related problem of Fort Sumter. Major Robert Anderson had earlier moved his small force from Fort Moultrie to Fort Sumter, and now needed the supplies that had been sent, but not delivered, during Buchanan's administration. Though Buchanan declined to make the seizure of some federal forts (including Castle Pinckney and Fort Moultrie in Charleston Harbor) a reason for war, he refused to surrender Sumter, which promptly became a divisive symbol between the two governments.

Meanwhile, Georgia troops seized Fort Pulaski in Savannah Harbor on January 3, and Alabama troops installed a strong garrison at Fort Morgan outside Mobile on January 4. At Pensacola, though Fort Pickens remained in Union possession, the federal navy yard and Fort Barrancas surrendered without a struggle to Alabama and Florida troops on January 12. Before Texas had even seceded, General David Twiggs, U.S.A., who was later dismissed from the army for his "treachery to the flag," delivered nineteen federal army posts to that state's secessionist authorities.[17]

In addition, a number of post offices, custom houses, hospitals, and other public buildings had been occupied. The New Orleans mint had been taken over; United States revenue cutters and other ships had been seized; and batteries in Charleston Harbor had fired on a schooner carrying the American flag. All these southern occupations of federal forts had occurred before Lincoln took office.

Although Lincoln had deliberately avoided threatening the repossession of places already taken by the Confederates, many northerners opposed further concessions to the South and looked on Sumter as a test of the president's commitment in his inaugural address that no more surrenders would take place. At the same time, southern Unionists insisted that the president abandon the forts to lessen any chance of a clash between the Confederacy and the Union.[18] Any bloodshed, these Unionists correctly reasoned, would make compromise impossible.

By March 1861, important northeastern business interests that earlier had favored compromise now were "forced back to the point where they found it necessary to 'take sides' for or against the Union." Holders of government securities "looked upon disunion as a menace to their investments"; other businessmen "believed that the reduction of the government to impotence would not only destroy its own credit but depress every form of private property." Those to whom southerners owed money feared the secessionists would make "depreciated paper money legal tender in payment of private debts"; manufacturers thought that the Confederacy, under its free trade policy, would no longer patronize northern markets but would buy directly from Europe. Faced with these economic realities, businessmen, "like other Yankees, . . . overwhelmingly chose the Union— even at the cost of war."

As northern opinion shifted to oppose further compromise, both Democrats and Republicans adopted the position that "only by preserving the Union could

Americans fulfill the promise of their Manifest Destiny." Nationalists accepted the view that the United States was an exceptional nation-state and held that "the preservation of America's political greatness was more than a duty they owed to themselves; it was a duty to mankind. . . . Many in the free states believed that the sectional conflict was itself a struggle between democracy and despotism." Though some antislavery spokesmen were willing to see the southern states depart in peace from the Union, "there were more abolitionists who desired a war against slavery than there were those who sought absolution from the national curse by speeding the departure of the South."[19]

Finally, amid the disparate views held by a northern population of twenty-three million was the perception that American society had become decadent and corrupt. To some, the possibility of moral regeneration through the discipline and self-sacrifice of war countered any compromising attitudes toward the South. Thus, for many different reasons most northerners hoped that the answer to a question posed by a Columbus, Ohio newspaper, "Have we a Government?" was yes—and one that would uphold the laws and protect the property of the United States.[20]

Despite this gradual hardening of northern sentiment, Lincoln was reluctant to abandon the idea of compromise. But the day after his inauguration, the president confronted Major Anderson's bleak assessment that he had only four to six weeks of provisions remaining. At first Lincoln's closest advisers advocated concessions to the South. General Winfield Scott, the veteran head of the army, argued that the sending of a sufficiently powerful force to supply or to reinforce was impracticable.

Turning to his Cabinet, Lincoln found that only Chase and Blair favored an expedition intended to supply food to the garrison. Blair was certain that such an expedition would demonstrate the "firmness" of the administration. Chase, though approving the expedition, believed such a move might begin a civil war. Seward blamed South Carolina for the "revolution," but declared that he "would not initiate war to regain a useless and unnecessary position. . . ." Cameron advised that an attempt to relieve the fort would be "unwise," as did Welles, Smith, and Bates.[21]

Such advice, to which the inexperienced Lincoln paid more attention than he would in later years, may have caused the president to reconsider his inaugural pledge "to hold, occupy, and possess the property and places belonging to the government" and to consider evacuating Fort Sumter. Such a move would encourage Unionists in the Upper South. In discussions with Unionist members of the Virginia secession convention, Lincoln may have made a conditional suggestion that he would "evacuate Sumter if they would break up their convention, without any row or nonsense." "A State for a fort," he is reported to have said, "is no bad business."[22] At the same time, the president considered the possibility of giving up Sumter and remaining "firm" at Pickens. In any case, on March 12 he ordered the reinforcement of the Florida fort.

Several developments during the early weeks of Lincoln's administration suggested that the government was planning the evacuation of Sumter. Indirect communications occurred between Seward, widely regarded as the "spokesman" of the administration, and Confederate commissioners in Washington. Though Seward did not actually "recognize" the Confederacy by receiving these commissioners officially, he did deal with them through Supreme Court Justices Samuel Nelson and John Archibald Campbell. To these emissaries, shuttling back and forth between the commissioners and himself, Seward, who was acting on his own, gave assurances in keeping with his own sincere wish that Sumter should be evacuated. Such information was regarded by the commissioners and by southern leaders as a "promise" that the garrison would be withdrawn, although Lincoln himself made no such commitment.

In the last few days of March a series of developments compelled Lincoln to abandon any idea of yielding Sumter. The president's ignorance about whether his order for the reinforcement of Fort Pickens had been obeyed obliged him to consider a new course.[23] Perhaps he also saw the hardening of northern opinion against further concessions to the South in the resolutions that Lyman Trumbull of Illinois introduced in the Senate on March 28: "[I]t is the duty of the President to use all the means in his power to hold and protect the public property of the United States."[24] The same day, Lincoln's faith in his military advisers was shaken when General Scott, on political grounds, advised yielding both Pickens and Sumter to the Confederates.

The next day, polling the Cabinet again, the president found a striking change in Cabinet opinion: only Smith and Seward were in favor of giving up the South Carolina fort, and the secretary of state forfeited much of Lincoln's confidence by making a bizarre proposal on April 1 to "Change the question before the Public from one upon Slavery, or about Slavery, for a question upon Union or Disunion" through making impossible demands upon Spain, France, Great Britain, and Russia.[25]

Ignoring the possibilities of unity through a foreign policy distraction, Lincoln ordered two relief expeditions to be fitted out, one intended for Sumter and the other for Pickens. On April 4 he placed Captain Gustavus Fox in command of the Sumter expedition and notified Anderson "the expedition will go forward," with the intention that once in Charleston Harbor, Fox would transfer the supplies to small, unarmed boats for delivery to Anderson in the island fort. Two days later Lincoln ordered a clerk in the State Department to travel to South Carolina and to inform Governor Pickens: "I am directed by the President of the United States to notify you to expect an attempt will be made to supply Fort- Sumter [sic] with provisions only; and that, if such attempt be not resisted, no effort to throw in men, arms, or ammunition, will be made, without further notice, or in case of an attack upon the Fort."[26]

Did Lincoln anticipate that sending this expedition to provision Fort Sumter would precipitate a civil war? Even at the time there were those who claimed that the president knew the consequences of his action and deliberately tricked the Confederacy into firing the first shot. "You and I both anticipated," Lincoln wrote to Captain Fox in May 1861, "that the cause of the country would be advanced by making the attempt to provision Fort Sumpter [sic], even if it should fail; and it is no small consolation now to feel that our anticipation is justified by the result."[27] Later, the president told his friend Orville Browning, "The plan [sending supplies to Major Anderson] succeeded. They attacked Sumter—it fell, and thus, did more service than it otherwise could."[28] Such evidence persuaded one southern historian that "Lincoln, having decided that there was no other way than war for the salvation of his administration, his party, and the Union, maneuvered the Confederates into firing the first shot in order that they, rather than he, should take the blame of beginning bloodshed."[29]

Today most historians feel that this is a distortion of Lincoln's motives. No pacifist, Lincoln was certainly willing to accept war rather than permit the dissolution of the Union. And though he understood the importance of the Upper South, he had never adopted a policy of concessions to the Confederacy. It is hard to see how, short of acquiescing in southern independence, he could have followed a more nonaggressive course. From the day of his inaugural to the time of the Confederate attack on Fort Sumter, he carefully refrained from any precautionary assembling of federal troops, from any issuing of belligerent public statements, and from any attempts to repossess federal property already taken over by the Confederacy.

So far as Sumter was concerned, the approaching exhaustion of supplies in the fort made some change in the situation inevitable. Lincoln's course offered the nearest approach possible to the preservation of the status quo. The expedition was directed not to reinforce but to provision Major Anderson's men; it was not stealthily sent, but notice of its pacific purpose was given to the governor of South Carolina. Of course Lincoln was aware that sending provisions to Sumter might provoke hostilities, but that is not to say that he desired war. And to argue that Lincoln meant that the first shot would be fired by the other side if a first shot was fired by no means the same as arguing that he deliberately maneuvered to have the shot fired.

On the other hand, the belligerence of the Confederacy has been underestimated. Many Confederates were anxious to make the war that Lincoln would accept. As Lincoln's actions emerged from an intensifying desire in the North to keep the nation whole, so too in the nascent Confederacy southern nationalism directed the government toward war. Jefferson Davis had encouraged commanders in local areas to initiate military actions against federal installations, and in

Florida to reduce Fort Pickens before any relief expedition arrived; nevertheless, like his counterpart in Washington, he did not want to fire the first shot. The Confederate president cautioned commanders not to fire on Sumter until Confederate diplomats had failed in their efforts to achieve a peaceful takeover of the fort. But Davis and the Confederate Cabinet faced their own set of dilemmas: the growth of southern Unionism if nothing was done at Sumter, the fear that states would take things into their own hands, and the need to bring a hesitant Virginia into the Confederacy.[30]

To some southerners, Lincoln's plan to relieve the installation seemed a challenge and a breach of faith. To others it appeared as the opportunity to avoid a feared reconstruction of the Union. "Sir, unless you sprinkle blood in the face of the people of Alabama they will be back in the union in less than ten days," worried one southerner before Sumter.[31] After the Confederate Cabinet had anxiously consulted in Montgomery, Secretary of War Leroy Walker directed General Pierre G. T. Beauregard, in command at Charleston, to demand the evacuation of the fort, and, if the demand was refused, to "reduce it." The excited temper of South Carolina made it inevitable that any attempt to provision the fort would precipitate an attack. There was apprehension that, in the absence of orders from Montgomery, the state might take the initiative, thus embarrassing the infant Confederacy by a conflict between state and federal authority.

On the afternoon of April 11 a boat carrying Colonel James Chesnut, the recently resigned United States senator from South Carolina, and Captain Stephen Lee, visited Fort Sumter under a flag of truce and conveyed Beauregard's demand for its surrender. Anderson refused, but remarked to the others that he would "await the first shot" and that in any case his garrison would be "starved out in a few days."[32] Only if Anderson surrendered could war have been avoided. As Secretary of War Walker advised Beauregard on the afternoon of April 11:

> Do not desire needlessly to bombard Fort Sumter. If Major Anderson will state the time at which . . . he will evacuate, and agree that . . . he will not use his guns against us, unless ours should be employed against Fort Sumter, you are authorized thus to avoid the effusion of blood. If this, or its equivalent, be refused, reduce the fort. . . .[33]

During the night of April 11–12, three officers visited the fort and informed Major Anderson of their orders from Montgomery. After a conference with his officers, Anderson responded that he would evacuate by noon on April 15.[34]

Without waiting to transmit this reply to Beauregard for further instructions, the aides, at 3:30 A.M. on April 12, served notice on Anderson that the general would open fire in one hour. Much has been made of this incident, for it appears that these three young men settled the fate of the country. The fact that the aides gave the order for the firing of the signal gun that was to begin the bombardment, instead of leaving the final order to Beauregard, does seem extraordinary. But the essential fact was that the Confederacy was demanding evacuation of a fort that Lincoln had decided not to evacuate. Moreover he had dispatched a provisioning expedition that southern authorities regarded as a ruse to permit the reinforcement of the garrison. When these Confederates rejected Anderson's reply, they were merely following established policy.[35]

At 4:30 A.M. on April 12, 1861, the firing began, and Sumter came under cross fire from a number of batteries in the harbor. After a bloodless bombardment of forty hours, during which the walls were wrecked, the ammunition was nearly exhausted, and extensive damage was done by fire, Major Anderson surrendered the fort on April 13. His garrison was permitted to depart after saluting the flag. Meanwhile, the relief expedition commanded by Captain Fox—consisting of the *Baltic*, the *Pawnee*, and the *Harriet Lane* but weakened by the absence

From housetops in Charleston, South Carolina, women watch the firing on Fort Sumter. For many southern women, the outbreak of war would bring change to their daily lives. Some women moved from the household to the work force as teachers or nurses.

Following forty hours of bombardment, the walls and interior of Fort Sumter were extensively damaged. When Major Robert Anderson surrendered on April 13, the Confederate flag was hoisted in the air. Following the attack on Fort Sumter, four more states (Virginia, Arkansas, Tennessee, and North Carolina) seceded.

of the *Powhatan* and unassisted by the necessary tugs, which had been detained by a gale—found itself powerless to do more than carry off Anderson and his men after the surrender.

## REACTION IN THE UPPER SOUTH TO WAR MEASURES

After receiving word of the surrender of the fort, President Lincoln, on April 15, issued a proclamation calling forth "the militia of the several States of the Union, to the . . . number of seventy-five thousand," to suppress "combinations" in seven states "too powerful to be suppressed by the ordinary course of judicial proceedings." In the same proclamation the president summoned Congress to meet in special session on July 4. Soon after, he launched other war measures.

Had there been a formal declaration of war, the effect could not have been more instantaneous and widespread. Within weeks of the firing on Sumter and Lincoln's call for troops, Virginia, Arkansas, Tennessee, and North Carolina seceded. In the case of Virginia, state commissioners were in Washington conferring with Lincoln when the Sumter bombardment began. On April 17 the Virginia convention organized in January voted 88 to 55 to secede, a vote that, once the outcome was certain, later changed to 103 to 46. Put to referendum, this decision was ratified five weeks later by the commanding majority of 128,884 to 32,314.

In Virginia as elsewhere in the Upper South, individual choices were influenced by region and class. In the northwestern counties of the Allegheny region (soon to become West Virginia), three of every four voters opposed secession; in the plantation counties with high proportions of slaves, the figures were reversed.[36] But even before this referendum, Virginia's state government agreed to place its militia under the command of President Davis.

After the firing on Sumter and Lincoln's call for seventy-five thousand militia, Arkansas also quickly moved to join the Confederacy. In that state on May 6, a reassembled convention voted 65 to 5 for secession, but the convention refused to submit the question to a popular vote. The governor had already placed the state militia under Confederate authority, and these militia units quickly seized federal arsenals. As in Virginia, "anti-secession sentiment found its strongest support from largely slaveless subsistence farmers in Northern and Western Arkansas, an area populated mostly by settlers from Missouri, Kentucky and Tennessee who showed a strong attachment to the Unionism of Henry Clay and Andrew Jackson."[37]

At the time of Lincoln's mobilization order, Tennessee had no convention in session, and the idea of holding such an assembly had been decisively rejected by voters. But Tennessee's Unionism did not include placing its militia in the service of Lincoln and the federal government. In these circumstances the governor and the legislature took matters into their own hands. Governor Isham Harris dismissed Lincoln's call: "[I]n such an unholy crusade no gallant son of Tennessee will ever draw his sword."[38] On April 25, the governor addressed a special session of the legislature urging union with the Confederate States. On May 6 the assembly, deliberating behind closed doors, directed that an election be held on June 8 to ratify or reject a declaration of independence and an ordinance dissolving the union between Tennessee and the United States.

Governor Harris had already appointed commissioners who signed a military "treaty" with the Confederate States, providing that in the interval before Tennessee formally joined the Confederacy the state would be under "the direction of the President of the Confederate States, upon the same basis as if the state were now a member of said Confederacy." This arrangement was ratified by the legislature which also authorized the governor to raise a force of fifty-five thousand men, funded by state bonds.

On election day, many Tennessee Unionists found themselves with a formidable army as well their state treasury in the hands of a secessionist governor. "Nothing they could do would free them from the military government imposed on them. The secret session of the Legislature and the Military League had turned the state over to the Confederate army which immediately took possession."[39]

Yet the people of Tennessee were not so much tricked by their legislature and governor as they were caught in the inescapable dilemma of the Upper South, which gave them no opportunity to promote measures for the peaceful restoration of the Union. Instead they were forced to an immediate choice between two unpalatable alternatives when their preference was probably for a border-state convention. When the vote was taken on June 8, 104,913 Tennesseans favored separation to 47,238 for staying in the Union.

Most Unionist sentiment was concentrated in the eastern counties, where opposition to secession was so strong that a movement to organize a coalition of counties to stay in the Union seemed possible. This movement was never realized, in part because Confederate forces soon occupied the area. Before they did so a Unionist convention in Greeneville adopted a list of grievances against the secessionists for their violations of free speech and free elections. In any case, the secessionist government of Tennessee was short lived. When Fort Donelson on the Cumberland River fell to Union forces in February 1862, Lincoln appointed Andrew Johnson the military governor in Nashville.

In North Carolina similar reactions to the firing on Fort Sumter and Lincoln's call for troops quickly eradicated Union sentiment. Governor John Ellis indignantly replied to Lincoln's troop requisition by claiming that he could not be a party "to this wicked violation of the law of the country and to this war upon the liberties of a free people. You can get no troops from North Carolina."[40] Promptly he called the legislature into extra session for the purpose of summoning a convention. When the ordinance of secession was put to a vote in this convention, which had authority from the people to make the decision, it passed on May 20 without a dissenting vote.

Jonathan Worth, a former Whig and opponent of secession who declined to be a candidate for the convention, displayed the anguish of North Carolina Unionists in a letter to a friend written on the day the secession ordinance passed:

I still firmly believe in the wisdom of the early promoters of our government and that no other divided government can ever be built up so good as the united one we are pulling down—and hence I abhor the Northern Abolitionist and the Southern Secessionist, both cooperating with different objects, to break up the Union, but the whole nation has become mad. The voice of reason is silenced. Furious passion and thirst for blood consume the air. . . . Nobody is allowed to retain and assert his reason. . . . The very women and children are for war. Every body must take sides with one or the other of these opposing factions or fall victim to the mob. . . . I think the annals of the world furnish no instance of so groundless a war. . . . but let us fight like men for our own firesides.[41]

With similar dilemmas and internal divisions but by different paths, the states of the Upper South made their choice. In contrast to the Deep South, non-slaveholding Democrats in the Upper South had, for a time, shifted to the anti-secessionist position, at least until Lincoln issued his call for troops in response to the Confederate firing on Fort Sumter. What the Upper South prayed for resembled the intention of Buchanan's and Lincoln's policies: peace, conciliation, and respect for some southern rights, such as the protection of slavery in the organized states. There was resentment against both those who agitated for secession and those who supported abolition. As a result, instead of taking bold measures, the Upper South had waited, hoping that time would alleviate the divisive issues driving North and South apart. The similarity of sentiment during this period in the Upper South and the border states, such as Maryland and Kentucky, is significant. Yet the enterprise that might have transformed this sentiment into policy—a national convention or the border-state convention planned for Frankfort in May—came too late.

## EFFECTS OF THE MOBILIZATION ORDERS IN THE NORTH

The president had declared an insurrection, which in practical effect, though not in legal theory, was a virtual declaration of war. Amid the storm of mutual indignation that shook both sections, preparations for war were vigorously pushed.

In the North the patriotic response included Democrats as well as Republicans. The attitude of Stephen Douglas was especially significant. When campaigning for the presidency in 1860, he had been asked in Norfolk, Virginia whether he would advise resistance by force if the South seceded after Lincoln's inauguration. He replied:

> I answer emphatically that it is the duty of the President of the United States, and all others in authority under him, to enforce the laws . . . passed by Congress. . . . [A]nd I, as in duty bound by my oath of fidelity to the Constitution, would do all in my power to aid the Government of the United States in maintaining the supremacy of the laws against all resistance to them, come from what quarter it might.

On the question of whether he would participate in an effort to dissolve the Union if Lincoln were elected, Douglas answered: "I tell them, 'no—never, on earth'!"[42]

Douglas, who both reflected and shaped northern opinion especially among Democrats, opposed extremists on both sides. On July 5, 1860, he had written, "We must make the war boldly against the Northern Abolitionists and the southern Disunionists and give no quarter to either."[43] When South Carolina withdrew from the Union, Douglas denounced secession and supported the

Crittenden plan, the Seward compromise resolutions, and the constitutional amendment to protect slavery in the states. In March, while Lincoln seemed to vacillate, Douglas indicated "that he would harass the Administration mercilessly unless it sacrificed almost everything for peace."[44]

At the same time he criticized the uncompromising leaders of the South. When Breckinridge declared in the Senate that southerners must be conceded the right to emigrate into all the territories, and that slaveholding southerners must be granted at least an equitable partition of the national domain, Douglas (referring to the territorial governments of the Dakotas and Colorado, organized without the Wilmot Proviso) answered that, with Republican consent, the South already had the right.[45] When Senator Louis Wigfall of Texas demanded that Douglas state what he would advise the president to do with regard to Fort Sumter, Douglas parried with a question as to whether the senator from Texas felt bound by his oath to support the Constitution of the United States.

But with the firing on Fort Sumter, all doubts as to Douglas's stand disappeared. On April 14 Douglas called on President Lincoln, pledged his aid for the preservation of the Union, and encouraged Lincoln to call up two hundred thousand rather than seventy-five thousand volunteers.[46] He then devoted himself to the task of rallying his own state to the support of the government. His influence was felt throughout the "Democracy" of the North; in Illinois it operated effectively in "Egypt," the southern region of that state where John Logan, later a distinguished Union general, was resisting the government. Douglas died in June 1861, but following his example, Democratic editorials took a strongly pro-Unionist position, applying the words *traitor* and *rebellion* to the Confederates and their attack on the flag.[47]

Now the North faced eleven states of the Confederacy. Four slaveholding border states did not secede, and their decisions were vital to the outcome of the Civil War.

## CHAPTER 8

# The Border States

T he Civil War cannot be understood without studying the border region that stretched from the Atlantic Ocean to the Missouri River and from the southern counties of the free midwestern states to northern Tennessee and Arkansas. This vast swath of land cut across state boundaries to include all of Kentucky, Missouri, western Virginia, Maryland, Delaware, and the southern portions of Ohio, Indiana, and Illinois. More white Americans lived in this section of the country than in the Confederate South, and the region's economy flourished through trade along the Ohio River and its tributaries.[1]

Unified in part by the southern origins of many of its residents, who had crossed the Appalachian Mountains of North Carolina and Virginia to settle on the western reaches of its prairies, meadows, and plateaus, the borderland hoped the sectional conflict could be resolved through mediation. For years the border states had provided the nation's most dedicated compromisers, among them Henry Clay and John Crittenden of Kentucky and Thomas Hart Benton of Missouri. Throughout the region, there was little desire to fight the South. On the other hand, there was no sympathy with the aggressive behavior of the Confederacy. Instead, compromise came naturally to those who knew their homes and farms could become the bloody cockpit of any civil war.

Like the states of the Upper South, those on the border were thrown into turmoil by the events of 1861—the creation of the Confederacy in February, followed by the appearance of commissioners urging secession, Lincoln's inaugural address, the attack on Fort Sumter, and Lincoln's mobilization of the militia. Ultimately the decisions not to secede made in Kentucky, Maryland, Missouri, Delaware and the northwestern counties of Virginia demonstrated the effect of geography and economics. Not only did these states have closer ties to the North through proximity and trade, but compared with the Lower South, they had adopted the markers of modernization—roads, industry, railroad lines, and cities. Baltimore, with over two hundred thousand residents in 1860, and St. Louis with 160,000, along with Kentucky's Lexington and Louisville and Delaware's Wilmington, were important commercial centers.

In these four border states the average slave population was only 10.8 percent, ranging from Kentucky's 19.5 percent to Delaware's 1.6 percent, and in all four states slavery was declining while the proportion of free blacks was growing. In the seven southern states that originally formed the Confederacy, the comparable average of slave population was 46 percent, and in the upper southern states of Virginia, Arkansas, Tennessee, and North Carolina which seceded only after Lincoln's mobilization orders, the figure was 28.5 percent. Clearly it was not military repression that determined the border's allegiance, as Confederate enthusiasts sometimes charged, but rather the weak identification of these states with slavery and the economic system of the South. With Unionists persistently dominating the political process in Delaware, Maryland, Kentucky, and Missouri even after Lincoln's mobilization order, the Confederacy had lost crucial territory and resources before the fighting even began.

## KENTUCKY'S ATTEMPTED NEUTRALITY

Nowhere were the special problems of the border more clearly revealed than in Kentucky. The birthplace of both Lincoln and Davis and a state where one of every five inhabitants was a slave and where slave markets flourished, Kentucky had obvious ties with the Confederacy. Yet its nationalism and its relations with the Union were more important. The state's significance as a link between North and South was illustrated by the large number of Kentuckians in northern states by 1860: sixty thousand in Illinois; sixty-eight thousand in Indiana; fifteen thousand in Ohio; and thirteen thousand in Iowa. So evenly was the balance struck between North and South that a slightly different turn of events might have drawn Kentucky into the Confederacy, making the Ohio River the boundary of the warring sections.[2]

But in 1860–1861 Kentucky had no heart for secession. Its favorite son, John Crittenden, put the Union first. Although the state legislature had upheld states' rights in its well-known resolutions of 1798—which declared nullification by states to be a remedy for federal encroachments—Kentucky history testified to the degree to which, at least until 1861, support of the South was not incompatible with nationalism. Yet as in Maryland, Delaware, and Missouri, the percentage of slaves and the power of slaveholders was not sufficient to dominate the behavior of the state and warrant secession. In the presidential campaign of 1860, Kentucky Democrats had refused to bolt the Charleston Convention, and the vote of the state registered its predominant Union support. The combined Douglas and Bell vote of ninety-one thousand was nearly twice that cast for Kentucky's own John Breckinridge. As for Lincoln, although the differences between his position on slavery and that of the northern abolitionists were acknowledged in some Kentucky newspapers (as was not the case farther south), he received only 1,364 votes.[3]

As the secession movement intensified, Kentucky was unwilling to choose between the Union and the South. The Democratic governor, Beriah Magoffin, was a Confederate sympathizer and favored a convention of southern states, but the efforts of Senator Crittenden for a compromise that would avert a civil war generally expressed the feelings of the entire border region. Breckinridge himself opposed secession (though secessionists outside Kentucky looked to him as a leader), and he used his influence as Buchanan's vice president to promote the Crittenden compromise. A few active secessionists maneuvered for a state convention that they hoped would sever the state from the Union in a process similar to that which was occurring in the Lower South, but Unionists opposed the calling of such a convention. Garrett Davis, an influential congressman from Bourbon County, declared that Kentuckians should resist with arms any legislative action for secession without a referendum.

Throughout this tense period of early 1861, suggestions for a national or border-state convention eclipsed discussion of a separate state convention and weakened the secessionist movement within the state. The Unionist victory came when the legislature adjourned in February without summoning a state convention, though the legislature did call for a meeting of the border states to be held in Frankfort, the state capital, in May.

Then in April came the firing on Fort Sumter and Lincoln's call for troops—actions that in Virginia, North Carolina, Tennessee, and Arkansas precipitated secession. But in Kentucky they led instead to a short-lived policy of neutrality that was based on the conviction that the state should take no part in any war but instead should stand between the sections as a neutral broker for peace. Meanwhile Magoffin refused to cooperate with Lincoln, claiming that "Kentucky would not join in the wicked purpose of subduing her sister Southern states."[4] Secretly the governor permitted southern military recruiters into the state, but he refused to send Kentucky forces to Harpers Ferry as requested by the Confederate government.

Many Kentuckians rallied around the unrealistic policy of armed neutrality. By a vote of 69 to 29, the Kentucky House of Representatives resolved on May 16 "that this state and the citizens thereof shall take no part in the civil war now being waged, except as mediators and friends to the belligerent parties." Writes one historian of this resolution: "A bewildered observer from abroad might well have concluded that the United States had become three countries: the Union, the Confederacy, and Kentucky."[5]

Expressing majority opinion in the state, neutrality and a policy of no secession meant, in practical terms and in the absence of any border-state confederation, that Kentucky was still in the Union.[6] During this period the correspondence of Crittenden, the state's respected senator, served as a barometer of public opinion. It included suggestions from Kentuckians for obtaining an armistice, encouraging the intervention of England and France and, especially from the women of Kentucky, praise for Crittenden's efforts to prevent war.[7]

Kentucky's neutrality lasted only four months—from May to September 1861. Once the war began on a large scale, young Kentucky males who prided themselves on their fighting spirit enlisted on one side or the other. In the special congressional election of June 20—held to replace those representatives who had joined the Confederacy—the Unionists won an overwhelming victory as well as three-quarters of the seats in the House and two-thirds of those in the Senate.

Meanwhile, Lincoln respected the neutrality of his native state. Declaring on April 26 that he had no military plan then in mind that required sending a force through Kentucky, the president indicated that he would not take any aggressive action against the state if it committed no hostile action against the national government. Lincoln confirmed this prudent policy in a letter to Crittenden in July: "I solemnly desire that no necessity for it [sending an armed force into Kentucky] may be presented; but I mean to say nothing which shall hereafter embarrass me in the performance of what may seem to be my duty."[8]

Though an impractical policy, Kentucky's self-proclaimed armed neutrality registered the distaste of many citizens who rejected both secession and war. Neutrality offered a temporary solution to internal friction at a time when men were arming on both sides.[9] Still, the time eventually came when Lincoln denounced this neutral position, which, he said, would "do for the disunionists that which . . . they most desire."[10]

When both sides established military camps within the state and violated Kentucky's neutrality by sending in arms, the rush of events and the strategic importance of the state forced an abandonment of neutrality. Any hope for Kentucky's role as an arbitrator mediating between North and South ended on September 4, when the Confederates seized Columbus, an important rail center and river port located on a high bluff overlooking the Mississippi River. In response, Union forces under Brigadier General Ulysses S. Grant, who had resigned from the army in 1854 but had been recommissioned in 1861, occupied Paducah.

On September 11, the Kentucky legislature demanded the withdrawal of the Confederates and requested federal protection from a southern invasion. At this point some prominent Kentuckians emigrated to the Confederacy, but opinion mostly supported the Unionists who had respected the state's neutrality. Even the quasi-secessionist Magoffin bowed to popular will. A week later the legislature created a military force to expel the Confederates, thus placing the state unequivocally and permanently in the Union.[11]

As in other border states, the decision for the Union did not end internal division. Nearly every town had flagpoles flying the banners of both North and South; families were divided, and the expression "the brothers' war" held concrete meaning in Kentucky. Crittenden, for example, had sons in both armies. After some initial difficulty in raising the 42,000 troops Lincoln called for in 1861 and 1862, Kentucky eventually furnished seventy-five thousand Union enlistments (of one hundred thousand requested). The Confederacy reported 7,950 Kentucky recruits in 1862, after which Confederate recruiting in the state slowed.[12]

After the Confederate general Edmund Kirby Smith's 1862 invasion of the state, Kentucky Confederates did form their own rump state government. Its shadowy existence continued until the end of the war, although it "was never quartered in the state long enough to develop any qualities of permanency."[13] Kentuckians, in fact, sat in the Confederate Congress, and one of the stars in the Confederate flag represented the state.

As the war progressed, complications concerning slavery and anger at the arrest of leading Kentuckians encouraged anti-Lincoln feelings. Denunciations of the Lincoln government and the Republican party became the order of the day. Military developments led to the proclamation of martial law in Kentucky, further angering the state's Democrats. In the election of 1864 the Democratic candidate McClellan received sixty-one thousand civilian votes to Lincoln's twenty-six thousand; the soldier vote, a stunning reversal of the choice of most Union soldiers, was 3,068 for McClellan and 1,205 for Lincoln.[14] When the war ended, prosouthern sentiment had become so strong that wartime exiles such as William Haldeman, editor of the pro-Confederate Louisville *Courier*, were welcomed home as leaders of the postwar Democratic party.

## MARYLAND'S CONTESTED UNIONISM

Like that of Kentucky, Maryland's strategic location made the state critically important to both Union and Confederacy, and as was the case in Kentucky, a vigorous minority tried to push the state into secession against the desires of the majority. Because Maryland nearly surrounded the nation's capital and because Baltimore was an important port, the stakes were high. Although the overwhelming majority of Marylanders opposed secession, there was Confederate sympathy in the city of Baltimore, on the Eastern Shore, and in the slaveholding regions of southern Maryland.

Again as in Kentucky, a third group sought to solve the sectional disagreements through a policy of armed neutrality that depended on persuading other border states to create a regional alliance. Political leaders such as the former congressman John Pendleton Kennedy argued that if the border states failed to bring about the restoration of the Union, they should form their own confederation and work for the reconstruction of the Union.[15]

When Federal soldiers from the Sixth Massachusetts Regiment moved through Maryland on April 19, 1861, they were met at the Camden Street Depot by a mob of southern sympathizers who threw stones at the soldiers. Firing began, and four soldiers and twenty-two civilians were killed.

Both neutralists and Unionists were fortunate that Thomas Hicks was governor. A former Know-Nothing, Hicks was a friend of the Union who feared that Maryland would be forced into secession through some mistake. Therefore the governor refused to call the legislature into special session until April 1861. Then he convened it in the northwestern town of Frederick, rather than in the state capital of Annapolis, where antiwar sentiment was rampant and mob violence was possible.

Once assembled, the Maryland assembly displayed few secessionist tendencies and did not follow the path of its neighbor Virginia. Instead it passed a resolution imploring the president "to cease this unholy war." Even this proclamation was qualified by the condition "at least until Congress assembles," as indeed that body did in July. With the movement of Union troops through the state and the stationing of a regiment on Baltimore's Federal Hill fresh in everyone's mind, the legislature protested what it called a "military occupation of Maryland." But what the legislature did *not* do displayed the state's true allegiance: it did not establish any mechanism for convening a future convention to consider the question of secession. An effort to do so was buried in committee.[16]

Among the legislature's resolutions was a protest against the movement of Union troops through Maryland, a protest that like so many positions in this border state was hedged by disapproval of "the violent interference with the transit of Federal Troops." The reference was to the armed clash that had taken place in Baltimore three weeks earlier. On April 19, a mob had tormented the soldiers of the Sixth Massachusetts Regiment when they changed stations in Baltimore en route to Washington. Stones, epithets, and finally gunfire had been exchanged in a riot that ended with four soldiers and twenty-two civilians dead.[17] Led by merchants, their sons, and Democratic party customs officials concerned about the prospects of Lincoln's controlling the patronage, the rioters attempted to install a policy of "armed neutrality," similar to that of Kentucky.[18] In any case, the first casualties of the long war had occurred in a border state that would serve as a battleground for thirty-two more engagements. After this confrontation Governor Hicks, although he asked for a halt to federal recruiting and the passage of troops through the state, conferred with Lincoln on ways to ensure Unionist support.

Although staunchly Unionist (sixty-one thousand Marylanders fought in the Union army and navy, compared with fewer than twenty thousand in the Confederate forces), Maryland continued to harbor activists with prosouthern and neutralist sentiments. Unionist war measures such as the seizure of property, the arrest of citizens, and the suppression of newspapers kept alive resentment of Lincoln and his government. This resentment signaled the desire in Marylanders to prevent any violations of their rights as Americans. They were especially angered by the actions of General Benjamin Butler, who stationed troops in Baltimore and seized the Annapolis and Elkridge Railroad. And because of Maryland's location, when southern sympathizers engaged in guerrilla activities such as destroying railroad tracks, the Lincoln government necessarily acted to preserve its authority.

On April 27, 1861, Lincoln suspended the writ of habeas corpus (a writ used to prevent illegal imprisonment) in an area stretching from Washington to Philadelphia. This irritated Marylanders, who considered such a surrender of the privileges of free men unnecessary. When the saboteur John Merryman blew up railroad bridges in Baltimore County to prevent the movement of Union troops, he was arrested by the military and imprisoned in Baltimore's Fort McHenry. In order to move jurisdiction into civilian courts, Merryman's lawyers applied for a writ of habeas corpus in federal court, but military authorities refused to honor it, citing the president's suspension of the writ in parts of Maryland. Merryman's lawyers then appealed to the Supreme Court, and eventually the case of *ex parte Merryman* led to a legal controversy over whether the president or Congress held the constitutional power to suspend the writ of habeas corpus. After seven weeks Merryman was released and indicted in civil court for treason, but his case never came to trial. To some residents of a border state, the military's refusal to turn Merryman over to civilian courts became a flagrant example of the trampling on American liberties that characterized Lincoln's approach to the Civil War.[19]

Well aware of the importance of Maryland to the Union cause, the Lincoln administration closely watched the Maryland elections, in the fall of 1861, which pitted the Unionist party against that of a newly formed States Rights party. Although southern sympathizers complained of electoral interference—and did so throughout the war without convincing evidence—the military had little effect on the outcome. In the June election for the special session of Congress, which was to meet on July 4, the Unionists, a wartime amalgam of former Whigs, Know-Nothings, Unionists, and Democrats, won 72 percent of the vote and elected five of six members of their party to the Congress that convened in Washington in July. In the fall gubernatorial elections, the Unionist candidate Augustus Bradford received 57,502 votes (including those of furloughed soldiers) to his opponent's 26,010. After these elections, there was no more uncertainty about whether Maryland was a loyal state.[20]

## DELAWARE'S UNQUESTIONED ALLEGIANCE

There was never much doubt about the allegiance of Maryland's neighbor, the tiny state of Delaware. Surrounded by the Union states of Maryland, Pennsylvania, and New Jersey, Delaware had few points of identification with the South. Slaves represented only 1 percent of the population, and as was the case in Maryland, slavery was declining in Delaware. This brought with it proportional increases in the free black population, which by 1860 was ten times that of slaves. Yet though there was never any real danger of Delaware's secession, there was "abundant pro-Southern feeling and a possibility that armed conflict might break out between friends of the North and South."[21]

Having extended to Judge Henry Dickinson, a commissioner from Mississippi, the courtesy of listening to his address urging the state to join the proposed southern Confederacy, the legislature, on January 3, 1861, unanimously expressed its "unqualified disapproval" of such a course. Earlier, in an address to the legislature, Governor William Burton did not even offer a proposal of secession. Yet many state leaders—especially in the Democratic party and especially in Sussex County, where nearly 80 percent of the state's slaves were located—were unwilling to "coerce" the seceded states. As the Delaware secretary of state inquired, "Why not let them depart in peace and save the horrors of a Civil War?"[22]

When the war did break out, Union meetings were organized throughout the state, but especially in Wilmington, where mass assemblages supported Lincoln's call for troops and cheered Major Anderson. Delaware women were active in their support of the cause, providing uniforms, blankets, and even shoes for the early Delaware regiments, made up of volunteers. In the southern part of the state, some communities were divided. "The boys, as well as the men, the grown up women as well as the young girls . . . arrayed themselves against each other in bitter hostility," a contemporary recalled, "and it was some times said, one half of the town did not speak or associate with the other half."[23]

Governor Burton recommended the formation of "volunteer companies for . . . protection of the people of this State against violence of any sort." He added that such companies might have the "option of offering their services to the general government for the defense of its capital and the support of the Constitution and laws of the country."[24] In all, Delaware supplied twelve thousand enlistments to the Union armed forces.

## VIOLENCE IN MISSOURI

In Missouri the conflicts among unconditional Unionists, conservative Unionists, supporters of a border state confederacy, and secessionists produced confusion and violence. In 1860 Missouri voters had cast a bare plurality of their ballots for Douglas over Bell, with Breckinridge running a distant third. Like that of all border areas, Missouri's allegiance was crucial for both sides, especially since St. Louis held one of the largest arsenals in the country. Leading the movement for secession, Governor Claiborne Jackson warned that if the Union used force against any seceded state, Missouri should join the Confederacy. While the governor began strengthening the militia, he also persuaded the legislature to call a convention. But when this convention was chosen, its members were so overwhelmingly Unionist that it adjourned on March 22, 1861 without passing the ordinance of secession the governor desired. A few weeks later, Jackson rejected Lincoln's call to arms as illegal and unconstitutional. On his own authority, the governor not only organized a plan to seize the arsenal in St. Louis, but also wrote to Jefferson Davis for arms.

The Jackson and Union factions were soon aligned in opposing armed groups, and violence erupted when a force accused of being pro-Confederate formed Camp Jackson in St. Louis. At the same time and in the same city Nathaniel Lyon, an army captain from Connecticut, commanded a pro-Union force that he had organized. Though the officers and men of Camp Jackson professed their support of the Union, a skeptical Lyon surrounded them and forced their surrender on May 10, 1861. Street fighting then erupted in St. Louis between Union soldiers and citizens, resulting in twenty-eight deaths. Reports spread of a "massacre" of defenseless civilians. This volatile situation was further complicated by clashes between pro-Union, antislavery Germans and former Know-Nothings who mixed their cries of "Damn the Dutch" with "Hurrah for Jefferson Davis."

Governor Jackson promptly organized a state military force, putting it under the command of the former governor Sterling Price, who had served in the Mexican War. Price had been a Unionist while presiding at the convention that had repudiated secession, but now he became so outraged at the conduct of Lyon and

Unionists such as Frank Blair that he joined the secessionists. Internecine war resulted, despite an agreement between federal and state forces that relegated to the latter the sole function of keeping order in Missouri. At the battle of Wilson's Creek on August 10, 1861, Federal troops were defeated. Seven months later, on March 6–8, 1862, Union forces, in a smashing victory at Pea Ridge in northwestern Arkansas, pushed Confederate troops out of Missouri and ended Confederate hopes that the state would aid the South. After Pea Ridge, all except a small portion of the territory of the state now fell under Unionist control.[25]

But Missouri remained internally divided. The violence at Wilson's Creek precipitated an avoidable civil war in Missouri. Unlike other border areas in Maryland and Kentucky, local conflicts, bushwhacking, sniping, and guerrilla fighting marked this period of Missouri history. "When regular troops were absent, the improvised war often assumed a deadly guerrilla nature as local citizens took up arms spontaneously against their neighbors. This was a war of stealth and raid without a front, without formal organization, and with almost no division between the civilian and the warrior."[26]

The situation further deteriorated when troops from Kansas intervened. Free-state men of this adjacent state feared and despised their slaveholding neighbors across the border. Remembering the intervention of the Missouri "border ruffians" in their affairs in the 1850s, Kansans waited "for the opportunity to take revenge for real and fancied wrongs that had occurred in the five years before

Guerrilla warfare raged in Missouri. Kansas "jayhawkers," led by James Lane and Charles Jennison, engaged in violence with citizens of Missouri. This photograph shows a dead Confederate guerrilla.

Charles Jennison led the Kansas "jayhawkers" on vicious raids into Missouri. He sometimes boasted that Missouri mothers quieted their children with the mere mention of his name.

1861."[27] Led by the notorious James Lane and Charles Jennison, these Kansas "jayhawkers" descended upon the Missouri border with the cry, "Everything disloyal . . . from a Durham cow to a Shanghai chicken, must be cleaned out."[28] Even Union officials in Missouri complained that these Kansas volunteers were "no better than a band of robbers."[29]

Pro-Confederate forces reciprocated, and their retaliation culminated on August 21, 1863, when the bloodthirsty Confederate guerrilla captain William Quantrill, with a force that included the young Jesse James, descended on Lawrence, Kansas, and in a "wholesale and indiscriminate slaughter" killed 150 men and wounded thirty others in what has been called "the most atrocious act of the Civil War."[30] In response, Union authorities issued General Orders No. 11, which commanded approximately twenty thousand Missouri residents in Jackson, Cass, and Bates counties and half of Vernon County to leave their homes in two weeks. These counties were the strong guerrilla areas from which the Lawrence raid had been launched, but the angry outcry against this drastic measure led to its suspension.[31] Along with the forced removal of some of its citizens, Missouri was repeatedly placed under martial law. Military courts were busy with cases of civilians charged with burning bridges, tearing up railway and telegraph lines, and other acts of sabotage.

The legal basis for Union authority was a state convention that performed the fundamental functions of government after the governor and most of the legislature abandoned their offices to set up a prosouthern lawmaking body and in some cases to join the Confederacy. The convention—first organized in March 1861 and soon dubbed the "Long Convention" to establish a connection with the "Long Parliament" during the seventeenth-century English Civil War—administered state affairs throughout the war.

In the early summer of 1861—even before the military confrontation at Wilson's Creek in August—this convention declared the executive and legislative offices of the state vacant and filled the executive offices itself, after decreeing loyalty to the Union a prerequisite for holding office. Hamilton Gamble was chosen governor, and the Lincoln administration cooperated with him in a manner that avoided offending state pride. When, for example, the governor organized the state militia as home guards, Lincoln selected the head of the militia to command Federal forces in Missouri. The Lincoln government also supplied arms to state troops, together with two hundred thousand dollars to be used for equipping and maintaining them. When Gamble died in January 1864, his duties were assumed by Lieutenant Governor Willard Hall, who was also appointed by the state convention.

Meanwhile, a shadow pro-Confederate state government was maintained. On August 5, 1861, at New Madrid, General (formerly Governor) Jackson proclaimed the independence of Missouri "as a sovereign, free, and independent republic." In November a remnant of the "deposed legislature" (a phrase used by the legislators to suggest their illegal removal by the Long Convention) met at Neosho, decreed the secession of Missouri from the United States, and established a government that was admitted to the Confederate States. Jackson served as governor of this political entity until his death in 1862. The office was later held by Thomas Reynolds, and Missouri was thus represented by this minority as one of the states in the "Western section of the Confederacy" which would never "seek any destiny separate from that of our [Confederate] sisters east of the Mississippi."[32] Yet the true division of sentiment in the state is suggested by enlistments: 109,000 Missouri men joined the Union army, whereas about thirty thousand fought with the South.

## WEST VIRGINIA'S SECESSION FROM THE CONFEDERACY

The formation of West Virginia, which in effect seceded from Virginia, demonstrated split allegiances within a Confederate state. For decades before the war sectional differences had festered within the Old Dominion.[33] The tidewater, middle, Piedmont, and Shenandoah Valley regions looked to the seaboard and the South. Here the concentration of slaves was high and the influence of planters significant.

In the thirty-five counties of the northwest and those of the panhandle west of the Shenandoah Valley and north of the Kanawha River, the general outlook was, as the rivers flowed, toward the Ohio. This region of western Virginia had gradually developed grievances against the older counties, which had retained political power disproportional to their numbers. Discrimination in favor of slaveholders in taxation and representation in the state assembly, along with favoritism in the distribution of government benefits for roads and improvements, provided the sources for complaints from residents of the Kanawha region, who felt that they were at a disadvantage compared with the "aristocrats" of the east. Other states suffered similar sectional differences without disruption, but in Virginia the approach of a civil war precipitated a political division.

When Virginia seceded on April 16, 1861, only five of thirty-one delegates from this western region voted for an end to the Union. On April 22, a mass meeting took place in Clarksburg, where activists resolved to summon a prelimi-

When Virginia voted to secede, only a small number of delegates from the western region voted to withdraw from the Union. At the Custom House in Wheeling, Virginia, delegates denounced secession and established a Unionist government. Eventually, West Virginia would be formed as a separate state that joined the Union in 1864.

nary convention of delegates to meet in Wheeling in May to consider what emergency steps should be taken to uphold the Union in Virginia and to oppose the heresy of secession. This convention passed resolutions denouncing secession and summoning a general convention to meet in June, also in Wheeling, to take action for Virginia as a whole.

This latter "reorganized government of Virginia," made up of delegates chosen at Union mass meetings, appointed Francis Pierpoint as provisional governor, along with other state officials. Although the convention spoke for all Virginia, in fact only twenty-six counties of the fifty that became the war-born state of West Virginia were represented. It adopted an ordinance of secession from Confederate Virginia that was ratified by popular vote. The June convention also adopted an ordinance making loyalty to the Union a requirement for holding state office. Then, on August 20, the convention agreed to a resolution that decreed that "a new State, to be called the State of Kanawha, be formed and erected," to consist of forty-eight designated counties. This ordinance was crafted by an active group of separationists and anti-Confederates in the counties near Pennsylvania and Maryland and was put in place without a popular referendum. Later the counties of Berkeley and Jefferson, in the area of Charles Town and Harpers Ferry, joined.

In the meantime, the Union army had driven back a Confederate force that might have undermined this secession from Virginia. Troops from Ohio under the command of George McClellan had entered the state in May in order to control the critical Baltimore and Ohio Railroad junction at Grafton, a town fifty miles south of Wheeling. Having already cut this railroad line, Confederate troops retreated as McClellan's twenty-thousand-man force outflanked them in the region of Laurel and the Rich Mountains. The ensuing Confederate retreat removed any opposing military force from northwest Virginia.[34]

By October 1861, the "reorganized legislature" of Virginia, constituted according to a pattern devised by the June convention, elected Waitman Willey and John Carlisle as United States senators from Virginia (not West Virginia) in place of James Mason and Robert Hunter, adherents of the Confederacy whose seats had been vacated. The new Union government for Virginia was established in Wheeling. This ended an awkward period between June and October 1861, when the absence of a legitimate local government encouraged bandits and guerrillas who roamed about, shooting citizens, ravaging farms, and easily evading the home guards and impromptu military forces dispatched to disperse them.

On October 24, 1861, in accordance with the ordinance of the Wheeling convention, an election for a constitutional convention to frame an instrument of government for the new commonwealth was held. At the same election the people within the predetermined boundaries of the proposed new state voted as individuals and not by counties in a referendum on the question of whether the new state should be created. The vote of 18,408 "yea" to 781 "nay" did not reflect the normal vote of the region, for it was virtually limited to Unionists. Confederate sympathizers and those opposed to the new state boycotted the election.

This constitutional convention met in Wheeling in November and wrote a formal charter for West Virginia, dropping the picturesque name of Kanawha. On April 3, 1862, the male residents of the designated region of fifty counties voted 18,862 to 514 to ratify a constitution that by the narrowest of margins did not include a gradual emancipation clause. On May 13, 1862, the "restored" state legislature at Wheeling, acting for all Virginia, gave its "consent" to the formation of the new state.

This legislature consisted of thirty-five members of the lower house and ten in the upper, though the full membership according to the Virginia constitution should have been 152 delegates and fifty senators. Except for the "eastern shore" and a limited area opposite Washington, the constituencies represented were entirely in the northwest. And even there, many counties were not represented; nor was all of Confederate Virginia. It was by this legal fiction that the consent of Virginia was obtained in compliance with the provision in the United States Constitution that no state could be created within the limits of an existing commonwealth without the consent of the latter's legislature.

The matter now came before the United States Congress, which passed the bill admitting West Virginia to the Union, though many Virginia Unionists opposed its admission. For senators such as Pennsylvania's Thaddeus Stevens, "the absolute power ... of the laws of war provided justification."[35] Lincoln disapproved of the bill, and Senator Willey believed he would veto it.[36] But in the end the president's reluctant consent was obtained. It took some months to complete the conditions of statehood, and it was not until April 20, 1863, that President Lincoln issued a proclamation declaring the state of West Virginia admitted to the Union as the thirty-fifth state. The admission of the new state, whose capital was at Wheeling and whose first governor was the Pennsylvania-born Arthur Boreman, left the Pierpoint government high and dry. It continued to exist, however, transferring its seat to Alexandria under Union control, as it sought to carry on the government of a Unionist Virginia.

Thus in the vast borderland that separated North and South the predominant allegiance was for the United States. Maryland, Delaware, Kentucky, and Missouri all chose the Union, depriving the Confederacy of crucial human and material resources as well as a much stronger territorial position from which to fight the war. The border states along with West Virginia provided over three hundred thousand Union soldiers as well as significant numbers of horses and mules and amounts of food and war materials. And through a war-driven expediency the new state of West Virginia was added to the twenty-three supporting the Union. As a result of the Unionism of these areas, it was the southern boundaries of the border states that marked the official division between the Union and the Confederacy when the war began.

CHAPTER 9 | # First Campaigns

Wr is never simply a matter of battlefield encounters and military operations, and this is especially true of a civil war. Political decisions about how to raise troops, how to pay for the war, and what kinds of domestic policies to follow inevitably influence the military outcome. So too do the resources of the opposing sides. To continue this analysis we must define certain concepts.

In the following chapters, the term *military operations* refers to the ways in which the Union and Confederate armies were used to obtain strategic goals through the organization and conduct of large-scale campaigns. The term *tactics* defines the arrangement and maneuvering of armies and navies in specific battles. The concept of *military strategy*, as the historian Joseph Glatthaar writes, "refers to the art and science of using the armed forces of a nation to achieve policy objectives by the application of force." On the national level, strategy refers to "developing and using the political, military, economic, and psychological powers of a nation to further national interests." This chapter focuses on military strategy.[1]

## RESOURCES, GOALS, AND MILITARY STRUCTURES

When the alignment of states finally stabilized into a northern and a southern nation, the superior strength of the North was obvious. With twenty-three states and a population of more than twenty-two million (minus about six hundred thousand southern sympathizers), the North confronted an enemy of eleven states with a population of just over nine million, more than a third of whom were slaves. A symbol of the differences between the two warring sides, these slaves who remained for the most part on the South's farms and plantations in the early stages of the war permitted a high proportion of white male Confederates to serve in the military. But soon transformed into a morale-threatening source of anxiety for those left on the home front, slaves became an unstable labor force that disappeared at the approach of the Union army.

Both sides included individuals and regions of uncertain allegiance, but overall the North had a 4:1 population advantage. Among white males between eighteen and forty-five, the North could draw from a pool of approximately 3,500,000 to which could be added, as the war continued, increasing numbers of freed southern blacks and the one hundred thousand white southerners who fought for the Union.[2] The South had a "military population" of approximately one million—a figure that omits black males, whom neither side initially used. Potentially, the Union had three and a half times as many men available for its armed forces as did the South.[3]

The North's economic strength and more modern infrastructure of communication, transportation, and industrial facilities—including the largest arms manufacture in the nation in Springfield, Massachusetts—were vastly superior to those of the Confederacy. In 1860 the North had 110,000 manufacturing establishments employing 1,300,000 industrial workers; the South was at a distinct disadvantage with its 18,000 manufacturing establishments and 110,000 workers. The value of manufactured products produced annually in the state of New York alone was more than four times as great as that of the entire Confederacy. By every comparison, whether of miles of railroads or the manufacture of firearms, pig-iron, and cloth or even the number of draft horses, the North had at least a seven-to-one, and often a nine-to-one, advantage.[4] The North had not only greater material resources, but also other elements of industrialization and financial organization. Even southern banking and foreign exchange—centered in New York. Moreover, the North had an existing government with its official machinery and prestige that was already established at home and overseas, whereas the Confederates had to create a national government (and military force).

To contemporaries, the war did not appear as unequal as this comparison would suggest. The Confederate general Pierre Beauregard believed that

> No people ever warred for independence with more relative advantages than the Confederates; and if, as a military question, they must have failed, then no country must aim at freedom by means of war. . . . The South, with its great material resources, its defensive means of mountains, rivers, railroads, and telegraph, with the immense advantage of the interior lines of war, would be open to discredit as a people if its failure could not be explained otherwise than by mere material contrast.[5]

Certainly the nature of the war was such that the South needed fewer men. Confederate armies repeatedly managed to resist superior numbers. As was obvious from the failure of frontal assaults during the Mexican War, any successful attack on Richmond would take more men than were needed to defend it. Thus the disparity of numbers between the sections must be measured against the Confederacy's defensive position; the increasing use of entrenchments further evened the balance. Not only did the North have to expend its manpower in heavy battle losses, but the necessity of enlarging its area of invasion and holding occupied territory required more men than would battles on equal terms.[6] Given the North's goal of restoring the Union, its armies must invade the South and occupy its land, unless the Confederates themselves decided to give up the rebellion. Even the sheer size of the South provided a military obstacle.

The South also had the psychological advantage of fighting for independence—for something bold and positive—although the North's intention of restoring the Union and, as time went on, overthrowing a slave regime, served as an emotional counterpart. And the South gained a slight advantage from a railroad network that, however limited in comparative terms, was useful for establishing interior lines. In addition, the Confederacy's long coastline provided possibilities for foreign trade with the European nations that Jefferson Davis anticipated would promptly recognize and aid his new government. Confederate sentiment ran high in New York and many other northern centers, as well as in parts of some border states. Union sentiment in the Confederacy, though by no means nonexistent, was inarticulate at the beginning. The Washington establishment was southern, and its sympathy with the Confederate cause was potentially damaging to the Union.

Highlighting its traditional values, the South believed that it had more martial spirit and patriotism than the North. Its young men had given more attention to military training, and, like many northern boys, were handy with horse and rifle. Its generals were among the finest products of West Point. When to these factors is added the surrender of federal forts and arsenals, the advantage of Confederate troops fighting on interior lines in their own "country," and the rapid mobilization by May 1861 of sixty thousand troops, perhaps the Confederates seem less unreasonable in their expectations of winning a short war. The unequal weight of resources against them was not so great as in the case of the American colonies in their rebellion against the British, nor of other peoples who have achieved independence against heavy odds, whether the Dutch against the Spanish in the sixteenth century or the Vietnamese against the French and later the Americans in the twentieth century.[7] Still, these successful revolutions received outside aid that the Confederacy never obtained.

Both sides predicted a short war. Lincoln's call for seventy-five thousand militia men implied that the "insurrection" would be "suppressed" in three months, although on May 3, 1861, the president called for forty-two thousand three-year army volunteers and eighteen thousand sailors. In April, Lincoln issued two blockade orders for the southern coast, and by May the navy had armed ships patrolling Confederate waters.

In the South there were confident expectations of capturing Washington and driving out the "Black Republicans" by early summer. In fact, both sides were initially unprepared for four years of brutal conflict. Neither the Union nor the Confederacy had a general staff, and the chaotic war preparations in the early months were characterized by state and local activity more than by the effective

Both the North and the South turned to symbols to support their cause. This "Spirit of the Union" sheet-music cover shows a woman dressed in white proudly holding the flag with a bald eagle by her side. The Confederate cover depicts a soldier holding a Confederate flag reading "God Save the South."

use of national powers. In the South, such activity was even more locally inspired and driven.[8]

While both governments were taking the initial steps to organize their military forces on paper, individuals enthusiastically vented their pent-up feelings in an emotional release that followed months of uncertainty. Mass meetings in both North and South intensified patriotic spirit as young men on both sides, reminded of the heroic days of the now idealized Revolution, pledged their lives, fortunes, and sacred honor to the cause. In Goodhue County, Minnesota, a war rally, typical of many throughout the United States, was held in the courthouse. The next day there were enough recruits to fill several companies of the First Minnesota Volunteers. In Virginia, a classics professor signed up seventy-three students from his Greek classes at Washington College in Lynchburg for what became the Liberty Hall company.[9]

There were, it is true, some dissenters to whom the thought of civil war in America was a nightmare. "The shame, the folly, the outrage, seemed too great to believe," observed Ohio's general Jacob Cox, "and we half hoped to wake from it as from a dream."[10] But such forebodings were lost in the clamor. As volunteering, drilling, parading, and organizing camps of instruction proceeded, military men became the center of attention, while civilians rushed about in a hectic impulse to "do something." On both sides anyone who wished could advertise his intention to raise a company, and notices were everywhere for all who wanted to join up to come on a certain morning to some tavern, hotel, or public hall.

The three branches of American military service that had been established in previous wars now provided patterns for enrollment in the North. The militia, though organized by congressional statute and subject to federal mobilization by the president in extraordinary circumstances, was in peacetime a state institution under the control of governors who appointed its officers and paid its expenses. In most communities it was a paper organization. In Minnesota, for example, the militia supposedly included twenty-six thousand men, but in fact there were only 147 active officers and two hundred privates.[11] In July 1862 Congress standardized some features of the militia service, requiring the enrollment of all able-bodied men from eighteen to forty-five (thus establishing an implicit draft) and providing that the president might specify the period of such service, which was not to exceed nine months.

The second branch of the military was the regular army of the United States, consisting of slightly more than sixteen thousand regular officers and men in March 1861. Of 1,105 officers, 296 left the army, some resigning their commissions, others dismissed for possible disloyalty. Of these, 270 joined the Confederate military forces. Of the 15,259 enlisted men, most of whom were foreign-born, fewer than four hundred left for the southern army, a figure that indicates the success of an effort by the army to retain professional soldiers.[12]

At the beginning of the war, most army regulars were scattered throughout the West—inadequate in numbers, according to General Winfield Scott, even for peacetime troubles with the Indians. The navy had twenty-three active ships, with only ten warships immediately available for duty along with twelve hundred officers and seven thousand men, though the United States had a large merchant marine.

The initially decentralized method of raising troops prevented the use of the regular army as a nucleus. Considering the regular army his mainstay, General Scott refused the requests of army officers who desired leaves of absence so that they could direct the organization of the state militia and volunteers. As a result these younger professionals did not serve as field officers among the new regiments, where their training would have been beneficial for the amateurs soon to do battle.

Later the Union general Jacob Cox acknowledged this mistake: "There can be no doubt that the true policy would have been to encourage the whole of this younger class to enter at once the volunteer service. They would have been field-officers in the new regiments, and would have impressed discipline and system upon the organization. . . . The Confederates really profited from having no regular army. . . . Less than a year afterward we changed our policy but it was then too late to induce many of the regular officers to take regimental positions in the volunteer troops."[13]

The third branch of the military was the volunteers, who, stimulated by the patriotic fervor of their communities and families, hurried to sign up. During the Mexican War these volunteers had numbered about seventy-three thousand, compared with a temporary increase in the regular army of thirty-one thousand.[14] Such dependence on volunteering reflected the widely shared sentiments of Americans who, since before the American Revolution, had held that a large standing army could be dangerous to the liberties of the people, and that citizen-soldiers, like George Washington, must defend the nation in times of peril.

Once mustered into companies, troops were organized in traditional patterns. On paper each regiment of ten companies was made up of one thousand men; roughly four regiments made up a brigade; two or three brigades or sometimes more made a division. In July 1861, divisions were first organized into a corps, with two corps necessary to make up the units commanded by a major general. After the fighting began, units had fewer men.

In the South the formula was the same, although consistent with that society's culture, cavalry regiments often were larger (twelve rather than ten companies) and were independent units operating outside of any permanent attachment to a brigade. In 1864 the Union army followed this type of deployment. Overall 80 percent of all military personnel (75 percent in the Confederacy) were infantry troops, 14 percent were cavalry, and the remaining 6 percent served in the artillery.[15]

The border and Upper South promptly became the principal theaters of war, as Missouri, Kentucky, Tennessee, and Virginia bore the brunt of the early campaigns in the East. Some of the first military maneuvers took place in the portion of Virginia that bordered Ohio and Pennsylvania and that became West Virginia in 1863. Thus the areas that showed the least enthusiasm for secession at first witnessed the most severe fighting. Later the war moved southward into the heart of the Confederacy.

In general terms the northern strategy was to capture and hold Missouri, Kentucky, and Tennessee; to control the Mississippi River, thereby detaching the Southwest from the main part of the Confederacy; to protect Washington; to direct offensive campaigns toward Richmond; and to blockade southern coasts and push Confederate gunboats up the inland rivers. Unionists hoped General Scott's Anaconda Plan—based on a strategy of occupying the line of the Mississippi River from Cairo, Illinois to the Gulf of Mexico with sixty thousand troops and blockading southern ports—would induce first southern Unionists and then all Confederates to rejoin the nation. In Scott's thinking the Union should minimize the destruction of southern resources in order to accomplish what at this stage many Americans thought was a realistic goal—the voluntary return of southerners to the Union.

Meanwhile the South sought to protect Richmond while threatening Washington. In theoretical terms of larger war goals, it could fight a passive war and defy the North's ability to conquer it. Or, cognizant of its enemy's superior resources, Jefferson Davis could try to strike quickly before these material advantages could be organized. And like the North, the Confederacy could hope that public opinion in the border states could broker an agreement guaranteeing its independence. Throughout the war the South anticipated uprisings in the border states as it awaited a hoped-for demoralization of the North. It also anticipated recognition, and possibly aid, from France and Great Britain.

On the principle that Providence favors the strongest battalions, each side sought by scouting, rapid movement, and surprise maneuver to confront its opponent at decisive points with superior numbers. The capture and destruction of armies was an objective along with the control of territory, but few battles were decisive. Given the losses, commanders were usually unable to follow up any victory with the exhausted remnants of their regiments. Thus after a battle had been "won," the defeated enemy would regroup, shift position, and re-form its lines for another encounter. Discouragement on both home fronts resulted from the circumstances of an apparently interminable war punctuated by bloody battles.

Each side harassed the other, raiding its territory, destroying its military stores, smashing its bridges, wrecking its railroads, and cutting off its communications. Aside from the exceptional case of Sherman in Georgia and the Carolinas, each army, when conducting major military operations as distinguished from mere raids, established at its rear a base with telegraph, roads, railroads, and depots. Sieges were few, although those at Vicksburg in Mississippi and Petersburg in Virginia were important both strategically and psychologically. Trench warfare, though not unknown, was at first rare. The traditional pattern of warfare fought by soldiers arranged in formal lines who fired and then withdrew to the back of the column mostly disappeared.

These new tactics on both sides were shaped by the introduction of new technology, especially the rifled musket. An advance over the smooth-bore musket, this development in small arms was available before the Civil War but awaited a more efficient bullet—the minié ball—which was developed in the 1850s by the French army captain Claude Minié. By the 1860s, although muzzle loading still limited the capabilities for rapid fire, the precision and range of the rifle musket permitted soldiers who in the Revolution had an effective range of one hundred yards to hit targets at three to four hundred yards.

The combination of longer effective range of shoulder arms and a soft lead bullet led to high casualty rates and changes in how infantry fought. No longer was it effective to concentrate troops and fire in a tight parade of soldiers; now infantry units were more efficient if they broke ranks, sought cover, and reloaded as they confronted the enemy in looser fighting arrangements. As Edward Hagerman has described, "[the] devastating increase in firepower doomed the open frontal assault and ushered in the entrenched battlefield. . . . Offensive infantry tactics led to the extended skirmish order and . . . assaults by rushes, with the spade accompanying the rifle."[16]

Most battles lasted no more than one or two days. Yet the number of brief engagements with sniping, bushwhacking, guerrilla activity, and armed confrontations ran into the hundreds. Less effective than infantry and artillery in the new kind of fighting that developed, cavalry usually scouted, reconnoitered, and raided instead of engaging in the head-on charges that had been the practice in the past. In the face of accurate fire from rifled muskets, cavalry units often dismounted and fought on foot.[17] The use of balloons, the reliance on the telegraph, and experimentation with submarines made the American Civil War seem modern, although to a later generation accustomed to airplanes, tanks, and missiles, it may seem archaic. On most battlefields the armies used the same means of communication as Alexander the Great; many a courier lost his way on unfamiliar terrain. Staff organization, which relied on the personal direction of the army commander, precluded any synchronization of strategic planning, ancillary services, and field command in the kind of operations familiar in World War II. In an era before radio communications, it was impossible to coordinate some engagements. And frequently the influence of public opinion and politicians overrode military considerations.

## EARLY BATTLES: WEST VIRGINIA
## AND BULL RUN

In the first weeks after the attack on Fort Sumter in April 1861, northerners worried about Washington. Inadequately protected by fortifications and militia, and with Confederate flags flying across the Potomac, the capital city of the Union was exposed. Later, in the postwar battles for reputation that marked the refighting of the war in the history books, some authorities declared that Pierre Beauregard missed an opportunity by not moving his army of nearly twenty thousand rapidly northward from South Carolina after Sumter and seizing Washington before Union troops arrived and defensive outposts were prepared. After the arrival of the earliest military contingents—notably a few companies from Pennsylvania, the Seventh New York Regiment and the Sixth Massachusetts—the president, government officials, and citizens breathed easier. Reaching Washington in late April after their harassment by a Baltimore mob, the soldiers were quartered in the Capitol. By June, Maryland offered no serious resistance to the reinforcement of Federal troops, though Washington remained a possible target for a Confederate attack throughout the war.

Western Virginia, strong in Unionist sentiment and exposed to attack, witnessed an early campaign in May and June that produced celebration in the North and made George McClellan a hero. Born in Philadelphia, educated at the University of Pennsylvania, and trained at West Point, McClellan had served with distinction in the Mexican War and had been a military observer in the Crimean War. Retiring to civilian life as many underpaid army officers did, he became an officer of the Illinois Central Railroad and later president of the Ohio and Mississippi Railroad in Cincinnati. At the beginning of the war he was given the rank of major general and was put in command of the military department of the Ohio. Trained in the Corps of Engineers, he favored field maneuvers over direct frontal attacks.

A Virginia force of ten thousand had already taken up a strategic position in the Kanawha Valley in northwestern Virginia and had seized Harpers Ferry with its valuable machinery and federal arsenal. It was here that Thomas J. Jackson, temporarily in command at Harpers Ferry, saw his first action in the Civil War. The lines of the Baltimore and Ohio Railroad connecting Washington with the West were temporarily cut, and Jackson managed to capture much-needed rolling stock for the South. He was then superseded by Joseph E. Johnston, who withdrew from Harpers Ferry to a more tenable position in Winchester. Harpers Ferry was then reoccupied by a Federal force under General Robert Patterson.

Intending to use tactical maneuvers rather than throwing "these men of mine into the teeth of artillery and entrenchments," McClellan and the nearly twenty thousand troops under his command entered western Virginia in late May for a campaign that lasted a month.[18] Partly in response to pleas of Unionists who were trying to establish a new state government and partly for strategic reasons, he intended to move up the valley of the Kanawha River to secure the area for the Union. With both military and political goals, his movement was timed to coordinate with a movement in the western theater to control the Mississippi.

When the Confederates pulled back from the Baltimore and Ohio junction at Grafton to Philippi, a small town fifteen miles south, McClellan's forces followed, routing the Confederates in small engagements in which he used turning maneuvers to force the Confederates out of their positions. But on June 3 a Union attack on Philippi failed. Next McClellan tried to surround the Confederate general Robert Garnett's small force at Laurel Hill near Rich Mountain. Exhibiting the caution that marked his approach to battle, the Union commander failed to launch an offensive at a crucial time when the Confederates were evacuating their position. By July, although their army had not been destroyed, Confederate resistance had ended in most of west Virginia.

McClellan, who had earlier announced to West Virginians that they must end their connections with traitors, addressed his soldiers with the grandiosity that characterized his personality and in the early days of the war brought him admiration:

> Soldiers of the Army of the West! I am more than pleased with you. You have annihilated two armies, commanded by educated and experienced soldiers, intrenched in mountain fastnesses, fortified at their leisure. You have taken five guns, twelve colors, fifteen hundred stand of arms, one thousand prisoners, including more than forty officers. . . . You have killed more than two hundred and fifty of the enemy, who has lost his baggage and camp equipage. All this has been accomplished with the loss of twenty brave men killed and sixty wounded on your part.
>
> You have proved that Union men, fighting for the preservation of our Government, are more than a match for our misguided and erring brethren; more than this, you have shown mercy to the vanquished. . . . I have not hesitated to demand courage of you, feeling that I could rely on your endurance, patriotism, and courage.[19]

The message conveyed the general's egotism, but also his ability to inspire his men.

One hundred twenty miles to the east, in July 1861, the Union general Irvin McDowell guarded the capital from an entrenched position near Centreville, twenty miles southwest of Washington. The main Confederate army under Beauregard was stationed nearby in Manassas, where the Orange and Alexandria Railroad joined a rail line from the Shenandoah Valley. Beauregard's force, besides threatening Washington, occupied a junction vital for the protection of Richmond. Under pressure from public opinion as well as newspapers whose reverberating slogan "On to Richmond" soon became a battle cry, McDowell reluctantly planned an advance. Though he had, for the most part, merely a collection of civilians in uniform, he had a few regulars, and his opponents' forces were as raw and "green" as his own, circumstances his commander in chief Abraham Lincoln pointed out. McDowell's campaign was based on the false premise that the Confederate force under Joseph E. Johnston, then at Winchester, would not join Beauregard. Meanwhile, Confederates profited from information about McDowell's advance provided by their Washington-based spy Rose O'Neal Greenhow.

Isolating Johnston's forces was the task of sixty-nine-year-old General Robert Patterson, who was to engage Johnston and keep him occupied. Even if defeated in such an engagement, Patterson would have strengthened McDowell by preventing the reinforcement of Beauregard. But Johnston was allowed to slip away. His main force joined Beauregard on July 20, on the eve of McDowell's attack, which was planned as a flanking movement, not a frontal assault.

The next day—July 21, 1861—McDowell's attacking force of ten thousand men at first dislodged the Confederates who were positioned along the south bank of the Bull Run River that named the battle for the Union. (For this and several other engagements, the Confederates used the name of towns, in this case Manassas.) Mistaking the thrust of the Union attack, which was expected toward the railroad, Beauregard was surprised by McDowell's offensive on his left, not right, flank. Until mid-afternoon the Union soldiers, having forded Bull Run upstream, had the better of the fight.

The southerners, however, had several advantages. They had only to defend their position on a hot day and not undertake long advances under fire. Furthermore, reinforcements arrived when most needed, whereas two Union reserve brigades were never deployed. In short, quick assaults during which the Yankees, for the first but not last time, heard the fury of the "rebel yell," the Confederates drove the Union forces back. Rallied by Johnston and Beauregard, the commands of Barnard Bee (who died in the battle), Edmund Kirby Smith, and Thomas J. Jackson distinguished themselves; it was at Manassas that Jackson earned his nickname "Stonewall." The conduct of this one commander did much to prevent a Confederate rout, while Johnston's reinforcements contributed the added factor needed for victory. In fierce fighting the Union army was driven from Henry Hill, and McDowell was forced to retreat toward Washington.

The retreat was at first orderly, and at Centreville the Federals blocked the Confederate pursuit. But when the soldiers were fired on in the road and became entangled in a mass of camp followers, congressmen, and picnicking spectators, the army disintegrated into a mob that fled toward Washington. According to a congressman from Ohio who observed the retreat:

> There was never anything like it for causeless, sheer, absolute, absurd cowardice, or rather panic, on this miserable earth before. Off they went, one and all; off down the highway, over across fields, towards the woods, anywhere, everywhere, to escape. Well,

the further they ran the more frightened they grew, and although we moved on as rapidly as we could, the fugitives passed us by scores. To enable them better to run, they threw away their blankets, knapsacks, canteens, and finally muskets, cartridge boxes, and everything else. We called to them, tried to tell them there was no danger, called them to stop, implored them to stand. We called them cowards, denounced them in the most offensive terms, put out our heavy revolvers, and threatened to shoot them, but all in vain; a cruel, crazy, mad, hopeless panic possessed them, and communicated to everybody about in front and rear. The heat was awful, although now about six; the men were exhausted—their mouths gaped, their lips cracked and blackened with the powder of the cartridges they had bitten off in the battle, their eyes starting in frenzy; no mortal ever saw such a mass of ghastly wretches.[20]

Bull Run seemed a defeat for the Union, but like most battles of the Civil War, it produced no decisive results or significant military disadvantage for the North, nor gain, except in terms of pride and the emergence of Stonewall Jackson as a hero, for the South. Union casualties, including prisoners of war, were approximately three thousand, while those of the Confederacy numbered less than two thousand. Since the grim realities of the battle served to stimulate war preparation in the North while causing overconfidence in the South, the benefit probably belonged to the Union. The spirit in which the North received the humiliating news of the battle was typified by a postbattle memorandum in which President Lincoln called for tightening the blockade around the South; drilling new volunteers; strengthening the commanders in the Shenandoah, Robert Patterson and Nathaniel Banks; reorganizing the forces engaged at Bull Run; keeping the lines open from Washington to Manassas and from Harpers Ferry to Strasburg, Virginia; and initiating an advance in the West in order to shake the Confederate hold on Tennessee.

Meanwhile McDowell was so discredited by Bull Run that Lincoln replaced him with McClellan. With the retirement of General Scott on November 1, 1861, McClellan became general-in-chief of the army at a time when the matter of greatest concern to the Union government was the exposed condition of Washington. Ever alert to defense rather than offense, McClellan complained about the hasty entrenchments and lack of "any general defensive line." Positions from which the enemy could have commanded Washington were open for their occupation, and the city, he objected, was "full of drunken men in uniform," with McDowell's army so demoralized that its officers and men were deserting their camps.[21]

The two critical tasks to which the new commander at once addressed himself, and for which he was particularly fitted, were the preparation of adequate defenses to protect the capital and, more especially, the drilling of the new re-

General George McClellan replaced Irvin McDowell after Bull Run and became the general-in-chief of the army. Although McClellan trained his troops well, his leadership was one of hesitancy. On numerous occasions, he failed to advance his troops in a successful movement.

cruits into disciplined units. McClellan proved a brilliant organizer, but he became so absorbed in preparing and training the army that he attempted no forward movement until the spring of 1862. Fortunately, the Confederates, at this critical stage of the war, never seized the opportunity to attack Washington.

In the South, according to Joseph E. Johnston, the army was "more disorganized by victory than that of the United States by defeat."[22] President Davis, who harbored notions of leading Confederate troops into battle, had arrived on the Bull Run battlefield and had rallied demoralized troops with his exhortation "I am President Davis. Follow me back to the field." After the battle Davis was accused of having opposed a coordinated movement by Johnston and Beauregard that would have caught McDowell before his advance to Manassas. In fact the Confederate president's orders for a joint effort had been imprecise.[23] Some officials in Richmond complained that a pursuit after Bull Run would have resulted in the capture of Washington and the "liberation" of Maryland. Davis's defenders, on the other hand, claimed that he supported plans for a pursuit that night, but that Johnston "was decidedly averse to an immediate offensive, and emphatically discountenanced it as impracticable."[24] In any case Confederates could not have followed up their victory; a pursuit would have required the fresh troops they did not have.

## EARLY CAMPAIGNS IN THE WEST

A period of military inactivity followed in the East as the war moved to the West, where the organization of both armies was slowly proceeding. Chief command of the Union forces in Kentucky had been assigned to Brigadier General Robert Anderson of Fort Sumter fame, who relinquished it to General William Tecumseh Sherman. Conferring with Secretary of War Simon Cameron in Louisville in October 1861, Sherman argued that, for effective offense, a force of two hundred thousand men was needed in the West. Sherman's supposedly irrational request was reported in the East, where primary attention would remain focused until 1864 on the Virginia front. The general's "insanity" became a bit of gossip fostered by newspapers. Shortly thereafter Sherman was relieved of command of the Department of the Cumberland and placed in a subordinate position. For Confederates the strategic options were limited by the extent of the territory to be defended. Rivers—the Ohio, the Tennessee, the Cumberland, and the Mississippi, which earlier had linked North and South—now emerged as avenues of entry into the Confederacy.

The year 1861 passed without major confrontations in Kentucky, but in January 1862, a clash developed between the Union commander (and future president) James A. Garfield and the Confederate general Humphrey Marshall near Prestonburg in the eastern part of the state. Both commanders withdrew from the field, each claiming victory. This often-overlooked battle was important because it established the Union hold on eastern Kentucky. Shortly afterward one of the ablest Union commanders, George H. Thomas, defeated a Confederate force commanded by General George B. Crittenden at the battle of Mill Springs on January 19, 1862. Thomas's victory opened the road for an invasion into eastern Tennessee, where there was considerable support for the Union. But despite the president's agreement to such an advance, the difficulties of transportation and provisioning prevented such a movement.

In 1862 the Union launched its successful river war, a combined operation of armies and gunboats on large inland streams. Both sides understood the value of controlling these strategic points in the border areas of Kentucky and Tennessee. While the North mounted its attack from Cairo, Illinois, General Albert Sidney Johnston defended the entrance to the Confederacy's west by placing his seventeen thousand troops along the eight-hundred-mile border of Kentucky and Tennessee. The Confederates were well positioned, entrenched, and armed at Columbus, Kentucky, on the Mississippi River, at Fort Henry on the Tennessee River, and at Fort Donelson on the Cumberland River, although the latter fortification remained little more than a stockade. But at each location the Confederates had built their installations too close to the rivers to protect them from northern gunboats.

After a coordinated land-and-water effort under the army's Ulysses S. Grant and the navy's Andrew Foote, Fort Henry in Tennessee surrendered on February

Commodore Andrew Foote used Union ironclads to capture Fort Henry in February 1862. The gunboat pictured here was the first to fire a shot at Fort Henry.

6, 1862. Its capture occurred after a short battle between the fort and the fleet. Losses were light. Then Grant turned his fifteen thousand troops, now increased to twenty-five thousand, on Fort Donelson, which fell on February 16, 1862, but only after heavy fighting between the Confederate forces under Gideon Pillow, John Floyd, and Simon Buckner. Again, the infantry and artillery on land coordinated their movements with the gunboat flotilla under Foote. With the fall of Forts Henry and Donelson, the Union had begun its campaign to control the Mississippi River.

The northern victory at Donelson resulted from a combination of factors. Confederate strategy mistakenly permitted most of its troops to be bottled up by the Union's three-sided deployment. The Confederates also used a "cordon defense," with separate detachments not viewed as a whole but deployed where needed.[25] Throughout there was a lack of collaboration between the southern commanders. The Confederates also failed to attack before Grant's ten thousand reinforcements arrived. Nor did they effectively use the reinforcements that Johnston sent.

An important element in the Union victory was the boldness of Grant, who, though absent during the earlier hours of fighting on a gunboat of Foote's, correctly concluded that the enemy was in worse condition than he was, and ordered a charge on the left. Although superior in numbers and position in the earlier stages of a battle that began on February 13, two days later the Confederates

This painting shows Ulysses S. Grant on horseback, watching the fighting at Fort Donelson. Grant not only ordered the charge that surrounded the weakening Confederate forces but also demanded an unconditional surrender. His aggressive stance (which earned Grant the nickname "Unconditional Surrender") was instrumental in the capturing of Fort Donelson.

took refuge within their works and were promptly surrounded. That night Floyd, Pillow, and Buckner decided that further resistance could only result in needless slaughter and that the fort must be surrendered.

After Floyd and Pillow fled during the night, the surrender was left to Buckner, who proposed an armistice while terms were discussed.[26] Responding to the Confederate general's proposal, Grant announced that "no terms except an unconditional and immediate surrender can be accepted. I propose to move immediately upon your works," to which Buckner agreed, but only after complaining of "ungenerous and unchivalrous terms." On the 16th Grant, who earned his nickname "Unconditional Surrender" at this battle, reported the capture of an important Confederate position, along with a force of approximately fifteen thousand men and forty artillery pieces.

Following months of discouraging news the reports of the river war encouraged the North; optimists thought the end near at hand. "After this, it certainly cannot be materially postponed," predicted the *New York Times*. "The monster is already clutched and in his death struggle."[27] Beyond its celebration as a Union victory, the capture of Forts Henry and Donelson was strategically important because it cut the rail communication between Johnston's force at Nashville and Confederate armies along the Mississippi. Other fruits of the Union victory became evident with the evacuation of the Confederate position at Columbus in early March and the retreat of Albert Sidney Johnston, the ranking Confederate general in the West, who was forced not only to abandon his Kentucky front but to evacuate Nashville as well.[28] "The Tennessee and Cumberland rivers," Grant noted, "from their mouths to the head of navigation, were secured."[29]

The Union commander was soon to find, however, that a new Confederate line was forming farther south and that a powerful enemy effort focused on regaining everything that had been lost. This aggressive southern campaign rejected any cordon defense or defensive strategy of trading land for an extended war in which the North would become demoralized and seek terms. Instead the Confederates began to move fifteen thousand troops from New Orleans and Mobile, Alabama, by train to Corinth, a railroad junction in northern Mississippi. With forty thousand troops available, Johnston intended to strike Grant before the Union general was reinforced.

A brutal battle at Shiloh, thirty miles north of Corinth in southwestern Tennessee, took place on April 6–7, 1862. Though fought nearly a year after the war had begun, the battle was notable for the inexperience of the troops and the ease with which the whole Union war machine was thrown into confusion by a sur-

On April 6, 1862, Confederates, depicted charging in this print, attacked inexperienced Union troops and occupied Union camps in the beginning stages of the bloody battle of Shiloh in southwestern Tennessee. Soon Union troops rallied and drove the Confederates back to Corinth.

prise attack. This Confederate assault also found Grant unprepared, and he has been criticized for his management of the army.[30]

At the time he was planning his own offensive and was acting on his famous maxim that a successful general must think more about what he will do to the enemy than what the enemy will do to him. Although his main army was at Pittsburg Landing on the west bank of the Tennessee River, he had his headquarters in Savannah nine miles farther north on the opposite side of the river. Here he awaited General Don Carlos Buell and thirty-five thousand reinforcements. His army "had no line or order of battle, no defensive works of any sort, no outposts, properly speaking, to give warning, or check the advance of an enemy, and no recognized head during the absence of the regular commander."[31]

The most exposed position at Shiloh Church, about three miles west of Pittsburg Landing, was held by the rawest of the troops, commanded by Sherman. Many Union soldiers had just received their muskets and hardly knew how to load them. Others had only been introduced to military discipline through the interminable drilling that characterized army training. Suddenly, the Confederates struck in an attack that constituted the main feature of the first day's battle. As Sherman later explained, the place could easily have been made impregnable by defensive works. But because of the inexperience that characterized this early period of the war and the fact that the Union army was advancing, this precaution was neglected.

A tumultuous battle raged on Sunday, April 6, and by nightfall the Confederates occupied the Union camps. The Federal line had been pushed a mile behind the position it had held in the morning. Troops lost touch with their units. Fragments of broken regiments and companies joined any command they happened on. Only one of Sherman's brigades retained its organization. Two colonels, as Grant explained, "led their regiments from the field on first hearing the whistle of the enemy's bullets."[32] At one stage during the battle Grant found over four thousand stragglers lying panic stricken under cover of the river bluff. Union cavalry, useless in front, was employed to stop stragglers, who were quickly shifted to that part of the line where reinforcements were needed. Among other Union difficulties on Sunday was the delay of General Lew Wallace in bringing up reinforcements. Because of his confused orders he took a wrong road, moved only a short distance, and arrived after the first day's fighting was over.

Grant, who had suffered a painful fall from his horse, was ten miles away when the firing began, but he rushed by steamer to the front. Military historians disagree about the effectiveness of his leadership in the battle of Shiloh. Some believe that he did little beyond his appearance. Others conclude that "if this half-crippled man, who on the night of the 6th–7th slept among his men in torrents of rain and could get no rest because his ankle was much swollen had not acted as he did, the battle would have been lost."[33]

Of course the critical issue beyond the personal reputation of the generals centered on the failure of the Confederate armies to follow up after Beauregard was blocked by Union artillery and stopped fighting late Sunday afternoon. As a result, Grant was able to rally his troops. Although victorious in the first day's battle, the Confederates suffered a serious loss when their commanding general, Albert Sidney Johnston, was hit in a leg artery and died from loss of blood, leaving Beauregard in command. As Grant's recent biographer William McFeely explains, Beauregard's soldiers were "weary rather than triumphant; [they] wanted not to finish the job, but to sleep—some of them in the tents of the men they had driven out at the start of the day."[34]

When the battle resumed on Monday, the Union soldiers had been strengthened by reinforcements under Buell and Wallace. With fresh troops Grant was able, after ten hours of bitter struggle, to drive the enemy back toward Corinth. Shiloh passed into history, to be refought endlessly in post-mortem reviews and divisional reunions. On both sides losses were heavy, with Confederate casualties numbering 10,699 and those of the Union 13,047, more wounded and killed in two days than Americans had lost in the Revolution, the War of 1812, and the Mexican War combined. As Herman Hattaway and Archer Jones conclude, "despite the essentially stalemated engagement, the North had turned the southern response to its western concentration into a strategic victory; the South had hoped to destroy Grant's force and threatened to recapture western Tennessee but Grant had now exhausted these hopes."[35] There would be no more significant Confederate efforts to retake western Tennessee and prevent the inexorable Union movement into the heart of the Confederacy.

Paralleling the Henry-Donelson-Shiloh campaign on the line of the Tennessee River, another Union army under General John Pope had been operating on the Mississippi. Leadership of all the western armies rested with General Henry Wager Halleck, whose headquarters were in St. Louis. Halleck intended to push the Confederates out of their territory by waging war on their communications and attacking the middle of the Confederate line. Naval cooperation was again supplied by the flotilla of gunboats and mortar boats under Admiral Foote. After the evacuation of Columbus, Kentucky, the Confederates took their stand just below that city on a turn of the river known as "Madrid Bend," with an army under Generals Leonidas Polk and Pillow, and with batteries commanding the river both on the shore and on Island Number Ten.

After a long and useless naval bombardment, part of the Union fleet slipped past the batteries of the island, while transports carrying the troops moved through a specially cut canal. Pope's army of twenty thousand thereby maneuvered into a commanding position below the bend. Already partly cut off by the swampy approaches to the shore and surrounded by Halleck's lines, the Confederates were caught in an indefensible position. "Halleck had intelligently concentrated his forces first in Missouri and then on the Tennessee and Cumberland Rivers, the line of operation where the enemy was weakest and the fruits of success most promising."[36] The Confederates abandoned New Madrid on March 14. Island Number Ten, with its garrison of over five thousand, surrendered without bloodshed on April 7, 1862. In addition to the garrison, artillery, ammunition, and provisions fell into Union hands.

The Shiloh campaign ended in May 1862 when Union forces, now commanded directly by Halleck, captured Corinth, the position that Beauregard had occupied following Shiloh and that he evacuated before Halleck's attack.[37] The place fell before the heavy guns and superior force of the Army of Tennessee. The first phase of the western war, with its steady Union advance, came to a close. Now Union armies would suffer delays and setbacks before winning further victories at Vicksburg and Chattanooga. By that time the war in the East had become the focus of presidential and congressional attention.

## CHAPTER 10

# The Virginia Front, 1861–1863

## MᴄCʟᴇʟʟᴀɴ ɪɴ Cʜᴀʀɢᴇ

Following the battle of Bull Run on July 26, 1861, there was a lull on the eastern front. All was quiet along the Potomac, according to dispatches to the War Department.[1] Lincoln had placed McClellan in charge of the newly named Army of the Potomac, and in November McClellan was appointed general-in-chief. When Lincoln asked the new commander if he was overextending himself by becoming both the general of the Army of the Potomac and all the armies of the United States including Don Carlos Buell's Army of the Ohio, he replied, "I can do it all."[2]

Heated controversies have raged about McClellan's personality and career.[3] His supporters have emphasized his success in shaping an army of amateurs into a fighting force that undertook an offensive against the Confederacy in 1862 and whose success was wrecked, as was McClellan's whole career, by interference from Washington.

Critics of the general have interpreted the same events as a record of failures: "McClellan was not a real general. McClellan was not even a disciplined, truthful soldier. McClellan was merely an attractive but vain and unstable man, with considerable military knowledge, who sat a horse well and wanted to be President."[4] According to his recent biographer Stephen Sears, "He believed beyond any doubt that his Confederate enemies faced him with forces substantially greater than his own. He believed with equal conviction that enemies at the head of his own government conspired to see him and his army defeated so as to carry out their traitorous purpose. . . . When he lost the courage to fight, as he did in every battle, he believed he was preserving his army to fight the next time on another and better day."[5]

Even McClellan's critics admit that he was an excellent coordinator and trainer of troops, though he was unable to organize them for the next step—fighting a battle. From July 1861 to March 1862, he devoted his time to organizing the army for an advance that he expected would end the war with a definitive campaign. Believing that Union strategy required the destruction of the Confederate army in an overwhelming defeat on the battlefield, McClellan assumed that all Union operations must be secondary to his.[6] A trained army of a quarter of a million men, drilled and organized after European models, with a formidable fleet for support, was what he intended.

As the months passed, he concerned himself with devising plans for western and naval operations as well as for those of his immediate army; giving advice on foreign affairs; overseeing the defenses of Washington; perfecting the organization of divisions, brigades, and regiments of his infantry; determining the proper proportion of artillery pieces to infantry units; building up his staff of adjutants and inspectors; marshaling his engineers, quartermasters, and commissaries: and assembling his gas-filled observation balloons and his telegraph operators. Throughout his career McClellan was preoccupied with the development of communication and military signals. His days were spent in the saddle, his nights in office work, attending to the infinite details he deemed had to be re-

This political cartoon, entitled "Masterly Inactivity, or Six Months on the Potomac," refers to the inability of both George McClellan and Pierre Beauregard to advance their armies. McClellan became too involved in training his troops and failed to make any forward movement, while Beauregard, with a lack of manpower, failed to lead an immediate move for Washington.

This oil painting depicts the Army of the Potomac, led by the colorfully uniformed Zouaves, marching up Pennsylvania Avenue in Washington in 1861.

solved before operations in the field could even be considered. Much of his time was devoted to reports that would record for posterity that this general had left nothing undone.

Meanwhile Lincoln, under pressure from the public and Congress, was eager that something be done or else, he is reported to have said, "the bottom would drop out of the whole concern."[7] Inexperienced as he was in such matters, the president had been devouring military treatises, poring over maps, attending war councils, and issuing repeated calls for troops. Lincoln, it seems, had a natural flair for strategy, although his occasional interference on the eastern front soon clashed with McClellan's campaign plans.

McClellan found it "perfectly sickening" to be obliged to listen to the president's advice on military matters, and he rapidly concluded that his civilian superiors were motivated by "hypocrisy, knavery, and folly."[8] Believing that the country's safety rested on his shoulders, he displayed what Lincoln's secretary John Hay called "the unparalleled insolence of epaulettes."[9] He snubbed the president, wrote complaining letters, and disregarded his commander in chief's requests. With Congress and the public demanding an offensive, Lincoln decided to force his slow-moving general into action. In January 1862, he issued a

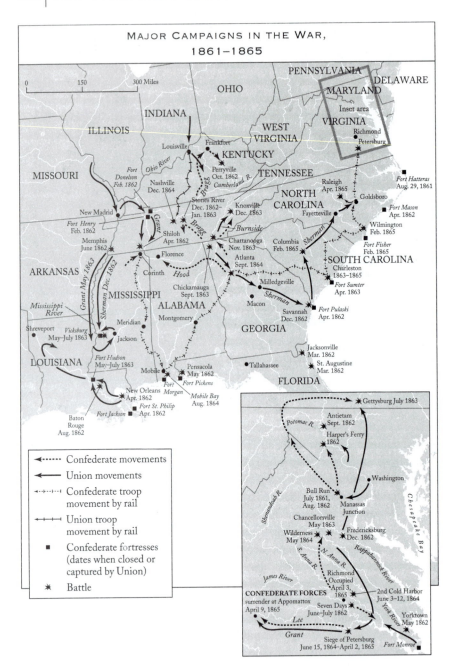

## MAJOR CAMPAIGNS IN THE WAR, 1861–1865

0    150    300 Miles

PENNSYLVANIA
OHIO
DELAWARE
MARYLAND
INDIANA
WEST
VIRGINIA    Inset area
VIRGINIA
ILLINOIS
Richmond
Petersburg
Louisville    Frankfort
KENTUCKY
MISSOURI
Perryville
Fort    Ohio River    Oct. 1862    TENNESSEE    Raleigh    Fort Hatteras
Donelson    Nashville    Cumberland R.    Apr. 1865    Aug. 29, 1861
Feb. 1862    Dec. 1864    NORTH    Goldsboro
New Madrid    Stones River    Knoxville    CAROLINA    Fort Mason
Fort Henry    Dec. 1862–    Dec. 1863    Fayetteville    Apr. 1862
Feb. 1862    Jan. 1863    Wilmington
Memphis    Burnside    Feb. 1865
June 1862    Chattanooga    Columbia    Fort Fisher
Florence    Nov. 1863    Feb. 1865    Feb. 1865
ARKANSAS    Corinth    Hood    Atlanta    SOUTH CAROLINA
Sept. 1864    Charleston
Chickamauga    Milledgeville    1863–1865
MISSISSIPPI    Sept. 1863    Fort Sumter
Mississippi    ALABAMA    Macon    Apr. 1863
River    Meridian    Savannah    Fort Pulaski
Shreveport    Vicksburg    Montgomery    Dec. 1862    Apr. 1862
May–July 1863    Jackson    GEORGIA
LOUISIANA    Fort Hudson    Jacksonville
May–July 1863    Mobile    Pensacola    Mar. 1862
New Orleans    Fort    May 1862    FLORIDA    St. Augustine
Apr. 1862    Morgan    Fort Pickens    Tallahassee    Mar. 1862
Fort St. Philip    Mobile Bay
Baton    Apr. 1862    Aug. 1864
Rouge    Fort Jackson
Aug. 1862

- - - - ▶ Confederate movements

——▶ Union movements

- ·-·-·-▶ Confederate troop
movement by rail

——+—+— Union troop
movement by rail

■  Confederate fortresses
(dates when closed or
captured by Union)

✳  Battle

Gettysburg July 1863
Potomac R.    Antietam
Sept. 1862
Harper's Ferry
1862
Washington
Shenandoah R.    Bull Run
July 1861,
Aug. 1862    Manassas
Junction
Chancellorsville
May 1863    Fredericksburg
Wilderness    Dec. 1862
May 1864    Rappahannock River
N. Anna R.    Chesapeake Bay
S. Anna R.    Richmond
James River    Occupied    2nd Cold Harbor
April 3,    June 3–12, 1864
CONFEDERATE FORCES    1865
surrender at Appomattox    Seven Days    Yorktown
April 9, 1865    June–July 1862    May 1862
Lee    York River
Grant    Siege of Petersburg    Fort Monroe
June 15, 1864–April 2, 1865

special command, designated as the "President's General War Order No. 1" for a general forward movement of the Union forces to take place on February 22.

At this time, and for months before, the Confederate general Joseph Johnston's army was at Manassas—the railroad junction in northern Virginia where Union and Confederate forces had clashed seven months before. Nearby McClellan faced him with a force three times as large, although McClellan's imagination had transformed Johnston's army of fewer than 45,000 into an impregnable force of 170,000. Lincoln, of course, expected a direct movement against the Confederates at Manassas.[10]

McClellan, ignoring the president's "war order" to advance, decided on an oblique advance to Richmond by way of the peninsula between the York and James rivers, a plan that offered military advantages but which Lincoln considered would leave Washington vulnerable to attack. After promising to leave sufficient forces to protect the capital, McClellan organized a troop embarkation with the cooperation of the Potomac flotilla. By placing his army between Johnston's forces and Richmond, McClellan intended to reach Richmond before Johnston could maneuver southward. Alternatively, if he could not capture Richmond, he hoped to force a battle in an advantageous location. By May 1 McClellan, in a large operation displaying northern resources and organizational potential, was safely on the peninsula with an army of 112,000 men, 44 artillery batteries, 1,150 wagons, and 25,600 horses and mules.[11] From its base at Fort Monroe, the army now prepared for an advance on Richmond, the Confederate capital.

## THE PENINSULAR CAMPAIGN

At Yorktown, a Confederate force was entrenched at the mouth of the York River and along a fortified line from the city across the peninsula to the James River. It would have yielded quickly to Union assaults, yet McClellan devoted a month to a siege, after which, having occupied the abandoned Confederate works, he announced on May 4, 1862 that "Yorktown is in our possession." Later, the Confederate commander Johnston remarked of this delay, "No one but McClellan could have hesitated to attack."[12]

Retreating up the peninsula between the York and James rivers toward Richmond, the Confederates delayed the Union pursuit at the battle of Williamsburg on May 5, where James Longstreet, commanding the Confederate rear guard, fought off a large Union force. This action upset McClellan's plan to assault the main Confederate army under Johnston. When the Confederates evacuated Norfolk after first burning the naval yard, the James River was opened to a repetition of the Union's land-and-water operations, successful in the West. But on May 15, eight miles from Richmond at Drewry's Bluff, where there were batteries on high bluffs and the river narrowed, the Confederates obstructed the passage with sunken obstacles, and Union gunboats were stopped.

From his headquarters at White House Landing on the York River, McClellan now planned a cautious advance on Richmond. He anticipated a decisive battle, as he moved to within seven miles of the Confederate capital. Reporting that he had only 80,000 men (40,000 fewer than he actually had) and desiring to overawe the "enemies of the Constitution" with the largest possible force, he urged his army's reinforcement. Because he had inflated the Confederate army to 185,000, more than twice its actual size, McClellan now demanded Washington's cooperation in concentrating under his command all available Federal forces in Virginia.

It is unclear whether, with this cooperation and an increased force, he could have taken Richmond, although most historians believe that a more aggressive commander would have done so.[13] It is possible, however, that if McClellan had moved into the Confederate capital, Confederate troops would have attacked the rear of the Union army and cut its communications, isolating McClellan in hostile territory.[14] On the other hand, had the Union held Richmond for even forty-eight hours, the destruction to manufacturing and transportation as well as the psychological impact of having lost its capital would have been devastating to the Confederacy. In any case McClellan was consistent in his approach to tactics when he refused to storm the Richmond defenses.

Cooperation in Washington, however, was withheld. Under pressure from McClellan's opponents, who worried that not enough troops had been left to defend Washington, Lincoln removed McClellan from supreme command and reorganized the army under corps commanders. In fact McClellan had inflated the number of troops he had left behind to defend the city from the actual figure of twenty-six thousand to forty thousand, most of them untrained. Because Lincoln and his secretary of war, Edwin Stanton, insisted on "covering" Washington by keeping McDowell directly between the two capitals, the president on April 3 ordered McDowell's corps held back in Fredericksburg to defend the capital. Meanwhile, to take the pressure off Richmond, Stonewall Jackson's army began diversionary moves in the Shenandoah Valley, threatening Washington by way of Harpers Ferry. In response, Lincoln detailed McDowell's corps to chase Jackson—a move McClellan considered a colossal blunder. McClellan argued that Washington was virtually defended by his offensive on the peninsula and that in any case the Confederates were not attacking Washington by way of Fredericksburg.

Jackson's sixteen thousand troops were eventually covered by nearly forty-five thousand Union troops under different commands. Jackson's strategy was not to fight a major battle or to win and hold particular places, but rather to attack Union commanders before they could unite, to create panic in Washington, thus preventing what would best capture Richmond—the reinforcement of McClellan.

In carrying out this assignment, Jackson was notably successful. By successive assaults on the Union commanders James Shields, Robert Milroy, Nathaniel

Banks, and John Frémont in the battles of Kernstown, McDowell, Winchester, Cross Keys, and Port Republic in northern Virginia in late May, Jackson had Union leaders mystified as to his movements. Northern newspapers complained that Washington was in danger. Alarmed governors called for increased mobilization.

Lincoln, however, was not frightened. Anticipating an opportunity to trap Jackson in the Shenandoah valley, he detached McDowell's corps from McClellan's army. The result was to deprive McClellan of forty thousand men at the moment when his advance on the Confederate capital was about to materialize. And when Union troops failed to cut off Jackson, the Confederate commander moved quickly to return his forces to the main Confederate defense for the decisive battles in front of Richmond.

In the end only one division of McDowell's forty thousand men actually joined the now resentful McClellan in his attacks on the Confederate capital. Such confusion displayed the early uncertainty of an immature Union army command system that suffered from "insufficient topographical information, problems of coordinating field operations with the extended line of a mass army, and McClellan's special inability to delegate authority."[15]

As a result of the collaboration between Lee and Jackson in the late spring of 1862, the Confederates had about eighty-five thousand men to defend Richmond, while McClellan had approximately one hundred thousand on the peninsula. The first major battle in the peninsular campaign took place on May 31–June 1 at Seven Pines, also called Fair Oaks, an engagement fought before

On May 31, Fair Oaks, also known as Seven Pines, became the first major battle in the peninsular campaign. Here Union troops of the 104th Pennsylvania drive Confederate forces back toward Richmond.

Jackson returned to Richmond. The battle was a tactical defeat for the Confederates, who wished to drive McClellan back and prevent a possible siege of their capital. "When McClellan's army reached the outskirts of Richmond, it so menaced the capital that it compelled the Confederates to attack him, thus enabling him to fight Johnston's force with all the tactical advantages of being on the defensive."[16] Thus the Union attacker had become the attacked, with the advantages of that position in terms of commensurately lower casualties.

At this time the Union army straddled the Chickahominy River, with more than 40 percent of its forces north of the river, connected to the main part of the army only by a few insubstantial bridges. Recognizing his advantage, Johnston struck south of the river in an assault that took place after ferocious rain storms raised flood waters and destroyed these bridges. McClellan's force of about 39,000 was separated by the raging river when Johnston attacked near Fair Oaks in the early morning of May 31. About 12,000 Union troops and 9,500 Confederates were involved in heavy fighting. Both President Davis and General Robert E. Lee were under fire in this battle, though at the time Lee had no field command and was on staff duty in the Confederate war department. By the end of the day the Confederates had retreated and their commander lay wounded. On June 1 Davis replaced the incapacitated Johnston with Robert E. Lee, who now became the commander of the southern armies in eastern Virginia and North Carolina.[17]

## ROBERT E. LEE

Lee, the son of "Light Horse" Harry Lee, was born in Westmoreland County, Virginia in 1807. He graduated from West Point, served in the engineers of the regular army, and distinguished himself in the Mexican War. He served as a superintendent of West Point and had commanded the small Federal force that captured John Brown at Harpers Ferry in 1859. Married to Mary Custis, the daughter of Washington's adopted son, he inherited her father's Arlington, a stately mansion opposite Washington, D.C., along with sixty-three slaves. Just after Lincoln's call for troops, Scott offered him the command of the armies of the United States; as an officer of the United States whose flag he had sworn to defend, Lee faced a critical dilemma.

In Texas on military duty when the secession crisis developed, Lee opposed the secession of the Lower South, which he thought foolish and short-sighted, and he hoped for some peaceful resolution of the crisis. He was by no means a proslavery radical, supporting instead gradual emancipation. But he believed the institution should be allowed to expand, and that the South was justified in complaining about northern aggression, especially as practiced by the abolitionists. Writes Douglas S. Freeman, "if secession destroyed the Union, Lee intended to resign from the army and to fight neither for the South nor for the North, unless

In the spring of 1862, Jefferson Davis brought Robert E. Lee, the Confederacy's most famous general, to Richmond to direct military operations in the armies of the Confederacy. In June, Lee became the commander of the southern armies in eastern Virginia. He was the architect of the South's most aggressive strategic offensives.

he had to act one way or the other in defense of Virginia." When Virginia joined the Confederacy, Lee is said to have remarked that he could not "see the good of secession."[18] But his state's departure and his own views on sectional loyalty determined his course. Two days after he resigned his commission in the United States Army, despite his comments about not wanting to draw his sword again, he had agreed to lead the armed forces of his state.[19]

Lee's dilemma illustrated the plight of other southern officers of the United States army and navy. David Farragut, George H. Thomas, and Winfield Scott were among the 162 (of 308) southerners of slave-state origins who faced the same question and remained loyal to the Union. Many military men felt that blundering politicians had forced the country into a situation that imposed a terrible choice on them. It was a matter of conflicting loyalties, and the decision was rendered in the court of individual conscience.

Lee's skill as a general was immediately apparent in his tactical abilities to position inferior numbers and resources for the protection of Richmond against McClellan and his successors, and in the spirit he infused into the Army of Northern Virginia. His tempered control of the army was not the result of a general's authority; rather, his discipline depended on morale. With an unusual memory for names and faces, he knew and loved his army. Though viewing him at something of a distance, his troops reciprocated with an affection that amounted to hero worship.

Yet recent historians have found that his predilection for the offensive, learned in the Mexican War, linked to Confederate conceptions of honor and grounded in his conviction that the South must destroy the North's will to fight, was costly. "Lee took longer to learn from his experience that the frontal assault contributed only to attrition without victory than any other field commander in the Civil War."[20] On the other hand Lee's aggressiveness sustained the morale of the Confederacy, and in the early years of the war he, almost alone of the commanders on both sides, was able to develop a course of action, shape a campaign, and fathom the enemy's response.

## THE SEVEN DAYS' CAMPAIGN

By mid-June 16, 1862 Lee, now the field commander of the Army of Northern Virginia, believed Jackson could no longer serve as a diversion in the Shenandoah Valley and also join in any timely defense of Richmond. He informed Jackson "the sooner you unite with this army the better."[21] With considerable secrecy, sometimes by railroad, sometimes by rapid marches, Jackson moved his army of 18,500 east. Lee's plan was to get at "these people" (as he habitually called the Union troops) not through a frontal assault against the well-defended Federal force across the Chickahominy River but by a flanking movement from the left by Jackson, aided by J.E.B. ("Jeb") Stuart, against Fitz John Porter's Fifth Corps, while Lee himself attacked from the right.

After the union of Lee's and Jackson's forces on the battlefield for the defense of Richmond, the opposing armies clashed in the Seven Days' battle from June 25 to July 1, 1862. Before this, battles in Virginia had been short, usually lasting only a day or two. But the military engagement known as the Seven Days' campaign was a week-long event. A hiatus developed in the fighting after the first engagement at Oak Grove when McClellan delayed because of muddy roads and the reorganization of his army. It permitted the adventuresome twenty-nine-year-old Jeb Stuart and his cavalry to survey the deployment of Union troops, while riding around the Union army gathering intelligence for Lee, his new commander. What Stuart learned was that the Union had not anchored its flank and that Lee could turn it.

Then beginning at Mechanicsville (Beaver Dam Creek) on June 26 and continuing through Gaines's Mill on June 27, Savage Station on June 29, and Frayser's Farm on June 30, the great armies fought each other in an exhausting series of encounters. McClellan, retiring from the Chickahominy, changed his base from White House Landing on the York River to Harrison's Landing on the James. Near Harrison's Landing on the broad plateau at Malvern Hill on July 1, the final bloody conflict of the Seven Days took place. The engagement

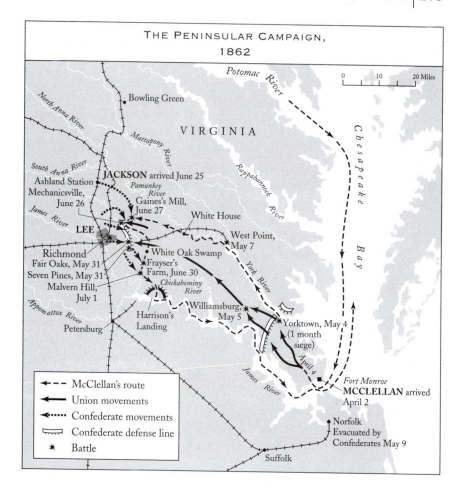

stands as a Union victory, as massed artillery with overwhelming firepower decimated Confederate infantry. It was not war, observed the Confederate general D. H. Hill, "it was murder."[22] Over five thousand bodies lay strewn over the slope of the hill by the end of the day.

Yet McClellan had not taken Richmond in the peninsular campaign.[23] This failure disappointed the North, which had anticipated an end to the war from this venture. Actually the campaign also displayed the same factors that would make the American Civil War so long and brutal: the advantage of a tactical defensive, the difficulty of the terrain, the invulnerability of both armies to a death blow because of their size and organization into divisions and corps, and the incredible destruction of men and material in the face of withering firepower. In just a week the Union army sustained sixteen thousand casualties and the Confederates sustained twenty-one thousand—the higher percentage of southern killed and wounded were the result of its offensive maneuvers as Lee sought to drive McClellan from Richmond.

Lincoln now pondered the twin problems of replacing McClellan and of removing the Army of the Potomac from the peninsula. Visiting McClellan's headquarters on July 8, he interrogated his generals. He inquired about the health and numerical strength of the army, the whereabouts of the enemy, and the desirability of "getting the army away from here." He was informed that McClellan had about seventy-five thousand or eighty thousand men, that the enemy was four or five miles away, and that the army was probably "safe" with the help of the navy.

From his questioning the president deduced that 160,000 men had gone into McClellan's army, that 86,500 remained, that no more than 23,500 had been killed or wounded, and that 50,000 had "left otherwise." The figures gave dramatic testimony to the other scourge of Civil War armies—sickness and disease. If these men could be brought back, Lincoln surmised, McClellan might be in Richmond in three days. Meanwhile, the general rationalized his lack of success in the Peninsula campaign as partly the result of "a command procedure which prevented the coordination of [his] troop movements in the forests of the Peninsula."[24]

At this time Lincoln confronted other problems, including Britain's possible recognition of the Confederacy, the growing congressional demand for emancipation and confiscation of slaves as rebel property, and the Republican party's uncertain prospects in the coming elections. On July 8, 1862, McClellan added to the president's dilemma by handing him his "Harrison's Landing letter," which instructed Lincoln on political matters. Opposing military excesses on the civilian population and aware of a punitive confiscation bill under consideration in Congress, McClellan warned that arbitrary arrests could not be tolerated, and he advised that war be conducted "upon the highest principles known to civilization."

It "should not be . . . a war upon population, but against armed forces and political organizations," wrote McClellan, who espoused conservative views that were rapidly fading in importance. Seizing southern property, including slaves, concluded the Union general, should not even be considered. The "forcible abolition of slavery" would unquestionably lead to the disintegration of the army. Like many northerners at this time, McClellan favored a limited war which would defeat the Confederate army and oust its leaders, but not necessarily overturn its social structures.[25]

Now Lincoln decided that the time had come to try new commanders in the eastern theater. The president had already reorganized the Army of the Potomac into quasi-independent corps, an arrangement that McClellan had bitterly protested. Bringing John Pope from the West, Lincoln placed him in command of the scattered forces of Frémont, Banks, and McDowell, with orders to operate in central Virginia and the Shenandoah Valley. The bearded, imposing Pope, a West Point graduate and veteran of the Mexican War, would command approximately forty thousand men. Relinquishing duties that he and Stanton had performed since March, on July 11 the president conferred the rank of general-in-chief of the Union armies on Henry Halleck, who was fresh from victories in the West.[26]

McClellan was ordered to move his army from the peninsula to Aquia Creek on the Potomac, where it could support Pope. In vain McClellan protested. The Army of the Potomac was in fine condition, he asserted. "Here," he said, is the "true defense of Washington"; in front of his army was the "heart of the rebellion." Withdrawal, in his opinion, would be disastrous.[27] His advice, however, was disregarded. He was denied command of an active army, as units as large as corps were transferred from the Army of the Potomac to Pope's command.

The promotion of Pope to command of the major Union force in Virginia was partly the result of pressure from Republicans. They appreciated his complaints of McClellan's "incompetency and indisposition to active movements," his bold promises to take "the most vigorous measures in the prosecution of the war," and his predictions that "slavery must perish."[28] Though associated with victories in the West such as Island Number 10, Pope's aptitude for supreme command had by no means been demonstrated. His supplanting of McClellan as the dominant Union general revealed the inevitable intermixing of politics and war. Some thought it a reward for his criticisms of other commanders before a House and Senate committee investigating the defeats at Ball's Bluff and Bull Run, the Committee on the Conduct of the War. To this group he had confidently announced that if he had been in charge in the West in March, nothing could have prevented his marching to New Orleans.

## SECOND BULL RUN

The manner in which the Confederates disposed of Pope remains a striking episode of the war. It went far toward fixing Lee's reputation as a daring strategist who was willing to divide his army and employ bold flanking movements. Lee used his understanding of the Union need to cover Washington, the failure of its armies to coordinate, and his expectations of Jackson's effectiveness. It is doubtful whether similar methods would have worked against Grant or Sherman.

First there was a minor attack on a dangerously detached portion of the Union army, then a flanking movement and a raid on the rear, then a maneuver against the main force. Next, eight miles south of Culpeper at Cedar Mountain (also called Cedar Run) on August 9, Jackson, with superior numbers, struck Nathaniel Banks. The results of the hard-fought engagement were indecisive. Although Banks suffered heavier casualties and Jackson was left in possession of the field, tactically the Confederate leader "badly botched" the fighting and southerners received a "significant rebuff."[29] Yet the Confederates had also undermined Pope's resolve to hold the initiative.

By a march on Pope's right flank involving a risky splitting of the Confederate forces, Jackson now swept north away from Lee, through Thoroughfare Gap in the Bull Run Mountains, to reach Pope's rear. There he disrupted Pope's communications. At this point two regiments under General Isaac Trimble and Stuart's cavalry undertook a daring raid on the federal base at Manassas. In two days Jackson had traveled fifty miles, wrecked several Union trains, and captured Federal troops, cannon, and supplies. Still, his departure left the Confederates vulnerable. But Pope failed to exploit this weakness, and instead the Federals made a shift that Lee had anticipated, allowing Jackson to slip back to precisely the place where Lee needed him.

In the two-day battle of Second Bull Run that followed on August 29–30, Union assaults were repulsed. Pope's offensive on the 30th failed not for any lack of Union fighting spirit but because of the general's errors. Lee patiently waited for an opportunity to counterattack and then launched the largest attack he would mount during the war,[30] led by his corps commander James Longstreet. The struggle closed with Lee's counterstroke on a retreating enemy.

In these operations, McClellan's force at Aquia was not used, demonstrating again communication failures, McClellan's uncooperativeness, and the associated inability to deploy available troops when and where they were needed.[31] Second Bull Run also revealed "the mid-nineteenth-century army's virtual invulnerability to destruction in the open field."[32] But individuals were not invulnerable. The week's casualties numbered for the Union sixteen thousand of sixty-five thousand, and for the Confederates ten thousand of fifty-five thousand—a differential of 7 percent that, multiplied over time, drained manpower the Confederacy could not afford to lose.

Thus, at the beginning of June 1862, McClellan was in front of Richmond, Jackson was menaced in the Shenandoah Valley by three strong Union forces, and western Virginia was in Union hands. Three months later western Virginia was nearly evacuated, the main Union army was retreating toward Washington, and "the only Federals closer than 100 miles to Richmond were prisoners . . . and men . . . preparing to retreat."[33] Lee, at the height of his reputation, had taken over an army defending Richmond and through a series of successful fights and maneuvers had moved the attackers backward until now the Confederates seemed on the brink of overrunning Washington.

## ANTIETAM

The state of the Union after the disaster of Second Bull Run was critical. Pope's army, demoralized and badly beaten, was retreating toward Washington, with thousands of stragglers clogging the roads. Military direction in Washington was confused, with Secretary Stanton, General Halleck, and even congressmen and senators urging their schemes on the president. Fearing that Lee would capture the capital, Lincoln and Halleck had little confidence that they could even save the city. Pope's failure left the Union armies in Virginia split between his forces and those of McClellan, at a time when the Confederate army, enthusiastic after recent successes, enjoyed high morale under the leadership of Lee and Jackson.

The choice of a successor to Pope could not be delayed. McClellan, the best general then available to command the Union army in the East, had been reduced to the command of the small forces assigned to the immediate defense of Washington. In this crisis Lincoln, who understood McClellan's popularity with his soldiers, asked him to accept command of all forces in the Virginia-Washington area. Although the request came from the president, the only published order was that of September 2, which read: "Major-General McClellan will have command of the fortifications of Washington and of all the troops for the defense of the capital."

Later McClellan was accused of assuming command without authority, and in fact he believed that he fought the forthcoming battles of South Mountain and Antietam "with a halter around my neck." "I was fully aware of the risk I ran, but the path of duty was clear and I tried to follow it." The wild cheers that greeted him as he met the retreating force gave evidence of that confidence in "Little Mac" that the soldiers of the Army of the Potomac never lost. "Men threw their caps high into the air, and . . . frolicked like school-boys. . . . They cheered and cheered again. . . . A great crowd continually surrounded him, and the most extravagant demonstrations were indulged in. It was like a great scene in a play, with the roar of the guns for an accompaniment."[34]

But even as McClellan revamped the army and began to move them onto the field, Lee, with an audacity beyond that of other generals, had decided to ignore the poor equipment of his ragged army and to invade the North. Hoping to draw Union forces out of Virginia during the fall harvest while his soldiers lived off of the produce of Maryland and Pennsylvania farmers, he intended to return to Virginia by the winter. Lee also planned to threaten vital Union lines of supply by attacking the Baltimore and Ohio Railroad. Finally, he intended to turn northern opinion against the Republicans in the impending Congressional elections, and as he informed the people of Maryland, to liberate a "sister State" which had been "reduced to the condition of a conquered province." He would "aid" the state "in throwing off this foreign yoke."[35] As Lee soon discovered, he had miscalculated. Maryland supported the Union, and his offensive proved a costly error. He also believed that his campaign would encourage recognition of the Confederacy by foreign governments, and this assumption proved incorrect as well.

Crossing the Potomac near Leesburg, Virginia on September 4, Lee occupied Frederick, Maryland on the 7th, causing northerners from New York to Washington to fear that the capital would soon be surrounded. But the president saw the rebel advance as an opportunity for a decisive victory. And Lee's army, on paper a fighting force of seventy thousand, was poorly equipped. At least ten thousand of them were shoeless, hungry volunteers subsisting on daily rations of eighteen ounces of flour and ten ounces of bacon, supplemented by Maryland corn and green apples.

With McClellan slowly moving his force between Washington and the Confederates, Lee took a dangerous gamble. He had expected that Harpers Ferry, the gateway to Maryland from the Shenandoah Valley, would be evacuated by the Yankees. When this withdrawal did not occur, he divided his army in the face of a superior enemy, sending Stonewall Jackson in command of twenty-five thousand men, with the cooperation of Lafayette McLaws and J. G. Walker, to capture Harpers Ferry, while his own force proceeded toward Hagerstown, in the west-central part of the state.

McClellan had intended to evacuate Harpers Ferry and use its garrison of ten thousand men and thirteen thousand small arms as reinforcements. But he was overruled by Halleck, a decision which had unintended results.[36] Obliged to dislodge the Harpers Ferry garrison before concentrating his forces west of the South Mountain range, Lee was placed at a disadvantage. Halleck's tactical error unwittingly helped determine the outcome of the Confederate offensive.

By chance, a Union private discovered Lee's orders detaching Jackson. Wrapped around three cigars and lying in the grass, the Army of Northern Virginia's Special Orders No. 191 had been dropped by a Confederate officer. McClellan, still under delusions as to the enemy's strength, now knew the exact status and intentions of Lee's army. "Here is a paper," said McClellan at the time, "with which if I cannot whip Bobbie Lee, I will be willing to go home."[37] But with his habitual slowness, he lost his chance of striking rapidly at a divided army, shattering Lee's depleted forces, and preventing their return to Virginia.

Confederate strategy at Harpers Ferry was to occupy the heights, to surround the Union positions, and to force a capitulation without an assault. Instead a brief battle ensued, with A. P. Hill's infantry advancing under cover of artillery fire from Confederate batteries. On September 15 the Federals surrendered the garrison, with its rich transportation and quartermaster stores, along with those in Winchester and Martinsburg. While he awaited the return of Jackson, who had learned of McClellan's discovery of his orders, Lee was able to delay the Union advance by an engagement in the passes at South Mountain.[38]

Even so, the Confederate commander was caught in a serious situation. His force was far inferior to McClellan's. And the Union army had punched through at Crampton Gap. Needing time and aided in this by his opponent McClellan, Lee now faced battle with the Potomac River at his rear and with the danger of losing his whole force in case of defeat. Realizing belatedly the threat to his dispersed army, Lee planned to retreat across the Potomac back to Virginia. But

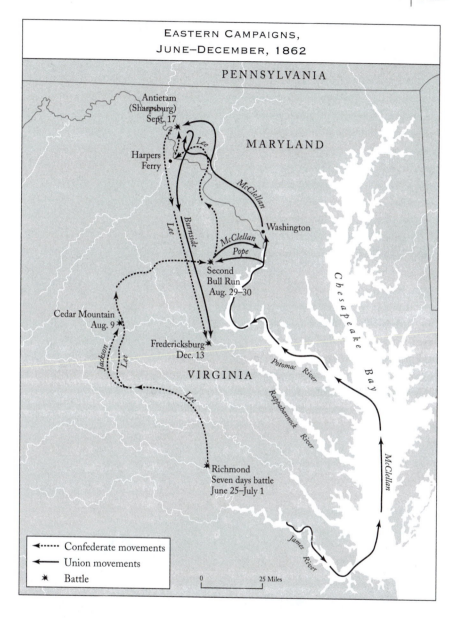

EASTERN CAMPAIGNS,
JUNE–DECEMBER, 1862

PENNSYLVANIA

Antietam
(Sharpsburg)
Sept. 17

Lee

MARYLAND

Harpers
Ferry

McClellan

Lee

Burnside

Washington

McClellan

Pope

Second
Bull Run
Aug. 29–30

Cedar Mountain
Aug. 9

Jackson

Lee

Fredericksburg
Dec. 13

VIRGINIA

Lee

Potomac River

Rappahannock River

Chesapeake Bay

McClellan

Richmond
Seven days battle
June 25–July 1

James River

◄----- Confederate movements
◄───── Union movements
✳ Battle

0        25 Miles

when Jackson returned from Harpers Ferry, the intrepid Confederate commander decided to stay and fight.

Lee had the advantage of choosing his ground, when McClellan spent an entire day reconnoitering. On September 17th, the Union forces attacked an enemy positioned on a three-mile ridge along Antietam Creek, north of Sharpsburg, Maryland. The Union battle plan involved flanking attacks that would put the Confederate force of thirty-five thousand in a vise. McClellan, the supreme planner, had even developed fixed positions for each division of his army of seventy-two thousand.

But the battle plan was poorly executed. In the morning the attacks undertaken on the right by Joseph Hooker and Edwin Sumner were piecemeal and disjointed. In the absence of a coordinated Union effort, Lee was able to shift his forces as needed from one part of the line to the other and compensate for his smaller number of troops. When the Confederate lines buckled in the center and fierce fighting developed along a sunken country road later to be renamed Bloody Lane, McClellan refused to send in reserves from Fitz John Porter's corps. In all, only forty-six thousand Union troops saw action, circumstances that neutralized the significant Union manpower advantage.

Meanwhile on the left, the Union corps commander Ambrose Burnside struggled to secure the little stone bridge across the swollen Antietam River, an advance necessary for his assault. By the afternoon he was successful, and now pouring across the bridge, his soldiers seemed about to split the southern line of retreat when A. P. Hill's division, hurrying back from Harpers Ferry, arrived on the battlefield. Moving his soldiers at a rapid pace, Hill had covered seventeen miles in seven hours, violating Jackson's standard of ten minutes rest after every fifty minutes of marching.[39] Hill's brigades turned the tide as Union lines broke. By dusk Burnside was begging for reinforcements from McClellan, who declined to give them; the Union commander was eventually rolled back to the bridge he had taken only hours before.

Ambrose Burnside's Union troops launch an attack by crossing the stone bridge over Antietam Creek. Burnside's advance was successful until A. P. Hill's Confederate troops arrived from Harpers Ferry and pushed Burnside's troops back to the creek.

Antietam claimed more soldiers' lives than any other single day's fighting in the Civil War. After twelve hours of combat, 12,401 Union troops lay dead, wounded, or missing—a quarter of those who went into action and nearly double those on D-Day during the Second World War. The Confederates lost fewer, having fewer to lose—10,318, or 31 percent of those on the front lines.[40]

After the battle McClellan, announcing he had fought the battle "splendidly," claimed victory. The Union forces did control the battlefield when Lee withdrew. But they did not soon renew the fighting. Convinced that McClellan would hesitate before pursing him, Lee waited a day before retreating across the Potomac River.

At Antietam the Union army had stopped the first major Confederate offensive into the north. But if McClellan's advantages—especially his numerical superiority and his knowledge of Confederate plans—are measured against the outcome, his results were disappointing. "McClellan failed to employ his cavalry either to gather intelligence or to protect the flanks of his army against surprise attack. He put his troops into action in driblets. . . . He failed to get all his men to the battlefield and in any case held back a third of those who were available to him."[41] Moreover, he permitted Lee to cross the Potomac River back to Virginia on the night of September 18–19. After this dismal outcome became known in the north, McClellan's critics attacked the general, even questioning his loyalty.

Yet Lee had also failed, for his ambitious offensive had accomplished none of its goals. On the Confederate side, however, Antietam was not a demoralizing failure, for the attack-minded Lee remained close to the south side of the Potomac, where he could enter Maryland again and attempt to occupy the significant flank position he had originally chosen and indeed would try to use again. But Lee had failed in his political objective of influencing northern elections, and the bedraggled condition of his army, some of whom were said to look like "a most ragged, lean and hungry set of wolves" encouraged northern morale.[42]

Still, the aggressiveness of the South contrasted with McClellan's caution. Again, Jeb Stuart had ridden his cavalry around McClellan's army as he had done during the Peninsular campaign in June. With a cavalry force of twelve hundred, moving with swiftness and secrecy, he rode around the Federal right far to the rear and returned by the left flank, covering eighty miles in twenty-seven hours. Considered a perilous endeavor by military experts, Stuart's exploit encouraged his supporters. While its main purpose was to bring information to Lee as to the size and disposition of McClellan's forces, its exaggerated retelling in Confederate papers thrilled southerners.[43]

In a larger sense the Confederates began to appreciate the cavalry's strategic benefit in fostering communication and command procedures. No longer were cavalry routinely used in battle charges, although removing cavalry from the battlefield for raids could be detrimental. "Lee's organization of a separate cavalry corps was perhaps the most dramatic organizational recognition of the revised strategic role for cavalry."[44]

In late September, when McClellan reported that the horses of his cavalry were too fatigued to move, Lincoln sarcastically asked "what the horses of your army have done since the battle of Antietam that fatigues anything."[45] The president's patience was obviously near the breaking point. After five weeks of delay, McClellan at last moved. He began crossing the Potomac on October 26; by November 7 his army was massed in the neighborhood of Warrenton, ready for battle. In his memoirs he concluded that his army was in the best condition of its history to fight a great battle.[46]

Lincoln continued to urge McClellan to capitalize on his advantage, but when McClellan asked for more men and animals, Lincoln could tolerate his general with "the slows" no longer.[47] On November 5, just before a proposed movement, the president gave command of the Army of the Potomac to General Ambrose Burnside, who had been a corps commander at Antietam. Having waited for the midterm elections, Lincoln, who had tolerated his critic McClellan for so long, now dismissed him. The army was distressed at the news; but McClellan, taking his leave, was careful to assist his successor.[48]

## BURNSIDE AND FREDERICKSBURG

Mutterings of Republican discontent as McClellan took his farewell were mingled with fear about the future. Such apprehension was soon justified. Less than six weeks after Burnside assumed command, he committed one of the colossal blunders of the war at Fredericksburg in northern Virginia. Lacking pontoons, Burnside missed a chance to strike Jackson and Longstreet, Lee's corps commanders, separately from an advantageous position. Several days later on December 13, 1862, he instead attacked the united Confederate forces at Fredericksburg, where his preponderance of numbers (he had 110,000 men in his army to the Confederates' 75,000) was neutralized by disadvantageous topography.[49] The Confederates had placed part of their force in an almost impregnable position on Marye's Heights west of the city, where the brigade of General T. R. R. Cobb, together with some of Joseph Kershaw's and J. R. Cooke's forces, maintained an "unapproachable defense" behind a stone wall in a sunken road at the base of the hill.[50]

The main battle resolved itself into a series of forlorn, desperate Union charges against the withering rifle and artillery fire of the Confederates in what amounted to a death trap. Still, some units—among them the Irish brigade, shouting "Erin go bragh!" and waving green banners—advanced to within twenty-five feet of the wall, only to be shot down by the 24th Georgia, whose forces included many Irish-born as well. Hopeless as was their situation, Union soldiers charged up the hill with magnificent determination until they retired at nightfall, leaving the field strewn with their dead, piled three deep in places. Later a member of the First Minnesota Volunteers acknowledged that "It was murder to attempt such an assault, but the orders were obeyed."[51]

Union troops charge forward, attempting to penetrate the Confederate defenses at Fredericksburg, Virginia, in December 1862. Although Burnside had 110,000 men (compared with Lee's 75,000 Confederate soldiers), he suffered great losses as a result of the placement of Confederate soldiers behind a stone wall at Marye's Heights. The desperate Union charges, such as this one by the 114th Pennsylvania Zouaves, were halted by Confederate soldiers who held a strong defensive position behind the wall.

But these thirteen Union assaults in front of Marye's Heights on the Confederate left were only a part of the battle. On the Confederate right there were heavy Union attacks against Jackson. Hopeless efforts to penetrate a swampy but lightly defended part of Lee's line failed. Quickly the Confederate batteries responded as gaps were cut in the charging columns. The toll was heavy after the Confederate infantry opened fire.[52]

Burnside's combat strength at Fredericksburg had numbered nearly 106,000 to Lee's approximately 75,000. But the Confederates were positioned so that they could have succeeded had they been outnumbered two to one. Burnside lost 12,600 men, of whom 1,284 were killed and 9,600 wounded, the remainder being unaccounted for—in all more than 10 percent of his total force. Lee's dead numbered about 600, and his total loss was about 5,300.[53] This battle elicited Lee's confession to Longstreet as he observed an especially ferocious Confederate assault: "It is well that war is so terrible—we should grow too fond of it." And when the Federal army withdrew from the field, Lee chose not to counterattack. His troops were too exhausted to do so.[54]

After the failure at Fredericksburg, northern morale plunged to its lowest point. Sorrow caused by the death or mutilation of thousands of brave men turned into rage as Americans wondered how so fine a fighting instrument as the Army of the Potomac had been used with such stupidity. The slump in public credit was evident in the sharp depreciation of government-issued paper money. Many believed that the South was ready for a reasonable peace and that it was only the obstinacy of the Lincoln administration that prolonged the war. Others demanded a "more vigorous" policy, for which Lincoln was considered incompetent.

With the army so distrustful of its commander that it seemed on the verge of disintegration, the feckless Burnside asked Lincoln to dismiss or demote some of its best officers, including Joseph Hooker, John Newton, John Cochrane, and William Franklin. Their only offense was lack of faith in Burnside, a sentiment that pervaded the whole army and indeed Burnside himself. Eager to atone for his rout at Fredericksburg, the Union commander now considered another thrust across the Rappahannock River, but his chances were so doubtful that the president restrained him. When Halleck's evaluation of Burnside's plan was slow, an exasperated Lincoln complained, "Your military skill is useless to me if you will not [evaluate this plan]."[55] Halleck's subsequent resignation was not accepted, and Burnside's crossing of the Rappahannock was approved.

It resulted in nothing except a wretched "mud march" that began on January 21 amid a terrible rainstorm. "The Virginia mud . . . does not appear to soak water or mingle with it, but simply hold it, becoming softer and softer," reported a Union soldier, as vehicles and men became stuck in the morass. An army bent on attacking Lee now floundered in floods of rain and seas of sticky clay without making any progress.[56] Another change was imperative. On January 25, 1863, Lincoln removed Burnside and placed General Joseph Hooker in command of the Army of the Potomac.

In the spring of 1863 Americans looked back on two years of bungling and bloody warfare. Neither of the struggling sections could point to gains commensurate with the losses incurred. The conflict had reached unimaginable proportions. Modern warfare had supplied a ghastly sequel to the confident predictions from politicians in 1861. Neither side could see its way clear to a termination of the struggle, although with its superior resources the North held the advantage. As to generals, the advantage was clearly with the Confederacy, at least on the important Virginia front. At a time when southern enthusiasm for Lee and Jackson was unbounded, Lincoln wrote his new army chief Joseph Hooker a curious, fatherly letter in which he confessed that he was "not quite satisfied" with him, counseled him to "Beware of rashness," and wistfully encouraged him to "go forward, and give us victories."[57]

CHAPTER 11 | # Union Measures and Men

Behind the tales of valor and gore on specific battlefields rest the routine, often invisible bureaucratic tasks of organizing a huge army. Its effectiveness in recruiting, training, equipping, and deploying hundreds of thousands of men was a crucial part of the Union's success. The rapid change from the amateurs at Bull Run to the professional troops of the Army of the Potomac and the western armies of the Cumberland, the Ohio, and Tennessee reflected other war-generated transformations in administration along with a centralization of authority.

## MILITARY STRUCTURES

In a society that distrusted standing armies as remnants of British tyranny and that faced no threat of a foreign invasion, the army and the War Department were unprepared for war. As noted earlier, there were three different military structures: the regular army, a force made up of approximately sixteen thousand professionals after southerners resigned; the militia, an instrument of state law subject to nationalization; and, most important for the expansive needs of the Civil War, the United States volunteers. From 1861 to 1863 the government operated within the bounds of these three structures, although it was volunteers who filled the regiments spontaneously organized by communities and states across the United States.

Three weeks after his initial April call for seventy-five thousand militia men to serve ninety days, Lincoln appealed for forty-two thousand three-year army volunteers and eighteen thousand sailors. As no federal mechanism existed, state governors supervised the recruitment of these men, some of whom signed up for two rather than three years. State governors, not the War Department, appointed regimental officers below the rank of colonel, though governors did not have exclusive control over this process. In a practice deplored by professional soldiers, many units elected their officers. State delegations in Congress, alert to the possible expansion of patronage, recommended generals to the president, as the struggle for control of the officer corps pitted state and national politicians against army professionals.[1]

Filled with men from the same state and usually the same county, these regiments were inspired by state pride and the understanding that whatever they did under fire would affect not strangers, but often relatives and friends from their communities. A powerful incentive to perform well, such an arrangement sometimes meant disproportionate casualties for towns and rural districts. Units carried names such as the 69th New York, 104th Illinois, and 1st Maryland, affiliations that in later American wars would be subsumed under national labels.[2]

Men also enrolled, as James McPherson's study of a sample of their letters has shown, because they felt it was their duty. Many connected their personal sense of honor with a commitment to the cause of saving the Union and preserving the intangible commitment to liberty that the United States inspired. "We fight for the blessings brought by the Treasure of our Fathers," wrote one Missouri enlisted man to his parents. "I will fight till I die if necessary for the liberties you have so long enjoyed."[3]

In the spring of 1861 so many northern men volunteered that states chafed at the slowness of the federal government in arming and supplying them. Massachusetts governor John Andrew was especially efficient in directing the recruiting of his state's early regiments and the appointment of their officers. Andrew chartered steamers and railroad facilities for their transportation and raised emergency funds in his state to pay for their supplies. For several weeks after Massachusetts sent four thousand men south, the state provided the resources to maintain them in the field.

In the early months of the war, supply outran logistical support. While Governor Richard Yates of Illinois was working day and night to raise Union troops, word came from Washington that the War Department could handle no more than twelve regiments. Similar situations occurred in Massachusetts and other states, as the federal government struggled to manage its available manpower.

Although it produced administrative tangles, state activity brought results. Within two weeks of Lincoln's first call, fifty-five thousand men were either in Washington, on the way, or ready to come. But the volunteer system had drawbacks, principally that once depleted, its units could not be reinforced from the same source. Instead completely green regiments were raised in a system that prevented the more practical arrangement of mixing veterans with new recruits.

By early 1862 more than seven hundred thousand troops had been enrolled in the Union army. They would not be sufficient, and in the dreary days following the Seven Days' campaign in June 1862, the War Department called for three hundred thousand new men to serve for the more realistic three-year term, which had replaced the optimistic ninety-day enrollment.

Changes were also made in the structure of the militia. In July 1862 Congress passed the Militia Act, which provided that the president might specify the period of such service (not to exceed nine months) and issue regulations for enrolling in the militia "all able-bodied male citizens between the ages of eighteen and forty-five." Laying the groundwork for the recruitment of black soldiers, its discriminatory provisions stipulated that blacks would be paid three dollars less than white soldiers.[4]

The Militia Act, with its implicit draft an effort to force states to fill their quotas, had many defects. One was its federal nature. Although Congress had the power to support armies, governors had the power to raise them.[5] In Indiana, for example, Governor Oliver Morton devised a scheme whereby commissioners he appointed created lists of those to be enrolled in each county and township. Under this system, Morton had his own appointees deal with widespread disaffection without relying upon local sheriffs. Although the changes in the Militia Act created a precedent for enhanced national authority, a minor modification of the militia could not create a huge emergency army. Moreover, the Lincoln government gave informal guarantees that some units would not serve out of state.[6] Overall only a small part of the militia was ever called into national service, although between 125,000 and 200,000 men in state organizations provided a useful supplement to Federal troops by guarding the coastline and Canadian and Indian frontiers, protecting factories important for the war effort, and guarding prisoner-of-war camps.[7]

## CONSCRIPTION

The disappointing results of the July 2, 1862 call for new volunteers left the War Department in need of three hundred thousand more troops. With the most fervent patriots already in the army, a more coercive system would now be installed. But not until 1863 did Congress, spurred by the need for more troops after the war had seemingly stalled on both the eastern and western fronts, pass a national conscription law. The pool of volunteers had dried up, and Lincoln argued that in fighting an enemy that made use of every able-bodied man it would be unwise to "waste time to re-experiment with the volunteer system, already deemed by congress, and palpably, in fact . . . inadequate."[8]

This act of March 3, 1863, passed the House in a party vote—Republicans mostly in favor, Democrats opposed. It held that all able-bodied male citizens

Americans did not lose their sense of humor during the war. Here a likely recruit who wants to be a "peace commissioner" is about to become a soldier who fights for peace on the battlefield.

between twenty and forty-five, and those who had sworn their intention to be naturalized, were "to constitute the national forces," and were liable for military service. Exemptions were granted to the mentally or physically unfit, certain high officials of state and federal government, the only son of a widow dependent on his labor for support, and the only son of infirm parents. By early 1864, after harsh treatment of several Quakers, conscientious objectors were treated as non-combatants if drafted and were assigned to duty in hospitals or given the opportunity to pay three hundred dollars for the benefit of sick and wounded soldiers—the latter an alternative to the more general option of paying a three hundred dollar fee "to commute" service in the army.[9] Federal machinery for enforcement was provided, including enrollment officers organized by congressional districts, boards of enrollment, provost marshals, and a provost marshal general in Washington.[10]

Men who were enrolled were subject to be called into the military service of the United States, with their service not to exceed three years. Conscripts received the same advance pay and federal bounties as three-year volunteers. The president fixed state quotas in his calls, of which there would be four in October 1863, in March and July 1864, and finally in December 1864.[11] Volunteer enlistments were to be credited to the state's quota, and only the "deficiency" was to be made up by conscription. This arrangement served the dual purpose of stimulating voluntary enlistment and equalizing the burden among states. Two legacies from the old militia system were incorporated into the new act, relating to substitutes and commutation money. If a drafted man furnished an acceptable substitute, he would be exempt from service. Such exemption could also be purchased for three hundred dollars—the approximate yearly wage of a typical worker and therefore well beyond the means of most men. In fact the system worked as a form of taxation until commutation was ended in 1864 except for conscientious objectors.

In the two years during which the conscription act operated, over three-quarters of a million names were enrolled. But only 46,347 entered the army as draftees. Another 73,607 found substitutes; 86,724 paid a commutation fee; and untold others avoided the draft by volunteering. Others did not qualify on med-

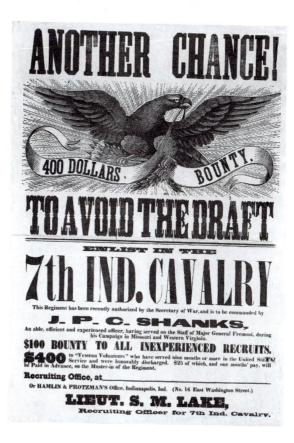

Men were encouraged to volunteer to join the army in order to avoid the draft.

As evident in this portrayal of a call for volunteers, cash incentives were offered to promote recruiting. Eventually, large sums of money were spent on these bounties.

ical grounds, and still another group was exempted for family reasons. Clearly the draft served as a stimulus for volunteering, not a direct means of obtaining soldiers. Encouraged by federal, state, and local bounties, a man could receive one thousand dollars for signing up and sometimes more. Much of this money was raised by local communities, which solicited private funds and supported increased taxes and bonded indebtedness so that their district might fill its assigned quota. In time, recruiting became a lucrative business; because individuals often lacked information about available bounties, brokers came to control the process of supplying substitutes and volunteers.[12]

City, county, and state authorities, along with private organizations, created an elaborate system of paying bonuses to recruits, and it was not long before the federal government adopted the practice. On July 22, 1861 Congress, sanctioning an already established War Department practice, added a bounty of one hundred dollars over and above the regular pay of volunteers. By 1864 the federal bounty for new recruits had increased to three hundred dollars, with an additional one hundred for veterans. Eventually the sums spent grew enormous, as the system encouraged bounty jumpers who often enlisted, took the bounty, and disappeared.

In Cook County, Illinois, for example, the local government spent nearly $3 million for bounties. The New Jersey legislature passed nearly one hundred laws in one session authorizing various districts to undertake such obligations. Claremont, New Hampshire, a small community of four thousand, spent $74,468 on bounties and another $26,356 on aid to families of soldiers for a cost per family of over a hundred dollars. Philadelphia's city council allocated $500,000 to spur enlistment in 1862, a figure that was increased by subscriptions of nearly $160,000 later that year.[13]

Commutation and substitution clearly favored the middle and upper classes. But legislating for a society in which the draft was a controversial innovation, many congressmen wanted to soften its impact on the civilian population. The two systems of avoiding service were linked together and should have been retained or abandoned together. Yet when complaints against commutation and its implicit favoritism of the rich grew, the three-hundred dollars clause was dropped while substitution was allowed to continue. This arrangement caused substitute prices to rise drastically, which in turn gave new impetus to draft jumpers and brokers.[14]

**SCENE, FIFTH AVENUE.**

HE. "Ah! Dearest ADDIE! I've succeeded. I've got a Substitute!"
SHE. "Have you? What a curious coincidence! And *I* have found one FOR YOU!"

This cartoon depicts a woman supporting enlistment in the army and discouraging a man from finding a substitute in what has sometimes been called a "rich man's war and a poor man's fight."

Democrats especially objected to the enrollment act, complaining that its co-ercive system of drafting manpower enhanced the power of the state and denied the rights of "freemen." In some areas of the North the drawing of names from the wheel was the signal for violence. Enrolling officers were attacked and physi-cally harassed. In other places Federal troops and state militia had to be called to put down resistance. In Holmes County, Ohio, arrests were made for resistance to conscription. Outbreaks occurred in Kentucky, where a special military force protected enrolling officers. In Wisconsin, "in one county the boxes containing names of potential draftees were destroyed, and it became extremely hazardous for the draft officers to serve notices personally. In Ozaukee County a mob as-saulted a commissioner."[15] Draft-related rioting also took place in cities such as Troy, Albany, and Newark, as well as in rural communities in Missouri, Ohio, Indiana, and Illinois.

It was in New York that the largest, most vicious disturbance occurred. There had always been a strain of southern sympathy in the city, and influential papers such as the *World* and the *Journal of Commerce* were outspoken in their criticism of Lincoln, emancipation, and the Union government. Opposed to abolition, the New York Irish were notoriously hostile to African Americans. The Tammany leaders Fernando Wood and A. Oakey Hall opposed Lincoln, as did the state's Democratic governor, Horatio Seymour. In a partisan speech in Albany on July 4, 1863, Seymour attacked the Lincoln government for its alleged violation of individual liberty. His reaction encouraged popular beliefs that conscription was unconstitutional, that Democratic districts furnished more than their share of conscripts whereas Republican areas got off lightly, and that African American suffrage was manipulated for party gain.

The drawing of the first draftees' names, on July 11, 1863, set off what has been called "New York's bloodiest week." First the provost marshal's head-quarters at Third Avenue and Forty-sixth Street was stoned and burned. Then telegraph wires throughout the city were cut. Next, the mob fought pitched bat-tles with the police. When the police superintendent tried to calm the rioters, he was beaten and dragged through the streets by his hair. Crying "Down with the rich!" the mob plundered houses and rifled jewelry stores.

Soon African Americans became the special objects of attack. "A Negro cart-man, trying to escape under cover of darkness, was caught by a gang of men and boys and hanged from one of the fine spreading chestnut trees on Clarkson Street." The rioters destroyed and then burned the Colored Orphan Asylum, where the children barely escaped the torches of the mob. For a week anarchy prevailed, until on July 16 army units sent from New York to fight at Gettysburg returned. With the help of a company from West Point they dispersed the mob.[16] In all 119 New Yorkers were killed; over three hundred African Ameri-cans were wounded, at least eleven killed by rioters; and thousands of African Americans were forced to flee the city.

On July 11, 1863, "New York's bloodiest week" began. Several Democrats, including New York's governor, Horatio Seymour, believed that Lincoln was unfairly trying to draft working-class whites and use African American suffrage to benefit the Republican party. Rioters targeted African Americans and burned the Colored Orphan Asylum on Fifth Avenue, as illustrated here.

Governor Seymour's role in the draft riots remains controversial. Although he did call for an end to the rioting, which had made African Americans scapegoats, he asked Lincoln to suspend the draft pending a court test. Seymour also demanded that New York's quotas be lowered. Anxious to avoid further conflict, Lincoln reduced the number of conscripts required from New York and consented to a Democratic-controlled commission to study the draft in New York. On August 19, 1863, the New York draft was resumed, and it proceeded calmly with Governor Seymour advising, on the one hand, peaceful submission to conscription and, on the other, a legal test of the constitutionality of the law.[17]

One concern raised by Seymour and the Irish rioters was the differential impact of the draft on the rich and the poor. As Iver Bernstein has written, "the provisions of [the conscription act of 1863] highlighted three explosive issues in mid-century New York city: relations between the wealthy and the poor, between blacks and whites, and between city and nation. . . . The burden of the March Act fell heavily on the poor, and among the poor it singled out young men and women and families economically dependent on the young male conscript."[18]

The issue of whether the Civil War was a rich man's war and a poor man's fight was a divisive matter in both the North and the South. At the time,

Democrats thought the draft singled out the poor, and the party emphasized that point in popular antidraft slogans such as "$300 or Your Life." Still it is hard to argue that the poor were disproportionally drafted when, "only ¼ of 1 percent of the total population of the North in 1860 entered the war as conscripts." In all, only 2 percent of the Union army were draftees. Moreover, systematic comparisons of the occupational backgrounds of recruits do not support the contention that the poor did not have the money to hire substitutes or that wealthy professionals were underrepresented in the army, especially if the effect of age on wealth is factored into such comparisons.[19]

Moreover, isolated examples of opposition to conscription, whether individual or collective, tend to distort the degree of compliance with an arrangement that, even if indirectly, raised the necessary manpower to win the war. What appears as resistance to the draft must also be placed in the context of community tensions, as in New York. In another example, in mining areas of Schuykill County, Pennsylvania, where provost marshals were closely allied with mine owners, the use of conscription became a means of squelching union activity. Hence the objections of miners were played out in the local framework of labor-management relations. "Wartime outrages," writes Grace Palladino, "have more to tell about the development of the capitalist industrial system, its relation to class conflict, and the process of building a nation state than they do about disloyalty."[20]

Clearly the structure of the draft was flawed, and it did not fulfill the expectation that draftees could be integrated into battle-decimated regiments with veterans. Still, despite commutation and substitution, which were traditions incorporated as palliatives into an innovative effort to raise a huge army, and despite the unfairness of the bounty system and its opportunities for fraud, the draft was the catalyst for the enlistment of over one million men in the last two years of the war. In all over one million whites and 179,000 blacks served in the Union army, a war characterized, as Maris Vinovskis has written, by "high rates of participation, high rates of disability and death, widespread desertion, and service in locally based units."[21] Within a year the federal government had established the principle and the reality that it could raise and support armies without state assistance.

## IMPROVISED WAR: INITIAL EFFORTS AT SUPPLYING THE ARMY

Besides raising an army, the War Department had to supply and run it. The sudden demand for equipment, munitions, food, and animals, the competition with Confederate as well as state agents in European markets, the claims of rival suppliers, the strain of production on factories, the operations of speculators—all led to inefficiency and corruption in a nation that was unprepared for the mobilization of men and resources required by a war of this magnitude.

Lincoln's first secretary of war was poorly equipped for the challenge. Simon Cameron was a self-made businessman and politician who had become a leader of the Democratic party; after shifting to the Republican party, he had won a U.S. Senate seat from Pennsylvania in 1857. As a result of bargains made in the Chicago nominating convention of 1860, Lincoln was committed against his will to appointing Cameron to some cabinet post. The president reluctantly took the Pennsylvanian into the Cabinet as Secretary of War.

Cameron's administration of the War Department produced one of the most controversial episodes of the Lincoln presidency. While officials in Washington struggled to organize, governors "became war lords" and pushed ahead "as if there was not an inch of red tape in the world."[22] John Andrew of Massachusetts, Andrew Curtin of Pennsylvania, and Oliver Morton of Indiana simply assumed the supply functions that the War Department later controlled. So uncertain was the relationship between the state and federal governments that as late as January 1862 Governor David Tod of Ohio inquired of the War Department whether he had control of state troops in camp and in the field after they had been mustered into federal service; what his duties in the procuring or issuing of military supplies were; and whether the federal government would refund to the states "*all* the money expended directly and indirectly in the raising, equipping, sustaining and mustering of the troops."[23]

In the early days of the war, governors even sent state agents abroad to obtain arms and supplies. Serving as a state agent for Indiana, Robert Dale Owen purchased rifles, carbines, and revolvers abroad. He forwarded arms from New York to Fort Monroe as well as to Indianapolis; he procured coats, blankets, and equipment; he visited Indiana regiments in the field; and he even signed contracts for the state, although the bills were ultimately paid by the federal government. On one occasion he wrote to Governor Morton: "I fear that if you trust wholly to the [federal] Government to send you what more guns we may need, you will be likely to get trash. I hear very poor accounts of the purchases made by the Government agent in Europe."[24]

The efforts of such state agents embarrassed the Washington authorities. Bidding against the federal government in foreign arms markets, they not only added to the overall national expense, but they also laid the basis for thousands of postwar claims arising when the national government made good its pledge of compensating the states for war expenditures.[25]

When the governors implored Secretary of War Cameron for instructions and arms, he pleaded for more time. Not only was his administration marked by confusion, but by haste in outfitting the armies. The outmoded procurement procedures followed by the War Department afforded an opportunity for speculators to gain from their country's misfortunes. The case of General Frémont in Missouri was typical. In his military district, rules and regulations were replaced by an orgy of expenditure that made it necessary for Lincoln to appoint an investigating committee. Among the questionable transactions was a contract of $191,000 to build five forts, $111,000 of which went as profit to the contractor.[26] But at the time, St. Louis had to be defended, and Frémont's ill-equipped troops had to be armed. The failure of the national treasury to supply the necessary funds compelled the general to rely on credit and as soon as that happened, "control over prices passed into the hands of banks, brokers, speculators, and moneyed merchants, the intermediary links between the army and its sources."[27]

Throughout Cameron's tenure during what Allan Nevins has called the "Improvised War," the dealings of the War Department with businessmen exhibited a similar negligence. Not only did Pennsylvanians receive a suspicious number of contracts, but the secretary of war also awarded contracts without any competitive bidding. Thousands of pistols were sold to the government at $25.00 each, when a fair price would have been $14.50. Horses that could be bought for $60 were sold to the government for $117, and many of these were not fit for army use. Austrian muskets, rejected by the Ordnance Bureau at a price of $5.50, were bought by a government agent at $6.50.[28]

Finally Cameron was removed. Lincoln accepted the resignation of Kentucky's Cassius Clay as minister to Russia (Clay was anxious to return home for military service), and Cameron, resigning the war portfolio in January 1862, was appointed to this diplomatic post. Thaddeus Stevens advised Lincoln to warn the czar to hide his jewelry from the avaricious Cameron, who subsequently resigned the ministership in November 1862.[29] Meanwhile, the House of Representatives condemned his management of the War Department, specifically censuring actions "highly injurious to the public service."[30]

Before Cameron resigned, he made his greatest contribution to the department by encouraging the appointment of a competent successor. On January 20, 1862, the former Democrat Edwin Stanton took charge of the War Department, where he remained secretary until after the Confederate surrender at Appomattox. Stanton also had difficulties with such matters as contracts and inspection; he stumbled badly when, in April 1862 in his General Orders 33, he inexplicably discontinued recruiting.[31] Still, the army improved under his administration. He was an excellent manager; he supervised the endless contracts promptly; and he knew how to use his powers. When Congress in January 1862 gave the president authority to take over the railroads when the public safety demanded, Stanton used this lever to force companies to give military needs priority. A department that Stanton earlier had dismissed as a "source of weakness rather than strength" changed from "an insignificant clerical convenience" to an effective agency overseeing a vast institution made up of over one million men.[32]

An additional reason for the improvement rested with the organizational ability of Montgomery Meigs, the efficient quartermaster general of the army. Trained at West Point, Meigs had served in the Corps of Engineers, and his approach to logistical problems reflected this discipline's precision. Struggling to

Although Edwin Stanton, Lincoln's secretary of war, was not popular in the War Office, he did earn a reputation for efficiency and improving the army.

set standards for crucial logistical decisions such as how many supply wagons should accompany each regiment, how many rations should be available for each soldier, how much forage to send with each horse and mule, and how to get men and materials to where they were needed, Meigs proved a masterful coordinator of supplies. His success in delivering superior Union resources to the nation's troops in the field was a significant reason for the Union victory.[33]

## A SOLDIER'S LIFE

Reflecting the superior resources of the Union in such vital matters as food, clothing, and bedding, Federal soldiers were the best supplied in the world—by the standards of the period. Billy Yank had "the most abundant food allowance of any soldiers in the world" at that time, certainly more than the Confederates usually had. Bread, meat, and coffee were the staples of the army diet, with vegetables and fruit always in short supply. Like soldiers in all wars, Union troops complained about the quality of their staple food, hardtack—the square, usually stale, nearly unbreakable cracker. "The boys say that our '*grub*' is enough to make a *mule* desert, and a *hog* wish he had never been born," an Illinois corporal complained in 1862. Another soldier counted "32 worms, maggots etc." in a single piece of his hardtack. Salt pork, called "sowbelly" or "salt horse," seemed at times "so strong it could almost walk itself."[34] In enemy territory, Union soldiers, who seldom suffered from hunger no matter where they were, foraged for food, sometimes supplementing their diet with potatoes, fruit, sheep, and hogs.

During the first months of the war, army uniforms were made of "shoddy," which, to quote a contemporary writer, consisted of "the refuse stuff and sweepings of the shop, pounded, rolled, glued, and smoothed to the external form and gloss of cloth."[35] When it rained, the soldiers "found their clothes, overcoats, and blankets, scattering to the winds in rags, or dissolving into their primitive elements of dust."[36] But after the first year, supply contracts improved, and Union soldiers had little basis for criticism of the durability of army-issued uniforms. Still, there were legitimate complaints about the standard wool uniforms in the South's summer heat.[37]

As to munitions, at first Union soldiers were supplied with virtually every kind of small firearm in existence. So difficult was it to purchase equipment that thousands of men were initially given smooth-bore muskets, hastily converted from flint to percussion locks. Others received outmoded European firearms. As the war continued, the standard infantry weapon became the Springfield or the rarer Enfield rifle. In all, 1,600,000 Springfields, with their long thin barrels and spinning grooved track, were manufactured during the war. These weapons were accurate and reliable but difficult to load. Here is a description of the time-consuming process of loading and firing the regulation Springfield muzzle-loading rifle, and indeed all muzzle loaders:

> Reaching into his cartridge pouch, the soldier took out a paper cartridge containing the powder charge and the bullet. Holding this between his thumb and forefinger, he tore it open with his teeth. Next he emptied the powder into the barrel and disengaged the bullet with his right hand and the thumb and two fingers of the left. Inserting the ball point up into the bore, he pressed it down with his right thumb. Then he drew his ramrod, which meant pulling it halfway out, steadying it, grasping it again and clearing it. [Soldiers in fixed positions often plunged the ramrod into the ground for greater convenience.] He rammed the ball half-way down, took hold of the ramrod again, and drove the ball home. He then drew the ramrod out and returned it to its tube, each movement again in two stages. Next he primed his piece by raising it, half cocking it, taking off the old cap, taking a new one out of the pouch and pressing it down on the nipple. At last he cocked the gun, aimed it and fired.[38]

At best, muzzleloaders could be fired only two or three times a minute; it was rather the tenfold increase in the effective range of rifles that transformed the way the war was fought by soldiers.

Easier to load, breech-loading rifles were not supplied, except in small numbers and to select groups of sharpshooters and cavalrymen. Some authorities believe that had the War Department introduced the breech loader the war might have ended in the first year. President Lincoln continually pressured the resistant Chief of Ordnance James W. Ripley, who opposed an untried innovation that might delay production of a known quantity.[39] In 1861 the breechloader was an untested and imperfect weapon that, in any case, was not mass-produced in either America or Europe. Though useful for mobile troops, the breechloader, at this stage of its development, had serious disadvantages for the ordinary infantry-man. The War Department believed it too intricate for general use, although the muzzleloaders obviously had problems as well. After the battle of Gettysburg, for example, twenty-four thousand loaded muskets, mostly muzzleloaders, were recovered from the battlefield, half of them jammed by double loads inserted by soldiers too excited to realize that the first charge had not exploded.[40]

Soldiers' pay, though high in comparison with European armies, was far below prevailing civilian wage scales. At the beginning of the war a private earned thirteen dollars a month plus food and clothing; by 1864, sixteen dollars, with African American soldiers regardless of rank earning three dollars less, minus three dollars for clothing. Any increase was offset by inflation. One soldier, after receiving his wages for two months, predicted that "our children's children will never have it in their hearts to say of us we were governed by mercenary motives."[41]

Low pay, the daily hardships of war, homesickness, forced marches that exhausted even the most vigorous men, thirst, suffocating heat, delay in pay, impatience at the monotony between campaigns, and panic on the eve of battle—all these factors led to desertion.[42] Many men left after first encounters with military discipline or because they resented control by outside authorities. Others, thrown in crowded camps into contact with new bacteria and viruses to which they had no immunity, fell victim to measles, malaria, and smallpox. Dysentery, diarrhea, and typhoid—the soldiers' scourge from contaminated water—haunted army camps. Such lethal infections accounted for the deaths of twice as many Civil War soldiers as died from wounds received in combat. In the twentieth century availability of antibiotics and understanding of germ theory lowered the proportion of those dying from battle wounds to fewer than 1 percent. In the Civil War the northern figure was 14 percent—and was higher in the Confederacy.[43]

Many soldiers left the army voluntarily. As James Robertson has explained, "desertion followed a natural and chronological pattern in the Civil War. On both sides the desertion rate was lowest at the beginning, then increased steadily until it reached the highest levels in the last year of hostilities."[44] In all, over 200,000 men deserted from the Union army enlistments, compared with 104,000 from the million Confederate enlistments, roughly the same proportion as in the Confederate army and for the same reasons. "I tell you," wrote one Michigan soldier to his wife after the battle of Fredericksburg in 1862, "Patriotism *played out* with me some time ago, and more so after the battle over the River." Three weeks later this soldier deserted.[45]

The sense of war weariness, the lack of confidence in commanders, and the discouragement of defeat and even stalemate led to lower morale among replacements. Often the latter were substitutes and bounty soldiers who "skedaddled" in disproportionate numbers, leading hardy combat veterans to scorn these new men. General Hooker estimated in 1863 that 85,000 officers and men had deserted from the Army of the Potomac; in December 1862, 180,000 of the soldiers listed on the Union muster rolls were absent, with or without leave.[46] Abuse of sick leave and furloughs—a practice that became known to later generations as being AWOL—were among the chief avenues for desertion. Throughout the war the overwhelming number of deserters left (as depicted in the popular 1997 novel *Cold Mountain*) while they were patients in hospitals.[47] Other methods included slipping to the rear during a battle, inviting capture by the enemy (a method by which honorable service could be claimed), and leaving when on picket duty. A few deserters on both sides went over to the enemy not as captives but as soldiers; others left for the frontier. Some went to Canada; some appeared at home and were shielded by their neighbors and families. Many were caught and returned to the army.

Overall, desertion never crippled the war effort in the North, and many divisions in the Union armies, especially in the Army of the Potomac, maintained sufficient morale to become tough, proud instruments of battle. Nowhere is their patriotic allegiance more obvious than in the overwhelming soldier vote for Lincoln, their commander in chief, in the 1864 election. And in the spring of 1864 when the three-year men's enlistment time ended, many veterans remained in the army.[48]

## THE UNION COMMAND SYSTEM

Management of the Union army evolved over the course of the war. At the war's beginning, there was no general staff: army administration resembled that of Washington's day because a permanent staff corps reminded Americans of their British enemies during the Revolution. Instead, according to two modern authors, "the American staff concept remained primarily the performance of necessary special staff housekeeping chores, vaguely coordinated by the commander himself with the help of his personal aides." Such a system, which lacked a management team to oversee and coordinate personnel, intelligence, operations, and logistics was inadequate on the expansive Civil War battlegrounds, where the rapid deployment of troops and supplies was critical.[49]

Under the Constitution the president was commander in chief of the army and navy, but Lincoln did not lead the army into battle. The president's principal military adviser at the outbreak of the war was General Winfield Scott, whom Lincoln respected. But Scott, who had been a brigadier general in the War of 1812, was older than the national Capitol and was physically incapable of commanding an army in the field. Consequently he was obliged to delegate actual battle operations to subordinates such as General Frémont in Missouri and General McDowell in Virginia.

The staff of the army, if it can be called that, consisted of Scott and a few heads of departments and bureaus, such as the quartermaster general, the adjutant general, and the chief of ordnance. At the divisional level the army was especially deficient in intelligence-gathering capability as well as in coordinating field operations. The need for maneuverability led Union commanders to develop their own staff systems and to reorganize the cavalry and artillery. "The traditional forms of command and control," writes Edward Hagerman, "which focused on the personal direction of the army commander, had served mass armies in the past. . . . [But] fighting for the first time with mass armies in American terrain . . . required new staff procedures. There was need for a comprehensive doctrine to coordinate strategic planning, bureau organization, and operational command and control of armies in the field."[50]

The first battle of Bull Run had revealed the consequences of dividing responsibilities among Cabinet officers and the military. The confusion led to Lincoln's summoning McClellan to Washington, where he worked under Scott's direction at first, reveling in the deference shown him. "I seem to have become *the* power of the land," he informed his wife. But "Little Napoleon" soon came to regard the old general as incompetent and began dealing directly with the president and the cabinet, ignoring his military superior.[51] After Scott retired on November 1, 1861 and McClellan became general-in-chief and commander in chief of forces in northern Virginia, "Little Napoleon"'s extraordinary powers were gradually whittled away.

In early March 1862, Lincoln, against McClellan's wishes, reorganized the Army of the Potomac by grouping its divisions into corps commanded by generals chosen by the president. As McClellan prepared to begin the peninsula campaign, Lincoln relieved him of his duties as general-in-chief, restricting his role to that of commander of the Department of the Potomac. Henceforth commanders of the departments were ordered to send their reports to the Secretary of War rather than to McClellan.[52]

While McClellan was fighting on the Peninsula, Lincoln and Stanton attempted to exercise central direction over the war effort as an army staff might, notably in their effort to trap Stonewall Jackson in the Shenandoah Valley. Painfully aware that he was "the depository of the power of the government and had no military knowledge," the president turned to the elderly, retired, and ailing General Ethan Allen Hitchcock, who, much against his will, accepted an ill-defined staff appointment as adviser to Stanton and Lincoln.[53] The administrative machinery was further complicated when Stanton created an "army board," composed of chiefs of various bureaus of the War Department, over which Hitchcock was to preside.[54]

Confusion in the management of the army persisted. There was neither unity of command nor general-in-chief of the army; Stanton and his bureau heads still performed functions that a general-in-chief should have executed; Lincoln, under political pressure, proclaimed army movements that were never carried out. Notoriously, in 1862 the president detached units from McClellan's main force. Meanwhile, corps commanders continued to report first to the president, then to the secretary of war, then to the army board. Councils of generals miles from the field of operations were consulted on difficult operations; and, through it all, the Joint Committee on the Conduct of the War tried to serve its congressional function of investigating the reasons for failure on the battlefield.

Order began to emerge when Lincoln, on July 11, 1862, appointed General Henry Halleck to command the whole land force of the United States as general-in-chief.[55] Though Halleck exhibited none of the bold decisiveness that Lincoln had desired and though the general—who was the author of the influential *Elements of Military Art and Science*—was reluctant to accept a post with such ill-defined functions, Halleck did have "the happy faculty of being able to communicate civilian ideas to a soldier and military ideas to a civilian and make both of them understand what he was talking about."[56] In time his tiny office staff, which initially had only seven officers and sixteen enlisted men, gave some measure of central direction to war strategies, as Halleck worked for the more professional army he believed undermined by "political wirepulling in military appointments."[57] As a result Secretary Stanton, who understood the necessity for more centralization and for specialized departments managed by his assistant secretaries, began to devote his abundant energies to problems of procurement and supply. But Lincoln was never a man to revere any table of organization, nor was he "satisfied to sit back and merely watch attentively."[58]

Not until 1864 did Lincoln solve the problem of running the Union armies. On March 12, Lincoln brought Grant from the West and, naming him lieutenant general, assigned him to command the armies of the United States. Halleck, who resigned as general-in-chief, became chief of staff of the army, with a staff of twenty-three officers acting as a modern group of senior advisors and administrators might. Halleck now served as an effective strategist and coordinator of staff bureaus, though he had little to do with raising troops and though Grant and Sherman usually shaped strategy.[59] This arrangement of commander in chief, general-in-chief, and chief of staff gave the United States a modern system of command. And Halleck's staff, the coordinators of diverse policies and functions, was able to provide the North with clear superiority in its logistical ability to deliver men and materials to the front and to achieve Halleck's (and Lincoln's) specific battle goals to "turn the enemy's works, or to threaten their wings or communications; in other words keep the enemy occupied till a favorable opportunity . . . to strike a decisive blow."[60]

## HANDLING PRISONERS OF WAR

The war command on both sides immediately faced the prisoner of war issue. Because issues of exchange, parole, release, and the Confederates' treatment of black soldiers (who were accepted into the Union army after the passage of the

Militia Act in 1862), were entangled in the issue of the Confederacy's belligerent status, no single policy lasted the duration of the war.[61]

Early in the war a Union threat to treat Confederate privateers who preyed on northern shipping as pirates—which meant the death penalty—was countered by southern talk of retaliation against selected northern hostages. Later it was decided that privateers would be treated as prisoners of war. Troops surrendered to the enemy by their commanders were not taken into custody, but were instead given their parole and authorized to return home or to parole camps where they were to await notification that they had been exchanged, whereupon they could return to the ranks.[62]

In the North, parole camps were established in Columbus, Ohio, at Benton Barracks, Missouri, and at Annapolis. Order in the parole camps was hard to keep. Paroled prisoners expected to be sent home, not to camps, and some soldiers deliberately fell into the hands of the enemy, knowing that they would be exchanged.[63] Then the South unilaterally broke the agreement by declaring many of its parolees exchanged and thus eligible for military service, when in fact no exchange had taken place. Desperately needing manpower, the Confederacy returned these men to service. The Confederacy's refusal to exchange black soldiers further violated the compact.[64]

The Confederate policy regarding black Union soldiers led to a complete breakdown of the exchange system. When Jefferson Davis refused to consider African American troops as legitimate soldiers and threatened to execute or enslave captured blacks and prosecute their white officers for inciting insurrection, Lincoln responded by threatening to execute a rebel prisoner for every such atrocity and to give hard labor to Confederates, man for man, for each black soldier restored to slavery. Though there was no systematic enforcement of the southern threat, the Confederacy did execute black Union soldiers, the most brutal instance occurring at Fort Pillow, Tennessee, on April 12, 1864, where 292 black soldiers died, as many as thirty after they had surrendered. There is also evidence at Fort Pillow of both burying the wounded alive and the deliberate burning of hospital tents.[65]

As a result the system of exchanges failed, just as the number of prisoners on each side was burgeoning. Some exchanges were made later in the war; there was also a Confederate attempt to negotiate a new agreement through Vice President Alexander Stephens, as well as endless negotiations between Robert Ould, the Confederate agent of exchange, and W. H. Ludlow, the Union agent. All this, however, failed to bring a restoration of any formal system. Then in 1864 General Grant ordered that no more exchanges of Confederate prisoners would be permitted until the Confederates stopped discriminating against African American prisoners and released enough Union prisoners to offset the paroled men of Vicksburg and Port Hudson, who had violated their paroles. Various proposals for even exchange, man for man and officer for officer, continued until January

1865, when Grant, with the war nearly over, consented to the policy of even exchange.[66]

According to official reports, the Confederates captured 211,000 Federal soldiers, of whom 16,000 were released on the field. The Union captured 462,000 Confederate soldiers, of whom 247,000 were paroled on the field. Subtracting those paroled on the field, the Confederates took nearly 195,000 Unionists and the Unionists took about 215,000 Confederates. The South, especially in the latter part of the war, was unable to care for these captives at a time when its own transportation and supply system was breaking down, when Sherman and Grant were hammering at its interior, and when effective officers and men were desperately needed at the front. As a result, horrifying conditions of poor sanitation, malnutrition, and inadequate shelter existed inside the prisoner of war camps.[67]

Andersonville Prison in southwestern Georgia was especially notorious. Until the soldiers built huts for themselves, the Confederate prisoner-of-war camp was only a stockaded enclosure of sixteen and a half acres. Here mosquito-infested tents, myriad maggots, a contaminated water supply, unbaked rations, inadequate hospital facilities, and lack of sanitation led to high death rates. When Union captives attempted to tunnel their way to freedom, they were hunted down by bloodhounds. The Confederate government attempted a defense in a report of the Confederate Congress, claiming that "rations furnished to prisoners of war in Richmond and Belle Isle have never been less than those of the soldiers

Located in Georgia, Andersonville was one of the worst prison camps. Close to thirteen thousand Union prisoners of war lost their lives there. This picture shows how close the prison tents were to each other and how crowded the conditions were.

who guarded them."[68] In the first six months of 1864 the prison population at Andersonville grew to thirty-one thousand. In August nearly three thousand prisoners were reported to have died at the rate of approximately one hundred a day. Some figures are unreliable, but prisoners' graves in the Andersonville cemetery number 12,912.

In Richmond's Libby Prison, at Belle Isle (a misnamed island in the James River near Richmond), and at minor southern prisons in Macon, Salisbury, Columbia, Charleston, Savannah, and Florence, conditions were slightly better than at Andersonville. Yet for all Andersonville's notoriety, the mortality at the Salisbury, North Carolina camp, where overcrowding led to several epidemics, was 34 percent compared with Andersonville's 29 percent.[69] Still, it was Andersonville's commander Henry Wirz who became the only Confederate to be tried and executed after the war for what amounted to war crimes.

Northern prisons included facilities at Johnson's Island (in Lake Erie near Sandusky, Ohio); some barracks at Elmira, New York; various forts such as Fort Lafayette in New York Harbor; Fort Warren in Boston; Fort McHenry in Baltimore; Point Lookout in St. Mary's County, Maryland; Rock Island Prison in Rock Island, Illinois; and various camps named for public figures, such as Indiana's Camp Morton outside of Indianapolis, Ohio's Chase in Columbus, and Illinois's Douglas in Chicago. Poor conditions in northern camps, especially at Camp Randall in Wisconsin, certainly killed their quota of Confederates. At Elmira, for instance, 775 of the 8,347 prisoners died of disease within three months, as the river that flowed through the grounds was "green with putrescence, filling the air with its messengers of disease and death." At Rock Island, doctors reported "a striking want of some means for the preservation of human life which medical and sanitary science has indicated as proper." At Camp Douglas "filth, poor drainage, and overcrowding created a horror."[70] However, in this as in other aspects of the war, the North's greater resources and its enhanced logistical capability to build housing and distribute supplies for its war prisoners meant that death rates in the northern camps were lower than those in the Confederacy.

Sites of human suffering, prisoner-of-war camps became propaganda tools used by both sides to fuel war spirit. Unionists and Confederates hated each other all the more when they read tales of the suffering in prison camps. Secretary of War Stanton employed a familiar idiom when he connected the brutality of war camps to the expected cruelty of those raised in a slave system. "The enormity of the crime committed by rebels toward our war prisoners . . . cannot but fill with horror the civilized world when the facts are revealed." In the South, E. A. Pollard blamed conditions in Confederate camps on the North and wrote of the Yankees' "cruel purpose to let their prisoners rot and die."[71] The impact of these charges would resonate long after the war itself had ended.

Although students of the conflict between the North and the South often concentrate on events on the battlefield, the Civil War involved more than just military engagements. It involved enrolling volunteers and later conscripts in a vast organization where they must learn the rudiments of soldiering; it involved supplying these new soldiers and sailors with weapons, clothes, and food; it meant creating a command system to oversee and coordinate personnel. And as the war continued, it required handling prisoners of war. No one in the United States had experience in such military matters, and both the Union and the Confederacy—to which we turn now—struggled to deal with these issues.

## CHAPTER 12

# Problems of the Confederacy

## MOBILIZING THE CONFEDERATE ARMY

Although the first two years of war brought some military success to the Confederacy, especially in the East, the aspiring nation faced many challenges on the home front. At the beginning of the war, the most urgent task was to raise, equip, and train an army. Even before the attack on Fort Sumter, the Confederate Congress had created both a regular army, which remained only a paper force throughout the conflict, and a provisional force, which actually fought the war.

The Confederate Congress initially authorized the recruitment of one-hundred thousand troops to serve either six months or a year, but after the war began, the number was increased to four hundred thousand men to serve either for three years or for the duration of the conflict. According to this legislation: "A person might become a member of the Provisional Army either as a volunteer without passing through the hands of a governor or as a member of state militia offered by the governor; and his term of service might be for the duration of the war however long it might last, for the duration if not over three years, for three years, for twelve months, for six months, or possibly for any intermediate time."[1] At first such inconsistencies seemed unimportant, as able-bodied white males rushed to enlist.

As in the North, Sumter became a rallying cry. In the Confederate version, Lincoln had refused to listen to southern peace proposals, after which, according to Jefferson Davis, there was "no alternative but to direct that the fort should be at once reduced." In his war message Davis described the Confederacy as a peaceful nation drawn into a purely defensive war "by aggression from without."[2] Fearing the North's denial of their right of self-government and an associated loss of their privileges as free men, southerners saw themselves as fighting for lib-

In this Currier and Ives lithograph, the allegorical Columbia, dressed in Revolutionary War–era garb and armed with sword and flag, inspires citizens to embrace the Union cause.

erty. "They fight for dominion," wrote the Georgian Susan Cornwall Shewmake about the North. "We fight for our liberty and our constitutional rights."[3]

Inspired by similar patriotic fervor along with fears of a northern invasion, individual southerners took up arms for the same mix of personal reasons and grand principles as did northerners. One Virginian reported to his governor, "All of us are ripe and ready for the fight. I shall be shoulder to shoulder with you whenever the fight comes off. I go for taking Boston & Cincinati [sic]. I go for wipeing them out." So great was the flood of volunteers that the government could not arm or equip them all. "From Mississippi I could get 20,000 men who impatiently wait for notice that they can be armed," President Davis reported. "In Georgia numerous tenders are made to serve for any time at any place and to these and other offers I am still constrained to answer, 'I have not arms to supply you.' "[4] Secretary of War Leroy Walker estimated that he rejected two hundred thousand volunteers during the early months of the war. Even so, this rapid enrollment depleted the southern labor supply necessary to run farms and factories. But left at home were nearly eight hundred thousand male slaves who were the mainstay of the Confederacy's agricultural work force and whose presence permitted the government to mobilize 75 to 80 percent of its white male population of military age.[5]

These patterns of volunteering generally followed those of the North, as did the organization of Confederate military commands. Prominent citizens usually raised companies among their neighbors and then initiated them into the mysteries of elementary army tactics. An election followed to choose company officers, with the person most active in raising the company usually elected captain. The men brought whatever arms and equipment they could find, including shotguns, flintlocks, and even swords used in the Mexican and Revolutionary wars. An important aspect of this preliminary stage was the choosing of a company name, and like those of Yankee units, the choices were often picturesque: Tallapoosa Thrashers; Southern Avengers; Bartow Yankee Killers; Chickasaw Desperadoes; Dixie Heroes; Southern Rejecters of Old Abe; Cherokee Lincoln Killers; and South Florida Bull Dogs.[6] Once organized and christened, the company tendered its services to the state governor or directly to the Confederate authorities, and if accepted, marched away to the mingled cheers and tears of the families left behind.

Having absorbed a sense of honor from antebellum southern culture, white males were enveloped in a domestic society that required military service. For young men, the decision to volunteer was not a private choice. Southern women played an instrumental role—both consciously and unconsciously. Women came to represent the vision of home and family for which soldiers fought. In the towns, rural crossings, and cities of the South, women joined the crowds that

Determined-looking Confederate volunteers stack arms and pose for the camera in northern Virginia in the early days of the war. Note the variety of hats and uniforms.

gathered after the firing on Sumter. Writes Drew Faust, "Patriotic addresses were the order of the day and the soldiers marched off . . . pelted with fruit, cards and notes from the throngs of ladies."[7]

Yet some women were troubled by the call for soldiers. Often overlooked in the masculine setting of war, women had ambivalent reactions not so much to the political choice of secession as to its successor—war. Torn between their patriotism and their fears for family members, Confederate women rationalized their dilemma by coming to believe that "the very value of these men was inseparable from their willingness to sacrifice their lives in battle."[8]

After the first rush to the colors, volunteering slowed. In time, finding soldiers became a significant problem for the Confederacy. The most devoted enlisted at the outset; those who remained behind lacked a sense of southern nationalism or had inescapable duties at home.[9] Many southerners thought the war was won at First Bull Run and saw no further call for their services after July 1861. Moreover the Confederates viewed Yankees as cowards who "did not want to fight, could not fight, and would not fight if forced into a major confrontation."[10] Volunteering was also discouraged by reports from men in the army that soldiering was not all "fun and frolic" but was instead drill, spit and polish, military discipline, and more drill. Reflecting the southern understanding that personal autonomy was a necessary component of freedom, one disillusioned Alabamian wrote home: "A soldier is worse than any negro on the Chatahooche [sic] river. He has no privileges whatever. He is under worse taskmasters than any negro. He is not treated with any respect whatever. His officers may insult him and he has no right to open his mouth and dare not do it."[11]

After the miserable winter of 1861–1862, when northern and southern armies faced each other in sullen idleness, many Confederate twelve-month volunteers prepared to return to their homes when their enlistments expired in the spring. Just as McClellan was about to begin his peninsular offensive in the early spring of 1862, the Confederate armies seemed to be melting away. So severe was the crisis that the southern Congress hurriedly passed an act to encourage reenlistments by granting generous furloughs and bounties to veterans who promised once more to volunteer.

Even so, it was clear that the volunteer system was breaking down, and under pressure from President Davis, who declared compulsory service "absolutely indispensable,"[12] the Confederate Congress on April 16, 1862 passed its first conscription law (and the first in American history), requiring white men between eighteen and thirty-five to serve. This act was later amended to broaden the age limits from thirty-five to forty-five; those under eighteen and over forty-five constituted a reserve for state defense, which was not required to go beyond its state's limits. In February 1864, when a depleted South faced another spring of military campaigns, a further extension of the most unpopular legislation of the Confederate government stretched the age limits to seventeen and fifty.[13]

These measures had numerous defects. The most objectionable were the exemptions that allowed a man to avoid military service by hiring a substitute or to avoid service if he was the schoolteacher of twenty pupils, a minister, or a college professor; a druggist; a mail carrier, postmaster, or civil officer of a state government or the Confederacy; a railroad employee, ferryman, or telegraph operator; an employee in a cotton or woolen mill, mine, furnace, or foundry; a shoemaker, blacksmith, tanner, miller, or saltmaker; or a printer or newspaper editor. The exemption that caused the greatest outcry and that significantly eroded morale was that of one overseer or slaveowner to every twenty slaves, a provision that actually freed only a few hundred men from military service but that spurred the protest that it was "a rich man's war and a poor man's fight."[14] As one soldier wrote home, "I do not think it is right for me to go through the hardships of camp life and the dangers of Battle [with] others living at home enjoying life because they have a few negroes."[15]

It is difficult to judge how effective Confederate conscription was. Compared with that in the North it came earlier and, given the large categories of those exempted, was more selective. After the passage of the 1862 draft law and during a year in which Confederate casualties reached 75,000, the number of men in the Confederate army increased from approximately 325,000 to over 450,000. In four years of war between 800,000 to 900,000 men (80 percent of potential white manpower) served.

Although the authorities in Richmond claimed to be satisfied with the draft, the constant modifications made in the laws indicated that the results left something to be desired. For example, in December 1863, the system of hiring substitutes was abolished after as many as fifty thousand substitutes had been recruited; in February 1864, all industrial exemptions were ended, although soldiers were to be detailed to war industries, and other exemptions were drastically reduced. Yet in the same month the "twenty Negro law" became the "fifteen Negro law," to appease smaller plantation owners.

Precisely how many conscripts the draft laws brought into the Confederate armies is uncertain. In fact, a chief function of this legislation was not so much to draft men as to force them, through volunteering, to avoid the disgrace of being conscripted. One authority concludes that, directly or indirectly, conscription was responsible for the enlistment of three hundred thousand soldiers, a third of the entire Confederate fighting force.[16]

This system of forced service upset southern notions of patriotism and undermined the common soldier's morale. A Texan noted the necessity of shooting "twenty-five conscripts for mutiny, whipp[ing] and shaving the heads of as many more for the same offense." Another soldier believed that "the conscript act will do away with all the patriotism we have. Whenever men are forced to fight they take no interest in it. Knowing that, let them do as well as they can. It will be said they were forced and then bravery was not from patriotism. . . . A more oppressive law was never enacted in the most uncivilized country or by the worst of despots."[17]

The draft system also revealed the tensions within the Confederacy—a society built on a value system that heralded the importance of states' rights, personal freedom, and economic and social inequalities. Such views were not always compatible with the revolutionary military demands of a society struggling against an enemy with far superior resources.[18] Some southerners, including highly placed, influential leaders, refused to compromise. As Georgia's Governor Joseph Brown pondered the dilemma: "What will we have gained when we have achieved our independence of the Northern States if in our efforts to do so, we have . . . lost *Constitutional Liberty* at home."[19]

## SUPPLIES AND RESOURCES

It was even more difficult for the Confederacy to supply these troops than to raise them. At the beginning of the war the government seized about 190,000 small arms of all descriptions from federal arsenals in the South, and there were probably 300,000 more, "of varying degrees of antiquity and disrepair" that the states owned. Yet in the entire South in 1861 there were only two small, inactive powder factories to provide ammunition.[20]

That the South was not hindered more by its shortage of arms and ammunition was largely the work of Josiah Gorgas, a Pennsylvanian who accepted an appointment as the Confederacy's chief of ordnance. Quiet and unassuming, Gorgas was little known to the public, but because of his efficient labors the South rarely, if ever, lost a battle through lack of munitions. During the first two years of the war, imports from Europe formed the principal source of supply. In all, blockade runners brought in 330,000 arms for an ordnance bureau that was chronically short of funds. Another 270,000 were supplied by states and private individuals. Another large source was the capture of northern arms on the battlefield; for example, southern soldiers obtained 35,000 Federal small arms in the Seven Days' battles and about 20,000 more at Second Bull Run.

Increasingly, however, the Confederacy relied on its own factories for arms and ammunition. Through Gorgas's industry large arsenals were set up in Richmond, Fayetteville, Augusta, Charleston, Columbia, Macon, Atlanta, and Selma. Foundries were established in Macon, Columbus, Augusta, and elsewhere; and, under the expert supervision of Colonel George W. Rains, a huge powder mill was built in Augusta. In addition, government contracts were given to privately owned factories, notably to the Tredegar Iron Works at Richmond, which "made torpedoes, submarines, plates for ironclad ships, propeller shafts, cannon, the great Brooke rifled naval guns, machinery for war production."[21] By 1863 Gorgas confidently reported, "We are now in a condition to carry on the war for an indefinite period."[22]

The quartermaster corps was less well managed. Under Abraham C. Myers, there were too many bureaucratic regulations. One of Myers's chief duties was to procure millions of uniforms and shoes for the army. Since no factories in the South were capable of handling orders of such magnitude, the Confederate government set up its own clothing and shoe factories, a startling departure from the norm of private enterprise. By late 1861 some government-owned factories made army clothing, and the war also spawned a few privately owned establishments.

In most cases the Confederate government "loaned contractors money to meet start-up costs and limited the profits these government-sponsored enterprises could make." Because the government controlled manpower (through conscription laws) as well as the railroads, it could foster the development of war industries such as those producing or refining sulfur, niter powder, clothing, and shoes.[23] Ironically, the war to save slavery, the Old South, and a traditional style of living rapidly pushed the Confederate government to try to create those elements of transportation and industrialization that the North had earlier developed. To do so required (as it did not in the more developed North, where facilities remained in private hands) the intervention of the national government. So much of this Confederate activity was government induced and controlled that several historians have labeled these efforts state socialism.[24]

Another of Myers's functions was to procure the horses and mules needed in the Confederate army for the cavalry and artillery as well as those for the transport of supplies, a task that became increasingly difficult as Union forces occupied the horse-breeding areas of Kentucky and Tennessee. After the battle of Chancellorsville in May 1863, Lee's army never had enough horses, although it mustered twenty-eight thousand for the battle of Gettysburg; in late 1864 more than one-fourth of the Confederate cavalry fought dismounted because of the shortage. So desperate did the problem become that in February 1865, General W. N. Pendleton, Lee's chief of artillery, believed that "the question of our horse supply is hardly second to that of supplying men for the army, or food for the men."[25]

The commissary general of the Confederate army, Lucius B. Northrop, was one of the most incompetent men in the government. For example, in 1862 Northrop was responsible for importing tons of beef through the blockade for Texas, where the ranchers' corrals were crowded with cattle.[26] Often misusing his powers, Northrop became the most abused man in the southern forces. To most Confederates it seemed preposterous that, in a fertile agricultural area like the South, there should be shortages of food for the armies, and they naturally blamed Northrop. George Cary Eggleston summarized their complaints:

[A]t Manassas, where the army was well-nigh starved out in the very beginning of the war, food might have been abundant but for the obstinacy of this one man. On our left lay a country unsurpassed, and most unequaled in productiveness. It was rich in grain and meat. . . . The obvious duty of the commissary-general, therefore, was to draw upon that section for the supplies which were both convenient and abundant.[27]

Many historians agree with Richard Beringer that "no Confederate army lost a major engagement because of the lack of arms, munitions, or other essential supplies. . . . Nor is there evidence that Confederate armies suffered from starvation or even malnutrition."[28] Yet the issue was often not one of actual deprivation, but rather the growing perception of undeniable hardships. Such attitudes sapped morale and were especially enervating when victories on the battlefield became scarce. Eventually, persistent shortages, government mismanagement, and the removal of resources by Union occupation, sieges, and destruction undermined the earlier optimism of both civilians and soldiers. This continual interplay of domestic and military circumstances weakened the Confederacy psychologically and militarily.

Northrop's incompetence should not obscure the obstacles he faced. Among these was the inefficiency of the South's transportation system, itself a result of the comparatively retarded advancement of the industrial South. In 1861 the Confederate railroad network was composed mostly of short lines, inadequately financed by local capital, and very poorly equipped and constructed.[29] At the outbreak of the war few leaders in the Confederacy had any comprehension of the role railroads would play in the conflict. Almost none understood, as did Brigadier General J. H. Trapier, that "Railroads are at one and the same time the legs and the stomach of the army,"[30] necessary for the transport of troops, supplies, and munitions.

The Davis administration at first relied on informal agreements with the private railroad managers rather than coercion. Under this system, there was a persistent lack of supervision, coordination, and centralization, although by 1863 Davis had the power to seize railroads that failed to give priority to military shipments. In 1865 the Confederate Congress granted authority to the secretary of war over the transportation of troops, supplies, and munitions, a power that included the authority to place railroad and navigation companies under military officers.[31]

But by this time it was too late. Not only did the Union control sufficient territory to threaten all but the shortest lines, but also the deterioration of rails, engines, and rolling stock destroyed the effectiveness of the system. Nevertheless, because their lines of communication between the eastern and western theaters of war were shorter than those of the Union, the Confederates did use the railroads for troop movements. In these efforts the line from Chattanooga to Richmond was of critical importance. And Corinth, the railroad junction in northern Mississippi, became an important deployment point for forty thousand troops and a Union target because the Confederacy's principal north-south, east-west lines intersected there.

## FINANCING THE WAR

The problems of the Confederacy were aggravated by the difficulties of financing a costly war without much gold and silver, without a financial plan, and without a community resolve to use taxation as an economic tool. When Christopher Memminger, who had little comprehension of either economic theory or financial practice, became secretary of the treasury in 1861, the treasury had no money in it. Only loans from the state of Alabama and from banks in New Orleans enabled the Confederate States to begin the war solvent.

Memminger, a South Carolinian of German birth, relied on his own limited experience as chairman of the South Carolina legislature's House Ways and Means Committee and on the advice of leading bankers in devising a makeshift policy. A proponent of hard money and stringent taxation, he was forced to depend heavily on paper money and loans rather than taxes.

The principal requirement of any wartime treasury is to determine how to find adequate revenue to fund the war. But the Confederacy was hindered by a long antebellum tradition of hostility to certain sources of revenue. Although Memminger considered several options—including customs duties, which had

In this lithograph entitled *The Lost Cause*, leaders of the Confederacy are pictured in the center of a ring of Confederate currency, which became worthless after the war. In nostalgic fashion, Confederate triumphs during the war are pictured along the border.

been anathema in the Old South and a high-profile source of conflict with the North—loans and treasury notes became the principal sources of wartime revenue. The secretary's challenge was soon complicated by the printing of nearly a billion and a half paper dollars, secured only by a promise of postwar redemption in gold and silver. As the Confederacy became a money factory unable to print currency fast enough, its reliance on paper money fueled an inflation that undermined its economy and demoralized its civilians.

Despite the urging of Secretary Memminger, the Confederate Congress was reluctant to levy taxes. Southerners had not been accustomed to paying heavy taxes; taxation might impose too heavy a strain on loyalty to the Confederacy; and taxes were difficult to collect because parts of the richest areas of the South were soon controlled by northern armies. As the editor of the Wilmington (N.C.) *Journal* declared: "The burden of taxation, State and Confederate, should be laid as lightly as possible on our suffering people. We of today are paying the price of our righteous war of defense in blood and wounds and death . . . and it is but just and right that posterity should pay in money the price of that heritage of freedom, property, and glory which we will bequeath them."[32]

There was little revenue from tariffs, in part because the northern blockade limited imports and exports. But tariffs would not have provided much revenue in any case. In February 1861, when Memminger took office and transferred the U.S. customs houses to the Confederacy, "the potential volume of revenue was limited by the fact that only $4 million of U.S. customs receipts were collected at southern ports." With southern commerce so meager, and southern hostility to taxes so strong, the secretary's options were limited. However, his own failure to dissuade either Congress or the people from their "ignorant optimism" about the chances of Confederate success also contributed to the deficit spending of the Confederacy.[33]

Thus, a direct tax enacted on August 19, 1861, which imposed a one-half percent tax on major categories of assets such as real estate, slaves, and other property, was weakened by the provision that the states might avoid its imposition if they paid the required amounts in Confederate treasury notes or in specie (money in coin). Relying on precedent, southern states avoided payment by borrowing the amount due and transferring the proceeds to Richmond. "They followed the precedent of the States during the Revolution in meeting their quota of the [continental] taxes . . . not by raising the amount by taxation, but by issuing bonds or paper money." In all only $17,500,000 was raised in 1861–1862, at a time when the annual Confederate budget was over $160 million.[34]

Though the direct tax was obviously defective, the Confederate Congress did not try to remedy the situation until April 1863, when it adopted a more comprehensive tax law that combined the features of an income levy, a license tax, and a general internal revenue measure. The duties imposed by this law included, among other things, an 8 percent levy on salt, wines, liquors, tobacco, cotton, wool, flour, sugar, molasses, syrup, rice, and all other agricultural products; a license tax, of varying amounts, on bankers, brokers, auctioneers, wholesale and retail dealers in liquors, pawnbrokers, distillers, brewers, innkeepers, theater and circus owners, jugglers, butchers, bakers, apothecaries, physicians, tobacconists, peddlers, lawyers, photographers, and confectioners; and a graduated income tax, ranging (after an initial exemption of one thousand dollars) from 1 percent on the first fifteen hundred dollars to 15 percent on all incomes over ten thousand dollars.

No tax was imposed directly upon land or slaves, because the Confederate Constitution required that such direct taxes be apportioned according to population. But no census had been taken, and given the manpower shortage, there was no way to take one. To circumvent this restriction, a tax in kind was imposed. After reserving certain amounts of food for his own use, each farmer and planter was required to pay to the government one-tenth of his wheat, corn, oats, rye, buckwheat or rice, sweet and Irish potatoes, cured hay and fodder, sugar, molasses, cotton, wool, tobacco, beans, peas, and bacon.[35]

This new legislation was very unpopular, especially among the farmers, who compared their 10 percent duties with the low taxes on other forms of income and protested that the tax in kind was "oppressive, and a relic of barbarism, which alone was practised in the worst despotisms." In North Carolina there was open opposition, and in Richmond a clerk in the War Department observed that "farmers are making preparations for only so much corn as will suffice for their own use. . . . The instant impressment of flour, corn, and meat as soon as they are brought to . . . towns to be put in the market is causing universal withholding of surplus-secreting and non-production."[36] Though some areas such as the trans-Mississippi region seem to have complied more readily, this and subsequent efforts to strengthen tax provisions were too little, too late. One historian calculates that the Confederacy raised only about 1 percent of its revenue in taxes, as the government's fiscal policy drifted far too cautiously given the rampant inflation.[37]

Nor was the Confederacy much more successful in its loans, which taken together raised $712 million, or 39 percent of the government's total revenues.[38] From the start there was not enough gold and silver in the South to serve as the collateral that would make large loan subscriptions possible. Later, when the South was awash in vast quantities of depreciating paper money, citizens preferred fluid currency, real estate, or gold to bonds with fixed rates. The chief borrowings included the $15 million loan, the $100 million loan, the Erlanger loan, and the produce loans. The $15 million domestic loan, authorized on February 28, 1861, was mostly subscribed by November of that year, with nearly two-fifths of the amount taken up by banks in New Orleans. Its proceeds constituted one of the few sources of specie for the Confederate government. The $100 million loan of August 19, 1861 was floated chiefly among planters and was paid in part by paper money (treasury notes and bank notes) and in part by produce.

Early in the war this idea of a "produce loan" was introduced into southern fiscal schemes. In later loan measures this type of borrowing came to be especially significant, although the South never adopted Alexander Stephens's daring proposal. The vice president proposed to issue 8 percent bonds up to $100 million on the cotton crops of 1860 and 1861, buy ironclad steamers, and send the cotton to Europe. There it would be stored until its price reached fifty cents a pound, when it would be sold at ten times the value of the bonds.[39]

The produce loans had the planters, in effect, turning over their cotton and other commodities to the government in specified amounts in return for Confederate bonds. Because of the reluctance of some planters to part with their cotton for government paper, and also because of the difficulty of getting specie for cotton, the produce loans proved disappointing.

The most famous of the foreign loans was floated with Émile Erlanger, a French financier whose son was romantically involved with the daughter of the Confederate minister to France, John Slidell. In return for Confederate bonds backed by cotton, Erlanger, who was secretly promised a handsome profit, agreed to market a loan abroad. The subscription books were opened on March 18, 1863. Since at this point the bonds were exchangeable for cotton at a price far below the current market price for that commodity, the whole scheme was actually a speculation in cotton. In addition, the Erlanger firm was given a commission of 5 percent as well as Confederate funds with which to sustain the market—Erlanger having demanded that the Confederates offer a price support so that subscribers would not forfeit their subscriptions.[40] Eventually the profits of the firm were enormous, running to nearly thirteen and a half million francs. The Confederacy realized 1,458,678 British pounds in this single loan operation, which inexplicably was not repeated. Having fluctuated wildly during the war, the bonds became worthless after the collapse of the Confederacy, though the ever hopeful bond holders kept pushing their schemes for payment.[41]

As both loans and taxes proved insufficient amid continuously burgeoning war expenditures (which reached half a billion dollars by 1863), a public debt of the same proportions, and an empty treasury, the Confederacy turned to its last resource, the printing press. At first, only small sums of paper money were authorized in order to provide sufficient circulating currency and to pay the outstanding debts of the new government. Virtually every responsible leader of the Confederacy realized the perils of fiat currency; Memminger himself declared that printing money was "the most dangerous of all methods of raising money."[42]

Nevertheless, the commercial need for currency, the inadequacy of other fiscal measures, and the readiness of the southern Congress to take the easiest road led to the issuing of immense quantities of treasury notes. The Richmond government promised to pay a specified dollar amount to the bearer "two years after the ratification of a treaty of peace between the Confederate States and the United States of America." Unlike northern greenbacks, Confederate paper money was never made legal tender, for both Davis and Memminger resisted the arguments of several congressmen that a legal-tender law would increase the value of the notes.[43]

As more and more treasury notes rolled from the printing presses, all other forms of official currency were quickly driven into hiding. Small coins disappeared, as Confederates tried to use postage stamps in their place. Shinplasters, that is, "small paper notes, generally in denominations from five cents to fifty cents . . . were issued illegally by merchants, railroads, taverns, saloons, butchers, bakers, almost every other kind of business, and even by individuals." Since Memminger never moved to outlaw these alternatives, the Confederacy was plagued by the lack of a uniform currency. There was also a great deal of counterfeiting, both of local and state currencies and of Confederate treasury notes.[44]

By the end of the war the Confederacy had issued $1,554,000,000 in paper currency, over three times the total amount of northern greenbacks. Though the gold value of these Confederate notes stood at 90 percent of their face value in 1861, it declined to 82.7 percent in early 1862, to 29 percent in early 1863, and to 4.6 percent in early 1864. So desperate did the situation become that the Confederacy resorted to a partial repudiation. After April 1, 1864, and July 1 west of the Mississippi, treasury notes had to be exchanged for 4 percent bonds. Thereafter larger bills would be gradually reduced in value until they were worthless, while small bills could be exchanged at two-thirds of their face rate. A new, presumably less depreciated paper currency was to be issued. But this scheme only further eroded confidence in the treasury and ultimately in the Confederacy itself. By early 1865 these notes were worth only 1.7 cents on the dollar.[45]

In June 1864 Memminger, the architect of these proposals, resigned under fire. Even granted the difficulty of financing the war in a society hostile to taxes, still Memminger mismanaged the Treasury Department. He neglected the currency needs of the Trans-Mississippi Department, whose supply of money was disproportionately low and whose soldiers and suppliers often remained uncompensated. In the East, his failure to distribute funds efficiently also left the army unpaid, without food, clothing, or shelter. He failed to understand the need for revenue in an economy engaged in deficit financing. And in a very dispiriting situation for providers of goods and services, the Confederacy ended the war with three hundred and fifty million unpaid requisitions. Nor did the secretary make any effort to persuade the public of the importance of making sacrifices, as the Confederate economy rapidly deteriorated.

George A. Trenholm, one of the wealthiest men in the South, succeeded Memminger. Trenholm, a member of the financial firm of Fraser, Trenholm, and Company of Charleston, did not alter his predecessor's financial policies, but he did try to change the direction of the treasury's appeals. Instead of aiming principally for planter, merchant, and banker support, he sought to cement "the natural alliance that exists between a people and their treasury" and to bolster general public confidence. He was, however, far too late to remedy a bad situation.[46]

The Confederacy's reliance on paper money spurred inflation, as citizens bought today, knowing that their money would be worth less tomorrow. From October 1861 through March 1864, prices consistently rose at a steady clip of 10 percent a month. Although prices fell in the summer of 1864, in the winter they rose again, unaffected by the government's partial repudiation of its treasury notes—a plan that only caused southerners to reduce their cash balances by spending, thereby increasing the rate of inflation. By the end of the war the general price index stood at ninety-two times its prewar base.[47]

Inflation brought suffering and misery to many, especially to women, who participated in the marketplace principally as consumers. As early as July 1862, the French consul in Richmond reported that, aside from potatoes, there were "no vegetables except cabbages and one cabbage, one single cabbage, costs $1.25."[48] In October 1863, Robert Kean, head of the Confederate Bureau of War, described the impact of inflation on his income:

> My salary of $3000 goes about as far as $300 would do in ordinary times in purchasing all the articles of household necessity, the average of prices being about ten fold. The consequence is that with an income from all sources of at least $6000 and a good deal of help from my father-in-law, my family is reduced to two meals a day . . . and they are of the most plain and economical scale. Wood for fuel is $38 per cord, butter $4 per pound, coal $1.25 per bushel, calico $4.50 a yard.[49]

Seven months later another War Department official recorded the following prices in Richmond: "boots, $200; coats, $350; pants, $100; shoes, $125; flour, $275 per barrel; meal, $60 to $80 per bushel; bacon, $9 per pound; no beef on the market; chickens, $30 per pair; shad, $20; potatoes, $25 per bushel . . . butter, $15 per pound; lard, same; wood, $50 per cord."[50] By the end of the war, flour sold at one thousand dollars a barrel in Richmond.

Except for debtors and speculators, everyone in the South suffered from the rampant inflation. Poor families and those on fixed incomes, such as government workers, were hardest hit. Planters, too, were affected, for their crops, normally exported, declined in real value. Creditors actually avoided the payment of debts in the Confederacy's worthless paper money. Professionals were badly hurt; some doctors resorted to a barter arrangement, offering their services at 1861 rates "to those who will furnish . . . grain or forage AT OLD PRICES."[51] A teacher in Georgia discovered after paying her rent that she had nothing left over for her food, and concluded, "everything in the Confederacy was rising in price except teaching."[52]

For laborers, real wages declined by a third. As one group of workingmen complained to Secretary Memminger, wages were "totally inadequate to afford us the merest necessities of life—plain food, shelter, fuel, and clothing. We are literally reduced to destitution."[53]

The families of soldiers were especially hard hit by inflation since the monthly wages for privates remained fixed at eleven dollars a month—when they got paid. "Unheard of prices . . . for provisions of almost every kind," lamented the *Eastern Clarion*, a Mississippi newspaper, in 1862, "are fast reducing a large class of our population to the condition of paupers."[54] States tried to care for these indigent families, undertaking government-financed welfare programs at odds with the South's laissez-faire heritage. Most states appropriated large sums for direct relief. Louisiana "adopted a systematic pension system, providing for the payment of $10 monthly to wives or widows of soldiers . . . the same amount to dependent parents, and $5 each to children and dependent younger brothers and sisters of soldiers."[55]

Georgia was especially active in trying to alleviate the deprivation of its yeomen farmers and soldier's families. Many of the conflicts between Governor Joseph Brown and the government in Richmond had their origin in "the [state's] simple desire to relieve their hard-pressed citizens"[56] But the relief was minimal in terms of purchasing power, and repeatedly the complaint arose:

> There is no doubt an ample sufficiency of Corn in this country for its consumption; but holders can't be moved to sell for less than the most exorbitant prices & many women & children are entirely without. Now just let this news reach our Soldiers in the Army whose families are thus oppressed, & I should not be surprised to hear any day that many of them had laid by their arms and marched off home.[57]

## ALIENATION IN THE CONFEDERACY

During the war Confederates experienced material and psychological hardships involving almost everything from the death of family members and the destruction of farms, houses, railroads, and roads to inadequate diets and even the grotesque features of a war that found pigs rooting amid unburied soldiers. Although some historians have discovered a remarkable persistence of loyalty to the Confederacy, others have located in these discomforts the source of civilian disaffection and the erosion of female patriotism. In turn the loss of morale has become an explanation for the southern failure to win the war.

As Drew Faust has written, "At the beginning of the war middle and upper-class women sought active means of expressing their commitment," by sewing uniforms, writing patriotic songs, and even creating special talismans from the hair of Confederate generals. As their economic condition deteriorated and their families were destroyed, Confederate women experienced emotional and physical deprivation. The absence of their promised male protectors—in New Bern, North Carolina, for example, only twenty white men remained of a prewar white population of 250—meant that women did arduous physical labor in the fields. One Alabamian informed the governor at the beginning of the harvest season

This Confederate woman is reading a letter from a soldier. As the war dragged on, some southern women withdrew their support and urged their husbands and sons to return home.

that hundreds of women would be seen for the first time "between the handles of the plow." [58]

Joined by women from yeomen families, some informed both their states and the Richmond government that they would urge their husbands and sons to desert if their basic needs for family subsistence were not met. Others signed petitions asking for economic assistance. Some fled North to relatives, while others who remained barely survived. Some became forlorn refugees, forced to abandon the former focus of their lives—home and family.[59] A few turned to petty shoplifting and large-scale robbery, along with trading with the enemy. Others encouraged the desertion of their relatives—a circumstance that led one military official to urge the secretary of war to censor the mails to prevent such subversion. As one North Carolina editor bluntly explained, "Desertion takes place because desertion is encouraged. . . . the ladies are responsible."[60]

Besides women, there were other groups of alienated Confederates, and their numbers increased as large parts of the South endured a hated occupation. At first, southerners greeted Yankee soldiers with bitter hostility, bristling with the sense that their nation had been violated, polluted, and degraded. "It makes me so mad," said one woman who noted that the invaders were unmolested. In time the weakness of their own military forces and the removal of important territory from the Confederacy eroded the earlier fierce commitment to the cause.[61]

There can be no doubt that suffering and the need to make sacrifices for their new nation brought out the fundamental disunity of the Confederacy. The South had never been unanimous in support of secession, and its nationalism had the fragility of novelty. Every state, with the possible exception of South Carolina, held vigorous Unionists. In the Appalachian mountain region, opponents of the Confederacy were probably in the majority throughout the war.

In other areas Unionists, though in a minority, continued to challenge the Confederacy. In the hill country of Alabama, for example, hundreds agreed with one small farmer's verdict that the war was a slaveholder's plot: "[A]ll they want is to git you pupt up and go to fight for there infurnal negroes and after you do their fighting you may kiss there hine parts for [all] they care."[62] The Ozark region of Arkansas was strongly opposed to the war, and among the German population of Texas, possibly one-third of the people "remained neutral and one-third, actively or passively, gave support to the Federal cause."[63]

At the outbreak of the war, Unionists agreed, with varying degrees of reluctance, to go along with their state's effort at independence. The hard shocks of war revived uncertainties and persistent grievances. Next to inflation, economic

In the Tennessee Mountains, pro-Union guerrillas fire at Confederate cavalry attempting to track down army deserters. The Conscription Act angered many southern soldiers and led them to desert.

hardship, and the various tax and currency policies, the operation of the conscription act did the most to turn southerners against the Confederacy. Some opposed the draft because it seemed a step toward military despotism.

The exemption of one slaveholder or overseer for every twenty (later fifteen) slaves was especially objectionable to the small farmers of the South. "Never did a law meet with more universal odium than the exemption of slave owners," wrote Senator James Phelan of Mississippi to Jefferson Davis; "its injustice, gross injustice, is denounced even by men whose position allows them to take advantage of its privileges. . . . It has aroused a spirit of rebellion . . . and bodies of men have banded together to desert."[64]

In North Carolina citizens angrily opposed conscription on the basis that their state had provided its proper share of soldiers.[65] Many outraged southerners shared the opinion of a North Carolina draftee who paid his respects to President Davis as he deserted:

> Your happy conscript would go to the far-away North whence the wind comes and leave you to reap the whirlwind with no one but your father the devil to reap and rake and bind after you. And he's going. It is with intense and multifariously proud satisfaction that he gazes for the last time upon our holy flag—that symbol . . . of an adored trinity, cotton, niggers, and chivalry . . . Behind he leaves the legitimate chivalry of this unbounded nation centered in the illegitimate son of a Kentucky horse-thief. . . . And now, bastard President of a political abortion, farewell. . . . Except it be in the army of the Union, you will not again see the conscript."[66]

Sometimes these deserters formed guerrilla bands that hid in the hill country of the Confederacy. In Washington County, in southwestern Virginia, deserters "roamed over the country and robbed citizens indiscriminately of money, clothing, horses, saddles, grain and forage."[67] In some areas of northwestern Georgia the conscription law was suspended for twelve months before the end of the war because "tories and bushwhackers" made the region "a theater for the lawless depredations of prowling bands of cavalry."[68] If Confederate officers halted these disloyal citizens and asked for their authority to be absent from their commands, they patted their guns and defiantly said, "This is my furlough." [69]

Deserters moved with impunity through the backwoods areas of the Confederacy because the large majority of the population in that region shared their disaffection toward the Richmond government. Throughout the South secret peace societies sprang up. In Arkansas poor, nonslaveholding whites banded together as early as 1861, vowing "they would never muster under the d——d nigger flag, but if any one would just come along with the stars and stripes that they would arise at midnight and go to it, and they would fight for it too when they got there."[70] Using the elaborate rituals of fraternal organizations, the Peace Society also flourished in Mississippi, Alabama, Georgia, eastern Tennessee, and Florida. In Alabama members claimed that they furnished the Federal armies with critical information in the successful Union campaigns in 1863 at Vicksburg and Chattanooga.

Similar societies flourished in Virginia and in the Carolinas. William W. Holden, the most influential editor in North Carolina and candidate for governor of that state in 1864, was a member of the secret peace society called the Order of the Heroes of America. Holden regularly used his newspaper, the Raleigh *Standard*, to attack the Confederate government and to advocate a separate peace. "North Carolina is true, and will be true to the Confederate government as it was formed, in its integrity and purity," he argued, "but she would not be bound by a government which had lost its original character and had been perverted to despotic purposes against her own rights and the rights and liberties of her citizens."[71]

Many disaffected southerners expressed their disloyalty by refusing to serve in the Confederate armies and disobeying Confederate laws. Others took more active steps of opposition, openly trading with the enemy or giving Federal troops information as to the whereabouts of Confederate forces. Some idea of the extent and importance of opposition in the Confederacy can be gained from the fact that after the war, 22, 298 persons put in claims for over $60 million against the United States government for reimbursement for quartermaster and commissary supplies they declared they had furnished to the advancing Federal armies in the South. That such an equivocal commitment was not confined to the poor and economically deprived classes of the South is evidenced by the fact that 701 of these professed pro-Union southerners made claims totaling ten thousand dollars or more each.[72]

## OPPOSITION BY THE STATES TO THE CONFEDERACY

Internal opposition within the Confederacy was evident on many fronts, as states' rights often proved a hindrance in a war that made some centralization imperative. On the other hand, a case can be made for the alternative position that state governors performed some beneficial services for the Confederacy, such as raising troops, providing effective local defenses, and especially taking on the administration of welfare services crucial for morale.[73] Thus the net effects of states' rights may not have been to hinder the military effort, although the influence of its outspoken advocates certainly did not inspire confidence in the Confederacy. The two states in which independence from the Richmond government was most conspicuous were Georgia and North Carolina, where governors Joseph E. Brown and Zebulon Vance emerged as opponents of Jefferson Davis.

Brown took state sovereignty seriously. After the secession of Georgia, when technically the state was an independent nation, he even sent a diplomatic officer abroad. On January 30, 1861, he appointed T. Butler King commissioner to the government of Queen Victoria, to the emperor Napoleon III, and to the government of the king of Belgium, with instructions to explain Georgia's secession and to "ascertain from those Governments whether it will accord with their policy, to immediately acknowledge the Government of Georgia as that of an independent State." On February 5, Brown ordered the seizure of ships in Savannah harbor belonging to citizens of New York as a reprisal for the seizure of Georgia guns by the New York police.

After Georgia entered the Confederacy Brown was intensely loyal to the cause of southern independence, at the same time that he tangled with the authorities in Richmond. His policy was that Georgia should look to its own defenses, raise huge war chests, develop its own foundries, raise and maintain state troops (referred to as "the Georgia regular army"), "prevent the Confederate tax-gatherers from making their appearance among us,"[74] and in general promote the southern cause by state measures with as little obedience as possible to the increasing efforts, albeit often mismanaged, of central direction from Richmond.

As the war dragged on, Brown's devotion to the Confederacy diminished, and he began to think about making a separate peace treaty between Georgia and the United States. He vigorously opposed the Confederacy's Conscription Acts, believing that such measures contradicted the "constitutional liberty which so many Georgians have died to defend." He believed that "conscription strikes down the sovereignty of the state, triumphs upon the constitutional rights and personal liberty of the citizens and arms the President with imperial power."[75]

Only when judges on the state supreme court decided unanimously in favor of the constitutionality of conscription did Brown permit the Confederacy's second conscription act to go into effect. And even then he used the exemption clauses to the fullest, declaring that over fifteen thousand Georgians, mostly in the militia, were indispensable state officers not subject to the draft.[76]

In North Carolina's Governor Vance, the Davis administration found a different kind of critic. A soldier himself and an effective administrator, Vance never wavered in his loyalty to the Confederacy, even when Holden, his principal backer, and large segments of the Conservative party joined the peace movement. "I will see this Conservative party blown into a thousand atoms and Holden and his understrappers in hell . . . before I will consent to a course which I think would bring dishonor and ruin upon both State and Confederacy," he declared. At the same time that he supported the Confederacy, Vance insisted "that the Richmond authorities should exert their war power with due regard for the rights of North Carolina and with especial consideration for her civil law."[77]

Whenever the governor thought that the Confederate government was infringing on the sovereignty of his state or that it was mistreating its citizens, he protested heatedly to President Davis. At one point his language in objecting to alleged discriminations against North Carolina became so intemperate that Davis stiffly replied, "I must beg that a correspondence so unprofitable in its character, and which was not initiated by me, may here end, and that your future communications be restricted to such matters as may require official action."[78] Like Brown, Vance did not approve of the conscription acts, and through the use of liberal state exemptions, he kept many North Carolinians at home. Overall he deprived the Confederacy of more than ten thousand troops, at the same time that his state spent $1,500,000 aiding the destitute families of soldiers. Both Vance and Brown were alert to issues of morale and the well-being of their citizens and tried to sustain them through state welfare.[79]

In other states besides North Carolina and Georgia there was official opposition over laws passed in February 1862, which gave the president the power to suspend the privilege of the habeas corpus writ. At various times Portsmouth, Salisbury, Norfolk, Mobile, Petersburg, New Orleans, and the entire state of Texas were under Confederate martial law. But Brown and Vance were the most outspoken critics. Brown so furiously opposed a military order placing Atlanta under martial law that the order was annulled after his opposition:

> We were recently informed that a [Confederate] military commander . . . had issued an order declaring the city of Atlanta to be under *martial law*, and had appointed a Governor and his *aides* to assume the government of the city. The order was issued without any conference with the Executive of this State . . . and the Governor appointed by the General assumed the Government and control of the city. . . . I consider this and all like proceedings, on the part of Confederate officers not only high-handed usurpation . . . without the shadow of constitutional right, but dangerous precedents, which if acquiesced in by the people of this State, tend to the subversion of the government and sovereignty of the State, and of the individual rights of the citizen.[80]

State judges also released prisoners held under Confederate authority. For example, Chief Justice Pearson of the Supreme Court of North Carolina granted writs—that is, legal orders—to all who applied, discharging one reluctant conscript after another. Yet the state's supreme court eventually upheld the habeas corpus act as constitutional, giving the Confederate government broad powers of arrest. In Georgia, however, the legislature declared the act unconstitutional, and a commissioner, appointed to execute the act in 1864 concluded that enforcement in Georgia was impossible.[81] Extended throughout the Confederacy, the effects of wartime control and centralization "shocked, amazed, disillusioned and angered significant segments of the southern community. The mobilization of both men and resources necessary to wage war successfully proved a good deal more rigorous than Confederates ever had dreamed."[82]

## PROBLEMS OF LEADERSHIP

In Richmond, Jefferson Davis provided a target for Confederate discontent throughout the war. Although he was popular enough in the early days of the war, his opponents questioned his fitness for the post when the conflict proved a long one and things did not go well for the Confederacy. T. R. R. Cobb, the Georgian who had helped draft the Confederate Constitution, called him the "embodiment of concentration of cowardly littleness;" James L. Alcorn agreed that the president was a "miserable, stupid, one-eyed, dyspeptic, arrogant tyrant"; Linton Stephens, brother of the vice president of the Confederacy, termed Davis "a little, conceited, hypocritical, snivelling, canting, malicious, ambitious, dogged knave and fool." Seeing his "country dying from the incompetency of its presumptuous chief," Congressman William W. Boyce lamented, "It looks to me like we are going under the Jeff Davis lead very fast over the precipice. His intermeddling with the armies is usually disastrous, and he has no diplomacy. I don't see how we can come without ruin if the matter is left entirely to Davis."[83]

Some complaints against Davis were justified. For a man who had made an enviable record as secretary of war in the Pierce administration, he was an astonishingly bad administrator. He spent far too much time on details, on "little trash which ought to be dispatched by clerks in the adjutant general's office."[84] Secretary of Navy Stephen Mallory thought he "neither labored with method or celerity himself, nor permitted others to do so for him." Conducting a revolutionary enterprise as though it were a leisurely southern debating society, Davis insisted on holding prolonged cabinet meetings, but, as Mallory lamented, "from his uncontrollable tendency to digression,—to slide away from the chief points to episodical questions, the amount of business accomplished bore but little relation to the time consumed; and unfrequently [sic] a Cabinet meeting would exhaust four or five hours without determining anything; while the desk of every chief of a Department was covered with papers demanding his attention."[85]

Another of Davis's weaknesses was his effort to combine the civilian and military leadership of the Confederacy, a combination delegated in both the United States and the Confederate Constitutions to the president as commander in chief. He would have preferred a military command to his political position, and he never gave up thinking that if he and Lee could jointly lead the armies, they would sweep to victory. Whenever there was a possible battle near Richmond, he rushed to the front, where he hoped to perform as a brilliant field commander. "A strict constitutionalist, he found it difficult to yield any prerogatives. Because the president was entrusted with military leadership, he must exercise it, and from his point of view, of course, it was fortunate that he had had professional military training. In reality it was an inestimable curse."[86] His belief in his own military competence even delayed the appointment of a general-in-chief as well as the consideration of a staff to coordinate and supervise the handling of a huge army.

More critical, Davis's military background blinded him to civilian issues and public opinion as he attempted to answer questions of morale with victories on the battlefield. Underestimating the importance of civilian disaffection, even as Confederate armies were increasingly unable to provide patriotism-infusing victories on the battlefield, Davis was, for example, unmoved by arguments for lower postal fees so that soldiers could stay in touch with their families. He also vetoed a bill to permit free mailing of newspapers to the front.[87] Though he could be warm and even humorous in private conversation, his public manner was cold and haughty.[88]

As Bell Wiley has written, "Davis neither realized the importance of cultivating good will nor was he willing to pay the price of being a popular leader." Sure of his own rectitude and of the justice of his cause, he never believed it necessary to coax men to do their duty.[89] And though he displayed in his messages to the Confederate Congress some grasp of what was necessary to win the war and though he cannot be held solely responsible for the failure of Confederate nationalism, still he had none of the characteristics of a great national leader.[90] At a time when it was necessary to use persuasion with Congress, Davis vetoed thirty-nine bills (compared with Lincoln's six), and he became so unpopular that congressmen talked openly of deposing him.

Associated with this insensitivity was Davis's loyalty to his friends even after they had lost the confidence of the public. In 1862 when Judah Benjamin, as acting secretary of war, came under severe congressional criticism following the loss of Forts Henry and Donelson in the West and Roanoke Island on the east coast, Davis promoted him to secretary of state.[91] Similarly, Davis clung to unpopular commanders such as Braxton Bragg and John B. Pemberton, even after defeat had cost them the support both of the public and of the army, and he insisted on keeping the notorious Northrop as commissary-general.

Other charges against Davis are less justified. Although he neglected the concerns of Confederate citizens, he made tours through the South, speaking effectively and with tremendous earnestness. For example, in late 1862 the president returned to his home state of Mississippi and in a moving address to the state legislature urged them to continue the grim struggle against "a power armed for conquest and subjugation." In this address he vowed that the South could never reunite with the North.[92] But such a call to arms left no room for the conditional surrender that might have saved at least a part of the Confederacy.

The Confederate president was clearly not the ideal leader for a revolutionary cause because he was traditional in his ideas and precedent minded in his actions. Indeed he reflected the values of the society that chose him, though never in a competitive election, to be its leader. However, Davis did have a comprehensive strategic plan for the Confederacy based on "the offensive-defensive," a technical phrase meaning that "the Confederates would stand on the defensive because they had fewer men and feebler resources than the Yankees. On the other hand, they would exploit every chance to counterattack, to take the initiative, and to carry the war to the enemy." Such a plan was probably the best strategic theory of the day considering the Confederacy's political ideas along with its economic and military circumstances.[93] But the offensives were costly, and given the general commitment to retain the South's entire territory, Davis insisted on defending all of the Confederacy. Davis also understood the necessity of gaining support from Europe and emphasized the importance of alliances, but they were not to be.

On the positive side Davis was honest, courageous, and dignified. Beset with health problems, he nonetheless looked the part of the leader. As a Confederate lieutenant described him, "He bears the marks of greatness about him beyond all persons I have ever seen—A perfect head, a deep set eagle eye, an aquiline nose, and mouth and jaw sawed in steel—but above all, the gentleman is apparent, the thorough, high-bred, polished gentleman."[94]

Much of the criticism of the Confederate president fails to take into account the insuperable difficulties of his position and to realize that no other southern political leader even approached Davis in stature, although it is clear that the southern people never loved Davis as they did Lee. What the Confederacy required was a hero who transcended the talents of most mortals—able to negotiate with a prickly Congress, evaluate and shape military policy, choose effective generals, and gain the devotion of a people unprepared for war and with fewer resources than their enemy. Jefferson Davis was not that man.

## CHAPTER 13

# The Union
# Government at War

A s it faced the challenges of war, the Union government had the advantages of nearly eighty-five years of history and the respect of citizens for a familiar enterprise. But the familiar would not suffice during the Civil War. Northerners quickly had to accept innovations in the level of federal activity, the extent of its impact on individual citizens, and changes in the relations among the three branches of government.

## EARLY PRESIDENTIAL DECISIONS

In planning for a three-months' war, Lincoln acted without Congress, which was not scheduled to meet until December 1861. New to the duties of high office, the president was reluctant to incur the complications of an immediate congressional session. Furthermore, an unusual situation existed in Kentucky and Maryland, where special elections were to be held for members of the Thirty-seventh Congress. Lincoln was glad to allow time for the development of a Union party, the wartime coalition that the president hoped would foster Unionist sentiment in the South and provide a meeting ground for Republicans, Democrats, and residents of border states.[1] Hence he did not call a special session of Congress until July 1861.

The interval of eighty days between the beginning of the war and the assembling of Congress gave the president a monopoly over certain emergency powers. Using language reminiscent of Washington's at the time of the Whiskey Rebellion, he announced the existence of an "insurrection," called out the militia, and on April 19 announced a blockade of the seven states of the Confederacy; on April 27 it was extended to Virginia and North Carolina.[2] In theory the Union government did not regard the Civil War as similar to a conflict between independent nations, which under Article I, Section 8 of the U.S. Constitution required a declaration of war; it was, as the official records gathered after the war labeled it, a war of rebellion—an internal affair and therefore a civil war. (Southerners thought of it as a "war of independence" or a "war between the states.") Most northerners denounced southern belligerency as a rebellion conducted by individuals against the nation's constituted authorities, although in practice belligerent rights were conceded to the Confederate armed forces. When captured, Confederate soldiers were treated as prisoners of war; crews of Confederate privateers were treated as naval prisoners, not as privateers; southern citizens supporting the war were not punished for treason, and the conflict, with some exceptions, was conducted according to established procedures of international law regarding war.

Although the president would later be criticized, especially by members of the Democratic party, for extensions of his power—such as initiating the blockade, nationalizing the militia, and delaying the convening of Congress—the rush of patriotic activity left no time for deliberation as to legal authority. "These measures," Lincoln declared in his July 4, 1861 message, "whether strictly legal or not, were ventured upon, under what appeared to be a popular demand, and a public necessity; trusting that then as now, Congress would readily ratify them."[3]

In this spirit Lincoln authorized citizens of his own choosing to make arrangements for transporting troops and supplies. Doubting the loyalty of some government officials, he directed the secretary of the treasury to advance $2 million of unsecured public money to three wealthy New York businessmen to pay the expenses of "military and naval measures necessary for the defense and support of the government."[4] Yet the Constitution provides that "No Money shall be drawn from the Treasury, but in Consequence of Appropriations made by Law." Conscious of the irregularity, Lincoln believed the emergency excused its illegality; later he would justify exceptional uses of his authority as warranted under his role as commander in chief.

On April 27, the president suspended the writ of habeas corpus along the railroad lines threatened by possible saboteurs through Maryland and Pennsylvania. Habeas Corpus is the ancient legal right that a person held in custody must be granted a hearing. In absorbing an authority defined in Article I of the U.S. Constitution, where legislative duties and rights are considered, the president greatly expanded the executive power. Historians have explained Lincoln's actions as justified by the wartime emergency. Most believe his transgressions, considering the threat, were limited and appropriate; others note that his exposure to activist Whig principles encouraged him to view the Constitution as an agent of change.

In the Prize Cases, argued during the war, the Supreme Court retroactively considered the legitimacy of the president's actions—specifically whether the war measures taken between April 15, 1861, the date of Lincoln's proclamation of insurrection, and July 13, 1861, when Congress passed an act recognizing the existence of the insurrection, were legal. The point at issue had to do with Confederate ships captured for violating the blockade proclamations. Since there had been no congressional declaration of war, war did not legally exist when the captures were made. Hence the ships could not be legally forfeited. While the case was pending, Richard Henry Dana, the Massachusetts writer, complained of the absurdity of the situation: "In all States but ours . . . the function of the Judiciary is to interpret the acts of the Government. In ours, it is to decide their legality. . . . Contemplate a Supreme Court, deciding that this blockade is illegal! It would end the war, and how it would leave us with neutral powers, it is fearful to contemplate!"[5]

In a five-to-four decision handed down on March 10, 1863, the Supreme Court held that domestic war may begin without a declaration, that the president was bound to act without waiting for Congress "to baptize it with a name," and that the presidential proclamations were valid. Implicitly recognizing the dual nature of the war, the Court agreed that a civil conflict did not have to be declared and that Lincoln's acknowledgment of the insurrection constituted its beginning. Four justices—including eighty-six-year-old Chief Justice Taney, who still presided over a court with six members who had participated in the *Dred Scott* decision—entered the dissent. They held that the president's power of

Chief Justice Roger B. Taney, who wrote the *Dred Scott* decision, continued to preside over the Supreme Court during the war. Eighty-six years old in 1863, he dissented in the Prize Cases, arguing that the president's power of suppressing an insurrection did not justify the executive's waging a civil war.

suppressing an insurrection is not tantamount to the power of initiating a legal state of war and that civil war cannot begin with merely an executive proclamation.[6] There would be other judicial deliberations on the military actions of commanders, but the Prize Cases represented the greatest challenge to the legal legitimacy of the Lincoln government's early actions.

## THE THIRTY-SEVENTH CONGRESS

The Thirty-seventh Congress convened on July 4, 1861. With the exception of some members from Virginia and Tennessee, the states of the Confederacy were not represented. The strong-minded Thaddeus Stevens of Pennsylvania soon became one of the leaders of the lower house, guiding it toward effective war measures. Other important Republicans in the House included Owen Lovejoy of Illinois, brother of the abolitionist martyr; George Julian and Schuyler Colfax of Indiana; Frank Blair, Jr., of Missouri, a friend of Lincoln's and a future general; and, from Pennsylvania, William Kelley and John Covode. Among the prominent Democrats were William Richardson and John Logan of Illinois, the latter soon to become a general and a staunch Republican; Daniel Voorhees of Indiana; George Pendleton, Clement Vallandigham, and Samuel Cox of Ohio; and Erastus Corning of New York. Most of the lower house, as always, consisted of men who followed their leaders and did not contribute to the development of policy.

The party distribution in the House followed sectional and geographic lines. The Republican party dominated the New England, New York, and Pennsylvania delegations. The Democratic party showed some strength among the Illinois, Ohio, and Indiana delegations without controlling them; the Democrats, old-line Whigs and Know-Nothings, and the new hybrid faction of Unionists controlled the border states of Kentucky, Maryland, and Missouri. Among the moderates of the border states none was more notable than seventy-five-year-old John J. Crittenden, whose service in the Senate had started during James Monroe's presidency and had ended with Lincoln's inauguration. Now he brought to the House his Unionist, border-state ideals of Henry Clay and the Bell-Everett Constitutional Union party.

In the Senate there was much the same party and sectional division. Most of the senators from the free states, with the exception of five from New Jersey, Indiana, Oregon, and California, were Republicans. New Englanders, because they held the important committee chairmanships, shaped vital war policies. For example, Charles Sumner of Massachusetts was chairman of the committee on foreign relations; Henry Wilson, also of Massachusetts, headed the committee on military affairs; the naval committee was headed by John Hale of New Hampshire; and the finance committee, which dealt with crucial matters of revenue and expenditure, was chaired by William Fessenden of Maine.

Although earlier historians emphasized the divisions among the majority Republicans, who held 105 seats compared with the Democrats' 43, more recent studies find that senators' "conceptions about their obligations to party, to section, to their own ideology shaped their legislative behavior in ways that were anything but chaotic." Moreover, the image of vindictive Radical Republicans pitted against the more sensible coalition of Democrats and conservative Republicans overlooks the level of agreement among "the earnest men who served in the Civil War Senate." Developed by enemies, the stereotype emerged over issues relating to ending slavery, which was still a radical notion among lawmakers in 1861. And the alliance among senators who voted together on issues involving slavery and race disappeared in economic roll calls, when geography became the determining factor.[7]

Seward, Cameron, and Chase had left the Senate to join Lincoln's Cabinet. Of the thirty-one Republican senators who remained, Charles Summer was the most prominent. This eloquent son of Massachusetts had gained national attention after his vicious caning at the hands of a South Carolina congressman, Preston Brooks, in 1856. But Sumner was also respected for his antislavery convictions, as northerners increasingly came to believe that slavery was a morally unacceptable practice and that it had produced an oppressive, undemocratic society.

The Democrats, so recently the dominant party, were reduced to only ten representatives in the Senate. John C. Breckinridge represented Kentucky in the upper house. During his campaign for the presidency in 1860 and in the winter crisis of 1860–1861, he worked not for secession but for a compromise that

Going against the wishes of his own state, Kentucky's Senator John C. Breckinridge did not resign from the United States Senate, but instead entered the Confederate army.

would avert it. Now, "his loyalties, his prejudices, and perhaps his ambition pulled him in diverse directions." Like many Confederates, Breckinridge admitted that he "infinitely preferred to see a peaceful separation of these States than to see endless, aimless, devastating war, at the end of which I see the grave of public liberty and of personal freedom."[8] One of the dramatic incidents of the summer session of 1861 was a disagreement between Breckinridge and Edward Baker of Oregon, a close friend of Lincoln's, who appeared on the Senate floor in the uniform of a Union army colonel and criticized Breckinridge for his support of the enemy. Pro-Confederate in his post-Sumter attitude, Breckinridge now found himself opposed to the prevailing policy and opinion of his own state, whose legislature requested that he and his colleague, Lucius Powell, resign their seats. Without the formality of such a resignation Breckinridge entered the Confederate army; the Senate expelled him in July along with others from seceded states.[9]

In contrast to Breckinridge, Senator Andrew Johnson of Tennessee was a southerner who opposed secession. Born in Raleigh, North Carolina, the son of a hotel handyman, Johnson never attended school and began his career as a tailor's apprentice before becoming active in Tennessee politics. Elected to Congress in 1842, Johnson championed generous land policies and other help for the farmer. As that congressional rarity, a self-made man though a slaveholder, he spoke for the yeoman farmers of the South. While in the Senate, he became a persistent champion of the Homestead Bill.[10]

The border-state senators, chiefly Democrats, Know-Nothings and old-line Whigs, included James Bayard and Willard Saulsbury of Delaware, James Pearce and Thomas Hicks of Maryland, and Garrett Davis of Kentucky, who replaced Breckinridge after his expulsion. Generally theirs was the role of a loyal opposition, as they voted against much of the Republican program.

In a message sent to the members of this special session of the Thirty-seventh Congress on July 4, Lincoln reviewed the Sumter crisis, recounted the emergency measures he had taken, justified the war against the South, and appealed for the ratification of executive measures taken without congressional authority. Nearly a third of his remarks were devoted to a constitutional defense of his actions, but the president also placed the war in a larger, more democratic framework that eloquently defined Union war goals and defended the actions he had taken before Congress assembled:

> This [said the president] is essentially a People's contest. On the side of the Union, it is a struggle for maintaining in the world, that form . . . of government, whose leading object is, to elevate the condition of men—to lift artificial weights from all shoulders—to clear the paths of laudable pursuit for all—to afford all, an unfettered start, and a fair chance, in the race of life. . . .
>
> Our popular government has often been called an experiment. Two points in it, our people have already settled—the successful *establishing*, and the successful *administer-*

*ing* of it. One still remains—its successful *maintenance* against a formidable [internal] attempt to overthrow it. It is now for them to demonstrate to the world, that those who can fairly carry an election, can also suppress a rebellion—that ballots are the rightful, and peaceful, successors of bullets; and that when ballots have fairly, and constitutionally, decided, there can be no successful appeal, back to bullets. . . . Such will be a great lesson of peace; teaching men that what they cannot take by an election, neither can they take it by a war—teaching all, the folly of being the beginners of a war.

Commenting on the international significance of the existing struggle, Lincoln also expressed his views on the exceptionalism of the United States and its mission in the world:

> And this issue embraces more than the fate of these United States. It presents to the whole family of man, the question, whether a constitutional republic, or a democracy—a government of the people, by the same people—can . . . maintain its territorial integrity, against its own domestic foes. It presents the questions, whether discontented individuals . . . can . . . break up their Government, and thus practically put an end to free government upon the earth. It forces us to ask: Is there, in all republics, this inherent, and fatal weakness? Must a government, of necessity, be too *strong* for the liberties of its own people, or too *weak* to maintain its own existence?[11]

Viewing the war from such a perspective, Lincoln felt that out of necessity he must use the war power of the government and resist force employed for its destruction. Heeding the president's request that his emergency acts be ratified, Congress responded with the following resolution:

> [B]e it . . . *enacted*, That all the acts, proclamations, and orders of the President . . . [after March 4, 1861] respecting the army and navy of the United States, and calling out . . . the militia or volunteers from the States, are hereby approved and in all respects legalized and made valid . . . as if they had been issued and done under the previous express authority and direction of the Congress of the United States.[12]

In addition to this endorsement of the president's actions, the special session of July–August 1861 considered other emergency war measures. Congress passed a law recognizing that an "insurrection" existed, which amounted to a congressional declaration of war.[13] The effect of the Bull Run disaster appeared in congressional proceedings. One day after the battle, on July 22, 1861, worried about border state sentiment and anxious to win proslavery support for the Union, the House of Representatives passed the Crittenden resolution, which declared:

> That the present deplorable civil war has been forced upon the country by the disunionists of the southern States, now in arms against the constitutional Government . . . that this war is not waged on [Congress's] part in any spirit of oppression, or for any purpose of conquest or subjugation, or . . . overthrowing or interfering with the rights or established institutions of those States, but to defend and maintain the *supremacy* of

the Constitution, and to preserve the Union with all the dignity, equality, and rights of the several States unimpaired; and that as soon as these objects are accomplished the war ought to cease.[14]

If this resolution meant anything, C. Vann Woodward remarks, it meant that, "so far as both President and Congress were able to formulate war aims, this was a war of narrowly limited objectives and no revolutionary purpose. It was to be a war against secession, a war to maintain the Union—that, and nothing more."[15] But this solemn declaration, though probably reflecting the prevailing sentiment of the nation at the time, marked a passing phase in the development of legislative policy, and indeed of national war aims, which would change during the coming months.

Of more significance than the Crittenden resolution was another bill that Congress passed the day following Bull Run. It was an act authorizing the enlistment of five hundred thousand volunteers for a period of not more than three years nor less than six months. Overnight Congress had altered its conception of the struggle from a three-months' war to a three-years' war. A few days later, on July 25, the question of the length of service was more satisfactorily resolved by a supplementary act providing that volunteers be mustered to serve "during the war."

## INVESTIGATIONS BY THE THIRTY-SEVENTH CONGRESS

The attention of the Thirty-seventh Congress was not limited to legislation about the war. The manner in which it used its investigative functions, as well as its role in executive matters, is illustrated by the Joint Committee on the Conduct of the War. The committee has been criticized as an example of the intervention of politicians in military affairs and even as "a mischievous organization which assumed dictatorial powers." Such complaints ignore the fact that in a democratic society civilians exercise control over the military, that Congress's investigative power is an important tool of that body, and that the executive power is properly balanced by congressional committees.[16]

Pressure for the creation of this investigative committee came from a small group of the so-called Radicals—or Jacobins, as their enemies called them in language borrowed from the French Revolution. These Republicans were angered during the autumn of 1861 by McClellan's failure to use his army to defeat the Confederates. They visited McClellan's camp, remonstrated with him, and voiced their complaints to Lincoln. Their feelings were further aroused by the disaster at Ball's Bluff, a minor engagement that occurred on October 21, 1861.

Thirty-five miles northwest of Washington, a brigade of General Charles Stone's division, under the command of Colonel Edward Baker, attempted to cross the Potomac and was attacked by superior Confederate forces. Baker had

On October 21, 1861, Confederate troops attacked General Stone's Union division along the Potomac River. What transpired at Ball's Bluff, depicted here, helped lead to the creation of a congressional committee to report on the conduct of the war.

exceeded his instructions "to make a slight demonstration." The resulting Union losses of 49 killed, 158 wounded and 714 captured or missing mark it as a small confrontation compared with later battles, but in these early stages of the war the casualties seemed heavy and needless. And the proximity to Washington, the reliance placed on Stone's troops for the defense of the capital, the inevitable comparison of Ball's Bluff with Bull Run, and especially the death of Colonel Baker, Lincoln's close friend and recently a member of the Senate, caused legislators to demand closer congressional supervision of the war effort.

When Congress convened in December 1861, the House of Representatives unanimously passed a resolution introduced by New York's Roscoe Conkling requesting the secretary of war to report on the Ball's Bluff disaster. Additional resolutions calling for investigations by Congress were also discussed, until both houses adopted a resolution creating a committee "to inquire into the conduct of the present war." This committee consisted of three senators (Senators Benjamin Wade of Ohio, Zachariah Chandler of Michigan, and Andrew Johnson of Tennessee) who were appointed by Vice President Hannibal Hamlin, and Representatives Daniel Gooch of Massachusetts, George Julian of Indiana, John Covode of Pennsylvania, and Moses F. Odell of New York, who were appointed by Speaker of the House Galusha Grow of Pennsylvania.

Most of the committee's work was routine. Members performed useful investigations of scandals in connection with such matters as "light-draught monitors, ice contracts, heavy ordnance, employment of disloyal persons in government work, hospitals and the treatment of the wounded, and illicit trade with the Confederates." The committee, declares one scholar, "brought speed and efficiency into the conduct of the war . . . they ferreted out abuses and put their fingers down heavily upon governmental inefficiency; and . . . they labored, for a time at least, to preserve a balance and effect a co-operation between the legislative and executive departments."[17] Members also investigated abuses of military power that might well have gone unnoticed. Among them was the November 1864 Sand Creek, Colorado massacre of Arapahoes and Cheyennes who had surrendered to military authorities and were peacefully camped near Fort Lyon when a unit of Colorado militia attacked them without warning.

Assailed by opponents for its partisanship, the committee tried to remove politically conservative generals like McClellan from active command, and as one student has concluded, "was always committed to an all-out war that included the abolition of slavery as soon as possible."[18] Overall the impact of the committee came through its influence on political and military decisions and its circulation of influential pamphlets, designed to stir the North to patriotic support of the war. Yet the committee will doubtless remain best known for its investigations of Union generals.

Illustrative of this aspect of its work was its investigation of the alleged responsibility of General Stone for the Union defeat at Ball's Bluff. Stone had a fine military record. A Californian, he had been trained at West Point and had served in the Mexican War. At the request of General Scott in 1861, he was given the important task of raising, organizing, and commanding the militia and volunteers in Washington on whom the defense of the national capital first rested. Later he was promoted to the rank of brigadier general and given a division command under McClellan.

The Ball's Bluff affair was chiefly attributable to the rashness of Colonel Baker, who had exceeded instructions. But a living scapegoat was demanded. So the Committee on the Conduct of the War examined Stone's conduct, raising questions about his alleged disloyalty, his treasonable correspondence with the enemy, and his supposed contacts with Confederate officers. Wade conducted the inquiry in a manner that showed he had prejudged the case.[19] The "evidence" was kept secret; Stone was not permitted to know the charges against him or the names of the witnesses. The committee never reached any conclusion, and Stone's persistent demand for a proper military court of inquiry was refused. Yet on the strength of unsupported rumor and false testimony, he was placed under arrest in 1862 by order of Secretary Stanton and was imprisoned for over six months without a trial. Such imprisonment was contrary to the existing Articles of War, under which an officer, when arrested, was entitled to a prompt trial and a copy of the charges against him. Only in February 1863 did the committee mildly censure Stone who, a victim of both the committee and the War Department, resigned from the army in 1864.

## AN ACTIVIST CONGRESS

More important than its investigating committees was the Thirty-seventh Congress's role in formulating the public policies that taken together have been called "a second American Revolution." Just as the pressure of total war compelled the Confederate government to abandon its commitment to states' rights, so, too, did the federal government move toward increased centralization. As Leonard Curry has written, "the Thirty-seventh Congress was active in drafting the blueprint for a new social order." Emerging from prewar northern proposals and ideas for development, these legislative changes amounted to an economic transformation of lasting importance. Naturally some congressional actions such as the Confiscation Acts were war inspired, but all grew out of the same expression of developing nationalism, belief in the power of Congress and the Constitution to effect social and economic change, and a desire for further modernization. Both wartime congresses, but especially the Thirty-seventh, passed legislation accurately characterized by Senator John Sherman as "covering such vast sums, delegating and regulating such vast powers and so far-reaching in their effects, that generations will be affected well or ill by them."[20]

Among these policies were the Confiscation Acts. On August 6, 1861 Congress passed a first confiscation measure which provided for the seizure of all property used for "insurrectionary purposes." Only property used to aid the rebellion could be taken under this act, and in the justification offered by Stevens, "If their whole country [i.e., the South] must be laid waste, and made a desert, in order to save this Union from destruction, so let it be. I would rather, sir, reduce them to a condition where their whole country is to be repeopled by a band of freemen than to see them perpetrate the destruction of this people through our agency."[21] It was a political statement of the total war that would soon mark military strategy.

A year later, on July 17, 1862, the Republicans passed a more sweeping measure known as the Second Confiscation Act. The law covered three main subjects: the punishment of treason, the confiscation of property, and the emancipation of slaves. Persons convicted of treason against the United States were to be punished by death or fine and imprisonment; those concerned with "rebellion or insurrection" were to be subjected to fine, imprisonment, and the liberation of their slaves. As for confiscation, the main provision was immediate forfeiture to the United States of all real and personal property of officers of the Confederate government and a similar forfeiture, after sixty days' warning, in the case of all other persons who supported the rebellion.

Conservatives such as Browning of Illinois, Davis of Kentucky, Collamer of Vermont, and Henderson of Missouri urged that such a drastic program would ruin many civilians. Others believed that it was unjustified even as a war measure, that it was forbidden by the Constitution (which specifically prohibited the punishment of treason by the forfeiture of property beyond the lifetime of the offender), and that it amounted to a legislative bill of attainder (as opposed to a judicial action) hurting many who supported the Union. After complicated legislative maneuvers and many compromises, the final bill passed by the decisive majority of 28 to 13 in the Senate and 83 to 21 in the House, a vote that illustrated the broad agreement among the Republicans, who provided nearly all the affirmative votes.

Meanwhile Lincoln, displaying characteristic moderation, prepared a veto message of this legislation, remarking that "the severest justice may not always be the best policy." The president pointed out that the bill was unconstitutional because it declared forfeitures beyond the lives of the guilty parties and because, by legal proceedings, it "forfeited property . . . without a conviction of the supposed criminal or a personal hearing in any proceeding."[22] Eventually Congress included an explanatory joint resolution to the effect that the law was not to work forfeiture beyond the life of the accused. Because this caveat met some of his objections, Lincoln signed a measure of which he fundamentally disapproved.

In fact, the bill was something of a paper tiger. Few condemnations of property took place through proceedings in United States courts; only such rebel property as was subject to attachment by reason of location within the jurisdiction of some federal court—that is, southern-owned property within northern judicial reach—was legally confiscable. Moreover, proceedings depended largely on Attorney General Edward Bates, who made no serious effort to enforce the act, and as a result a relatively small amount of property was seized.

In a more familiar area, the lawmakers used tariff legislation to move toward a policy of government-subsidized industrialization, in marked contrast to the tendency of preceding decades, when southerners in Congress had persistently fought higher tariffs. By the 1860s most northerners had embraced a capitalistic creed that affirmed the authority of the federal government to promote development and that viewed protection as a cure for many economic ills. As Lincoln argued, higher tariffs would "secure to the workingman liberal wages, to agriculture remunerative prices, to mechanics and manufacturers an adequate reward for their skills, labor and enterprise and to the nation commercial prosperity and independence."[23]

Earlier, the tariff had entered national politics as a sectional issue, generally separating low-tariff southerners from the rest of the nation. With the Tariff of 1842 duties on imports became more a partisan than a sectional measure. The Walker Tariff, sponsored by Democrats and designed with a view to abandoning the principle of protection altogether, passed in 1846. In 1857 the tariff was further lowered, owing to the ascendancy of free-traders, southerners, and a surplus of federal revenue from existing duties. In the closing days of the Buchanan administration, the Morrill Tariff passed. Introduced by Justin Morrill of Vermont and favored by the Republicans, even this moderate, revenue-raising measure would never have been accepted had southerners been in Congress.

The year 1861 marked a new orientation toward the tariff. Though a majority of northern manufacturers were either indifferent or opposed any further changes in the tariff, the iron interests, hard hit by the Panic of 1857, demanded protection. Their pleas gained credibility when it became obvious that mounting deficits required increases in revenue. Using the principle of protection that was part of their Whig inheritance, the Republicans had earlier promised duties encouraging the development of the industrial interests of the country. Their tactics were successful in some northeastern states; "Republican and Democratic campaign managers agreed that the tariff issue enabled Lincoln to carry pivotal Pennsylvania."[24]

Then during the war, the Republican Congress, as part of its efforts to raise money, revised the tariff upward several times, motivated first by the need for additional revenue and later by the quite different principle of "compensatory" duties—that is, high tariff rates to protect American manufacturers from foreign competition during any period when companies were subjected to high internal taxes. The tariff act of August 4, 1861, with its duties on coffee, tea, sugar, spices, India rubber, and other necessary imports, was distinctly revenue producing. The act of July 14, 1862 increased the rates on articles of non-American production, gave protective increases to many articles that could be produced at home, and reduced the list of free items, which could be imported without any duties.

Compensatory protection because of wartime taxation was the chief feature of the tariff act of June 30, 1864. The nature of this tariff can be partly judged by the fact that imported tobacco was taxed at 35 cents a pound, beer at 35 cents a gallon, and brandy at $2.50 a gallon. The war ended with some duties as high as 100 percent and with the general average at about 47 percent, more than double the average in 1857. Though not all Republicans supported these high tariffs, the concept of protection was accepted by most. So too was the notion that high tariffs protected workers' jobs by restricting foreign competition and helping American industry. But the transformation of American industry, which remained in the hands of individual firms, should not be exaggerated.

Even during the war, the development of the Far West, so significant in the 1850s, continued with government aid and encouragement. Railroads were organized; Indians were progressively "eliminated" as obstacles to settlement; generous aid was given to the homesteader. Expansion in the 1840s and 1850s, the Mexican War, and the discovery of gold and silver in California and Colorado, together with fears of a sporadically threatened independent West Coast should

Congress refuse to act, had earlier led to discussions about a railway that would link the East with the Pacific coast. Ideas for a transcontinental railway by a southern route had been among the favorite projects of the Pierce administration, which bought a strip of land known as the Gadsden Purchase from Mexico in 1853. Pierce's secretary of war, Jefferson Davis, had vigorously promoted this project through government surveys and reports. Owing to sectional rivalry, however, no definite steps had been taken.

Not only did competition between the North and South obstruct progress, but so too did the clamoring of particular cities such as New Orleans, St. Louis, Memphis, and Chicago for selection as the eastern terminus. Indeed, the promotion of transcontinental railroads was one of Douglas's motives in introducing the Kansas-Nebraska Act, though during the Buchanan administration plans for a railway across the continental United States remained dormant.

After southerners left Congress, Republicans who were committed to the policy of a transcontinental railway seized their opportunity. The plan finally adopted was to create a federal corporation, the Union Pacific Railroad Company, charged with building a line westward from Omaha, then only a village. At the same time a California railroad, the Central Pacific, was to be built eastward until the tracks met. The purposes of this grand scheme were to "form a continuous line of railroad from the Missouri River to the navigable waters of the Sacramento . . . and thereby to unite the railroad system of the Eastern States with that of California, strengthen the bonds of union between the Atlantic and Pacific coasts, develop the immense resources of the great central portion of the North American continent, and create a new route for commerce from the Atlantic and Europe to the Pacific and Asia."[25]

To this end, in 1862 federal statutes guaranteed rights-of-way, extinguished Indian titles, and delivered millions of acres of public land to a privately owned venture. As Philip Paludan has written, "such generous grants to private corporations inspired some harsh criticism." But the practice of trading land for railroad building was "another mixed heritage of the war, reflecting the ambiguous nature of an economy just entering the modern age . . . The wartime mentality made it easy to equate the benefits that rails would bring to the nation with the profits to be made by government-encouraged private industry."[26]

Also critical to westward development was the Homestead Act. Before the war the federal government had become increasingly generous in the disposal of the public domain at cheap rates to homesteaders. The government had also, with less justification, permitted the private exploitation of its vast stores of timber and mineral wealth. The plan to "give every poor man a home" had seized the imagination of pioneers, whether from older settlements in the United States or from Europe. Certainly the Republicans had attracted many votes with the homestead plank in their 1860 platform. Illustrative of the effectiveness of this issue was an article in a Nebraska paper in September 1860. Under the heading "Let It Be Remembered," the writer protested that neither the Douglas nor the Breckinridge Democratic platforms mentioned a homestead bill, and that the Douglas convention, while ignoring this vital subject, had passed a resolution favoring the acquisition of Cuba, thus "saying to the farmer on the Western frontiers, 'we care nothing about you or your rights, all we desire is to extend the area of slave Territory.'"[27] But on a positive note, railroad advocates who shared the nationalistic views of the Republicans insisted that a transcontinental railroad would make the United States "the greatest nation on earth."[28]

In 1860 President Buchanan, questioning the power of Congress to give land to individuals, also objected that homestead legislation discriminated against previous settlers whose property would be depressed in value, and favored farmers over mechanics. For these reasons he vetoed the homestead bill. Two years later in May 1862, the Homestead Act became law by a vote that reflected sectional as well as political tensions. In the final version a quarter section of 160 acres of unoccupied land was to be given to homesteaders for nominal fees after five years of actual residence. During the year ending June 1864, farmers settled on 1,261,000 new acres under the operation of the act, and thereafter the law provided land for thousands of farmers. Yet much of the land homesteaded was either too dry or too small for cattle operations or in other ways insufficient to support the intended purpose of supporting a family farm. In fact, speculators acquired nearly fifty million acres between 1864 and 1869. Thus "the act fostered the illusion that the United States was a nation of sturdy, independent yeoman farmers while in actuality the nation was rushing headlong toward industrialism."[29]

Another wartime measure of lasting importance which was passed by Congress in June 1862 established state "agricultural and mechanical colleges" through the aid of federal land grants. Dedicated to the development of higher education, the bill was called the Morrill Land-Grant Act after Justin S. Morrill of Vermont, who sponsored the movement in Congress, though the final bill was introduced by Senator Wade of Ohio. Three features of the plan, which had been developed originally by Jonathan Turner, a professor at Illinois College, were crucial: first, the federal government must donate land, not money; second, all states must be treated alike in proportion to population, the older states having the same consideration as those in which public lands were still unsold; and third, beneficiaries must emphasize practical education for agricultural and industrial pursuits.

From 1857 to 1862, Morrill had struggled for the adoption of a congressional measure incorporating all three aspects of Turner's plan. Such a plan passed the House in 1858, but was delayed in the Senate by the opposition of mostly southerners, including Jefferson Davis of Mississippi, Clement Clay of Alabama, and James Mason of Virginia. Clay objected particularly to the fact that it "treats the

States as agents instead of principals, as the creatures, instead of the creators of the Federal government." Finally the bill passed the Senate in 1859 but was vetoed by President Buchanan, whose constitutional objections were intensified by the existing depression with its resulting governmental deficits.

By the act's provisions established during the war, each state was granted thirty thousand acres of public land for each senator and representative in Congress. Proceeds from sales were to support colleges "to teach such branches of learning as are related to agriculture and the mechanical arts." Though the benefits of the act were at first confined to the Union states, its terms were later extended to all states. In time the effects of this legislation on American higher education were profound. Some states used the land to create new schools. Twenty-two states added the money from land sales to existing schools.[30] In this way important state institutions such as Cornell, the University of Wisconsin and the University of California were established or improved.

Overall the Thirty-seventh Congress, which adjourned in March 1863, enacted a program that had been discussed in some form for several decades. But during the war intentions became realities as public policies extended and consolidated the power of the central state. It is possible to exaggerate the impact of this program during a period in which the federal government continued to depend on market forces and the private sector, with the outstanding exception being the federally administered arsenals that produced tents and uniforms.[31] Still, most historians agree that the second session was one of the most productive in American history because of its adoption of legislation that approved land-grant colleges, a Pacific railroad, a Homestead Act, and the high tariffs that displayed the understanding that government assistance would be at the service of entrepreneurs and private interests.[32] In nearly every instance of progressive legislation, Congress, not the president, took the initiative, although Lincoln generally supported this program.

Of course the Civil War was not the only war in which business and government have linked hands. But as part of this new understanding of American nationalism, congressmen, like other Americans, expressed their faith in the Union's future. Thus, the act for the Pacific railroad was described as "striking proof of the unconquerable determination of the nation and an unfaltering faith in its ability to preserve its territorial integrity." According to Secretary of the Interior John Usher, "Had it been deemed possible that our country could fall a prey to rebellion and its dissevered parts become subjected to . . . separate and alien governments, the construction of such a work would never have been undertaken and its execution would have been impracticable."[33] Even in a republic threatened by disruption and ruin, the lawmakers thought in terms of an enduring nation. In a variety of ways, Lincoln and the Thirty-seventh Congress laid the foundation for a new United States.

## OPPOSITION TO THE GOVERNMENT

Not every northerner accepted either the president's extensions of executive authority or the congressional program enacted by the Republicans. Democrats especially believed that the Lincoln administration violated the principle that the government itself is always under the law. No matter what the circumstances, it must not be arbitrary; its agents, including Union commanders, must be held punishable or liable for damages if they wrongfully invaded private rights. Even during a civil war the government, according to this position, must not overstep international law or violate treaties; it must keep within what are called the "laws of war"; it must not ignore certain rights of enemy citizens during military occupations; it must not destroy the civil liberties of its own people.

The Civil War caused the Lincoln administration to challenge these standards, engendering criticism that should be evaluated in the context of partisan denunciation by Democrats, some of whom regretted a war they blamed on the Republicans. The most outspoken critics of Lincoln were conservative Democrats who exaggerated the growing power of the federal government into a tyrannical oppression. In some states this partisan opposition was fueled by the farmers' concern over the eastern industrialists' apparent domination of the nation's economic policies.[34] In Indiana Lincoln's opponents gained control of the legislature, forcing Governor Oliver Morton to find unofficial ways of obtaining funds. In Illinois the "Copperheads" (the contemporary term of reproach for those Democrats who were outspoken in their opposition to the Lincoln administration) controlled the 1863 legislature. Though they denounced secession and supported the Union, they so embarrassed Governor Richard Yates with their agitation for an armistice that the governor prorogued (discharged) the legislature.

The most extreme of these Democrats, along with various adventurers and crackpots, organized associations that were promptly exaggerated into large-scale conspiracies by Republicans. While Republicans were forming their own associations called Union Leagues, Democrats particularly in Ohio, Indiana, and Illinois established an organization variously known as the "Knights of the Golden Circle," the "Order of American Knights," and later the "Sons of Liberty." With the passwords that typically characterized such male fraternities, they carried on their activities in supposed secrecy. In fact both the federal and state governments had infiltrated informers who reported on their activities. It is now clear that the main purpose of the "Knights" was to promote the success of the Democratic party, and today's historians do not accept the view that the group was dangerous.

At the time, however, according to a report by Judge Advocate General Joseph Holt, these secret societies, magnified into a membership of hundreds of thousands of members, were communicating with the enemy and were also seeking to promote Union defeat and to overthrow the government. Holt estimated that there were 75,000 to 125,000 members in Indiana, 100,000 to 140,000 in Illinois, and perhaps as many as 200,000 in other states. Such exaggerations led overzealous provost marshals to arrest civilians on the basis of signed affidavits, sometimes prepared for the sake of settling a wartime grudge. Others were arrested for aiding desertion, discouraging enlistment, resisting arrest, destroying enrollment lists, and circulating disloyal literature. More serious accusations included recruiting for the enemy, distributing arms and ammunition so that "rebel" raids in the North might be assisted from the rear, plotting the release of Confederate prisoners, and planning the creation of a "Northwest Confederacy" that by dividing the North would promote Confederate success. Though some of the bolder schemes of the Knights seemed treasonous, their leaders, such as Clement Vallandigham, denied any disloyal activity. And certainly the main interest of the Order was to oppose Republican control of the government and to urge peace with reunion through negotiation.

In addition to these southern sympathizers, agents of the Confederacy were also occasionally caught committing sabotage against Unionists in border states and the Midwest by stealing military supplies, destroying bridges, engaging in bushwhacking, mapping fortifications, intimidating voters, and otherwise assisting the enemy. In time the Copperheads became a "secret society scarecrow," leading naive army commanders to extend their authority over civilians. "The Republican-constructed myths about copperhead secret sources served [the party's] purposes well," writes Frank Klement. "It was a political apparition which appeared on the eve of elections. Lincoln's supporters had succeeded in stigmatizing the opposition party and at the same time, they made a contribution to American mythology."[35]

Responding to these challenges, Congress passed the Conspiracies Act on July 31, 1861, and the Treason Act (also known as the Second Confiscation Act) on July 17, 1862. The Conspiracies Act established fines and imprisonment for those who plotted to overthrow the government or opposed governmental authority. The Treason Act softened the existing death penalty for treason to imprisonment and fine. Neither of these laws, however, effectively punished antiwar activities in the North.

Throughout the war the application of the Treason and Conspiracies acts was limited and restrained. Certainly some overzealous grand juries brought unnecessary indictments, but the typical procedure was to keep such indictments on the docket from term to term, while the offenders remained free. Eventually the indictments were dropped. Attorney General Bates had no interest in such prosecutions. In fact he resented the use of the courts for proceedings in which a conviction would be difficult to obtain. Moreover, such a verdict, by rendering the victim a martyr, might be more embarrassing than an acquittal.

Instead of enforcing statutes and conducting prosecutions in the courts, Lincoln suspended the habeas corpus privilege and resorted to arrest by executive authority. In the early part of the war suspensions were restricted to definite locations specified in presidential proclamations, beginning with that of April 27, 1861, which covered an area from Washington to Philadelphia. Later in 1861 Secretary Seward, who controlled a secret service organization with agents located at strategic points to seize suspected persons, took charge of these arrests. Passports were required of anyone entering or leaving the country, and those persons considered dangerous were intercepted. Prisoners were not told why they were seized, and often Seward's department never brought charges.

In February 1862 two important steps were taken. As part of an effort to reorganize procedures and end any arrests on vague charges of disloyalty, a sweeping order provided for the wholesale release of political prisoners. The control of arrests was now transferred from the State Department to the War Department under Stanton. A special commission, consisting of Judge Edwards Pierrepont and John A. Dix, was appointed to operate under the secretary of war in order to examine individual cases. On the recommendation of this commission many prisoners were released in 1862.

On September 24, 1862, Lincoln issued a general proclamation providing that during the existing "insurrection" all persons discouraging enlistment, resisting the draft, or guilty of any disloyal practice were subject to martial law and liable to trial by court-martial or military commission. The number of arrests under this order and others that involved the withholding of normal constitutional guarantees has recently been revised downward to 5,443. The earlier figure of 13,535 civilian military arrests, apparently included individuals who "would have been arrested whether the writ was suspended or not. [Arrests] were caused by the mere incidents or function of war which produced refugees, informers, guides, Confederate defectors, carriers of contraband goods." Such persons were hardly "political," nor were their arrests "arbitrary." "In fact," writes Mark Neely, "many detentions involved both former citizens of Confederate states and army deserters."[36]

## THE MERRYMAN, VALLANDIGHAM, AND MILLIGAN CASES

Several famous controversies symbolizing the nature of the opposition to Lincoln resulted from military arrests. In Maryland in the spring of 1861, John Merryman, an officer of a secessionist drill company, was arrested, taken into military custody by order of General George Cadwalader, commander of the department, and confined in Fort McHenry. After a petition for a writ of habeas corpus was presented to Roger Taney, the chief justice caused the writ to be served, directing Cadwalader to produce Merryman in court so that the case for imprisonment might be judicially examined. Cadwalader's instructions, however, were to hold persons whose offenses were like Merryman's and to refuse to produce prisoners where habeas corpus writs were issued. Citing the president's suspension of the writ, he refused to produce the prisoner. Taney then issued a writ of attachment for contempt against the general, but the marshal seeking to serve this writ was refused entrance to the fort.

The next stage in this confrontation between judicial and military authority occurred when the chief justice prepared an opinion denying the president's right to suspend the writ, and insisting on the chief executive's obligation to enforce the "civil process of the United States." The right to suspend, he declared in an opinion while on circuit duty, belonged only to Congress; the president had no power to effect such suspension himself. Since civilian courts were open, Taney maintained that any suspected treason should have been reported to the district attorney and dealt with by judicial process. Denouncing Lincoln's act as usurpation, he challenged the president to maintain constitutional guarantees. As a legal matter the case rested there. Merryman, who was never charged, was free six weeks after his arrest.

Following his criticism of the war, Clement Vallandigham (seated in the center) was arrested and tried by a military court. After Vallandigham's sentence was commuted by Lincoln from imprisonment to banishment to the Confederacy, Vallandigham went to Canada.

Although the Merryman case did not reach the Supreme Court and only the opinion of one member is on record, another case involving the suspension of civil liberties—that of Clement Vallandigham, a Democratic politician from Ohio—did. On May 1, 1863, Vallandigham delivered a speech in Mount Vernon, Ohio, asserting that the war could easily have been concluded by negotiation or by the acceptance of French mediation, but that the administration needlessly prolonged the bloodshed. The war, he said, was not for the Union, but for the liberation of blacks and the enslavement of whites. After his speech Vallandigham was arrested for violating General Order No. 38. Under the military prerogative of generals to control local opposition to the draft, General Ambrose Burnside on April 19, 1863 had issued a broad command that "the habit of declaring sympathies for the enemy [would] be no longer tolerated" and that offenders would be punished by military procedure.[37]

Many Democrats argued that Vallandigham had not denounced Burnside, and that he had neither advocated resistance to military orders nor attacked conscription. Instead he counseled resistance to the Lincoln administration by means of the ballot and free discussion.[38] Nevertheless, by Burnside's order, Vallandigham was placed under military arrest under provisions of Lincoln's proclamation of September 24, 1862, which authorized military trials for those who obstructed the war effort. Denied the protection of habeas corpus, he was tried by a military commission. Though the former congressman denied the jurisdiction of the military court, the judge advocate entered a plea of not guilty, and the trial proceeded with the safeguards for the accused that are customary in such military proceedings. The commission found Vallandigham guilty of declaring disloyal opinions with the object of weakening the government, and he was sentenced to prison. Making full use of his notoriety, on May 5, 1863 Vallandigham issued from "a military bastile" in Cincinnati a stirring appeal "To the Democracy of Ohio," in which he summarized his position: "I am a Democrat—for the Constitution, for law, for the Union, for liberty—this is my only 'crime.' "[39]

An embarrassed president understood the potential harm of Vallandigham's martyrdom to his party and nation and advised Burnside: "All the cabinet regretted the necessity of arresting . . . Vallandigham, some perhaps, doubting, that there was a real necessity for it."[40] On the other hand, the administration wished to guard against the effect of an immediate release that might be interpreted as weakness. Lincoln extricated himself from the dilemma by commuting Vallandigham's sentence from imprisonment to banishment to the Confederacy. Later Vallandigham was delivered across the lines to a startled Confederate captain. The famous Democrat knew his role. Proclaiming himself a citizen of Ohio and the United States, he surrendered as a prisoner of war.

By summer Vallandigham was in Canada where he issued proclamations denouncing "the despots in Washington" and asserting his determination "to recover the liberties of which he had been deprived . . . or perish in the attempt."

Nominated by the Democratic party for the governorship of Ohio, he became the first American to campaign for public office while in exile. For the rest of the war his case served northern Democrats as a popular symbol of Republican tyranny. Vallandigham was routed in the gubernatorial election, but his circumstances—the supposedly illegal arrest, the military trial, and the unusual punishment—provided a partisan focal point for Democrats' opposition to the war.

The case also revealed the inherent conflict between Lincoln's executive power to authorize military trials and congressional directives in the form of the Habeas Corpus, Indemnity, [and] Removal Act of March 3, 1863. The latter required that all political prisoners be brought before federal civilian grand juries within twenty days of their arrest. It also required that the secretary of state and the secretary of war furnish federal judges the names of northerners under arrest and that military officers having custody of such prisoners obey the orders of the civil courts.[41]

Meanwhile, the Vallandigham case came to the Supreme Court on a motion to review the sentence of the military commission. The defense counsel argued that the prisoner had been tried on a charge unknown to the law; that the military commission had exceeded its jurisdiction; and that the Supreme Court of the United States, as the only remedy for such excess of authority, had the power to review the proceedings. In an opinion taken from the argument of Judge Advocate General Joseph Holt, in 1864 the Supreme Court refused to review the case, declaring that its authority, derived from the Constitution and the Judiciary Act of 1789, did not extend to the proceedings of a military commission.[42]

After the war, however, a different opinion emerging from a different case was issued by the Supreme Court. The case originated in the arrest in Indianapolis on October 5, 1864 of Lambdin Milligan, who with several associates was sentenced to be hanged. A member of the Order of American Knights, Milligan was accused of taking part in a conspiracy to release Confederate prisoners and then march with this anti-Union force into Kentucky and Missouri. His hanging was set for May 19, 1865, but execution was postponed pending an appeal to the United States Supreme Court.

On April 3, 1866, in an opinion written by David Davis, the Court decided that Milligan's trial by military commission was illegal. "Martial law cannot arise from a *threatened* invasion. The necessity must be actual and present; the invasion real, such as effectually closes the courts and deposes the civilian administration. . . . Martial rule can never exist where the courts are open, and in the proper and unobstructed exercise of their jurisdiction. It is . . . confined to the locality of actual war."[43] No doubt such a conclusion was easier to entertain during peacetime.

At the same time the Supreme Court did not question the suspension of the writ of habeas corpus during the war—an outcome feared by Attorney General

Bates—or the arrests of uncharged civilians. After this decision Milligan was re-leased. Later he pressed for damages in a civil suit against General Hovey, under whose order he had been arrested, though the damages awarded were minimal. The practical implications of *ex parte Milligan* were few, and the case had, ac-cording to a recent evaluation, "little effect on history,"[44] although it had impor-tant implications for the use of military commissions in the South during Reconstruction.

## MEASURING LINCOLN'S ACTIONS

Ever respectful of the opposition, Lincoln defended his extraconstitutional measures in his message to Congress on July 4, 1861, as well as in several letters, especially the "Birchard letter" and the "Corning letter." His main explanation was to argue the critical nature of the emergency and the inability of the courts to deal with organized rebellion. When citizens protested the arrest of an agitator, Lincoln referred to the death penalty for deserters and then asked, "Must I shoot a simple-minded soldier boy who deserts while I must not touch a hair of a wiley [sic] agitator who induces him to desert?" Any extreme methods, Lincoln showed, were not for partisan advantage, not even for punishment, but for a pre-cautionary purpose. In contrast to judicial prosecutions intended in peacetime as punishment for deeds committed, he held that arrests in cases of "rebellion" were made "not so much for what has been done, as for what probably would be done." The purpose, he explained, was "preventive," not "vindictive."[45]

Other Republicans, including Attorney General Bates and the distinguished Philadelphia lawyer Horace Binney, justified the president's course.[46] In their view, there was no violation of the Constitution, since that instrument permits suspension of the habeas corpus privilege when the public safety requires it dur-ing a rebellion. Nor did the Constitution specify which branch of the govern-ment is to exercise the suspending power. Although the habeas corpus clause appears in Article I, the legislative article, this was not evidence that the original intention of the founding fathers meant such suspension to belong exclusively to Congress, inasmuch as the clause was debated at the Constitutional Convention with judicial issues and was grouped with the legislative clauses as an after-thought by the committee on style.

The question of arbitrary arrests was not entirely clarified by the Habeas Cor-pus Act of March 3, 1863, a measure that left the main issue—the president's right to suspend—precisely where it had been before. This law provided that "during the present rebellion, the President of the United States, whenever, in his judgment, the public safety may require it, is authorized to suspend the privi-lege of the writ of habeas corpus in any case throughout the United States, or any part thereof."[47] Thus the president's authority to suspend was recognized, while in the future lists of political prisoners were to be sent to the federal courts, and if grand juries found no indictments against them, they were to be released. Yet officials often were negligent in furnishing lists of prisoners to the courts, and courts in some areas did not control the situation.

Despite the exaggerations of biased postwar accounts such as John A. Marshall's *American Bastile*, which estimated that "military prisons contained ten to twenty thousand men, besides women and children,"[48] Lincoln hardly behaved like a dictator. He did not think of suppressing Congress and governing without it. He did not pack Congress or eject the opposition. There was nothing in his administration comparable to a Napoleonic *coup d'état* or a Cromwellian purging of Parliament, and sometimes the excesses were those of military commanders acting without consultation. No party emblem was adopted as the flag of the country. No rule for the universal saluting of Lincoln was imposed. There was no Lincoln party constituting a superstate and visiting vengeance on political opponents, although for the first time in American history, there was "a nearly complete fusion of party and state."[49] Criminal violence was not employed after the fashion of modern dictatorships. No advantage was taken of the emergency to force arbitrary rule on the country or to promote personal ends. Lincoln even expected to be defeated in 1864. The Constitution was stretched, but it was not subverted.

Nor did the president extinguish freedom of speech and press. Although Vallandigham was banished in 1863 for making a speech, he spoke with equal violence in 1864 without penalty. There were a number of instances of suppressing newspapers. The Chicago *Times*, an anti-Lincoln paper, was suspended by General Burnside's later military order in June 1863 because of "disloyal and incendiary sentiments," but Burnside's order was promptly revoked by the president. In May 1864, the New York *World* and the *Journal of Commerce* were suspended for publishing a bogus proclamation of the president calling for four hundred thousand men and naming a day of public humiliation and prayer. This hoax was not so much a deliberate falsification by the management of the papers (though their antiadministration bias was evident) as it was a trick to rig the stock market. Three days after the suspension, the papers were allowed to resume. Various other newspapers, including the Louisville *Courier*, the New Orleans *Crescent*, the *South* of Baltimore, the Baltimore *Gazette* and the Philadelphia *Evening Journal*, were temporarily suppressed or suspended.

The larger fact, however, is that the government generally refrained from controlling the news. It did not force the publication of planted articles; nor did it censor. Scores of newspapers throughout the country, including some prominent ones, continually published abusive articles about the Lincoln administration without being shut down. Lincoln expressed his views as to the appropriate course to be taken toward newspapers in a letter to General Schofield: "[You] will only arrest individuals, and suppress assemblies, or newspapers, when they may be working *palpable* injury to the Military in your charge; and, in no other case will you interfere with the expression of opinion in any form, or allow it to be interfered with violently by others. In this, you have a discretion to exercise with great caution, calmness, and forbearance."[50]

As the Civil War was unique in American history, so was the Lincoln administration unique in its methods. That it departed from some aspects of civil liberty is obvious; that it stretched and at times seemed to ignore the Constitution is evident. The arbitrary arrests cannot be passed over lightly; to do so would devalue civil guarantees. On the other hand, even with an enemy on the country's borders and subversive individuals and organizations inside its boundaries, Lincoln never considered the overthrow of the civilian government. Leniency tempered even the harshest of regulations, and the president was generous in releasing political prisoners, whom he refused to treat as war criminals. Despite the provocation, constitutional government survived the war.

## CHAPTER 14

Financing the
War in the North

The Civil War was an expensive proposition for both sides, but the North held significant advantages in its ability to pay wartime costs. Its Treasury Department was already established, with dependable sources of revenue in custom duties and land sales. But such peacetime means did not suffice, and the story of financing the war involved efforts to find other means of financing the conflict that would bind citizens to the cause, enable the government to pay its bills, and prevent the rampant inflation that demoralized the Confederates.

Struggling to meet its costs, the government faced the critical issue of extracting more funds from its citizens than it had in the prewar period. In the 1850s the federal government never took in more than $63 million annually, with expenditures in the same range. By 1862 the costs of the war were $2 million a day. In the four years of the war the costs to the Union were roughly $3.4 billion, as the annual national budget grew to twelve times that of a typical year a decade earlier.

In trying to finance the war, the federal government faced difficulties imposed by a political and economic system marked by unregulated capitalist markets. The control of banking by individual states and privately owned banks as well as the absence of any easily expandable source of revenue also challenged the efforts of policy makers to pay for the war. In time the federal government developed many methods of raising money, and to some degree these arrangements changed the nation's political economy.[1]

## GENERAL ISSUES AND PROBLEMS

In 1861, the American economy, despite important pockets of industrial development, was basically agricultural, with manufacturing its fastest-growing segment.[2] National income, estimated at $4.3 billion, amounted to $140 per capita, and there was neither sufficient private investment nor personal savings for the government to borrow. The nation's inelastic revenue system, which did not include either excise or income taxes, depended on customs duties and the sales of public land. There was no central bank to oversee borrowing. On the contrary, sixteen hundred state banks issued their own currencies; this paper money, added to those of private concerns, amounted to seven thousand different kinds of bank notes circulated.[3]

Attempting to meet its wartime needs, Lincoln's administration resorted to every available method of raising money: borrowing, taxing, issuing paper money, finding markets for Union bonds through a new federal banking system, and eventually creating a huge national debt of $2.6 billion. Although the amount of change should not be exaggerated, the creation of a large national debt altered the banking system, as well as the makeup and structure of the nation's investment sources. It also fostered the emergence of a new class of financiers who were dependent on the effectiveness of federal fiscal operations.[4]

In the short run, the United States government financed the war chiefly by loans and paper money that inflated the currency. In comparison to the amount obtained from these sources, the sum collected through taxes was small. In the first year of the war, loans exceeded taxes eight to one. As the war progressed, however, the ratio of loans to taxes decreased, until by 1865 it was less than three to one.[5] Overall, in a difference that reflected and in turn affected civilian morale, the Union raised 26 percent of its revenues through taxes, compared with the Confederacy's 1 percent.

War loans took various forms, constituting a miscellaneous indebtedness that required a thorough "refunding" after the war. The most crucial features of the wartime borrowing were the immense issues of paper money and the numerous short-term loans at high interest rates. The obligations for three years at 7.3 percent interest[6] added considerably to the cost of the war because the terms were so disadvantageous to the government. The total amount received from loans, including treasury notes for the four fiscal years from 1862 to 1865, was $2.6 billion, as compared with $667 million received from taxes.[7]

## TREASURY DEPARTMENT PROPOSALS FOR TAXES AND LOANS

For the head of the Treasury Department, Lincoln had made a political choice. Ohio's Salmon Chase was an antislavery leader, a free-soil organizer, and an anti-Douglas Democrat who had joined the Republican party over the slavery issue. Chase, who lacked financial experience, had no sooner taken office than he discovered that the treasury faced a fiscal crisis. Since 1857, declining tariff revenues had obliged the government to resort to deficit financing, and so great had been the distrust of Buchanan's administration in financial circles that Chase's predecessors had been obliged to make short-term borrowing the principal fea-

Once chosen for Lincoln's cabinet, Salmon P. Chase inherited the problems of the Treasury Department. Chase was able to maintain national credit and raise money to continue funding the war. Although political disputes with Lincoln forced Chase to resign as secretary of the treasury, Lincoln named him chief justice.

ture of government finance.[8] Facing a nearly empty treasury and a mounting pile of requisitions, Chase soon learned the hazards of his position.

A successful wartime secretary of treasury would have to consult with congressmen about financial bills, obtain money from bankers and investors, prepare estimates of revenue and expenditure in a time of uncertainty and of unscientific budgets, devise new schemes of currency and banking, and administer confiscation laws for the seizure of captured and abandoned property in the South. To Chase fell the principal responsibility of persuading government officers as well as American citizens that some financial sacrifices were necessary, that these must not hurt morale, and that certain fiscal operations must be centralized. He was aided by a group of Republican lawmakers who asserted the power of the federal government to control the nation's finances and who implemented this necessity by creating financial institutions such as a national banking system and currency.[9]

Chase's first report as secretary of treasury had an unfortunate effect. Bankers had hoped that he would outline an adequate tax program. Instead he indicated that the government would rely on borrowing. At this moment, in December 1861, a storm broke over the *Trent* affair, with its threat of war with Britain over the seizure by Union forces of Confederate envoys aboard a British ship. Although this international emergency was entirely beyond Chase's control, it had economic repercussions. National credit declined; government securities could not be sold through the banks; depositors withdrew their funds. Meanwhile, under the terms of the 1846 Independent Treasury Act, New York banks, some of which did buy government bonds in 1861, were forced to pay in gold and transfer $63 million worth of their bullion reserves to federal vaults. In December 1861 they ran out of money and suspended specie payments.[10]

Unable to sell government bonds in the New York and Philadelphia markets after this, Secretary Chase made Jay Cooke and Company the major subscription agent for the distribution of United States bonds to the public at large. The firm was to be paid one-fourth of 1 percent of the value of its bond sales, a rate that made Cooke rich and established him as the most important financier of the Civil War. Benefiting from Cooke's agencies throughout the country, his lavish use of newspaper advertising, and his vivid appeals to workingmen to put their savings into government bonds, the loans were quickly marketed. In less than a year Cooke had sold more than $320 million of these securities.

Some Americans objected to the influence of a private citizen over public fiscal concerns, and others grumbled that through syndicates of wealthy bankers, East Coast purchasers held a disproportionate percentage of the bonds and interest-bearing notes, which in time would become an excellent investment. The Democratic New York *World* questioned Chase's giving Cooke "a monopoly of the five-twenty funding instead of doing business by accredited assistant treasurers in the different cities."[11] Yet, at the beginning of the war, Chase and the Treasury

Jay Cooke was the most important financier of the Civil War. His company distributed U.S. bonds—which totaled well over $1 billion—to the public.

Department were compelled to accept the adverse conditions imposed by Cooke and the bankers, partly because Chase repeatedly subverted an attempt by Congress to suspend the hard-money provisions of the Independent Treasury Act.[12]

Making an arrangement with Cooke and other financiers to retail bonds was not the only innovation in federal financial policies forced by the bankers' suspension of specie payments in December 1861. Expecting a short war and reluctant to burden citizens, Congress at first levied inadequate taxes. But in time Congress installed far higher taxes than Chase had originally recommended. The legislature also authorized the printing of unbacked paper money to substitute for gold.

Since customs duties, which in the past had raised 90 percent of the nation's revenues, were now insufficient, the chief taxes were internal. The "direct tax" law of August 5, 1861 reflected the government's initial approach to the process of extracting financial resources. Each state was given its quota of the tax, apportioned by population, as provided by the Constitution. By basing the tax on numbers, not ability to pay, this system raised only $17 million of an anticipated $20 million. The federal government even tried to collect the tax in the South and to enforce penalties for its nonpayment by southerners.

The income tax, which from a modern point of view should have been the mainstay of the treasury, became another new revenue source. Passed overwhelmingly in August 1861, the first bill set a very low, fixed rate of 3 percent on all incomes over eight hundred dollars a year, lowered in 1862 to six hundred dollars.[13] On June 30, 1864, the rates were raised and slightly graduated so that incomes from six hundred dollars to five thousand dollars carried a rate of 5 percent (with an exemption of $600). On incomes from five thousand dollars to ten thousand the rate rose to 7½ percent, and to 10 percent on amounts over ten thousand dollars. Anxious to offset the irritation of farmers over land taxes, Congress was reluctant to go further in taxing income, despite its conviction that any wartime taxation policies must be dependent on the ability to pay.[14]

This first income tax ever levied by the United States government collected $346,911,760 in the decade from 1863 to 1872.[15] The sum collected between 1863 and 1865, however, amounted to only $82,000,000 because of the high exemption levels, the low rates, and the deductions, which included any income from federal securities. The income tax had a distinctly regional impact, with residents of the Northeast paying nearly three-quarters of the revenues in 1864. In a reflection of the distribution of personal income throughout the Union, residents in just three states—New York, Pennsylvania, and Massachusetts—paid 60 percent of the tax.

Clearly the income tax, which helped convince the financial community that the government could pay interest on its bonds, was an expandable precedent for raising money, just as it represented a more modern, progressive form of public finance. It also marked a significant feature of the Civil War in the North—the

THE IMPACT OF INCOME TAXATION:
GEOGRAPHIC DISTRIBUTION OF INCIDENCE
OF INCOME TAX, 1864

*Percent of National Total*

| State | | Region | |
|-------|------|--------|------|
| New York | 34.3 | Northeast | 74.9 |
| Pennsylvania | 13.8 | New England | 20.0 |
| Massachusetts | 13.2 | Middle Atlantic | 54.9 |
| Ohio | 7.4 | Midwest | 14.6 |
| Illinois | 3.6 | Great Plains | 2.8 |
| Maryland | 3.4 | South | 3.0 |
| California | 3.2 | Far West | 3.6 |
| Connecticut | 3.0 | | |
| New Jersey | 3.0 | | |
| Rhode Island | 2.4 | | |

Source: From Robert Stanley, *Dimensions of Law in the Service of Order: The Origins of the Federal Income Tax* (New York, 1993), 41.

increase in congressional power and the expansion of the state into the financial lives of Americans, as congressional Republicans used the authority of the federal government to extract more financial resources from its wealthier citizens. After the military and naval departments, the Internal Revenue Service, soon organized into 185 collection districts, became the government agency that most touched northern lives. Americans who had no previous contact with their central government except for the postal service now had to reveal information about their income; if it was over six hundred dollars, they were compelled to pay a tax to the United States Treasury.[16]

Other important wartime taxes included various internal revenue duties. The excise was a subject about which the American people held bad memories, their hostile attitude reaching back through the 1794 Whiskey Rebellion into colonial days. Despite this heritage, excise taxes provided the bulk of the federal tax revenues. The Internal Revenue Act of July 1, 1862 had been broadly written as an attempt to tax everything, and it included some elements of a contemporary value-added system. With regard to a carriage, for instance, the leather, cloth, wood, and metal were taxed as raw materials; the manufacturer was taxed for the process of putting them together; the dealer was taxed for selling the carriage; and the purchaser, having paid a price sufficient to cover these various levies, was additionally taxed for its ownership. So it went with other materials, as well as banks, insurance, and railroad companies. Butchers paid thirty cents for every cow slaughtered, and through the necessity of purchasing licenses even the professions were subject to this far-ranging form of taxation. All sorts of manufacturers contributed 3 percent in a system that relied on tangible forms of wealth.

After mostly partisan votes as it moved through the House and Senate with Democrats in opposition and Republicans in favor, the internal revenue bill, in its final form, enumerated various taxes on everything from professional services to inheritances to "sin" taxes on liquor, tobacco, and playing cards.[17] Rates of taxation were later raised. As a result, in 1864–1865, the internal revenue system, including the income tax, produced $209 million, in all a quarter of its needs.[18] Accustomed to a weak federal government from the administrations of Polk, Taylor and Fillmore, Pierce, and Buchanan, Americans now encountered a more powerful state, whose tendency was, in both the Union and the Confederacy, to augment its power in this emergency, to centralize its activities, and to appropriate an increased share of the economy to public uses.

In addition to taxes and loans, the government issued large amounts of paper money. The dislocation caused by the suspension of specie payments at the end of 1861 convinced Chase and members of the House Ways and Means Committee to look elsewhere than to hard-money methods for the solution of fiscal problems. With the treasury nearly empty, financial markets shaken, foreign bankers unsympathetic, taxation inadequate, and loans unmarketable except at a discount, paper money became a necessity. Without consulting the Treasury Department, Representative Elbridge Spaulding of New York introduced a bill for the issuance of treasury notes to be made legal tender in payment of all debts except for the interest on the national debt and customs duties.

Democrats in Congress promptly raised questions about this measure. Was it necessary? Would not patriotic Americans supply the treasury as they filled the armies? Was not the issuing of irredeemable paper money as legal tender a breach of contract? Since gold was the foundation of the nation's prewar money supply, would it not be bad faith to introduce paper for the payment not only of government obligations but of private debts, including debts bankers owed their note holders and depositors? What about the rights of creditors who had paid out gold, only to be repaid in paper? Was it not a forced loan that diminished the value of credit? Would not such action injure public credit and seriously embarrass sounder schemes of financing by the treasury? And would not this display of "government bankruptcy" encourage the enemy? Besides, where was the constitutional power in Congress to make paper money legal tender?

In support of the measure, Republicans argued that there was no choice. The bill was a necessity, a war measure that would not have been considered in peacetime. The treasury was facing staggering expenditures, and the war effort would be hampered if this important power were withheld. Since bonds could be purchased with legal tender notes, issuing them, in an attractive feature for bankers, could rejuvenate bond sales. Any alternative arrangements between the Treasury

Department and leading bankers would take too long to implement. And banks might refuse the notes unless they were made legal tender.[19] Such arguments were convincing, because in a time of unsound bank currency, the legislation legalizing paper notes, with the faith of the government and the wealth of the nation behind them, seemed preferable to the flood of irredeemable banknotes with which the country was then plagued.

After some disagreement among the Republicans, the Legal Tender Act was passed on February 24, 1862. Lincoln signed it the next day. It authorized the issuance of $150 million in non-interest-bearing "United States notes," soon to be dubbed "greenbacks" because they were printed in green ink. Such notes were vague promises to pay hard money, although no provision was made for their actual redemption on demand, in the present or future. They were receivable for internal taxes to the United States and for obligations of the United States except for interest on bonds, which was to be paid in coin. The notes were declared to be legal tender in payment of all debts, public and private, within the United States, except duties on imports and interest on the public debt. When received into the treasury, they were to be reissued. The same law provided for $500 million in "five-twenty" bonds bearing 6 percent interest and graced with the visages of Chase and Lincoln.[20] Again, Congress took a different approach from the Confederacy, which refused to make their paper money legal tender, thereby destroying any confidence in it.

Like so many northerners, Chase had been overly optimistic about a quick victory. For this reason he had at first opposed the measure, but the demands of the war changed his mind. To set any doubts at rest he advised the House Ways and Means Committee that because of the government's financial difficulties it was necessary to use United States notes. A few months later the secretary asked Congress for more paper money; Congress responded with the act of July 11, 1862, authorizing an additional $150 million in greenbacks and lowering the minimum denomination from five dollars to one dollar. A further increase was approved in 1863, so that by the close of the war a total of $450 million legal tender notes had been authorized, although the actual issues reached $432 million.

## GOLD

With the introduction of greenbacks, the United States now had two currencies—one to use in foreign exchange and the other in domestic markets. The inevitable differentiation between greenbacks and gold produced many problems bound up with the operations of the "gold exchange." An importer of goods paid his foreign creditor in gold, or, what amounts to the same thing, in a bill of exchange on a gold basis. The requirements of international trade, involving contracts to pay in gold after sixty or ninety days, created a legitimate demand for future gold, and a class of brokers promptly arose to handle these dealings in "gold futures." Throughout the war the value of gold in relation to greenbacks rose and fell, and though many northerners believed that speculators caused the depreciation of greenbacks, in fact "the short-term fluctuations of greenbacks were often related to how well the Union armies were doing in the field."[21]

If brokers had not assumed the risk of gold futures, such speculation would have fallen back on dealers, importers, and anyone who had need for gold in future business operations. Gold traders, presumably equipped with expertise, enabled dealers to plan ahead. Moreover, the New York Gold Exchange, which developed during the Civil War, helped to translate American paper dollars into foreign currencies. It became an important institutional clearinghouse and exchange for both domestic and international dealings and was another example of the North's war-driven economic development. In this regard, when compared with antebellum fiscal organization, the changes seem to have been extensive. But when measured against the future, everything from the mobilization of labor to the reliance of the military on small private firms to the types of northern occupations and the short duration of the income tax suggest limited change on the road to centralization.[22]

According to one banking expert, "all the foreign trade of the country, both imports and exports was regulated by the daily and hourly quotations of the Gold Room. This trade could not have been carried on otherwise. The wholesale prices of all importable and exportable commodities were regulated by the quotations. Retail prices were affected at longer range. . . . The Gold Exchange . . . was accordingly indispensable."[23]

Besides this legitimate service that the gold brokers performed, the system opened the way for abuse and speculation. A smart broker could make handsome gains; with no way of limiting gold operations to the necessary uses of legitimate commerce, anyone might take a chance on the gold market as on the stock or grain markets with the hope of making a killing. Congress decided to intervene. On June 17, 1864, when the ratio of paper to gold was approximately two to one, Congress passed the Gold Act, forbidding any purely speculative trading in gold futures, and making it unlawful for anyone to contract for subsequent delivery unless he possessed gold to that amount at the time the contract was made. For violation of the act penalties of fine and imprisonment were imposed.[24] But the law did not achieve its intended purpose.

On June 18, 1864, the gold premium stood at 95¼, that is, it would require $1.95¼ in paper to purchase one dollar in gold. A week later the premium had risen to 150, making it necessary to pay $2.50 for each gold dollar. Congress stepped into this intolerable situation after legislators had been deluged with complaints. But on July 2, fifteen days after it had been passed, the Gold Act, intended to stop speculation, was repealed and the previous free-market system returned.[25]

Throughout the war the relationship of gold to paper currency responded to events on the battlefield. Indeed, while the exchange's bears sang "John Brown," the bulls, who stood to gain from Union losses, whistled "Dixie."[26] For example, when the forces of the Confederate general Jubal Early were near Washington in July 1864, the paper price of gold reached $284, whereas in January 1862, according to the comptroller of the currency, gold in New York was at the very low premium of 1½ percent, or $150. "On the 1st of January, 1864 [continued the comptroller], it opened at 52, went up to 88 on the 14th of April, and fell to 67 on the 19th of the same month. . . . On the 1st of July it was forced up to 185, but on the day following (the gold bill having been repealed) it fell to 130. On the 11th of the same month it went up again to 184; on the 15th it fell to 144, and after various fluctuations dropped on the 26th of September to 87." Such wide variations afforded risk-taking capitalists opportunities for quick profits.[27]

Of course other influences produced gold fluctuations. Indeed, the gold market was about as thoroughly attuned to the political and economic pulse of the country as was the stock market. Changing currents of fiscal policy, debates in Congress, international crises, market fluctuations in United States bonds, changes in government personnel, preelection news, and many other factors affected the price of gold and the associated degree of the greenback's depreciation.

## BANKS AND THE CURRENCY

At the beginning of the Civil War the United States lacked a uniform system of banking and banknote currency. Thus the necessity of creating such a system became one of the immediate matters of war finance. Chase had early seen the need for reform in this field. In his December 1862 report, he outlined a plan for national banks and a national currency that evoked a favorable response in the East. According to New York City mayor George Opdyke, the report was an "admirable . . . state paper—clear in statement, sound in theory, logical in argument, and most comprehensive in its grasp."[28]

What Chase proposed was a system of federally supervised national banking associations that would issue currency, including greenbacks, based on their holdings of United States bonds and guaranteed by the federal government. In making this proposal he intended to correct the evils of the existing state banknotes. These were of bewildering variety and great redundancy; the security behind them was often flimsy; they were subject to wide and eccentric fluctuations; and so long as such an unstable currency existed, any plan for an adequate national currency was doomed.

After some delay, Chase's proposal for a centralized monetary system controlled by the government was promoted by influential congressmen and senators such as New York's Elbridge Spaulding and Ohio's John Sherman. Sherman especially saw its implications. In a speech before the Senate, the Ohio senator, arguing for a "sentiment of nationality," noted that "all private interests, all local interests, all banking interests, the interests of individuals, everything, should be subordinate now to the interest of the Government."[29] Though opposed by influential Democrats and some western Republicans, a banking act passed on February 25, 1863. Because this legislation had certain technical defects, Congress modified the statute in 1864.

This law of June 3, 1864 became the legislative basis of the post–Civil War national banking system. During the war it answered the need to centralize financial operations and create a market for bonds. Banking associations under national charters could be created anywhere in the United States. Their organization and management were to be supervised by a bureau of the Treasury Department, headed by a newly created officer to be known as the comptroller of the currency. The minimum capital for each association was specified, varying with the population of the city or town in which the bank might be located. Each shareholder was made doubly liable for the obligations of that bank. Every such bank was required to purchase United States bonds of not less than thirty thousand dollars, or less than one-third of its paid-in capital.

These bonds were to be deposited in the United States Treasury, where they earned interest in gold for the bank. The comptroller of the currency was to issue the notes to the national banks, and they were to be equal in amount to 90 percent of the value of the United States bonds received. The maximum amount of such banknotes was fixed at $300 million, and thereby a more uniform form of currency known as "national banknotes" was created.

Other provisions of the act concerned the maintenance of a required reserve in both specie and greenbacks against both banknotes and deposits; the depositing of such reserve in "reserve cities" (which permitted the concentration of bankers' funds in New York City and the resulting encouragement of a financial partnership between a group of clients and the central government); the appointment of receivers under national supervision in the case of failed banks; and the use of the banks as depositories and financial agents for the government. As a method of stimulating, or rather requiring, the sale of United States bonds, the National Bank Act became an essential feature of Civil War finance.

Organization of these new banks proceeded slowly at first. New York, Boston, Philadelphia, and Baltimore financiers were initially hostile to the new arrangement. Some large eastern banks that did not rely on note issues for their profits had little to gain by joining the system. As late as 1864 the New York Clearing House challenged the law with its resolution that all National Bank currency be discounted "unless the bank in question redeem at par through a member of this Association." Many western bankers, who believed the new system would lessen their profits through its restraints on the issuing of notes, also hesitated to support the national banking system.[30] Not until after March 3, 1865, when Congress placed a 10 percent tax on state banknotes, did most state banks join the national system.[31] That year, 1,014 new national banks were organized, bringing the total number to 1,601.

When fully in operation, this new national banking system did much to bring order and a degree of stability out of the previous financial chaos. The new national banknotes, based on adequate reserves, were in every sense superior to the fluctuating and unreliable state note issues they replaced. On the other hand, the arbitrary limit placed on the amount of the national banknote circulation, the ir-redeemability of eventually $450 million greenbacks in specie, and, especially, the concentration of a large part of the nation's banking reserve in New York for use on the call loan market contributed heavily to the periodic financial panics in postwar decades.[32]

Another of the inequities of the system was the favoritism shown after the war to the eastern states, which received the lion's share of the $300 million bank-notes assigned by law as the maximum for the whole country. "For the older ma-ture regions of the country the national bank system was a comparatively safe method of mobilizing and exporting capital through the New York money mar-ket into western development," writes Richard Bensel.[33] But as a result some areas were currency deprived, a circumstance that hindered their economic devel-opment. Every state in the New England and Middle Atlantic regions obtained an amount of banknotes in excess of its quota, whereas not a state in the South received an amount equal to its quota. For example (though this was irrelevant during the Civil War and only became an issue during Reconstruction), Massa-chusetts received the circulation that would have been necessary to raise Virginia, West Virginia, North and South Carolina, Louisiana, Florida, and Arkansas to their legal quotas. And Connecticut had more national banknote circulation than Michigan, Wisconsin, Iowa, Minnesota, Kansas, Missouri, Kentucky and Ten-nessee combined. Moreover, the per capita figures reinforce the differential, with no state in the Middle Atlantic or New England having less than eleven dollars per capita, and no state outside the East having more than eight dollars.[34] Clearly the most developed regions in the United States obtained disproportionate amounts of the currency needed to facilitate their economic operations.

With some modifications the national banking system continued for half a century. Considered a necessity during the Civil War, it had the positive effect of bringing order to the heterogeneous system of state and local banks. In time, de-spite its merits, it proved inadequate, especially because it lacked an elastic cur-rency arrangement, and was superseded by the Federal Reserve Act of 1913.

## EVALUATION OF THE TREASURY DEPARTMENT

Chase's performance as Secretary of the Treasury was mixed. All authorities admit that he was energetic, and virtually all stress his incorruptibility, although by modern standards he violated his fiduciary trust in his close relationship with Henry Cooke, Jay Cooke's brother, and with Jay Cooke himself, who became Chase's personal broker.[35] But later economists have generally condemned his fi-nancial policies, particularly his support for issuing paper money; his objection to the option by which the holder of legal tender notes could exchange them for 6 percent government bonds payable in gold; his refusal to insist on prompt, stiff taxation; and especially his sudden contraction of the supply of greenbacks in 1863. Chase's annual reports seem naive today in terms of their assessment of the seriousness of the financial situation.[36] When he did recommend new revenue programs, he was hesitant. Other experts blame Chase's ignorance and inexperience for the decision to issue legal-tender notes, which "increased the debt incurred during the war by a sum running into hundreds of millions."[37]

Recent historians have tied the treasury's incapacity to manage the financial system not to Chase individually, but to the party system, which made appointments even to the critical post of assistant treasurer dependent on partisan patronage rather than financial competence.

Yet such criticisms fail to take into account the magnitude and urgency of the problems the secretary faced; he "was operating with untested assistants to meet unascertained demands from uncertain resources."[38] He had raised funds sufficient to finance over a million troops and a navy equal to that of Great Britain, and he had accomplished this without a devastating inflation rate or government controls.[39] Moreover, much of the abuse of Chase is by scholars who have made sound money and a balanced budget cardinal articles of economic faith and have accordingly denounced Civil War finance as an unwholesome aberration. Such judgments overlook the historical context in which Chase operated—a society with little experience or toleration of the operation of national taxation and a rapidly centralizing state. And even during the war the federal government continued to rely on the private sector and market forces.[40]

Experiences during the New Deal, the Second World War, and the Vietnam War in managed currency and deficit financing have caused some economists to revise their judgment of Chase. When compared with those of World War I and World War II, the Union debt incurred during the Civil War, as a fraction of national income, was not excessive, nor does the interest charge on it seem to have been exorbitant.[41] (There were differences in the percentages of tax revenues raised to pay for the war effort, with that during the Civil War being the lowest at 20 percent.) On the whole, inflation was more effectively curbed during the Civil War than during the Second World War.[42] Indeed, it is noteworthy that, without rationing, price controls, or central banking, Chase could have managed the federal economy as well as he did during the Civil War.

In comparative terms, which is the best measure, the Union government experienced less inflation, raised more money by taxation, relied on loans for nearly 70 percent of its revenues (compared with 38 percent in the Confederacy), and had almost no unpaid requisitions by 1865 (compared with the Confederacy's $350 million.) As southern morale declined because of a poorly managed treasury and insufficient efforts to pay for the war, more and more northerners were incorporated into a national economy they had every reason to support.[43] As one Republican senator said of the convictions behind the bank bill: "This is our country. Let it have one national Government—one destiny."[44]

CHAPTER 15 | The American
Question Abroad

While the Union government struggled with internal challenges, it also
faced serious threats from overseas. Until 1863, one of Lincoln's
greatest fears was that Great Britain would recognize the Confederacy, an act that would not only give creditability to the Davis regime and boost
morale in the South, but would inevitably lead to a break in diplomatic relations
between London and Washington.[1] At a time when interventionist policies
still appealed to European statesmen and when the countries of most concern to
the United States—Britain and France—were led by Lord Palmerston and
Napoleon III, to whom international affairs had become something of a specialty, the diplomatic decisions made in London and Paris were critical to the
Union's future.

After 1861 what Europeans called the American question could not be
evaded; nations had to choose between intervention and neutrality. Yet neither
the Union nor the Confederacy wanted Great Britain or France to be strictly
neutral. The United States expected European nations to go further than neutrality and reject belligerent status for the Confederacy, the latter classification
establishing what the Union denied—that this was a conflict between two independent nation-states, rather than the insurrection Lincoln claimed it to be. On
the other hand, the Confederacy sought the opposite—recognition followed by
assistance and foreign intervention similar to France's support of the United
States during the American Revolution. Throughout the Civil War both sides
maneuvered for international advantage. Eventually, though neutrality was the
course adopted, the war ended with both the Union and the Confederacy nursing major grievances against Britain and France, and neither side satisfied with
the conduct of those powers.

## EUROPEAN ATTITUDES TOWARD THE NORTH AND SOUTH

Influenced by the changing tides of military success between the combatants, European attitudes toward the Civil War shifted. At the outbreak of the conflict most Europeans were poorly informed about the United States. Although Britain had already fought two wars with the United States, as one Englishman acknowledged in 1865: "The name of America five years ago, called up to the ordinary English mind nothing but a vague cluster of associations, compounded of Mrs. Trollope, Martin Chuzzlewit, and *Uncle Tom's Cabin.*"[2]

Impressed by the rabidly prosouthern *Times* of London as well as by the Confederacy's publicity agents who often exaggerated the South's military strength, most upper-class Britons sided with the Confederacy.[3] For years the Old South had been affiliated with Great Britain in both business and society, and it was easy to find in southern planters an equivalent of the English gentry. British aristocrats such as the marquis of Lothian, the marquis of Bath, and Lord Robert Cecil believed that the success of the Confederacy would give a much needed check to democracy, both in America and in Europe. "I fancy," wrote an approving marquis of Lothian (founder of the Southern Independence Association), "that there is in some of the Southern States what may be called an approach to an aristocratic class ... who hold the same land as their grandfathers held and can pretend to something like a pedigree."[4]

Even more liberal Britons favored the South, on the basis that its efforts to escape northern "tyranny" were comparable to the aspirations of Italian and German nationalists, who sought to end the political domination of their countries by Hapsburgs and French relatives of Napoleon. The reputations of Confederate leaders inspired respect abroad, and the chivalric bearing of Robert E. Lee and Stonewall Jackson enlisted admiration. From the outset of the war, the aristocracy in Britain was "anxious to see the United States go to pieces."[5]

On the other hand, though at first not so articulate, distinct segments of British society favored the Union cause. Many British manufacturers and shippers had strong commercial ties with the North. Workers in the wool industry supported the Union for a combination of reasons growing out of self-interest and conviction. The drought-shriveled European harvests of the late 1850s made northern grain exports more important, and appreciated, than ever.

The powerful British reform movement, especially the antislavery societies, found it impossible to sympathize with the Confederacy. Friends of democracy and proponents of republicanism saw in the United States a model to be cherished. John Bright, the powerful leader of the British radicals, spoke eloquently of the "odious and ... blasphemous" attempts of the Confederates to divide the United States. He looked to the day when America, with "one people, and one language, and one law, and one faith," would become "the home of freedom, and a refuge for the oppressed of every race and of every clime."[6]

The principal leaders of the British labor movement also supported the North, finding in the prosouthern sympathies of the "millionaire aristocrats, venal politicians, and some of the press, led by the great bully the *Times*," a "hatred of freedom, jealousy of the growing power of the United States, and a desire to see democratic or republican institutions overthrown or brought into disrepute."[7] At the beginning it was uncertain that these latter sentiments, resting on the pro-Unionism of the British masses, would triumph. Attitudes were in fact divided, as a significant body of working-class opinion supported southern independence. Such views had little influence on the government, but they did exist.[8]

At first the North seemed to lose every opportunity to gain popular support. Already fearful of northern economic competition, which threatened the supremacy of the British merchant marine and challenged the preeminence of their manufactures, the British middle classes were alienated by the Republican-sponsored Morrill Tariff of 1861, which made English goods more expensive in the United States. Northern appeals to British idealism were also undercut when Secretary of State Seward, early in the war, declared that the conflict was not being waged over slavery and that it would not disturb the South's peculiar institution. Even such a staunch friend of the Union as the duke of Argyll concluded "that the North is not entitled to claim all the sympathy which belongs to a cause which they do not avow; and which is promoted only as an indirect consequence of a contest which (on their side at least) is waged for other objects, and on other grounds."[9]

The British viewed the leaders of the northern cause with suspicion. Lincoln was an unknown quantity, whom even the friendly member of Parliament Richard Cobden dismissed as "a backwoodsman of great sturdy common sense, but . . . unequal to the occasion."[10] The British assumed (as did some Americans) that Seward, who was distrusted abroad after some careless criticism of Britain, would run the administration.[11] And the British also recalled that Seward had boasted to the duke of Newcastle, during the Prince of Wales's American visit in 1860, of his intention to twist the lion's tail once he assumed high office. When news leaked out about his startling proposal of April 1, 1861, to demand explanations from Great Britain, France, and Spain for their interference in Santo Domingo and Mexico, European fears were confirmed. Even the secretary of state's careful handling of the crisis over the prosouthern consuls in the fall of 1861 (when Seward demanded their recall but did not prosecute them for activities bordering on spying) did not restore his credibility overseas.[12]

The Confederates were not unrealistic in their hopes for recognition followed by aid. A month before the war started, the southerners William Yancey, Pierre Rost, and A. Dudley Mann traveled to England, France, Russia, and Belgium. Their instructions from Secretary of State Toombs were to explain to these governments the nature and purposes of the southern cause, to open diplomatic relations, and to "negotiate treaties of friendship, commerce and navigation."[13] This effort was the first of a series of diplomatic and commercial missions that, as the war continued, represented the Confederacy throughout the world—in Spain, at the Vatican, in Mexico, and in British dominions such as Canada, Ireland, and various West Indian colonies.

In the diplomatic game, the enterprising Confederates took the first trick. On May 13, 1861, Queen Victoria issued her proclamation of neutrality, recognizing the Confederates as having belligerent rights, thereby giving to that government the right to make contracts, purchase supplies, and commission cruisers to search and seize Union ships. The significance of these initial concessions to the South is best measured by the reaction in Washington, where Seward asserted that the war was a domestic question and that belligerency should not be accorded to a fictitious southern government. Seward could not overlook the fact that the queen's proclamation, a proper one under international law that was imitated by other countries, involved a recognition of Confederate belligerency. In the eyes of Europe the Confederate States of America, though not yet a member of the

With the blockade of southern ports, the South was no longer viewed solely as an insurrectionary power. Blockades were focused on major ports such as Charleston (shown here), where cotton exports and various imports aided the South's war effort.

"family of nations," appeared to be a responsible, autonomous government conducting war.

Ironically, the blockade was a paradox for both sides. The South undermined its status as a belligerent in calling the Union effort to choke off its trade a "paper blockade" (a classification with which the British minister to Washington, Lord Lyons, at first agreed) and advising Europeans that it should not qualify under international law as a true blockade. Yet when Lincoln proclaimed the blockade in April 1861, he promoted the Confederates to the standing of a belligerent, entitled to those rights and subject to well-understood obligations.

Given the importance of status in international law, the refusal of Europe to adopt the northern interpretation of the war as an irresponsible insurrection by southerners was damaging to the North. Indeed, in being recognized as a belligerent, the South came close to drawing Great Britain into the conflict on its side. On the other hand, the decisions made by the British inevitably followed their own interests. In the case of the blockade this meant that Britain, whose power rested with its navy, saw the danger of any precedent that might undermine any blockades it might declare in the future.

Fortunately for the Union, Lincoln had made one of his best appointments for the ministry to Great Britain. Indeed the talents of Charles Francis Adams may have been as valuable as some Union military victories. As a member of the prominent Adams family, Charles Francis Adams was already acquainted with Europe. With his mother he had made an arduous winter journey by carriage from St. Petersburg to Paris to join his father, John Quincy Adams. Passing through the Allied lines, he reached Paris just after Napoleon's return from Elba in 1815.

After attending a grim English boarding school whose master he detested, Adams graduated from Harvard in 1825 and studied law under Daniel Webster. By 1861 he had served as a Massachusetts legislator, had become a prominent leader of the "conscience Whigs" and the free-soilers. He had been a vice presidential candidate on the Free Soil ticket in 1848. Later, Adams served as an influential moderate Republican in the House of Representatives from 1859 to 1861. He did not support Lincoln for the Republican nomination in 1860, although he accepted the appointment as minister to England and loyally served the Lincoln administration.[14]

Arriving in Britain on the day of the queen's proclamation of neutrality, which he had wanted to prevent, Adams had hardly settled in London when Seward's "bold remonstrance" (Dispatch No. 10 of May 21) claimed his attention. In this dispatch Seward instructed Adams to have no relations whatever with the British government so long as it continued to interfere in American domestic questions, and to discontinue relations if Foreign Secretary Lord John Russell continued to negotiate with Confederate diplomats.[15] Fortunately Lincoln had softened this dispatch, and Adams, without committing himself to complete compliance with

Seward's instructions, handled the matter so deftly as to avoid a clash. Meanwhile he won from Russell an agreement that the secretary would hold no more interviews with southern commissioners.[16]

During the Yancey-Rost-Mann mission—that is, from March 1861 to January 1862—the South failed in its objective of achieving recognition as a nation. Yet the commissioners, one a fire-eater, the other without serious qualifications, and the third, "like a Polonius, full of words and wind,"[17] did gain the attention of the London public and obtain recognition of the Confederacy's belligerency. But they were unsuccessful in securing a treaty of amity and commerce and in persuading the British to denounce the blockade on the basis that British textile factories needed southern cotton. Nor did the British agree to provide access to their ports for Confederate privateers, much less intervene militarily as allies.

Although Russell granted interviews to the southern commissioners on May 3 and May 9, the conversations were unofficial. Thereafter southerners were requested to put their communications in writing. As time passed, Yancey became bitterly antagonistic toward Britain and asked to be relieved of his duties. Differing among themselves, the commissioners felt snubbed. With the arrival of new commissioners in January 1862, their mission came to an end.

## THE *TRENT* AFFAIR

For its continuing diplomatic efforts to obtain full recognition from France and Great Britain and to press for a disavowal of the northern blockade of its ports, the Confederate government selected two experienced politicians—James Murray Mason of Virginia for London and John Slidell of Louisiana for Paris. But the most significant aspect of their diplomatic mission turned out to be their initial voyage, which raised such controversy as to bring Great Britain and the United States to the brink of war.

The U.S. navy had failed to intercept their ship after it ran the blockade off the Charleston coast. At the Spanish port of Havana the southern commissioners had taken passage on a British merchant ship, a mail packet named the *Trent*. The day after leaving port, on November 8, 1861, the vessel was stopped, after the conventional signal of a shot across her bow, by the *San Jacinto*. This warship of the United States was commanded by Captain Charles Wilkes, a distinguished explorer, author, and naval officer. The two commissioners, with their secretaries, were arrested and removed to the *San Jacinto*. The searching party "met with some difficulty," according to Wilkes's report, and "a force became necessary to search" the ship. Though the envoys were "treated with every possible courtesy by Captain Wilkes and his officers," they were confined to Fort Warren in Boston Harbor as political prisoners.

The news of this seizure created a sensation. Northerners applauded the actions of Wilkes, and Secretary of the Navy Welles approved them. American newspapers treated Wilkes like a hero, and the House of Representatives joined in the acclaim with a ringing resolution of support.[18]

Amid the jubilation, however, some northerners raised questions. Was it valid to assume that the Confederate ministers lacked diplomatic immunity because the Confederacy had not been recognized and its agents only meant to obtain aid for an insurrection? What, after all, was to be gained by sustaining Wilkes's act? Since he had acted without instructions, shouldn't the government save face by disowning his actions entirely? Would the seizure not be a foolish renunciation of America's traditional defense of neutral rights at sea? If war between Britain and the United States followed, would not Mason and Slidell have accomplished, from the enemy's perspective, infinitely more than they were likely to accomplish by proceeding on their mission?

As to the legal merits of the *Trent* affair, the point at issue was not just a matter of searching a neutral ship. The right of search, related to the right of capture where contraband is found or violation of a blockade is involved, was clearly recognized. The well-known American legal authority Joseph Storey had declared that the right of search was allowed by the general consent of nations in time of war. Nor was the right to seize and condemn contraband on board a neutral vessel in question. The offense to Britain instead consisted of impressment—that is, the fact that certain individuals had been "forcibly taken from on board a British vessel . . . while such vessel was pursuing a lawful and innocent voyage—an act of violence which was an affront to the British flag and a violation of international law."[19]

And Wilkes had not exercised the right of search properly; instead he had impressed persons from a neutral ship. Even admitting the right of the United States to take Mason and Slidell (on the doubtful grounds that persons could be deemed contraband, or as Wilkes put it "embodiments of despatches") it was clear that Wilkes's method was incorrect. If any part of the ship's "cargo" was to be condemned, this action could be done only by sailing the ship into a port of the United States, submitting the case to a prize court, and carrying out the forfeitures as the result of a regular judicial decree in compliance with procedures of international law. The heart of the matter, according to the British, was that "Wilkes had undertaken to pass upon the issue of a violation of neutrality on the spot, instead of sending the *Trent* as a prize into port for adjudication."[20] In London the *Chronicle* went further in its condemnation: "Mr. Seward . . . is exerting himself to provoke a quarrel with all Europe, in that spirit of senseless egotism which induces the Americans, with their dwarf fleet and shapeless mass of incoherent squads which they call an army, to fancy themselves the equals of France by land and Great Britain by sea."[21]

Beyond its breach of international practice, Wilkes's actions challenged Britain's national honor. When he heard the news, Palmerston burst out in a Cabinet meeting, "You may stand for this but damned if I will!"[22] The British people seemed to share his rage, as angry placards posted in British cities proclaimed an "Outrage on the British Flag—the Southern Commissioners Forcibly Removed from a Mail Steamer."[23] War preparations included sending eight thousand troops and supplies to Canada, readying a fleet, and prohibiting the exportation of munitions. Henry Adams wrote from Britain to his brother: "This nation means to make war. . . . A few weeks may see us . . . on our way home." Meanwhile his father, the ambassador, was "indescribably sad" as he decried "the exultation in America over an event which [bade] fair to be the final calamity in this contest."[24]

Despite the initial overheated reactions, the affair was satisfactorily settled. The first letter of instructions from the British cabinet to its minister in Washington, Lord Lyons, was softened by the royal tact of Prince Albert who, on the eve of his death in December 1861, advocated compromise. Lincoln's ignorance of the refinements of international law was more than offset by his innate common sense, which led the president to turn to arbitration if diplomacy should fail. In an exchange of letters Senator Sumner and the British reformers John Bright and Richard Cobden acknowledged the desire of reasonable men on both sides for a peaceful settlement. At a time when the recently broken Atlantic cable required that messages travel by sea, the length of time necessary to communicate cooled fiery tempers on both sides and encouraged compromise.[25] Meanwhile, both Seward and Adams made clear that Wilkes had acted without authorization.

The Cabinet in Britain, avoiding an ultimatum, first demanded an apology, but then reconsidered and accepted in its place an admission that Wilkes had acted without authority. Finally the matter was thrashed out in a meeting of Lincoln's Cabinet on Christmas Day, 1861, in which Sumner read friendly letters from Bright and Cobden. After a long discussion, according to one Cabinet member, "all yielded to the necessity [that war with Britain must be avoided], and unanimously concur[r] ed in Mr. Seward's letter to L[or]d Lyons."[26]

In this letter Seward ended the incident by stating that the prisoners would be "cheerfully liberated." The now accommodating secretary of state nevertheless included touches intended for the home front. After analyzing the relevant questions of international law, Seward, who was well aware that the principal source of saltpeter for Union gunpowder was British India and that the British had frozen this export during the crisis, conceded the main point by declaring that Wilkes had erred in arresting the prisoners instead of sending the vessel into port for adjudication.

This concession, however, was so phrased as to put Britain in the wrong for its traditional stance favoring impressment and to call attention to America's high-minded role as a champion of freedom of the seas. Finally, in a passage that one biographer has characterized as "sheer impudence," Seward gratuitously added that "if the safety of this Union required the detention of the captured persons it would be the right and duty of this government to detain them."[27]

In this cartoon, Secretary of State William H. Seward holds out his hand, returning the two Confederate commissioners (Slidell and Mason) who were seized from the British ship *Trent*. Lord Russell, on the left, is satisfied with Seward's action, but Jefferson Davis, on the right, marches off in frustration because Britain did not enter the war against the Union.

So completely did the release of the envoys close the incident that by the end of January, when Mason and Slidell finally arrived in Britain, there was little public interest in them.[28] The sense of relief felt in the American legation in London appeared in the Adams letters. Pessimistic in December about the possible effects of the crisis, by January Charles Francis Adams concluded that "Captain Wilkes has not positively shipwrecked us. . . . The first effect of the surrender of Messrs. Mason and Slidell has been extraordinary. The current which ran against us with such extreme violence six weeks ago now seems to be going with equal fury in our favor."[29]

In retrospect some observers believed that the hostilities between Britain and the Union were lessened by the favorable resolution of a crisis that had initially heightened them.[30] The *Trent* crisis ended without recognition of the Confederacy, but it did not dissuade British leaders who wanted to intervene for humanitarian or economic reasons.[31]

## THE FAILURE OF COTTON DIPLOMACY

In the early days of the war southern diplomats relied on the presumed economic magic of "King Cotton" as a tool in their diplomatic campaign. In general, southerners followed two strategies. Confident that the disappearance of an

INDIAN COTTON DEPÔT

The Confederacy grossly miscalculated when it expected that Great Britain would have to rely so heavily on southern cotton production. As evident in this political cartoon, with the Civil War discouraging Great Britain from trading with the South, India eagerly awaited taking over the trading.

industry on which nearly five million British citizens depended would force Britain to recognize their new government, Confederates believed that withholding cotton would be a lever to win that nation's support. But some members of Jefferson Davis's Cabinet proposed that the government purchase as much cotton as possible, ship it immediately to England, and use it as the basis for Confederate credit.[32] Such a strategy was theoretically possible in the early days of the war when, according to Secretary of War Benjamin, the blockade was a farce, with the Union squadron able to maintain only one ship for every three hundred miles of coast.[33] But advocates of such a policy were never able to obtain effective legislation, and without it the alternative policy of an international boycott that would starve Britain's cotton supply gained in popularity.

Both the French and the British initially worried about the impact of a cotton shortage, though the highest priority of both countries was to avoid an American war. But the dominance of King Cotton in prewar international trade had produced a surplus in British factories by the time the war began. Only in the summer of 1862 was the pinch felt as the number of bales in Britain fell to one-sixth that of 1861. As a result, approximately two million people were out of work at the height of the "cotton famine" in late 1862.[34] But the next year, ominously for the South, the industry picked up, owing to higher prices and the opening of other sources of supply in India and Egypt.[35] By December 1863, 180,000 textile workers were on poor relief, compared with 485,000 the year before; by the end of the war the number of unemployed was down to 75,000, compared with 48,000 in normal times.[36]

The Confederacy's cotton diplomacy was based on the miscalculation that a shortage of cotton would determine British and French diplomacy. In fact, during this time of crop failures in Europe, Britain needed wheat from the North as well as cotton. As a result, prosouthern demonstrations in Britain were offset by protests that emphasized that "an adequate and cheap food supply concerned the masses of people . . . no less than . . . the cotton supply."[37] Moreover, linen and woolen mills expanded at the expense of those processing cotton. Meanwhile British munitions manufacturers reaped profits from their sales to both sides, and the British merchant marine benefited from the decline of American commercial shipping. Such advantages would be lost if the British government recognized the South. To the extent that economic elements determined British policy, in sum, the balance of these forces tilted toward the North. By 1863 cotton diplomacy had failed.

## CRISIS OVER RECOGNITION

Through these and other diplomatic issues ran the central question of recognition of the Confederacy and related concerns over mediation, intervention, and the demand for an armistice. Had the South won on any of these points, the war's outcome might have been different. With Confederate commissioners pleading for recognition while Adams was instructed to break relations if this should happen, the British Cabinet confronted a delicate situation. Recognition had been avoided in 1861; with the *Trent* affair satisfactorily adjusted and the effect of any cotton shortage declining in significance, the diplomatic prospects of the Union in England seemed brighter.

But in the summer of 1862, a crisis loomed over the issue of Confederate recognition. This policy was seriously considered by the British Cabinet in view of the failures of the Union generals McClellan and Pope and the prospects of Lee's offensive in Maryland. In September 1862 Prime Minister Lord Palmerston's and British Foreign Secretary Lord John Russell's deliberations had reached the point where Palmerston suggested that England and France "address the contending parties and recommend an arrangement upon the basis of separation."[38] Russell believed that the time had come "for offering mediation . . . with a view to the recognition of the independence of the Confederates." He added that in case of the failure of mediation, Britain should recognize the South.[39]

In early October 1862 the chancellor of the exchequer, William Gladstone, publicly announced that "Jefferson Davis and other leaders of the South have made an army; they are making, it appears, a navy; and they have made what is more than either,—they have made a nation.... We may anticipate with certainty the success of the Southern States so far as regards their separation from the North."[40] Delivered without ministry approval, this speech forecast a policy that had some adherents but not a consensus of policy makers.

Gladstone's position encouraged Russell's efforts to bring the American question to a head. On October 13 the foreign minister sent a memorandum to the Cabinet proposing an armistice between the Union and Confederacy so that peace could be considered. At this point Russell also launched a mediation plan involving joint action by Britain, France, and Russia. Although French support was certain, the Russians would not agree. Russell's plan constituted a dangerous crisis for the Union. Even without the support of other European countries, if Great Britain had promoted an official mediation proposal to divide the Union, the United States would probably have ended diplomatic relations with Britain. Conflict with the British as their navy confronted Union blockaders would have led to war.

At this critical point, however, counterforces restrained the British. Lee's setback at Antietam and Lincoln's Emancipation Proclamation (though its significance was discounted by the British Cabinet) had their influence. One member of the Cabinet urged a continuance of strict neutrality, and others immediately backed him up. Having doubts about the Confederacy's military strength, Palmerston delayed, advising on October 22 that "we must continue to be lookers-on till the war shall have taken a more decided turn."[41]

The Cabinet postponed its consideration of the question, set for October 23, and by October 31 the tension between the United States and Britain had relaxed so much that Confederate officials believed the British ministry unfriendly to the Confederacy.[42] On this day Benjamin advised Mason to address a formal protest to Russell (on another matter) and hinted that the Confederacy was considering the propriety of expelling British consuls. Throughout this dangerous period Charles Francis Adams, keeping silent about his instructions to leave if Britain recognized the Confederacy, made just enough references to packing his carpetbag and trunks to make Russell cautious. And Adams made it unmistakably clear that Washington would not accept mediation.

For two years Britain had tilted toward and then away from intervention. But just at the moment when the British ministry seemed most disposed to a policy of mediation—a course that was greatly feared by the Union government—Lee had followed his success at Second Bull Run with an invasion of the North. Accordingly the British decided to wait and see if the war might not end without any intercession. Subsequent military events dampened British support of any intervention. By 1863 "the likelihood of conflict with the North outweighed the attraction of intervention," especially as Canada, the obvious theater for any Anglo-American war, seemed indefensible to British military planners.[43]

## CONFEDERATE WARSHIPS AND RAMS

In July 1862, a powerful warship known as the *Enrica* or the "290" steamed down Britain's Mersey River. Not yet supplied with war equipment, the ship had left Liverpool supposedly for a trial run, but instead had headed for sea. Reaching an appointed rendezvous off the Azores, this British-built vessel took on British-supplied arms, provisions, and coal, and was boarded by the Confederate commander Raphael Semmes, who had already achieved naval success with the C.S.S. *Sumter*. As the illustrious *Alabama*, the "290" launched its career as a Confederate cruiser, destroying or capturing sixty-four Union merchant ships before being sunk by the U.S.S. *Kearsarge* off France in 1864.

The story of the *Alabama* and others like it is one of the most serious chapters in Anglo-American diplomacy. British laws were designed to prevent unneutral activities within its jurisdiction. The law forbade the fitting out, equipping, or arming of vessels for warlike operations in any war in which Great Britain was neutral. Yet in some tortured interpretations the law was not violated if the equipping and arming of the vessel were accomplished as distinct operations separate from its building, even though the whole process involved British aid. The building of the *Alabama*, along with other warships, had been promoted by Captain James Bulloch of the Confederate navy, who was in England for the purpose. So transparent was the concealment that there had never been any mystery about the ship, whose future as a Confederate cruiser had been unmistakable.

Nor was the *Alabama* an isolated case. In March 1862 the *Oreto* (soon to be renamed the *Florida*) had been allowed to depart from Liverpool, had disappeared for a time, and had later turned up in Nassau to receive her equipment and arms from British sources.[44] Adams and Thomas Dudley, the United States consul in Liverpool, presented irrefutable proof of British involvement to the British ministry, which neglected to seize or detain the ships. While work continued on a project that threatened broken relations at the least between Great Britain and the United States, and while Captain Bulloch was sufficiently in touch with developments to choose his time for the flight of the *Alabama*, Russell advised Adams that the matter had been referred to the "proper authorities."

Adams persisted. Despite the evasion and delay, the proof was so overwhelming that the Crown's legal officers recommended the seizure of the vessel, and Russell ordered the *Alabama* detained. But this order arrived too late to prevent departure of the Confederate raider. With vital interests at stake, American authorities characterized the attitude of the British government as one of negligence and even connivance, although at least four cabinet ministers regretted the *Alabama's* escape.

Meanwhile, two powerful ironclads, to be delivered in 1863, had been ordered from the Laird firm in Liverpool. If these "Laird rams," intended to challenge the Union blockade, had been allowed to depart following the *Florida* and *Alabama*, a diplomatic break might have occurred. The seriousness of the matter was apparent to Assistant Secretary of the Navy Gustavus V. Fox, who ordered the Union navy to stop the rams "at all hazards."[45] So fundamental to Seward's policy was the conviction that Britain dreaded a war with the United States that he instructed Adams to warn Great Britain that the proceedings relative to the fitting out of ships for the Confederacy could "complicate the relations between the two countries in such a matter as to render it difficult . . . to preserve friendship between them."[46]

Yet Adams and Russell wanted to avoid conflict, and on April 5, 1863 the British government took possession of the *Alexandra*, a raider intended for the Confederacy.[47] Such a seizure, on the grounds that the ship was "apparently intended" for the Confederacy, reversed the earlier policy of allowing the *Alabama* and the *Florida* to escape for lack of "conclusive" evidence. Such a shift signaled the British government's efforts to enforce neutrality.

As to the Laird rams, it still seemed possible that they might escape on the pretext that they were intended for France or for Egypt. Not until five months after the *Alexandra* seizure was the matter settled. During this time the Union victories at Gettysburg and Vicksburg took place; a parliamentary motion for recognition of the South failed. Through it all, Adams kept presenting affidavits relating to the true purpose of the rams, at the same time emphasizing the serious nature of a controversy affecting Anglo-American relations. The affair was finally decided in the United States' favor on September 9, when the British placed the rams under surveillance. In October they were seized.

Some attribute the British compliance to Adams's famous letter of September 5, 1863 to Russell. Informed of the expected departure of the rams and that the government could not detain the ships on the basis of existing information, but would be ready to stop them if new evidence showed any violation of neutrality, Adams warned: "It would be superfluous in me to point out to your lordship that this is war."[48] Actually, Russell had moved toward detaining the rams before receiving Adams's note. The foreign secretary had arrived at his new policy during the *Alexandra* affair, and had pledged to Seward that he would not abandon it.

After the controversy over the rams was settled in the fall of 1863, relations between the United States and Great Britain improved. Conversely, the Confederacy became increasingly displeased with the British when it failed to win recognition, and in late 1863 Davis expelled British consuls from the South. As one Confederate agent in Europe admitted, "Diplomatic means can now no longer prevail and everybody looks to Lee to conquer recognition."[49]

So crucial was French and British support that Davis tried a final time to obtain diplomatic recognition. In January 1865 he dispatched Duncan Kenner, a Louisiana congressman and one of the South's largest slave owners, to Europe with a proposal that the Confederacy would emancipate its slaves if France and Great Britain recognized its government. By that time Confederate defeat seemed so certain that even this astonishing offer could not change British policy, which throughout the war had been rooted in a sense of *Realpolitik* and practical politics.[50]

## RELATIONS WITH OTHER NATIONS

Although the international concerns of both the North and the South centered on Great Britain, relations with France, Russia, and Spain about the "American Question" were also consequential. In the case of France, that nation and Great Britain collaborated, and in June 1861, Edward Thouvenel, the French foreign minister, issued a declaration of strict neutrality. Earlier, Spain had invaded Santo Domingo and France had been meddling in Mexico. In Seward's view, foreign intervention in hemispheric affairs violated the Monroe Doctrine and threatened the Union. It was in the context of these threats, which included the sending of warships to the American coast, that Seward issued his blustery memo to Lincoln on April 1, 1861 for explanations from Spain and France, "which if not received should be followed by convening Congress and declaring war against them."[51]

The Confederates also had agents in France and as in Britain, French textile mills suffered from a shortage of cotton, which the Confederates hoped to use as a lever for obtaining recognition.[52] In Rouen, according to one resident, the cotton weavers were eating grass and "mothers register their daughters as prostitutes."[53] The flamboyant Napoleon III often expressed sympathy with the cause of the South, as did the French people. But strong antislavery sentiment, the fear of war with the United States, and a prudent tendency to follow Britain's lead worked for the Union.

As was the case with Britain, Confederate military reverses hurt the chances for recognition, even as Henri Mercier, the French minister in Washington, offered to serve as a mediator between representatives of the Union and the Confederacy. Seward dismissed this offer, noting that the Union would neither consider suspending the war nor implicitly accept the Confederacy's legitimacy by meeting with southerners in such a peace conference.

Relations with France were further complicated by that nation's continuing intervention in Mexico. When the Benito Juárez administration in Mexico was unable to pay its European debts in 1861, the French, British, and Spanish sent an expedition of ten thousand troops to collect their claims. After the British and Spanish departed, the French made additional demands on the Mexican government. In 1863 France installed a puppet government under the Austrian archduke Maximilian, who with his wife Carlotta landed at Vera Cruz in May 1864. Napoleon's imperial ambitions in the New World and rumors that the French might even try to seize Texas drew warnings from Secretary Seward: "The President does not allow himself to be disturbed by suspicions so unjust to France . . . but he knows, also, that it is out of such suspicions that the fatal web of national animosity is most frequently woven."[54]

Meanwhile Confederate diplomacy focused on an opposite strategy—how to use Mexico as a pawn to obtain recognition. The most effective southern argument was that Napoleon's Mexican state could not possibly succeed unless the

Confederacy succeeded, and on this basis the Confederate government offered to support Maximilian in return for French recognition. But despite Maximilian's sympathy with the Confederates and sustained lobbying in Paris, Napoleon was unwilling to take such a bold step. So the war ended without the Confederacy gaining the support of any European nation.

With Russia, the other great European power, the Union had no major problems, although Baron Edward de Stoeckl, the Russian minister in Washington, believed American politicians contemptible demagogues. Like those of other European nations, Russia's policies were determined by self-interest. The Russians understood that the destruction of the Union would threaten European equilibrium if the United States was no longer a power capable of challenging Great Britain. Not only did a long-standing friendship exist between Russia and the United States, which Prince Gortchakov, the Russian foreign minister, acknowledged. But Russian-American friendship was also based on a mutual rivalry with Great Britain. The sending of Russian warships to American waters, though motivated by European considerations and the Russian desire to avoid having its navy trapped in its home waters by the powerful British fleet, had the effect of emphasizing this friendship.

By 1863 the diplomatic stakes had been won by the Union. Generally the outcome reflected changing economic patterns that made northern exports of grain as important as southern cotton. Neither economic interest nor sympathy with the South was strong enough to cause Britain or any other European country to go beyond a recognition of Confederate belligerency, and the Confederate failure to win sustained military victories prevented any diplomatic success. Viscount Palmerston was aware that recognition of the southern government might upset the European balance of power, precipitating a world war. And despite French adventurism in Mexico, Napoleon was reluctant to act independently. Gradually the influence of Lincoln's emancipation policy and northern military advances had an impact abroad, as all the European powers, no matter what their opinion before the war, moved away from any support of the Confederacy.

CHAPTER 16 | # Emancipation: The War Redefined

S lavery, the root cause of the war, soon became the subject of rapidly changing policies on the battlefield, in Congress, and in the White House. The conflict continually produced issues relating to the status of individual slaves as well as to the future of the peculiar institution as a regional system and to the effect of its termination on the war. No understanding of the Civil War is complete without an account of the profound social revolution of emancipation and the roles played in that process by slaves themselves, by Congress, by the military, and by the president.

## INITIAL ATTITUDES

At the outset of the conflict, the Lincoln administration made it clear that the object of the war was to preserve the Union and not to change the existing social or political order. In his March 1861 inaugural address, Lincoln sought to quiet southern fears about emancipation with this disclaimer:

> There has never been any reasonable cause for such apprehension. Indeed, the most ample evidence to the contrary has all the while existed. . . . It is found in nearly all the published speeches of him who now addresses you. I do but quote from one of those speeches when I declare that 'I have no purpose, directly or indirectly, to interfere with the institution of slavery in the States where it exists.' I believe I have no right to do so and I have no inclination to do so.[1]

Nor did the Republican party intend abolition in the South. Lincoln was merely following his party's 1860 platform, which held that states had the right to control their own domestic institutions—of which slavery was one. Congress concurred. Just before Lincoln took office, it had passed an amendment guaran-

This northern poster reflects the patriarchal attitude held by many
white northerners. A white Union soldier raises his sword and a
flag to symbolize freedom and public education to former slaves.
The slaves are depicted as powerless and hailing the Union
soldiers as their saviors.

teeing slavery against any interference from the federal government. Forty percent of the Republicans in that session had voted for this proposed amendment.
On July 22, 1861, a new Congress resolved that the war was not being prosecuted with the intention of overthrowing the "established institutions" of the
states.

Behind such disclaimers lay the conviction held by both northerners and
southerners that federal authority was limited by the United States Constitution.
Control over domestic institutions such as slavery belonged exclusively to the
states. In reality slavery was also protected by the racial animosity of whites toward African Americans, which was especially virulent among Democrats. In
any case, the Republican party did not plan to make slavery a matter of congressional legislation, except to prevent its extension into national territory. And
even on this matter the reprehensible judicial doctrine of the *Dred Scott* decision
stood in the way.

But Americans who opposed slavery, including the nation's nearly half million free blacks, immediately saw in the war a powerful new reason to challenge the traditional states' rights protection of slavery as a domestic institution. They transformed their moral outrage against an inhumane practice into pragmatic arguments about the necessity of undermining the enemy's labor force. Northern abolitionists such as Frederick Douglass promptly linked the slaves' coerced contribution to the Confederate cause to the need for emancipation. In June 1861 Douglass declared that "not a slave should be left a slave in the returning footprints of the American army gone to put down this slaveholding rebellion. Sound policy, not less than humanity, demands the instant liberation of every slave in the rebel states."[2]

Those who view emancipation solely as a public policy debate emerging from Washington and the state capitols of the border slave states or as a change accomplished by Lincoln overlook the process of self-liberation by slaves themselves. As Ira Berlin has written,

> [S]laves had a different understanding of the sectional struggle. Unmoved by the public pronouncements and official policies of the federal government, they recognized their centrality to the dispute and knew their future depended upon its outcome. Lacking political standing or public voice, forbidden access to the weapons of war, slaves nonetheless demonstrated their readiness to take risks in the service of the Union. In so doing they gradually rendered untenable every Union policy short of universal emancipation.[3]

Large numbers of southern slaves acted to free themselves, some by escaping from the plantations. Here slaves escape by boat.

Before long, the front lines of the Union armies extended into areas where many slaves lived. Such circumstances forced the Union government to make decisions about slavery and the African American population. One immediate issue involved the status of fugitive slaves who found their way to northern lines.

Confronted with this question in Virginia, General Benjamin F. Butler, the commander at Fortress Monroe, refused on May 24, 1861 to give up three slaves, declaring that he needed workmen, that the slaves were building enemy batteries, and that the Fugitive Slave Act of the United States did not extend to a foreign country, which Virginia claimed to be. Butler was supported by Secretary of War Simon Cameron, who referred to the "alleged masters of slaves,"[4] though the legal status of those who were everywhere called contrabands was not immediately clear.

The events of war quickly outran government policies as thousands of African Americans flooded into Washington and into military installations in Virginia, Kentucky, and Missouri. Some came by boat; others, despite intimidation, marched boldly into Union camps. Nearly all declared their willingness to work for the army. In Missouri where guerrilla war raged in 1861, African Americans gave valuable information to Union forces, and such support directed Union soldiers who still disliked blacks to link slavery to their enemy and consider it treason. As one Union soldier acknowledged, "The inexorable logic of events is rapidly making abolitionists of every soldier."[5]

In August 1861, General John C. Frémont proclaimed martial law in Missouri. He stipulated that the property of all persons resisting the United States was to be confiscated and their "slaves declared freemen." Lincoln's secretaries believed Frémont's announcement a clumsy bid for popular favor at a time when the general's prestige was waning. In fact, the proclamation emerged from the need to control guerrilla warfare and to win favor with antislavery Republicans as much as from any high-minded motives about freeing human beings. Whatever Frémont's motives, he had exceeded his military authority by dealing with matters of public policy. Lincoln promptly ordered Frémont to show leniency as to martial law, to shoot no man without the president's approval, and to modify the confiscatory and emancipating order so as to conform to existing law.

The Frémont episode had wide repercussions. Worried that Fremont's order would "alarm" the slave border states and southern Unionists, Lincoln believed that the Kentucky legislature—then in session—"would not budge till that proclamation was modified." He also feared the reaction of some Union soldiers: "on the news of General Frémont having actually issued deeds of manumission, a whole company of our Volunteers threw down their arms and disbanded."[6] Sensitive to the effect of emancipation on the border states, which were crucial to the president's strategic considerations, Lincoln overruled the proclamation. The president was also embarrassed by his general's defiance, together with complaints about his military incompetence, and on November 2, 1861, he removed Frémont from his command in St. Louis.

Lincoln applied his policy of not permitting military commanders to force his hand in the matter of emancipation again in May 1862, when he overruled an order of General David Hunter freeing "persons in . . . Georgia, Florida, and South Carolina—heretofore held as slaves." Problems of military emancipation, said the president, "are questions which, under my responsibility, I reserve to myself."[7]

## CONGRESS AND EMANCIPATION

While the president was confronting the slavery question because of the abolitionist orders of two of his generals, Congress was considering applications of the Confiscation Act of August 6, 1861. This legislation mandated that when slaves were engaged in hostile military service, their owners' claim to their labor was forfeited. The law, representing a stage in the development of legislative policy toward emancipation, was vague as to the manner of forfeiture, although enforcement was clearly located in the federal courts. In practice, it rested with the Union army.

The second Confiscation Act of July 17, 1862 went further. It provided that the slaves of all persons supporting the rebellion should be "forever free of their servitude, and not again held as slaves." This law also included slaves of rebel owners in the border states. In addition, the Militia Act of July 17, 1862 freed slaves and their families owned by the enemy. Freedom was later extended to "slave-soldiers of loyal owners," with bounties promised to their owners.[8] By the act of March 13, 1862, Congress, responding to the reality of slaves' making their way to the Union army, prohibited their return by the military.

Although most Democrats in Congress voted against such measures and some Republicans were also opposed, an impressively unified coalition of Republicans "pressed the logic of the situation to its conclusion." Testifying to the shifting opinions of many northerners about the illegitimacy of slavery, these measures were broadly supported in Congress. They were not merely the work of a small group of extremists. Instead, the philosophical unity of moderates and so-called radicals fostered agreement on a congressional version of emancipation.[9]

In other measures relating to emancipation, Congress took the lead, abolishing slavery in the District of Columbia on April 16, 1862. Earlier, in June 1861, Congress passed legislation freeing slaves in the territories without compensation to their former owners, fulfilling a Republican pledge, with all Republicans in favor and nearly all Democrats opposed. But the Fugitive Slave acts of 1793 and 1850 were not repealed until 1864. The Lincoln administration, with congressional approval, also negotiated a treaty with England for the suppression of the slave trade. Since 1820, importing slaves had been a crime punishable by death, but the law was rarely enforced. Now such laxity ended. On February 21, 1862, Captain Nathaniel P. Gordon, the commander of a slave ship, was executed in New York City.

Eventually, the president's emancipation policies outshone those of Congress in the minds of Americans, but before Lincoln's preliminary emancipation proclamation of September 1862, Congress had done as much, on paper, as was accomplished by the president's proclamation. Indeed, with its territorial exceptions, even the final emancipation proclamation fell short of the clause in the Confiscation Act of July 17, 1862, which declared that "all slaves of persons who shall hereafter be engaged in rebellion against the Government of the United States, or who shall in any way give aid . . . within any place occupied by rebel forces and afterwards occupied by the forces of the United States . . . shall be forever free."[10]

Such was the difficulty of enforcing this legislation, and so great the lack of coordination between the president, who considered freeing the slaves as a military measure, and the Republican Congress, which saw freedom as necessary on many grounds, that Lincoln issued his edict as if Congress had done nothing.

## LINCOLN AND EMANCIPATION

As the war progressed, Lincoln pondered the military, legal, and moral implications of the slavery question. Lincoln abhorred slavery, but as a pragmatist he sought a way to devise its destruction without upsetting the fragile coalition that sustained his administration. Initially Lincoln supported compensated emancipation by the states followed by the colonization of freed blacks in central America, the latter an impractical solution to an anticipated mass black migration northward. As he informed a delegation of African Americans in 1862, "On this broad continent not a single man of your race is made the equal of a single man of ours. . . . It is better for us both, therefore, to be separated."[11] According to Richard Current, Lincoln's early plans had five elements:

> First, the states themselves must emancipate the slaves, for in his opinion slavery was a "domestic" institution, the concern of the states alone. Second, slaveowners must be paid for the chattels of which they were to be deprived. Third, the Federal government must share the financial burden by providing Federal bonds as grants-in-aid to the states. Fourth, the actual freeing of the slaves must not be hurried; the states must be given plenty of time, delaying final freedom as late as 1900 if they wished. Fifth, the freed Negroes must be shipped out of the country and colonized abroad, but they must be persuaded to go willingly. Federal aid, gradual emancipation, and voluntary colonization—these were the indispensable features of the Lincoln plan.[12]

In an effort to initiate his program, Lincoln drafted a plan that would free Delaware's slaves, with federal compensation to owners at the rate of four hundred dollars per slave. But opposition in Delaware proved too strong for its passage.[13] He then called a conference of the congressmen from the Union slave states of Maryland, Delaware, Kentucky, and Missouri, pleading with them to support this measure which, in his mind, could both shorten the war and destroy slavery. Responding to complaints that his scheme of compensation cost too much, Lincoln pointed out that compensation at the rate of four hundred dollars each for all Delaware's slaves at a total cost of $719,200 was insignificant in comparison with one day's war expenses of $2 million.[14] At $174,000,000, the cost of eighty-seven days of the war would more than pay for all the slaves of Delaware, Maryland, the District of Columbia, Kentucky, and Missouri.

The president was convinced that such steps toward abolition would discourage the efforts of southern leaders to add the border states to the Confederacy. "To deprive them of this hope substantially ends the rebellion, and the initiation of emancipation completely deprives them of it," he declared. "I say 'initiation' because, in my judgment, gradual, and not sudden emancipation, is better for all."[15] But the result of the border-state conference among apprehensive congressmen was disappointing.[16] Despite criticism from abolitionists that he was too preoccupied with the rights of loyal masters and that it was slaves who should be compensated, Lincoln encouraged Congress to pass a resolution in April 1862 approving his plan in principle.

In his annual message of December 1, 1862, the president proposed three war-influenced constitutional amendments to Congress: one, which acknowledged the reality of slave self-emancipation, guaranteed the freedom of all slaves "who enjoyed actual freedom by the chances of war"; the second authorized congressional appropriations for colonizing "free colored persons with their own consent" outside of the United States; and the third authorized compensated emancipation through federal bonds issued to states abolishing slavery by 1900.[17] But the scheme for state emancipation with federal compensation failed because of the intransigence of the border states.

Ever sensitive to the precariousness of the slave border states—"the fire in the rear"—and anxious that the war not "degenerate into a violent and remorseless revolutionary struggle," Lincoln later returned to his compensation scheme. But influenced by abolitionists in Congress, the course of the war, changing public opinion, slave self-emancipation, and his own repugnance against slavery, he began to move beyond the conservative position that the power to overthrow slavery did not lie within his grasp. Earlier he had replied to a religious delegation from Chicago: "What *good* would a proclamation of emancipation from me do, especially as we are now situated? I do not want to issue a document that the whole world will see must necessarily be inoperative, like the Pope's bull against the comet!"[18]

He had even taken the position that slavery was peripheral to the war, with the cause of the Union primary and vital. To Horace Greeley, who in his "Prayer of Twenty Millions" had reproached the president for not striking at slavery, Lincoln gave his classic reply on August 22, 1862: "My paramount object *is* to save the Union, and *is not* either to save or to destroy slavery. . . . What I do about slavery, and the colored race, I do because I believe it helps to save the Union; and what I forbear, I forbear because I do *not* believe it would help to save the Union." Having struck this note of expediency, he went on to say the following, in a sentence that is often omitted from this quotation and that displays the conflict between his personal wishes and his presidential duties: "I have stated here my purpose according to my view of *official* duty; and I intend no modification of my oft-expressed *personal* wish that all men could be free."[19]

But by the summer of 1862 the cautious Lincoln had in fact made up his mind to issue a proclamation of military emancipation, informing Secretary of Navy Welles and Secretary of State Seward on July 13, 1862 that he had "about come to the conclusion" that a proclamation of emancipation was "absolutely essential for the salvation of the Union."[20]

At Seward's suggestion, Lincoln laid his emancipation proclamation aside, waiting for a military victory, because he did not want emancipation to appear as "a last shriek on the retreat." And he wanted to be certain that the border states, so much in the forefront of his thinking, were secure.[21] His initial poll of his Cabinet revealed that only Postmaster General Montgomery Blair opposed his plan on the partisan grounds that the Democrats, who had taken 44 percent of the northern vote in 1860, would gain in the fall elections after such a revolutionary pronouncement. The Marylander Blair also worried about the effect of emancipation on the border states. The president then waited two months. Five days after Lee's northern invasion had been stopped at Antietam, he told his Cabinet that the time had come to issue the preliminary proclamation on September 22.

The proclamation began by repeating that the purpose of the war was the restoration of the Union. Reaffirming his intention to work for compensated emancipation, Lincoln nevertheless declared that on January 1, 1863, slaves in rebellious states or parts of states should be "then, thenceforward, and forever free." The South had until January 1, 1863 to rejoin the Union or face the freeing of its slaves. He added that "the executive government of the United States will do no act . . . to repress such persons . . . in any efforts they may make for their actual freedom," a clause that southerners interpreted as inciting the slave insurrections they had long feared.

On January 1, 1863, acting on his authority as commander in chief, Lincoln issued a final proclamation. Its provisions expressed the president's view that his military powers extended only to slaves in enemy territory, not to those within Union lines or those in border states, where civilian governments must determine slavery's future. For Lincoln, by 1863 emancipation was a military necessity, an act of justice, and an end to his placating approach to the slave border states. For although the proclamation did not interfere with what he considered the domestic institutions of Maryland, Delaware, Kentucky, and Missouri, slavery, now surrounded everywhere by freedom, was in fact fatally compromised. The chief provision held that in regions then designated as in rebellion (with

Lincoln and members of his Cabinet discuss emancipation. Lincoln declared that on January 1, 1863, slaves in rebellious states would be "forever free."

certain exceptions) all slaves were free. The exceptions included the state of Tennessee, the Union slave states, and parts of Virginia and Louisiana within Union military lines. The proclamation also invited black men to join the army and navy, their service to be limited to "garrison forts, positions, stations, and other places and to move vessels." Freedom was thus decreed only in regions then under Confederate control, a point noted by Lincoln's detractors.

"The President has purposely made the proclamation inoperative," declared the Democratic New York *World*, "in all places where we have gained a military footing which makes the slaves accessible. He has proclaimed emancipation only where he has notoriously no power to execute it. The exemption of the accessible parts of Louisiana, Tennessee, and Virginia renders the proclamation not merely futile, but ridiculous."[22] "We show our sympathy with slavery," Seward agreed, "by emancipating slaves where we cannot reach them and holding them in bondage where we can set them free."[23]

The London *Spectator* declared on October 11, 1862, "The government liberates the enemy's slaves as it would the enemy's cattle, simply to weaken them in the conflict. . . . The principle is not that a human being cannot justly own another, but that he cannot own him unless he is loyal to the United States." At the very time when his government was considering recognizing the Confederacy, Lord Russell agreed: "The Proclamation . . . appears to be of a very strange nature. It professes to emancipate all slaves in places where the United States authorities cannot exercise any jurisdiction but it does not decree emancipation . . .

in any States, or parts of States, occupied by federal troops . . . and where, therefore, emancipation might have been carried into effect. . . . There seems to be no declaration of a principle adverse to slavery in this proclamation."[24]

No matter what the international criticism, Lincoln's proclamation effectively destroyed any possibility of European recognition of the Confederacy. Judah P. Benjamin, the Confederate secretary of state, acknowledged as much. He sent new instructions to southern agents abroad proposing Confederate emancipation of African Americans if such action improved the prospects of recognition. The fact that recognition was not obtained whereas before it seemed probable was attributable partly to Lincoln's proclamation and partly to the observable reality of slave self-emancipation.[25]

Among northern whites there was no unanimity about the Emancipation Proclamation. Northern Democrats were especially hostile to emancipation, though their successes in the 1862 fall elections, when they gained thirty-five seats in the House, were as much the result of discontent with other administration policies and the normal swing of American electoral politics in nonpresidential years as the specific effect of the preliminary proclamation. But after 1863, Democrats such as Clement Vallandigham angrily denounced the war as a battle to free blacks and enslave whites, a message that found a receptive audience among their constituents. In Illinois the proclamation was attacked by members of that party as a "gigantic usurpation," unwarranted by either military or civil law.[26] Some found emancipation an executive acknowledgment of reality; others feared that freed blacks would now find their way north, to which the administration responded that emancipation ensured that blacks would stay in the South.

Of course the proclamation and the president had many supporters. "How decent Abe grows," declared Wendell Phillips, while Horace Greeley cheered "the beginning of the life of the nation." Despite the limitations of the proclamation, abolitionists celebrated the occasion with gratitude that the war against slavery had gained a significant victory. For northern African Americans who also did not quibble about the document's limitations, the day was one of jubilation. In Washington Henry Turner, a prominent African American minister, witnessed processions of black people marching in front of the White House until the president came to the window and made responsive bows. In Boston a large crowd awaited the news sent by telegraph from Washington, after which they adjourned to the Twelfth Baptist Church, singing "Old John Brown," "Marching On," and "Blow Ye Trumpet Blow." Blacks in the border areas, uncertain about the war's outcome, now demanded certificates of freedom from Union officers under the authority of "a proclamation of his excellency Abraham Lincoln."[27]

No matter what others said, Lincoln justified his act as a war measure issued "by virtue of the power in me vested as a commander-in-chief by the Army and Navy . . . and as a fit and necessary war measure." "I think the Constitution invests its commander-in-chief with the law of war, in time of war." The president found another justification in history, explaining that "armies the world over destroy enemies property when they cannot use it." Still, he worried about stretching his powers into what he called "the boundless field of absolutism," fearing citizens in the border states would now anticipate a presidential order freeing their slaves. Thus Lincoln explained this enduring symbol of his presidency—an act that he himself came to see as the crowning achievement of his administration—as constitutionally justified on the grounds of military necessity.[28]

Although constrained by law and by his own moderation, Lincoln, like other Americans, was also influenced by principles of democratic majority rule and republican self-determination. Slavery notably violated the rights of individuals; it denied essential American values such as the equality of human beings and the understanding of freedom as the consent of the governed. If liberty and freedom were right, slavery must be wrong. So although Lincoln relied on temporary war powers, the Emancipation Proclamation rested on abiding national principles. Moreover, the proclamation, as James McPherson has written, "announced a revolutionary new war aim—the overthrow of slavery by force of arms if and when Union armies conquered the South."[29] In an explicit way the Emancipation Proclamation acknowledged that the war was about slavery.

Like the restoration of the Union and the destruction of the Confederate government, the overthrow of slavery now became a northern war objective. Lincoln recognized this change, eloquently absorbing this new goal into what had been a war for the Union. In his second inaugural address, delivered in March 1865, Lincoln said that "if God wills that [the war] continue until all the wealth piled up by the bond-man's two hundred and fifty years of unrequited toil shall be sunk, and until every drop of blood drawn with the lash, shall be paid by another drawn with the sword . . . so it must be."[30]

Senator Charles Sumner immediately understood the need for Congress to ratify the president's proclamation. "I wish to see emancipation placed under the guarantee of an act of Congress. I do not wish to see it float on a presidential proclamation," said the Massachusetts senator. By a vote of 78 to 51, the House approved a resolution that the Emancipation Proclamation would hasten peace. In the Senate, when that body was later considering the Wade-Davis Bill, establishing procedures to restore states to the Union, Sumner successfully included a provision that "all persons held to involuntary servitude in the seceded states were emancipated and discharged therefrom, and their posterity shall be forever free."[31] Here again, Congress had moved beyond Lincoln to free those slaves exempted by the Emancipation Proclamation and to guarantee, even in this late stage of the war, that slaves who came into Union lines were free.

## BLACKS AND EMANCIPATION

The Emancipation Proclamation held different meanings for different groups of African Americans. In areas penetrated by the Union army, the effect was dramatic as slaves moved as close as possible to Union camps. On African Americans in the Deep South, the decree had a less immediate effect, though blacks everywhere, but particularly in the border regions, continued to walk to freedom. Over the grapevine telegraph the news spread, in turn stimulating the process of self-emancipation. A few former slaves, including Harriet Tubman, "traveled hundreds of miles into the Confederate interior, threading their way through enemy lines, eluding Confederate pickets, avoiding former masters, and outrunning the slave catchers hired to track them down" in order to bring the news of liberation.[32] Behind Confederate lines the information was shared in secret meetings in swamps under cover of night; it "could not be prevented," reported an angry Confederate general.[33] In states such as Maryland, where slavery remained legal, men left farms and plantations, women being tied to home as child raisers. One Marylander believed that "if their families could be cared for or taken with them the whole slave population of Maryland would make its exodus to Washington."[34]

With the announcement that emancipation would take effect on January 1, 1863, black soldiers on Port Royal Island in South Carolina hold United States flags in celebration of Lincoln's proclamation.

When slaves escaped from the South, they often traveled in secrecy to avoid capture. Here fugitive slaves enter Union lines.

But the reaction of border-state slaveholders, who had no compunctions about searching military camps, even for slave children, suggests how entrenched slavery was. Near Memphis, Tennessee, a Confederate sympathizer, accompanied by a Union general's aide-de-camp, rode through Camp Holly Springs in the spring of 1864, searching for slaves. When they found three weeping children, they delivered them to their former owner, though their father was at the time a Union soldier.[35] Freedom for many blacks remained conditional and hung on the proximity of the Union army. In Kentucky, for example, slaveholding Unionists reclaimed their property when the Union army retreated from the central part of the state in the fall of 1862.

When the Union army appeared in the interior of the South, as it increasingly did in 1864 and 1865, more slaves left plantations and farms. As Bell Wiley writes, blacks "generally engaged in the seizure and distribution of property and a general celebration of the advent of freedom." Freed women sometimes adopted symbolic badges of their liberation, carrying parasols and wearing the veils previously denied them.[36] Yet many blacks in the interior of the Confederacy remained in bondage—some hurriedly removed to Texas, where as many as 150,000 were sent during the war.[37]

Though the Confederates detected constant plotting among slaves, in fact few organized uprisings took place during the war. One exception occurred near Culpeper, Virginia, with the result that seventeen slaves, several with copies of the Emancipation Proclamation in their pockets, were executed.[38] Those who remained, especially the less mobile women and children, were often held by force on plantations. Frequently the measure of freedom was independence from white domination as former slaves rebelled against overseers, talked back to female plantation managers, took what would earlier have been forbidden trips to be with their families on distant plantations, and complained to Union army officials about their mistreatment.[39]

As the war continued and the army moved farther into the interior of the South, Union generals faced the necessity of providing shelter and protection for former slaves. Federal legislation and executive proclamations changed the way they dealt with African Americans, as the commanders of the Union army no longer deferred to slaveholders and what the latter considered their rights. In the process, the Civil War was redefined.

In Tennessee and Mississippi, Ulysses S. Grant found that, as his army approached, African Americans "flocked in vast numbers—an army in themselves—to the camps of the Yankees." Here was a slave population "forsaking its local traditions and all the associations of the old plantation life ... with feet shod or bleeding, individually or in families—an army of slaves and fugitives, pushing its way irresistibly toward an army of fighting men." In 1863 a congressional committee representing freedmen's aid societies found "the late glorious victory near Chattanooga has, probably, loosed fifty thousand freedmen." For every mile of Grant's advance "ten thousand freedmen drop their chains." Some estimates placed the number of homeless African Americans at over one hundred thousand in Louisiana alone, although these slaves were soon sowing subsistence crops in weed-choked fields of sugarcane and corn.[40]

To deal with the former slaves, Grant ordered Chaplain John Eaton of the Twenty-Seventh Ohio Infantry Volunteers to supervise those whom he still referred to as "contrabands," though they were legally free persons. According to Grant, his own troops had to be protected from disease, and humanitarian considerations dictated that care be given to the new citizens, as they were declared by Attorney General Edward Bates. To this end Eaton established camps, cared for the sick, and organized the able-bodied for military labor, which included picking and baling cotton.

By July 1864, Eaton had over one hundred thousand African Americans under his supervision. Most of these were earning their own subsistence: 41,150 in military service as soldiers, laundresses, guides, cooks, officers' servants, and laborers; 62,300 in private employment as mechanics, draymen, hackmen, barbers, hired laborers, and nurses. The numbers suggest the military significance of denying the labor power of African Americans to the Confederacy and adding it to that of the Union.

In 1863 General Butler created a similar system in parts of Virginia and North Carolina, appointing a "general superintendent of Negro affairs," with other officials directed to take a census, provide shelter, medical care, and other welfare to freedmen; supervise labor contracts; allot lands to blacks; and attend to their training.[41] In Corinth, Mississippi, blacks ran their own camp.[42] Everywhere Union military lines served as the boundary between slavery and freedom.

Confederates continued to warn their slaves to stay away from the Yankees, but few did so. Susie King Taylor, a fourteen-year-old slave from Georgia, came to Fort Pulaski after its capture in 1862, and was soon sewing and teaching reading to other slaves on Saint Simon's Island. Informally enlisted along with her family in Company E of the 33rd Regiment of the U.S. Colored Troops, she worked as an unpaid nurse, tending wounded soldiers.[43] In such individual stories the meaning of emancipation emerged for nearly four million slaves.

Meanwhile the white South continued to oppose the Emancipation Proclamation. On October 1, 1862, the Richmond *Whig* denounced the "fiend's new programme," describing the proclamation as "a dash of the pen to destroy four thousand millions of our property, and . . . a bid for the slaves to rise in insurrection."[44] To the Richmond *Examiner* it seemed the "most startling political crime . . . yet known in American history."[45]

Referring to the proclamation in his message to the Confederate Congress on January 12, 1863, Jefferson Davis declared that "a restitution of the Union has been rendered forever impossible by the adoption of a measure which . . . neither admits of retraction nor can coexist with union." Edward Pollard, who later published a defiant justification of the Confederacy, described emancipation as the "triumph of fanaticism under a false pretense." Worth "no more than the paper on which its bold iniquity was traced," the Emancipation Proclamation, according to Pollard, held as its fundamental principle "an act of malice towards the master rather than one of mercy to the slave."[46]

## BLACK SOLDIERS

The participation of blacks in the army both preceded, and was stimulated by, public policies relating to emancipation. In turn, serving in the armed forces became an opportunity to enact freedom for former black male slaves as well as a potent catalyst for ending slavery. In many cases black soldiers encountered possibilities for demonstrating the manhood and patriotism denied earlier to both slaves and free blacks. Yet at first most white northerners who were willing to accept blacks as laborers in the army were reluctant to accept their participation as equals in combat. Lincoln considered any premature organizing and equipping of African American troops as potentially counterproductive, believing it would not be sustained by public opinion.[47] In time, northern attitudes shifted as the recruitment of blacks came to be seen as a way to fill state quotas and keep fewer whites from being drafted.

African Americans, slave and free, North and South, knew otherwise. As the black corporal James Henry Gooding of the Massachusetts 54th wrote, "The

Hubbard Pryor of Georgia is shown as a slave and then as a Union soldier. Several former slaves joined the Union army to fight against slavery and the Confederacy.

American people, as a nation, knew not what they were fighting for 'til recently, and many have different opinions now as to the ends and results of the contest." But blacks had a clear duty to liberate their race and to demonstrate that they could become "something more than hewers of wood and drawers of water all their lives."[48]

Sentiment supporting black soldiers grew among whites, even as blacks continued to press their claims to join the military in order to, in Frederick Douglass's words, "help raise aloft their country's flag." Since 1861 Douglass, along with other black northerners, had been demanding that the war be carried "into Africa. Let the slaves and colored people be called into service, and formed into a liberating army to march into the South and raise the banner of Emancipation among the slaves." As Ira Berlin explains, "the enlistment of black soldiers provided a powerful instrument in the war against slavery. Even before they had seen active service, news of black men in uniform had an electrifying effect on those still in bondage, encouraging many to strike out for Yankee lines."[49]

Several Union commanders had not waited for the president to act, but on their own initiative had recruited black troops. On April 12, 1862, General David Hunter, commander of the Department of the South, had organized the first unofficial regiment of black troops, composed of former slaves from Georgia, Florida, and South Carolina. A few months later, after the occupation of New Orleans, General John Phelps began equipping five black regiments for his Louisiana command. At first opposed, a month later General Benjamin Butler called on the free "colored" militiamen of Louisiana to enroll in the volunteer forces of the Union; some of these units of the Louisiana Native Guards were led by black officers. In theory all who joined Butler's troops were to be free, but in practice no one asked these volunteers if they had ever been slaves. Meanwhile, in Kansas General James Lane had earlier recruited black soldiers who had been among the first African Americans permitted to fight for their own freedom. When the War Department notified him twice that he had no authorization to raise a black unit, Lane simply ignored the order "in the best frontier fashion."[50]

On August 25, 1862 the War Department officially sanctioned the recruitment of black soldiers, authorizing General Rufus Saxton, who replaced Hunter in the Department of the South, to organize and equip no more than five thousand black volunteers. Lincoln's Emancipation Proclamation also encouraged the enlistment of African American males into the armed forces. By 1863 the formation of black units became commonplace, as former slaves, aware of the opportu-

Provost guard of the 107th Colored Infantry at Fort Corcoran, part of the defenses of Washington.

nity to have a part in emancipating themselves and others of their race, joined up. Not all, however, were volunteers, as some were coerced by army officials.

By the end of the war nearly 179,000 black soldiers and ninety-five hundred black sailors had served in Union forces. Some thirty-four thousand had been free blacks before the war; the rest were counted as slaves in the official records. Thus, nearly one of every ten Union soldiers was an African American, with the proportion even higher in the war's last two years.[51] This force saw action on widely separated fronts—in South Carolina, and Florida, at Fort Hudson, at Petersburg, at Olustee, in Kansas, Missouri, and Virginia—indeed everywhere that the Union Army fought.

"Let any Union man who complains of [black troops]," wrote their commander in chief in 1864, "test himself by writing down in one line that he is for subduing the rebellion by force of arms; and in the next, that he is for taking these one hundred and thirty thousand men from the Union side and placing them where they would be but for the measure he condemns."[52]

Cautious at first, Lincoln was soon praising black troops. Writing to General John Dix in January 1863, the president concluded that since the restrictions of the Emancipation Proclamation (and the limitations on his power as commander in chief) had to be endured, its benefits should also be grasped. Two months later he spoke of black troops as "very important, if not indispensable." Soon after he expressed satisfaction at the conduct of these troops and noted that "the raising of colored troops . . . will greatly help [in] every way." Some, he said, considered "the emancipation policy and the use of colored troops . . . the heaviest blow yet dealt to the rebellion." The president also pointed out what the soldiers themselves already knew: that they could not be reenslaved. "Should I do so, I should deserve to be damned in time and eternity."[53]

But national prejudices required that black soldiers be commanded by whites, and the War Department opposed the appointment of black officers. Nevertheless, about one hundred African Americans held commissions at various times, mostly in the Department of the South.[54] Yet it was generally whites who led the black regiments into battle. The most famous white officers were Robert Gould Shaw of the Massachusetts 54th and Thomas Higginson, also of Massachusetts, who accepted the colonelcy of the First Regiment of South Carolina Volunteers. After leading this unit in raiding operations up the St. Mary's and Edisto rivers, Higginson explained his motives: "I had been an abolitionist too long, and had known and loved John Brown too well, not to feel a thrill of joy at last on finding myself in the position he only wished to be."[55]

Shaw's troops were the first black regiment of the North to go to war. In a heroic attack on Fort Wagner in Charleston Harbor on July 18, 1863, Shaw died, as did nearly one-half of his regiment, while advancing under a barrage of Confederate fire. Although few of these black soldiers left accounts of their service, Corporal Gooding on nearby Morris Island recalled that "mortal men could not stand such a fire, and the assault on Wagner [which he called the Sebastopol of the rebels] was a failure."[56] Later, a black sergeant who survived Fort Wagner wrote his company commander that he was "more Eager for the struggle than I ever yet have [been], for I now wish to have revenge for our galant Curnel and the spilt blood of our Captin. We expect to Plant the Stars and Stripes on the Sity of Charleston."[57]

Gooding and other black soldiers understood the importance of fighting a war they saw less as one to restore the Union than to end slavery. Serving in thirty-nine major battles and 449 smaller engagements, charging through the crater at Petersburg and flanking the Confederate army at Nashville, through it all blacks sang with special meaning the Civil War song, "We'll rally around the flag boys, we'll rally once again, shouting the battle cry of Freedom." Two black amputees later linked manhood, freedom, and patriotism in sentiments common to blacks: One, surveying the stump of his arm, said he would like to have his arm whole again, but he didn't begrudge it; the other, who had lost a leg, replied, "Well, 'twas lost in a glorious cause, and if I'd lost my life I should have been satisfied. I know what I was fighting for." And after the war had ended the black chaplain of the 28th U.S. Colored Infantry gave a final assessment that the pens of historians "cannot fail to locate us among the good and the great, who have fought and bled upon the alter [sic] of their country."[58]

Throughout the war black soldiers were discriminated against with regard to pay, bounties, reenlistment bonuses, and even medical services, the latter's deficiencies being one reason for the high percentage of black casualties. In the beginning of the war, racial hostility required that blacks fight in subordinate positions with picks and shovels, but not guns. In time, northerners came to see black soldiers as a proper substitute for whites. In the words of a contemporary song, "I'll let Sambo be murdered instead of myself."[59] Clearly the unequal treatment of blacks in the military, vociferously protested by some, was a preview of their postwar status in both the North and South.

The War Department's assurance of equal pay was persistently violated. Until 1864 even noncommissioned black officers received seven dollars a month, the same as black privates but four dollars less than whites in similar positions.[60] The outspoken Corporal Gooding took his complaints to the president: "Now the main question is are we soldiers or are we laborers? We are fully armed and equipped, have done all the various Duties pertaining to a soldier's life, have conducted ourselves to the complete satisfaction of general officers who were . . . prejudiced against us. Would it not be well and consistent to set the example . . . by paying all soldiers alike?" Others protested the predominance of their details to "hard fatigue work and bone labor" which made them feel as if they were slaves again.[61] Not until June 1864 did the federal government end this policy of discrimination in the pay of black troops, who remained in segregated units until after World War II.[62]

The use of black troops brought threats of retaliation from the South, where the practice was denounced as a barbaric departure from the laws of war. On August 21, 1862 Jefferson Davis ordered that the Union Generals David Hunter and John Phelps be treated as outlaws and executed as felons because they used slaves as soldiers. Later Davis declared that Lincoln was trying to encourage a slave rebellion and the slave soldiers and Federal commissioned officers serving with them should be turned over to the southern states, where of course they would be put to death or reenslaved. And the Confederate Congress agreed in a resolution passed in April 1863.[63]

On July 3, 1863 Lincoln reacted by ordering that the Union would respond in kind for every soldier killed in violation of the laws of war. For every black soldier reenslaved, a rebel prisoner "shall be placed at hard labor . . . until the other shall receive the treatment of a prisoner of war."

Yet overall the president handled Confederate atrocities timidly, even the brutal affair at Fort Pillow, Tennessee. There on April 12, 1864, General Nathan Bedford Forrest allowed the murder of the surrendering black troops who constituted a part of that garrison. Forrest's forces massacred several hundred African American Union soldiers instead of taking them prisoner, as would have been the case had they been white. A United States Senate investigating committee concluded that the Confederates had killed three hundred men "in cold blood after the post was in the possession of the rebels, and our men had thrown down their arms."[64]

Unlike Congress, Lincoln remained uncertain about the events at Fort Pillow, urging a further investigation and announcing only that he did not "know that a colored soldier, or white officer commanding colored soldiers, has been massacred by the rebels when made a prisoner."[65] There were other instances of the murder of black troops, which often solidified support for black units on the battlefield among white soldiers and civilians. "Remember Fort Pillow" became a call for retaliation and refusal to surrender.[66]

## EMANCIPATION BY STATES
## AND THE THIRTEENTH AMENDMENT

Although blacks, encouraged by public policies, continued to liberate themselves, other forms of emancipation initiated by white leaders were also required. In the border states exempted from the Emancipation Proclamation, ending slavery became a political issue often separating the Republican and Democratic parties. In order for West Virginia to be admitted to the Union, the state constitution of 1863 included a clause providing gradual emancipation. The Maryland constitution of 1864 officially freed that state's slaves, and in Tennessee an amendment to the constitution in early 1865 accomplished the same purpose. In Missouri slavery was abolished by an ordinance passed by a state convention in

January 1865. In Louisiana, Lincoln appointed a military governor in 1862 and impatiently awaited a new constitution written in April 1864, which freed slaves but did not enfranchise blacks.[67] Delaware and Kentucky, however, clung tenaciously to the dying institution, and the war ended with slavery still technically legal in those states.[68]

Closure to formal emancipation—a process that had been handled piecemeal by the president, Congress, and state legislatures—came in the form of a constitutional amendment reported from the Senate Judiciary Committee in the first use of the amending process to accomplish a specific reform on a nationwide scale. Since 1862, Republicans had argued that Congress, through the Declaration of Independence and its war powers, had the authority to end slavery by statute. To prevent any doubt, the 1864 Republican National Convention had endorsed an abolition amendment, even as Democrats held to the traditional view that domestic institutions such as slavery should be subject to state law and that the U.S. Constitution should not be altered during the war.

Such was the opposition to the amendment that when first brought to a vote in the spring of 1864, it failed to achieve a two-thirds majority in the House, although it did pass in the Senate 38 to 6. The results of the election of 1864, the success of the war, and Lincoln's personal lobbying and use of patronage changed several minds. On January 31, 1865, the amendment was carried, 119 to 56, 8 not voting, before an audience of cheering African Americans.[69] State ratification of the amendment followed during the early stages of reconstruction.

The passage of the Thirteenth Amendment was the necessary culmination of the North's antislavery program. It would enable a reunified nation to move beyond an issue that had dominated the political agenda since 1818. Yet until a clear federal policy outlawing slavery was installed, the possibility of repealing wartime confiscation acts or overriding the Emancipation Proclamation remained. In Kentucky the Thirteenth Amendment's impact was immediately felt by African Americans, who had been required to produce passes in order to ride on public transportation facilities. By order of the commanding general of Kentucky, "from henceforth colored people will be under the general laws of the land, and if owners or operators of Boats or Rail Roads shall disregard their undoubted right to travel at pleasure . . . they are advised to apply promptly to the Courts for Redress."

Yet freedom from slavery did not imply citizenship. Many legislators who opposed slavery also opposed black equality. Despite the amendment, several states such as Maryland prohibited former slaves from owning businesses or riding on trains. African American children were required to be apprentices in situations that violated their freedom. According to some border-state residents, legislatures could continue to pass restrictive laws regulating all blacks.[70]

Late in the war Frederick Douglass had proclaimed the wartime intentions of nearly four million slaves. Said Douglass, "I end where I began; no war but an abolition war; no peace but an abolition peace, liberty for all, chains for none; the black man a soldier in war; a laborer in peace; a voter at the South as well as the North; America his permanent home, and all Americans his fellow country-men."[71] Ultimately emancipation would bring different futures for individual slaves.

But to the extent that Douglass's mission had been accomplished, it had been achieved by African Americans themselves, by the thrust of war, by the increasingly anachronistic situation of slavery in a growing industrial nation, and by the policies of the Republican party, including Abraham Lincoln, who came to believe that "the emancipation policy, and the use of colored troops, constitute the heaviest blow yet dealt to the rebellion" and that important successes "could not have been achieved . . . but for the aid of black soldiers."[72] The process of emancipation redefined the meaning of the war, and that redefinition was echoed on the battlefield.

CHAPTER 17 | # The War's Middle Phase

I n many ways 1863 was the most critical year of the war. Controversies continued to swirl around the Lincoln administration's policies of emancipation, conscription, and financial management, as events on the battlefield were influenced by these political decisions. Both governments continued to concentrate men and materials in the more prestigious eastern theater, but there was growing recognition, as Lee acknowledged, that the loss of the Mississippi valley region would bring a Union victory.[1] In Richmond a political bloc composed of southwestern representatives, along with the efficient postmaster general, John Reagan of Texas, continually pressured Davis to concentrate on the West. This internal struggle often led to arguments about and delays in deploying troops.[2]

Although 1863 opened unfavorably for the Union armies, it ended with significant military victories in both the eastern and western theaters. As the Union armies penetrated vast portions of the Confederacy, 1863 came to mark "the emergence of large-scale destruction carried out, in fairly routine fashion, by large bodies of troops."[3] The Union occupation, which by the end of 1863 included enclaves on the North Carolina coast, Tennessee, most of Arkansas, and swaths of territory along the Mississippi River in the states of Louisiana and Mississippi, increasingly cost the Confederacy critical resources.

While there was continuity in the Confederate commanders in the East, Lincoln struggled to find a competent general to lead the Army of the Potomac. In January the president replaced the disgraced Burnside with Joseph Hooker, who had a reputation for aggressiveness and who exuded confidence with his bombastic comments about bestowing no mercy on Lee. Soon the two clashed in that corridor of northern Virginia where so much of the Civil War was fought.

President Lincoln appointed Joseph Hooker commander of the Army of the Potomac in 1863. Following his defeat at Chancellorsville, Hooker was relieved of command at his own request.

## CHANCELLORSVILLE

After their success at Fredericksburg in December 1862, the Confederates, as was often the case with both armies, had failed to destroy Burnside. That general's shattered army, according to the Confederate writer Edward Pollard, was cowering beneath the houses of the northern Virginia town. Pollard added that the southern public "waited with impatience to hear that Gen. Lee had assumed the offensive."[4] But Union artillery emplacements as well as various logistical challenges caused Lee to fear further attacks. He kept his defensive position, advising Jeb Stuart that "no one knows how brittle an army is."[5]

Avoiding any direct movement against a numerically superior enemy, the southern commander divided his army, sending James Longstreet south toward Suffolk, Virginia, where the Union general John Peck had thirty thousand troops.[6] Lee believed that the position was being developed as a point from which to strike at Richmond. To prevent this possibility and to gather supplies, he detached Longstreet's troops from his main army facing Hooker, positioning them between Suffolk and the Confederate capital. These maneuvers gave Hooker a significant advantage, with about 133,000 well-trained troops of the Army of the Potomac facing Lee's 60,000, although when Hooker attacked, Longstreet was ordered to rejoin Lee.[7] Hooker's cavalry of 11,000 was nearly triple that of Lee, who had 4,450 mounted troops.

According to Hooker's plan to destroy the Confederate army, John Sedgwick's two corps were to threaten Lee's right below Fredericksburg; Hooker's own force of seventy thousand, moving westward after crossing the Rappahannock River, was to strike Lee from the direction of Chancellorsville, a little country crossroads fifteen miles west of Fredericksburg. George Stoneman's cavalry, organized for the first time in one concentrated force, was to imitate Stuart's exploits by sweeping around the rear of the Confederate force and wrecking communications with Richmond as well as confusing Lee. Intending a pincer action, the Union commander divided his army into two wings, with the enemy, though it was no ordinary one, between them.[8]

Aware of Hooker's positions and plans, Lee again audaciously divided his force, even in the face of Union forces double his in numbers. Believing that an army inferior in size must compensate by taking risks, Lee kept a force of ten thousand under Jubal Early at Fredericksburg. Then he sent Stonewall Jackson with about thirty thousand men on a wide, sweeping movement to strike Hooker's right flank, commanded by O. O. Howard. Lee himself with about fourteen thousand troops was to hold Hooker and lock the Union army into the bushy terrain of the Wilderness, where rapid movements were impossible. In the battle of Chancellorsville, May 1–3, Lee succeeded in controlling Hooker's turning movement, and Confederate troops followed by attacking the Federal force on its flank.[9]

After a march of twelve hours on May 2, Jackson surprised Howard, whose men, with their arms stacked, were cooking supper. In the 75th Ohio regiment, a private with a fiddle had just began singing the doleful song "Tell My Mother When You See Her" when the shout went up, "Johnnies, the Johnnies are coming."[10] Separated from the main force under Hooker and without advance warning, Howard was caught with significantly fewer numbers and was rolled up in a sharp attack from the front and sides by Jackson's troops. In the confusion of combat Union soldiers fled, with Jackson's pursuing troops slowed only by darkness and exhaustion. In this action the Confederates applied the classic principle of concentrating their strength against the weakest point of the enemy. But by the second day of battle the Confederates had failed to push all the way to the Rappahannock and were threatened by the possibility of a Union counterattack.

Meanwhile Lee's demonstration with a thin line of troops farther to the east had deterred Hooker from promptly sending reinforcements. Although he had reports that Confederate troops were sliding across his stationary front, the Union general known as "Fighting Joe" did little. Howard was held responsible for the Union withdrawal because he failed to reconnoiter his position. But Hooker, who had lost his nerve, shared this responsibility because he never attacked, though his forces outnumbered Lee's. Some authorities believe that Hooker commanded a larger force than he was capable of handling.[11] In fairness it must be said that he had been wounded and was out of command for part of the engagement.

By May 6 Hooker had retreated across the Rappahannock River, a movement that the Confederates had achieved at great cost. The battle has been acknowledged as Lee's tactical masterpiece and the high point of Confederate military fortunes, but southern forces sustained thirteen thousand casualties, a higher proportion of those engaged than the Union's seventeen thousand. In time such losses would deplete an unreplenishable resource—the South's manpower.

Chancellorsville was also Stonewall Jackson's last battle. The southern hero had ridden out with staff officers beyond his lines, and his party was mistaken for Union cavalry by soldiers of the 18th North Carolina. The victim of friendly fire, Jackson died, following the amputation of his left arm, of pneumonia, the bacterial infection that proved fatal to one of every six Confederate wounded. On his deathbed he received Lee's congratulations on the victory, "which is due to your skill and energy." Lee, at the Confederacy's high noon, had now lost his "right arm."[12] The South had lost a revered symbol of its manhood and purpose.

Jackson combined a commitment to drastic war making and a self-discipline that became the measures of the courage in battle admired by both sides. An evocative figure for the Confederacy from the beginning of the war, Stonewall Jackson favored a destructive war aimed at decisively defeating the northerners. He believed that aggressiveness was the only way for the Confederates to win against a stronger enemy. Several times he had called for invasions across the Potomac, not so much for the purpose of striking at the Federal army as to undermine the will of northern citizens to continue the war. He intended to make the struggle for independence a relentless operation, believing like many southerners, according to Charles Royster, "that aggressive war offered the best means of establishing this new nation swiftly and conclusively. After decades of sectional crises, years of threats to secede, and months of debate between eager and reluctant secessionists an assault on the North would demonstrate at once the reality of the Confederacy and the power of its new citizenry."[13]

The results of Chancellorsville were inconclusive, as stalemate continued to prevail in Virginia. Hooker, putting the blame on subordinates, was still a formidable enemy in command of a powerful army. For Lee the main questions were whether to fight south of the Potomac or to carry the war north, and whether to send a part of his troops west to relieve Pemberton and Bragg, who were trying to save Vicksburg from Grant's closing vise.

## GETTYSBURG

A month later, the offensive-minded Lee decided to invade the North and not to send troops west. For this decision, and for the continuing priority given to the eastern front as vast portions of the West were compromised by Union armies, he and Jefferson Davis are often criticized.[14] During June, both Washington and Richmond were exposed, as both armies marched and maneuvered. But the "swapping of queens" represented by the capitals did not occur; as Lincoln informed Hooker, "I think Lee's army and not Richmond is your true objective point."[15] At the end of the month Lee crossed the Potomac and swung his

MAJOR CAMPAIGNS IN THE EAST,
1863

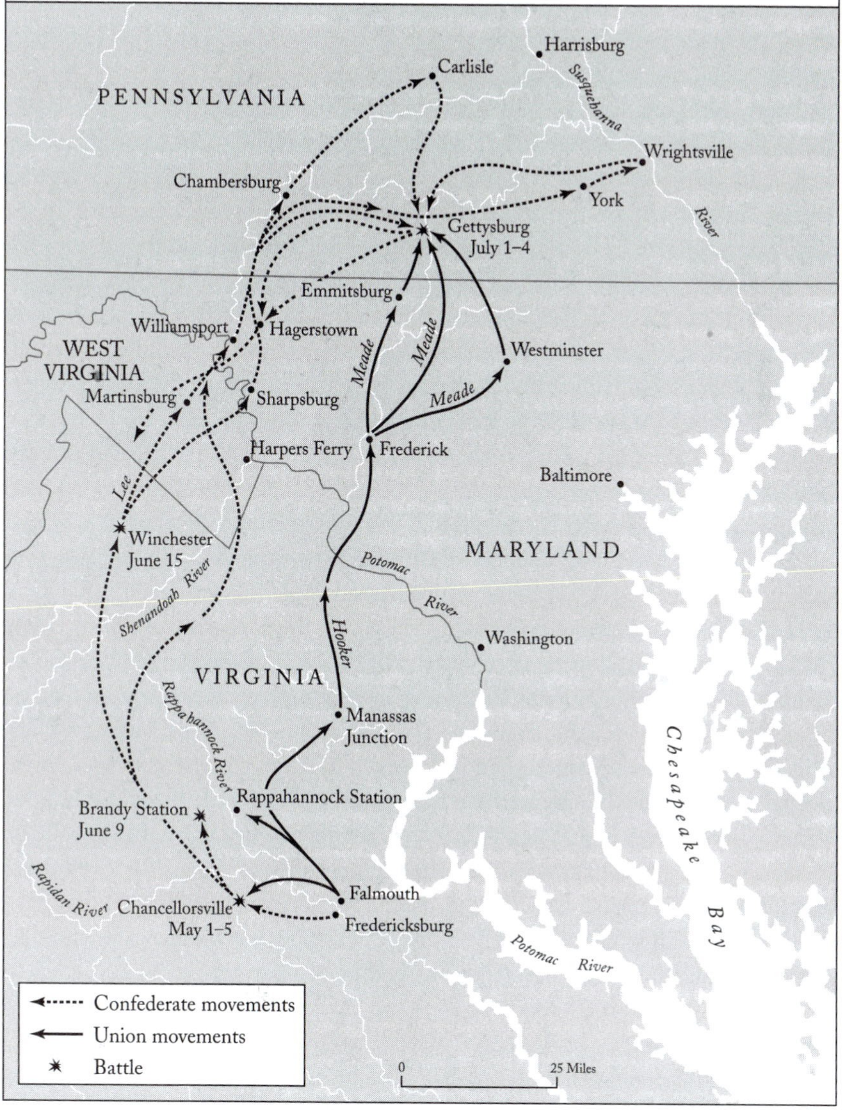

Confederate movements

Union movements

Battle

0    25 Miles

corps under Longstreet, Richard B. Ewell, and A. P. Hill northward. His objectives were both political and military. He hoped to resupply his army, to dampen
northern morale before the fall elections, to draw a Union attack in favorable circumstances, and to influence the campaign around Vicksburg by his success.

On the first three days of July the greatest battle of the war was fought at Gettysburg. On both sides its location was unpremeditated. Lee was moving north

to threaten Washington and other cities, even planning at one stage to push Ewell as far as Harrisburg, the capital of Pennsylvania. Meanwhile Hooker marched north over a more easterly route to keep his forces between Washington and the Confederates. Lead elements of both armies collided outside Gettysburg on July 1, and the battle began.

Four days earlier Lincoln had removed Hooker as commander of the Army of the Potomac had appointed George G. Meade, whose rise to high command was as much a surprise to himself as to the army, many of whom still preferred McClellan. Meade had trained at West Point and had distinguished himself in the Virginia campaigns. The Union force under his command numbered approximately eighty-eight thousand to Lee's seventy-five thousand. From Meade's perspective his operational objective was to force Lee to fight before he could cross the Susquehanna River. For Lee, battle was necessary. He was conducting an offensive with a confident army; he could not retreat without fighting. It was Meade's purpose to see that the location and the conditions of battle were as favorable as possible to the Union army. Meanwhile in Washington, Lincoln saw Lee's raid as "the best opportunity we have had since the war began" because it afforded the possibility of destroying the Army of Northern Virginia.[16]

Abandoning any plan to attack Harrisburg, Lee recalled Ewell and was concentrating his forces at Cashtown in southern Pennsylvania, when, on July 1, Henry Heth's Confederate division of Hill's corps engaged John Buford's Union cavalry, together with the advance infantry of the Federals, led by John Reynolds. Other troops, Union and Confederate, were now rapidly converging on Gettysburg. Each hour brought changes in the positions of corps, divisions, and brigades. On the first day the Union forces, in a sharp engagement, were overpowered by superior Confederate numbers. By falling back in relatively good order, although five thousand soldiers were captured, they were able to rally on Cemetery Hill south of town, and with the help of new troops under Howard and Winfield Scott Hancock to hold that important position. In this first day's fight, General Reynolds was killed by a sharpshooter. Hancock—who had trained at West Point and had served in the Peninsula campaign, at Antietam, at Fredericksburg, and at Chancellorsville—took his place.

In the land around Gettysburg, flat fields alternated with ridges, rock formations, hills, and small mountains. West of the town stood the Lutheran seminary, from which extended a stretch of high ground called Seminary Ridge. About a mile east of this position was Cemetery Ridge, with its parallel ridges slightly higher than the intervening plain. The cemetery was just south of town. Farther to the east was Culp's Hill. About two miles south of Cemetery Hill were two small, spherical mountains called Round Top and Little Round Top. As the Union position developed after much shifting, it presented a fishhook formation with the eye of the hook the Union left on Round Top, the main part of the position along Cemetery Ridge, and the right barb of the hook on Culp's Hill.

It was a strong defensive position, assumed more by accident than by the foresight of Union generals. Opposite, on Seminary Ridge, waited the Confederates. Instead of giving battle under such circumstances, Longstreet urged Lee to swing around the Union left and by slicing between the Union army and Washington, dislodge Meade, select a good position, force Meade to make the attack, and defeat the Union army, as had occurred at Fredericksburg. But with Union reinforcements rushing into position, Lee feared Longstreet might become isolated and overruled his plan as impracticable.[17]

The events of the second day took place chiefly on the right and left of the Union positions. On the left, Longstreet, who commanded the First Corps of the Army of Northern Virginia, and A. P. Hill hurled their forces against the exposed Union position below the Round Tops. Brutal fighting in the Peach Orchard and the Devil's Den ended with the Den and the field at the foot of the Round Tops held by the Confederates. Yet the high ground of the Round Tops remained in Union hands. Earlier, General Gouverneur Warren, to whom Meade had entrusted the operations on his left, had found Little Round Top unoccupied. Believing it the key to the whole position, he urged Meade to send troops there. Infantry and artillery rushed to the heights, arriving in time to beat the Confederates back in a close encounter. Thereafter both Round Tops remained Union strongholds.

A Confederate soldier lies dead in the jagged rocks in Devil's Den at Gettysburg.

At the other end of the battle line, at the close of the second day, Ewell's troops assaulted the Union right. Jubal Early struck on East Cemetery Hill without capturing the position. Johnston's division did better, seizing Union entrenchments at Culp's Hill. This position, however, was recovered the next day.[18]

Some experts attribute the Confederate failure to crack the Union left on July 2 to Longstreet, whose assault did not begin until mid-afternoon. Others explain the late attack as the logistical result of the distance to be covered and the fact that the roads were blocked by other units. Lee himself noted that Longstreet—a general many Confederates believed after Jackson's death "the best fighter in the whole army"—had not completed the operation as quickly as expected, forcing Lee to change his battle plan.[19] In his official report, Lee also drew attention to the earlier absence of the cavalry, since Jeb Stuart had chosen to attempt another ride around the Union army as he had done twice in 1862. Lee's orders on June 23 had left Stuart some latitude on the issue of when and where "to pass around their army without hindrance."[20] Still, his absence left Lee without essential reconnaisance information.

On the night of the second day, Meade held a council of war, where it was decided to hold the existing Union position, remain on the defensive, and await Lee's attack. When that attack came, it was directed against the Union center. Delayed until the afternoon of July 3, the charge marked the climax of the battle and the high-water mark of the Confederacy. Impressed with the strength of the enemy's position, Longstreet urged that this frontal attack be avoided and that an attempt be made to turn the Union position by a maneuver on Meade's left. Again he was overruled, as Lee ordered an advance into the center of the Union line. The celebrated charge of three divisions, led by forty-five hundred troops of Pickett's division, was thus ordered in the hope that by a supreme effort the Union center could be broken and the army routed.

But Meade had anticipated this assault on his center and had concentrated his first and second corps there, with Hancock in command. The position was secured by defensive fortifications and artillery placements. Reserves were close by; the cavalry was stationed in the rear with orders to shoot stragglers. About one o'clock, the Confederate guns opened fire with the largest bombardment ever witnessed on American soil. Answering Union batteries caused the scene to resemble a "furious thunderstorm."[21] Confederate ammunition was low, however, and the bombardment overshot its target. Meade's artillery was far from silenced. Though it "seemed madness to launch infantry into that fire," three divisions of mostly Virginians and North Carolinians—about thirteen-thousand men—moved forward to cross a mile of open terrain separating the two armies.[22] They were led by George Pickett with his long ringlets, astride a shining black horse, wearing brightly polished boots, and carrying a crop, joined by troops under James Pettigrew, Cadmus Wilcox, and Isaac Ridgeway Trimble.

Their advancing lines crumpled, reformed, and pressed ahead under intense fire from Union batteries. The chaos made even veterans caught up in the action

In this painting of the battle of Gettysburg, Union troops defend Cemetery Ridge from Pickett's charging troops. Very few Confederate soldiers were able to penetrate the Union defense and reach the top of the ridge. One of the soldiers who was successful was a woman disguised as a man.

forget to fire their muskets before reloading. As the troops approached the Union position, they endured concentrated infantry volleys aimed with sharp-shooters' precision. In past wars such an attack might have succeeded, but by 1863 the long range of rifles kept attacking cavalry at a safe distance and permitted defenders to remain in whatever natural fortifications were available or in trenches they made.[23] Of thirteen thousand who charged, over half were killed or wounded.[24]

At the peak of the attack the Confederate general Lewis Armistead fell at the moment when, with a hundred men, he had momentarily pierced the Union position at a "bloody angle" on the crest of the ridge. As a sergeant in the 14th Connecticut Volunteer Infantry described the scene to his wife two days later, "I saw the Rebels in 3 lines of Battle moving to attack us. we had but one line to oppose them with but we had a low stone wall behind which we laid, until the Rebels got within 30 Rods of us, then such a Volley of rifles we gave them you can not imagine. soon the first line was shattered to pieces, and with shouts of Derision we awaited the next, served them the same way and soon the whole were Flying from whence [they] came, leaving behind Hundreds of Killed and Wounded."[25]

The bleeding fragments of Pickett's division staggered back to Seminary Ridge. Lee, whose thoughts may have anticipated Appomattox, met them with

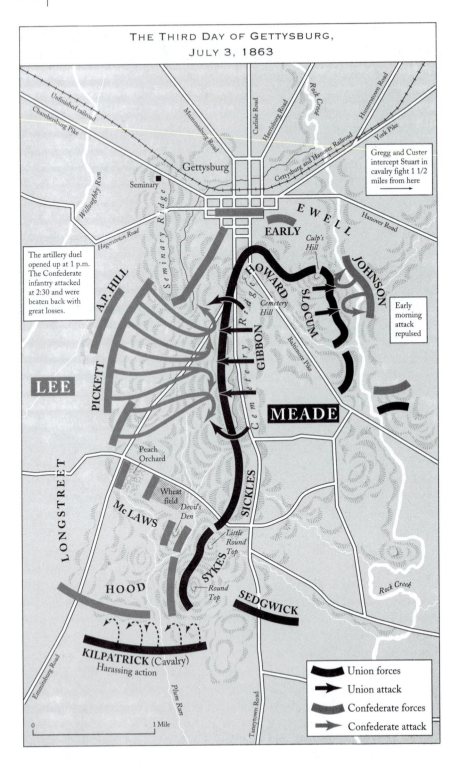

THE THIRD DAY OF GETTYSBURG,
JULY 3, 1863

Gregg and Custer
intercept Stuart in
cavalry fight 1 1/2
miles from here

The artillery duel
opened up at 1 p.m.
The Confederate
infantry attacked
at 2:30 and were
beaten back with
great losses.

Early
morning
attack
repulsed

Union forces

Union attack

Confederate forces

Confederate attack

self-composed dignity. In a letter to Jefferson Davis on July 31, Lee wrote that he alone was to blame for the defeat, perhaps "expecting too much of the prowess and valour" of his army. Indeed, the southern commander seemed to rely too much on his infantry to achieve an impossible victory, though he believed it had achieved "a general success."[26] Meanwhile Meade withheld the countercharge that the southerners feared, and the battle of Gettysburg was over. Next day the armies lay facing each other "like spent lions nursing their wounds." In three days the Union army of eighty-five thousand had sustained twenty-three thousand casualties; twenty-eight thousand of the Confederates' seventy-five thousand were wounded or killed—figures that suggest the heavy losses throughout the battle, not just on the last day of fighting.

The exhausted survivors in Meade's army neither attacked, as Lincoln wanted, nor immediately followed as Lee retreated into Virginia.[27] Having halted his army at Williamsport, where he waited for the Potomac to subside, he crossed on the night of the 13th. Meade's opportunity to catch Lee at a disadvantage, with a swollen river at the back of his retreating army, was lost. That failure prolonged the war, but Lee's defeat had severely reduced the Confederates' chance of winning it. A disappointed president advised General Halleck that "Meade's movements seemed more connected with a purpose to cover Baltimore and Washington and to get the enemy across the river . . . than to prevent his crossing and destroy him."[28]

## EARLY OPERATIONS IN THE WEST

In the heartland of the Confederacy, the Union was operating a two-pronged strategy. One was a drive to control the entire Mississippi River from Memphis, which was taken in June 1862, to New Orleans, the Confederacy's largest city and principal port, which had surrendered to a Union flotilla and fifteen thousand troops two months earlier. In Edward Pollard's glum assessment, "It annihilated us in Louisiana . . . and led to our virtual abandonment of the great and fruitful valley of the Mississippi."[29] A second effort depended on an advance through Kentucky into Tennessee, a state that produced large quantities of essential war materials such as iron, gunpowder, and salt.[30]

The Union army's 1862 campaigns at Forts Henry and Donelson as well as at New Orleans, Island Number 10 (the tenth island in the Mississippi south of Cairo, Illinois), and Shiloh on the Tennessee River had demonstrated the importance of joint military and naval operations on the western rivers. By the beginning of 1863 the Union controlled much of the Cumberland and Tennessee rivers (though not Chattanooga) and the upper Mississippi (though not Vicksburg).[31]

Henry Halleck, who was generally given credit for these western advances, moved to Washington as general-in-chief in July 1862. Grant, whom Halleck had displaced as field commander after Shiloh, was now in overall command of the forces in western Tennessee and northern Mississippi. Besides his own Army of the Tennessee, he had authority over William Rosecrans, who had succeeded John Pope as commander of the Army of the Mississippi. Like many Union generals, Rosecrans had graduated from West Point, but had left the army for a career in business. Don Carlos Buell, who had chosen the Union over his native Virginia, now commanded the Army of the Ohio and was entrusted with operations in central and eastern Tennessee, the latter important to Lincoln because of its readiness to cooperate in the process of reconstructing the Union.

The keys to western strategy were Chattanooga and Vicksburg. As a result of both topography and rail connections, Chattanooga formed a doorway into the Confederate heartland. Its value rested in the fact that the only railroads linking the eastern and western parts of the Confederacy intersected there. Vicksburg not only commanded the Mississippi River, but had rail connections to Texas by means of the Vicksburg, Shreveport, and Texas Railroad line. And parts of Texas, where the Union blockade had only a limited effect, remained sources of much-needed food and munitions for the Confederate armies in the East. The loss of Chattanooga or Vicksburg would sever vital transportation arteries, and the Union seizure of both in 1863 had as much to do with sealing the doom of the Confederacy as did the defeat of Lee at Gettysburg.

On the Confederate side, Braxton Bragg—a West Point–trained veteran of the Mexican War—had succeeded P. G. T. Beauregard as general commander of the forces between Virginia and the Mississippi River. He transferred his army to Chattanooga, leaving the defense of Vicksburg and the operations in northeastern Mississippi to Earl Van Dorn and Sterling Price. Other Confederate armies in the West were those of Humphrey Marshall, soon to move into Kentucky from western Virginia, and Edmund Kirby Smith, who commanded an important force at Knoxville and who stood ready to cooperate with Bragg on the eastern Tennessee and Kentucky fronts. It was Jefferson Davis's policy to separate his military departments, and the resulting lack of collaboration among specific army corps in the West remained a handicap throughout the war.[32]

Buell, who had organized his troops into a well-disciplined army, had only tenuous control over central Tennessee. Although he held Nashville and Murfreesboro, his communications through the Louisville and Nashville Railroad were difficult to maintain in a region of hostile civilians and guerrilla bands. He was also hampered by the destructive operations of two skillful and aggressive Confederate cavalry commanders, Generals John Hunt Morgan and Nathan Bedford Forrest, the latter a former slave trader. With two thousand cavalry, Forrest descended on Murfreesboro on July 13, 1862 and captured a force of brigade proportions under General Thomas Crittenden, the son of the well-known Kentucky politician John J. Crittenden. At about the same time, Morgan's cavalry struck the line of the Louisville and Nashville in Kentucky, surprising small Union detachments, cutting railway tracks, wrecking bridges, capturing military stores, interrupting telegraph communications, terrorizing small villages, and creating general havoc along the widely stretched Federal lines.

This three-week raid by Morgan in July was followed by another in August near Nashville, where isolated Union forces were dispersed and a large cavalry unit captured.[33] Meanwhile, guerrillas engaging in plunder, assassination, and random acts of violence terrorized soldiers and civilians in Tennessee. In the summer of 1863 Morgan, distinctive among southerners for the plumed hat he wore into battle and his lax discipline over his often unruly men, pushed into Ohio, where his twenty-five hundred guerrillas pillaged, captured horses, and destroyed bridges. But despite boosting morale in the South, these dramatic episodes had little effect on the war's outcome.

The western campaigns of the summer and fall of 1862 were indecisive. In retrospect it is clear that the Confederate units needed more support from the Richmond government to offset the Union strategy which, if successful, would carve the Confederacy into untenable thirds. This part of the war resolved itself into three main phases: Bragg's invasion of Kentucky, which was intended to turn the war around in the West after the disasters suffered during the winter and spring of 1862; second the Iuka-Corinth campaign of Rosecrans against Price and Van Dorn in the fall of 1862; and finally, the initially unsuccessful movements of Grant and Sherman against Vicksburg.

On August 28, 1862, Bragg began a northward march from Chattanooga which developed into an ambitious invasion of Kentucky. Earlier in the year his wife had expressed the growing dissatisfaction of many Confederate women: "in truth, we cannot retreat much more without coming on the enemy in the Gulf. . . . We women had better take the field and send [the Confederate soldiers] home to raise chickens."[34] If successful, Bragg's offensive would have significant political and military implications. Reaching Glasgow, Kentucky in mid-September, he pressed on and seemed on the point of taking Louisville, when he swung his columns toward Lexington. In response, Buell promptly entered Louisville, where fresh recruits joined his army. Bragg, on the other hand, was strengthened by Edmund Kirby Smith's forces moving from Knoxville. Entering Kentucky near the Cumberland Gap, he defeated a Union force at Richmond, Kentucky.[35]

The climax of this campaign occurred at the battle of Perryville on October 8, 1862. The night before, Bragg, who intended to retake the state, had gone to the capital of Frankfort to participate in the inauguration of Richard Hawes as the secessionist governor of Kentucky.[36] The approach of the army interrupted this ceremony, and "Governor" Hawes fled. In the Perryville engagement three of Bragg's divisions under General Leonidas Polk, a West Point graduate and in peacetime Louisiana's Episcopal bishop, attacked part of Buell's army. The brunt of the attack fell on Alexander McCook's corps. His troops were surprised in a furious assault by superior numbers and driven back with great losses. Part of the

Union line in this battle stood fast: the center, under Philip Sheridan, secure in its entrenchments on Chaplin Heights, remained unshaken by Confederate assaults and counterattacked.[37]

But half the Union army did not take part because Buell did not learn of the battle until two hours after it began. Unusual atmospheric conditions, which made it difficult to hear, as well as an ineffective communications system prevented the delivery of vital information. Neither side could count the battle as a clear victory, but as was the case at Antietam, since the invading Confederate army was forced to withdraw, the advantage was with the North. On the other hand, the Union armies had failed to crush Bragg, although the Confederates now abandoned Kentucky, whose residents had generally been indifferent to their Confederate liberation. Now Bragg entered Tennessee by way of the Cumberland Gap, and Buell moved toward Nashville and another showdown.

In the battle of Iuka, at a small railroad junction in northern Mississippi on September 19, 1862, Rosecrans defeated Price, who had earlier led Confederate forces in Missouri at Wilson's Creek in August 1861 and Pea Ridge, Arkansas in March 1862. Again, poor coordination between the Confederate generals Van Dorn and Price prevented an opportunity, through collaboration, to launch a successful offensive. More successfully coordinated in the battle of Corinth on October 3–4, which was fought in ninety-degree temperatures, the Confederates still failed to drive Rosecrans out of his position.[38]

Meanwhile, Lincoln had become dissatisfied with Buell, who had failed to anticipate Bragg's invasion of Kentucky and then had not pursued the Confederates after Perryville. On October 23, 1862, Lincoln replaced him. Rosecrans now became the commander of the Army of the Ohio, as Lincoln sought concerted action on every front, with Grant moving in Mississippi and Hooker attacking in Virginia. But Rosecrans was slow to organize his forces. At the end of 1862, commanding what was now called the Army of the Cumberland, Rosecrans moved out of Nashville to strike Bragg's forces near Murfreesboro, forty miles south of Nashville along Stones River. The Confederates had been weakened by the detachment of a whole division for operations in Mississippi. Rosecrans had about forty-three thousand effective troops, Bragg about thirty-eight thousand in his reorganized Army of the Tennessee, which had been admired by Jefferson Davis in a recent trip to the front lines.

When Rosecrans moved to within two miles of Bragg's lines, a fierce battle at Stones River ensued. Beginning on December 31 and continuing until January 2, it ended indecisively. Its results were nevertheless important because Bragg now evacuated Murfreesboro, and middle Tennessee remained in Union hands. But the Union army that achieved this withdrawal did not strike again for six months.[39]

When the Army of the Cumberland did engage the enemy, it was in the relatively bloodless and therefore sometimes overlooked Tullahoma campaign from June 23 to July 3, 1863. In this series of actions undertaken at the same time as Vicksburg and Gettysburg, Rosecrans, urged on by Lincoln and Halleck, sought to prevent Bragg from sending reinforcements to Pemberton at Vicksburg. Strengthened by fresh troops after the battle of Stones River in January, 1863, Rosecrans's Army of the Cumberland was located at Murfreesboro, while the Confederates under Bragg held a fortified line from Shelbyville to Wartrace, Tennessee. Rosecrans broke through the Confederate lines and by June 26 was threatening Bragg, who pulled back to Tullahoma. Then Rosecrans sent a force to strike at the railroad in Bragg's rear; when Bragg hastily withdrew to a new position behind the Tennessee River, the Union purpose was achieved.[40]

## VICKSBURG

The most important event in the West in 1863 was Grant's remarkable Vicksburg campaign—an enterprise that only a daring and resourceful general could have carried to a successful conclusion. For Confederates, the fortified town, whose garrison and nearby troops were under the command of General John B. Pemberton, was essential in order to keep open at least part of the Mississippi. For the Union, Confederate control remained an impediment to naval ascendancy on the river. With Vicksburg, the Confederacy could still mount raids and interdict Union military activities in the area.

Located on a high bluff, this so-called Gibraltar of the West commanded a hairpin bend in the Mississippi. The surrounding topography made it virtually unapproachable except from the south and east. On the west the Confederate batteries blocked the river approach, while on the north the region of the Yazoo delta constituted an impenetrable tangle of wetlands, lakes, swamps, bayous, and wooded bluffs. Throughout May and June of 1862, a naval expedition under Admirals David Farragut and David Porter tried unsuccessfully to capture the city.

Vicksburg remained impregnable even after another Union effort in December. According to this plan, Grant was to engage Pemberton's Confederate forces near Grenada, while Sherman and Porter surprised Vicksburg from the Chickasaw Bayou. But Confederates under Van Dorn destroyed Grant's depot at Holly Springs on December 20. With the navy struggling to maneuver its vessels in the tree-clogged passages of the Yazoo Delta, Sherman concluded that any attempt on Vicksburg from this direction was "hopeless."[41] In the assault at Chickasaw Bluffs on December 29, 1862, the Union troops lost twelve-hundred killed and wounded. Vicksburg thus continued to be impervious to Union attempts either to invest or reduce its fortifications. Other unsuccessful efforts to move a force in front of it included the construction of a canal to divert the Mississippi River, the breaking of a levee to form a channel from the Mississippi to the Yazoo River, and an attempt to push through the bayous to the Yazoo above Haynes Bluff.

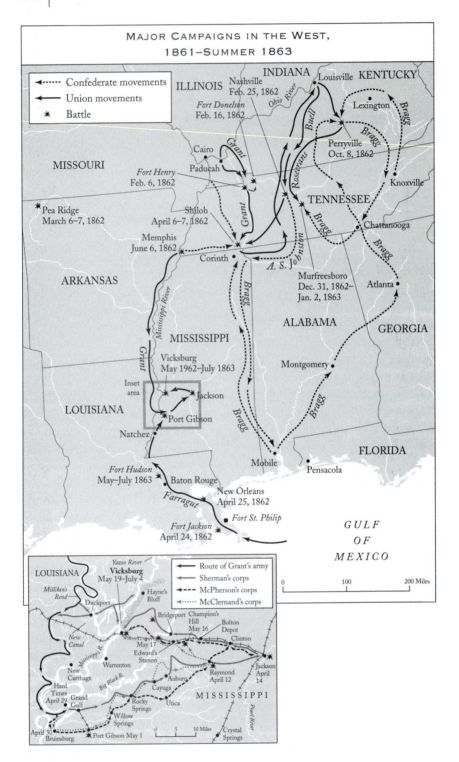

### MAJOR CAMPAIGNS IN THE WEST, 1861–SUMMER 1863

- ◄----- Confederate movements
- ◄───── Union movements
- ✳ Battle

INDIANA

ILLINOIS

Nashville
Feb. 25, 1862

Fort Donelson
Feb. 16, 1862

Ohio River

Louisville    KENTUCKY

Lexington

Bragg

Buell

Bragg

Cairo

Paducah

Grant

Perryville
Oct. 8, 1862

MISSOURI

Fort Henry
Feb. 6, 1862

Rosecrans

Bragg

Knoxville

✳ Pea Ridge
March 6–7, 1862

Shiloh
April 6–7, 1862

Grant

TENNESSEE

Chattanooga

Memphis
June 6, 1862

Corinth

Bragg

A. S. Johnston

Bragg

Murfreesboro
Dec. 31, 1862–
Jan. 2, 1863

Atlanta

ARKANSAS

Mississippi River

ALABAMA

GEORGIA

Grant

MISSISSIPPI

Vicksburg
May 1962–July 1863

Bragg

Montgomery

Inset
area

Jackson

LOUISIANA

Port Gibson

Natchez

Bragg

Mobile

FLORIDA

Pensacola

Fort Hudson
May–July 1863

Baton Rouge

Farragut

New Orleans
April 25, 1862

Fort St. Philip

GULF

OF

MEXICO

Fort Jackson
April 24, 1862

0        100        200 Miles

---

**Inset:**

LOUISIANA

Yazoo River

Vicksburg
May 19–July 4

Milliken's
Bend

Duckport

Hayne's
Bluff

- ───── Route of Grant's army
- ───── Sherman's corps
- ----- McPherson's corps
- ·····◄ McClernand's corps

New
Canal

Bridgeport

Champion's
Hill
May 16

Bolton
Depot

Mississippi R.

May 17

Clinton

Edward's
Station

Warrenton

Big Black R.

New
Carthage

Auburn

Raymond
May 12

Jackson
April
14

Hard
Times
April 29

Grand
Gulf

Rocky
Springs

Cayuga

Utica

MISSISSIPPI

Willow
Springs

Pearl River

April 30

Bruinsburg

Port Gibson May 1

Crystal
Springs

0    5    10 Miles

In April 1863 Grant gambled on a risky, but ultimately successful, plan of operations. Discarding military theory, Grant cut loose from his distant base at Memphis and launched the arduous campaign that stands as his greatest achievement. First he moved his army to Milliken's Bend above Vicksburg, where he met the fleet, which had to run the fortification's batteries and ferry his men to a location south of Vicksburg. While Sherman's forces created diversionary attacks around the city to confuse Pemberton, Grant's twenty thousand men twice crossed the river in Porter's gunboats and transports, ending on the Mississippi side at Bruinsburg on May 1. "The enemy is badly beaten, greatly demoralized and exhausted of ammunition. The road to Vicksburg is open," Grant reported to Sherman.[42]

Grant was now cut off from his supplies, operating in enemy territory over difficult terrain. Yet within twenty days he dominated the entire Vicksburg area after a series of brilliant victories, finally closing in on Pemberton with a grip that could not be broken. On May 1—the same day that the battle of Chancellorsville began—he captured Port Gibson. Then he took Grand Gulf at the confluence of the Mississippi and and the Big Black River. General John Gregg was defeated in the battle of Raymond on May 12, as beleaguered Vicksburg called for more support. Troops were pulled from the East, especially from the Charleston area, to hurry—too late as it turned out—to Vicksburg. Eighty miles to the east, Jackson, the capital of Mississippi, fell on May 14 to Union corps commanded by William Sherman and James McPherson. The noose around Vicksburg was tightening. On May 16 and 17, Grant defeated Pemberton in the battle of Champion Hill and Big Black River Bridge.

Ironclads contributed to the siege of Vicksburg. On April 16, 1863, the ironclad *Lafayette* was taken past the Vicksburg batteries in order to support the troops crossing below the city.

This hill facing Vicksburg was lined with Union shelters. James Shirley, who owned the house at the top of the hill, supported the Union cause and aided the soldiers who camped on the hillside.

Joseph E. Johnston, recovered from his wounds at Fair Oaks in 1862, was now ordered by Jefferson Davis to assist Pemberton. But after Grant's campaign around Vicksburg, Johnston could get no closer than Jackson. Now Pemberton fell back to the earthworks on Vicksburg's outskirts, which Grant with a total force of forty-five thousand futilely assaulted for three days. Then the siege of Vicksburg began.

For over six weeks the two armies faced each other at a distance of six hundred yards or less. There was much fraternizing as well as some Confederate desertion to the Union lines. "Sometimes," wrote an Illinois soldier, "one party would tell the other they were going to shoot when bang would go the gun and then the one shot at would laugh and tell the other he shot too high or too low. . . . They would curse and blackguard each other all the time they were firing."[43] After constructing mines near the Confederate fortifications, Union engineers exploded powder charges on June 25.

Meanwhile the inhabitants of Vicksburg had been living largely underground. Citizens and soldiers were on short rations; mules and rats served as food, and the city was constantly shelled from gunboats and Grant's artillery. Finding himself bottled up by land and prevented by the fleet from escaping across the river into Louisiana, Pemberton surrendered thirty thousand troops on July 4, 1863.[44]

Grant first fed these Confederate soldiers and then released them as paroled prisoners of war, the latter a formal system of prisoner exchange based on a man-for-man trade. Any excess soldiers on either side promised not to take up arms until officially exchanged. The fall of Vicksburg, coming simultaneously with the Union victory at Gettysburg, encouraged the North, impressed Europe with the strength of the United States, and put an entirely new face on the war, which only a few months before had seemed to tilt to the Confederates' favor.[45]

As Lincoln noted, "The Father of Waters again goes unvexed to the Sea," with the military effect that Texas, Arkansas, and Louisiana were isolated from the rest of the Confederacy. But Bragg's army was still intact, operating south and west of the Tennessee town of Murfreesboro.

## THE BATTLES OF CHATTANOOGA AND CHICKAMAUGA

Ranking in importance with the capture of Vicksburg were the conflicts at Chattanooga and Chickamauga. Their outcome made 1863 a decisive year for the Union in the West. Lincoln wanted to pressure the Confederacy on all fronts. The president hoped that Rosecrans could take Chattanooga and cut the railroad connection between Atlanta and Richmond at the same time that Nathaniel Banks, operating in the lower Mississippi, secured that area and moved into Texas. In June 1863, after months of inactivity and urgings from Lincoln, Rosecrans moved his army out of Murfreesboro. By September 9, he had occupied Chattanooga without a battle.

By this time Bragg had lost the confidence of his soldiers and subordinate generals. He lacked the resourcefulness, dash, and craftiness of Lee; his system of scouts was inefficient; and he was perplexed by the appearance of Rosecrans's various units in different places and bewildered by "the popping out of the rats from so many holes."[46]

Meanwhile the Confederate General Simon Buckner had been drawn out of Knoxville, which was promptly occupied by Burnside, now in command of the Department of the Ohio. Burnside, however, failed to join Rosecrans, although Buckner did coordinate with Bragg. In an action that acknowledged the impor-tance of the West, Lee, who still hoped for a decisive battle in the East, reluc-tantly detached eleven thousand troops from his theater and sent them with Longstreet by railroad to reinforce Bragg in the forthcoming showdown in the West. Given the deterioration of the Confederacy's few railroads, it took ten days to make the 952-mile trip from Richmond to northern Georgia, but these reinforcements made a difference in the forthcoming battle.

The armies met in a valley at Chickamauga—which means "River of Death" in Cherokee—ten miles south of Chattanooga. A month earlier Rosecrans had found an unguarded ferry on the Tennessee River. With the aid of pontoon bridges constructed by the Corps of Engineers as well as some rafts, he had crossed thirty miles below Chattanooga, compelling Bragg to abandon the city. But on September 19–20 the Confederates counterattacked. With the high screeching rebel yell that the poet Sidney Lanier described as "a howl, a hoarse battle cry, a cheer, and a congratulation all in one," Longstreet's troops struck a weak portion of the Federal right, made a gap, and broke through with two corps in a rout similar to the first Bull Run.[47] Rosecrans, who knelt and prayed to "His Most Sacred Heart to pity us," then retreated to Chattanooga, where he reorganized his army to make another stand.[48] On the Union left George "Pap" Thomas, a native southerner who had remained in the Union army, knew nothing of this reversal and stood fast against attacks by superior numbers, saving the Union army from complete disaster.

As a slaughterhouse, the battle at Chickamauga compared with Gettysburg and Antietam. As a victory for the Confederates, the engagement was an empty one. As a lesson to Rosecrans, the battle revealed the ability of the Confederates to counterattack. The Union army suffered approximately sixteen thousand casualties of fifty-eight thousand troops engaged; the Confederates a total of nearly eighteen thousand, with nearly twenty-three hundred killed of sixty-six thousand.[49] Bragg now commanded the railroads entering Chattanooga and had his enemy penned up.

But at the moment when Rosecrans, paralyzed by the effect of Chickamauga, seemed to be waiting for his army to starve, the Union general George Thomas, "the Rock of Chickamauga," superseded him as commander of the Army of the Cumberland. At the same time, Grant was elevated to supreme command of Union operations in the West, save for those of Nathaniel Banks in Louisiana.

Now the Union army was besieged in Chattanooga. They were short of food and supplies, and Jefferson Davis predicted that the Yankees would soon be compelled to evacuate the city—a Vicksburg in reverse. Moreover, the Confederates had the advantage of occupying the main heights facing the city—Missionary Ridge and Lookout Mountain—together with extended positions that blocked Union navigation on the Tennessee. When he arrived in Chattanooga, Grant's first problem was to open up a line of supply; his next was to coordinate his scattered forces; his third, to strike the Confederate army under Bragg. He began with supplies.

River access through Bridgeport was opened after a minor operation at Brown's Ferry below Chattanooga. Steamers could now ply this part of the Tennessee River; the army had its "cracker [supply] line." Then reinforcements were brought up, including two army corps under Sherman, who worked his way eastward from Memphis. His advance depended on rapid railroad repair because the enemy had wrecked the tracks, captured or destroyed cars and locomotives, and demolished the bridges. This phase of the campaign was chiefly the work of General Grenville Dodge, who had "every branch of railroad building . . . going on at once."[50]

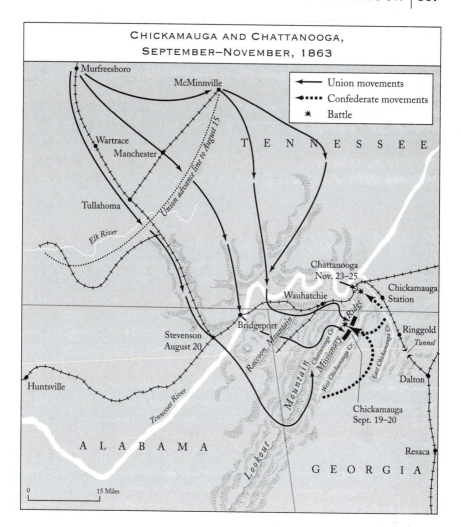

With the Army of the Potomac inactive in Virginia, two corps under Hooker were transferred by rail via Cincinnati, Louisville, and Nashville to cooperate in the Chattanooga campaign. Accomplished in eight days, this movement was the largest redeployment of troops between theaters in the entire war. It revealed the increasing importance of railroads in the Civil War, not only to move large contingents to battle in distant places, but afterward to transfer them to hospitals miles from the scene of battle.[51]

While Grant was consolidating his forces, there was mismanagement on the Confederate side. A controversy between Bragg and his subordinate generals over the conduct of the recent battle distracted the Confederate high command. "There sits Bragg," noted the acerbic Richmond insider Mary Chesnut in her diary, "a good dog howling on his hindlegs. . . . He always stops to quarrel with his generals."[52] As Longstreet informed the secretary of war: "I am convinced that nothing but the hand of God can help us as long as we have our present commander."[53] In the hope of settling the quarrel, President Davis visited the army but, even after hearing the complaints of Bragg's subordinates, he kept Bragg.

In a fateful decision dividing Bragg's already small force, Longstreet, at Davis's suggestion, moved off with one-third of the troops in a pointless operation to capture Burnside's army at Knoxville, where he was driven back. From the outset this campaign was bungled by the Confederates; Longstreet "allowed himself to go off on an expedition into an unknown part of the country with less than fifteen thousand men in an attempt to capture or defeat a large force, with little or no control over transportation and less over the system of supply."[54] Thus a movement depending on rapidity slowed to a crawl, and although Longstreet's First Corps made several attempts to advance, he was never able to organize a major campaign.

Meanwhile, Grant's seventy thousand troops attacked the main body of Bragg's army of forty-seven thousand in the three-day battle of Lookout Mountain on November 23–25, 1863. The battle had three main phases. First Thomas sent two divisions to attack near Orchard Knob, a position they took with little opposition. On November 24, the blue-clad troops under Hooker crossed Lookout Creek and struck the opposite extreme flank of the Confederates on Lookout Mountain. In the "battle above the clouds," they repulsed a few Confederate skirmishers and captured this mountain position. Bragg's army was now concentrated on Missionary Ridge, but Sherman's assault against northern Missionary Ridge had not shaken the Confederates seriously. By mid-afternoon of November 25 the battle had not yet been won.

Finally, the main engagement of the battle developed in the afternoon of November 25, when two of Thomas's divisions moved out for what was intended to be a "demonstration" to assist Sherman by relieving the pressure in this area. According to Grant's plan, the movements of Thomas against the Confederate center and Hooker against the left were to be subordinate to those of Sherman against the right.

The soldiers' orders were to seize the rifle pits at the foot of the ridge. But after they accomplished this, the men who were told to await orders pushed on, to the surprise of their generals. After the Union divisions forced their way over rough ground up the ridge, Confederates at the top panicked. Confederate entrenchments were improperly located by Bragg's engineers, and for cover northern soldiers took advantage of the dips in the terrain slope. The battle went so quickly that Confederate gunners had to withhold their fire or shoot their own men. After hard fighting, the panting and exhausted Unionists clambered up the two-hundred-foot ridge and carried the crest against Confederate troops who seemingly could have stopped them, but who instead broke and ran.[55]

Soldiers sit on Umbrella Rock on Lookout Mountain above Chattanooga and the Tennessee River. Union troops drove Braxton Bragg's men from the ridge.

A Union colonel stated that after the battle General Gordon Granger rode along the Union lines, calling to the troops: "I am going to have you all court-martialed! You were ordered to take the works at the foot of the hill, and you have taken those on top! You have disobeyed orders, all of you!"[56] They had, however, produced a splendid victory at the cost of Union losses of 5,824, compared with 6,667 for the Confederates. Chattanooga and Tennessee were in Union hands, as the third year of the war ended with significant northern victories. In Richmond Mary Chesnut described "gloom and unspoken despondency hang[ing] like a pall everywhere."[57]

| Military Campaigns in 1864

In the spring of 1864, the war entered a new phase. Union victories in the West had eroded the Confederacy's economic and military strength and had boosted morale in the North. Grant and his lieutenants were now associated with victory, though Grant did not merit all the acclaim for the victories achieved in the West. In fact Rosecrans initiated some of these tactical movements, and such events as the charge at Missionary Ridge were an unpredictable development for which no general could take credit. But Grant's famous commitment was to take his troops wherever the enemy went. Under such a leader the circumstances had arrived in which the combination of northern manpower and resources, Confederate depletion and failure to get European aid, and Grant's aggressiveness created the essential conditions for Union triumph.

On March 9, 1864, President Lincoln rewarded Grant with a commission as lieutenant general, a rank newly restored by Congress. The president gave him general command of the Union armies with the stipulation that he come east to confront Lee. Grant held as his first priority an eastern strategy based on crushing Lee's army and preventing him from sending reinforcements elsewhere, at the same time that Union forces undertook an offensive from Chattanooga and Mobile against Atlanta, an invasion of North Carolina from the sea, and movements to cut the railroads in Virginia.[1] Such a plan, according to Grant in a letter written to Halleck in January, would give the Union the initiative, preventing "the enemy from campaigns of their own choosing, and for which they are prepared . . . [moving] them to new lines of operations never expected to become necessary."[2]

But almost immediately public pressures during an election year forced Grant with his numerical superiority into a frontal assault against Lee, rather than the war of maneuver he sought. In Virginia he lost an enormous number of men, but he reduced the Confederate forces as well. Meanwhile, in the Lower South, Sherman destroyed vast amounts of food and other supplies in his march through Georgia and the Carolinas. Grant's raids against railroads, roads, and other resources were a series of unceasing blows at the heart of the Confederacy. They brought a stalemated war to an end in the spring of 1865.

## THE SOLDIERS' LIFE

In retrospect the Civil War seems a series of campaigns punctuated by battles involving huge armies. Yet in small engagements as well as larger confrontations, an ethic of proper behavior by those in command on the battleground prevailed. Although official reports covered tactics and logistics, for the soldiers themselves the ideal deportment was not necessarily the collective success of turning a flank or carrying a position. Rather it was individual courage defined as "heroic action undertaken without fear." Soldiers on both sides measured their own—and their fellows'—honor by actions that either fulfilled or violated the decorum of discipline and fearlessness. Officers such as Carl Schurz and Philip Sheridan or Jeb Stuart and Lewis Armistead, who boldly exposed themselves to death, provided models of the coolness under fire that, according to Gerald Linderman, linked command to compliance. Efforts to attain such bravery made it possible for young men to detach themselves from the gruesome sights of battle during a war that was no longer a summer's outing.[3]

But Civil War soldiering was not just a matter of fighting the enemy. In every winter of the war, before the weather improved and military action became possible, the tedium of camp life provided an unappealing counterpoint to the terror of combat. During the winter and early spring soldiers in camps across the nation felt they were literally deteriorating, and many did take sick from microorganisms causing potentially lethal dysentery, measles, malaria, and diarrhea. In the Union army, disease killed 224,580 soldiers, compared with the 110,000 who died in combat. In a three-month period during the spring of 1863, a private in the 1st New York Engineer Corps stationed on the coast of South Carolina noted the death of one soldier from scurvy, another from "unclean habits" (probably from syphilis), and a third from fever—all within his company.[4]

Makeshift hospitals and negligent medical care further demoralized soldiers on both sides. "Particularly after a battle, when the surgeons spent a long night in ill-lit hospital tents amputating the arms and legs of wounded men in an assembly-line procedure, medical care impressed the soldiers not only as dubious and painful, but as dehumanizing."[5] Overworked medical personnel carelessly threw body parts anywhere; the dead, believed by their compatriots to merit at least the decent burial they expected for themselves, were dumped in great heaps.

Union soldiers play a game of baseball. When idle time fell on the battlefield, soldiers looked for different ways to occupy themselves. During the winter, they would often participate in snowball fights.

Along with sickness and the callous treatment of the wounded and dead, soldiers complained of monotony and the tedious duties associated with army life. Between engagements John Beatty, a lieutenant colonel in the 3rd Ohio, had "hardly enough to keep me awake. Bugles, drums, drills, parades—the old story over and over again." The daily routine of Civil War soldiers consisted of roll call at six, breakfast at seven followed by drilling until the noon dinner, and more drill in the afternoon. There were, of course, extracurricular activities. "Soldiers established Masonic Lodges, built chapels, competed in running, wrestling, boxing and jumping, organized debating societies, temperance meetings, prayer groups, singing classes, reading clubs, spelling schools, theatrical troups and grand balls (with some of the men appearing in hoop skirts)."[6]

Many soldiers found solace in organized religion, their spiritual needs attended to by over two thousand chaplains, theoretically one for each Union regiment at the beginning of the war. Later, religious volunteers from various Protestant denominations spread the gospel during their visits to camps, encouraging conversions along with the building of makeshift structures in which to worship during the winter. Among Confederates especially, a popular revival of evangelical religion meant that most soldiers in a brigade heard their chaplains' increasingly grim warnings that "the military reverses proved that Jehovah was angry with the Confederacy."[7]

To be sure, soldiers on both sides also visited prostitutes in brothels or enjoyed what were called "horizontal refreshments" with female camp followers—white and black—who tagged along behind the lines.[8] Some even established their own tents and opened for business. Wrote one Minnesota soldier, "We have about forty women in the regiment, some of them make lots of money nature's way."[9] Reported instances of rape were not unknown, and some Union soldiers were court-martialed for rape.[10] In 5 percent of the military trials surveyed by one author, more than thirty were rape trials with black women the principal victims. The number of unreported rapes will never be known.

Whatever the diversion, at times most soldiers agreed with a lieutenant from Massachusetts that "it is awful dull here . . . It seems to me I never was so sick of this life and yet I dread the spring."[11] When spring came and the military campaigns started up again, soldiers were often sent into battle after pep talks delivered by their officers. "Thirteenth New Hampshire! You love your country, you are brave men, and you came out here to fight for her. Now go in! Forward!" went a typical encouragement from a major before his regiment surged into battle.[12]

Besides discipline and leadership, there were other motivations to fight. Some men had a consciousness of duty and its behavioral cousin honor, the latter embodying their public reputation. Others found in the war an opportunity to participate in a masculine right of passage, while still others found purpose in the

During the war, many soldiers found meaning in religion. These photographs show two regiments attending Sunday morning mass, the 9th Massachusetts (left) and the 69th New York, the "Fighting Irish" (right).

White Union soldiers gather around two black men preparing birds for a cockfight. Many white northerners heed paternalistic attitudes toward blacks. Notice the chain whip in the hands of the man on the far left.

brotherhood of their comrades. But it would be a mistake to overlook the patriotic motives that sustained commitment.

In a sample of the letters of over one thousand Confederate and Union soldiers, two-thirds expressed some sense of love of country as a motivating factor. As a sergeant from Illinois explained of his company after the battle of Stones River, "They are too patriotic to be cowards and are willing to do or suffer anything for their country."[13]

Sometimes principles, calls to duty, and even the examples of heroes were not sufficient. Under heavy artillery fire, the 17th Georgia suddenly broke and ran at Chickamauga. "If you are going back to Georgia," shouted one of their officers, "wait and I'll go with you."[14] After the same battle, a southern soldier confessed that "we made a perfect stampede. It was a disgraceful affair."[15]

Units on both sides occasionally refused to fight. Such instances were rare and usually occurred after heavy casualties had been sustained, when there had been no opportunity to assimilate new men, and when a regiment was exhausted and could not move. In the case of the Union Second Corps during Grant's 1864 Virginia campaign, the 12th New Jersey endured all these circumstances. Ordered to attack across an open space of two hundred yards, the troops "had lost too many comrades and realized that no fresh troops were ready to support their attack. . . . [According to an officer], our men have so much experience that they understand what they can and cannot do."[16] Even when twice ordered by their officers to advance, these men refused to move.

Still, motives to fight survived the brutality and made it possible for many men to find a high-minded rationale for their efforts. Union soldiers retained their attachment to the nation. An officer from New Jersey fought because "I love my country and its institutions and am willing to sacrifice much—even life itself—to sustain our glorious country and the best Government in the world."[17] As they gained in soldierly competence, men measured their standards of conduct not only by their leaders' conduct but by an inherited notion of the Revolutionary generation, who had also sacrificed their lives.[18] A soldier from Ohio recalled Valley Forge, when "our fathers in coldest winter marked the road they trod with bleeding feet . . . so that we might enjoy the blessings of free government."[19]

Not all these soldiers were men, as a few women also joined the war as combatants. Along with their more familiar roles as laundresses, cooks, and nurses, women "donned the breeches" and enlisted in both the Confederate and Union armies. Perfunctory physical exams, the youth of other male recruits, the gender-neutral exercises and training, the casual attitude toward uniforms, and the strongly implanted sentiment that women couldn't—and wouldn't—serve as soldiers permitted an acceptance that, in some instances, survived several campaigns. Like the other sex, women soldiers fought for many reasons—to uphold political principles, to enjoy the drama of battle, to support themselves, and to accompany their loved ones.[20]

By 1864 some Union soldiers had an additional reason to fight—for emancipation, although others were horrified by the idea of an antislavery war. One Union soldier supported "old Abes emancipation proclimation" because "as far as I can see there is no other cause for this war but Slavery and the sooner it is done the better for us."[21]

In this unusual photograph, Union soldiers watch a minstrel show performed by blacks.

## The Wilderness Campaign

After the winter's encampment of 1863–1864, Grant, planning for the spring campaigns, saw both hopeful and disheartening signs. On the one hand, the Mississippi River was in Union hands; Tennessee, West Virginia, and Virginia north of the Rapidan River were held by Federal forces; most of the coastal fortresses along the Atlantic and the Gulf were in northern hands; Louisiana was largely under Union occupation. And northern morale and expectations were high.[22]

On the other hand, vast portions of the Confederacy were untouched in a war that required the Union to occupy the South or to obtain an unconditional surrender from the Davis government. The Confederacy held the rich Shenandoah Valley, and two powerful armies—Lee's in Virginia and Johnston's in northwestern Georgia—were battle ready. The Confederacy also had smaller but still intact forces led by two capable commanders in the trans-Mississippi region of Texas and Louisiana—Edmund Kirby Smith and Jefferson Davis's brother-in-law Richard Taylor.

Meanwhile the three-year enlistment of many veterans in the Union armies would end just as military operations began. Some of the men enrolled in 1862 and 1863 reenlisted, but almost a half were replaced by inexperienced recruits. It was these new men who would fight in the forthcoming Union campaigns of 1864, when Grant accompanied Meade, who continued to command the Army of the Potomac operating against Lee, and Sherman moved against Johnston. By the summer Sheridan was operating in the Shenandoah Valley. Instead of attacking Mobile as Grant wished, Nathaniel Banks, the commander of Union forces in Louisiana, was moving in a northwesterly direction up the Red River toward Texas.

Grant first engaged the Army of Northern Virginia in a series of bloody encounters in the wooded region near Fredericksburg known as the Wilderness, the site of a previous battle in December, 1862. At the outset of this Virginia campaign, Grant's main force, assembled north of the Rapidan River with headquarters at Culpeper, numbered approximately 118,000. Benjamin Butler, with about thirty-six thousand troops at Fort Monroe, was expected to threaten Lee's supply lines by disrupting the railroads between Petersburg and Richmond. Lee faced Grant's main army with about sixty thousand men, while Beauregard commanded a supporting force of some thirty thousand in the region of Richmond and Petersburg.[23]

On the early morning of May 4, 1864, the Army of the Potomac, inactive since Gettysburg except for bloodless maneuvering in late 1863, began to move across the Rapidan River. Grant had hoped to get through the Wilderness into open country before giving battle. But the late arrival of wagon trains delayed his movements, and on the 5th and 6th, in dense thickets of brush and scrubby pines that neutralized Grant's numerical advantage and artillery superiority and ren-

In the battle of the Wilderness on May 5, 1864, Richard B. Ewell's men put up breastworks to strengthen their position. Grant was surprised to learn that Ewell's troops were continuing to advance.

dered orderly battle plans impossible, Lee attacked. The two armies clashed in some of the most horrendous infantry combat of the war. Union losses approximated eighteen thousand, of whom over two thousand were killed, many of them burned to death by brush fires as they lay wounded. Confederate losses exceeded ten thousand.

Undeterred by the casualties, Grant did not pull back as other Union commanders had, but instead launched another movement that Sherman judged "the supreme moment of his life."[24] Some experts believe Grant's continued advance on May 7th down Brock Road toward Spotsylvania when he could have retreated toward the Rapidan one of the turning points of the war. In a Confederate's ironic assessment:

> [S]urprise and disappointment were the prevailing emotions when we discovered, after the contest in the Wilderness, that General Grant was not going to retire. . . . We had been accustomed to a programme which began with a Federal advance, culminated in one great battle, and ended in the retirement of the Union army, the substitution of a new Federal commander for the one beaten, and the institution of a more or less offensive campaign on our part. . . . But here was a new Federal general, fresh from the West, and so ill-informed as to the military customs in our part of the country that when the battle of the Wilderness was over, instead of retiring to the north bank of the

river and awaiting the development of Lee's plans, he had the temerity to move by his left flank to a new position, there to try conclusions with us again. We were greatly disappointed with General Grant, and full of curiosity to know how long it was going to take him to perceive the impropriety of his course.[25]

In close, sometimes hand-to-hand fighting near Spotsylvania Court House from May 5 to May 12, Grant lost over fifty-five hundred killed and wounded. Yet with grim resolve to fight it out on this line "if it takes all summer," he pushed on to Cold Harbor, where he made a costly error. With Lee's army protected by strong entrenchments, hastily constructed in the day's delay when General Hancock's troops arrived late, Grant hurled three corps against an enfilading cross fire from the enemy on June 3, 1864, losing more men in these eight minutes of bitter fighting than in any similar period in the war. The twelve thousand killed and wounded in operations from June 1 through June 12 (and seventy thousand in the six weeks from early May to mid-June) produced a shudder in the North and intensified the peace movement and the opposition to Lincoln during an election year. Before they entered battle, as they had in other encounters, soldiers grimly wrote their names and addresses on strips of paper and pinned them to their coats so that their bodies might be identified afterward.[26]

Later Grant indicated that he would not have fought the battle of Cold Harbor again given the circumstances, and in his memoirs he expressed regret that the assault was ever undertaken.[27] Subsequent observers see the campaign as one of Grant "frustrating Lee's attempt to force him to give battle against entrenched defensive positions, as Lee was frustrating Grant's attempt to win by maneuver ... The battle of Cold Harbor, lasting from May 31 to June 3, showed that both armies had learned their lessons in field fortification to near-perfection."[28] And although offensive entrenchments as forward positions from which to launch an assault had been used from the war's beginning, in the Wilderness campaign field fortifications, no longer laid out by engineers but by soldiers in the field, became increasingly commonplace.[29]

Hunger, as well as Grant's army, now stalked Lee's soldiers. George Cary Eggleston, whose artillery company received less than a half-pound of cornmeal a day, described the effects of that enemy: "Hunger ... is a great agony of the whole body and of the soul as well. It is unimaginable, all-pervading pain inflicted when the strength to endure pain is utterly gone."[30]

In the month-long campaign from the Wilderness to Cold Harbor, Union dead, wounded, and deserted were approximately fifty-five thousand (of some 118,000 men present for duty), nearly as many as Lee's entire army of sixty-four thousand, which had suffered twenty-four thousand casualties. Grant, however, could find new, if inexperienced, recruits, and he had sufficient food and equipment. As a defensive accomplishment in fighting off superior numbers, the campaign stands as a significant chapter in Confederate annals. Later, Grant pointed out the enemy's advantage of fighting in familiar territory with short supply lines and concluded that "all circumstances considered we did not have any advantage in numbers."[31]

Nor did the Union general have the advantage of a coordinated series of successful movements against the Confederacy. Franz Sigel, one of the political generals chosen as much for his leadership of the German community as his tactical prowess, had been repulsed at New Market in the Shenandoah Valley, and although Benjamin Butler had landed his forces south of Richmond on May 5, he had failed to advance.[32]

## CONTINUING BATTLES IN NORTHERN VIRGINIA

Grant reconsidered his determination to fight it out "on this line." The struggle to defeat Lee north of Richmond had continued for forty days of human sacrifice. Now he transferred his whole army south of the James River, with the purpose of moving on the Confederate capital from the rear in order to accomplish what Butler and Sigel had failed to do—separate Lee from the rest of the Confederacy and sever the railroad links to Richmond. But the rivers of northern Virginia were a persistent impediment to Union offensives. Any crossing of the Chickahominy and James rivers in the face of possible attack by Lee required difficult engineering techniques as well as complex movements of troops in marshy terrain with inadequate guides and maps. The operation led by Grant stands as one of the most important feats of the Army of the Potomac. Beginning on June 12, Grant completed the crossing of the James in four days and surprised Lee, who thought the reported Union tugs and transports were those of Butler.[33] By the 17th Union soldiers were surging against the defenses of Petersburg.

While the main armies under Lee and Grant fought north of Richmond, Butler's subsidiary campaign against Beauregard continued below Richmond. Grant had expected Butler to advance up the James, approach Richmond, prevent reinforcements from reaching Lee, and sever Confederate communications. His advance, an essential part of the Union's 1864 strategy, was timed to coincide with Grant's forward movement through the Wilderness. But Butler's incompetence proved as striking as his pomposity. He moved from Fort Monroe, easily seized City Point and Bermuda Hundred, and moved up as far as Drewry's Bluff, taking enough time in the process to permit Beauregard to assemble his forces. Then he entrenched at Bermuda Hundred in a neck of land between the James and the Appomattox Rivers, where he was penned in by the Confederates, who also used trenches.

"If someone had capably managed Butler's big army, it certainly could have taken Petersburg, perhaps have reached the south side of the James, and possibly even have taken Richmond," conclude two modern scholars.[34] Instead his army, though secure, was "as completely shut off from further operations directly against Richmond as if it had been in a corked bottle. It required but a comparatively small force of the enemy to hold it there."[35] Butler's release came only when the Confederates, hard pressed by the main Union drive south of the James, themselves uncorked the bottle.[36]

The defense of Petersburg now became essential for the southerners, as they struggled to stop the Union advance. Had Butler not been confined, there was a reasonable expectation that an entryway to Richmond could have been seized. From the 15th to the 18th of June, the Confederate lines at Petersburg were assaulted by Union forces. Against heavy odds Beauregard's men held their positions. Then Lee arrived with his army, and for the time Petersburg and Richmond were saved for the Confederacy. Spades replaced guns as Grant settled down to a long siege. He had fought his last large-scale battle with Lee.

After other attempts to carry the city failed, the Union army constructed an elaborate mine from the center of Burnside's position to a point twenty feet under the Confederate works in an effort to breach the Confederate defenses. The mine extended more than five hundred feet in length. Once it was completed, eight thousand pounds of powder were deposited. On July 30 the fuses were lit. As huge masses of earth shot into the air, "men, guns, carriages, and timbers," during what one soldier recalled as a "grand convulsion," were hurled aloft and buried in a shapeless ruin.[37] The explosion left a "crater" 30 feet in depth and 170 in length. In the desperate Battle of the Crater that followed, northern units piled into the cavern, fighting hand to hand against Confederates who had quickly recovered and now surrounding them on the rim of the crater shot the Union soldiers like fish in a bowl.

Foremost in the attack after the assault by white regiments bogged down were black and Native American troops. They had trained to make the first assault but, in a command decision evidently based on the fear of political repercussions if the endeavor failed, they were replaced by whites.[38] Despite a temporary break in the line, Confederate artillery continued to rake the front and flank of Union troops in the huge crater, and soon the Confederates recovered sufficiently for a lethal counterattack. The 29th Regiment of United States Colored Troops, which numbered 450 soldiers before the Crater, lost 322 men. One Illinois soldier, a chaplain from the 28th United States Colored Troops, described the scene: "For several rods the dead lay thick, both white and colored, Union and rebel. It was a sad sight. Recollect the colored troops went as far as they were ordered to go—both in going in and remaining there."[39]

Later Grant called the operation a "stupendous failure," and the Union commander became convinced that the war could be won only by using the rat-filled trenches lacing the Virginia landscape where infantry troops took cover from lethal rifle fire.[40] Grant had lost four thousand men; Lee, whose army continued to erode, lost fifteen hundred.

## OTHER VIRGINIA CAMPAIGNS, MAY–SEPTEMBER 1864

As part of Grant's strategy for a coordinated campaign in Virginia, elaborate cavalry operations developed, involving such Confederate leaders as Jeb Stuart, Jubal Early, and John Mosby, and on the Union side Philip Sheridan, David Gregg, James Wilson, and a youthful George Custer. When Grant launched his Wilderness campaign against Lee in May, the thirty-three-year-old, West Point–trained Sheridan, who had served at Chickamauga, moved south with twelve thousand men from the Rapidan in a swift raid toward Richmond. He intended to get behind Lee's army, cut his communications, draw off Confederate cavalry, and contribute to Grant's success in the major attack. On May 9, 1864 he turned directly toward Richmond.[41]

Jeb Stuart, at first pressing on Sheridan's rear as the Union cavalry advanced toward the Confederate capital, abruptly changed course and after a hard march placed his force between Sheridan and Richmond at Yellow Tavern, six miles north of the city. In a sharp engagement on May 11, the Confederates were attacked by superior numbers. They held the Unionists in check, but Stuart, having "saved Richmond," was killed.

In June of 1864, Grant studies a map at his field headquarters. Behind him are Lieutenant Colonel Bowers (standing) and General John Rawlins.

CAMPAIGNS IN THE EAST,
1864–1865

Legend:
← Union movements
◀······ Confederate movements
+—+—+ Railroads
✳ Battle

Sheridan did not push his raid into the city of Richmond, where panic prevailed. Although he informed his aides that he could take the Confederate capital, he also believed that he could not hold it.[42] Instead, penetrating the outer fortifications of the capital, he swept east and south, reached the James River at Haxall's Landing on May 14, turned his prisoners over to Butler, and started on his return march to join the Army of the Potomac, knowing neither its location nor its fortunes. Crossing the Pamunkey River on an improvised bridge, he rejoined the main army on May 24 on its march from North Anna to Cold Harbor. He had partly relieved Grant of harassment by the enemy's cavalry. In addition, Sheridan had destroyed scarce provisions and munitions and had temporarily broken up the railroad connections between Lee and Richmond, all the while improving the morale of his troops. But in the battle of the Wilderness he had failed to screen the army's west flank and had not located two Confederate corps approaching on a large thoroughfare.[43]

Sheridan's "Richmond raid" was followed by his "Trevilian raid," an episode occurring twenty-eight miles east of Charlottesville in early June 1864. Sheridan severed railroad connections. In retaliation hostile Virginians cut the throats of unwary stragglers and left them hanging from trees with warnings to the Yankees that such was the fate of foragers.[44] In his report on the raid, Sheridan echoed Grant and Sherman: "I do not believe war to be simply that lines should engage each other in battle and therefore do not regret the system of living on the enemy's country. . . . As war is a punishment, if we can, by reducing its advocates to poverty, end it quicker, we are on the side of humanity."[45]

Sheridan maintained that civilians who waited at home "in peace and plenty" would continue to support their government. "Sheridan held that reduction to poverty brought prayers for peace more surely and more quickly than does the destruction of life."[46] Such sentiments mirrored Grant's idea that the Union armies should give the Confederates no rest. "If the war is to last another year, we want the Shenandoah to be a barren waste."[47]

In the Shenandoah Valley Franz Sigel's Union divisions had been operating around New Market on May 15, 1864, when the Confederates under John Breckinridge counterattacked in an engagement that has loomed large in Confederate mythology because of a gallant charge by four companies of young cadets from the Virginia Military Institute.[48] After this encounter, instead of his intended advance up the Valley, Sigel retreated to a position behind Cedar Creek near Strasburg. Then followed a campaign between his replacement, David Hunter, and Jubal Early, whom Lee had detached with a corps from the main Confederate army to drive Hunter from outside of Lynchburg, which had been surrounded by Union troops on June 16.

As Hunter withdrew toward West Virginia, Early seized the opportunity for a bold raid on Washington. Crossing the Potomac into Maryland, he turned east toward the federal capital. At Monocacy near Frederick, Maryland on July 9, 1864, he encountered a hastily improvised Union division under Lew Wallace, whose defeat saved Washington because it gained valuable time for the troops that Grant quickly dispatched to protect the capital. Early got within sight of the United States Capitol, and some of his troops, in an example of the Confederate version of "total war," burned Chambersburg, Pennsylvania at the end of July.[49] But now hearing of the approach of troops sent by Grant and finding "impregnable works" as far as "the eye could reach,"[50] he gave up any hope of capturing Washington.

Before Early did so, residents panicked despite energetic efforts to protect Washington. On July 10 President Lincoln wired a group of Baltimoreans: "Let us be vigilant, but keep cool. I hope neither Baltimore nor Washington will be sacked."[51] At the same time the president described Washington's uncertain defenders—the "hundred-day men" (whom he had requested from states as far away as Massachusetts), the invalids, the "odds and ends" assembled under Wallace, and the troops "scarcely . . . worth counting" from New York and Pennsylvania. He noted as well the "vague rumors" reaching the capital, and the urgency that Grant, who was then at Petersburg, come "personally" to protect the city.

The troops that Grant sent—the Nineteenth Corps, just arrived from New Orleans, and two divisions of the Sixth Corps—came in time to meet Early in the suburbs of Washington and drive him back to Virginia after the last of the offensive-minded Confederacy's invasions of the North.

Grant now sent his ablest cavalry commander, Sheridan, into the Shenandoah Valley to dispose of Early. After sharp fighting at Winchester near Opequon Creek on September 19, 1864 and at Fisher's Hill on September 22, Early retired southward down the Valley. It was a campaign of constant movement and fighting. "I do not advise rashness," Sheridan had told his staff, "but I do desire . . . actual fighting with necessary casualties, before you retire. There must be no backing and filing by you."[52] The troops complied. In twenty-six engagements during this period, aside from the battles, the Union cavalry lost 3,205 men and officers.[53]

Sheridan now made a quick trip to Washington for consultation with Halleck and Stanton. Returning, he found his troops retreating, with hundreds of stragglers displaying the unit's confusion. Hearing the noise of battle at Winchester, where he had stopped overnight, Sheridan hurried to the battlefield and succeeded in rallying his demoralized men, who gave him a wild cheer as they reformed their lines for a new attack, which reversed the tide of battle. A message to Grant from Sheridan's chief of staff included the description, "We have just sent them whirling through Winchester." The phrase "whirling through Win-

Sheridan's men cheer as he rides to the battlefield. Sheridan's presence turned the tide at the battle of Cedar Creek on October 19, 1864.

chester" caught the public's attention, although it exaggerated Sheridan's command of the military situation.[54]

After the Union disaster at Cedar Creek, where Confederate troops surprised and routed Sheridan's men on October 19, 1864, Sheridan, despite Grant's urging, failed to push southward. Instead the Union commander and Early confronted each other without serious fighting until winter. Aside from the damage inflicted on the enemy's armies, Sheridan's efforts in the Valley featured aspects of the destruction of civilian property concurrently used by Sherman in Georgia. The burning of houses and barns, the destruction of food, and the removal of slaves and animals brought the war home to southern civilians. Violence to persons was, however, avoided and rarely was any family left entirely without subsistence.

## SHERMAN'S CAMPAIGN

While Lee was contending with the demoralization of his ill-fed and poorly provisioned troops in Virginia, another distinguished Confederate commander, skilled in defensive generalship, was guarding the gateway to the lower South against Sherman's veterans.[55] At Dalton, Georgia, Joseph E. Johnston with fifty-three thousand men faced Sherman's ninety-eight thousand troops. By this time the comradeship of Sherman and Grant mirrored the high morale in Union ranks. They were "as brothers," said Sherman, both trained as professional soldiers but shaped on the anvil of war, both associated with western victories, each giving credit to the other and ready to cooperate in the closing strokes of a well-planned, comprehensive strategy. Defined by Grant in April of 1864, Sherman's mission was "to attack Johnston's army and destroy it, to capture Atlanta and hold it, and to get into the interior of the enemy's country as far as you can, inflicting all the damage you can against their war resources." The first blow was the march through Georgia.[56]

Certainly Sherman—a scrawny, forty-four-year-old West Point graduate with a permanently furrowed brow—did not easily smash his way through the heart of the Confederacy. He was operating in rough country, where marching a hundred thousand men through a narrow mountain pass was a slow and dangerous business. His lines of communication, extending over a shaky railroad five hundred miles to Louisville, were, as he expressed it, exposed to the guerrillas of an "exasperated people."[57] At the beginning of May, as Grant moved south from the Rapidan River, Sherman launched the campaign against Johnston that resulted in the capture of Atlanta on September 2. At first he was held in check by the defensive skill of Johnston, with whom he fought a series of battles at Resaca from May 13 to 16, at New Hope Church, May 25–28, and, disastrously, at Kenesaw Mountain on June 27.

By retreating slowly and in good order, destroying bridges and railway tracks, keeping his antagonist constantly on the move, avoiding open warfare, fighting

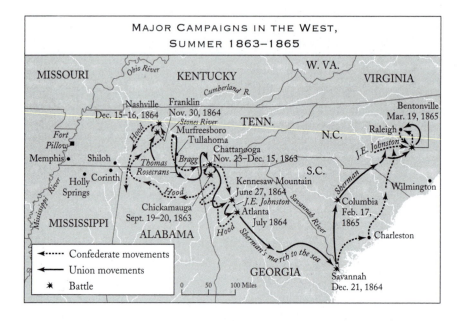

from behind entrenchments, and not permitting Sherman to attack with his superior numbers, Johnston tested Sherman's veterans. These soldiers, nearly 80 percent of whom had enlisted in 1861 and 1862 and 50 percent of whom had reenlisted in the same companies in 1864, understood that they must defeat a despised enemy who by this time they held responsible for the war's carnage.[58]

In mid-July the Confederate commander was ready to strike the Yankees while they divided in order to cross Peachtree Creek, after which Johnston intended to stand and fight within the city of Atlanta. His resistance to Sherman was comparable with Lee's performance in delaying Grant, although, as one scholar has joked, if Davis had left Johnston in command, the decisive battle might have been fought in Key West, Florida.

At this stage, however, the Confederate government removed the defensive-minded Johnston, whom Davis had disliked for years.[59] Mindful only of the fact that Sherman had been allowed to approach Atlanta instead of being pushed back into Tennessee, and that the uncommunicative Johnston had expressed "no confidence" that he could defeat or repel his antagonist, the War Department in Richmond required that Johnston hand his command over on July 17, 1864 to John Hood, who was less skillful and cautious—"all lion, none of the fox," as Lee once said.[60]

Hood, who had lost his right leg at Chickamauga and the use of his left arm at Gettysburg, left his entrenchments to fight a losing battle at Peachtree Creek on July 20. In a week of fighting, Hood lost over thirteen thousand men to Sherman's six thousand. Hood then withdrew to a defensive line outside Atlanta.

As the weeks wore on, Sherman extended his lines around Atlanta and succeeded in cutting off all rail communication. Not prepared psychologically for
the necessary trench warfare, Hood and his troops became demoralized. Confederate desertions increased, and disagreements erupted between Governor Joseph
Brown of Georgia and Jefferson Davis. South of Atlanta, Sherman placed most
of his troops between the city and William Hardee's corps, which Hood had sent
to defend the railroad. Cut off from half of his army, Hood had to evacuate and
joined Hardee south of the city. Now Sherman entered the city. "Atlanta is ours
and fairly won," he proudly telegraphed Washington. Promptly he ordered the
evacuation of Atlanta by all citizens. When Hood protested, the northern general responded, "You cannot qualify war in harsher terms than I will. War
is cruelty, and you cannot refine it. . . . You might as well appeal against the
thunderstorm as against the terrible hardships of war." Then in order to destroy
property of military value, his men burned the city.[61]

The war brought extensive damage to Atlanta. Both the Union and the Confederacy
contributed to this destruction. Refusing to allow the factory just beyond the Georgia
Central tracks to come under Union control, Hood's retreating troops blew it up
themselves.

To northerners, weary of hope deferred after years of losses, the fall of Atlanta was exhilarating. For Lincoln and the Republicans, success in the presidential election was ensured. To Halleck, who had at first objected to the raiding strategy of Grant and Sherman, the future was certain: "Deprived of the grain, iron and coal of Northern Georgia, Alabama and Mississippi . . . [the Confederates] can hardly hold out in strong force another year. Your mode of conducting war is just the thing we want. We have tried the kid gloves policy long enough."[62] For Grant, the fall of Atlanta provided another example of the Union's power, especially since Davis had publicly announced that Atlanta would cause the North the same kind of military overextension that Moscow had created for Napoleon.[63]

The military situation that developed after the Confederate evacuation of Atlanta was one of the war's curiosities. The main armies, so long in contact, withdrew in divergent directions. Hood believed that if he operated in Sherman's rear and struck his lines of communication he could, even if unable to beat him, at least prevent an invasion of central Georgia. Hood's army, which was never captured by Sherman, now numbered about forty thousand, and it continued to threaten the railroad from Chattanooga to Atlanta. Its morale improved when it took the offensive, and it caught something of Hood's confidence as he dreamed of drawing Sherman after him into Tennessee and Kentucky and even of defeating him in battle.[64]

In early November Sherman's "march to the sea" began. As to the advisability of this plan, Lincoln was "anxious, if not fearful"; Grant, who approved of the plan once it began, thought Hood should be destroyed before Sherman struck

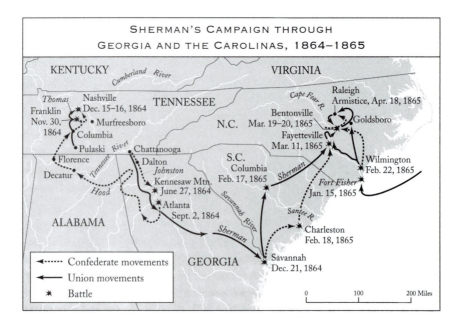

SHERMAN'S CAMPAIGN THROUGH
GEORGIA AND THE CAROLINAS, 1864–1865

William T. Sherman's greatest accomplishment during the Civil War was his march across Georgia, "from Atlanta to the sea." Sherman has been called the first modern general because of the way he waged war against civilian morale.

south.[65] Sherman, however, felt that he could not turn back. He judged that "no single army [could] catch Hood,"[66] and he was convinced that his best plan was to frustrate Jefferson Davis's plan of maneuvering him out of Georgia. Abandoning his lines of communication and supply, he lightened his baggage and lived off the land. As for Hood, George Thomas was to pursue that Confederate general's forces.

Sherman's purpose in waging a relentless war was to make Georgia and South Carolina "howl," and this strategy emerged from his conviction, shared by soldiers and officers under his command, that "we are not only fighting hostile armies, but a hostile people and must make old and young, rich and poor, feel the hard hand of war, as well as their organized armies."[67] And in the campaign that followed, his soldiers, inured to disease and hardship and motivated by a strong commitment to the cause of the Union, fought and pillaged with a stern conviction that the South was responsible for the war and must be punished. In denying Confederate citizens the protection that Jefferson Davis had promised and in marching audaciously through their interior, they further demoralized the rebels.

Many southerners could hardly believe it. In some southern newspapers Sherman's campaign was treated as a Union confession of failure and as an opportunity for the Confederates to destroy his army. Newspaper editors and politicians throughout the South exhorted citizens to revive the spirit of 1861 and defy Sherman. "Our own citizens without guns can conquer the enemy," wrote the editor of the Augusta, Georgia *Constitutionalist*, while in the fantasies of the Richmond *Enquirer*:

> Never was there presented an opportunity so promising for the ruin of an army as Sherman now offers in Georgia. He has abandoned Atlanta, not by retreating backward toward his former base, but by a forward movement to a new base on the coast. It is . . . a confession that Atlanta could not be retained. . . . Rather than make the open confession of a failure by a retreat into Tennessee, the enemy have determined to keep up appearances and to march on, not to subjugation and conquest, but to devastation and ruin, as far as possible, and to a new base on the coast.[68]

With no Confederate army opposing him, Sherman's famous 163-day march from Atlanta to Raleigh, North Carolina began in mid-November. The entire operation, from his move from Chattanooga into northwestern Georgia until the end of the war when he was in North Carolina, lasted eleven months. His forces, "detached from all friends," numbered about sixty-five thousand. By field orders his army, stripped of noncombatants, advanced fifteen miles a day on four parallel roads, sometimes in a horizontal line stretching over five miles. His troops foraged the country, destroyed mills, houses, and cotton gins, and, when obstructed by guerrillas, enforced a "devastation more or less relentless."[69] Soldiers were ordered to leave enough resources for each family to survive and were forbidden to enter private houses, trespass, or use threatening language, though these orders were occasionally violated.

In general, Sherman's army treated southern civilians well, although after the war southerners conveyed the image of not a house standing, family treasure remaining, or field not scorched. In Savannah, some wives and families of Confederate generals stayed in Union-occupied areas, suggesting their confidence that troops would treat civilians properly.[70] But there was undeniable terror and hardship for Georgians and South Carolinians living in Sherman's path.

"Sixty thousand of us witnessed the destruction of Atlanta, while our post band and that of the 33d Massachusetts played martial airs and operatic selections. . . . At last came the familiar 'fall in'; the great 'flying column' was on the march, and the last regiment in Atlanta turned its back upon the smoking ruins," wrote a captain in the Massachusetts volunteers.[71] Once Atlanta disappeared, however, the march through Georgia sometimes degenerated into a wild holiday. There was a discrepancy between the commander's orders and the performance of his men, and thereafter Sherman bore the blame for the abuses of his army.

In Milledgeville, the Georgia capital and briefly the capital of the Confederacy, Yankee officers held a mock session of the legislature in which they repealed

As part of the destruction which occurred during the march through Georgia, railroad tracks were bent into "Sherman's hairpins." Four years of fighting destroyed or crippled more than half of the South's railroads.

the ordinance of secession. Some public buildings, including the arsenal, were destroyed, but private residences and property were not. According to the measures applied in modern rules of warfare, Sherman rarely violated the standard of proportionality—that is, using more force than is necessary to achieve an objective. Moreover, he differentiated between combatants and civilians. Viewed overall, more than 90 percent of the casualties during his march were soldiers, and the postwar images of Sherman and his depredations—so resonant in southern memory because they supported the view that Confederates had fought more honorably than the Union—exaggerate reality.

There were exceptions to Sherman's moderation and violations of his restrained orders. Along his route, the destruction of military material was accomplished with an expert thoroughness. In destroying a railroad, for instance, the rails were loosened from the ties; the ties were placed in piles with the rails on top; the piles were set on fire; and the heated rails then bent and twisted with specially constructed hooks so they could never be repaired. Bridges were destroyed, railroad cars burned, driving wheels and trucks broken, axles bent, boilers punctured, cylinder heads broken, connecting rods bent and hidden.[72] Public buildings were sometimes destroyed. Food stores were taken; horses, mules, and livestock were removed. Special details were sent out to forage, the men selected for this speciality nicknamed "bummers."

Along with the systematic business of foraging, there was occasional plunder and vandalism. Dwellings were burned; family silver was seized; wine cellars were raided; property that could not be carried away was ruined by Union veterans who felt little remorse. "It seems hard for the women and children," wrote one soldier to his family, "but this rebellion must be put down and we are doing it."[73]

Northern civilians and soldiers had, by 1864, adopted the policy of "hard war." Hard war—as opposed to the earlier conciliatory policies—was not a creation of Sherman's. It had always been present, but under him it became a systematic and official program. The conviction spread that actions against the enemy should be aimed at demoralization and must go beyond raids, minor engagements, and large, inconclusive battles if war was to end in the Confederacy's unconditional surrender.

Sherman's march brought bitterness to the invaded. But the dragon's teeth had been sown when the Confederates started a conflict that had been raging for three and a half years. By the fall of 1864 neither government could accept any compromise. Indeed, once the appeal to arms had been made, the motive of winning, and winning completely, became the dominant purpose on both sides. Such was war's grim nature that the struggle had to go on from slaughter to slaughter until one side or the other was defeated. To fight to the end and die in the last ditch might make even defeat honorable. To quit while there still remained a shaky line of ragged troops would seem a dishonor. And as Charles Royster has written, although the intention of this campaign was not mayhem, "destruction accompanied Sherman's army everywhere it went. For Sherman the long marches achieved important effects by being unstoppable. They could go on indefinitely; they could become harsher; they represented dramatically the sure coming of the South's defeat."[74]

After moving in a southeasterly direction, Sherman established his headquarters in Savannah on the coast, where his soldiers were ordered to refrain from "unsoldierly deeds," and his presentation of the city as a "Christmas gift" to Lincoln thrilled the North. By reaching the sea, he had accomplished the strategic objective of joining up with the navy, which had successfully blockaded the southern coast. He had not, however, destroyed Hardee's small force.[75] Yet Sherman's numerical superiority and ability to fool the enemy with rapid movements permitted him to push forward largely unimpeded. After a month in Savannah, his army of sixty-two thousand moved northward through the Carolinas, now followed by seven thousand black refugees.[76]

From the northern point of view, South Carolina, the chief offender in causing the war, deserved more vengeful treatment than Georgia. As Sherman wrote:

> Somehow our men had got the idea that South Carolina was the cause of all our troubles; her people were the first to fire on Fort Sumter, had been in a great hurry to precipitate the country into civil war; and therefore on them should fall the scourge of war in its worst form. Taunting messages had also come to us, when in Georgia, to the

effect that, when we should reach South Carolina, we would find a people less passive, who would fight us to the bitter end, daring us to come over, etc.; so that I saw and felt that we would not be able longer to restrain our men as we had done in Georgia.[77]

Earlier Halleck had advised Sherman: "Should you capture Charleston, I hope that by some accident that place may be destroyed; and if a little salt should be sown upon its site, it may prevent the growth of future crops of nullification and secession."[78] To which Sherman replied, "I will bear in mind your hint as to Charleston, and don't think salt will be necessary. The truth is the whole army is burning with an insatiable desire to wreak vengeance upon South Carolina."[79] As it turned out, Charleston was located off the main line of the march northward and was left untouched by his army. As in Georgia, Sherman's route was determined by topography, railroads, and manufacturing sites. In South Carolina, the towns of Robertsville, Grahamville, McPhersonville, Barnwell, Blackville, Orangeburg, Lexington, Winnsboro, Camden, Lancaster, Chesterfield, Cheraw, and Darlington, among others, were consumed in a series of fires, until the chimneys left standing were referred to as "Sherman's toothpicks."[80]

The worst destruction occurred in the burning of Columbia, the state capital and a haven for refugees fleeing the Yankees, where Sherman had anticipated a climatic battle. In his memoirs Sherman explained that the fire was accidental and that it began when Confederates under General Wade Hampton set fire to bales of cotton before retreating from the city. Others maintained that unruly, drunk Union soldiers had begun the fire. Sherman specifically ordered his forces to spare the city.[81] For Sherman, who told one resident that "hardship was the fortune of war," the issue was not whether his troops or the enemy had begun the fire but rather that the Confederates learn the lessons of war's horror.

The war had now entered its final phase. With Grant undermining the Confederate hold upon Petersburg, with Sherman swinging north into North Carolina to subdue Johnston and join Grant if necessary, with Sheridan's forces about to turn from destructive raids to cooperation in the main theater of war against Lee, with the Confederacy blockaded and Union forces supreme on the water, the surrenders of Lee and Johnston, signifying the military ending of the war, were not far distant. And such an ending was advanced by the supremacy of the Union on the seas.

## CHAPTER 19

# The Naval War

From the beginning of the war, when Lincoln announced a blockade of the South four days after the attack on Fort Sumter, leaders on both sides recognized the importance of the naval theater. The struggle to control seas and rivers affected every aspect of the conflict from diplomacy to resources to military strategy and morale. As in other arenas, both sides were unprepared, and both eventually contributed to new naval technology—whether it was armament on ships, shell guns, or new types of propellers. The four principal aspects of the encounters between the two navies were: the Union blockade of southern ports; the fighting along the river lines, especially of the Mississippi and Tennessee Rivers; the efforts of Confederate raiders on the high seas to hinder the U.S. merchant marine; and coastal operations in North Carolina, South Carolina, Mississippi, and Alabama. So significant was this warfare that Union victory without the contribution of its navy seems inconceivable.

At the start of the war both sides scrambled to meet the needs of hastily created navies. As was the case in so many aspects of the Civil War, the North quickly outdistanced the South in the size and effectiveness of its fleet. At no time was the Confederacy able to transport many troops by water, whereas the Union, demonstrating a superior flexibility of movement from the war's beginning, was able to ferry troops from southern Illinois along the Ohio, Tennessee, and Cumberland Rivers as early as the fall of 1861. And although Confederate commerce raiders harassed the U.S. merchant marine, such activity did not influence the outcome of the war to the degree that the Union blockade did.

## ORGANIZING THE CONFEDERATE
## AND UNION NAVIES

In another example of the devastating effects of its comparative backwardness, the Confederacy began the war without a navy and without the apparent means of constructing one. "The South," writes one historian, "had neither shipyards save Norfolk, which was soon lost, and Pensacola, which was inadequate and also captured, nor workshops, steam mills or foundries, except on the most limited scale.... There was not, in the whole Confederacy, the means of turning out a complete steam engine of a size suitable for ships. The timber for the potential Confederate ships still stood in the forests; the iron required was still in the mines ... the hemp required for ship ropes had actually to be grown.... There was not a rolling mill capable of turning out two-and-a-half-inch plate. There was not a sufficient force of skilled mechanics."[1]

Confronting these deficiencies, Confederates displayed great ingenuity, although the material contrast between their navy and that of the Union remained significant. The Confederate secretary of the navy, Stephen Mallory, was a man of ability. As a United States senator from Florida before the war, he had been chairman of the Naval Affairs Committee. Through his efforts to upgrade the United States Navy, he revealed his interest in new advances in design and construction as well as in ordnance. In the Confederate Cabinet he quickly came to understand the complexity of his task, which began with a shortage of cash and a navy of only ten vessels.[2]

The Confederate naval strategy involved defending the thirty-five hundred miles of southern coastline against Union attack, challenging the Federal block-

When the Civil War began, the Confederacy had no navy. This northern political cartoon, entitled *Master Jeff—and his Navy*, depicts Jefferson Davis preparing to launch a toy sailboat in a barrel of water. This image was printed on envelopes by patriotic northerners.

Stephen Mallory, the Confederate secretary of the navy, used innovative techniques to build the Confederate wartime navy from virtually nothing. He employed such devices as underwater explosives, ironclads, and even a submarine, the C.S.S. *Hunley.*

ade of southern ports, encouraging privateers to prey on Union shipping, and destroying enough of the northern merchant marine so that "the Federal government would be forced to withdraw numerous ships from the blockading squadrons in order to pursue the 'highwaymen of the sea.'"[3] In these endeavors Mallory, assisted by other Confederate naval leaders, including James Bulloch and Raphael Semmes, achieved some success despite the lack of material and financial resources. One historian concludes that Mallory's "results were little short of phenomenal."[4]

Recognizing that the only way in which the Confederates could challenge northern naval superiority must be through innovative approaches, Mallory supported new methods of sea warfare. In defending the Confederate coastline, for example, he and his torpedo bureau developed elaborate systems of mines and underwater explosives that prevented the U.S. Navy from easy access to harbors such as Wilmington, North Carolina; Charleston; and Mobile. As a result blockade runners were able to continue trading with Bermuda, Nassau, and Havana for some time. Under Mallory's direction southerners even devised a primitive submarine, the C. S. S. *Hunley*, whose attack on the Union blockading sloop *Housatonic* outside Charleston harbor in February 1864 marked the first sinking of a warship by a submarine.[5]

Mallory also recognized that ironclads would have an immense advantage over the wooden ships of the Union blockading fleet, and he made the construction of these armored vessels an essential part of his shipbuilding strategy. Some of these new ships, such as the *Merrimack*, which was rechristened the *Virginia*, were fitted out in southern shipyards, but Mallory looked to Europe for the heavy rams and cruisers that he hoped would break the blockade and drive the northern fleet from the seas. What Mallory did not do was organize a transport fleet of steamers capable of moving Confederate troops up the Mississippi to Missouri or even across the Potomac to Washington.

The task of the United States Navy was the reverse of that of the Confederates. The Union had to maintain a blockade of nearly two hundred bays, river mouths, and inlets, especially those leading to the Confederacy's ten major ports. The U.S. Navy also had to conduct operations on the southern coasts while combating Confederate cruisers and privateers, and protect the ocean commerce of the United States. The navy started the war with relatively few ships for the job it had to do. On March 4, 1861, naval vessels of all classes numbered ninety, with only half available for service.[6] Mostly overseas, these obsolescent sailing ships required overhauling. In fact, just ten ships were immediately available for service along the coast.

The responsibility for making this feeble force into a powerful fighting operation fell to Secretary of the Navy Gideon Welles—who looked like Neptune with his white whiskers and wig and who was soon nicknamed "The Old Man of the Sea"—and his able assistant, Gustavus Fox. Welles, whom Lincoln appointed partly for political and geographical reasons to head his Navy Department, was an able and vigorous administrator. He made no pretense to a technical knowledge of the navy, but was an efficient executive who expanded

In terms of designing the navy, the Union's secretary of the navy, Gideon Welles, was not so creative as Stephen Mallory. Still, the Union navy was able to dominate vital positions on the southern coasts and to close off southern trade with a blockade.

the service with remarkable vigor. Within weeks of Lincoln's April 19 proclamation establishing a blockade, Welles had purchased and armed dozens of merchant vessels that patrolled southern waters.[7]

After the war began, the United States Navy repaired and fitted out every available vessel on its idle list. The department purchased or chartered merchant ships and hastened construction of new warships in private shipyards. Compared with forty-five ships in March 1861, the secretary reported eighty-two vessels in commission by July 4, 1861, 264 in December 1861; 427 in December 1862; 588 in December 1863; and by December 1864, 671, a list that included every type of ship.[8] Annual naval expenditures rose during the same period from $12 million to $123 million. "By the end of the Civil War the U.S. Navy had become arguably the most powerful sea force in the world with a total of 670 ships led by an impressive fleet of turreted, iron class monitors, equipped with 8-inch rifles and 15-inch smoothbore cannon, unmatched afloat. The original 1,500 officers and 7,500 enlisted men of 1860 had increased sevenfold."[9]

In addition to the creating of a navy, new designs for fighting and cruising had to be evaluated. During this transitional period in naval technology, sailing ships were rapidly giving way to steamers, ironclads were displacing wooden vessels, and inventors and naval architects were revolutionizing construction. The Swedish-born inventor John Ericsson's design for a hull covered with iron plate and overlaid with iron-plated decks, sitting low in the water and armed with a revolving turret, transformed the nature of naval warfare, just as rifling did the land war.

Besides deciding on the best designs for the navy, Welles and his assistants had to supervise expenditures and contracts. Naval bureaus and branches had to be organized; skilled mechanics had to be hired; sailors to man the new navy had to be recruited and drilled. And after 332 southern officers resigned from the U.S. Navy to join the Confederacy, new naval commanders had to be trained to replace them.[10]

In addition to these challenges, the United States did not possess a single coaling station beyond its own coasts for the necessary refueling of this generation of steamships. To deal with this handicap the navy's best resource was the construction of large, swift steam-and-sail cruisers that did not use much coal but could carry a plentiful supply.

Immediately after the war began, the Union navy tried to blockade the entire coast of the Confederacy. At first the Union fleet was unable to make its blockade effective, and as late as 1864 there was still some running of supplies into the South, including essential military materials such as rifles, lead, and saltpeter. Although this seaborne lifeline continued throughout the war, Union success in closing southern ports and sinking blockade runners (eventually two-thirds of some three-hundred vessels) strangled the Confederacy, most critically the Army of Northern Virginia, which depended on these materials.[11] By late 1863, Welles correctly believed that his ships were cutting off the Confederacy's trade in heavy goods. As he had reported earlier on December 1, 1862:

> These [four blockading] squadrons have been incessantly maintaining a strict blockade of such gigantic proportions that . . . foreign statesmen . . . denounce it as "a material impossibility"; and . . . [they] admit . . . that the proof of the efficiency of the blockade was conspicuous and wholly conclusive, and that in no previous war had the ports of an enemy's country been so effectually closed by a naval force. . . . The proof of the fact abounds . . . in the . . . industrial and commercial condition of the insurgent region.[12]

## BATTLES OF THE IRONCLADS

Early in 1862, the importance of the ironclad became apparent in a famous battle along the coast of Virginia in the body of tidal waters known as Hampton Roads. After seizing the Norfolk naval yard in April 1861, the Confederates salvaged the powerful steam frigate the U.S.S. *Merrimack*, which Union forces had sunk after they evacuated. Confederates promptly raised it, and after armoring the vessel with iron plate, added a cast-iron ram to its stem. On March 8, 1862, this iron giant, renamed the *Virginia*, steamed down the Elizabeth River under the command of Captain Franklin Buchanan for an attack on the Union blockading squadron in Hampton Roads—where McClellan planned to land his army for the peninsular campaign. "I am going to ram the *Cumberland* [a Union ship]. . . . The moment I am in the Roads I'm going to make right for her and ram her," announced Buchanan.[13]

In the subsequent unequal contest, the fire from U.S. wooden ships blockading the entrance to the James River had little or no effect on the *Virginia*. With astonishing ease the *Virginia* rammed and shelled the *Cumberland*, whose crew stayed heroically with the sinking vessel and went down with flags flying. As Union sailors on other ships apprehensively watched, their cannonballs bounced off the *Virginia*'s iron plates. The *Congress* was then destroyed with heavy casualties, and the U.S.S. *Minnesota* became an easy target after it ran aground. Southerners were jubilant as their newspapers predicted the raising of the Union blockade; an attack on Washington; the leveling of New York, Boston, and Philadelphia; and even the end of the war after these naval victories. But the *Virginia* proved unseaworthy, its patched-up engines unfit for any ocean cruises.

Still, the news of the destruction of the *Cumberland* and *Congress* caused panic among officials in Washington and residents of northern seaboard cities. "We shall have a cannon-ball from one of her guns in the White House before we leave this room," warned Secretary of War Stanton.[14]

But Welles had learned of the existence of the *Virginia/Merrimack* and had already contracted for several new types of ironclads. One of these, the *Monitor*, had been launched in January 1862; after tests and improvements, it was immediately ordered to Hampton Roads. Resembling a "tin can on a shingle," it featured advanced engineering techniques.[15] Its distinguishing characteristics were its small size; its low-slung hull, only a few inches above the water line (the deck was always awash in high seas); its surprising mobility given its design; and its central revolving gun turret, which proved impregnable against ten-inch shot at close range. This new design was used for other ships until the word *monitor* became a generic term for this class of vessel. Although the rate of fire from the two guns on all monitors limited their offensive capability, the Union's industrial capacity to produce ironclads in great numbers threatened the Confederate navy and ultimately gave the Union superiority in controlling coastal operations.

On March 9 the *Virginia*, under the command of Lieutenant Catsby Jones (who had replaced the wounded Buchanan), set out to attack and destroy the wooden frigate *Minnesota* and other Union ships below Fort Monroe and thereby break the blockade. But the Confederate vessel was challenged by Ericsson's "tin can," commanded by Lieutenant John L. Worden. There followed hotly contested duel at close quarters in which the *Monitor* protected the *Minnesota* from the onslaught of the Confederate ironclad. Neither vessel did much damage to the other, and after several hours of fighting, with only one casualty, both quit as if by mutual agreement.

The *Monitor* withdrew temporarily because its commanding officer, Worden, was partially blinded by a shell. The leaking *Virginia* turned back to Norfolk and eventually was scuttled by the Confederates when it proved too large to negotiate

On March 9, 1862, at Hampton Roads, Virginia, the Union's *Monitor* and Confederacy's *Merrimac* (renamed the *Virginia*) fired at each other at close range in the famous battle of the ironclads. Shown in the background of this painting is the wooden frigate *Minnesota*.

the passage up the James River, where it was needed to assist in the defense of Richmond. But this small engagement had important strategic results for the Union. Clearly the blockade would continue and with it the chances for European intervention diminished.

Meanwhile, the *Monitor* accompanied the Union squadron operating up the James River and protected the transports unloading McClellan's soldiers—an operation that took three weeks. Several months later, when McClellan withdrew from the Peninsula after his unsuccessful campaign, the vessel went to Hampton Roads, then to Washington for repairs, and then back to Hampton Roads. During the night of December 30–31 1862, on its way to Beaufort, North Carolina, the celebrated vessel sank in a gale off Cape Hatteras along with twenty-one men.

Though the epoch-making character of the *Monitor-Virginia* duel has been exaggerated, the fight did mark a definite trend in naval warfare. The Union fleet had been saved at a threatening time by an ironclad whose design heralded a change for all navies. More ironclads were added to the Union navy, as the value of the turret was repeatedly demonstrated. Federal naval supremacy continued.[16]

## THE UNION'S COORDINATED ARMY-NAVY OPERATIONS

The Union navy quickly captured important positions on the southern coasts. In August 1861, a joint military and naval expedition seized Forts Clark and Hatteras. Soon after, the inlets into the Pamlico Sound fell under Union control. In February–March 1862, another combined force of the army and navy under General Ambrose Burnside and Commodore Louis Goldsborough seized the fortified Confederate positions on historic Roanoke Island and at New Bern. With these inner coastal positions in Union hands, a much tighter blockade of North Carolina could be maintained than by operations outside the sound.

Farther south, after an expedition led by Flag Officer Samuel F. Du Pont in the fall of 1861, the Union controlled the Port Royal entrance, including Beaufort, South Carolina, together with the Sea Islands of Hilton Head and St. Helena. Fort Pulaski, outside of Savannah at the mouth of the Savannah River, fell to the Union in April 1862. By then the Union dominated the coast, achieving its early strategic plan of having operating bases on the Confederacy's Atlantic seaboard. Only Charleston, Mobile, and Wilmington remained important ports still in Confederate hands.

The most impressive of the Union's combined land-and-water expeditions was that which ended in the capture of New Orleans in April 1862. The largest and wealthiest of the Confederacy's cities, New Orleans had strategic and prestige value. To seize the city by land attack from the North was impossible. On the other hand, a naval assault would not be sufficient because the city would have to be occupied. Although the Navy Department at first did not realize this, the undertaking required a coordinated military and naval expedition. The city was defended by an army of three thousand under General Mansfield Lovell of the Confederate army; on the gulf approach by two powerful forts, St. Philip and Jackson; and seventy-five miles below the city, by a Confederate fleet of armed steamers and ironclads.

Flag Officer David G. Farragut, born in Tennessee of Spanish-American heritage, commanded the attacking squadron. The adopted son of Commodore David Porter of the United States Navy, Farragut saw action as a midshipman on the *Essex* under Porter and later in the Mediterranean. As a young officer he was in the "mosquito fleet" directed to end piracy in the Caribbean. After many years of uneventful naval service, the outbreak of the war found him in Norfolk, where the influence of his wife and his associates as well as his southern antecedents might have drawn him into the Confederate navy. Instead he insisted that Virginia had been "dragooned" out of the Union and promptly left for the North. Applying to Washington for orders, he was given a desk job weeding out incompetent officers.[17]

Sixty years old when appointed to the command of the West Gulf Blockading Squadron, Farragut was a natural leader and a good choice for the hazardous enterprise of capturing New Orleans. Commander David Dixon Porter, his brother, accompanied him with a fleet of mortar vessels, while Major General Benjamin Butler, with an army of eighteen thousand, stood ready to hold the

In the battle of New Orleans, David Farragut's fleet passed the forts below the city. Like many other engagements, the capture of New Orleans involved a coordinated military and naval expedition.

city once it had been seized. Farragut sailed from Hampton Roads on February 2, and had great difficulty in maneuvering his heavy vessels across the bar at the mouth of the Mississippi River. After approaching the installations protecting the mouth of the river, for six days beginning on April 18, Porter's mortar flotilla blazed away at the masonry Forts St. Philip and Jackson with little effect. Then Farragut ran by the forts, pushing his vessels against a strong current under the terrific fire of one hundred shore guns while giving battle to the Confederate fleet. Farragut's flagship, the *Hartford*, beached upon a shoal, and was set ablaze by a fire raft. The ship was struck thirty-two times with a loss of three men killed and ten wounded, but Farragut extinguished the fire.

Having passed the forts and destroyed the Confederate river fleet, the Union commander steamed up the river and out of danger. On the 25th his squadron, which had suffered only one lost ship and three disabled vessels, faced the proud city of New Orleans. Forts Jackson and St. Philip surrendered, and by the 29th the city was in Union hands. The South had lost its most important port.

Although an angry crowd of civilians confronted the landing force, street fighting was avoided when the Confederate general Lovell withdrew his army. By May 2 General Benjamin Butler had landed his troops. "Laden with the breath of those invaders, I am sick at heart," wrote a defiant sixteen-year-old, Clara Solomon, who wore black mourning clothes for the duration of the occupation. "What a victory. The taking of N. O. The Fed. Flag over the Custom House."[18] So began an occupation in which the city's women fought the Yankees symbolically—with snubs, small Confederate flags pinned to their dresses, spitting, and even chamber pots dumped on the heads of Union soldiers.[19]

Farragut's fleet continued up river, capturing Baton Rouge and Natchez. But he could not take Vicksburg with the eighteen hundred troops that accompanied his warships. Meanwhile on June 16 at Memphis, the Mississippi River Flotilla with several ironclads, under the command of Flag Officer Charles H. Davis, confronted a Confederate fleet. Despite citizens lining the banks of the Mississippi to cheer their fleet on and smoke so thick it was impossible to pick out individual vessels, the Union "turtles" (squat ironclads) devastated the Confederate fleet. Memphis, the fifth largest city in the Confederacy and a communications center at the junction of four railroads as well as a naval center, now fell into Union hands.

Union leaders increasingly applied the valuable lesson of close cooperation between military and naval forces—on inland rivers and during the campaigns for Forts Henry and Donelson, New Madrid, Island Number Ten, and Vicksburg. The seizure of Memphis, the expedition against Arkansas Post, the movement on the Yazoo, the attempt of Farragut to force his way up the Mississippi, the successful operation of Porter in running the Confederate batteries at Vicksburg and in transporting Grant's army across the river illustrated the remarkable activity of the Union fleet in the West. With the fall of Port Hudson on July 9, 1863, the North had won the battle for the opening of the Mississippi.

## P R I V A T E E R S   A N D   C O N F E D E R A T E   R A I D E R S

Since the Confederate navy lacked not only ships but the materials to build and equip them, it expended its effort chiefly on raiders and a few powerful cruisers. As Jefferson Davis expressed it:

> At the inception of hostilities the inhabitants of the Confederacy were almost exclusively agriculturists; those of the United States, to a great extent, mechanics and merchants. We had no commercial marine, while their merchant vessels covered the ocean. We were without a navy, while they had powerful fleets. The advantage which they possessed for inflicting injury on our coasts and harbors was thus counterbalanced in some measure by the exposure of their commerce to attack by private armed vessels. . . . The value and efficiency of [privateers] . . . is [sic] strikingly illustrated by the terror inspired among the commercial classes of the United States by a single cruiser of the Confederacy.[20]

In such circumstances, the South revived the dying practice of privateering outlawed by the Declaration of Paris in 1856, an international agreement that the United States had refused to sign. Agreeing to abide by the principles of the declaration with the exception of those relating to privateering, the Confederate Congress authorized its president to issue letters of marque and reprisal [authorizations for action] against "the vessels, goods and effects of the government of the United States, and of the citizens or inhabitants of the states thereof"[21] Appropriate for its circumstances, Confederate law recognized the doctrine of "free ships, free goods," which meant that noncontraband private property on a neutral ship was exempt from capture. The statute also recognized the exemption of noncontraband neutral property on any enemy vessel. Neutral rights were safeguarded: to prevent any tendency toward piracy, each captain of a privateer was required to keep a journal of his cruises and to deliver it to a Confederate collector of customs.

Patriotism, the thirst for adventure, and the hope of profit stimulated privateering in the South, whereas in the North, despite legislation authorizing the issuing of letters of marque, the practice was of little importance. Confederate ships ranged from the tiny *Sea Hawk* with its crew of nine to the formidable blockade runner *Isabella* with its force of over two hundred. Confederate privateering, by means of licenses given to owners of private vessels to hunt down Union shipping, was mostly confined to 1861. Thereafter, Lincoln's threat to treat the crews of captured vessels as pirates and the jailing of a number of sailors curtailed the escapades of those after booty. By 1862, not only were Confederate ports closed to southern privateers by Federal fleets, but such was the effectiveness of the blockade in shutting off foreign markets that southern ships could serve more effectively by running the blockade with needed materials than by trying to interrupt northern shipping. As it became increasingly difficult for large Confederate privateers to get into ports monitored by the Union blockades, smaller ships unable to carry large cargoes but able to hide in small inlets served as a diminishing supply line.

The naval war raised legal questions about the international standing of the Confederacy. In many of its early public declarations, the Lincoln government was reluctant to commit itself officially to ascribing full belligerent status to the South. Various threats were made as to punishing southerners for treason or "piracy." In fact, on April 19, 1861, President Lincoln issued a proclamation that declared the crews and officers of Confederate warships and privateers to be pirates, and there were several abortive trials of those captured. But a storm of abuse ensued in Europe over this interpretation of maritime law, and in retaliation Confederates seized northern sailors and held them as hostages, to be treated like captured crews in northern jails. In the case of the *Petrel*, a Confederate privateer whose crew was indicted for piracy in Philadelphia in 1861, Supreme Court Justice Robert Grier, serving on circuit duty in his native state, complained:

> Why should this difference be made between men captured on land and on the sea? Why not try all those taken on land and hang them? That might do with a mere insurrection; but when it comes to civil war, the laws of war must be observed, or you will lay it open to the most horrid reactions that can possibly be thought of.[22]

The first commerce-raiding cruiser to fly the Confederate flag on the high seas was the five-hundred-ton steamer *Sumter*.[23] After cruising for six months in the Caribbean and the Atlantic, receiving hospitable treatment in neutral ports, and capturing eighteen merchant vessels (eleven of which were released, ransomed, or recaptured), the ship was blockaded at Gibraltar by pursuing Union warships and was abandoned by its officers after the discharge of the crew. It was later sold to the British, became a blockade runner, and was finally lost in the North Sea.

The *Sumter*'s commander, Raphael Semmes, was the most distinguished naval officer in the Confederacy. For many years he had been an officer in the United States Navy, and had seen action in the Mexican War before resigning on February 15, 1861 to follow his state of Alabama into rebellion. No officer was more ardent in his southern sympathies, and none more savage in his denunciation of Yankees than the doughty Semmes.[24] His great cruise was with the famous *Alabama*. This vessel, notable for the international controversy which it occasioned, had been built at Liverpool under an arrangement made by Captain James D. Bulloch, a Confederate naval agent in England. Secrecy had accompanied the transfer of the ship to the Confederates. It was a powerful vessel of a thousand tons, over two-hundred feet long, armed with eight guns and equipped with two engines of 300 horsepower each. Its crew of twenty-four officers and 120 men, "made up from all the seafaring nations of the globe, with a large sprinkling of Yankee tars,"[25] was mostly British and included very few southerners.

The vessel left Liverpool as a private ship, the *Enrica*, and sailed to the Azores, where, on the high seas, it received its equipment, its complement of men, and its stores. Off the island of Terceria on August 24, 1862, Captain Semmes took command of the vessel, and for two years it ranged over the seas, playing havoc with Yankee commerce. The *Alabama*'s best-known cruise took it to the Newfoundland Banks, to the Caribbean, to the vicinity of Galveston, Texas, to the Cape of Good Hope, then through Asian waters as far as Singapore, back to Cape Town, again to the Azores, and finally to the French coast. In the course of this voyage the *Alabama* sank the U.S.S. *Hatteras*, which was one hundred tons larger, and captured sixty-two merchant ships, most of which were burned.

During these cruises the *Alabama* found a haven in friendly British ports, where Captain Semmes obtained fuel and supplies, discharged prisoners, and made repairs. Finally the vessel was trapped by a Union cruiser, the *Kearsarge*, commanded by Captain John A. Winslow, in the French port of Cherbourg. In the ensuing fight, celebrated in naval annals, the *Alabama* was sunk on June 19, 1864.[26] Other Confederate cruisers, such as the *Shenandoah*, the *Florida*, the *Tallahassee*, and the *Georgia* similarly preyed on Union vessels. They managed to drive northern merchant shipping from the world's sea lanes, hindering American seaborne commerce, "though it is doubtful whether the commerce-raiding campaign affected the outcome of the Civil War by as much as a single day."[27] Building and outfitting these ships was expensive and "did not contribute much to the strategic interests of the Confederates."[28] But by forcing insurance costs in the North to prohibitive levels, these raiders did restrain the postwar development of a large American merchant marine.

## UNION COASTAL OPERATIONS AFTER 1862

Coastal operations in the latter part of the war resulted in some of the Union navy's most courageous assaults. Earlier, the seizure of outer positions on Pamlico Sound, the operations against Roanoke Island and New Bern, the reduction of Port Royal and Fort Pulaski, the seizure of Norfolk, the occupation of Florida ports, and the reduction of New Orleans had given the United States important coastal strongholds. Nevertheless the year 1864 opened with four important ports—Charleston, Mobile, Wilmington, and Galveston—in southern hands. With the blockading of these ports an essential element in Federal naval strategy, the ability of the Confederates to hold them as long as they did is surprising.

In the case of Charleston, Union efforts failed. Entrenched on the land side, the city was fortified by harbor defenses, which included Forts Sumter, Moultrie, and Johnson as well as Castle Pinckney. On April 7, 1863, with a powerful fleet of seven monitors carrying thirty-four guns, Du Pont attacked Sumter, encountering such accurate fire from Confederate batteries that he withdrew his squadron. This result—so different from northern expectations, given the Union navy's reliance on what it considered its invincible monitors and given the fact that in New Orleans Farragut's wooden fleet had swept past the forts—shocked military officials. Other attempts, both by land and sea, were directed against Charleston in July and August, 1863 and led to Du Pont's dismissal. Attempts by John Dahlgren also failed. In 1864 Major General Quincy Gillmore tried to reduce the city by siege operations and infantry assaults on Battery Wagner. The city itself was shelled, and Fort Sumter was subjected to a seven-day military bombardment. None of these efforts, however, succeeded as P. G. T. Beauregard's men held fast. The assaults on entrenched Confederate positions were turned back, and neither side was able to move the other from its established positions. Although Sumter was shattered and its guns silenced, the Confederates held the ruins until February 1865, when the position was finally abandoned.

Further naval operations occurred in the Red River expedition, the assault on Mobile, and the reduction of Fort Fisher. The Red River expedition in March 1864 proved a costly fiasco for the Union. It was a huge land-and-water enterprise under General Nathaniel P. Banks and Admiral David Dixon Porter whose main object was, by proceeding up the Red River in western Louisiana, to clamp the Union vise on Louisiana and East Texas and simultaneously to dampen the French emperor Napoleon III's ambitions in Mexico. An incidental purpose was to seize quantities of cotton. In its strategic object the expedition failed completely. As for the cotton, southerners destroyed it as Union forces approached. The army units in this expedition numbered about thirty thousand, while the navy used over twenty ironclads and gunboats in addition to a large number of transports.

Between the time that Porter's fleet entered the mouth of the Red River on March 12, 1864, escorting a detachment of Banks's army, until May 21, when the squadron and transports returned dejectedly to the Mississippi, the force encountered not only the Confederates but the "treacherous nature of this crooked, narrow, and turbid stream, whose high banks furnished the most favorable positions for artillery and for the deadly sharp-shooter."[29] Shreveport was not captured; the southern military force was undefeated. In fact Edmund Kirby Smith, the Confederate general in charge of the trans-Mississippi Department, did not surrender until May 1865. Confederate strength in the Southwest had hardly been shaken, and Sherman had been deprived of a powerful force in his Atlanta campaign. Moreover, Banks had suffered two defeats at Sabine Cross Roads and Pleasant Hill in Louisiana, and the fleet had narrowly missed being stranded in the falling river. Along with the military, the hordes of speculators accompanying the army had indignantly retired without the cotton they anticipated.

The naval assault in Mobile Bay was much more successful. The city, defended by shore forts and a fleet that included the famous ram *Tennessee*, was captured in August 1864. In this action Farragut was piloting a fleet of fourteen wooden ships and four ironclads toward the passage past the fort when the leading ironclad in the battle line, the *Tecumseh*, struck a mine and sank. At a critical moment Farragut, lashed to the rigging to prevent his falling into the sea as he directed operations aboard his flagship the *Hartford*, decided that he must lead across the mines, yelling to his crew , the captain of another vessel, and posterity, "Damn the torpedoes! Four Bells. Full speed ahead!" Once past the forts and into Mobile Bay, Farragut accepted the surrender of the forts and the Confederate fleet commanded by Franklin Buchanan. The city, now of little importance without access to the sea, remained in Confederate hands until the end of the war.

For an assault on Fort Fisher, which guarded Wilmington Harbor, the Union planned a formidable military and naval attack. But in December 1864, the North Carolina garrison, with its elaborate coast defenses, held out against a combined but poorly coordinated effort by the navy under Porter and the army under Benjamin Butler and Godfrey Weitzel. A second expedition in January 1865—a huge armada under Porter and a military force of nearly eighty thousand under General Alfred Terry—destroyed the fort, chiefly by a bombardment that silenced its guns. "Its capture [wrote one of its southern defenders], with the resulting loss of all the Cape Fear River defenses, and of Wilmington, the great importing depot of the South, effectually ended all blockade-running. Lee sent me word that Fort Fisher must be held, or he could not subsist his army."[30] Another lifeline of the Confederacy was closed off, though the effect was limited in the closing days of the war.

The war came to its end with the Stars and Bars still flying over Galveston. So far from the major Confederate armies, this port in the southwest did not surrender until June 2, 1865. But its fall may be regarded as the final act in the struggle on the seas that took place all over the world but which was won by the Union navy.

This navy made two critical contributions to the Union victory. One was to deploy an increasingly tight blockade that cut the South off from essential imports such as blankets and shoes as well as war materials such as guns. The blockade destroyed 221 of three hundred steamers sent to test it. As the war continued with the U.S. Navy able to patrol in wider and wider arcs around southern ports, the Confederacy was sealed off, with devastating results for its war economy and civilian morale. Though it cannot be argued that any southern army lost a battle because of the lack of such supplies, nevertheless the cumulative effect, especially on the Army of Northern Virginia, was demoralizing.[31]

The other essential contribution of the Union navy was to transport troops to beachheads along the coast and especially on the inland rivers that served as highways into the Confederacy. The artillery support from these armadas was crucial to the success of the Union army.[32]

CHAPTER 20 | # Northern Politics, 1861–1864

I f war is politics carried on by other means, then wartime politics both reflects the fortunes of war and influences military events. In the North, the Civil War transformed party choices even as the institutions and practices of the nation's public culture mainly stayed the same. In one example of war-induced change, the Republicans emerged as the majority party. Their candidates controlled the presidency and Congress, with few exceptions, into the twentieth century.

In turn, the Democrats—who had been the dominant party before the war and who, even in 1862, would have won control of Congress if the Confederate states had rejoined the Union before the November elections—became the minority party. Secession had cost the party an irretrievable half of its congressmen. Thereafter brushed with the label of treason, Democrats elected only Grover Cleveland to the presidency in the next forty years, as Republicans hammered their rivals as the party of "Dixie, Davis, and the Devil."

At the same time that Republican domination changed the partisan landscape, the procedures of American politics survived the challenges of war. Lincoln did not administer a one-party government, despite the efforts of some to install a Union party. Instead, Democrats came to define their role as that of a loyal opposition, considering themselves as challenging, within acceptable limits of disagreement, the policies of their opponents. Democrats also believed their name conveyed a special commitment to the principles of self-government within a two-party system.[1]

Because partisan differences within such a party system had become institutionalized, elections were held—no matter how chaotic the circumstances. Patronage, platforms, and the rituals of party affairs from election parades to stump speeches survived in border states despite the war raging nearby. The importance of voting was never more obvious than to northerners of the 1860s, who in nineteen states passed legislation permitting either voting in the field or absentee balloting so that soldiers could participate in elections.[2]

## THE REPUBLICANS

The transformation of the Republicans into the dominant party was as significant a development as the survival of democratic practices. Only six years old when the war began, the new organization was threatened by factions. Even before his inauguration, Lincoln encountered disagreements with party leaders over his policies and personnel. Some Republicans demanded the removal of his secretary of the state, William H. Seward. On March 2, 1861, a group of Seward's supporters informed Lincoln that the New Yorker would not serve in the Cabinet with Salmon P. Chase, Lincoln's choice for secretary of treasury.

The sources of this division among Republicans were twofold. First, Chase and Seward competed as ambitious party leaders who sought control over the organization. Second, the two men approached the secession crisis differently. Seward believed that he had a responsibility to save the country through conciliation with the South. Chase, on the other hand, opposed any concessions to the South. Both men agreed, however, that the inexperienced Lincoln was incapable of dealing with the crisis, and Seward went so far as to call the administration "a doubtful experiment."

For the president-elect, the intransigence of Seward and his New York supporters, led by Thurlow Weed, produced a dilemma. When Seward asked to withdraw from the Cabinet, Lincoln shrewdly realized that the Seward-Chase rift made it politic to have both factional chiefs in his official family. Unwilling for Seward to "take the first trick," Lincoln thus launched his administration with a hybrid Republican Cabinet of mutually suspicious former Whigs and Democrats who also disagreed over slavery.

These factional dissensions intensified after Frémont's proclamation freeing the slaves of rebels in Missouri. When Lincoln, mindful of border state sentiment, first overruled Frémont and then removed him from command in November 1861, he nearly fractured his party over an issue that would continue to divide it. The president's conservative friend Orville Browning warned him that Frémont's removal would be "damaging both to the administration and the cause."[3] But at this point in the war, the president wanted to shape his party into a voting coalition that would include Unionists from the south and Democrats from the north.[4]

On the other hand, friends of Chase supported Frémont and criticized the president for his appeasement of "the contemptible state of Kentucky when the free states may want a little conciliation."[5] In a struggle that had implications for

Lincoln removed John C. Frémont from his command in November of 1861 because of Frémont's proclamation freeing the slaves of rebels in Missouri. Frémont ran for president in 1864, but withdrew one month before the election.

the postwar period, northern Republicans in Congress opposed Lincoln's efforts to attract border-state residents (and later those of occupied Tennessee and Louisiana) to their party.[6]

By 1862 the opposition to the Lincoln administration from both the Democrats and from within the Republican party had grown. Military failures and the calls for more troops deepened the impression of incompetence in Washington. The year's disastrous offensives—beginning with the peninsular campaign and climaxing with the fighting during the Seven Days and Second Bull Run and the failure to pursue the Confederates after Antietam—had partisan repercussions. While alienating antislavery men, Lincoln had also irritated those who, unconcerned about emancipation, demanded a prompt Union victory.

## OPPOSITION TO LINCOLN

Lincoln was also under fire from Democrats. His suspension of habeas corpus and the arrests of civilians, although greatly exaggerated by his opponents, became partisan evidence of the president's tyrannical suppression of civil liberties. Though in 1861 some Democrats, including Andrew Johnson, had been attracted to a bipartisan coalition called the Union party, others resisted what one

With Washington burning in the background in this 1862 painting, a Copperhead of
New York's Tammany Hall chains Lincoln to the Constitution as Lincoln hacks at the
Confederate dragon. Although the Democrats supported the Union, they did not
approve of the Republican administration.

described as being "swallowed up."[7] Instead, Democrats retrieved their ancient
dogma that the best government is the least government and held Republicans to
be meddling oppressors. The Democrats also held fast to their opposition to any
change in the status of African Americans.

In the election year of 1862 Democrats vehemently opposed Lincoln's September proclamations—on emancipation and two days later, the general suspension of habeas corpus and the use of military trials to suppress disloyalty.
Enunciated shortly before the midterm elections, both policies infuriated Democrats and conservative Republicans. Such support as Lincoln gained among
abolitionists was more than offset by the defection of those who favored restoring the Union and avoiding issues relating to slavery. John T. Stuart of Illinois,
Lincoln's former law partner, considered the proclamations "most unfortunate";
even Maine's Republican Senator William Fessenden deplored the habeas corpus
edict as "an exercise of despotic power" and "very dangerous."[8]

As the congressional elections approached, discontent spread. Iowa's Senator
James Grimes wrote, "We are going to destruction as fast as imbecility, corruption, and the wheels of time, can carry us."[9] Lincoln's friend Lyman Trumbull
thought the war would never end unless a different approach was taken. The Illi-

nois senator complained of the "lack of affirmative, positive action & business talent in the cabinet."[10] To Governor John Andrew of Massachusetts it seemed that "the President [had] never yet seemed quite sure that we were in a war at all."[11]

In the fall of 1862 no faction seemed pleased with Lincoln. Many abolitionists, though partially appeased by the Emancipation Proclamation of September 22, still attacked the administration for what they regarded as weakness and incompetence. They discovered in Congress's confiscation policies more effective measures for freeing the slaves and defeating the South than those proposed by the president. The preliminary Emancipation Proclamation, accompanied by the president's promise of compensation to slave owners in loyal states, also irritated them. Meanwhile the harassed Lincoln, without winning the support of abolitionists, alienated moderate Republicans.

## THE 1862 ELECTIONS

In 1862 the Democrats revived their party. Some had simply let local elections in 1861 go by default; others had worked with the Republicans under the label of the Union party. The main purpose of this Republican-managed Union party initially had been a vigorous prosecution of the war and an unyielding suppression of the rebellion. These, indeed, were the broad purposes of the northern people, and they served admirably as party slogans. In opposition to the Unionists of 1861 stood the regular Democrats, who were outspoken opponents of the administration. Since this faction preferred to preserve its organization intact, a mistaken view that these were antiwar Democrats has emerged. Generally this characterization was not true, although Republicans found in the label Copperhead an effective smear.[12]

The regular Democrats supported the government of the United States against the Confederacy. But they wished to follow a different direction in the prosecution of the war, and they wanted to replace the existing Republican administration. Indeed, Democrats declared that Union success in the war could never come along the lines proposed by the Lincoln government. The party's leaders fanned the fear among white laborers of economic competition with emancipated blacks, who, it was assumed, would flood the North. The Democratic claim that "every white laboring man who does not want to be swapped for a nigger should vote the Democratic ticket" attracted some voters, as did the slogan that summarized the party's platform: "the Constitution as it is, the Union as it was, and the Negroes where they are."[13]

In the fall congressional elections, Lincoln and the Republicans nearly lost control of Congress. In the Thirty-seventh Congress after the withdrawal of its Confederate members there were 106 Republicans, 42 Democrats, and 28 Unionists. In the Thirty-eighth Congress, elected in 1862, the Democrats gained 35 seats from the Republicans and Unionists. The composition of this House was 103 Republicans, 77 Democrats and 3 Unionists. Democrats also won the important governorships of New York and New Jersey.

Changes that exceeded the traditional turnover in off-year congressional elections voting reveal the extent of Republican losses. Five states (Pennsylvania, New York, Indiana, Illinois and Ohio) that had voted Republican in 1860 now delivered slender Democratic majorities. In New Jersey the Democratic majority increased, and in four other states (Massachusetts, New Hampshire, Maine and Michigan), large Republican majorities fell to narrow margins. Almost everywhere these reversals reflected a dramatic drop-off in the Republican vote in 1860, rather than an increase in Democratic support.[14]

The Republican defeat in Lincoln's home state was a notable feature of this election. In September 1862, an anti-Lincoln paper in Springfield denounced the "party of unscrupulous demagogues" who controlled the United States Congress and pointed to the reign of terror in the North stoked by the administration's illegal arrests.[15] The most striking aspect of the election in Illinois, which was one of the most competitive party states in the Union, was the contest in the Eighth Congressional District, where John Todd Stuart, a cousin of Mary Todd Lincoln, ran as the Democratic candidate against Leonard Swett, the Republican nominee. Stuart was one of those Whigs who, in the redrawing of party lines, had not joined the Republicans. He had supported Fillmore in 1856 and Bell in 1860.

In 1862, while supporting the war and professing respect for Lincoln, whose political mentor and close friend he had been, Stuart urged the maintenance of the Constitution and the Union without "resort to revolutionary means." Democrats accepted him on this platform. Here, then, were two of Lincoln's close friends at odds: Stuart opposing Lincoln; Swett championing Lincoln's policies. After a heated campaign in which pamphlets denounced Lincoln's suppression of civil liberties, the final vote stood at Stuart, 12,808 to Swett, 11,443. Eight other Democrats won congressional races in Illinois; only five Republicans did so. In addition, Lincoln's opponents obtained control of the Illinois legislature. "Badly beaten by the Democrats," admitted a glum Orville Browning. "Just what was to be expected from the insane ravings of the *Chicago Tribune, Quincy Whig.*"[16]

Lincoln had clearly become a lightning rod for discontent in the North. According to the *New York Times* on November 5, 1862:

> The heaviest load which the friends of the Government have been compelled to carry through this canvass has been the inactivity and inefficiency of the Administration. . . . The country has given the Government over a million of men, and all the money they could possibly use.

Two days later under the headline "The Vote of Want of Confidence," the *Times* held the president responsible for the resurgence of the Democrats:

The very qualities which have made Abraham Lincoln so well liked in private life . . . his kindheartedness, his concern for fair play, his placidity of temper . . . unfit him for the stern requirements of deadly war. Quick, sharp, summary dealings don't suit him at all. He is all the while haunted with the fear of doing some injustice, and is ever easy to accept explanations. The very first necessity of war is extreme rigor, and yet every impulse of our constitutional Commander-in-Chief has been to get rid of it. . . . There is not a purer patriot in the land. And yet there is something beyond this which we miss—the high sacred vehemence, inspired by the consciousness of infinite interests at stake.

## THE CABINET CRISIS

Infuriated by the losses in 1862, Republican Congressmen looked for a scape-goat on whom they could place blame and found Lincoln. A few spoke of a cau-cus or directory to replace him. Most knew, however, that they had to live with him until the 1864 election. A rift in Lincoln's Cabinet helped them to locate a surrogate for more immediate punishment—Secretary of State William Seward.

Chase, always more radical than Lincoln on the need to end slavery quickly, shared his growing disappointment in the president with Republican senators. In these conversations the secretary of the treasury pointed to what he believed were the president's errors, especially with regard to Lincoln's revoking General David Hunter's order to free slaves in his military Department of the South, consisting of South Carolina, Georgia and Florida. Chase also argued that the president had been far too slow to remove General George McClellan from his command in 1862.

By this time Chase believed in his own superior ability to conduct the nation's affairs. Though never reaching the point of actual disloyalty to his chief, the sec-retary of the treasury became, because of his personality and position, the center of an anti-Lincoln movement. With Chase castigating Lincoln and his special ally in the Cabinet, Seward, some Republican senators continued to whisper of a directory that would assume Lincoln's powers.[17] Eventually a committee urged "such selections and changes [in the Cabinet] . . . as will secure to the country unity of purpose and action."[18]

This Cabinet crisis placed Lincoln in a dilemma. Although giving little out-ward evidence of emotion, he revealed his inward turmoil to his friend Brown-ing, who has quoted him as saying, "What do these men want? . . . They wish to get rid of me, and I am sometimes half disposed to gratify them. . . . Since I heard of the proceedings of the caucus I have been more distressed than by any event of my life."[19]

Lincoln's way of confronting the issue displayed the president's characteristi-cally adroit handling of those situations involving personnel that often test American presidents. Before his first meeting with the senatorial committee,

Lincoln received word of Seward's resignation. When the committee met with him, Vermont's senator Jacob Collamer read a statement in which Republican senators urged a vigorous prosecution of the war and a unified Cabinet that agreed with the president in political principle and general policy—conditions that the Senate did not believe currently existed. Finally, they encouraged a Cabinet "exclusively composed of statesmen who are the cordial, resolute, unwavering supporters" of prosecuting the war "with energy" and suppressing a "causeless and atrocious rebellion."[20] Republicans who were more progressive on the emancipation issue appeared to be on the point of remaking the Cabinet. Clearly the president's leadership was at stake. Lincoln's next move was to call another meeting of the senatorial delegation to confer with him. When they met, they were surprised to find that the president had shrewdly arranged to have the whole Cabinet present except for Seward.[21] If they were surprised, Chase was mortified.

Confronted with his Cabinet colleagues, the senators, and the president, Chase now found it necessary to state "that the cabinet were all harmonious." Previously he had said to these same senators "that Seward exercised a backstair and malign influence upon the President, and thwarted all the measures of the Cabinet."[22] The result was that Chase as well as Seward resigned. "I can see my way clear. Now I can ride. I have a pumpkin in each end of my bag," said the delighted president, who refused to accept either resignation.[23] So the crisis passed, the cabinet continuing as before, the senators somewhat chagrined, Chase embarrassed, and the president maintaining what some believed a lack of system in dealing with his advisors.[24]

## THE DEMOCRATIC CHALLENGE IN 1863

More serious than the bickering within Lincoln's party and the obvious threat to the president's renomination was the growing challenge of the Democratic party, rejuvenated after its successes in 1862. From its traditional belief in the sovereignty of the people, the rights of the states, and a light and simple government, the Democrats in 1863 fashioned an indictment of the Republicans that they retained after the war ended. Their objections continued to center on Lincoln's supposedly unconstitutional measures. They also held as unacceptable the dogma, sometimes quoted by Republicans, that in wartime the laws must sometimes be silent. By 1863 Democrats found in the drafting of soldiers a violation of American liberties. According to one party member, "all conscription or other forced service of the citizens to the state is contrary to the genius and principles of republican government."[25] In the same vein Horace Greeley informed Secretary of War Edwin M. Stanton that "the people have been educated to the idea of individual sovereignty and the principle of conscription is repugnant to their feelings and cannot be carried out except at great peril to the free states."[26]

Along with conscription, Democrats made partisan issues of such wartime extensions of federal authority as the printing of greenbacks, the centralization of banking functions, the suspension of specie payment by banks, and the power of the provost marshals—all of which they considered unconstitutional subordinations of the separate states and of the rights of individuals to the government in Washington. "Shall we sink down as serfs to the heartless speculative Yankee for all time, swindled by his tariff, robbed by his taxes, skinned by his railroad monopolies?" wondered one Democrat.[27] By no means did war justify these encroachments in the view of those who saw the restoration of the Union—not the emancipation of slaves—as the sole condition for peace.[28]

Included in Democrats' complaints was a strident opposition to the Emancipation Proclamation which, to them, summarized the excesses of the Republicans. While both parties opposed equality for blacks, in 1863 Democrats played the race card more than the antiabolitionist card, charging that Lincoln had "nigger on the brain." For the black, said one Democrat, "you will destroy the country. For him you will allow the liberties of the white man to be stricken down and every sacred guarantee of liberty in the Constitution put under foot without a whimper or a censure."[29] Yet for all their complaints, most Democrats stopped short of subverting the war effort and acknowledged, even as their own legitimacy was challenged, allegiance to the institutions of the government, but not to the current administration and its programs.

After their success in the congressional elections of 1862, Democrats anticipated gains in the eleven governor's races and in lesser state offices contested in the fall of 1863. Horace Greeley predicted that the identification of the Republicans with the Emancipation Proclamation would hurt that party at the polls. Yet the results proved otherwise. Democrats did not win any gubernatorial races; prominent Peace Democrats such as Ohio's Clement Vallandigham and Pennsylvania's George Woodward suffered especially large defeats. Thus an equilibrium between the parties was achieved, characterized as "a pattern of selective gains and losses, responses to particular and local situations, rather than any sustained national surge in the Democracy's favor [that] seemed to mark popular voting by 1863 . . . Democrats had become a respectable minority, a few of whose members sometimes moved beyond criticism to disloyal opposition to the war."[30]

As the 1864 Republican presidential nominating convention approached, the Radicals within Lincoln's party were ready to find another standard bearer. This discontent first took the form of the "Chase boom." As Chase had informed his son-in-law in 1863, "I think a man of different qualities from those the President has will be needed for the next four years. I am not anxious to be regarded as that man; and I am quite willing to leave that question to the decision of those who agree in thinking that some such man should be chosen."[31] By early 1864 many national leaders, such as William Cullen Bryant, Theodore Tilton, and Horace Greeley, also believed that the Lincoln administration was largely a failure and that, according to the Ohio senator John Sherman, there were far better men for president than Lincoln.[32]

The Chase boom was launched by a group of Republican leaders led by Senator Samuel Pomeroy of Kansas.[33] In the "Pomeroy Circular," they declared that the reelection of Lincoln was impossible, that the President's unfortunate "tendency toward temporary expedients" would become stronger during a second term, and that Chase combined more of the necessary qualities for an effective war president than any other available candidate.

When Chase made his embarrassed explanation to the president denying his ambition, Lincoln refused to accept the resignation that Chase again offered and shrewdly managed to keep the secretary in the Cabinet, where he could do the least harm to the Lincoln cause. Before long the boom collapsed. Powerful as was the anti-Lincoln movement, bad management and poor timing hindered the efforts of Chase's friends.

## LINCOLN'S RENOMINATION

The political season began with some dirty politics when in May 1864 two New York papers—the New York *World* and *Journal of Commerce*—published a bogus proclamation attributed to Lincoln. In this statement Lincoln supposedly recounted recent disasters on the battlefield and called for four hundred thousand more soldiers. The forged, morale-deflating document led to a three-day suspension of the newspapers involved. Its more important long-term effect, however, was to erode confidence in the president's ability to lead the country and to stimulate rumors that Lincoln would become the dictator that, Democrats exaggerated, he already was.[34]

Yet Lincoln was too much the democrat to use such episodes as a reason to postpone this crucial election. Later Lincoln explained why elections, even in wartime, were a necessity. "We can not have free government without elections; and if the rebellion could force us to forego, or postpone a national election, it might fairly claim to have already conquered and ruined us. The strife of the election is but human nature practically applied to the facts of the case."[35] Amid challenges in 1864 from within his party, from the Democrats, and from advocates of peace without conditions, the president maintained this position.

Two weeks after the fraudulent Lincoln proclamation was printed, disaffected members of the president's party, led by B. Gratz Brown and Wendell Phillips, met in Cleveland. Unable to control the regular Republican machinery, delegates who included many German-Americans nominated John C. Frémont for president and New York's John Cochrane for vice president, after bitterly denouncing Lincoln and his administration.

But the president and his allies controlled the regular Republican organization, and they had been working through state conventions, where delegates to the national convention were instructed to vote for Lincoln. There was strong support for the president in the western states. Gradually state after state fell into line, many passing resolutions praising Lincoln's statesmanship. When the Republican convention met in Baltimore on June 7, the effectiveness of the regular organization was demonstrated. There was some opposition, and the presence of an anti-Lincoln delegation from Missouri that first gave its votes to Grant, drew some attention.[36] Yet Lincoln was unanimously renominated, even though some delegates preferred Grant, the only man in the country who could have defeated Lincoln for the nomination but who discouraged his supporters.[37]

Outwardly Lincoln kept his hands off the convention, but his private secretary John Nicolay was in Baltimore, functioning as a Lincoln scout and taking care that nothing distasteful to the president was done on such matters as the platform and the vice presidency. Behind the scenes Lincoln was reported as favoring former Democrat Andrew Johnson of Tennessee to replace Vice President Hannibal Hamlin, but officially the president took the position that the convention must settle this question for itself.[38] Largely through the shrewdness of Henry Raymond, the editor of the *New York Times*, Johnson's name was presented at the right moment. When the Tennesseean's nomination was made unanimous, most Republicans believed that Johnson's selection had strengthened the ticket because it recognized the Democrats and the South.

The 1864 Republican platform—officially, the party renamed itself the National Union party for this election—was one of the most progressive in the party's history. It resolved "for the unconditional surrender of the rebels," announced slavery as the cause of "this rebellion" and endorsed passage of the Thirteenth Amendment to eradicate it, urged the protection of black soldiers and encouraged immigration and the construction of a Pacific railroad. Republican-Unionists also praised the president for his "unswerving fidelity to the Constitution and the principles of American liberty," and approved his Emancipation Proclamation.

Yet in the weeks following the president's renomination, opposition within his party surfaced again when congressional Republicans passed the Wade-Davis bill on July 2, 1864. The immediate cause of its hasty enactment was the failure of the House to pass the Thirteenth Amendment at a time when northern Republicans wanted to enter a campaign with a concrete record of action against slavery. More broadly, however, the Wade-Davis bill detailed a more stringent, restrictive plan for bringing southern citizens and states back into the Union.

By 1864 Lincoln and the Republicans in Congress agreed on the need for a constitutional amendment ending slavery. As more areas of the South came under Union control, what increasingly divided them was the looming agenda of restoring the Confederacy to the nation. The Wade-Davis bill summarized these differences. This congressional measure required 50 percent (compared with Lincoln's 10 percent) of each state's voters in 1860 to swear an oath of allegiance to the United States government. It also required that a constitutional convention take place before the election of state officials, and it restricted the right to vote for convention delegates to men who could take an ironclad oath that they had never voluntarily supported the South's rebellion.

Such propositions reflected congressional Republicans' dissatisfaction with the terms of reconstruction of Confederate states that Lincoln had announced in December 1863 and especially with developments in Louisiana and Tennessee under Lincoln's policy.[39]

Lincoln could not approve such a plan. It seemed to him to perpetuate wartime bitterness, to deny the necessary flexibility of different arrangements for different states and therefore to retard the restoration of the Union. As president, Lincoln had rarely used the veto. But in this case he applied the pocket veto—a method by which presidents block legislation within ten days of congressional adjournment by not signing a measure. Such an unusual action gave Congress no opportunity to override his opposition.

In an explanatory document accompanying his pocket veto, Lincoln denied the right of Congress to control the process of Reconstruction, and he refused to be committed to any single plan. He also argued that the Wade-Davis bill would undermine the new constitutions and governments already in place in Arkansas and in Louisiana. In the context of electoral politics, Lincoln's explanation revealed his growing differences with more radical Republicans as well as his desire to defuse opposition in Congress and restore party unity at the beginning of the election campaign. But so bitter was this conflict that, on August 5, the two Republican sponsors of the bill—Ohio's Senator Benjamin Wade and Maryland's Representative Henry Winter Davis—issued a scathing "manifesto" to the press, denouncing the president who had just been renominated as their party's candidate.

Even before this rupture with congressional Radicals over Reconstruction, Lincoln had rekindled their suspicions by removing Chase, the Radicals' preeminent ally, from the Cabinet. On June 29, the secretary of the treasury once more gave his resignation to Lincoln, and to his chagrin, this time it was accepted. As Lincoln put it: "Of all I have said in commendation of your ability and fidelity, I have nothing to unsay; and yet you and I have reached a point of mutual embarrassment in our official relation which it seems cannot be overcome, or longer sustained, consistently with the public service."[40]

## THE PEACE MOVEMENT

If the Radicals' disaffection with Lincoln threatened to reduce his support among Republicans, growing war weariness seemed to boost his Democratic opponents. As the war dragged on during the election summer of 1864, it brought military disappointments to the North that culminated in Jubal Early's raid, the burning of Chambersburg, Pennsylvania, and the narrowly averted capture of Washington. Amid the clouds of defeatism, political opposition to the president deepened. In the South spirits rose at the possibility of Lincoln's defeat. Anticipating that the "tyrant at Washington" might lose, a Georgia editor wrote that a crisis had arrived "with our oppressors."[41] Meanwhile northern Democrats played a waiting game, postponing their convention until the end of August.

Agitation for peace and efforts at negotiation undermined Lincoln's position on unconditional surrender. The outspoken Clement Vallandigham, after escaping from the South and returning through Canada to Ohio, attacked Lincoln and urged peace. In Illinois James Singleton emerged as the leader of a group organizing peace demonstrations. Singleton promoted a convention in Peoria in early August that Republicans denounced as a Copperhead movement to make "peace with traitors." A "peace pow-wow" was held in Springfield on August 18. These efforts were closely associated with Democratic opposition to Lincoln's candidacy, and the connection of the movement with the Confederate-leaning Sons of Liberty further identified the peacemakers with those who wished to overthrow the existing administration.[42]

In a larger sense, however, the spread of the peace movement was the inevitable expression of a war-weary nation. Sincere northern patriots yearned for an end to the fratricidal slaughter. Even Charles Francis Adams, far removed in London, was willing to grasp at almost any hope for peace. Early in 1864, the American ambassador had entered into unofficial discussions with Thomas Yeatman of Tennessee, who pledged that Jefferson Davis would step aside as president of the Confederacy in order to allow the southern states to reenter the Union, provided that the Lincoln administration adopted a plan of compensated, gradual emancipation. When Yeatman's indiscreet behavior and his failure to produce credentials as a Confederate peace envoy caused Seward to drop the negotiations, Adams lamented that his government had failed to pursue "the heroic policy which would have smoothed the path to reconciliation."[43]

Adams's views were kept secret, but when Horace Greeley associated himself with the peace movement, the attention of the North focused on the subject. On learning from a self-constituted envoy named William C. Jewett that "two ambassadors of Davis & Co. are now in Canada, with full and complete powers for a peace," and that "the whole matter [could] be consummated by me, you, them, and President Lincoln,"[44] the editor of the *Tribune* referred the matter to Lincoln. "I venture to remind you [wrote Greeley to the president] that our bleeding, bankrupt, almost dying country also longs for peace; shudders at the prospect of fresh conscriptions, of further wholesale devastations, and of new rivers of human blood. And a widespread conviction that the government and its supporters are not anxious for peace is doing great harm."[45]

Lincoln, distracted at the time by Early's raid on Washington, replied to Greeley on July 9, promising to meet "any person anywhere professing to have any proposition of Jefferson Davis in writing, for peace, embracing the restoration of the Union and abandonment of slavery."[46] At the same time he made Greeley the intermediary for conveying the government's willingness to receive authorized negotiators. To show good faith, the president extended to three southern "commissioners" then in Canada a formal letter of safe conduct to Washington. In fact the purpose of these Confederate agents was to promote the Confederate cause in the North and stir up peace sentiment in the Union on the eve of the election.[47]

Caught up in a plan for which he now had no enthusiasm, Greeley traveled to Niagara only to find that the advertised diplomats had no credentials. Their mission was unofficial. Instead they offered, if granted safe conduct to Washington and Richmond, to obtain the needed authorization. The agents were primarily interested in peace agitation during a presidential election year: if Lincoln were made to appear resistant to legitimate appeals to negotiate, he might lose votes to the Democrats. The Niagara episode demonstrated that Lincoln's war goals were not just restoring the Union but also included freeing the slaves.

This fiasco was followed by another unofficial peace effort which seemed more promising—the Jacquess-Gilmore mission. James F. Jacquess was a Methodist clergyman and college president from Illinois, who had become the colonel of a volunteer regiment. James R. Gilmore was a writer and friend of Greeley's. Disturbed that Christians were killing one another, Jacquess had earlier entered Confederate lines under a flag of truce and asked to be taken to see Jefferson Davis. He did this without government authority, though Lincoln unofficially approved the mission, wishing to draw attention to southern intransigence on peace terms.

In Richmond the peacemakers conferred with President Davis and Secretary of State Judah Benjamin on July 17. But as in similar cases, the meetings broke down when the Confederate leaders indicated that Confederate independence was an indispensable condition. "We are fighting for INDEPENDENCE and that, or extermination, we will have," said Jefferson Davis, ending with this stipulation any possibility of a negotiated peace.[48] In his annual message to Congress in December 1864, Lincoln clarified the differences between the Confederacy and the Union: "Davis cannot reaccept the Union; we cannot voluntarily yield it. . . . Between him and us the issue is distinct, simple and inflexible. It is an effort which can only be tried by war and decided by victory.[49]

On July 22, 1864 the Boston *Evening Transcript* printed an account of the Jacquess-Gilmore mission in which Jefferson Davis was quoted as saying: "This war must go on till the last of the generation falls in his tracks . . . unless you acknowledge our right to self-government." Much the same result occurred in Toronto in August 1864, when Jeremiah Black met Jacob Thompson, his former colleague in the Buchanan Cabinet. Again the southern requirement of independence afforded no opening for a consideration of collateral points such as amnesty, state restoration, and compensation to slave owners, issues on which Lincoln stood ready to negotiate.

## FURTHER POLITICAL CHALLENGES TO LINCOLN

As these peace negotiations continued, some Republicans, during the dark summer of 1864 when Lee seemed so invincible and Grant so bogged down in Virginia, moved to replace Lincoln with a "more vigorous" candidate. With the press informing northerners that the South was anxious to negotiate but was rebuffed by a stubborn administration, dissenting Republicans secretly circulated a call for a convention to meet in Cincinnati in late September "to consider the state of the nation and to concentrate the union strength on some one candidate who commands the confidence of the country, even by a new nomination if necessary."[50] Though the projected convention never met, the call evoked surprisingly pessimistic letters from Republican leaders.

The influential Horace Greeley wrote, "Mr. Lincoln is already beaten. He cannot be elected. And we must have another ticket to save us from utter overthrow. If we had such a ticket as could be made by naming Grant, Butler, or Sherman for President, and Farragut as Vice, we could make a fight yet. And such a ticket we ought to have anyhow, with or without a convention." Baltimore's Henry Winter Davis concurred: "My letters from Maryland say Lincoln can do nothing there, even where the Union party is most vigorous, and everybody is looking for a candidate."[51] Richard Smith of the Cincinnati *Gazette* believed that the success of the Democrats would be the ruin of the nation, that the "peace party" was dangerously strong, that the "people regard[ed] Mr. Lincoln's candidacy as a misfortune," and that the best course would be the withdrawal of Lincoln and "the nomination of a man that would inspire confidence and infuse life into our ranks."[52]

Influenced by such sentiments, Lincoln expressed his pessimism in an August 23 memorandum: "This morning . . . it seems exceedingly probable that this Administration will not be re-elected. Then it will be my duty to so cooperate with the President elect, as to save the Union between the election and the inauguration. . . ."

After his reelection the president stated that he had been determined, in case of McClellan's election, to "talk matters over with him" and say, "General, the election has demonstrated that you have more influence . . . than I. Now let us together, you with your influence and I with the executive power . . . try to save the country. You raise as many troops as you possibly can . . . and I will devote all my energies to assist and finish the war." "At least," said Lincoln, who had believed he would lose the election but who never considered its postponement, "I should have done my duty and have stood clear before my own conscience."[53]

## THE DEMOCRATIC NOMINATION OF MCCLELLAN AND THE 1864 PRESIDENTIAL VOTE

In late August more than two hundred Democratic delegates met in Chicago. The convention represented both war Democrats and peace Democrats. The latter faction of purists refused any compromise that might help elect a Democrat.[54] The Democrats who supported the war and opposed any peace short of restoration of the Union nominated McClellan, the commander of the Army of the Potomac who had clashed with Lincoln so often, for the presidency and George Pendleton of Ohio for vice president. But the peace faction led by Vallandigham drafted the platform. After proclaiming "four years of failure to restore the Union by the experiment of war," this platform demanded the cessation of hostilities "to the end that at the earliest possible moment peace may be restored on the basis of the Federal Union of the States."[55]

This resolution was not a peace-at-any-price declaration; still, it unrealistically proclaimed reunion as the sole condition of peace. Its weakness lay in the assumption that an undefeated Confederacy, having achieved an armistice on the basis of what would have been considered a southern victory, would abandon the main purpose for which it was fighting. And the platform said nothing about emancipation.

Embarrassed by the peace plank, McClellan emphasized the Union as a "paramount consideration," and in his letter of acceptance wrote that there must

More than two hundred Democratic delegates met at the 1864 Democratic national convention in Chicago. At the convention, George McClellan was nominated to run for president on a disastrous peace platform.

be no peace, not even a temporary armistice, until reunion was assured.[56] He ran as a military leader: indeed, his war record was the reason for his appeal as a candidate. Nor did McClellan stand apart from other leading Democrats in his insistence on the preservation of the Union as the object of the war. Avoiding mention of the "peace plank," Democratic leaders generally inveighed against Lincoln's policies, denounced his acts of "usurpation," and called the Republicans unfit for the task of restoring the Union.

Until the beginning of September the political horoscope seemed to forecast a Democratic victory. On September 2, three important editors—Horace Greeley, Theodore Tilton, and Parke Godwin, representing New York's *Tribune, Independent* and *Evening Post*, respectively—signed appeals to northern governors, promoting the movement to discard Lincoln for some other candidate.[57] Dirty campaign tricks also hurt Lincoln when two Democratic editors produced a spurious pamphlet entitled "Miscegenation: The History of the Blending of the Races Applying to the American White Man and the Negro." Attributed to the Republicans, the pamphlet approved the mixing of the races. By implication Lincoln and his party were continuing the war so that in the future blacks and whites could intermarry, a red herring rejected even by abolitionists.

Gradually, however, the political horizon changed. The Democrats had stirred up resentment with their peace proposals, which the Republicans effectively denounced as a "Copperhead platform" negating the sacrifice of brave Union soldiers. With some success the Republicans countered the Democrats' peace message with a loyalty crusade.[58] Then in September Atlanta fell, giving Lincoln the military victory he needed, and Republicans carried state and congressional elections in Maine and Vermont. Promptly the plans for the Cincinnati convention melted away. Frémont withdrew from the race on September 22.

At the same time the retirement of Postmaster General Montgomery Blair from the Cabinet and the appointment of William Dennison, the war governor of Ohio, in his place appeased anti-Lincoln Radicals. Chase, with the possibility of appointment to the Supreme Court dangling before his ambitious eyes, even campaigned for Lincoln. Wade and Davis, seeing the hopelessness of displacing Lincoln, decided that it was expedient to support him. Republican ranks closed behind the president. "The multitudes rushing to McClellan" who had caused Henry Winter Davis so much concern drifted back to Lincoln.[59]

In the November election, only the votes in Union states were counted, though elections were also held in Louisiana and Tennessee, which Lincoln carried. Just prior to the election, Nevada was added to the Union, although in Colorado the process was delayed. The Nevada constitutional convention completed its work so that the state might be admitted prior to the election. On October 31, 1864, Lincoln proclaimed the admission of the new commonwealth. Eight days later he carried the state by a comfortable majority.

All except three states—Kentucky, Delaware, and New Jersey—gave Lincoln their electoral vote, while in the popular vote the incumbent president had a ma-

Here are two polling places in New York City as depicted by an
artist in the *Illustrated London News*. Note the class bias in terms of
the interpretation of American voting.

jority of four hundred thousand out of more than four million cast. Over 250,000
soldiers voted in their military camps, and thousands of others received furloughs
to return home to vote. Three-quarters of these voted for Lincoln, because they
identified the president with the goals they sought as Union soldiers. In the
154th New York Volunteers, about to begin the march to the sea in Georgia,
"not more than 5 or 6 vot[ed] for Mc. [Clellan] out of 150 . . . and these born,
raised and educated as Democrats," explained their major.[60] As one Union soldier from Connecticut acknowledged:

> The trial by ballot reached its crisis in the presidential election. In that most exciting
> canvass, conducted with the utmost license of speech and of the press even in the face
> of a great civil war, all the influences which could pervert the judgment, sap the loy-

alty, or shake the purpose of the people, culminated in a final appeal against the war and the administration. . . . [But] as at Gettysburg, the victory was . . . overwhelming; and the nation was saved in the trial of patriotism on the 8th of November, 1864, as decisively as on the 4th of July, 1863.[61]

After an analysis of the election returns among civilians, one scholar has concluded that

> Lincoln won the election because of the support given him by the agricultural areas inhabited largely by native-born citizens, former Bell-Everett voters, and the skilled urban workers and professional classes. McClellan drew his best support from the immigrant proletariat and from rural areas in which the foreign element predominated. Those who supported Breckinridge in 1860 seem in a large measure to have voted for McClellan in 1864. Most Protestant denominations urged support of the administration, while the Irish element of the Catholic church [which included many sailors] supported McClellan.[62]

Voter turnout dropped from over 80 percent in 1860 to 73 percent of the electorate in 1864, but Lincoln received 360,000 more votes than he had in 1860. Facing only one party and opponent, he now took 55 percent of the vote. There was no dramatic reconfiguration of voting preferences.

Although the election was hailed as a Lincoln "landslide," the large minorities for McClellan in New York, Pennsylvania, Ohio, Indiana, and Illinois suggested the durability of the Democrats, who remained competitive. According to the Illinois Democrat John Caton, the Democrats' loss in 1864 was due to the ambiguous expressions in their platform and to the questionable principles of their leaders at the Chicago convention. The Democrats, supporting the war but condemning the "radicalism of Lincoln," won the election of 1862; then in 1864, thought Caton, they failed because they took up the cry of peace, denounced all others as abolitionists, organized secret societies, and wrote a platform to conciliate a minor, though outspoken, faction that had assumed leadership.[63] Yet New York's Democrat Horatio Seymour announced he was satisfied with the result, which showed "our numerous strength."[64]

In fact, the election revealed the continuity of political behavior during wartime—in terms of nominating candidates, writing well-publicized platforms, choosing between Democrats and Republicans, and confirming a basic distribution of the vote that had taken shape during the party realignment of the 1850s. In the context of the war, Lincoln's reelection ensured that the conflict would not be interrupted by a cease-fire followed by negotiations, and in that sense was as important a Union victory as any on the battlefield; whereas in the Confederacy, the president's reelection ended any possibility that a demoralized North would seek a negotiated peace.

## CHAPTER 21

# The Home Front
in the North

P olitics was only one aspect of the Union home front during the Civil War. Domestic concerns such as rising prices, shortages of labor, family separations, and changes in religious faith affected the lives of northerners. Sometimes the historical attention devoted to Lincoln, his administration, and the generals who led the Union armies obscures the degree to which the Civil War had become, in Lincoln's phrase, "a People's contest." More distant from the battlefield than southerners, northern civilians experienced the Civil War less directly. Yet neither their zeal for the cause nor the transforming nature of their participation should be minimized. And though it is difficult to make generalizations about a population of twenty-two million living, in 1860, in twenty-two states and six organized territories, the northern home front is an essential part of Civil War history.

## EFFECTS OF MOBILIZATION
## ON NORTHERN WOMEN

The war's first impact came quickly in the effect of mobilization on communities and on individual families. With a population of 1,711,000 men, women, and children, Illinois furnished 259,000 enlistments; Massachusetts, with 1,231,000 residents, provided 146,000, and Michigan, with 749,000, sent off 87,000 men. Even the border state of Maryland furnished 60,000 soldiers and sailors to the Union forces and another 20,000 to the Confederacy from its population of 687,000.[1] Other states matched these proportions, until 37 percent of males of military age had served in the Union forces by May 1865 (a total of 2,778,304, although that number includes thousands of reenlistments as well as

This oil on canvas painting, entitled *The War Spirit at Home—Celebrating the Victory at Vicksburg*, demonstrates the extent to which the war affected life on the home front. In the games they played, children imitated the actions of soldiers.

some soldiers younger than eighteen and older than forty-five, compared with 87 percent of the Confederacy's white male population between eighteen and forty-five, for a total of 750,000 individuals).[2] Six percent of northern white males aged thirteen to forty-three never came home, and many who did were physically disabled (the *Medical and Surgical History of the War of the Rebellion* lists an unrealistically low thirty thousand amputations) and emotionally scarred.[3] Even for the families of those who survived, military service inevitably and variously affected their lives.

Some women lost fiancés; others husbands, fathers, and brothers as personal tragedy stalked the lives of those on the home front. Yet for many women war brought the opportunity to enter public life in their own right. At first twenty-one-year-old Ellen Wright of Auburn, Massachusetts reveled in her new war-related activities of sewing blankets and participating in a ladies aid society: "Away with melancholy is the tune for us women nowadays—Chirp up." But a year later when a suitor was killed, "nothing earthly" seemed worth his life.[4]

Wives of enlisted men often had to work, necessarily supplementing their husband's army pay of no more than twenty-two dollars a month, or typically for privates only thirteen dollars a month. Substituting for men in activities outside the home, women—previously invisible as workers though representing 11 per-

The women who fought for their causes had to dress as men in order to join the army. Frances Clalin was one of some four hundred northerners who dressed as male soldiers and fought for the Union.

cent of the paid labor force before the war—harvested wheat, labored in textile factories, and served as nurses. Many felt "an irresistible impulse," according to Anna Morris Holstein, "to do, to act."[5] As nurses, middle-class white women sought to move beyond the refined duties of lady volunteers who did little more than what members of the Women's Central Relief Association called the "mechanical and menial (and domestic) tasks" of serving food to the wounded and doing their washing.[6]

Thirty years old and single, Louisa May Alcott was typical of these women. In 1862 she decided to go to Washington and find a place in an army hospital. "Help needed," she reported in her journal, "and I love nursing and must let out my pent-up energy in some new way." Soon she was rushing "through the country all white with tents, all alive with patriotism, and already red with blood." But Alcott contracted typhoid fever, nearly died, and after returning home in 1863, began what became a successful career as an author—first of *Hospital Sketches*, based on her experiences as a war nurse, and then in 1868 of *Little Women*.[7]

In the beginning Alcott had wanted to be a soldier: "I long to be a man; but as I can't fight, I will content myself with working for those who can."[8] For one Vermont woman, "It seemed the greatest misfortune of my life that I was born a girl. . . . I would have given years off my life could I have taken a place in the ranks with my brother."[9] But at least four hundred women did join the ranks, cutting their hair, disguising themselves as men in caps and shirts, and joining the Union army. One young woman joined the Second East Tennessee Cavalry, accompanied the Army of the Cumberland to Nashville and subsequently fought at Murfreesboro, where she was wounded. Her sex was discovered while she was having her wound dressed, and by order of General Rosecrans, she was discharged. Promptly she reenlisted under a different name and served as a regimental bugler for the rest of the war.[10]

Others, according to Jane Schultz, found in hospital work a form of "surrogate soldiering," and though the role of middle-class female nurses in the Civil War is well documented, the work of thousands of working-class women, immigrants, and former slaves is less well known. These women, probably numbering over ten thousand, served as hospital workers—cooking, cleaning and doing the laundry.[11] A few northern women, notably Pauline Cushman, served as spies and messengers and were reimbursed for such activities.[12]

Meanwhile, male relatives worried that these wartime experiences, whether at the front or at home, would "coarsen" women and "deform their bodies."[13] Other women stayed closer to home but also moved across gender boundaries to manage stores and run businesses. Nearly five hundred women, often the sole breadwinners of their families, were employed as clerks in an expanding federal bureaucracy.

The Women's Central Relief Association became the most important agency coordinating the women's voluntary work on the home front. Throughout the North uncounted numbers of women, working within the social codes that prevented them from demonstrating their allegiance in the same ways as men did, served the Union. Producing uniforms, sewing head coverings, preserving fruits, sending boxes of supplies to the front, and organizing the popular fundraisers called sanitary fairs, these women applied their domestic arts to the cause in valuable activities for which the male-dominated United States Sanitary Commission often took credit.[14]

Northern children were also affected by the war, losing the financial support and companionship of fathers, sometimes permanently. Thousands of youngsters replaced men in factories until in one representative textile mill in Pennsylvania 22 percent of the workers who typically worked fourteen-hour days were sixteen and under.[15]

Losses of every kind were absorbed within the exalted sense of patriotism evoked by Walt Whitman:

"Long, too long O Land
Travelling roads all even and peaceful
You learn'd from joys and prosperity only
But now . . . to learn from crises of anguish . . .
And now to conceive, and show to the world, what your children en masse really are."[16]

When the war began, northerners characterized the conflict as a struggle between Richmond and Washington, and focused their attention on the Virginia front. Believing their sons, husbands, and brothers would be home by fall, civilians suffered the humiliation of Bull Run and then the long months of inaction. By 1862 some wondered whether McClellan would ever fight. At last McClellan moved; he came to the very outskirts of Richmond and was held back. Then a discouraging series of defeats—Second Bull Run, Fredericksburg, and Chancellorsville—shook northern optimism. Even the brighter news of Antietam and Gettysburg, and in the West Vicksburg and Chattanooga, was offset by the extent of northern losses, the failure to follow and destroy Confederate armies, and the invasion of the North. As casualties mounted, northerners rode a psychological roller coaster of hope and disappointment.

## THE NORTHERN ECONOMY

The war had begun during a period of recession and economic stagnation, which continued until 1862. Then a recovery set in, fueled by increased government spending and federal policies such as cutting off foreign imports by means of high tariffs and pouring money into war contracts. By 1862 business failures were down as a period of war-driven prosperity developed.[17] While profits mounted, orders flooded manufacturers of products from railroad cars, woolen goods, ships, and shoes to machine parts and guns. Banks began to extend their credit operations, and the role of the merchant as financier declined. Long-term capital, previously available only through patchwork arrangements of a proprietor's personal investment, was replaced by bank loans and mortgages on real estate, with the foundation of the nation's credit system coming to rest in specialized New York banks. Overnight the Civil War had become a catalyst for capital development; some invested in government bonds.[18]

In the kind of transaction taking place throughout the North, A. and W. Denmead, a nearly bankrupt Baltimore foundry and machine works firm in 1861, mortgaged its real estate to the Eutaw Savings Bank, used the capital to expand, and was able to return profits to its owners by 1863. The same year the economically cautious *New York Times* declared that "the greatest disadvantage of the war" was "the prosperity of the country."[19] By 1864 the New York *Herald*, recalling that yearly or semi-yearly dividends were customary practice, noted that a Colorado gold mine was paying monthly dividends. Railroad profits doubled and tripled annually. The earnings of the Erie Railroad, for example, leaped from $5 million in 1860 to $10 million in 1863, while its stock rose from 17 to 126½ in three years.

The owner of a Pennsylvania forge spoke for many when he said, "I am in no hurry for peace."[20] Though the war was responsible for much of this change, its financial derivatives—a national currency and banking system, and a concentrated credit system as state banks disappeared—shaped an economic environment from which, after the war, the Rockefellers, the Carnegies, and other plutocrats of the Gilded Age benefited. After describing a series of war-spawned business opportunities to a friend, Judge Thomas Mellon warned his son, who was getting started in the law, "Don't do it [enlist]. It is only greenhorns who do."[21]

Despite the hundreds of thousands of men in the service—from Ohio, Indiana, Illinois, Michigan, and Wisconsin, an estimated 680,000 farmers joined the army—prewar levels of crop production were sustained. Areas devoted to the production of grain increased in the midwestern states, as women and children worked in the fields. One New York family of a mother and seven daughters harvested a hundred acres of wheat, milked twenty-two cows, made butter and cheese, and still had time to lathe and shingle an addition to their home.[22]

Labor-saving machinery also helped to replace absent male workers. The necessity of substituting machines for human labor brought enormous profits to the manufacturers of reapers, threshers, and similar devices. Cyrus H. McCormick, the farm machinery magnate, continually reminded his Illinois salesmen that of the soldiers and militia forces leaving the state, most would be farmers, whose departure would encourage the use of his popular invention for cutting grain.

The war's disruptions spurred experimentation in cotton production in Kentucky, Missouri, and southern Illinois and Indiana. Other innovations were adopted in beet-sugar and sorghum farming. Canned fruits and vegetables appeared, as did canned milk and a machine for making cheese and butter, the latter freeing women from a tedious, despised task. A shortage of raw materials from the South stimulated production of wool, flax, and hemp as substitutes for cotton.

Isaac Newton, the first commissioner of the newly created Bureau of Agriculture, reported an increase in the total value of basic crops from $955 million in 1863 to $1,440 million in 1864.[23] Given both the domestic demands of feeding a great army and foreign demand, especially from Great Britain, prices increased. Between January and December 1862 wheat rose from $1.52 a bushel to $1.75; corn from 68 cents to 95 cents; barley from 80 cents to $1.55, increases that outran inflation rates.[24] Meanwhile, farmland in soil-rich states such as Illinois soared in price from ten dollars to one hundred dollars an acre.

The accelerating rise of agricultural prices—the greatest since the Revolution—remained a wartime trend. By 1864, the wholesale farm price index was double that of 1860. As all prices rose, inflation pinched especially the poor, whose wages had not kept pace with the spiraling prices of necessities.[25] Yet the overall northern increase of 80 percent over prewar prices should also be interpreted in the context of inflation rates ten times higher in the Confederacy and also in nearly all other American wars.

For investors, rising prices, mounting dividends, and gold fluctuations combined with the boom times of war to produce rapid changes in stock and gold prices. One aspect of gold speculation was that bad news increased the price of gold, whereas good news diminished it. Hence the bull-market speculator in gold, who benefited from rising prices profited from disaster or threatened disaster to the country, as during the summer of 1864 when Washington seemed about to be captured. Though most investors realized the speculative wave was temporary, such knowledge only increased gambling instincts. Warnings were given as the number of industrial issues listed by the New York Stock Exchange rose. Some predicted that the war would end suddenly, and speculators were advised to beware of the coming crash.

On the other hand, investors were also advised to "buy now," and their easily won fortunes often had more influence on speculators than sober warnings. Women as well as men caught the mania. Commenting on "Crinoline in Wall Street," the *Herald* noted that ladies were "fully alive to per cent," and were evaluating stocks with an animation that defied the traditional female concerns of domesticity.[26] In the North, the new rich were conspicuous in purple and fine linens, and expenditures for luxuries were described as "unexampled, even in the history of our wasteful people."[27] The city of New York, it was said, had never been "so gay . . . so crowded, so prosperous."[28]

The stimulation of business and the concurrent drain on civilian manpower produced a labor shortage, from which emerged, however, few benefits for the working class. Besides women, the most obvious source of replacement labor came from immigration, which in the early part of the war declined from the 1850s. Immigrants entering the country numbered only 142,000 in 1861, 72,000 in 1862, and 132,000 in 1863, as compared with 427,000 in 1854.[29] In

The number of women working in northern textile mills increased in the years prior to as well as during the war. By 1860, women represented 15 percent of the work force.

During the war, women continued to enter the work force. These women are making cartridges for the war effort under the supervision of a stern Union officer.

his annual message to Congress in December 1863, Lincoln noted "a great deficiency of laborers in every field of industry," and asked Congress to encourage immigration.

Congress responded by passing a bill on July 4, 1864 that established a contract labor system whereby workers could be imported according to regulations fixed by the commissioner of immigration. Under this legislation, immigrants could mortgage future wages and homesteads to ship companies to repay the cost of emigration to the United States. Partly as a response to this law, partly as a result of perceived economic opportunities, immigration in 1864 and 1865 rose to 191,000 and 180,000, though these figures fell considerably short of postwar immigration, which by 1866 reached 332,000. Though many newcomers became citizens or gained citizenship after joining the army, those who had not voted or declared an intention of becoming citizens were exempt from military duty.[30] Even so, the Union army gained an estimated 183,440 soldiers from an immigrant population that, by 1870, represented one-third of all U.S. industrial workers.

In the early days of the war, unemployment was high, but as prosperity spread and more workers enlisted in the army, there were jobs for all. Wages gradually increased but never as fast as prices. For example, carpenters' wages rose from a prewar daily minimum of $1.75 to $2.25; harness makers' from $1.40 to $2.00; blacksmiths' from $1.50 to $2.25; clerks' from $30 to $50 a month.[31] Such an apparent increase in wages was deceptive because the cost of living rose even more rapidly. Real wages, which define purchasing power, consequently declined

NORTHERN WAGES DURING THE CIVIL WAR

| | *Wage Indexes for*<br>*Nonagricultural Employments* | *Real Wages Indexes* |
|---|---|---|
| 1860 | 100.0 | 100 (January) |
| | | 100 (July) |
| 1861 | 100.8 | 102 (January) |
| | | 104 (July) |
| 1862 | 102.9 | 102 (January) |
| | | 101 (July) |
| 1863 | 110.5 | 89 (January) |
| | | 86 (July) |
| 1864 | 125.6 | 81 (January) |
| | | 71 (July) |
| 1865 | 143.1 | 67 (January) |
| | | 97 (July) |

*Sources:* The first column is from *Historical Statistics of the United States, 1789–1945* (Washington, D.C., 1945), Table D-108; the second is from Wesley Clair Mitchell, *A History of the Greenbacks* (Chicago, 1903), 342.

as necessities like eggs, bread, and fuel doubled in price. In some industries, especially factories employing large numbers of women, sweatshop conditions and starvation wages prevailed.

By 1863, female workers accounted for nearly 25 percent of all workers in manufacturing. "On the average," writes Philip Paludan, "[women's] wages increased by less than half that of men. In some businesses their pay actually went down as costs skyrocketed. Seamstresses in New York [employed in a piecework system], saw their wages go from 17 cents per shirt in 1861 to 8 cents per shirt in 1864. Women who worked a fourteen hour day at this job received on the average $1.54 per week."[32] *Fincher's Trades' Union Review,* the self-proclaimed "advocate of the rights of the producing classes," chronicled the growing dissatisfaction of women forced to work at "just such prices as employers chose to pay." Employers justified such treatment by arguing that women supported only themselves and were not family breadwinners. Yet such discrimination spurred women to organize a "Working Women's Protective Union" to help New York's thirty thousand working women.[33] A group of women textile workers in Cincinnati complained to Lincoln in March 1865 that they were unable "to sustain life" on their pay, while their employers "fattened on contracts" by "grinding immense profits out of the labor of their operatives."[34]

## THE LABOR MOVEMENT

At the beginning of the war only five national unions—the National Iron Molders and the unions of printers, stonecutters, hat finishers, and machinists—existed. Trade assemblies and local organizations also occasionally supported strikes and boycotts but more often operated as social organizations. Many of these local unions had not recovered from the depression of 1857, when factories closed and thousands of men and women lost their jobs. But as prosperity increased, the movement for organizing labor was renewed. One of the earliest signs of a revival was the formation of a city trades' assembly in Rochester, New York, on March 13, 1863.[35] Across the North, by December 1863, some twenty trade unions had been organized; by December 1864, 53 trades were organized, with 203 locals; and by November 1865, 69 trades had some formal structure, based on 300 locals.

National unions also sprang up, among them those of the iron puddlers, locomotive engineers, plasterers, cigar makers, ship carpenters, coach makers, house carpenters, bricklayers and masons, tailors, painters, and heaters. In September 1864, twelve delegates representing eight city trade associations met in Louisville and formed a national organization called the International Industrial Association of North America. By 1865 total union membership was estimated at two hundred thousand, but that figure represented less than 10 percent of all industrial workers.

Despite their limited gains, as David Montgomery has written, "military enthusiasm wrought havoc on the little trade unions of the time." Many closed their books for the duration, "until either the union is safe or we are whipped."[36] And there were other problems besides the war. William Sylvis, who became president of the National Iron Molders in 1863, complained of workers whose "vision is so contracted that they cannot see beyond the narrow limits of the village they live" and therefore did not pay dues to the national organization he tried to create.[37]

In every instance, no organizational gains came without bitter opposition from employers who "called to [their] aid every possible form of cheap labor." The use of blacks as strikebreakers led to race riots in New York, Brooklyn, and Cincinnati. Under pressure from businessmen, the Illinois legislature enacted a potent weapon against strikes called the "La Salle Black Laws," which held that "any person who by threat, intimidation, or otherwise sought to prevent another person from working, is guilty of a crime." Similar legislation was defeated in New York and Massachusetts largely because of labor's opposition.

During the war Federal troops were called in to break strikes, such as those of the gun workers in Cold Spring, New York, of the engineers on the Reading Railroad, and of the miners in Tioga County, Pennsylvania. In several instances the army arrested the leaders of strikes. In the anthracite regions of Pennsylvania, when miners "turned out" for wage increases and for the recognition of their union in 1863, a separate military district was created in order to establish law and order in the coal regions.[38] In Missouri in 1864 General Rosecrans, then commanding the Union forces in that state, prohibited the unionization of men engaged in war production; his orders were enforced against "striking coal miners, machinists, printers, and tailors." By the end of the Civil War, the workers' condition, concludes one scholar, "was undoubtedly worse than in 1860."[39]

## URBAN SOCIETY

For more affluent groups in northern society, increased prosperity was displayed in middle-class amusements. Immense crowds filled theaters in New York, turning them into firetraps by blocking the aisles. Barnum's "colossal museum and menagerie" with dog shows and huge serpents flourished, soon enhanced by war-related exhibits; bands played in Central Park.[40] In smaller communities public lectures continued to be popular diversions. Washington was gay with dinners, receptions, and elegant parties. These were often organized by First Lady Mary Todd Lincoln, who presided over a White House salon where literary men and public figures met to discuss the issues of the day. Organized baseball, introduced by Union soldiers to westerners and even southerners, spread across the land; prize fights entertained. One bare-knuckle event in rural Maryland, held ten days after the Battle of Chancellorsville, lasted sixty-two rounds.[41]

Comedy was in vogue, and the New York Academy of Music presentations of German grand opera competed with animal curiosities and minstrels. One much-publicized event, the wedding of the midgets "General" Tom Thumb and his bride, Lavinia Warren, took place in a Broadway church and was attended by General Burnside. It was followed by a reception at the Metropolitan Hotel where the happy couple, perched on a piano, received their guests. Each summer rich northerners, including the president's wife, flocked to resorts.[42] In saloons, winter gardens, skating carnivals, billiard halls, burlesque shows and cockfights, and in Bowery theaters where audiences gathered to eat peanuts, whistle, and yell, the people tried to forget the war.[43]

Along with indifference and frivolity came corruption. A popular novel, Henry Morford's *The Days of Shoddy*, published in 1863, not only used as its title the nickname bestowed on inferior textiles and cloth sold to the army; the novel also assailed war profiteers.[44] There were immense profits to be made, especially in whiskey and cotton. Most trading of the latter commodity, which in 1864 could be bought in the South at 20 cents a bale and sold for $1.90 in Boston, was illegal.

Yet many soldiers benefited, among them Colonel Andrew Butler, brother of the Union general, who was said to be in Louisiana "for the sole purpose of making money." According to Benjamin Butler, his brother's profits gained from buying up sugar and smuggling salt were close to two hundred thousand dollars. Others said the figure was in the millions.[45]

The enormous commissions bestowed on agents who obtained government contracts constituted a national scandal. After persistent exposés, the New York *Herald* condemned the "gross corruption prevailing in nearly every department of the government."[46] In one area, the government's excise taxes stimulated the hoarding of liquor stocks, resulting in unparalleled profits because of pent-up demand and rising prices when the liquor was eventually marketed.

Trade in whiskey and other commodities to the army and to the enemy was theoretically controlled by a system of presidential licenses. Yet even supposedly "legitimate" trade was often questionable. Evoking angry comments from Union generals, much of the traffic amounted to smuggling and giving aid to the enemy. General Stephen Hurlbut described the practice as "demoralizing . . . bribery and corruption [that] seem to go into every branch of service."[47]

General Grant believed that any trade with the enemy was wrong. Both he and Sherman sought to have it suppressed, and although most traders were not Jewish, on December 17, 1862, Grant ordered Jews "as a class violating every regulation of trade established by the Treasury Department expelled from the Department."[48] Lincoln rescinded Grant's order. Later, Grant acknowledged he was in the wrong, noting that he had worded the order as he did because of the greater efficiency of Jews engaged in these activities and their ability to trade with both sides, and because the preexisting business ties between Memphis and Cincinnati rested primarily with Jewish merchants.[49]

Most restrictions to regulate the traffic both with southerners and with Yankee soldiers by making it unprofitable served only to encourage dishonest men to go into it. "No honest man," concluded Grant, "has made money in West Tennessee in the last year [1862–1863], while many fortunes have been made there during the time."[50]

Despite the profiteers, most northern officials had high standards. Certainly General Montgomery Meigs, the quartermaster general in charge of quarters, supplies, and clothing, was incorruptible. Many northern civilians were financial patriots. For example, William Aspinwall, a prominent New York businessman, sent the government a check for over twenty-five thousand dollars as his share of the profit obtained on arms purchased by his firm for the War Department.[51] Although most of the nation's business was conducted honestly, the regulations about public transactions with private firms permitted legitimate profits out of proportion to the services rendered. Lobbying and bribes for government business were common. As to the administration, Lincoln was indisputably honest, as were his heads of departments, with the exception of Cameron.

Along with the attention they gave to corruption, northern newspapers often carried reports of the increase in crime during the war. In 1864 the New York *Herald* described murders, "revolting atrocities," burglaries, vice-protecting politicians, and drunken brawls. Recent crimes "would shock a congregation in Pandemonium." Yet statistical evidence suggests a different conclusion. Arrests for violent and nonviolent crime did not increase, but stayed roughly the same in the wartime North. On the other hand, the existence of "a high degree of public disorder" marked by drunkenness and brawls in cities is undeniable.[52]

## PRIVATE AND PUBLIC ASSISTANCE

Another face of the wartime North emerged in private humanitarian efforts and public welfare. In what became the nation's first old-age assistance and disability plan, the Pension Act of 1862 and its various amendments eventually provided benefits to 300,000 veterans and 220,00 dependents, requiring by 1866 disbursements of nearly $16 million. This legislation also awarded benefits for those disabled "as a direct consequence of military duty or after the close of combat, from causes which can be directly traced to injuries received or a disease contracted in military service."[53]

Many widows—of the war's approximately 108,000 in the North—were entirely dependent on the monthly welfare payments of eight dollars a month (for privates) provided by the 1862 Pension Act. This legislation, which was the beginning of national entitlement programs and which instituted "unprecedented expenditures by the federal government," extended pensions to widows, children, and other dependent relatives of soldiers who had either died in the service or

This is a portrayal of the April 26, 1861, Cooper Union meeting of the New York City women who formed the Woman's Central Relief Association, a critical component of the Sanitary Commission.

In 1863, Chicago hosted a successful Sanitary Commission Fair, raising seventy-eight thousand dollars. The second Chicago fair, shown here, was held in 1865.

who died of causes that could be directly traced to military service.[54] According to a recent student of veterans' benefits, Union pensions, unlike social programs in Europe, "were idealized as that which was justly due to the righteous core of a generation of men (and survivors of dead men) [who] ought to be generously and constantly repaid by the nation for their sacrifices."[55] The Union government also delivered far greater services in hospitalization and general care to its troops than in previous wars.

Despite these increases in public support, private organizations and especially the United States Sanitary Commission made important contributions to the well-being of northern troops. An outgrowth of the Women's Central Relief Association, the commission, which remained dependent on the work of thousands of northern women, coordinated relief efforts and provided nurses, hospital and ambulance services for wounded soldiers. Led by its officers, Henry Bellows and Frederick Law Olmsted, the commission served as a civilian auxiliary to the medical bureau of the War Department. The forerunner of the Red Cross, it did not confine its services to Union soldiers. Many wounded Confederate soldiers left on the battlefield without medical care or food were cared for by the Sanitary Commission.

Supplementing the work of the Sanitary Commission was the United States Christian Commission, which was organized and run by the "relief ladies" who brought everything from chicken soup to Bibles to wounded soldiers on the battlefield. The Christian Commission held as its twofold mandate "to serve the spiritual and temporal welfare" of the military. By 1863 these purposes included a "diet service kitchen" on wheels that efficiently dispensed millions of rations, along with mutton soup and fresh vegetables, to the soldiers in the Army of the James.

A soldiers' aid society meets in Springfield, Illinois. These women sewed and gathered canned goods and sundries for the soldiers on the front.

Contributions to both commissions were voluntary, as "sanitary fairs" held in large northern cities and organized by women developed into successful fundraising events. A fair in Chicago raised $78,000 in September 1863; a similar event in Brooklyn in October 1864, $400,000, and in New York in December 1863, one million dollars was donated. In Philadelphia the Central Fair of June 1864 mixed entertainment and philanthropy. After three weeks, 250,000 of the city's 600,000 residents had purchased tickets, and over a million dollars was eventually contributed.[56]

The leaders of the Sanitary Commission intended to centralize the delivery of their relief work and the entire process of philanthropy. No longer was the relief of suffering an end in itself, but rather, as one commission report acknowledged, the purpose was "to economize for the National service the life and strength of the National soldier." One historian has argued that the Sanitary Commission represented a new, war-tempered "capacity for organization," paralleling the degree to which an "improvised war became a disciplined effort."[57] But the change was not complete, as sentimental and localized responses especially by women to what was still characterized as benevolence to the needy survived the war.

Private funds to aid wounded soldiers were also raised by relief associations formed by workers who agreed to set aside part of their wages and by clubs, ballrooms, and theaters that gave benefit performances. During the war many private hospitals were opened, often under the name *infirmary*, to care for soldiers. Staffed by volunteer nurses, they supplemented the work of government hospitals. The noted reformer Dorothea Dix gave up her work with the insane to be a superintendent of army nurses, and the take-charge nurse Clara Barton also helped organize hospitals in the East.

The spirit of voluntarism amid war-created opportunities thrust women into public activities outside of their homes, though men continued to manage relief societies. Women were instead assigned the more menial tasks of selling tickets, writing letters for incapacitated soldiers, and making goods to sell.[58]

But women were in charge of one organization spawned by the war—the Women's National Loyal League, founded in 1863 by the suffrage leaders Elizabeth Cady Stanton and Susan B. Anthony, both of whom suspended their efforts to obtain woman suffrage and economic rights. Instead, for the war's duration, they devoted their considerable talents to petition drives and other propaganda intended to free the slaves and give them the vote.[59]

## SHAPING NORTHERN OPINION

Often characterized as the first modern war, the Civil War advanced the extent to which the government tried to shape opinion through the press and other agencies. Both the United States and the Confederate States had propaganda services poised to influence foreign sentiment, but for the most part morale on the home front was left to private initiatives. In the fall of 1861 Lincoln sent a mission consisting of the Catholic archbishop John Hughes, Bishop Charles McIlvaine of the Episcopal Church, and Thurlow Weed, the editor of the Albany *Evening Journal*, to France and Britain, in order to "bring the press and the clergy and then the people, to a correct understanding of the causes and purposes of the Civil War."[60]

At home both government and private sources sought to shape opinion. Propaganda clubs such as the Union League sprang into existence. The league began when sixteen men in Philadelphia, disgusted with the prosouthern sentiments of their clubmates, organized the Union Club of Philadelphia. Dedicated to the defense of the Union, the league movement spread to New York and Boston. Soon it appeared in Baltimore, Washington, and San Francisco. Within a year Union Leagues existed in over eighteen northern states, even appearing among the Unionists of the South.

Primarily the league was a rallying point for support of the Union cause. Literature about the war was distributed; holiday celebrations and parades, especially around Washington's birthday, connected civic spirit to the national cause; money was raised for soldier relief. Volunteering was encouraged, and several hurriedly recruited militia units served during crises such as the Gettysburg campaign and in Washington during Early's raid.

Soon the efforts of the League turned partisan as members not only supported the cause of the Union but the Republican party. In Pennsylvania the league actively supported Governor Andrew Curtin against Judge George Woodward in the state's gubernatorial campaign of 1863 and Lincoln against McClellan in 1864. After the war its main thrust was to oppose the policies of President Johnson and to function as an adjunct of the Radical wing of the Republican party.[61]

Republicans also organized the Loyal Publication Society of New York and a similar society in New England in response to the Democrats' creation of the Society for the Diffusion of Political Knowledge. After Fredericksburg, the latter flooded the defeated Army of the Potomac with antiwar, antiadministration literature. To counter this, the New York society, under the leadership of Charles King and Francis Lieber, raised thirty thousand dollars during the three years of its existence, published ninety pamphlets, and distributed nine hundred thousand documents. Generally it targeted pivotal groups, using the modern approaches of advertising by making special appeals "to Midwesterners, New Englanders, and New Yorkers; farmers, merchants, and bankers; Catholics and Protestants; people proud of their American ancestry, and recent German, Irish, and French immigrants. Even women were subject [to] an especial appeal."[62] Such organizations, through their distribution of printed matter, shaped the opinion of newspaper proprietors and also bolstered morale—an important service as the war continued.

President Lincoln's activity in promoting support for his administration did not take the form of deliberate propaganda. Nor was there any organized White House publicity. His characteristic manner of speaking to the people was through well-timed letters to individuals and comments to visiting delegations, which were intended for the nation's ear in general. The president's August 1863 letter to the unconditional Union men in Springfield, Illinois, his reply to New York's governor Horatio Seymour declining to suspend the draft, and his correspondence with Greeley concerning emancipation displayed his pithy, epigrammatic style and his common-sense reasoning. On the rare occasions during the war when Lincoln made public addresses, he sought to unite the northern people on the fundamental principles for which the conflict was being fought.

The most famous, his brief address on November 19, 1863 at the dedication of the national cemetery at Gettysburg, was a model of clarity. Lincoln gave meaning to the war's carnage by invoking the global implications of the contest over republican self-government. The Gettysburg Address has also been interpreted as an authoritative statement about a new America, one grounded in the egalitarian sentiments of the Declaration of Independence rather than in a constitution that tolerated slavery. Said Lincoln in a penetrating summary of the meaning of the war:

> Four score and seven years ago our fathers brought forth on this continent, a new nation, conceived in Liberty, and dedicated to the proposition that all men are created equal.
>
> Now we are engaged in a great civil war, testing whether that nation, or any nation so conceived and so dedicated, can long endure. We are met on a great battle-field of

that war. We have come to dedicate a portion of that field, as a final resting place for those who here gave their lives that that nation might live. It is altogether fitting and proper that we should do this.

But, in a larger sense, we can not dedicate—we can not consecrate—we can not hallow—this ground. The brave men, living and dead, who struggled here, have consecrated it, far above our poor power to add or detract. The world will little note, nor long remember what we say here, but it can never forget what they did here. It is for us the living, rather, to be dedicated here to the unfinished work which they who fought here have thus far nobly advanced. It is rather for us to be here dedicated to the great task remaining before us—that from these honored dead we take increased devotion to that cause for which they gave the last full measure of devotion—that we here highly resolve that these dead shall not have died in vain—that this nation, under God, shall have a new birth of freedom—and that government of the people, by the people, for the people, shall not perish from the earth.[63]

## Northern Newspapers during the War

As free agents conducted according to the philosophies of their editor-proprietors, northern newspapers were influential in shaping opinion during the war. Almost overnight the war fostered a new type of journalist—the war correspondent.[64] Only occasionally, as in Sherman's army, were journalists excluded from

Newspapers became a fixture on the battlefields. The government not only provided horses and wagons for transportation, but also allowed journalists to write what they wanted without much censorship. Here a group of New York *Herald* correspondents sit in front of their wagon.

military areas. Sherman had long distrusted newsmen and limited their access to his military operations.[65]

But usually, reporters were welcomed and given special privileges such as government passes. They had the use of government horses and wagons; they were given transportation on government steamers and military trains. Enjoying the confidence of admirals and army commanders, they even transmitted military intelligence. A New York *Herald* correspondent held a pass that entitled him "to accompany naval expeditions in any staff capacity to which the commanders might appoint him, provided they did not interfere with the regulations of the Navy." At Antietam a *Tribune* reporter delivered to other officers several of General Joseph Hooker's messages and orders.

Throughout the war, opposition to the government's policies and personnel, including the president, was freely expressed in speech and in print. Censorship, though not absent, was never systematic. There were some forced suspensions, especially of newspapers that discouraged enlisting, but there were many more examples of the government's restraint.[66] The Democratic press often viciously attacked Lincoln, even accusing him of supporting racial intermarriage. The New York *World*, discussing the president's emancipation policy, denounced the "crazy radicals" who were advising Lincoln and the "miserable balderdash" by which, the editor said, the country was governed.[67]

After defeating McClellan, Lincoln delivered his second inaugural address on March 4, 1865. In the address, Lincoln urged a restoration of the Union, asking for "malice toward none" and "charity for all."

Papers such as the *World, Journal of Commerce, Daily News* and the Columbus (Ohio) *Crisis* regularly criticized the Lincoln government; even friendly papers engaged in practices harmful to the war effort. They printed casualty lists; revealed the composition, location, and destination of military units; gave information about preparations for military and naval expeditions; indicated the places of rendezvous for supply vessels; and in fact functioned as inadvertent Confederate spies within Union lines. Lee regularly read the northern newspapers, and his confidential dispatches of the time reveal many items of valuable information gleaned from them.[68]

In other ways civilians in the North came into first-hand contact with the war. Trains brought soldiers' coffins back to every town and hamlet in America, although thousands of Union men were buried in the South or thrown into unmarked mass trenches to keep the vultures away. Matthew Brady, the great photographer of the Civil War who had learned his trade in the 1840s and 1850s, displayed gory images of dead soldiers in his studios across the United States. The violence displayed in these often arranged representations from the battlefield became "signs legitimating the Union."[69] "If [Mr. Brady] has not brought bodies and laid them in our dooryards, he has done something very like it," concluded one northern civilian.[70]

## RELIGION IN THE NORTH

Along with publication societies, government officials, newspapers, and even photographs, religion played a major role in shaping northern responses to the war. For generations Americans had divided their mostly Protestant religion into different denominations. Yet the similarities of their Christian worship and beliefs provided a core of national values that fostered common ideals of civic virtue and moral leadership. During the 1860s the doctrine of American exceptionalism merged with a muscular, war-driven Protestantism to serve as a powerful morale-building force in the North.

When the war came, it seemed to many northerners a judgment of God on a society that had, as Henry Ward Beecher preached, forsaken God's commandments for "luxury, extravagance, ostentation and corruption of morals."[71] By 1861, ministers linked God's purposes with those of the Union, and their messages afforded a powerful incentive for northerners to make the war a Christian crusade. "Strike for Law and Union, for country and God's ordinance of Government," inveighed Andrew Stone of Boston's Park Street Church. As Henry Ward Beecher put it, "God hates lukewarm patriotism, as much as lukewarm religion."

Armed with such sentiments, clerics even recruited troops. New York's Archbishop Hughes, who raised the American flag over the Catholic cathedral where he presided, took pride in the organization of the Irish 69th New York Regiment, just as Henry Ward Beecher did in the Protestant Brooklyn Phalanx. Hymns also linked God to the northern effort. "Stand Up, Stand Up for Jesus," with its martial images, became a wartime favorite. So too did the future suffrage leader Julia Ward Howe's popular "Battle Hymn of the Republic."

Such elevating and patriotic religious sentiment helped stanch the pain of war as casualties mounted. Commitment to a religiously underwritten national endeavor made the wartime losses easier to understand, if not endure. Many northerners placed renewed emphasis on the Christian doctrine of resurrection; others found solace in spiritualism. Lincoln, who so often summarized the highest ideals of the wartime North but who before the war had never claimed a church, adopted this political religion. In his second inaugural he placed the nation under God's providence, using explicitly theological language when he said, "The Almighty had His own purposes. . . . [T]he judgements of the Lord, are true and righteous altogether."[72]

From this political religion, northerners drew their understanding of the war's meaning and purpose, and though they did not always agree on the specifics of federal or state policies, they held a common sense of the "People's contest." The saving of the Union (an abstract entity to which northerners were attached as an expression of their nationalism), the survival of a political system based on a federal democracy capable of providing social and economic advantages in a modern society, and the freeing of the slaves had become God's intentions. Meanwhile visions of God's connections to the Confederacy also inspired the South. But in war there could not be two victors. As southern losses increased, faith in religion and God's providence shook Confederate morale, just as these same forces strengthened northern confidence.

## CHAPTER 22

# The Collapse
of the Confederacy

Southern civilians experienced the war more directly than those in the North. Large areas of the Confederacy were trampled by shifting armies, and other regions were occupied by the enemy. In Virginia, the town of Winchester changed hands so often that it became a shuttlecock between contending forces. Nearby, the shady village of Culpeper served both sides as their winter headquarters; when spring came, as a battleground; and after the battles, as a makeshift hospital in its churches, private homes, and even tobacco warehouses.[1] When the Union army approached, thousands of Confederates—usually wealthy planters' wives and children who relocated in cities—fled, joining other refugees in numbers that challenged the government's distribution and welfare services.[2] An estimated fifty thousand southern civilians died of war-related epidemics; a few died in battle, although not as many as existed in the memories of postwar southerners.

The story of the end of the war and the reason for the North's victory in 1865 can be told as a tale of northern superiority in numbers of everything from men and weapons to ships and shoes. A more modern society as well as a more populous one, the North eventually carried the day with its material supremacy. The defeat of southern armies was the result. Writes Gary Gallagher in this military explanation, "Soldiers laid down their arms at Appomattox and Durham Station when brought to bay by imposing Federal forces under the resolute command of U. S. Grant and William Tecumseh Sherman."[3]

But the defeat of the Confederacy might be attributed to other factors: the failure of the South to obtain aid from England and France; or the Union strategy of total war as implemented by the effective generals Sherman, Grant, and Sheridan. Their successes must be weighed against the failures of southern generals, including Lee, who lost men in costly tactical and strategic maneuvers. The defeat of the Confederacy might be considered the result of the effective leadership of Abraham Lincoln, compared with the fumbling direction of Jefferson Davis. The outcome might be viewed as influenced by the Confederacy's crippling commitment to states' rights in a challenging time that demanded disciplined nationalism. To different degrees, the accumulation of these factors eroded southern prospects and confidence.

Viewed from such a perspective, the collapse of the Confederacy, which is the concern of this chapter, can be traced to the wilting resolve of southerners in the face of military and political failures. Certainly there is important testimony to the steadfastness of some southern whites who, according to Gary Gallagher, "knew as a people they had expended blood and treasure in profusion before ultimately collapsing in the face of northern power sternly applied."[4] But there is also evidence of the declining support of southerners for what they apprehended, at differing points during the war, as a lost cause.

Confederate soldiers and civilians had always lacked the "emotional, in-group sense of distinctive, shared history, culture, and nationality."[5] This failure of Confederate nationalism sprang from the very elements of the region's distinctiveness. Southerners were more attached to their local communities, whether plantation, small farm, county and state, than northerners, who identified with the United States of America as much as with any smaller unit within the nation. Besides this limitation, it was impossible in a society whose entire history (save for two months) was spent at war with a stronger enemy to sustain allegiances to the new entity of the Confederate States of America. By 1865 even the soldiers of the Army of Northern Virginia fought out of personal devotion to their beloved commander, Robert E. Lee, rather than commitment to any abstract nation called the Confederacy.[6]

## NORTHERN OCCUPATION OF THE SOUTH

When the two contending armies proved unable to destroy each other's forces or to occupy the other's capital, in what future generations called a blitzkrieg, the Union gradually occupied parts of the South. This loss of territory demonstrated the North's power, demoralizing a society whose nationalism had been fired by a belief in its unique fighting abilities. Yet the Union occupation of at first Tennessee, southern Louisiana, parts of Virginia, and various coastal areas followed by extensive territory in Mississippi, Georgia, and South Carolina was different from any occupation by a foreign enemy. Fighting the war to "resposses" and "restore" territory seized by those in "insurrection," United States armies sought to recover the South from Confederate control and its hostile leaders. For as Lincoln once said, the whole Confederacy was in fact American territory.

Union forces did not consider themselves simply to be in enemy country; southern regions under the Union flag were generally administered as part of the

With Union victories on the battlefield came occupation of southern plantations and homes. This was the case for General Thomas F. Drayton, former commander at Port Royal, South Carolina. Union soldiers and former slaves occupy Drayton's home and land.

United States.[7] The occupation of New Orleans in April 1862 was not analogous to the occupation of Tampico by the United States in 1847. American authorities in Mexico looked forward to relinquishing their control after the signing of a treaty. In the case of New Orleans and other occupied districts of the South, no treaty was anticipated. What was expected was the removal of the Confederate government's authority over part of the United States and the restoration of local authority under national sovereignty.

In an early example of Union occupation, Lincoln chose Benjamin Butler to administer affairs in New Orleans, and Butler provided an example of the latitude given to individual commanders. Under Butler's orders, Episcopal clergymen were required to include in the morning prayer the words "for the President of the United States and all civil authority." When the rector of St. Paul's Church tried to evade the order by omitting this prayer, the church was closed by an officer of Butler's staff.[8]

Using the mansion of the Confederate general David Twiggs as a residence, Butler arrested prominent citizens, threatened women who insulted Federal troops with prosecution as prostitutes, suppressed newspapers, and seized property. Applying federal confiscation acts vigorously without regard for Attorney General Edward Bates's preference for enforcement through the federal courts,

Butler issued sweeping orders of confiscation and set up a commission to sell goods taken from Confederates and to administer estates now managed by loyal owners. President Davis responded by declaring Butler an outlaw and ordered his execution as a felon.[9] By this time Lincoln had replaced Butler with General Nathaniel Banks.

Most Union commanders in the South showed more leniency then Butler. Andrew Johnson, who became the military governor of Tennessee, despite resorting to arrest, seizure, and other severe measures, gave less cause for the complaints of local citizens. The administrations of Banks in New Orleans and John Geary in Savannah were restrained, too much so for some northerners who believed the South a "guilty land."[10] But everywhere as the Confederacy lost its land and resources, these Union occupations undermined the will to fight and to support the war in a crippling process that the famous Prussian strategist Karl von Clausewitz likened to a spreading "rot like a cancer."[11] "Oh what a horrid sight. What a degradation ... the hateful symbol of despotism," was the response of a disheartened Confederate woman to the raising of the United States flag over Columbia, South Carolina.[12]

In the middle counties of Tennessee, which were occupied for three years and where there was little damage from actual combat, the challenge to civilians came from both the uncertainty of what Federal troops might do and shortages of food and fuel. Throughout the state Yankee soldiers seized buildings for barracks, devastated plantations such as William Harding's Belle Meade, stripped

448        HARPER'S WEEKLY.        [JULY 12, 1862.

THE LADIES OF NEW ORLEANS before GENERAL BUTLER'S Proclamation.        After GENERAL BUTLER'S Proclamation.

Early in the war many women of New Orleans treated Union soldiers with contempt, insulting them verbally and spitting at them. After General Butler ordered that any women caught offending Union soldiers would be treated as prostitutes, their animosity became remarkably less overt.

As the war progressed, Union soldiers occupied not only Confederate towns and military positions, but also Confederate homes. Here Union soldiers and freed slaves occupy Jefferson Davis' plantation.

the land of fences and trees, and through attrition destroyed the will of residents to maintain civic institutions such as schools, churches, and courts. In time a dispirited population had little interest in continuing the war.[13]

## DESERTION

One manifestation of alienation was displayed in the increasing desertions of southern soldiers, which reached 104,000 by 1865—or nearly 10 percent of the total Confederate force.[14] The desertions reflect the conditions that made the war intolerable to thousands of civilians and soldiers. Backwoodsmen, the very young, residents of non-slaveholding regions, and those living near the Appalachians had been drawn into the military without much sympathy for slavery or for the independence of the Confederacy. After April 1862, conscription swept up other groups with little commitment to the Davis government or sense of southern nationalism—northerners living in the South and Mexicans, neither of whom had much attachment to what was becoming a lost cause.

Poor food and clothing, the lack of shoes and overcoats, and insufficient pay, often given out fourteen months later, inevitably produced disaffection. General John Floyd noted that the 51st Virginia Regiment had not received a dollar after their enrollment six months before. "They are generally poor men, entirely without support for their wives and little children, except their wages."[15] Sometimes a soldier on leave could not afford transportation to rejoin his command. Nor could he expect that his pay would support his family. Unsanitary camp conditions had their debilitating effect. While those in combat had the terror of battle as a reason to leave for home, inactive soldiers left because of homesickness, depression, and physical illness.

Often, the conflicting alternatives were neglect of family or departure from the army—a choice between two kinds of desertion. Men increasingly felt that their services were more needed at home than in the army, as the fragile nationalism erected by the Confederacy in 1861 shattered. Southern soldiers found themselves in the situation of an Alabamian who deserted when his wife wrote: "We haven't got nothing in the house to eat but a little bit of meal. . . . I don't want you to stop fighting them Yankees . . . but try and get off and come home and fix us all up some and then you can go back."[16] A group of Arkansas soldiers deserted when informed that Indians were threatening their homes. Two members of a crack South Carolina regiment abandoned their unit when they heard that Lincoln had been reelected and that they faced four more years of war.[17] "The whole country is full of men on horseback," wrote one southerner, referring to cavalry on both sides. "Can't you protect the families?" So widespread did desertion become that even the distinction between those absent without leave and those who never intended to return to military service disappeared. So too did the stigma of leaving the army that had previously served to inhibit desertion. "By the winter of 1864 as scores of miserable men crept away from the lines daily desertion had all but destroyed the Confederate armies and made their final defeat a matter of time."[18]

Angry at profiteering and dissatisfied with the class divisions papered over in the prewar South, soldiers became disgruntled at what many believed a "rich man's war and poor man's fight," especially after the "Twenty-Negro Law" exempted over five thousand planters, overseers, government officials, and those in specified occupations such as the ministry and undertaking. A Mississippian complained to Jefferson Davis that nine-tenths of the young men "whose relatives are conspicuous in society, wealth, or influence obtain some safe perch."[19] Though the Confederate army roughly conformed to the occupational categories of white southern society with some underrepresentation of skilled and unskilled laborers, it was the perception of inequality that contributed to declining morale.[20]

Extortion, a term with mostly legal applications before the war, emerged as a loaded word for Confederates. Among soldiers and civilians alike, the word summoned up excesses of greed and the penetration of a war economy with opportunities for corruption and profiteering. In the past the self-image of southerners held no room for the kind of sharp practices subsumed in the word *extortion*. But throughout the war, in a challenge to southern traditions of self-sufficiency, state legislatures passed legislation to prevent speculation, hoarding, and "extortion."[21]

As the war dragged on, the government, having in various ways failed to meet the expectations of its citizens, lost not only the allegiance of dispirited civilians but that of its soldiers. What Paul Escott has called "the quiet rebellion of the common people" led to the withdrawal of support and the erosion of the will to continue a brutal struggle.[22] From the trenches of Petersburg in 1865, a North Carolina soldier described the effects of this discontent: "It is useless to conceal the truth any longer. Most of our people at home have become so demoralized that they write to their husbands, sons and brothers that desertion now is not dishonorable."[23] A civilian agreed, locating the source of her alienation in the fact that "the brunt is thrown upon the working classes while the rich live at home in ease and pleasure."[24]

There were occasions, notably after 1863, when whole companies, garrisons, and even regiments decamped at a time. In one month between February 15 and March 18, 1865, Lee lost nearly 8 percent of his army.[25] In some cases deserters banded together, roaming the countryside, fortifying themselves in mountains, hiding in caves, stealing cattle, and robbing military stores.[26] Forces had to be detached from Confederate armies to run down such groups.

At critical times, absenteeism prevented the South from following up on victories or even field advantage, as desertion became both the cause and effect of lowered morale on the home front. As a young soldier wrote his father, "the men can't be prevented from deserting when they think there is no prospect ahead for getting home. . . . [A]mong the deserters are some of the bravest men of our army. . . . Our leaders do not seem to think that morale is as great a portion of an army, as Napoleon thought."[27]

## WOMEN OF THE CONFEDERACY

Active before the war in agricultural and household production as well as the domestic vocations of running their homes, raising their children, and nursing the sick, Confederate women bore added burdens as they struggled to manage the farms and plantations which supplied vital war needs. The traditional southern fears about their human property—that slaves were ever poised to rape, poison, pillage, and steal—intensified, especially among women on isolated plantations surrounded, as was Keziah Brevard of South Carolina, by large numbers of slaves. "I lay down at night and do not know what hour . . . my house may [be] broken open and myself and children murdered."[28] Having been considered inappropriate, unfit masters of slaves before the war, only with difficulty did women give up their understanding that slave management was a male endeavor and exercise direct control over their human property. "Where there are so many negroes upon places as upon ours," complained one Alabama woman to the governor, "it is quite necessary that there should be men who can control them."[29]

Women also confronted devastating family losses. Commenting on the collective ways in which grief universally afflicts women during war, Mary Chesnut wrote: "I know how it feels to die. I have felt it again and again. For instance, Someone calls out, 'Albert Sidney Johnston is killed.' My heart stands still. I feel

Southern women at the gravestone of Stonewall Jackson. The death of Jackson at the battle of Chancellorsville was one of the events that damaged the morale of the South.

no more."[30] On a single morning in January 1865 two of Chesnut's friends lost sons; others lost husbands, brothers, sons. "The thought that their lives had been given up in vain was very bitter to them. The besom of destruction had swept over every family."[31] Although mourning had been an expected sacrificial duty for Confederate women at the beginning of the war—"a glorious privilege," according to one newspaper—by 1864 the death of a relative was yet another factor in the growing despair that led many discontented Confederates to withdraw their support from the government.[32]

Like northern women, southerners had at first moved enthusiastically into new arenas during the Civil War. It was an exceptional woman, said the Confederacy's First Lady, Varina Davis, who did not nurse in a hospital or teach school or cut up a carpet for the troops. Mrs. Arthur Hopkins of Alabama, under fire while ministering to the wounded on the battlefield, received a wound at Seven Pines which lamed her for life. Other women volunteered for teaching positions, as a number of institutions, including Hollins College in Virginia and the North Carolina Female College, created new teaching departments. In a more typical experience, on Oakwood plantation in South Carolina Kate McLure began making decisions about crops, livestock, and slaves that had previously been the domain of her husband.[33]

These "mothers of invention," as Drew Faust calls them, also found themselves doing work they had never done before—whether it was the cooking, cleaning, and washing that slaves had earlier done for the mistresses of the planter class or whether it was the raising of corn and hogs that their male relatives had undertaken on the farms of yeomen. Maintaining their stricken households, organizing sewing circles and charity bazaars, supplying gaiety during "starvation parties," sometimes driving a team or following a plow so that men who before the war had served as their controlling protectors could be released for fighting, the women of the Confederacy suffered.

In time their initial dedication, which had been manifest in sewing flags and uniforms, nursing the wounded, and raising money for the cause through Ladies' Aid Societies, faltered. Mary Chesnut has left a vivid account of her growing defeatism. Having embraced the notion of a reciprocal protective paternalism, Confederate mistresses felt increasingly abandoned. "The social order they were determined to preserve offered them only the best of a bad bargain; the ideal of male strength and competence that justified the paternalistic southern world had been proven mythical."[34] The sacrificial role of a loyal Confederate woman was replaced by disgruntled apathy as "the ability of Southern men to meet the requirements for care and protection, to ensure the physical safety—and even the subsistence—of the civilian population had broken down . . . Hardship and loss were no longer sacred, no longer to be celebrated, but instead came to seem causes for grievance."[35] In turn the grievances of one-half the white population (slave women had never supported the Confederate war effort)[36] had an impact on the soldiers and the state and local governments to whom they complained.

Among the most frequent complaints on the home front were those involving food shortages, with the poor being the most deprived. The Union blockade, poor transportation facilities, the closing of the Mississippi River, and the Federal occupation of the breadbaskets of the Confederacy in the Shenandoah Valley, Tennessee, and Georgia led to considerable hardship. By the end of the war many staples had permanently disappeared from the southern diet; in 1864 an ounce of meat per person daily was considered ample. Rats became a familiar item in many diets. President Davis was quoted as saying that he saw no reason for not eating them, for he thought they would be "as good as squirrels." But rats never became as popular as mule meat.[37]

The shortage of bread was even more devastating. Food riots occurred in Macon, Augusta, Salisbury, Atlanta, Mobile, and Richmond. In Mobile women assembled under such incendiary banners as "Bread or Blood" and "Bread and Peace." In Richmond, the wives of artisans and factory workers looted warehouses for bacon and shoes. "Armed with knives and hatchets, [they] marched down Dauphine street, breaking open the stores . . . and taking for their use such articles of food or clothing as they were in urgent need of."[38] Riots were not confined to the cities, as country women attacked wagon trains.[39]

Throughout the war the Confederacy lived ersatz, relying on inferior substitutes. Tea was usually not available, and coffee became a rare luxury, replaced by unsatisfactory substitutes concocted from "parched corn, rye, wheat, okra

The Richmond bread riot in April of 1863 was one of many riots caused by food shortages. In Richmond, women marched through the streets and broke store windows in search of food.

seed . . . acorns, dandelion roots, sugar cane, parched rice, cotton seed, sorghum molasses, English peas, peanuts . . . and beans."[40] Some shortages were the result of poor distribution, inefficiency, and the rampant inflation rate (at 700 percent from 1861 to 1863) of an economy spinning out of control. The scarcity of clothing led to angry civilian raids on clothing shops and an army lacking uniforms and socks. As she watched ten thousand men marching along a road near Richmond in August 1863, Mary Chesnut compared their "rags and tags— nothing alike—most garments and arms taken from the enemy—such shoes" with the fresh, smartly uniformed regiments of 1861.[41]

Like many southern civilians, John Jones, a clerk in the Confederate War Department, came to blame the government, believing supplies were available if "the government would wake up. . . . the people here [in Richmond] are almost in a state of starvation in the midst of plenty, brought on by the knavery or incompetency of government agents." Public officials, he said, allowed forty thousand bushels of sweet potatoes to rot in depots between Richmond and Wilmington.[42] Much-needed leather was "held, like everything else, by speculators, for extortioner's profits." The government only aggravated the problem by "capricious seizures and tyrannical restrictions on transportation." Jones was not alone in finding a scapegoat among "Jew extortioners" who "injured our case more than the armies of Lincoln."[43]

## SHORTAGES AND NATIONALIZATION

The sharp-eyed Mary Chesnut observed the contrast between the elegance of rich ladies in fancy carriages "lolling in silks and satins with tall footmen in livery—driving up and down the streets—the poor soldiers' wives on the sidewalks." For Chesnut it was the familiar story of the rich and poor, but in the crisis of war, class divisions among whites increasingly sapped commitment to the Confederacy.[44] Also observing the distress of the poor, Governor Zebulon Vance of North Carolina blamed "the demon of speculation and extortion [that] seems to have seized upon nearly all sorts and conditions of men, and all the necessaries of life are fast getting beyond the reach of the poor."

Such deprivation touched farmers as well as town dwellers. In North Carolina, 20 to 40 percent of the population needed food and poor relief. The government's sporadic relief measures required that planters, who took the overseer's exemption from military service, turn over to the government each year a hundred pounds of bacon and beef for each able-bodied slave. In turn the government sold this food at artificially low prices to the poor. Such efforts suggested an awareness of civilian suffering. "Eventually," writes Paul Escott, "both state government and the Confederacy became involved in relief efforts, but the evidence leaves little doubt that they were not equal to the challenge."[45]

The Confederacy was especially short of iron and salt, the latter essential for preserving meat. Most salt came from the remote hamlet of Saltville in southwestern Virginia, where the salt works were destroyed by the Union army in 1864.[46] Lacking these and other necessities, the South nationalized existing factories. In Richmond the Tredegar Iron Works, the largest in the Confederacy, operated under a contract with the government. In Georgia the Augusta Powder

Southern refugees load their belongings on a wagon. Many refugees left the South because their houses were destroyed by the fighting.

Proud Secession Hall, the place where South Carolina
officially withdrew from the Union, was left in ruins following
the war. Referring to states' rights, Jefferson Davis said, "If the
Confederacy falls, there should be written on its tombstone:
died of a theory."

Works, which produced niter, lead, rifles, and even buttons, became the largest
state-owned factory system in the world, as the Confederacy emerged as an
ironic example of unpopular, war-engendered state socialism.

The Richmond government controlled railroads, confiscated private property,
and initiated an income tax.[47] It also created the machinery to mobilize both men
and resources on a scale seldom achieved in U.S. history.[48] Viewed in comparative terms, the Confederates were compelled to adopt such a centralized program
because their private economy was not as modern as the North's; in the process
of doing so, they contradicted the libertarian ideals of most southerners.

Efforts at regulation and the control of property affected every southerner,
mostly through the system of impressment which, as the war dragged on, provided a continuing source of friction between citizens and the Confederate government and between state governors and the Richmond bureaucracy. Agents
seized wagons, harnesses, forage, and slaves at prices considered confiscatory by
farmers. In 1863 the Confederate Congress placed a tax in kind on farmers, who
were required to deliver 10 percent of their produce to the central government.
Governor Thomas Watts of Alabama, a former Confederate attorney general,
warned Davis in 1864 to "consider well the disastrous policy of harassing the
producers . . . or else the consequences may be serious."[49]

Responding to what was considered both an unwarranted invasion of the individual rights of their residents and the constitutional authority of their states, governors protested, holding back men and materials. In a famous example of such obstruction, Governor Vance stockpiled uniforms, shoes, and blankets for the future needs of North Carolinians, while Confederate armies went barefoot. In some accounts of how the South lost the Civil War these frequent confrontations between states (especially Georgia and North Carolina) and the Richmond government have been exaggerated into single causes for a Confederate defeat that in fact had many explanations.

But such conflicts were important aspects of the Confederacy's disabling contradictions. What the Confederacy required during the Civil War was a commitment to nationalism and an acceptance of centralization. Instead, the principles that informed the behavior of most of its citizens were devotion to states' rights and an obsession with individual freedom for white males. Its intention of accomplishing a conservative revolution floundered on this paradox.[50] Although many controversies between the Richmond and state governments were resolved by negotiation, the state-federal tension remained one of several accelerating factors contributing to declining morale and the Confederate surrender.[51]

## SUBVERSION IN THE CONFEDERACY

The Union military advance in 1864–1865 intensified this demoralization. In areas where individualism and self-sufficiency were strong, as in the piney woods of Jones County, Mississippi, the Confederacy encountered growing opposition. Agitation for peace increased where state courts such as those in North Carolina and Georgia declared conscription unconstitutional. The Heroes of America, an anti-Confederate secret society, gained supporters in its efforts to negotiate a unilateral North Carolina peace with the Union. Peace efforts "ranged from ostensibly legitimate endeavors to overthrow the Davis government [and] make peace with the North, to secret plots and conspiracies to overthrow the Confederacy."[52]

In a society that had no established political parties, the 1863 congressional elections provided a measure of alienation from the Davis administration. In elections for the Second Regular Confederate Congress, the number of antiadministration representatives increased from twenty-six to forty-one (of 106). In North Carolina, eight of ten Congressmen opposed Davis; only one former Democrat was elected, and no original secessionists were members of this delegation. Overall, the government gained its strongest support from the border states and from soldiers who, as was the case in the North, voted in the field. In a legislature in which only twenty-seven congressmen (of 236) served in all three congressional sessions, including the Provisional Congress of February 1861, former Whigs and Unionists unseated representatives who favored Davis and who argued for cooperation with the Richmond government and more material sacrifices.[53]

Another symptom of the approaching collapse was the Richmond government's response to these political challenges. In November 1864, Davis advised

Congress that "a dangerous conspiracy exists in some of the counties of south-western Virginia, and in the neighboring portions of North Carolina and Tennessee, which it is found impracticable to suppress by the ordinary course of law."[54] He also noted "serious embarrassment" in Mobile, Wilmington, and Richmond as a result of spies working for the Union.

Despite strenuous opposition by those who insisted that habeas corpus was a sacred writ of liberty whose suspension was not justified by the circumstances, in February 1864 the Confederate Congress passed a third act for the suspension of the writ. This law prohibited a range of activities, including conspiring to resist the lawful authorities and to subvert the government, communicating intelligence to the enemy, attempting to liberate northern prisoners in the South, deserting and aiding deserters, trading with the enemy, advising or inciting others to abandon the Confederate cause, and attempting to destroy arsenals, foundries, or other property of the Confederate States of America. Its suspension, in a society whose civilian arrests approximated in number those of the North, prevented men from dodging the army. Drawing attention to its frequent use, one southerner noted that "in one year the Confederate States Attorney in Richmond tried eighteen hundred cases in that city [under] writs of habeas corpus."[55]

Uncertain about the extent of their personal liberties during the war, Confederates were also increasingly ambivalent about the prohibitions on trading with the enemy, which held all such contact to be corrupt and demoralizing. Planters continued to trade especially cotton and sugar with Yankee troops. For the Union the issue was corruption and speculative profits, but for the South, trading with the enemy, which was never entirely outlawed, worked against the war effort. The official government policy was an embargo—planters were to burn their cotton crops and then raise food. But the casual flow of contraband goods to the enemy undermined that policy. Southerners also saw that many planters who had been enthusiastic for secession were the very ones who, now protected by the enemy, traded across lines.

But even Davis and his War Department took a pragmatic view of the issue because trading brought currency and scarce goods into the southern economy. In a few instances the trading of cotton for greenbacks, which were then converted into supplies, kept troops such as those in General Earl Van Dorn's Army of the Mississippi in the field. But the compromise of engaging in illegal activities produced another tension into the South.[56]

Even Vice President Alexander H. Stephens challenged the administration of which he was a part and opposed attempts to give the president desperately needed emergency powers. If Davis was granted the right to suspend the writ of habeas corpus, Stephens predicted in 1864, "constitutional liberty will go down, never again to rise on this continent." "Far better that our country should be overrun by the enemy, our cities sacked and burned, and our land laid desolate," the vice president concluded with impractical intransigence, "than that the people should thus suffer the citadel of their liberties to be entered and taken by professed friends."[57]

Stephens even initiated a peace movement in Georgia, endorsing Governor Joseph E. Brown's rhetoric "about re-establishing the principles of the Declaration of Independence— 'the right of all self-government and the sovereignty of the States' by which [Brown] meant that each state, Northern and Southern, should 'determine for herself what shall be her future connection, and who her future allies.'" Nothing concrete came of Stephens's peace maneuvers. Still, by schooling southerners in the conviction that their president was responsible for their suffering and by playing on the traditional themes of southern concern with individual liberty, fear of political power, and a passion for self-defeating antistatism, the second-highest official in the Confederacy and the governor of one of its wealthiest states sapped the determination of the people.[58]

Such growing alienation included suggestions that Lee become a dictator or at least the supreme commander of all Confederate forces. President Davis was among the last to accept an idea the Union had adopted nearly a year before. In January 1865, the Confederate Congress passed, by a substantial majority, a bill to appoint a general-in-chief of the armies, defeating an amendment that would have guarded against interference with the military rights and duties of the president. On February 6, 1865, far too late for any advantage from this legislation, Lee was appointed to the highest military office.

Military pressure on the South was also demonstrated in legislation to use black troops. On November 7, 1864, President Davis approved the military enrollment of slaves as preferable to defeat. On February 20, 1865, the Confederate House of Representatives authorized the president, if he could not raise sufficient troops, to call for additional levies "from such classes ... irrespective of color ... as the authorities ... may determine."[59] Such legislation, which required the approval of states and individual owners, indicated a victory of southern nationalism over the Confederacy's secessionist motive to protect slavery, for it was widely agreed that enlistment would carry emancipation with it.

Lee agreed with the president and Congress. In early January, he urged the enlistment of slaves and the granting of "immediate freedom to all who enlist, and freedom at the end of the war to the families of those who discharge their duties faithfully."[60] The law, however, did not go into effect until March 20, 1865, and although a few black troops were recruited, none actually served in battle.[61]

## RELIGION AND THE CONFEDERATE COLLAPSE

As Confederate forces withdrew farther into the interior and earlier, morale-affirming battlefield victories gave way to Sherman's penetration of the South, the Protestant religion that had earlier enhanced the will to fight now came to undermine it. Most southerners believed that God intervened in human affairs, shaping events, rewarding the good, and punishing the bad. At first God had clearly seemed to prefer the South, validating the Confederacy's war goals. As one Georgia congressman predicted, "He would never desert a cause so pure as ours." But by 1864 white southerners lived a contradiction as it became clear that in providential terms it appeared that they were being punished. The Episcopal bishop of Virginia, John Johns, preached that "God's displeasure resulted from the collective guilt of Southerners and he expressed amazement that God had not punished His people sooner and more drastically." In the waning days of the Confederacy, the South's sin seemed obvious, as previously buried guilt over slavery surfaced. "Religion, which had originally buoyed up Confederate confidence not only no longer supported morale but even inspired in some Southerners a fatalism about defeat."[62]

Confederate soldiers were also influenced by religion as revivalism swept through their ranks, especially during the winter of 1863–1864. Not only did the promise of salvation on the eve of possible death provide an appealing consolation to Protestants, but celebrations of worship also linked soldiers' camps with home life. Conversions cemented fraternal bonds of solidarity among the troops. "When I go into a fite I say God be my helper and when I come out I say thank God I feel like he has bin with mee," explained a Tennessee soldier to his wife.[63]

Eventually in the same process as occurred with civilians, soldiers came to interpret defeat as God's verdict. "It seems," wrote one soldier who faced Sherman's army in the summer of 1864, "like the Lord has turned his face from us and left us to work out our own destruction."[64] Thus the same judgments of the Lord that encouraged religious northerners to await victory no matter how long it took and that Lincoln referred to in his second inaugural resigned southerners to defeat and in a self-fulfilling prophecy lessened their resolve. "If the South was right," concluded a Georgia planter's wife, "God would give it victory; if slavery was wrong, I trust that He will show it unto us."[65] And by 1865 many southerners, demoralized and debilitated, awaited as God's judgment their military defeat, which arrived in the spring of 1865.

CHAPTER 23 | # The End of the War

Hastened by declining morale in the Confederacy and the powerful Union armies, the end of the Civil War came soon after the winter ended and the spring campaigns of 1865 began. The surrender of the Confederacy was in stark contrast to the enthusiasm of both sides when the war began in 1861.

## MILITARY ACTIONS IN 1865

By January 1865, the only important military action was taking place in Virginia and the Carolinas. In the fall of 1864 when William T. Sherman had marched southeast toward Savannah, John Bell Hood had led his army the opposite way, in a northwesterly direction from Atlanta into Tennessee. The Confederate commander hoped to cut Yankee supply lines as well as to draw the war away from the Confederate heartland. On November 30, he caught up with Union forces under General John Schofield at Franklin, a town eighteen miles south of Nashville.

In a bloody encounter marked by the frontal assaults of Hood's troops against the entrenched Yankees, the Confederates suffered casualties of sixty-three hundred out of a total force of approximately twenty-seven thousand. Among the dead and wounded were six Confederate generals; killed were States Rights Gist, the rabid secessionist from South Carolina, and Patrick Cleburne, the Irish-born officer who had recommended using blacks as soldiers. Also killed or captured were fifty-four regimental commanders. Schofield lost over two thousand men as he hurriedly repaired bridges to get his wagon trains and men to Nashville, where General George Thomas, the "Rock of Chickamauga," had placed his troops in a semicircle around the city. Hood followed him there and attempted to mount a siege of the city, though his army was too small to do so.

In Washington and in Grant's headquarters there was impatience about Thomas's failure to attack, given his superior numbers, but in mid-December his forces surged out of the city to do battle. In two days of fighting in fog, sleet, and rain outside Nashville on December 15–16, Thomas's fifty-five thousand troops virtually destroyed Hood's army, whose lines gave way as soldiers fled, leaving six thousand of an initial force of twenty thousand dead, wounded, or captured. For all practical purposes, the war in the West was over, as Hood straggled across the Tennessee River with the shattered remnants of the army Johnston had turned over to him in Atlanta.

In one of Lee's most important actions as the Confederate general-in-chief, he replaced Hood with Joseph E. Johnston and assigned him the task of stopping Sherman with whatever troops he could gather. The advance of Sherman's columns, however, was irresistible. Leaving Savannah on February 1, the Union general reached Columbia, South Carolina, on February 17. Nowhere did he encounter much resistance, leading Governor Zebulon Vance of North Carolina to note of the civilian reaction to its invasion: "[T]hrough our own country not a bridge has been burnt, a car thrown from its track nor a man shot by our own people whose country has been desolated! . . . [The] greatest popular heart is not now and never has been in this war."[1]

Nor were Confederate troops under General William Hardee able to contain Sherman's troops, although there was a skirmish at Averasborough in North Carolina. No doubt a New York sergeant was correct when he noted that "the Confederates seem to have lost their vigor." Governor Vance linked this decline in fighting spirit to "the state of despondency that now prevails among our people [which] is producing a bad effect upon the troops."[2]

Throughout the South civilians gave up the cause. In Lynchburg, Virginia, when calls came for more soldiers, only a few twelve-year-olds responded. In Arkansas and Florida, the Union was able to raise sixteen regiments of white troops, many more than the Confederates had been able to enlist during their movements into the North.[3] Most of the population had heard of Sherman's invasion and preferred Yankee rule over the hardships of life as Confederates.[4] As the new year began in the capital city of the Confederacy, a Richmond editor concluded that "our people are subjugated in spirit. . . . They have not the heart to do anything, but meet together and recount their losses and suffering."[5]

Leaving much of Columbia in ashes, Sherman was in Fayetteville by March 10. Up to this point his direction had been toward Raleigh. Now he shifted to a more easterly course toward Goldsboro, near which point on March 19 he fought a sharp engagement with Johnston at Bentonville. Sherman did not overwhelm Johnston's inferior force of no more than twenty thousand men. But he did drive him back, taking Goldsboro and with it the railroads connecting to

Wilmington and Beaufort. Earlier Wilmington had been evacuated, and Johnston advised Lee that he could only "annoy" the enemy with his small force. Sherman now moved north to join Grant.

In the midst of these final campaigns, with Sherman pressing Johnston and with Grant threatening Lee at Petersburg, a peace conference was held after Lincoln consented to receive southern agents within Union lines. The president had already made clear his peace terms, indicating that reunion and abolition were indispensable.[6]

On February 3, 1865, Lincoln and Seward met with the Confederates Alexander Stephens, Robert Hunter, and John Campbell on the Union transport *River Queen*, lying in Hampton Roads. Lincoln's terms centered on three points: (1) reunion; (2) emancipation; (3) no temporary armistice. The last point represented an important difference between the two sides; Confederate leaders sought a "suspension" of hostilities if full peace could not be obtained, and possibly postponement of all matters of negotiation if such suspension could be obtained. The Union had always resisted a temporary armistice, considering it an admission of Confederate legitimacy and more dangerously, an arrangement that had the potential for permanence.

On collateral issues Lincoln was generous, assuring the Confederates that his executive policies would be lenient and remarking that he would, for himself, be willing to consider compensation to slaveholders. He continued to stress, however, that the reestablishment of the Union was an essential condition and that the disbanding of southern armies was required. These were unacceptable stipulations to the Confederates, and the conference adjourned without agreement.[7] When Davis reported to Congress, he advised them that "the enemy refused to enter into negotiations with the Confederate States . . . or to give to our people any other terms . . . than our unconditional submission to their rule."[8] After the conference broke up, a resigned Mary Chesnut acknowledged that "the inevitable Yankees seemed coming at last."[9]

During the Hampton Roads conference Union troops had been advised that there would be no letup in the war and that they must maintain their readiness to move on short notice. Six weeks later, Grant launched his final offensive. The Union general's efforts at Petersburg had been devoted to extending his lines and guarding against Lee's escape southward to join up with Johnston in North Carolina. By the end of March all the Union forces under Sherman, Sheridan, and Meade, with Grant in command, were now ready to cooperate in the closing campaign, details of which were discussed when Lincoln met Grant and Sherman in a historic conference on the *River Queen* on the James River at City Point on March 27–28. At this time Lincoln deplored further bloodshed and insisted that generous terms be offered the South.

The final campaign displayed the deterioration of the Confederate army. Lee's long line defending Richmond was now so thinly manned that a break was inevitable, whereas Grant was strengthened by the arrival of Sheridan, who had shifted his army southward from Winchester to join the Army of the Potomac. In the last important battle of the war, at a road junction called Five Forks on April 1, Lee's army was overwhelmed. After strong assaults on the Confederate lines covering Petersburg, large numbers of Confederate prisoners were taken. Richmond must soon follow.

On the night of April 2 Lee evacuated Petersburg. The next day the Union forces took possession of the city. It was now a matter of retreat and pursuit. Lee retreated westward toward Lynchburg. Grant believed that from this point on the Richmond and Danville Railroad, he might escape into North Carolina and join Johnston. Some of the most rapid movements of the war now occurred, with hard marching, sharp cavalry skirmishes, rear-guard actions, and sudden encounters at crossroads and bridges.

Meanwhile in Richmond, the government had collapsed. The president and Cabinet fled as regular contact between Davis and the starving army ceased. There was confusion in the army itself, with destruction of reports and public papers, with many of Lee's regiments lacking officers, and with Confederate troops deserting in droves. In a symbolic display of the meaning of the war, the first Federal troops to march into Richmond, on April 3, were African American members of the Twenty-Fifth Corps. "First the cavalry thundered at a furious gallop," recalled an eyewitness. "Then the infantry came playing 'The Girl I Left Behind'— then the negro troops playing 'Dixie.'" Lincoln followed the next day, sitting at Davis's desk, visiting Libby Prison, where thirty thousand Union soldiers had been held in conditions that visibly shook the president, and listening to former Supreme Court Justice John A. Campbell suggest that Virginia might rescind its ordinance of secession.[10]

Grant now pushed his columns to the point where Lee's escape was cut off. The diminishing Confederate army was not only trapped but was almost without food. On April 7 Grant initiated an exchange of notes with Lee, who at first declined to discuss surrender terms. But the next day, forty-eight months after the war had begun, Lee, reciprocating Grant's desire to avoid more bloodshed, asked for terms. On Sunday, April 9, in the McLean House in the village of Appomattox Courthouse, the opposing commanders met—Grant in a mud-splattered uniform resembling that of a private; his brown hair and beard showing no touch of gray; Lee with his distinguished gray beard and aristocratic head, erect military bearing, and faultless uniform.

Under the terms of surrender, the officers and men of Lee's command were to be released after giving their word not to take up arms against the United States. But their arms, artillery, and public property were to be turned over. Then Grant generously added: "This will not embrace the side arms of the officers, nor their private horses or baggage." According to an eyewitness, Lee was visibly touched by this concession, which he said would have a good effect on his men.

Union soldiers and civilians stand before the courthouse at Appomattox. Lee arrived at the McLean house wearing a clean gray uniform with an engraved sword by his side. Grant then arrived wearing a uniform covered in mud and did not carry a sword. Here Union soldiers have stacked their rifles and face the camera at a historic moment in U.S. history.

Still, Lee had a further point to mention. Not only his officers but soldiers in the cavalry and artillery owned their own horses, and he inquired whether they also could retain them. Grant replied that he would give orders that all the men who owned a horse or mule would be permitted to take them home "to work their little farms." Thus the commander of the Union armies avoided the rituals and signs of victory that would have further humiliated the Confederates.

Grant did not demand Lee's sword, and the Union commander promptly supplied twenty-five thousand rations to the hungry Confederates. Grant also agreed that Lee's troops could return to their homes and "not be disturbed by United States authority so long as they observe their paroles and the laws in force where they may reside," conditions that indicated there would be no treason trials and that set the stage for the initial period of Reconstruction.

Grant had no specific instructions from Lincoln about these minor matters relating to the surrender. He had, however, discussed the basic requirements for the emancipation of slaves and the restoration of the seceded states with the president at a meeting at his City Point headquarters in late March. There Lincoln had said "[L]et them once surrender and reach their homes [and] they won't take up arms again. . . . Let them have their horses to plow with. . . . Give them the most liberal and honorable terms." Grant, who usually deferred to his superiors, remembered these words as he listened to Lee's requests.[11]

This painting, entitled *Furling the Flag*, shows Confederates mournfully rolling up the Stars and Bars.

In the days preceding the surrender, Lee's forces had rapidly dwindled because of battle losses and desertions by many who anticipated the end of the war and were eager to get home.[12] Others were overwhelmed with emotions that ranged from humiliation to despair. A young Virginian wrote, "[L]ast night we were free soldiers of the Southern states. Tonight we are defeated men, prisoners of war of the northern states." To those who remained Lee expressed his appreciation for their "unsurpassed courage and fortitude." Riding back to camp, he bade them a personal farewell, then set out for Richmond. He had surrendered approximately twenty-eight thousand men.[13]

In retrospect, the defeat of the Confederacy, as Richard Beringer and others have written, was as much a result of the South's demoralization as a military achievement, although the two were closely intertwined. The subduing of the Confederate military occurred because the Union was a far stronger war power in terms of resources and because none of the possibilities that might have evened the odds had happened. Great Britain and France did not give aid to the Confederacy; the Confederates did not win those victories it needed in the North in 1862 and 1863 in order to inspire its people and demoralize the North. Nor was its military able to sustain the war long enough for the Union to become distracted and settle for a conditional surrender. Lincoln's Emancipation Proclamation, despite its opponents, had only increased the North's military strength, because it added to the North's physical resources and subtracted black labor from the South, and because it defined a noble goal beyond the restoration of the Union.

Moreover the Confederacy had been unable—and possibly unwilling—to give the resources and attention to civilians that it had given to the army. And though its military mobilization had been successful when measured from its beginnings, the true yardstick was to compare it with the North's experience. The North had gained in commitment and unity as the war continued, while in every way the South had weakened. Even border states like Maryland, Missouri, and Delaware had become firmly committed to winning the war, while the border areas that had chosen the Confederacy, such as mid-Tennessee, were now anxious to return to the Union.

After Lee's surrender, neither civilian nor military leaders encouraged a guerrilla war, though the Confederacy still had sixty thousand organized troops, mostly in the East.[14] To be sure, such strategies of modern liberation movements were foreign to the traditional nineteenth-century West Point notion of warfare, though the Confederacy had sponsored Forrest's and Morgan's raids, which might have provided a model for continuing the struggle. Sherman was among several Union officers who worried about the possibility of bands of "desperadoes"—groups that could have made any sustained Federal occupation impossible.[15] At least one member of Lee's staff suggested that the men take to the woods and begin a partisan resistance.

But Lee, who assumed that such a war would degenerate into criminality, rejected such an idea: "We would bring on a state of affairs that would take the country years to recover from."[16] Unlike the Boers in the South African war in 1900 or the Algerians and Vietnamese in the twentieth century, Confederate elites, as George Fredrickson writes, had reasons to hesitate. "Their authority and prestige would have been put at risk if bushwacking became the order of the day."[17] The United States was spared such a disruption, though southerners faced other kinds of conflicts during Reconstruction. So the tired, hungry Confederate soldiers went home and did not continue the war against the North. Eventually they became symbolic folk heroes of the South's lost cause, venerated for their courage and devoted service.

The Confederate capital, meanwhile, had fallen, its citizens as exhausted as the army. President Davis, still defiant and hoping for a miracle, and nearly all his Cabinet left by train on the night of Sunday, April 2. Next day they reached Danville. There they lingered for a week before making their way southward, the fugitive president and Cabinet constituting the remains of the Confederacy's civil government. On April 3 Union troops under General Godfrey Weitzel occupied Richmond, replacing the Stars and Bars with the Stars and Stripes. Fire broke out, and soon most of the downtown district was in ruins. The city was put under martial law, and Weitzel occupied the mansion just vacated by Jefferson Davis. There was, however, little friction. "The military was for the most part courteous and the people gladly cooperated . . . to restore order."[18]

After Lincoln returned to Washington and learned there of Lee's surrender, he became preoccupied with problems of reunion and reconciliation. Just a few

Two women dressed in black walk among the ruins at Richmond. For many southern women, the dedication they felt at the beginning of the war began to crumble as the Confederacy began to collapse.

weeks before, he had been inaugurated for his second term. His address on that occasion was notable both for what it included and omitted. The president made no attempt to review the successes of his administration; he said nothing against the enemy. On the contrary, Lincoln counseled citizens to "judge not that we be not judged." Forgiveness and good will were the themes of his brilliant peroration: "With malice toward none; with charity for all; with firmness in the right, as God gives us to see the right, let us strive on to finish the work we are in; to bind up the nation's wounds . . . to do all which may achieve and cherish a just, and a lasting peace among ourselves and with all nations."

On April 11 the president delivered his last public address, the subject of which was reconstruction. With Lincoln's support, the Thirteenth Amendment, outlawing slavery, had already been passed by Congress. Slavery would be prohibited when three-quarters of the states accepted the amendment. Now Lincoln asked for reunion and for limited black suffrage.[19] Two days later, he held a Cabinet meeting during which he spoke kindly of Lee and expressed his desire that there be no persecution of the southern people after the war.[20]

The next day the president lay dead. On the night of April 14, he was shot at Ford's Theater by the assassin John Wilkes Booth in what briefly seemed an organized conspiracy against the Union government. Secretary of State Seward was severely wounded by one of Booth's conspirators. Another conspirator had been instructed to kill Vice President Andrew Johnson, but lost his nerve. The joy of the Union victory was now tempered by sadness at Lincoln's death and apprehension, with Joseph E. Johnston's army still in the field.

Moving forward from Goldsboro, Sherman had occupied Raleigh on April 13, the day before Lincoln's assassination. Although Johnston's small army of twenty thousand was certainly capable of further resistance, it was melting away from desertion. Johnston reported to Davis that after the news of Lee's surrender swept through his army, as many as four thousand soldiers a day left, some even stealing army mules to hasten their progress home. Davis intended that Johnston escape to the west and join the forces of Edmund Kirby Smith (nominally an army of sixty thousand) and Richard Taylor's forty-two thousand men in Texas and Louisiana. But the more realistic Johnston knew the war was over.

President Davis continued to believe otherwise. On April 4 he had issued an address to the southern people in which he spoke of continuing the war by "operating in the interior . . . where supplies are more accessible, and where the foe will be far removed from his own base." He asked the people of the Confederacy for that unquenchable resolve which alone was needed to "render our triumph certain."[21]

The very day of the surrender at Appomattox, Davis had written Lee of the need to "win success North of the Roanoke." After Appomattox, his thoughts turned to the trans-Mississippi where he thought the Confederate government and army could continue the struggle. Reaching Greensboro, he conferred with Johnston and Beauregard, still talking in military terms of "whipping" the enemy. In his letter to Johnston on April 11 he wrote that the important question was "at what point shall concentration be made, in view of the present position of the two columns of the enemy."[22] But at the Greensboro conference Johnston spoke plainly to the Confederate president, telling him that the southern people were tired of war, that his men were rapidly deserting, and that the proper course was to consult Sherman as to terms.

When Sherman presented terms of capitulation so broadly phrased as to cover even political reconstruction, Johnston accepted. Neither lawyer nor politician, Sherman believed he was following the spirit of Lincoln's generous program of reconstruction, recently explained to him at City Point by the president himself. In fact Sherman's peace terms went far beyond anything Lincoln contemplated, for they inadvertently "guaranteed property in slaves, left a chance for the payment of Confederate war debts, recognized insurgent state governments, and might well have put in question the authority of seven Union state governments" already established in the South.[23]

Although Sherman thought that he had "obtained the surrender of all the remaining Confederate armies and not just Johnston's . . . and that he had prevented the Confederate army from breaking into guerrilla bands," the new president, Andrew Johnson, and his Cabinet promptly overruled the general, and Secretary of War Edwin Stanton ordered Sherman to set aside the agreement he had drawn up.[24] Sherman then arranged another conference with Johnston near Durham Station, North Carolina on April 26, where terms of capitulation similar to those accorded Lee at Appomattox were signed.

In the Southwest during these momentous days, General James Wilson was pursuing Nathan Bedford Forrest and had just captured Selma and Montgomery in Alabama when news came of Johnston's surrender. The disbanding of the remaining Confederate forces followed. On May 4 at Citronelle, Alabama, the Confederate general Richard Taylor surrendered to Edward Canby what remained of the forces east of the Mississippi, including those in Forrest's command. Three weeks later, on May 26 in New Orleans, Edmund Kirby Smith surrendered his forces beyond the Mississippi, and with this capitulation southern military resistance to federal authority ended. The Confederacy had expired.

## EPILOGUE

Ultimately, Confederate hostility toward the Yankees and devotion to a new nation erected on the distinguishing institution of slavery (for all northerners believed to some extent in states' rights) could not stoke and enduring martial commitment in a society outnumbered by the Union in every relevant category. Yet in 1861 the Confederacy had begun the war with certain advantages that evened the odds. Although the American Civil War is usually studied in isolation, the

With the end of the war, Union soldiers returned home. Note, in a symbolic representation of the future, the black porter in the background.

Black men collect the amputated limbs and skeletons from the battlefield at Cold Harbor in a grisly reminder of the physical cost of the war.

experience of other secessionist communities attests to the possibility of success for the South.[25] But instead reverses in the field, tension between state governments and Richmond, the failure of the central government to maintain the morale of the people—all sapped dedication to a cause that from the beginning had depended on a martial spirit and victories on the battlefield along with a dedication to the anachronistic institution of slavery for its inspiration.

More than four years after it started, the war that both sides had believed would last a summer finally ended. Whereas the North found the war's purpose in the restoration of the Union, the survival of its federal democracy, the freeing of four million slaves, and the bold new expression of nationalism exhibited in transcontinental railroads, a banking system, and new funding for public higher education, both black and white southerners faced a period of disruption and confusion.

Over 620,000 Union and Confederate soldiers had died during the war, or 182 of every 10,000 Americans, a far higher figure than the 30 of every 10,000 in World War II. Over three million Americans had enlisted to serve either the United States of America or the Confederate States of America.[26]

On an individual level, the impact of the war was apparent in severed limbs, disrupted families—the famous Mrs. Bixby, to whom Lincoln extended condolences, lost two (not five) sons—and if northern observers were correct, in a national schooling in the virtues of endurance, discipline, and service. By 1865 few Americans were left untouched by the experience of Civil War; few could remember the innocent hope of only a decade earlier that the crisis between North and South could be resolved.

In April 1865, a Confederate captain asked himself the hard questions to which white and black southerners (and all Americans) would continue to give different answers: "Who is to blame for all this waste of human life? And what does it amount to? Has there been anything gained by all this sacrifice? What were we fighting for, the principles of slavery?"[27] Northerners also puzzled over the meaning of the war to the nation. But any despair was tempered by the sense of American exceptionalism, which had grown from northerners' industrial prowess and pride in their cities and agriculture, and which had inspired their increasing devotion to the Union. Soon enough they would confront issues relating to their commitment to former slaves and to Lincoln's spirit of magnanimity as the process of Reconstruction began.

## CHAPTER 24

# The Challenge of Reconstruction: Legacies of the War in the North

C essation of armed conflict in the spring of 1865 forced Americans to confront the consequences of their long war. Internal social and economic changes in both the North and South required readjustments and, in the South, sustained efforts at economic rebuilding and revival. For authorities in Washington, the primary task was devising and implementing policies to restore the prewar relationship between the recent combatants, to reintegrate the former Confederate states into the Union, and to secure basic rights for the newly freed slaves. That governmental effort is known as Reconstruction, and though many important aspects of the Civil War reverberated well into the twentieth century, Reconstruction is normally dated from the spring of 1865 to the spring of 1877.[1]

The historian William Gillette has aptly called Reconstruction "essentially a postwar political and constitutional settlement—the peace treaty ending the Civil War—the terms of which would define and consolidate the gains of the victor over the vanquished."[2] Inextricably entangled in partisan conflict between the Republican and Democratic parties, Reconstruction policies were framed and implemented by the Republicans, who continued to dominate the national and most northern state governments after the war. To achieve their goals, Republicans ultimately would pass two federal civil rights laws and the Fourteenth and Fifteenth Amendments to the Constitution, four Reconstruction acts to redefine the participants in and contours of southern politics, and a series of federal enforcement acts to protect blacks' newly granted political rights. This experiment met resistance from President Andrew Johnson, northern Democrats, and most southern whites. Quite unlike the North's successful wartime military effort to restore the Union and free the slaves, Reconstruction ultimately failed to secure the goals of Republican policy makers. By mid-1877, they had abandoned the Reconstruction experiment, and all southern state governments were dominated by men who repudiated it.

Few episodes in American history have been so controversial as Reconstruction. Influenced by regional loyalties, by contemporary partisan agendas and ideological climates, and, sadly, for too many years by hostile racial stereotypes, historians since the late nineteenth century often treated Reconstruction as a morality play and differed primarily about who were its heroes and villains. They disagreed about the motives of the Northerners who formulated Reconstruction policies, about how harshly radical or shortsightedly timid those policies were, about their impact on black and white southerners and the achievements or sins of Reconstruction governments in the South, about the reasons for Reconstruction's failure, about what exactly defined that failure, and whether it should be celebrated or mourned.[3]

Subsequent chapters will examine all of these political aspects of Reconstruction. This and the next chapter, however, examine the economic, social, and ideological legacies of the Civil War in the North and South that provided the context for the experiment of political Reconstruction. Those legacies often seemed of more immediate relevance to people than did working out a peace settlement between the sections. How citizens of the two sections responded to those internal regional problems, therefore, often complicated the task of Republican policy makers.

The Civil War not only left a legacy of economic and social problems that required postwar readjustments. It also bequeathed precedents for dealing with many of them, including the reconstruction of intersectional relationships. Those precedents, as much as the problems themselves, would shape the subsequent course of Reconstruction by fixing patterns that closed off alternative solutions, by sowing suspicions and misunderstandings that bore later fruit, or by illustrating the need for fresh thinking and innovative action.

Since the term *Reconstruction* refers primarily to a readjustment between the North and South and of economic, social, and political relationships within the South, most historians would agree with Eric Foner's contention "that events in the South remain the heart of the Reconstruction drama."[4] Nonetheless, over three-fifths of Americans lived in the North, where much of importance occurred between 1865 and 1877 that ostensibly had nothing to do with race relations or the South. The experiences of that northern majority require assessment. Since the power base of the Republican politicians who undertook the reconstruction of the South lay in the North, they had to pay close attention to the demands and grievances of their northern constituents, lest they lose power to the Democrats. Thus northerners' reactions to their own postwar experiences often helped shape and complicate Republicans' attempts to formulate and implement Reconstruction policies. This chapter examines the Civil War's legacies in the North and their implications for the Reconstruction experiment. The next chapter undertakes a similar examination of the South, since conditions there also helped dictate the nature of Reconstruction.

## INITIAL POSTWAR ATTITUDES IN THE NORTH

The tremendous sacrifice of human and material treasure necessary to conquer the Confederacy and the war's traumatic emotional costs left northerners with mixed attitudes toward, and degrees of interest in, the impending challenge of Reconstruction. Contrasting partisan ideologies about race and government's proper role that had hardened during the war divided northerners over policies for blacks and the South. But an even greater chasm initially separated those whose interest in public affairs had been quickened by wartime sacrifices from those whose sense of civic obligation had been exhausted by the arduous conflict and who longed now to ignore political matters and focus exclusively on their own private affairs.[5]

Many northerners were determined that their hard-won achievement not be wasted, that the fruits of northern victory be protected in any peace terms authorities in Washington imposed upon the South. As the young French newspaper correspondent Georges Clemenceau reported, "When anyone has for four successive years joined in a struggle as that which the United States has seen . . . [he desires] not to lose the dearly bought fruits of so many painful sacrifices. When the war ended, the North was concerned not to let itself be tricked out of what it had spent so much trouble and perseverance to win."[6]

Northerners' expectations about the possible terms of Reconstruction and race adjustment differed, but those viewpoints reflected broader attitudes about the role of the state that had been instilled by the war. Those attitudes, in turn, influenced how northerners responded to economic and social conditions in the North as well as to possible federal policies for the South. Though most Democrats remained suspicious of active government at all levels of the federal system, many Republicans and social reformers took from the "sudden upsurge" of governmental activity after 1861 a conviction "that applied government power worked" and that "government on some level of the federal system could cope with what was wanted." Significantly, that wartime upsurge, as the historian Harold Hyman has remarked, involved "cities, counties, and states," as well as the national government, "in unprecedented scales of commitment and wholly novel functional areas." Because Republicans controlled the national government, most northern state governments, and, after 1867, most southern state governments as well, the Reconstruction experiment therefore included "many 'reconstructions' [occurring] simultaneously North and South, involving applications of government's powers, resources, and institutions on some level or several levels of the federal system, for improvement purposes." Republican-controlled state and local governments everywhere sought to promote and then regulate railroads, improve public health, charter charitable organizations, expand tax-supported public education, impose prohibition, and create state police forces to enforce it and punish other crimes. Willingness to support federal policies for the South and African Americans, in sum, was buttressed by confidence in local and state governments in the North; conversely, any loss of that confidence could erode that support.[7]

During the war black spokesmen and white abolitionists had also sought to use enhanced governmental authority to eradicate discrimination against the North's black minority, and they had won some victories that were of vast importance for the impending challenge of Reconstruction. Laws banning black testimony in court were repealed in California in 1863 and in Illinois in early 1865. In response to blacks' pressure, San Francisco, New York City, Cincinnati, and Cleveland desegregated their streetcars and Chicago, its schools. Impressed by blacks' service in Union armies, Republican leaders had often joined the drive to advance African Americans' rights in the North, and where they failed during the war, Republican-controlled state legislatures succeeded shortly after it. Pennsylvania's legislature banned discrimination on public transportation throughout that state in March 1867; Rhode Island's legislature outlawed school segregation in 1866, and Connecticut's followed suit in 1868.[8]

Inspired by this wartime drive for racial justice, proponents sought its extension during Reconstruction. During 1865 black public meetings in both the North and South demanded that the federal government grant equal civil and political rights to African Americans throughout the nation.[9] In 1865, Republicans in several northern states pressed for the enfranchisement of their black residents, but their first successes, in Iowa and Minnesota, came only in November 1868.[10] Most Republican politicians were not yet prepared to go that far, but even in 1865 some spoke of enfranchising southern freedmen, if not the North's blacks. Sharply distinguishing between political and civil equality, far more Republicans insisted by late 1865 that the new Thirteenth Amendment, which northern state legislatures ratified throughout that year, entailed not simply blacks' right not to be chattel property, but also "the rights of personal liberty and locomotion, property ownership, free labor and liberty of contract, freedom of speech and worship, the sanctity of family and the home, the right to bring suit and testify in court, and generally the protection of person and property that belonged to all freemen or citizens." If enforced, this Republican reading of that amendment, let alone black enfranchisement, portended sweeping changes in the South.[11]

War-inspired faith in government's ability to solve social and economic problems in the North and South coexisted in uneasy tension with equally powerful contradictory feelings that would limit the reach of Reconstruction. Racism still pervaded the North, and Democrats, who continued to attract 45 percent of the northern vote, were virulently Negrophobic and ideologically averse to governmental activism.[12] Equally important, many other northerners who had no sympathy for that party were simply weary of war. They yearned to escape its psychological, physical, and financial burdens and to return as rapidly as possible to normal peacetime conditions. They insisted that the huge Union armies be disbanded quickly and Yankee soldiers sent home to their families. They wanted relief from the heavy excise, income, and property taxes that local, state, and national governments had levied to raise supplies, offer bounties to recruits, pay soldiers' wages, aid their families, and meet interest payments on bond issues.[13] Rather than plotting government-imposed vengeance against the South or girding their loins for a renewed sectional struggle over the terms of Reconstruction, they wanted to forget the war and the South and to get on with leading their own lives with a minimum of government interference. Rather than worrying about the fate of ex-Confederates and black freedmen in the South, they wondered primarily how best to exploit the opportunities or evade the pitfalls of the new economic world the war had created in the North.

The rapid demobilization of Union armies after the war in response to pleas from soldiers' families and taxpayers seeking to slash the government's payroll illustrates how the desire to escape war's burdens influenced Reconstruction. Aside from the Freedmen's Bureau established by Congress in March 1865, the national government lacked any administrative bureaucracy capable of overseeing Reconstruction in the South other than the army. Yet within days of the Grand Review of Grant's and Sherman's legions in Washington on May 23–24, soldiers were mustered out and sent home. From a total strength of over a million active men on May 1, 1865, the army shrank to 152,000 by the end of the year, and to

The Grand Review of Union Troops in Victory, Washington, D.C., May 1865.

38,000, many of them posted on the Indian frontier rather than in the South, by the fall of 1867.[14] This rapid disbanding of northern armies not only restricted the federal government's options regarding Reconstruction policy. It also unleashed into northern society hundreds of thousands of men, who, like civilians, were eager to get on with the business of making a living.

## ECONOMIC LEGACIES OF THE WAR IN THE NORTH

Returning Yankee soldiers discovered a transformed northern economy that created opportunities for some and hardships for others. They entered this economy alongside two other groups with whom they were often in competition. Untouched by the war's hardships, new immigrants poured into the country again as soon as the shooting stopped. Legislation passed by Congress on July 4, 1864 to encourage European emigration to the United States through recruiting agents in Europe was not repealed until 1868, and it helped raise annual immigration rates from below 100,000 in 1861 and 1862 to 193,000 in 1864. But the jump to 248,000 during 1865 and the fact that new immigrants numbered over 300,000 in all but one year between 1865 and 1875 suggests that economic opportunity and the end of the war, not federal policy, attracted them.[15]

Women, many of whose sons, fathers, husbands, and brothers had been killed or so maimed that they could not earn a wage, also entered the postwar work force to help support their families. How many women were widowed by the Civil War can only be estimated, but as late as 1890 almost one-eighth of all widows in the United States had been married to northern soldiers who died during, or later from disabilities sustained in, the war. Frequently forced by war's impact to fend for themselves economically, they had more justifiable claims for aid from the government that had waged it than any other civilians in the North. According to a provision of a pension act for disabled veterans signed by Lincoln on July 14, 1862, such widows, as well as dependent mothers and sisters, were eligible for monthly payments from the government ranging from eight dollars to thirty dollars, depending upon the rank of their husbands, with an additional two dollars per month for each child under the age of sixteen. Those amounts were raised by revised laws in 1864 and 1868, the latter allowing a lump sum first payment of $480 in addition to the monthly payments. Widows quickly took advantage of this legislation. Between 1861 and 1885, 335,296 claims were filed on behalf of widows, minor children, and other dependent relatives, and 220,825 of those claims were allowed. In 1866, 58 percent of claims came from women, but, as more veterans themselves got on the pension rolls, that proportion declined to 19 percent by 1891.[16]

Pension payments generated considerable income for the women fortunate enough to get them. In 1881, for example, the average annual first payout to widows and other dependents of deceased soldiers was $1,022, more than twice the average annual earnings of all workers.[17] But such large sums were not typical of the late 1860s, and not all women deprived of breadwinners by the war got any pension at all. Thus they entered the work force to support themselves. Many northern women, of course, had long done wage work outside the household to supplement family incomes or establish their independence from parents, and the war increased opportunities for women who wanted to work, either replacing men who had gone off to fight or exploiting new opportunities such as shearing out greenbacks and national banknotes for the Treasury Department. Although returning soldiers sometimes displaced women from their wartime jobs, by 1870 one of every four nonfarm wage earners was female. Seven-tenths of these were domestic servants, but, according to the labor historian David Montgomery, "the 368,266 women among the industrial manual workers constituted over ten percent of the group."[18]

Women thus joined veterans, new immigrants, and male civilians who had avoided military service in contending with the vicissitudes of the postwar northern economy. Scholars still disagree about the extent to which governmental policies enacted during the war shaped that economy. Industrialization in the North had proceeded at a rapid rate with only minimal governmental intervention for two decades prior to 1861. By diverting investment capital, material resources, and human energy from peacetime pursuits to wartime uses, the war in fact kept the North's economy from growing as fast as it otherwise would have. By one estimate, for example, the pig iron used in the manufacture of small and heavy arms equalled only one-seventh of the iron that would have gone into railroad construction had the war not interrupted it, whereas boot and shoe production in Massachusetts fell from forty-five million pairs in 1855 to thirty-two million ten years later.[19]

Nonetheless, this lag proved only temporary, and in absolute terms even during the war years output increased and many people prospered. The substitution of mechanical reapers for laborers absent in the army allowed farmers to meet and profit from the burgeoning civilian and military demand for grain products and laid the basis for further postwar expansion. Despite heavy excise taxes, thousands of manufacturers also flourished. High wartime tariffs protected them from foreign competition, and the price inflation accompanying the infusion of over $400 million worth of greenbacks into the economy allowed their earnings to exceed labor costs. One index of the war's economic stimulus was that the sudden end of wartime demand in the spring of 1865 provoked a sharp, if brief, recession. As the economist Rendigs Fels has written of this wrenching transition:

A federal budget deficit of almost one billion dollars in the fiscal year 1865—perhaps one seventh of national income—dropped to less than zero in 1866. The wartime speculative boom in wholesale prices collapsed early in 1865. . . . Pig-iron production [geared to war contracts] . . . fell from 1,136 thousand long tons in 1864 to 932 in 1865. One and a half million men who had been directly or indirectly engaged in prosecuting the war were released to the working force. In addition, the working force had to absorb a stream of 300,000 immigrants in each of the fiscal years 1866 and 1867.[20]

Lasting from April, 1865 to December, 1867, this cyclical contraction had important implications for the government's monetary policy and diverted the attention of job-seeking northerners from conditions in the South. So did the northern boom that rapidly succeeded the recession and lasted until a new depression began in 1873. The number of miles of railroad track in operation in the nation, for example, leaped from 38,085 in 1865 to 81,747 in 1878. Largely because of the market for rails, pig-iron production, which had dropped by 20 percent between 1864 and 1865, doubled between 1865 and 1870.[21] By the 1870s output in both the manufacturing sector and the economy as a whole enjoyed annual rates of growth similar to those of the 1840s and 1850s.

Farmers fully participated in this restored prosperity. Between 1866 and 1878, agricultural production doubled in the United States, even more than doubling in the North. The output of wheat, the crop most suitable for harvesting by mechanical reapers, nearly tripled during the years of Reconstruction, soaring from 152,000,000 bushels in 1866 to 420,000,000 in 1878.[22] Much of the increase in grain output, and especially wheat, moreover, stemmed from newly cultivated acres in the beckoning West, a region that captured the imaginations of both veterans seeking a fresh start and foreign immigrants seeking their fortune.

Population movement demonstrated that the West, not the South, preoccupied many northerners after 1865. The Homestead Act of 1862 and railroad land grants enacted during the war encouraged the rapid settlement of the trans-Mississippi region. Hundreds of thousands of Canadian, Scandinavian, and other immigrants poured into Iowa, Minnesota, Kansas, Nebraska, and the Dakotas between 1865 and 1890. The population of the latter four alone jumped from approximately three hundred thousand in 1860 to over two million in 1880. Taking up homesteads by the millions of acres or buying land from the railroads or directly from the government, they planted it in corn, wheat, and other crops; by 1880 the two north central regions were producing 71.6 percent of the nation's entire wheat crop.[23]

Almost inevitably, the vast buffalo herds that had once roamed over the western plains and the Indian tribes who had hunted them became victims of this westward population movement. Indiscriminately slaughtered by commercial hunters seeking to sell hides to leather tanners and even occasionally by travelers taking potshots from passing railroad cars, millions of bison were killed in the 1870s, and farmers and cattlemen occupied their former grazing grounds.[24] The greed of white farmers, ranchers, miners, and railroad companies for Indians' land usually overcame the efforts of thoughtful statesmen to negotiate agreements that ensured justice to the Indians and instead occasionally provoked the

As migration west increased, the once vast buffalo herds fell victim to the new population. Here two men are skinning a buffalo in northern Montana.

tribes into armed resistance against the whites' incursion. Yet even Indian victories such as the Sioux massacre of George A. Custer and his 250 men at Little Bighorn in 1876 only temporarily stemmed the inevitable. By the end of Ulysses S. Grant's second term in 1877, most tribes were already confined to reservations, and the days of the free-roaming Plains Indians were over.

White settlement of the Great Plains helped spur the growth of Chicago, postwar America's most vibrant and fascinating city. Blessed with unparalleled access to both water and rail transportation routes that kept shipping costs to and from the city low, it served as middleman between western farmers and eastern markets and investors. With its fantastically efficient system of grain elevators, its ingenious futures market in grain prices that allowed certificates for grain deposits to supplement the city's currency and credit supply, its sprawling lumber and cattle yards, and its agents of eastern banking houses, it emerged by the 1870s as the nation's leading processor of grain, wood, and meat products and the manufacturing and financial epicenter of a regional economy that extended hundreds of miles to its east, west, north, and south.[25]

Railroad connections provided the key to Chicago's prosperity, and railroad expansion was perhaps the most notable feature of the postwar boom. The famous "driving of the last spike" linking the Union Pacific and Central Pacific Railroads near Ogden, Utah on May 10, 1869 ostensibly signaled the success of one of the United States government's greatest wartime ventures—the chartering and subsidization of those two companies, a policy extended after the war to other transcontinentals such as the Northern Pacific, Atlantic & Pacific, and

Driving of the last spike, Promontory, Utah, May 10, 1869

Texas & Pacific. Yet graft connected with the Union Pacific's construction would later discredit the federal government's promotion of railroading, and in any event, most of the track laid in the late 1860s and 1870s was not subsidized directly by the federal government or located in the West. Rather, railroad expansion primarily represented the construction of new lines chartered by southern state governments after the war and especially the extension of eastern trunk-line roads that linked the Atlantic Coast to cities such as Cincinnati, Chicago, St. Louis, Kansas City, Milwaukee, and Burlington.

Railroad construction and the rate wars between competing lines influenced the price of farm products, raw materials, and manufactured goods and also generated two profoundly important political issues. State legislatures chartered and determined the routes and other privileges of most new lines, and they and local governments also often helped finance construction through direct bond issues and stock subscriptions, public endorsement of railroad bonds, and tax breaks. Between 1866 and 1873, for example, "twenty-nine state legislatures approved over eight hundred proposals for local aid to railroad companies," with the three leaders, New York, Illinois, and Missouri, alone authorizing "over $70 million worth of aid."[26] Not just the actual and potential customers of rail lines but all taxpayers, in short, had a stake in their efficient construction and honest operation. Thus, the ease with which railroad men seemed to bend public officials to their will raised concerns about corporate power and governmental corruption. Precisely because the mania for railroad building seized both northerners and southerners after the war, hostility to railroads' corruption of government was indeed a sentiment shared everywhere and helped shape northerners' attitudes toward Reconstruction in the South.

Second, just as completion of the trunk-line railroads in the Northeast in the 1850s had spurred attempts at rate regulation and the abolition of kickbacks, rebates, and free passes in New York, Pennsylvania, and Massachusetts during that decade, so the expansion of the rail networks to the Midwest in the 1870s instigated the so-called Granger movement for railroad regulation in Minnesota, Wisconsin, Iowa, Illinois, and elsewhere. Pitting shippers in communities that had rail connections and wanted state regulations against shippers from communities without railroads who feared that rate laws would deter new roads from being built to them, these intrastate battles complicated the task of northern political leaders who sought to hold statewide party coalitions together.[27]

Well before the regulation and corruption issues associated with railroads erupted into the state and national political arenas in the 1870s, railroad building after 1865 contributed to a parallel postwar boom in manufacturing. In a few cases entrepreneurs used fortunes they had earned during the war to invest in or exploit the opportunities offered by railroads. The financier Jay Cooke, for example, sank so many of the millions he had made from marketing government bonds in construction of the Northern Pacific Railroad that he became overextended; the collapse of his banking firm would precipitate the Panic of 1873. Philip D. Armour, the Chicago meat packer who grew rich from government meat contracts during the war, took a safer route. Using refrigerated railroad cars to ship pork and beef eastward and displacing local butchering rivals between Chicago and the East Coast in the process, he and his postwar Chicago rival Gustavus Swift made their names synonymous with meat products.[28]

Andrew Carnegie, who helped transform the iron and steel industry, also exploited the opportunities created by railroad construction. Although the Kelly-Bessemer process of converting iron to steel had been invented before the war,

Andrew Carnegie

Americans still relied primarily on iron at its close, and the primary product for iron was railroad track. A telegrapher for the Pennsylvania Railroad in Pittsburgh at the start of the war, the youthful Carnegie served briefly in Washington under its vice president, Thomas A. Scott, an assistant secretary of war, before replacing Scott as superintendent of the Pennsylvania's western division. From these positions, he, like other railroad men, noted how quickly the heavy wartime railroad traffic wore out the iron rails, and after observing the Bessemer process during a postwar European trip, Carnegie recognized the potential bonanza to be reaped from manufacturing steel rails to replace the less durable iron. Assembling capital of over seven hundred thousand dollars, Carnegie launched the firm of Carnegie, McCandless, and Company. Near Pittsburgh in 1873 it opened the J. Edgar Thomson Works, named for the Pennsylvania's president, for whom Carnegie had worked, and the world's most efficient steel-making plant soon set production records.[29]

The degree of productive consolidation or competitive oligopoly that occurred in manufacturing and mining during the 1860s should not be exaggerated, however. Instead of concentrating production in a few large and efficient firms, the frantic scrambling of local, state, and national governments for arms, shoes, blankets, uniforms, tents, and other matériel during the war had enticed thousands of small new firms into operation. Some would be squeezed out of business during the postwar recession; others would go under during the prolonged depression between 1873 and 1878.

Nonetheless, by the end of the 1860s most mining and manufacturing firms were small, limited partnerships that competed fiercely in local and regional markets, not legally incorporated giants that monopolized market share nationwide. In contrast to the huge Cambria Iron Works at Johnstown, Pennsylvania, which employed 1,948 workers in 1860, for example, the average number of workers per manufacturing and mining operation in 1869 was still only 8.15. In contrast to the Pennsylvania, Erie, Baltimore and Ohio, and New York Central Railroads, which were capitalized between $17 million and $35 million by the mid-1850s, in 1870 the average capital investment per manufacturing establishment in Massachusetts was only $17,536, in Pennsylvania, $10,936, and nationwide, $8,400. In ironmaking, which along with textiles boasted the nation's largest manufacturing firms by 1870, the census still listed 808 firms employing 77,555 hands, whereas ten years later 792 firms would employ 140,798 workers. The 1870s, not the 1860s, saw the trend toward consolidation of productive capacity in fewer firms and the herding of most industrial workers into factories using power-driven machinery.[30]

In sum, economic conditions in the North after the Civil War still offered opportunities to ambitious entrepreneurs and skilled artisans who aspired to climb the socioeconomic ladder. Rigid class lines separating immensely wealthy employers from an unskilled, permanently immobile class of factory workers were hardening, but had not yet congealed. Though limited compared to other occupations, white-collar jobs in sales, clerical work, and what we would now call middle management—jobs that often required educational attainment rather than manual labor—grew as the economy expanded. These allowed men, and to a lesser extent women, to achieve or retain middle-class status, as did older, self-employed professions.[31] In short, those intent on forgetting the war and making a living found much in the North to absorb their attention.

## THE NORTHERN ECONOMY, POLITICS, AND RECONSTRUCTION

Two very different groups affected by governmental economic policies during the war made demands on government that became entangled in the northern response to Reconstruction. No occupational group suffered from wartime mobilization and the government's financial policies so much as skilled artisans and especially unskilled laborers. Conscription fell far more heavily on workers than on the wealthy, who could hire substitutes or pay commutation fees. Fledgling unions collapsed when workers marched off to war. Jobs for the remaining were plentiful, but wages lagged far behind prices inflated by greenback issues and excise taxes. Purchasing power of the average worker's annual pay in fixed dollars fell from $363 in 1860 to $261 in 1865, and some economists attribute manufacturers' wartime prosperity primarily to this slump in real wages. When workers protested this impoverishment and attempted to strike, state legislatures, like that of Illinois in 1863, passed laws prohibiting union organizing and strikes. Elsewhere state militias and federal troops were deployed to break strikes, as in Cold Spring, New York, in March 1864 and Pennsylvania's anthracite fields during the war and even after it in the spring of 1865.[32]

Workers, in sum, emerged from the Civil War with concrete grievances against their lot, against their employers, and often against Republican political officials, who had deployed the military and legal resources of the state against them. These grievances stimulated a labor reform movement organized in city-wide workers' assemblies and national organizations such as the National Labor Union. Formed in Baltimore in August 1866 as a coalition of established trade unions, the NLU eventually included unskilled workers of both races and sexes, land and labor leagues, and intellectuals; at its peak in the late 1860s it claimed between two-hundred thousand and four-hundred thousand members. Meeting in a series of annual national conventions until 1875, it pressured state governments for eight-hour laws and mine-safety legislation to improve working conditions. Supplementing these collective cross-occupational workers' organizations were craft-oriented trade unions, which flourished after 1865 in part because the Civil War mitigated the mutual suspicions that had isolated Irish Catholics from Protestant workers in the 1850s. These workers sought higher wages through pressure on employers, rather than the state. Between 1865 and 1873, in fact, a larger proportion of the industrial labor force joined trade unions than at any other time in the nineteenth century.[33]

Working-class militancy became linked with Reconstruction because of the lessons workers learned from the war and because of the appalled reaction to workers' demands by employers, the middle class, and the politicians who represented them. Resentful of the favoritism government had shown economic elites with protective tariffs, bond issues, the national banking acts, the conscription acts, and military intervention against strikes during the war and aware of the apparent willingness of Republicans in Congress after the war to grant blacks special legislative benefits, workers now demanded that the state also act specifically on their behalf. As the labor activist and eight-hour proponent Ira Steward told a mass meeting of workers in Boston in November 1865, "But while we will bear with patient endurance the burden of the public debt, we yet want it to be known that the workingmen of America will in future claim a more equal share in the wealth their industry creates in peace and a more equal participation in the privileges and blessings of those free institutions defended by their manhood on many a bloody field of battle."[34] By pressing for prolabor legislation that went beyond equal rights before the law, by running independent labor candidates for local offices, state legislatures, and even Congress in working-class strongholds, and by forcing the Republican and Democratic parties into a bidding war for labor's support, workers not only complicated the task of politicians seeking to gain or retain power in the North. Even more important, they alerted those politicians and their most influential constituents to the dangerous precedent-setting consequences of laws enacted on behalf of southern black freedmen. The resulting increased commitment of Republican policy makers to protecting the rights of private property owners would limit what those Republican congressmen attempted to do in the South.

The second northern economic interest group created by the war that became immediately and enduringly entangled with Reconstruction policy making consisted of bondholders, bankers, and other financial operators. Even without considering the aggregate bonded indebtedness of local and state governments, the debt of the national government at war's end stood at $2.6 billion, with maturity dates ranging from thirty days for some short-term treasury notes to forty years for some bonds and annual or accumulated interest rates varying from 4 to 7.5 percent.[35] Meeting those interest payments necessitated the high federal taxes during the war. To lower those taxes, everyone realized, the debt had to be either redeemed or refinanced at lower interest rates.[36]

That task, in turn, became entwined with other financial legacies of the war. Most bonds and treasury notes sold during the war specified that interest payments must be in specie (which effectively meant gold in this period), but it was unclear how the principal would be paid. Selling new bonds at lower rates of interest required assurances to potential purchasers that both the principal and interest would be paid in gold, yet the government, like private bankers, had abandoned the gold standard after December 1861. By June 1865 over $432 million worth of unbacked greenbacks were in circulation, and the $300 million worth of national banknotes authorized in the legislation of 1864 were backed by bonds, not specie. To persuade potential bond purchasers that they would be paid in gold or its equivalent, therefore, both bankers and the government had to "resume specie payments," that is, accumulate enough gold reserves to cover not only the principal and interest of the new bonds but also greenbacks and national banknotes. And that goal, most people believed, required contracting the amount of greenbacks and possibly national banknotes in circulation.

Eastern importing merchants who had to buy gold to meet customs duties and pay foreign suppliers were eager to do this, since the fluctuating price of gold increased their business risks on future contracts. So too were Protestant ministers, college professors, and other men who simply considered it immoral to stray from the gold standard. But even more powerful interests opposed a contraction of the currency supply.[37] For one thing, too rapid a contraction could force prices down, squeeze the credit that businessmen needed to stay in operation, and aggravate the hardship of recessions. This fact became clear when Treasury Secretary Hugh McCulloch, acting with authorization he secured from Congress in April 1866, attempted to reduce greenbacks in circulation to $356 million during the postwar recession. In response to popular protest, Congress forced him to suspend that contraction in a new law of February 1868.[38] In addition, midwestern and southern merchants, manufacturers, and railroad promoters opposed contraction because they were disadvantaged by the maldistribution of national banknotes to the Northeast. As state banks in their own regions were driven from business by Congress' 1865 tax on state banknotes, they were often dependent solely on greenbacks for a currency supply. Although farmers did not become intensely agitated by the money question until after the Panic of 1873, they disliked McCulloch's contraction since a devalued domestic currency increased their competitive edge in foreign export markets.[39]

Manufacturers, who enjoyed additional tariff protection from the premium on gold and who sought ample and cheap credit supplies to allow investments in their enterprises, also opposed currency contraction. Manufacturers actually preferred an expansion of the national banking system and a lifting of the $300 million cap on national banknotes to continued reliance on unbacked legal tender notes, but that goal was contested by other elements in the anticontraction, or "soft money," camp. Represented by midwestern Democrats in Congress and including newly militant labor leaders, these groups ideologically opposed the control bankers exercised over the money supply. They resented the immense profits that national bankers earned from the high interest rates on the bonds that backed national banknotes. In response, they insisted that greenbacks be substituted for banknotes and that bonds be redeemed in greenbacks rather than gold so bloated financiers did not get still richer.[40] Most manufacturers, who often owned bonds themselves, and the Republicans who represented them in Congress denounced that scheme as repudiation, but they continued to oppose contraction of greenbacks until expansion of the banking system became possible.

The "money question" during Reconstruction, therefore, was extraordinarily complicated and would not be resolved, even temporarily, until 1875. Discussion of that resolution must be postponed, but three implications of financial issues for Reconstruction in the South require emphasis here. First, merchants and financiers who wanted the nation to accumulate enough gold to return to a specie standard pressured the government to facilitate the revival of southern cotton production for export, since the balance of international payments directly affected the nation's gold supply. That pressure in turn affected the organization of postwar southern agriculture and helped inhibit governmental policies that might allow blacks to set up as independent small farmers.[41] Second, both the Democratic and Republican parties were split along regional and factional lines by the money question, just as they were divided by the new labor militancy and cries for railroad regulation. Those internal party divisions constantly complicated quarrels over Reconstruction policy among authorities in Washington.

Third and most important, whatever political headaches the North's wartime fiscal and financial policies had created, they helped expand the vast disparity of wealth between North and South. Retaining the regressive excise taxes on consumer goods and high tariff duties after war-related expenditures stopped, the federal government began to accumulate a surplus of revenue as early as 1866 that equaled 2.8 percent of annual gross national product between 1866 and 1872 and averaged 1.7 percent of GNP from 1869 to 1878. Postponing the resumption of specie payments on greenbacks and banknotes, it instead used the surplus to buy back bonds, thus pumping hundreds of millions of dollars into the North's private economic sector. Much of this government-supplied capital was invested in the large factories that transformed northern industry in the 1870s.[42] Since access to this cornucopia of cash, credit, and capital depended on the ownership of United States bonds, southerners were excluded from it. Thus the bonds' availability in the North and absence from the South were major causes of the dramatically different economic trajectories of the two regions after the war.

## THE CHALLENGE OF RECONSTRUCTION

Northern economic and ideological legacies from the Civil War complicated the task of Reconstruction. They caused some Northerners to focus on their own problems and opportunities rather than on the South. Republican policy makers could hardly ignore the demands those northern constituents made on government, lest Democrats exploit them to oust Republicans from office. At the same time, addressing their constituents' situation influenced how they thought about the South and Reconstruction policy. The North's postwar prosperity, for example, clearly made many Republicans and northern businessmen less empathetic to the economic needs of their defeated foes than they might otherwise have been; calls to reduce taxes, shrink the national government, disband the army, and protect property rights limited Republicans' options for Reconstruction. Yet Republican policy makers in Washington could hardly ignore the challenge of Reconstruction if only because they themselves, like so many Northerners, were determined not to lose the fruits of their victory in the war. In seeking an advantageous peace settlement, however, Republican policy makers knew they were certain to face intransigent opposition from Democrats whose dislike of activist government and problack measures had been intensified by the war. The threat that Democrats might stage a comeback if Republicans flouted northern attitudes inhibited what they could do.

If northern conditions, attitudes, and partisan conflict influenced Republicans' attempts at Reconstruction, however, postwar conditions in the South and the reactions of white and black Southerners to them necessitated their efforts. As the loser of the Civil War, the South, not the North, was the primary target of Reconstruction. And when Washington policy makers looked southward in the spring of 1865, they discovered that many of the problems they had to address in the former Confederacy were also legacies of the Civil War.

## CHAPTER 25

The Challenge
of Reconstruction:
Legacies of the War in
the South

Transformations in the former Confederacy caused by the war decisively
shaped the agenda of Reconstruction and southerners' reactions to it.
The South's economy had been devastated. The end of slavery, bringing
joy to blacks and shocked disillusionment to many whites, necessitated a renego-
tiation of relationships between the races. Of all the efforts of postwar Americans to deal with new conditions created by the war, indeed, none was more
important than ex-slaves' attempt to give meaning to their new freedom, to carve
out a modicum of social and economic autonomy, and to secure equal civil and
political rights. White southerners, in contrast, were the first Americans to taste
the bitterness of military defeat. Their varied responses to that trauma help explain their reactions to blacks' aspirations and to federal Reconstruction policies.

## IMMEDIATE POSTWAR CHAOS

In 1865 black and white southerners awaited the North's decisions about
them with a mixture of trepidation, uncertainty, and hope. Rifts between whites
and blacks and between Confederate loyalists and white Unionists portended
fractious political conflicts. Immediately after the war, however, most white
southerners were less concerned about the political requirements for restoration
to the Union than about more urgent problems. Their economy lay in shambles.
Emancipation jarringly destroyed the legal basis for a centuries-old, if hugely unjust, system of social cohesion and suddenly forced a rearrangement of economic,
social, and legal relations between mutually suspicious blacks and whites. Freedmen and freedwomen sought to express their new status through physical mobility, a search for land of their own to farm, and immediate demands for civil and

political rights. Many white planters, meanwhile, feared that the reopening of federal courts in the South would result in the confiscation of their land under the as yet unenforced Confiscation Act of July 1862.[1] Civil order itself temporarily dissolved into anarchy. Southern society appeared on the brink of distintegration, and though some looked northward for help to avert it, others believed that any Yankee intervention would aggravate southerners' difficulties.

With the status of Confederate state and local governmental officials in doubt until northerners determined it, civil government broke down in many places during the first months after April 1865, law and order collapsed, and a wave of property and violent crime swept the urban and rural South. As the year 1865 progressed, much of this reign of terror was inflicted by angry whites on freedmen, but initially it was often perpetrated by discharged Confederate soldiers against the residents of communities through which they passed on the way home. "We have no currency, no law, save the primitive code that might makes right," a terrified Georgia woman wrote in her diary, while on May 4, 1865 the Macon, Georgia, *Telegraph* shrieked that the people of the South "face a prospect of anarchy and barbarien [sic] warfare" with "every man . . . forced onto his own resources, without the protecting arm of the law."[2]

Chaotic population movement into cities—by white refugees, disgruntled Confederate soldiers, and former slaves looking for family members, seeking new jobs or protection from Yankee troops, or simply expressing their freedom by abandoning plantations—not only aggravated social disorder. Massive inmigration also swelled urban populations far beyond the capacity of cities, whose supplies of food had been disrupted, adequately to feed them. Unable to find work, subject to crime and disease, the most destitute quickly faced the prospect of utter starvation.

To meet these emergencies, restore law and order, and help rebuild local infrastructure, many southerners, both white and black, looked eagerly for aid from the occupying Yankee armies. Some small communities such as Lexington, Virginia never saw a federal military or civilian official after the war, and they were forced to reorganize local governments and police forces on their own.[3] In much of the South for most of 1865, especially larger cities, however, the United States army was virtually the only source of law enforcement, local government, and economic relief. In retrospect, indeed, the army's role in bringing order out of chaos and micromanaging local governments with martial law in 1865 marked the most successful direct federal intervention in the South during the entire experiment of Reconstruction. It vividly illustrates what might have been done had pressure from civilians not forced the rapid demobilization of northern armies and the redeployment of most remaining troops to the West.

Richmond can serve as an example of patterns that occurred in Lynchburg, Natchez, Atlanta, and elsewhere. Within days of occupying the Confederate capital, Federal forces established a relief commission that made house-to-house visits searching for the destitute. By April 21, 1865, 128,000 rations had been distributed, and almost fifteen thousand persons had been given relief. Military officials also took over the day-to-day running of the city in the absence of civilian officials, appointing provost marshals to suppress crime, promulgating market and sanitation regulations, and rebuilding bridges. Indeed, so dependent were Richmond's residents on federal intervention that even though federal authorities permitted the election of a city council in July 1865 and of a mayor in October, and even though army commanders sought for months to transfer the task of law enforcement to local authorities, it was not until December 28, 1865, that a 120-man city police force inherited it. Not until April 1866 did military authorities fully turned responsibility for municipal government over to city officials.[4]

## A SHATTERED ECONOMY

If many Southerners welcomed the Yankees' help in restoring order and providing emergency assistance, their shattered economy in 1865 seemed equally in need of northern aid. Large portions of Richmond, Mobile, Columbia, and Atlanta had been gutted by fire; Vicksburg, Petersburg, and other cities had been shelled during sieges. As a northern traveler wrote of Richmond's burned-out business district in July 1865, "For a quarter of a mile one passes nothing but toppling walls, forlorn-looking chimneys, heaps of bricks, with here and there a

The ruins of Richmond, 1865

ruined safe lying in the midst, warped and red from the effects of the intense heat."[5] Hundreds of miles of railroad track had been torn up by invading Yankee armies, and heavy wartime traffic had worn out much of the rest. The South's industrial capacity had enjoyed truly miraculous expansion during the war, but much of the new manufacturing plant was geared to a now obsolete market for arms and ammunition while many other factories had been destroyed.

Long depleted of specie reserves, the region's banks held only now worthless Confederate bonds and currency and were effectively stifled from issuing new banknotes by the 1865 revision of the National Banking Act. The dearth of cash with legal value spawned a widely noted collapse of retail sales during 1865 in many cities. As one furniture dealer in Mobile, Alabama complained to a northern traveler, "Everybody . . . wanted to buy and nobody had any money." Thus he refused to reopen business until customers had cash, for "if he refused credit, he would make all his old customers enemies; if he gave credit he would soon be bankrupt." Small towns such as Lexington, Virginia reverted to a barter economy, but larger cities had to await economic recovery.[6]

Agricultural production, too, had been devastated. Plantations abandoned by owners seeking to escape invading Yankees sometimes stood in weeds. Elsewhere output had slumped when slaves took advantage of the chaos of war to flee to the Union armies or simply to defy the pleas of women and overseers to work as hard as they once had for now absent "massas." Bereft of menfolk and determined to avoid the hated Confederate impressment acts and taxes in kind, non-slaveholding white families also slowed food production. Rural areas of Virginia, Tennessee, Mississippi, Georgia, and South Carolina, moreover, had been denuded of crops by crisscrossing armies. The interior of South Carolina in 1865, wrote Carl Schurz, "looked for many miles like a broad black streak of ruin and desolation—the fences all gone; lonesome smoke stacks, surrounded by dark heaps of ashes and cinders, marking the spots where human habitations had stood; the fields along the road wildly overgrown by weeds, with here and there a sickly looking patch of cotton or corn cultivated by negro squatters."[7] By one estimate, in 1866 the average value of land in the Carolinas, Georgia, the Gulf states, and Arkansas was less than one-half of that in 1860.[8]

Beguiled by opportunities in the North and West, most Northerners saw no reason to invest their capital or seek their livelihoods in so bleak a region. Others did. Northern retail merchants set up shop and artisans sought work in occupied southern cities during and after the war. More significant, Northerners, lured by soaring cotton prices and the potential fortunes to be made in planting, had begun to lease or buy plantations in the occupied areas of the South during the war, and additional thousands did so immediately after it. Between 1861 and 1868, estimates their leading historian, "anywhere from twenty thousand to fifty thousand northerners tried their hands at planting," and they invested thousands of dollars to buy land, purchase seed, and pay wage labor. Most would fail for many of the same reasons that native southern planters did: insect infestations and bad weather that ravaged crops; inadequate credit supplies and usurious interest rates; and an inability to manage black workers who loathed the plantation discipline they associated with slavery. Nonetheless, these northerners hardly fitted the negative stereotype so long associated with the Reconstruction legend. Labeled *carpetbaggers* by generations of hostile white southerners, northerners who came South after the war and supported southern Republican parties were supposedly penniless opportunists who arrived with empty satchels and who hoped to use political office to fill them with plunder. Reaching the South well before northerners had any chance of gaining political office there, those who experimented with planting, in fact, sought economic opportunity, not political spoils, and they sank their own money in the South rather than looting southern taxpayers.[9]

Neither the investments by these northern entrepreneurs nor the rapid establishment of national banks in some cities like Richmond by the end of 1865, however, supplied enough funds to meet the South's desperate need for cash and credit. Aside from the emergency relief dispensed by the Freedmen's Bureau and the army in 1865, the federal government refused to subsidize the South's economic recovery. When Georgia's constitutional convention petitioned Congress in February 1868 for a $30 million loan "to the impoverished planters of the South," they were spurned, and even the later election of Republican congressmen from the South failed to secure federal subsidies for the region.[10] Nor would New York's financial community answer a request from the American Cotton Planters' Association for a $1 million loan in September 1865, even though cotton planters were willing to pay effective interest rates of 33 percent to obtain it.[11] In part as a result of these refusals to aid agriculture, the South's economic recovery was decidedly uneven.

## AN INCOMPLETE ECONOMIC RECOVERY

Physically devastated cities, railroads, and factories were quickly rebuilt, and by 1870 the South's manufacturing and transportation sectors had regained their prewar levels of productivity and growth. Manufacturing output expanded rapidly between 1870 and 1900, but it remained marginal to the southern economy as a whole. Manufacturers employed only 3.8 percent of the work force in cotton-producing states in 1870 and 6.5 percent by 1900.[12] Nor could this growth keep pace with northern industrial expansion, which started from a much larger base. The southern proportion of the nation's railroad mileage dropped from 26 percent in 1856 to 19 percent in 1879. Similarly, the South's share of the nation's manufacturing firms fell from 14.7 percent in 1860 to 11.5 percent in 1880; capital invested in southern manufacturing declined from 9.5 percent of the national total in 1860 to 4.8 percent in 1880.[13]

Agriculture remained the dominant sector of the South's economy, and it experienced two profound transformations after the war. First, although the South as a region had been largely self-sufficient in food production prior to 1860, after 1865 much of the acreage once planted in corn was devoted instead to cotton. As a result, by 1880 per capita production of corn, other grains, and hogs had dropped to half the 1860 level, and the South could no longer feed itself.[14] Second, staple-crop production, the chief source of the South's antebellum wealth, suffered a prolonged slump despite the conversion of more acreage to it. The most capital-intensive sectors of southern agriculture—rice and sugar—were especially devastated in 1865 and 1866. Rice output in the Georgia and South Carolina low country never recovered its prewar levels. Sugar production in Louisiana did, but only because northern investors, who had sufficient funds to pay high wages for the gang labor peculiarly necessary to that crop, bought out many antebellum planters.[15] Annual per capita output of cotton, by far the South's largest export crop, also declined dramatically. According to the economists Roger Ransom and Richard Sutch, in the five major cotton-producing states—South Carolina, Georgia, Alabama, Mississippi, and Louisiana—output stood at only 29.8 percent of the 1859 level in 1866, 57 percent by the late 1870s, and 75 percent as late as 1900.[16]

This prolonged agricultural slump rendered the once-prosperous South an economic basket case for the remainder of the nineteenth century, compared

### RELATIVE PER CAPITA INCOME, 1840–1900
### (U.S. AVERAGE = 100)

| Region | 1840 | 1860 | 1880 | 1900 |
|---|---|---|---|---|
| Northeast | 135 | 139 | 141 | 137 |
| Midwest | 68 | 68 | 98 | 103 |
| South | 76 | 72 | 51 | 51 |
| West | — | — | 190 | 163 |

### TOTAL PERSONAL INCOME BY REGION, 1840–1900
### (PERCENTAGE DISTRIBUTION)

| Region | 1840 | 1860 | 1880 | 1900 |
|---|---|---|---|---|
| Northeast | 58 | 50 | 44 | 41 |
| Midwest | 13 | 20 | 34 | 36 |
| South | 29 | 26 | 15 | 15 |
| West | — | 4 | 7 | 8 |

Source: Richard Easterlin, "Regional Income Trends 1840–1950," in *The Reinterpretation of American Economic History*, ed. Robert Fogel and Stanley Engerman (New York, 1971), pp. 40, 44.

with the booming North. By one estimate, whereas the North reached its prewar trajectory of economic growth by 1879, the South could not do so until 1909.[17] Indices of the regional distribution of per capita and aggregate income generated by the economist Richard Easterlin also illuminate the disparities.

Measured differently, whereas the per capita income of northerners *increased* by an average annual rate of 1.5 percent for twenty years after the start of the war, climbing in constant dollars from $128 in 1860 to $173 in 1880, the per capita income of southerners in the same period *decreased* by an average annual rate of 0.8 percent, falling from $103 in 1860 to $88 in 1880.[18]

Economic historians agree that the South's postwar poverty was rooted in the dismal performance of its agricultural sector, but one of the liveliest debates in all the literature on the postwar South concerns exactly what or who was responsible for this long-term stagnation. Some historians blame the shift of antebellum non-slaveholding white families from food to cotton production at a time when worldwide demand for cotton rapidly declined after 1865.[19] Others cite planters' disincentive to make ex-slaves grow food once they lost their capital investment in them and point out the endemic underemployment in any agricultural economy.[20] Ransom and Sutch attribute the slump to blacks' refusal to work like slaves once they became free and to the expropriation of agricultural workers' income by country merchants under the postwar crop lien system.[21] Others point to the destruction of the gang system of labor, the source of prewar plantations' productive efficiency.[22] And Gerald Jaynes faults "the serious inefficiencies in the southern credit markets" coupled with "the extreme fiscal conservativism of a ruling political party facing a large public debt" in the North that failed "to construct a 'Marshall Plan' for the reorganization of the cotton economy on the basis of free labor."[23] Some combination of these factors undoubtedly produced the end result. Understanding why, however, requires closer examination of readjustments in both parts of the South's "dual" antebellum economy: the black-belt, staple-crop-producing plantation sector that relied on slave labor and the geographically separated upcountry regions populated primarily by non-slaveholding white families.

## THE REORGANIZATION OF SOUTHERN AGRICULTURE

Though spared the economic and emotional trauma of emancipation, non-slaveholders still suffered grievously from the war. Traditionally these small farmers had grown food to subsist their families rather than export crops. They tried to avoid the perils of a market economy that might force them into debt that could jeopardize their ownership of land. With men away in the armies and remaining family members unable to sustain crop production during the war, however, they often had to borrow money to buy food at its inflated wartime prices. Owed to merchants, shopkeepers, bankers, and other private individuals,

Initially, many freedmen hoped to grow food for their families rather than staple crops; the photograph at the top shows farmers planting sweet potatoes. But soon most returned to the production of cotton as tenants or sharecroppers, as shown in the bottom photograph.

these debts must be distinguished from the public debts contracted by Confederate state and national governments during the war. But they were debts, nonetheless. They forced small farmers into cotton production in order to obtain cash to pay them off, thereby drastically reducing corn and hog production in the South. By 1876 white farmers grew 40 percent of the South's cotton crop, whereas black laborers had cultivated 90 percent of it in 1860. Cotton growing, however, proved as risky as yeomen had always feared. By 1880 one-third of the white farmers in the cotton states were sharecroppers—that is, employed agricultural workers paid in a share of the crop they grew rather than cash—or tenants, not independent farm owners.[24]

But the root of the South's economic problem lay in the plantation districts, and there, emancipation made all the difference. To resume production at pre-war levels, planters needed control of black labor power, but the abolition of slavery ended their ability to coerce it and, equally important, to pay for it. Compulsory uncompensated emancipation was the largest governmental expropriation of private property this nation has ever experienced. According to Ransom and Sutch, for example, the two million slaves who resided in South Carolina, Georgia, Alabama, Mississippi, and Louisiana in 1860 were worth approximately $1.6 billion, or 45.8 per cent of the total capital assets of those states.[25] Extrapolating those estimates to the almost four million slaves living in all the slave states in 1860 meant that slaveholders lost over $3 billion, over two-fifths of the South's capital assets, as a result of emancipation.

Some have argued that the region as a whole suffered no net loss since the value of black labor power remained in the South, but labor power "owned" by millions of individual blacks was hardly the equivalent of the capital assets represented by slaves whose owners could sell them or use them as collateral for obtaining loans.[26] Market-oriented agriculture has always depended on the availability of credit to finance farmers while their crops are in the ground. Just as northern manufacturers needed an ample credit supply to meet weekly payrolls, so planters needed credit to grow cotton. As slaveholders, they could command it in ample supply because creditors knew that planters could sell slaves if necessary to pay their debts. Emancipation thus robbed slaveholders of a source of collateral while forcing them to find the means to pay free laborers.

The trajectory of economic organization in southern agriculture after the Civil War was thus the polar opposite of that of northern manufacturing. Northern industrialists such as Armour and Carnegie amassed capital resources during the war or after it and used them to expand and consolidate productive capacity and thereby achieve economies of scale. Thus, in the 1870s, the North's manufacturing sector evolved from lightly capitalized, small firms with tiny work forces to huge, capital-intensive factories that often employed thousands. Planters had possessed similar resources before the war, but now had lost them. Because postwar planters failed to obtain the credit from merchants, the New York money market, or Congress to pay the cash wages necessary to operate on a large scale, the organization of southern agriculture evolved "from a network of centralized plantation factories—operated with slave gang labor—to a network of decentralized *domestic* production units," the small farms tilled by white and black tenants and sharecroppers.[27]

By freeing blacks from the legal control of white slaveholders, emancipation spurred this transformation in other ways. No longer able to command or coerce black labor at will, white planters now had to bid for it. And the freedmen had their own ideas about whom they would work for, how they would work, and what they wanted to grow. Thus the reorganization of staple-crop southern agriculture was part of a larger process of renegotiating race relationships in the South that was central to Reconstruction and that was also vitally affected by what had already happened during the war.

## CONTESTED MEANINGS OF FREEDOM: BLACK ASPIRATIONS VERSUS WHITE EXPECTATIONS

From the moment that hundreds of thousands of slaves secured their freedom during the war by escaping to Union army lines, blacks and northern white military and civilian officials had divergent views of what that freedom meant. African Americans defined freedom not simply as an end to the brutalities of slavery and a chance to reunite families and educate children, but as independence from the domination and supervision of all whites, not just their former masters, and as autonomy both as individuals and as a black community.[28] As their burning of cotton gins on abandoned plantations indicated, moreover, if they remained farmers, they wanted to grow food for their families as white nonslaveholders once had, not staple crops for market. Above all, they wanted land of their own to farm, rather than to return to work for "whitey" on plantations with their coercive discipline and hated labor-intensive gang systems.

During the war, however, blacks who achieved freedom only by reaching Union army lines found these "expectations . . . foreign to those of Northern planters and military officers."[29] Rather than being allowed to move where they wanted and to do what they wanted and rather than escaping white control, they were herded into refugee camps, forcefully impressed as laborers for the Union army, and dragooned into Union army units. Others were assigned to plantations where they worked for northern planters who often hired their old overseers or occasionally for their former masters themselves. In short, northerners had no intention of honoring blacks' definition of freedom or allowing them to grow food. They wanted cotton and other staple-crop production resumed as rapidly as possible and were prepared to compel those blacks who were not used as soldiers or army laborers to do so. Equally important, as the historian Louis S. Gerteis writes, "The decisions made during the war concerning the treatment, organization, and employment of Southern blacks shaped postwar policies toward the freedman and in large measure precluded the possibility of radical social reconstruction in the South."[30]

During the war a few blacks managed to acquire land of their own, notably on South Carolina's Port Royal islands, which had been captured by Union troops in November 1861, or to farm free of white supervision, as on Jefferson Davis' own plantation in Mississippi. More common, however, was the experience of those in Louisiana and the lower Mississippi Valley. Compelled to work for planters under contracts whose terms were dictated by Union army officers—including first Ben Butler and then Nathaniel P. Banks in Louisiana—they were required to remain on plantations for the entire growing season, forcibly returned by Yankee soldiers if they tried to leave, and paid minimal wages, half of which were usually reserved until the crop was harvested. So reminiscent were these conditions of slavery that articulate free blacks in New Orleans accurately complained that "our freedmen, on the plantations, at the present time, could more properly be called, mock-freedmen."[31]

Blacks had more opportunities to express what they meant by freedom once the war ended and emancipation was completed. Geographic mobility was one. Within weeks, days, and even hours of achieving freedom, blacks by the thousands left the plantations on which they lived to look for family members, to seek excitement, jobs, or protection in cities, or simply to shun former masters for whom they now refused to work. They created separate black institutions that had been prohibited under the slave regime: churches, fraternal organizations and burial societies, and political associations. Hungry for education, blacks with the aid of northern benevolent societies and the Freedmen's Bureau also established their own schools, many of which were initially taught by idealistic northern women like those who had gone to the Port Royal islands during the war.[32]

War's end also improved blacks' chances to get their own land, for in early 1865 the federal government adopted two measures that betokened federal land distribution to the freedmen and generated widespread rumors that the government would give each black family forty acres and a mule. Anxious to free his army from the black refugees who had swarmed after it on his march across Georgia and reassured by Secretary of War Edwin Stanton's express approval, on January 16, 1865, General Sherman issued Special Field Order No. 15. This order set aside the coastal area running from Charleston south to Jacksonville, Florida and thirty miles inland for the exclusive settlement of blacks. Each black family was to be given a temporary "possessory title" to forty acres of land until Congress "shall regulate the title." Although the purpose of this measure may well have been to segregate the races by quarantining blacks in a small corner of the South, by June 1865 forty thousand freedmen had taken up farms in the area.[33]

Two months after Sherman's decree, in early March 1865, Congress created the Bureau of Refugees, Freedmen, and Abandoned Lands, popularly known thereafter as the Freedmen's Bureau, in the War Department to provide aid to the South's most destitute. In its first 15 months of operation it distributed over thirteen million free rations and established hundreds of schools and hospitals across Dixie. It was also empowered to distribute some eight hundred thousand acres of abandoned and confiscated land in forty-acre lots for rental and eventual sale with "such title as the United States can convey."[34]

As the first substantial piece of congressional legislation for Reconstruction that became law, this measure and the debate over it revealed ambivalent attitudes among northern policy makers about race and about enhanced federal power that would also dilute subsequent laws. Deleted from the abbreviated popular title, "Refugees" referred explicitly to whites who were included among the agency's beneficiaries because Republican congressmen, who raised the cry of "no discrimination according to color" during debate, adamantly refused to allow the government to give preferential treatment to blacks. Reflecting the determination to retrench government expenditures as well as fears that a permanent welfare agency would sap blacks' willingness to work for their living, the bill also stipulated that the agency could operate for only one year after the war ended, which meant it was due to expire during the spring of 1866. This time limit made the promises of three-year rentals and eventual purchase of government land hollow, and, in any event, attempts to distribute that land during 1865 proved stillborn.[35]

Rather than distributing land in small plots to individual black families, in fact, federal authorities in the South vigorously continued their wartime policy of compelling black workers to resume staple-crop production. No long needing black manpower, army officers now devoted their energies to keeping freedmen out of cities and forcing them back to the plantations. Thus their attempt to bring order out of chaos in 1865 consisted in part of denying rations to blacks to force them to leave cities, arresting as vagrants those who refused, and consigning them to planters who paid their fines. Freedmen's Bureau agents now mediated the contracts between planters eager for labor and blacks who often gave it only because starvation was the alternative. And those contracts imposed on freedmen once again required blacks to stay with the same employer for the full year for meager wages that often went unpaid.[36]

The insistence of federal authorities that blacks work on staple-producing plantations and the army's readiness to arrest blacks who resisted the plantation regime as vagrants taught southern planters, who attempted to follow the Yankees' example, two lessons. First, even though emancipation ended individual masters' ability to coerce labor, the coercive authority of the state might be substituted for it. Second, mistaking what the army did for evidence of what the northern public expected, white Southerners would make punitive and discriminatory vagrancy provisions that forced arrested blacks to work central features of the notorious "black codes," the laws enacted by southern state legislatures in 1865 and 1866 to regain control of the black labor force.[37]

If federal policies that negated blacks' definition of freedom gave desperate planters access to black labor, however, they failed to revive plantation production. Not only did many planters lack the cash to pay large labor gangs, but without the powers of physical coercion intrinsic to slavery, they often could not force blacks to work like slaves. Unable to farm independently, freedmen could still refuse to labor in gangs or for as many hours of the day or days in a month as they once had. Reuniting as nuclear families as rapidly as possible after the war, blacks initially also refused to allow women and children to work in fields as they once had. According to Ransom and Sutch, in South Carolina, Georgia, Alabama, Mississippi, and Louisiana this withdrawal of black labor power against the wishes of white employers resulted in a total decline of hours worked that ranged between 28 and 37 percent and that by itself accounted for the dramatic decline in per capita cotton output in those states.[38]

Planters' inability to afford or coerce gang labor and black families' refusal to work as hard as they once had forced a financial and physical reorganization of the cotton economy that began in some places as early as 1865 and 1866. Rather than a single unit characterized by a planter's or overseer's control over a concentrated pool of black laborers who lived together in slave quarters as in antebellum days, plantations were subdivided into scattered small plots, usually of less than forty acres. These were occupied and farmed by individual black families who set their own work rhythms, but who, once the system was in place, often returned women and children to the fields to work on crops just as white farm families did.

The rental arrangements for these plots and the autonomy black and later white families on them had in crop selection varied enormously. Some formal

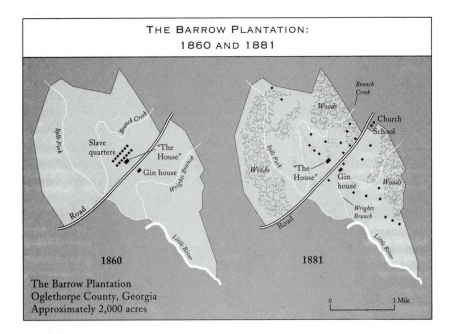

THE BARROW PLANTATION:
1860 AND 1881

1860

1881

The Barrow Plantation
Oglethorpe County, Georgia
Approximately 2,000 acres

0        1 Mile

leases required tenants to pay annual rents in cash or a share of their crops. More common were sharecropping contracts that usually called for dividing the crop into three equal shares. A third went to the planter, a third to the laborer, and a third went to whichever party provided the seeds, fertilizer, mules, and other farming equipment. When planters provided the seeds, they insisted that staple cash crops, not food, be grown since they wanted to maximize the cash return on their sole remaining capital asset, their land itself. If croppers supplied seeds, they theoretically could have grown only food. But they quickly became dependent for credit on small country merchants, who soon replaced large, urban factors as the South's chief credit suppliers, and who, like planters, insisted that sharecroppers and tenants grow cotton.

Never as efficient as the old plantations, this system represented a compromise for both white planters and African American laborers. Unable to obtain credit in sufficient amounts to resume the gang system with cash wages, planters effectively shifted the burden of credit and risk to the freedmen themselves, for they could not be paid until the crop came in. By making the freedmen's income dependent upon the size of the crop they grew, moreover, planters gave black families—men, women, and children—a powerful incentive to invest more collective hours in that crop. Though denied the independent ownership of land for which they yearned and forced to grow staple crops, the freedmen, in turn, obtained a degree of economic autonomy and freedom from the immediate, day-to-day white supervision and observation they had loathed under slavery.

## TOWARD POLITICAL RECONSTRUCTION

Much of the reorganization of southern agriculture occurred outside the political arena, but state power was hardly irrelevant to it. The struggle between blacks and whites over control of land and labor in the South could be influenced by governmental policies. Long before the process of agricultural reorganization was completed, planters and other white Southerners sought to apply the lesson they had learned from Yankee occupiers by substituting state power over blacks for individual masters' authority. Yet their ability to use local and state governments to accomplish that goal depended on whom the victorious Northerners allowed to run them. Thus what happened *within* the South could be determined by what happened *between* the North and South, by the peace terms that the Yankees imposed on their defeated foes. And just as legacies from the Civil War had shaped so many of the internal postwar social and economic developments in the two sections, so they set important precedents for Reconstruction as an intersectional political and constitutional settlement.

| # Presidential Reconstruction

As a political process, Reconstruction after the Civil War encompassed the efforts by Republican authorities in Washington to frame and implement a peace settlement for the defeated Confederacy. That program sought to secure the fruits of northern victory, protect the rights of former slaves, and restore seceded states to participation in national political life. Presidential Reconstruction usually refers to the phase of that process when President Andrew Johnson, rather than Congress, took the initiative in formulating the terms that Confederates must meet to achieve those goals.

Presidential Reconstruction, however, actually began in 1861 when the necessity of politically reuniting the nation and providing civil government to Union-occupied areas in the South first emerged. Wartime jousts between Lincoln and Congress over attempts to establish loyal pro-Union civilian governments in the seceded states raised questions about those states' constitutional status, jurisdictional authority over federal policy, and Reconstruction's purpose. Those quarrels set vital precedents for Johnson's subsequent program and his disputes with Congress over it.

## PRESIDENTIAL RECONSTRUCTION UNDER LINCOLN

In the spring of 1861, with Congress out of session, Lincoln inaugurated Reconstruction by encouraging developments in Virginia that he hoped residents of other Confederate states would soon emulate. At Lincoln's urging and with his promise of federal military protection from Confederates, western Virginians, who had strongly opposed the state's secession on April 17, quickly established a loyal state government for Virginia. A June convention at Wheeling representing some forty-eight counties, most from the trans-Allegheny region, elected Francis H. Pierpont governor of the "Restored Government of Virginia." State legislators from the same counties shortly thereafter chose two United States senators, John S. Carlile and Waitman T. Willey. Three Unionist congressmen elected during the earlier May congressional contests also sought seats in the House.

Even though only a minority of white Virginians supported Pierpont's government (a minority that shrank dramatically when West Virginia became a separate state in 1863), Virginia illustrated Lincoln's preferred mode of reconstruction. "Lincoln's wartime aim," according to the historian William C. Harris, "was to establish loyalty and civil government in the South as soon as possible."[1] Mistakenly convinced that the great majority of white southerners had been dragged into secession through the demagoguery of hotheads, Lincoln believed that loyalists would repudiate the Confederacy. He hoped that such men, once safe behind Union army lines, would create loyal state governments that would serve as nuclei around which other Unionists could rally. Insisting that individuals but not states had seceded, he sought the fastest possible *restoration* of southern states to their rightful place in Congress. He thereby hoped to avert a fundamental *reconstruction*, dictated from Washington, of their internal social, economic, and political arrangements *before* their readmission to Congress.

The promptness with which Unionist Virginians acted thus gratified him. In his July 4, 1861 message to Congress, Lincoln recognized Virginia's shadow government "as being Virginia," and to his joy Congress allowed the Virginia senators and representatives to take their seats. Even better, Indiana's Republican senator Henry Lane announced, "We expect soon to readmit Tennessee into the Union, as we have recently readmitted old Virginia; we expect soon to readmit North Carolina."[2] This attitude pleased Lincoln, for he consistently acknowledged the right of Congress, not the executive, to determine who could sit in that body. By eschewing sterner policies in favor of Virginia's rapid readmission, congressional Republicans appeared, if only briefly, to concur with Lincoln's commitment to "the principle of self-reconstruction controlled by southern white Unionists" and with his opposition to attempts by Congress to govern white southerners through edicts imposed from Washington.[3]

As soon as Congress reassembled in the winter of 1861–1862, however, a few Radical Republicans challenged Lincoln's conception and control of reconstruction. Senator Charles Sumner and Congressman James Ashley introduced bills insisting that Congress, not Lincoln, must set the terms of restoration. They argued that seceding states had reverted to a territorial status that Congress could govern directly by federal statute and insisted that emancipation, confiscation of rebels' land, and a permanent proscription of most Confederates' political rights must accompany any program of reunion. Those proposals were quashed, but over time congressional Republicans' complaints against Lincoln's policies increased.[4] Despite this mounting opposition, Lincoln retained the initiative until mid-1864.

Lincoln envisioned the restoration of Unionist self-government proceeding "simultaneously with the armed suppression of the rebellion."[5] As soon as Union armies invaded the Confederacy in 1862, therefore, he commissioned military governors to administer civil affairs in occupied areas and to launch the restoration process. Uncertain Union control over often small shards of territory and limited Unionist sentiment within those areas during 1862 prevented any attempt in North Carolina, Arkansas, and Texas to create loyal state governments. But in March, he installed Andrew Johnson in Tennessee and gave him "such powers as may be necessary and proper to enable the loyal people of Tennessee to present such a republican form of government, as will entitle the State to the guaranty of the United States therefor."[6] As early as July 3, 1862, Lincoln urged Johnson that "if we could, somehow, get a vote of the people of Tennessee and have it result properly, it would be worth more to us than a battle gained." He also clearly expected Colonel George Shepley, Louisiana's military governor, to arrange elections for a new state government as well.[7] Throughout 1862, however, Shepley did nothing, and Johnson, citing continued Confederate control of East Tennessee, the stronghold of die-hard anti-Confederate sentiment, refused to do so.[8]

Thwarted in his hope for the quick creation of loyal *state* governments, Lincoln in the fall of 1862 began to urge military governors in occupied areas to hold *congressional* elections to demonstrate those areas' loyalty to the Union. Here Lincoln's reconstruction policy became inextricably entangled with his movement toward emancipation. His appointed governors insisted that any move toward federally imposed emancipation would ruin the effort to create loyal state governments.[9] Lincoln therefore sought to keep proslavery southern Unionists "from deserting the cause and undermining his hopes for early restoration of the states to the Union." He explicitly promised in his Preliminary Emancipation Proclamation of September 22, 1862 that portions of rebel states represented by duly elected members in Congress on January 1, 1863 would be exempted from emancipation. Between September 22 and January 1, moreover, he repeatedly urged his governors and other federal officials to arrange congressional elections in occupied areas to exploit that escape hatch, and ultimately he exempted the occupied counties of eastern Virginia, occupied Louisiana, and all of Tennessee from his final Emancipation Proclamation.[10]

After January 1, 1863, however, Lincoln insisted that emancipation was a price of restoration, even in Tennessee and Louisiana, where he now pressed his governors and military commanders to secure abolition by state constitutional amendment. Congressional Republicans applauded that determination, but still they resented Lincoln's rush to restore self-government and congressional representation to men whose loyalty they doubted. Of the men chosen in the hastily arranged 1862 congressional elections in occupied areas, they seated only two representatives from Louisiana, where turnout approached antebellum levels, and then only for the few remaining days of the Thirty-seventh Congress. Meanwhile, Lincoln's and congressional Republicans' insistence on emancipation helped retard the creation of loyal state governments in Tennessee and Louisiana during 1863 since conservative slaveholding Unionists in each were determined to preserve the exemption from abolition granted by Lincoln in January.[11]

Frustrated by this delay, Lincoln announced a new policy in a Proclamation of Amnesty and Reconstruction on December 8, 1863.[12] Excluding some high-ranking civilian and military Confederate officials. Lincoln offered pardon to all Confederate supporters who took an oath of future allegiance to the United States and pledged to abide by all executive and congressional actions regarding emancipation. Amnesty carried with it the restoration of political rights to vote and hold office as well as property rights, except in slaves. He further stipulated that whenever the number of eligible white male voters taking this oath reached 10 percent of the number of votes cast in a state in the 1860 presidential election, those voters could "re-establish a State government which shall . . . be recognized as the true government of the State."

Though congressional Republicans cheered Lincoln's requirement of abolition for new state governments to receive recognition, other provisions of his policy challenged their expectations about Reconstruction. They had reached a consensus during the summer of 1863 that new state constitutions abolishing slavery must be adopted before elections of new state governments. Lincoln's December proclamation, significantly, did *not* require that sequence. In addition, Lincoln's provisions for pardon promised to spare Confederates' land from the Confiscation Act of July 1862 and to restore political rights to far more Confederates than many congressional Republicans thought tolerable. By "suggest[ing]" in his proclamation that the names and prewar boundaries of southern states should be retained, moreover, Lincoln also rejected congressional schemes for reducing Confederate states to territorial status.[13]

Finally, Lincoln's clear intention that only whites govern southern states angered the few Radical Republicans who were already clamoring that some, if not all, adult African American males be given suffrage. Indeed, he appeared to backtrack on emancipation itself. No doubt thinking about the labor arrangements for blacks that General Nathaniel P. Banks had worked out in Louisiana, which Louisiana's free blacks and many congressional Republicans were already protesting as a form of reenslavement, Lincoln seemed to endorse state-imposed apprenticeship systems in the South that might deny freedmen full freedom.[14]

Nonetheless, in December 1863 most congressional Republicans seemed prepared to let Lincoln have his way. Radicals and more moderate Republicans liked different aspects of the plan. With northern victory in the war apparently imminent at the end of 1863 and Lincoln's popularity correspondingly high in the North, moreover, few congressional Republicans had the stomach openly to challenge him. Only later in 1864, when Lincoln's popularity plummeted because of the military stalemate in Virginia and Georgia and when congressmen had seen how the 10 percent plan worked out in the South would their long-simmering grievances against Lincoln's attempt at presidential reconstruction boil over.

## THE 10 PERCENT PLAN IN OPERATION

Nowhere in the Confederacy did Lincoln's new program produce the results he sought. Virginia's already recognized, if woefully unrepresentative, "Restored Government of Virginia" had purposely been excluded from its terms. At Lincoln's urging, Pierpont called a constitutional convention consisting of only seventeen men from thirteen counties, and in March 1864 it issued a new state constitution for Virginia that abolished slavery and disfranchised all Virginians who voluntarily supported the Confederacy after January 1, 1864. This document remained Virginia's official state constitution until 1870,[15] but it was never submitted for popular ratification and the assemblage that wrote it hardly met Lincoln's minimal 10 percent test of loyalty. Aside from Senator John Carlile, himself a resident of West Virginia, moreover, Virginia had no representatives in the Thirty-eighth Congress. The full political reconstruction of Virginia awaited postwar developments.

Complete restoration also eluded Arkansas during the war. In January 1864 a convention representing twenty-three of the state's fifty-seven counties adopted a constitution that abolished slavery; in March it was ratified by a vote of 12,179 to 220, more than double the 10 percent requirement. On the same day, voters elected the staunch Unionist Isaac Murphy governor, as well as three congressmen and a new legislature that then chose two new United States senators. But congressional Republicans refused to seat Arkansas' representatives and senators, and in June, by a vote of 27 to 6, the Senate resolved that Murphy's state government was illegitimate because it was propped up by federal military support and therefore lacked the republican form guaranteed by the Constitution. This vote represented an explicit repudiation of Lincoln's policy.[16]

Nor did Lincoln's 10 percent plan lead to restored statehood for Tennessee. There the real problem was the growing division between ex-Whig Unionists from West and Middle Tennessee, who hoped to retain slavery, and the Democratic military governor Andrew Johnson, who had blocked an election in 1863 and who began that year to push for a new, antislavery state constitution. Throughout 1864 Johnson refused to administer the oath of allegiance prescribed by Lincoln, considering it far too lenient, or to hold elections for a new state government. In the 1864 presidential election, Johnson and his East Tennessee supporters confined the right to vote to those who subscribed to a draconian loyalty oath that proscribed all Confederate sympathizers. Though Lincoln criticized his running mate's heavy-handed intervention in arranging this election, some thirty thousand Tennesseans voted for Lincoln in November; five thousand defiant souls backed McClellan.[17]

With a new career in Washington beckoning, Johnson finally pressed ahead with the creation of a new state government. In January 1865, a state convention called and dominated by his die-hard Unionist East Tennessee supporters adopted a new state constitution abolishing slavery and invalidating the state's secession ordinance. It also stipulated that only those eligible to vote in the recent presidential contest—that is, no one who had ever supported the Confederacy in any way—could vote to ratify the new constitution and choose new state officers. In February the constitution won overwhelming ratification by the few Tennesseans who participated. On March 4, staunch anti-Confederate Unionists won control of the new state legislature, and William G. "Parson" Brownlow became the governor. Nonetheless, no Tennessean was seated in Congress until the summer of 1866, more than a year after Lincoln's assassination.[18]

## LOUISIANA AND THE CONGRESSIONAL BACKLASH AGAINST LINCOLN

Developments in Louisiana during 1863 and 1864 provoked congressional Republicans into an open break with Lincoln.[19] Throughout 1863 confused responsibility between the military governor, George F. Shepley, and the new military commander, Nathaniel P. Banks, prevented the calling of elections for a new state government. More important, Unionists from the sugar-growing parishes hoped to stop state abolition of slavery, whereas by the summer of 1863 those in heavily populated New Orleans, along with Lincoln, insisted on it. Further complicating this tangled situation was the labor policy that Banks imposed on the state early in 1863. It established a kind of quasi-freedom for blacks by requiring owners to pay them wages while forcing blacks to remain on plantations. Slaveholding Unionists denounced this as a step toward emancipation, and it increased their reluctance to support any movement to establish a free state. In contrast, New Orleans' well-educated free blacks and the many northern-born antislavery men in that city, who had the ear of Radical Republicans in Congress, complained that Banks was stopping emancipation to pacify slaveholders. In no Confederate state did the future status of blacks play so integral a role in wartime reconstruction as in Louisiana. By the fall of 1863 the most radical elements of the New Orleans antislavery Unionists, led by Thomas J. Durant, were demanding that at least free blacks be given the vote, a call applauded by some Radical Republicans in Congress.

The smear campaign against Banks became all important, for Lincoln, seeking to break the gridlock in Louisiana, sent Banks a letter on December 24, 1863 declaring him, not Shepley, "master of all" in Louisiana and ordering him to "give us a free-state reorganization of Louisiana, in the shortest possible time."[20] For over a year, grumbling about Lincoln's use of military governors who lacked statutory authority had been growing in Congress. By placing a military commander directly in charge of Louisiana's political reconstruction Lincoln increased congressional concern about military tyranny that subverted republican self-government.

Banks then compounded the damage. For months the New Orleans antislavery Unionists and especially Durant's radicals, like congressional Republicans, had insisted that a constitutional convention be held to abolish slavery, reapportion the legislature, and perhaps enfranchise blacks *before* any elections for state officials. Fearing that conservative sugar planters would boycott such a convention, Banks instead called for the election of a governor and other statewide officials under the terms of the antebellum constitution in February and the subsequent election of delegates to a constitutional convention that would abolish slavery. Now the Unionists split wide apart. The proslavery Unionists ran a gubernatorial candidate, but so did each of the radical and more moderate factions of the New Orleans Unionists. Banks openly supported Michael Hahn, the moderates' candidate and the eventual winner. Hahn endorsed emancipation, and his supporters subsequently abolished slavery in the new constitution. Long before that document was completed, however, Hahn's radical enemies in Louisiana demanded that Congress declare both Hahn's government and the new constitution invalid because of military intervention in the elections.

Further inflaming congressional reaction, Louisiana's reconstruction became entangled with the Republicans' struggle over the 1864 presidential nomination. Banks, Hahn, and the Louisiana moderates sided with Lincoln; Durant, Shepley, and the radical Louisianans sided with Treasury Secretary Salmon Chase and congressional Radicals who opposed Lincoln's renomination. In short, to his intraparty foes Lincoln appeared so eager to build a political machine among southern Unionists that he was prepared to accept unrepublican elections, to sanction an apprenticeship program like Banks's that denied full black freedom, and perhaps even to sacrifice constitutionally mandated state abolition.

In 1864, developments in Louisiana helped catalyze a backlash against Lincoln's policies. With elections impending in the fall, congressional Republicans were frustrated by Lincoln's easy renomination, by his apparent willingness to incorporate suspect southern Unionists into the newly renamed Union party, and by the as yet inconclusive results of the apparently polluted procedures in Louisiana. In retaliation, furious congressional Republicans passed the Wade-Davis bill on July 2, 1864 to provide an antislavery and stern anti-Confederate platform on which to go to the polls.[21]

Named after its chief House and Senate sponsors, Maryland's Henry Winter Davis and Ohio's Ben Wade, the Wade-Davis bill had four goals. It signaled unequivocally Congress's repudiation of reconstruction by executive proclamation and insisted that reconstruction rest on the authority of congressional statutes.[22] It sought to reassure civilian control of the process and to bring it into accord with the republican principle of majority rule by rejecting Lincoln's 10 percent formula. It tried to guarantee that abolition would precede restoration of congressional representation and internal self-governance for Confederate states. And, most important as far as Lincoln was concerned, it aimed at postponing political reconstruction until after complete Confederate defeat.

The bill emancipated *all* slaves within rebellious states, declared that "they and their posterity shall be forever free," and threatened any southerner who attempted to keep blacks in "involuntary servitude" with stiff fines and imprisonment.[23] The bill also called for Lincoln to appoint provisional civilian governors, who would require Senate confirmation, to administer civil government until the war was over. Once all military resistance to the United States had completely ceased within a state, its governor was to enroll all its white male citizens and to require them to take an oath of future allegiance to the United States. When the number taking that oath reached 50 percent of the total enrolled, then the governor was to hold elections for delegates to a constitutional convention. The new constitution must explicitly abolish slavery, repudiate state and Confederate bonds used to support the rebellion, and proscribe from the right to hold office in or vote for the new state government anyone who had held a state or national office under the Confederacy or a military commission at the rank of colonel or above.[24] Only after those constitutions were ratified by a majority of qualified voters could the president, "after obtaining the assent of Congress," recognize the new government as valid, and could the state elect members of Congress.

What made this bill so much more punitive than Lincoln's 10 percent plan, however, were certain other provisions. The bill stipulated that no one could vote for delegates to the new constitutional conventions, serve in those conventions, or vote in the ratification elections (which would also choose new state officials) who could not take the so-called iron-clad test oath that they had never supported or sympathized with the Confederacy. The bill, in short, would force the Confederate majority to turn control of their new state governments over to die-hard Unionists whom Confederates considered traitors to the South. It further stipulated that on the bill's enactment into law, anyone who continued to hold state or national office or high military rank under the Confederacy would be forever stripped of United States citizenship, whereas Lincoln's promise of future pardons had no time limit whatsoever. Finally, unlike Lincoln's amnesty proclamation, the bill made no mention of restoring property rights when one took an oath of allegiance.

Lincoln refused to sign the bill within ten days of Congress' adjournment, thereby killing it. He also issued an extraordinary public proclamation justifying his pocket veto on the grounds that he refused "to be inflexibly committed to any single plan of restoration," to recognize "a constitutional competency in Congress to abolish slavery in the States," or to discourage "the loyal citizens" of Louisiana and Arkansas by invalidating the free state governments they had already established. As if to mock the congressional Republicans he had stifled, Lincoln then called their procedure "one very proper plan for the loyal people of any State choosing to adopt it," and he promised to aid them in following it by appointing *military* governors to administer it.[25]

Recognizing the necessity of rallying behind Lincoln to stop Democrats from winning the presidential election, most congressional Republicans swallowed their anger and remained silent. Wade and Davis, however, published a "manifesto" in August denouncing Lincoln's pocket veto as a "studied outrage on the legislative authority." They flayed him for clinging to "the lawless discretion of Military Governors and Provost Marshals" and for failing to ensure emancipation or to deal with the issues of "the rebel debt and the political exclusion of rebel leaders."[26] Lincoln's successful reelection strengthened his hand within the party and his determination to win congressional recognition of the Louisiana government, but attempts at compromise between the two branches failed. At the time of his assassination in April 1865, Congress had refused to readmit anyone from Louisiana, Tennessee, Arkansas, and Virginia, but it had also failed to pass its own legislative program to guide the reconstruction process.

These controversies suggested that black suffrage might become a central and explosive issue of postwar Reconstruction. During the winter of 1864–1865 the most promising compromise between Lincoln and congressional Republicans coupled congressional recognition of the state governments in Arkansas and Louisiana with a requirement that other Confederate states must include suffrage for black soldiers, if not all black males, in their new constitutions before gaining readmission. The bill died in part because many Republicans and all Democrats found that requirement unacceptable. It was also defeated because Radical Republicans in the Senate, led by Charles Sumner, blocked Louisiana's readmission because its new constitution failed to give blacks the vote.

That failure was hardly Lincoln's fault. Seeking to neutralize congressional opposition and shore up Unionist strength in Louisiana, Lincoln in a private letter to Governor Michael Hahn on March 13, 1864 had "barely suggest[ed]" that the upcoming constitutional convention grant the vote to "some of the colored people . . . as, for instance, the very intelligent, and especially those who have fought gallantly in our ranks."[27] Hahn showed Lincoln's letter to delegates, and he and Banks lobbied the convention to heed Lincoln's wishes. But the best they could obtain, after a considerable struggle, was a clause in the new constitution authorizing the state legislature to enfranchise blacks who had served in the army, paid taxes, or were evidently intelligent. Though this authorization, along with other clauses providing for black education and equal rights for both races before the law, marked a considerable achievement for a former slave state, the subsequent legislature refused to enfranchise blacks or to provide for their schooling.[28]

Lincoln returned to the question of black suffrage in his last public statement about Reconstruction on April 11, 1865, three days before his assassination.[29] Dismissing the question of whether seceded states "are in the Union or out of it" as "a merely pernicious abstraction," he renewed his commitment to the Louisiana government. Even though "I would myself prefer" that the vote be granted to "the very intelligent" blacks and "those who serve our cause as soldiers," Louisiana deserved recognition. Continuing to deny Louisiana Unionists readmission would "reject, and spurn them," strip Louisiana's slaves of the freedom already granted them, and nullify a sure vote for ratification of the Thirteenth Amendment. "Can Louisiana," he asked, "be brought into proper practical relation with the Union *sooner* by *sustaining* or by *discarding* her new State Government?"

As for other Confederate states, Lincoln concluded, "so great peculiarities pertain to each state; and such important and sudden changes occur in the same state; and withal, so new and unprecedented is the whole case, that no exclusive, and inflexible plan can safely be prescribed as to details and colatterals [sic]." Thus, "it may be my duty to make some new announcement to the people of the South . . . when satisfied that action will be proper." What this new policy would have been can never be known, but there are indications of what it would *not* have been. Despite his apparent flexibility, Lincoln also insisted that "important principles may, and must, be inflexible." And one such principle was self-government through elections by southerners in the states as they had always existed. Thus, when Secretary of War Edwin Stanton, in a cabinet meeting on the very day Lincoln was shot, suggested "a project for military occupation as a preliminary step toward the reorganization of the Southern states, Virginia and North Carolina to be combined in a single military district," Lincoln instructed Stanton to revise the plan to make separate arrangements for Virginia and North Car-

Secretary of War Edwin M. Stanton

olina. "We can't undertake to run State governments in all these Southern States," he told the Cabinet. "The people must do that—though I reckon that at first some of them may do it badly."[30]

At the time of Lincoln's death, in sum, new loyal state governments had been established in four of the eleven Confederate states. Yet if those governments won Lincoln's approval, Congress had refused to recognize them or, with the exception of a single senator from Virginia, to admit representatives and senators elected since 1862 from any of the four states. But Congress had not yet legislated any Reconstruction program of its own, and the issue of enfranchising blacks in the South remained unresolved. This was the situation when Lincoln died in mid-April 1865, at a time, significantly, when Congress had adjourned and was not due to meet again until December.

## PRESIDENTIAL RECONSTRUCTION UNDER ANDREW JOHNSON

Lincoln's successor, Andrew Johnson, also believed that southerners should choose their own state governments to conduct affairs within the South. He too thought that the Civil War's primary purpose was preservation of the Union, not the remaking of southern society by federal dictation, and that Reconstruction was an executive prerogative. Rather than call Congress into special session, therefore, Johnson sought to complete Reconstruction through executive order before Congress reconvened in December. And Johnson, like Lincoln, wanted the fastest possible restoration of intersectional harmony, of self-government by

Andrew Johnson

white southerners within former Confederate states, and of those states' participation in national political life.

For that reason, he told Congress in December 1865, he had consciously rejected prolonged military governance of the South, since it would have fanned Southern resentment, "divided the people into the vanquishers and the vanquished," and "envenomed hatred rather than restored affection."[31] Rather than confront the defeated Confederacy with demands enforced by northern military might, in short, Johnson asked white southerners to comply voluntarily with conciliatory terms. By choosing on their own to accept what he offered, they would fulfill the test of self-governance. Yet as Lincoln had predicted, Southerners governed themselves "badly" at first, at least as far as congressional Republicans were concerned. Because of Congress's alarm at southerners' behavior, Johnson's experiment with Presidential Reconstruction proved no more successful than Lincoln's.

Johnson himself bore considerable responsibility for this result. Stubborn belligerence, prickly self-righteousness, and lifelong biases influenced his actions as president. Nonetheless, his Reconstruction program largely reflected the peculiar political situation he personally and the nation as a whole confronted in the spring of 1865. Although Johnson lacked Lincoln's political adroitness and would prove far readier than Lincoln to exploit the racist sentiments of many whites in the North and South, he was in fact a politician of long experience, enormous ambition, and considerable shrewdness. Hope of winning reelection influenced his Reconstruction policies as it had Lincoln's. Unlike the northerner Lincoln, an erstwhile Whig who embraced the Republicans' commitment to activist government, however, the southerner Johnson had always been a Jacksonian Democrat. He proudly announced his adherence to "limited government" and "the support of the State governments in all their rights,"[32] his detestation of privileged aristocrats, whether large planters or bankers, and his devotion to the welfare and values of white yeomen farmers and artisans. Most significant, he was a Democrat who had never joined the still exclusively northern Republican party of which he was now the nominal leader. That such a party might renominate him in 1868, as he hoped, seemed unlikely unless he embraced Republican policies or proved he could attract southern support to it.[33]

Winning southerners' allegiance in fact seemed vital in the spring of 1865 because of one the Civil War's greatest ironies. Slavery's abolition by the Thirteenth Amendment meant that now all the South's blacks, not just three-fifths of them, would count in the allocation of seats in the House of Representatives and votes in the Electoral College. Though defeated militarily, the former Confederate states would gain increased policy-making and electoral clout once they renewed participation in national politics, a fact of immense significance to both rival parties in the North. One of the central political necessities of Reconstruction, therefore, was the rearrangement of intersectional partisan coalitions between former enemies and, for northerners, identifying which southerners might constitute their most reliable partisan allies.

Many people assumed that white southerners would automatically align with northern Democrats against Republicans, but there were several reasons why this was not the case. Secession and Civil War had shattered the Democratic party along sectional lines, and animosities bred on the killing fields did not disappear instantly. Within the South itself, moreover, many people, including ex-Whigs who had opposed secession in 1861 and die-hard, non-slaveholding Unionists like Johnson's Tennessee supporters, blamed Democrats for causing secession and a disastrous war. Such men had little interest in joining a postwar Democratic party.

That aversion, however, hardly made them potential recruits for a Republican party determined to follow the punitive program betokened by the Wade-Davis bill and Radical demands for black suffrage and confiscation in the South. Indeed, southern suspicion of a blatantly antisouthern Republican party explains why anti-Confederate elements in both the loyal border slave states and the Confederate South had referred to themselves during the war as Union men or Union parties, not Republicans, and, in part, why the Republican party itself had adopted the Union label by 1864. The successful conclusion of the war, however, seemed to have resolved the question of union. Thus it was unclear in the spring of 1865 to which southerners, if any, northern Republicans might look for allies and on what basis they could recruit them.

With the war over, slavery's extinction certain, and a new political era apparently dawning, in fact, many people argued that neither the Republican party, which had been explicitly created to champion northern interests in a time of sectional crisis, nor the Democratic party, tainted as it was by charges of Copperheadism and Confederate sympathies, any longer served a useful purpose. Thus, such people contended, it was time for a complete realignment and partisan reorganization of the nation's political elements. "Since the slavery question is all over," wrote a Republican congressman in April 1865, "new parties must arise." Throughout 1865, a New York newspaper reported in December, the belief spread "that the old parties must soon give way to new combinations," and the following May Virginia's Richmond *Times* declared that "the welfare of the South can only be secured by the erection of a new, conservative party, upon the ruins of the old parties which agitated the slavery question for forty years."[34]

Ultimately Johnson tried to fulfill these predictions in shaping his southern policy and political strategy. On assuming the presidency after Lincoln's assassination, however, he first tried to shore up his relationships with the congressional Republicans who had blocked Louisiana's admission. Much about Johnson, in fact, initially pleased Radical Republican congressional leaders. He was an implacable Unionist who had spurned secession and served briefly on the Joint Committee for the Conduct of the War. As noted, he had resisted Lincoln's pressure for a fast restoration of self-government in Tennessee and had refused to administer Lincoln's generous amnesty oath, which restored political and property rights to most Confederates. As military governor and immediately after becoming president Johnson repeatedly threatened vengeance against secessionists. "Treason is a crime, and must be punished as a crime," he told a New Hampshire delegation in April. "Treason must be made odious and traitors must be punished and impoverished," he repeated in a meeting with Radical senators. Johnson "is as radical as I am and fully up to the mark," gushed Michigan's Senator Zachariah Chandler.[35]

Johnson's initial actions indicated his apparently punitive intentions, his desire to propitiate Republicans, and his determination to look for southern support exclusively among anti-Confederate Unionists like those who had backed him in Tennessee and whom even congressional Republicans admired. On April 21, he rejected the surrender terms Sherman had negotiated with Joseph E. Johnston because they recognized existing Confederate state governments as the legitimate civil authorities in the South. On May 9 he declared all Confederate authority in Virginia "null and void" and promised federal military aid to help Francis Pierpont's shadow government extend its administrative authority "throughout the geographical limits of said State."[36] More important, although many historians interpret Johnson's reconstruction policy as an attempt to follow Lincoln's, the terms for the Confederate states he announced on May 29, 1865 in fact more closely resembled the Wade-Davis bill that Lincoln had pocket vetoed.[37]

Johnson's policy was incorporated in a promise of amnesty and a plan for restoring civil government to North Carolina, the language of which was repeated virtually verbatim in subsequent proclamations for the six remaining Confederate states.[38] The first proclamation granted pardon to all supporters of the Confederacy who would take an oath of future allegiance to the United States and swear to obey all laws and proclamations regarding emancipation. That pardon would restore political rights and "all rights of property, except as to slaves and except in cases where legal proceedings" for the confiscation of land "have been instituted." Unlike Lincoln, who promised the return of land to those who pledged allegiance, Johnson in all seven proclamations declared the immediate reopening of federal courts and ordered the attorney general to "instruct the proper officials to libel and bring to judgment, confiscation, and sale property subject to confiscation."

It became clear from the list of those he excluded from his offer of pardon that Johnson intended the planter elite that had dominated antebellum and wartime southern politics to be the main targets of confiscation and loss of political privileges. Like the Wade-Davis bill, Johnson's policy denied amnesty to far more persons than had Lincoln in his 1863 proclamation. Johnson listed the same six exceptions as Lincoln, and then added eight other categories of Confederates. By far the most significant category designated all persons who had voluntarily supported the rebellion and who owned taxable property valued at twenty thousand dollars or more. In short, Johnson aimed at stopping the planter elite from regaining control of southern governments and at expropriating their wealth. Significantly, however, Johnson did promise "liberally" to pardon any individuals from the "excepted classes" who might apply to the president if such pardon was consistent with "the peace and dignity of the United States."[39]

The Reconstruction proclamations announced the appointment of a provisional civilian governor for each state, who was to cooperate with the state's military commander but whose primary duty was, "at the earliest practicable period," to arrange for the election of delegates to a convention that would rewrite the state constitution in order "to restore said State to its constitutional relations to the Federal Government." Only those who took Johnson's new oath of allegiance, thereby achieving amnesty, and were qualified voters under the antebellum constitutions (that is, only whites) could vote for or serve as delegates in these conventions. They or subsequent state legislatures could prescribe the eligibility for voting and officeholding in the new state governments, "a power the people of the several States composing the Federal Union have rightfully exercised from the origin of the Government to the present time."[40]

Several provisions of Johnson's plan closely resembled the Wade-Davis bill. Johnson's required civilian, not military, provisional governors. He specifically ordered military personnel "to aid and assist the said provisional governor in carrying into effect this proclamation." He too demanded a rewriting of the state constitution *before* any state or federal officials could be elected. He did not specify that the new constitutions abolish slavery, but that requirement was implicit, and later Johnson directed his provisional governors to require that the conventions or subsequent state legislatures ratify the Thirteenth Amendment, nullify the state's secession ordinance, and repudiate the Confederate debt.

Though Johnson's official proclamations contained no explicit provisions regarding the freedmen, he was hardly unsolicitous of their welfare. He instructed his provisional governors that the new state governments must protect blacks' basic rights as free workers through statutes, and he especially sought legislation authorizing blacks to testify in court. In August, he even urged Mississippi's provisional governor, William L. Sharkey, to have that state's constitutional convention grant qualified suffrage to blacks, since "as a consequence the Radicals, who are wild upon negro franchise, will be completely foiled in their attempts to keep the Southern States from renewing their relations to the Union by not accepting their Senators and Representatives."[41]

This hard-nosed advice reveals that propitiating Radical Republicans was not in fact Johnson's top priority. In part because he sought to restore harmony within southern states as well as between the sections and in part because he took seriously the widely bruited likelihood of a nationwide political realignment,

Johnson had no intention of handing control of southern governments to either blacks or the minority of die-hard anti-Confederate Unionists. Rather, he hoped to work with respected southern leaders, most of whom had supported the Confederacy, and to make them, as the historian Michael Perman puts it, "the instruments, not the objects, of Federal policy." Yet Johnson chose as his southern agents a particular type of Confederate—those who had opposed immediate secession in 1860–1861, most of whom were former Whigs who had long opposed the Democrats responsible for secession. To Johnson and to most white Southerners, the test of postwar unionism and loyalty was not which side one took during the war, but where one had stood on secession before it began.[42]

Winning over an influential base of southern supporters was important to Johnson because he wanted to create a national centrist coalition of moderates who agreed with his desire for a quick political reunion of North and South, who would rally behind his presidency, and who could quite probably reelect him to the White House in 1868. As Michael Perman and others have argued, this coalition would include northern Democrats who had joined the Union party during the war as well as other prowar northern Democrats who had remained with their old party, the moderate majority of Republicans, border-state Unionists, and southern opponents of secession in former Confederate states. Excluded from it would be extremists, whether "Copperhead" Peace Democrats, Radical Republicans of the Sumner-Stevens stripe, intransigent pro-Confederate Democratic secessionists, and unforgiving white southern Unionists who insisted on taking revenge against pro-Confederate whites.[43]

Though Johnson's intentions would not be made public until the summer of 1866, he sought to make the all-parties Union coalition that had been cobbled together during the war, often over the grudging opposition of Radical Republicans, into a permanent political party that could rule the nation.[44] Southern cooperation was imperative for the success of this scheme, but it seemed likely. As one Virginian assured Johnson in September 1865, by throwing the Radical Republicans "into a minority," he could "raise up a national party strong enough to support and sustain a conservative administration" that "will be so strongly attached to him that he may rely upon them in all straits and difficulties."[45]

Contrary to these rosy predictions, Johnson's strategy faced two potentially fatal pitfalls. First, despite his hope that white Southerners would act responsibly to appease the victorious North, he was in fact hostage to the actions and demands of the southerners on whom he depended for cooperation and, as he saw it, reelection. Second, his project for converting the wartime Union coalition into a permanent, centrist majority party virtually guaranteed the opposition of northern politicos bent on preserving the existing Republican organization. The combination of the two doomed both his political strategy and his attempt at Presidential Reconstruction.

## CHAPTER 27

Responses to
Presidential
Reconstruction

During the summer and fall of 1865 the seven remaining Confederate
states proceeded to reorganize state governments in accordance with
Johnson's policy. They held conventions, wrote constitutions abolishing
slavery, elected new governors and state legislatures, and joined Arkansas,
Louisiana, Tennessee, and Virginia in sending aspiring federal representatives
and senators to Washington in December 1865. From the start, however, white
southerners on whose cooperation Johnson depended diverged from his script. In
different states the constitutional conventions or subsequent state legislatures
balked at ratifying the Thirteenth Amendment, nullifying secession ordinances,
and especially repudiating the Confederate debt.[1] Southerners elected as convention delegates or later as government officials men who had been excluded from
Johnson's amnesty. These and other evidences of recalcitrance vexed Johnson,
and in some states he retained his appointed provisional governors rather than
allow newly elected governors to exercise power. By and large, however, he acquiesced because, as the historian Eric Foner puts it, "the support of prominent
Southerners seemed essential if Johnson were to fulfill his dream of a second
term in the White House."[2]

In August, he rendered confiscation and land redistribution a chimera by ordering the Freedmen's Bureau to return captured and abandoned lands in the
government's possession to all pardoned Confederates, and in the fall he required
the bureau's head, General O. O. Howard, to expel black families from the lands
along the southeast coast they had taken up under Sherman's Field Order 15.[3]
At the urging of his provisional and newly elected governors, moreover, he extended over seven-thousand individual pardons by the end of 1865 to men who
had been excluded from his general amnesty. The recipients included not only

elected officeholders but large planters with political influence, if not official portfolios. And in December, he called on Congress to allow all the former Confederate states "to resume their functions as States of the Union."[4]

By December, however, most congressional Republicans, like their northern constituents, were furious at what had happened in the South. They would insist on revising Johnson's program in 1866 before allowing the readmission of southern states, and in 1867 they replaced it with one of their own. These actions by Congress marked the end of Presidential Reconstruction and punctuated its failure. Clearly, white southerners' responses to Johnson's initiative helped produce this outcome. Their intentions and actions therefore require closer examination.

## THE SOUTHERN RESPONSE TO JOHNSON'S POLICIES

The success of Johnson's program depended upon the compliance of the great majority of white southerners who had supported the Confederacy. During 1865 and 1866, however, contemporary observers disagreed about former Confederates' readiness for loyal participation in the Union, and subsequent historians have echoed their different readings of southerners' mood.[5] Virtually all white southerners admitted that the Confederate cause was lost and shunned the thought of militarily renewing the rebellion. Nonetheless, resignation to being "whipped" was not synonymous with renewed loyalty to the United States. After a tour of the South in November–December, 1865, General Grant reported that "the mass of thinking men in the South" were "anxious to return to self-government within the Union as soon as possible."[6] In contrast, a traveler said of North Carolina in early 1866 that "the feelings of by far the larger proportion of this State are disloyal to the Govt.—and enamored of the bitterest hatred toward the North."[7] Similarly, although many historians contend that demoralized southern whites would have complied in 1865 with any reasonably firm application of Johnson's initial terms, Michael Perman insists that among Confederates "concession was regarded as capitulation and beyond consideration."[8]

If some Confederate supporters who were eligible for Johnson's pardon were prepared to acquiesce, the region's social, economic, and political elite resisted Johnson's demands with all the resources they could muster. There were two reasons for this resistance. First, wartime officeholders would not willingly abdicate political power, and many of the pro-Confederate yeomen and artisans on whom Johnson counted to elect new men continued to regard those politicians as natural leaders who deserved office. Second, planters, shorn of their slaves and facing possible confiscation, were desperate to regain control of black labor to begin economic renewal and sought to use the coercive power of the state to force blacks back onto the plantations. To exercise that state power, they needed men in office who shared their views, not hill-country Unionists who had long resented planters' domination of southern governments, let alone freedmen themselves. The antisecessionist ex-Whig businessmen, lawyers, and planters who controlled the constitutional conventions called under Johnson's policy and later, the elective offices, shared planters' commitment to controlling black labor.

In three ways the men who took power in the South in 1865 and 1866 flouted the expectations of the victorious North. First, northerners expected new, indisputably loyal men, not the antebellum and especially not the wartime political elite, to take the reins of governmental power in the South. For congressional Republicans, the litmus test of loyalty remained the iron-clad oath banning anyone from office who had ever sympathized with the Confederacy. Though less rigid than congressmen, the northern public demanded "the repudiation of the leaders of the Confederacy."[9] Yet in state after state southerners elected as governors, state legislators, congressmen, and U.S. senators men who had served as Confederate generals and Confederate congressmen. Georgia even tried to send Alexander H. Stephens, the Confederacy's vice president, to the Senate. "What scares" northerners, wrote a Chicago editor in September, "is the idea that the rebels are all to be let back . . . and made a power in the government again, just as though there had been no rebellion." Even Johnson was stunned. "There seems in many of the elections," he complained after surveying the results, "something like defiance, which is all out of place at this time."[10]

Second, northerners and especially Republicans expected protection of blacks' basic rights.[11] Aware of Republican feelings, Johnson himself had insisted on such protection in his private instructions to his provisional governors. Yet by the end of 1865 reports poured into Washington and northern communities from across the South that planters frequently cheated blacks out of the meager wages promised them in the contracts negotiated by the Freedmen's Bureau, that many planters continued to whip their laborers, and, worse still, that in rural areas out of view of occupying Union troops often lethal assaults on black men and women by whites had reached epidemic proportions. White terrorism against blacks would be more formally organized with the creation of the secret Ku Klux Klan in 1866, and it would spread when blacks gained the vote. But by the end of 1865 it was already evident that local white sheriffs, prosecutors, and judges elected under Johnson's policy in the South made little, if any, attempt to protect the freedmen or punish their tormentors.

Third, northerners insisted that there be no attempt to reenslave African Americans through systems of coercive or involuntary labor. Again, Johnson had recognized that expectation by urging the new southern state legislatures to pass formal statutory codes that protected blacks' basic rights of person, property, and voluntary labor. Yet these northern expectations came into direct conflict with planters' determination to force blacks back to work on their plantations as state after state enacted so-called Black Codes. These laws did recognize certain basic rights—for example, freedmen's right to own property, make contracts, marry, sue and be sued, and testify in court cases. Nonetheless virtually all of them criminalized vagrancy, that is, unemployment, and consigned those arrested to prison, hard labor on public projects, or involuntary labor for planters who paid their fines. Many restricted the right of blacks to hunt and fish by toughening trespass laws in order to force them to work in order to eat, authorized the involuntary apprenticeship of black children, and, now that ex-slaves were subject to a penal code formerly restricted to whites and free blacks, inaugurated a peculiarly heinous southern institution, the convict-lease system. Under this, prisoners were hired out by states to planters or other employers who subjected them to brutal work regimens. Mississippi's code required blacks to produce written evidence of employment at the beginning of each year, mandated that any blacks who left a plantation before the end of the year would forfeit their wages, fined any white who tried to hire someone else's field hand five hundred dollars, and forbade blacks to rent land in urban areas. South Carolina explicitly prohibited blacks from following any occupation other than farmer or servant except by paying a steep annual tax, required blacks to sign contracts mandating labor for a year from sunup to sundown, and formally defined relationships between black employees and white employers as one between "servants" and "masters."[12]

As overtly unfair as some Black Codes were, planters did not enjoy unalloyed success everywhere in the South in using the state to regain control of black labor. For one thing, by the end of 1865 only Mississippi, South Carolina, and Alabama had passed Black Codes. Subsequent laws in other states did not discriminate so blatantly against blacks on brazenly racial grounds. Some of the most egregious provisions of those three states' laws never took effect, moreover, because provisional and elected governors vetoed them or because northern military commanders such as General Daniel Sickles in South Carolina disallowed them.[13] Nonetheless, the terms of those laws, like other southern actions during 1865, deeply alarmed congressional Republicans that Johnson, willingly or inadvertently, was sacrificing the fruits of northern victory and that Confederates who had lost the Civil War might win the peace.

Ex-Confederates dared to take those actions for two reasons: a defiant refusal to be humbled by their Yankee conquerors; and their recognition that the success of Johnson's political strategy depended on their support, a dependence that seemed to ensure that Johnson would protect them from a congressional backlash. Here southerners correctly read Johnson's inclinations, but they exaggerated his ability to achieve them. When the Thirty-ninth Congress assembled in December 1865, with Republicans in overwhelming control of both chambers and the eleven Confederate states still unrepresented, changes in federal Reconstruction policy were certain.

## CONGRESSIONAL REPUBLICANS RESPOND TO JOHNSON'S PROGRAM

Were what happened in the South the only thing on northern Republicans' minds in December 1865, they probably would have immediately pushed Reconstruction policy in a far more punitive and problack direction. Certainly the most radical congressional Republicans, who had fumed for months about developments in the South and about Johnson's palpable retreat from his tough stance in April, were prepared to jettison Johnson's entire program. They wanted to block the admission of the southern representatives and senators chosen under it, replace the newly elected state governments with prolonged federal military rule, and enfranchise southern freedmen. A few even still spoke of confiscating planters' land and reselling it to help pay off the war debt.

In December 1865, however, Radicals formed only a minority of congressional Republicans. The majority, then as later, were more concerned about the potential reactions of their northern constituents to their southern policy than about the internal transformation of the South itself. Moderate Republicans opposed the Radicals' agenda as too controversial and expensive for the northern electorate to swallow. Voters across the North were crying for retrenchment of federal expenditures, and those in Connecticut, Minnesota, and Wisconsin defeated referenda on black suffrage in 1865. By December, even many Radicals agreed that black suffrage was temporarily impossible and that, in the words of Ohio Congressman James A. Garfield, they should instead "make a preliminary resistance to immediate restoration and thereby gain time."[14]

Most Republicans, moreover, had no intention of breaking with Johnson by repudiating his program wholesale. Instead, they expected to work with Johnson by amending, not ending, the initiative he had launched. This hesitance to declare open war against the president stemmed from two sources. First, Johnson seemed extraordinarily popular among their northern constituents. In 1865 virtually every northern Union/Republican state platform lavishly praised Johnson personally even as some demanded a more stringent Reconstruction policy than his.[15] Caution seemed the best policy, especially because northern Democratic platforms and newspapers gave additional testimony to Johnson's popularity by heaping praise on him throughout 1865. Just as congressional Republicans dared not challenge Lincoln in December 1863 when his popularity was high in the North, so most Republicans two years later shunned open warfare with Johnson.

Johnson's ostensible support from Democrats, indeed, was the second reason most congressional Republicans had no desire to antagonize him by totally rejecting his program. By December 1865 it was an open secret that influential Democratic politicos were courting Johnson, urging him to abandon his new Republican allies and return to the Democratic fold.[16] Given Johnson's evident popularity in both North and South, Republicans dared not let Democrats hijack their president, especially as Johnson had authority to replace virtually every federal appointed official in the North, patronage holders on whom congressional Republicans counted for help to win renomination and reelection.

Simultaneously, northern Democrats' ardent embrace of Johnson in 1865 gave congressional Republicans an incentive to change Johnson's reconstruction policies before the 1866 campaigns. Given the widespread commentary about the Republican party's obsolescence and cries for partisan reorganization, Republicans had to justify their party's continued existence. There was no better way to do so than by reemphasizing their differences from Democrats.

To define a distinctive Republican alternative on Reconstruction, therefore, congressional Republicans decided to revise, but not reject, Johnson's program in ways that would force Democrats into opposition against it and Johnson, so that Republicans could pose as the program's sole champions in the 1866 elections. Coupled with their genuine anger at the phoenixlike rise of Confederate leaders to political prominence and the maltreatment of freedmen, this partisan necessity helps explain what Republican congressmen did in the winter of 1865–1866. But partisan strategy also meshed with deeply held principle. By the end of 1865 virtually all Republicans were ideologically committed to the idea that black freedmen were citizens who must be guaranteed equal civil rights and the equal protection of the law, if not yet the political privilege of voting.[17] Since northern Democrats during the war had opposed even emancipation, congressional Republicans recognized that they could provoke Democrats into attacking any problack revisions of Johnson's program. They expected Johnson to realize that they were acting to save what the North had won in the war and that he would willingly accept their modifications of his program.

As soon as Congress met in December, the Republican caucus of representatives and senators agreed not to recognize the Johnson regimes in the ex-Confederate states or admit congressmen from them. By prearrangement, the clerk of the House of Representatives, Edward McPherson, excluded the southerners when he called the initial roll of members. Within days, Republicans in each chamber passed a resolution creating a Joint Committee on Reconstruction, consisting of nine representatives and six senators, that would investigate conditions in the South, consider all resolutions and bills pertaining to the terms of state restoration, and ensure that the House and Senate acted in tandem when admitting members from any ex-Confederate state. Though Democrats howled that this committee was a "revolutionary tribunal" or "star chamber," the idea of such a committee had in fact first been suggested by pro-Johnson newspapers. While Thaddeus Stevens, a leading House Radical proponent of confiscation and black rights, was a member, moderates predominated among Republican members. The chairman was Maine's moderate senator William Pitt Fessenden, already the Senate's chief Republican antagonist to the Radical senator Charles Sumner, who was denied a seat on the committee because he was considered too extreme.[18]

Afternoon at the Primary School for Freedmen, Vicksburg, Mississippi, June 1866

While the committee began to hear a string of witnesses who testified about the abuse of blacks, white Unionists, and northern travelers in the South, the moderate senator Lyman Trumbull of Illinois, chairman of the Senate Judiciary Committee, prepared two bills to provide greater protection of blacks' rights that almost all Republicans considered reasonable modifications of Johnson's program. Indeed, Trumbull and other moderate senators consulted with Johnson about the content of the two bills, and they were confident of his approval.

The first, passed by Congress with almost unanimous Republican support in February, extended the life of the Freedmen's Bureau. In March 1865 Congress had established the bureau but had limited its existence to one year after the end of the war. Providing food to the destitute of both races, establishing schools and hospitals for freedmen, supervising labor contracts entered into by blacks, and, at least initially, trying to place some black families on the abandoned and confiscated lands the government controlled in 1865, the bureau had constituted a crucial federal administrative presence in the South.[19] Most of its personnel were former Union army officers. Now, these assistant commissioners, assigned to each state, and their subordinates faced an excruciatingly difficult task in mediating between the expectations of African American freedmen, who sought the greatest possible economic autonomy, and the demands of white employers, who sought to reinstitute plantation discipline. Understandably, agents varied in how they coped with their jobs. Some curried the favor of local whites and allowed contract terms that granted black laborers little more than they had been given as slaves. Others, genuinely devoted to making freedom a reality for blacks, did their best to shield blacks from exploitation, thereby earning whites' execration. Johnson, once he had committed himself to seeking southern political support, responded to whites' complaints by removing many local bureau agents from office.

If the bureau's operation in the South varied, one fact was clear. In disputes with white employers, African American workers looked to the bureau's agents for protection and adjudication: with good reason, they distrusted the fairness of the white judges who staffed the civil courts reestablished under the terms of Johnson's policy. This preference outraged southern whites who, as the historian George R. Bentley has written, regarded the bureau as "virtually a foreign government forced upon them and supported by an army of occupation. They resented its very existence, regardless of what it might do, for it had power over them and it was beyond their control."[20] The overwhelming evidence of public and private discrimination against blacks, however, concerned congressional Republicans far more than

The Bureau as mediator between the races in the postwar South

The Democratic view

Contrasting Republican and Democratic images of the Freedmen's Bureau whites' resentment of the agency. As the historian Herman Belz has shrewdly pointed out, they passed the new Freedmen's Bureau bill in February 1866 precisely to confirm and extend the bureau's protective judicial function, which had not, in fact, been explicitly authorized in the original legislation of March 1865.[21]

Moderate Republicans saw Trumbull's bill as a necessary device for guarding freedmen's basic rights without overtly antagonizing the president. As the historian George Bentley has summarized, the bill provided "that the Freedmen's Bureau should continue its work indefinitely" and granted it power "to 'extend military protection and jurisdiction' over all cases involving discrimination against persons on account of race, color, or previous condition of slavery." It stipulated fines of one thousand dollars or one year's imprisonment or both for "any person who should, by reason of state or local law, or regulation, custom, or prejudice, cause any person to be deprived of any civil right." And it explicitly declared that the Bureau was "to take jurisdiction of . . . all offenses against this provision; and also of all cases affecting . . . persons who are discriminated against."[22]

Trumbull's second measure, later famous as the Civil Rights Act of 1866, was even more important to congressional Republicans. It explicitly asserted the right of the United States government to intervene in state affairs to protect citizens' rights. It also sought to transfer federal responsibility for protecting black rights from a presumably temporary military institution to federal districts courts and U.S. district attorneys, who were charged with prosecuting violators of the law exclusively in those courts. Thus it marked a step toward the expansion of federal judicial power that was a hallmark of Reconstruction policy.[23] Simultaneously, it nationalized civil rights by barring governmentally sanctioned racial discrimination in the North as well as the South.[24] Almost unanimously, Republicans passed Trumbull's bill over Democratic opposition in March, thereby signaling agreement with the assessment of a Republican newspaper in Massachusetts that the measure "follows from the rebellion . . . The party is nothing, if it does not do this—the nation is dishonored if it hesitates in this."[25]

Rejecting the racist doctrines of the *Dred Scott* decision, the bill declared that all persons of whatever color born or naturalized in the United States, except Indians not taxed, were citizens of the United States, and that such persons "of every race and color" had the right in every state to sue; to give evidence; to inherit, hold, and convey property; and to be entitled "to full and equal benefit of all laws and proceedings for the security of person and property, as is enjoyed by white citizens." Anyone who under color of state law, statute, ordinance, or custom deprived any citizen of such rights could be prosecuted in federal courts, which were granted exclusive jurisdiction over such cases; if found guilty, he or she was subject to fines and/or imprisonment.[26]

Most congressional Republicans expected Johnson to sign Trumbull's two bills, which seemed necessary to right the course of developments within the South during 1865. They also expressed the party's commitment to equal rights for all races under the law. Yet Johnson shocked, chagrined, and outraged Republicans by vetoing both of Trumbull's measures. Ignoring advice from his sagacious secretary of state, William H. Seward, that he should not unnecessarily offend congressional Republicans, Johnson seemed to go out of his way in his two veto messages to assail the idea that Congress had any voice in the Reconstruction process unless, and until, it readmitted the members already elected from ex-Confederate states.

In his message of February 19, 1866 vetoing the Freedmen's Bureau bill, Johnson complained that it established a "permanent" and unconstitutional military jurisdiction over matters that civil courts should adjudicate now that the Civil War was clearly over. He declared that the purposes of the original Freedmen's Bureau had already been fully accomplished, and, while referring to schools and hospitals for blacks, railed that the United States government had never spent similar money "for our own people,"—that is, whites. "A system for support of indigent persons in the United States," he maintained, "was never contemplated by the authors of the Constitution." Black freedmen, moreover, needed no such federal protection since southern states were avidly competing for their labor; indeed, the bill would only encourage an unhealthy dependence on federal assistance. What was worse, Congress passed the law when "loyal representatives" from the eleven ex-Confederate states in which it operated were excluded. Congress's unquestionable right to judge the qualifications of its own members, he added, "must not be construed as including the right to shut out in a time of peace any State from the representation to which it is entitled," no matter what its rebellious past.[27]

Johnson's long, dyspeptic veto of the Civil Rights bill on March 27, 1866, even more emphatically rejected as improper any congressional reconstruction effort so long as ex-Confederate states were denied representation. He denounced the effrontery of Congress' attempt to "establish for the colored race safeguards which go infinitely beyond any that the General Government has ever provided for the white race," thereby discriminating "in favor of the colored and against the white race." He denounced the unconstitutionality of extending the jurisdiction of federal courts over "relations existing exclusively between a State and its citizens, or between inhabitants of the same State." This unprecedented and unnecessary "assumption of power by the General Government," protested Johnson, would destroy the "federative system of limited powers" and "the rights of the States." If not resisted, it would lead inexorably "toward centralization and the concentration of all legislative powers in the National Government."[28] By posing as the champion of limited government, the white race, states' rights, and the South, Johnson rebuked the activist state and egalitarian program embraced by most Republicans.

As extraordinarily intransigent as the two veto messages were, an extemporaneous harangue Johnson delivered to a crowd outside the White House on the

Thomas Nast portrays congressional Republicans' anger at Johnson's defiance of Congress and his declaration of war against Radicals. Note that Thaddeus Stevens' head is on the chopping block and that Charles Sumner is third in line for execution. Note also the two allusions to Secretary of State William H. Seward as Johnson's closest advisor in the Union party scheme.

night of February 22, three days after his veto of the Freedmen's Bureau bill, declared open warfare against the Radical wing of his party. Reavowing his lifelong devotion to the Union and his determination to restore it, he reminded his audience of his struggle against Confederate leaders. Then he asserted that now some northerners were "still opposed to the Union" and "the fundamental principles of this Government." When the audience demanded that he name names, he listed the Radicals Thaddeus Stevens and Charles Sumner along with the abolitionist Wendell Phillips as the chief culprits.[29]

It is probable, as Johnson's biographer Hans Trefousse suggests, that Johnson was simply "carried away" by the enthusiasm of his audience when he made this outburst.[30] Commitment to states' rights and revulsion from a strong national government, a belief in white supremacy and aversion to government-mandated advancement of blacks, and sheer anger at congressional Republicans' refusal to accept his program clearly motivated him. Yet the speech and the language of his veto messages also revealed the political strategy that had been driving his actions since the summer of 1865. As a shrewd South Carolina observer in Washington correctly reported, Johnson hoped to provoke Radicals into opposing him, to isolate them from moderate Republicans, and to persuade the latter to "form a new party with the President."[31] As the historians Lawanda and John H. Cox put it,

"The war which President Johnson declared in February and March of 1866 brought to a climax the long-standing design to force the Radicals out of the Union-Republican party and inaugurate a reorganization of national parties."[32]

To build a reconfigured Union party, however, Johnson had to identify a plausible purpose for its existence now that the war itself was over. Defining that justification was the reason for the language that peppered his messages to Congress and his tirade on February 22. The Civil War had been fought to restore the Union, he insisted, but military victory alone did not secure the war's goal. Restoration of the Union remained incomplete until the ex-Confederate states were readmitted to Congress and to full participation in national political life. He sought that goal. So did the great majority of northern Democrats and Republicans, border state Unionists, and the "loyal" men who had been elected to office in the South under his program. Now the only people against the Union were die-hard Confederates and Radical Republicans, who because they put the interests of blacks ahead of whites' refused to admit the southern states. Through a kind of linguistic legerdemain, in short, Johnson attempted to redefine the meaning of disunionism from being pro-Confederate to opposing re-Union on his terms. It was precisely the capability for political obstructionism of such disunionists, he implied, that required the creation of a newly configured Union party to complete the mission of the Civil War. But in picking a fight with Radicals over measures designed to protect blacks' basic rights, Johnson also clearly intended to give the Union party an additional mission: the defense of white supremacy and black subjugation.

The key to the success of Johnson's strategy was holding the moderate majority of Republicans while he isolated the Radicals. But he had seriously miscalculated the line that divided moderate from Radical Republicans, for almost all Republicans considered the Freedmen's Bureau and Civil Rights bills necessary for the protection of blacks' civil rights. The Senate came within a few votes of overriding his veto of the Freedmen's Bureau bill,[33] and on April 9, 1866 both houses of Congress, with Republicans nearly unanimous in support, repassed the Civil Rights bill over Johnson's veto, thereby making it the law of the land.

That victory was important, for it showed congressional Republicans that they could enact a Reconstruction program of their own despite Johnson's opposition. Johnson continued to be a major player in the process of Reconstruction for the remainder of his presidency. His power to veto bills profoundly shaped what congressional Republicans did, because they knew Democrats and border state Unionists would vote to sustain those vetoes. And as commander in chief of the army he could influence the most important federal agency capable of implementing congressional policies in the South. But Johnson's role was now that of obstacle to, not initiator of, federal Reconstruction policy. From April 1866 on, Congress assumed chief responsibility for framing the constitutional and political terms of the North's peace settlement with the South.

## CHAPTER 28

Congressional
Reconstruction:
The First Phase

In attempting to separate non-Radical congressional Republicans from their
Radical colleagues with vetoes in early 1866, Andrew Johnson had miscalculated the line dividing them. Nonetheless, discernible Moderate and Radical
factions of the Republican party differed over federal policy for the defeated
South.[1] Squabbles between them continually shaped the formulation of Congress's Reconstruction program from 1866 to 1869. That program defined the
terms for restoring ex-Confederate states to the national polity, restructured the
balance of political power within those states, and, by vastly expanding blacks'
legal and constitutional rights, gave freedmen a chance to use local and state government to improve their social and economic condition. Thus congressional
policy making requires close investigation, and it can best be understood in two
phases separated by the congressional elections of 1866.

Historians once spoke of the statutes and constitutional amendments Congress passed during these years as epitomizing Radical Reconstruction. If viewed
from the perspective of white Southerners and the nation's long discriminated
against African American minority, those enactments did indeed promise fundamental change. From the perspective of the policy alternatives debated by congressional Republicans, however, their Reconstruction program did not primarily
reflect the Radicals' wishes. Rather it represented a series of compromises between Radicals and Moderates. The necessity of holding the party together in
order to overcome Democratic opposition and Andrew Johnson's vetoes forced
both groups to make concessions. Nonetheless, Moderates, not Radicals, generally got the better of the intraparty bargaining during both phases of policy
formation.[2]

## THE PROTAGONISTS: RADICALS
## AND MODERATES

Andrew Johnson was not the only one who had difficulty distinguishing Radical Republicans from their moderate and conservative colleagues. Just as white southerners and northern Democrats prior to the Civil War tended to label anyone who criticized slavery or slaveholders as an "abolitionist," so those groups, like Johnson himself after the spring of 1866, labeled all congressional Republicans "Radicals." As the historian Michael Les Benedict has astutely noted, therefore, "contemporaries used that term not to elucidate but to obfuscate the real alignments in the Republican party."[3] Efforts by subsequent historians to distinguish Radicals from Moderates in terms of the respective groups' occupational and regional backgrounds, economic interests, and even the character of their constituents foundered because there were too many exceptions to every such classification.[4] Almost every northern state, for example, sent both Moderates and Radicals to Congress, as did both rural and urban constituencies. Furthermore, the size and composition of each bloc varied from congressional session to congressional session, in part because the entire spectrum of alternative policies shifted toward the radical position over time. What was a radical option in the winter of 1865–1866, for example, had become the moderate option a year later.

Nonetheless, two conclusions about Republican factionalism, beyond its pivotal role in shaping Congress's Reconstruction policies, are warranted. First, the once prevailing Progressive interpretation of Radical Republicans as agents of northeastern businessmen whose primary goal was to protect the economic interests of their constituents from a renewed agrarian coalition of southern and western Democrats is untenable.[5] Aside from a marked factional disagreement over currency contraction, Radicals were divided internally over most economic issues, and many of them represented midwestern, not northeastern, interests. More important, intense ideological commitments concerning black rights and southern Reconstruction, not economic interests, defined the Radicals.

Second, what differentiated Radicals from Moderates was not so much a disagreement about the changes they sought within the South or on behalf of African Americans. Rather, they differed over the means of achieving those ends, over the acceptability of a permanent shift of power within the American federal system from states to the national government, and over the length of the Reconstruction process itself. And such disagreements stemmed less from regional or occupational background than from matters of temperament, the priority given to political prudence, and, in some cases, simply factional alignments within their state Republican parties.[6]

Radicals were always more proportionately influential among Republicans in the House than in the Senate, in terms of both numbers and important committee assignments. Among Radical leaders in the House were Pennsylvania's sar-

Radical leaders in the House of Representatives:

Thaddeus Stevens

James M. Ashley

George S. Boutwell

Benjamin F. Butler

William D. Kelley

Radical leaders of the Senate:

Zachariah Chandler

Henry Wilson

Jacob M. Howard

Benjamin F. Wade

donic Thaddeus Stevens and zealous William D. Kelley, ex-General Benjamin Butler and George S. Boutwell of Massachusetts, Ohio's Samuel Shellabarger and James M. Ashley, and Indiana's ex-Free-Soiler George W. Julian. In the Senate, Charles Sumner won a popular following across the North, even if his colleagues disdained his pomposity and inattention to legislative detail, while Ohio's Ben Wade along with Michigan's Zachariah Chandler and Jacob M. Howard proved tough and adept legislative managers. Their leading Moderate counterparts in the House were Ohio's John Bingham, Maine's James G. Blaine, and Henry L. Dawes of Massachusetts; in the Senate Maine's William Pitt Fessenden, Lyman Trumbull of Illinois, Ohio's John Sherman, and Iowa's James W. Grimes exemplified Moderate leadership.

In general, Radicals were long-time veterans of the political struggle against slavery before the Civil War. During the war they had been early proponents of emancipation, the use of black troops, and confiscation of Confederates' property. Thus they tended to be purist ideologues. They sought to extend the Republican party's egalitarian mission by seizing the opportunity offered by the North's victory to extirpate all legal and political discrimination against blacks throughout the nation. They also wanted to reduce, if not eliminate, the political influence and economic power of the South's planter elite. Of vast importance as well, as the historian Eric Foner contends, "more fully than other Republicans, the Radicals embraced the wartime expansion of federal authority, carrying into

Moderate leaders of the Senate:

Roscoe Conkling

Oliver P. Morton

John Sherman

James W. Grimes

Lyman Trumbull

Reconstruction the conviction that federalism and state rights must not obstruct a sweeping national effort to define and protect the rights of citizens."[7] As morally committed ideologues, moreover, Radicals disdained any compromises that might stop them from reaching their goals, compromises that Moderates often thought were necessitated by political realities. As Sumner once angrily retorted to Fessenden's call to limit Republicans' legislative agenda to what could realistically be passed, "Ample experience shows that [compromise] . . . is the least practical mode for settling questions involving moral principles. A moral principle cannot be compromised."[8]

Responding to Johnson's Reconstruction program, Radicals in early 1866 sought to deny ex-Confederate states representation in Congress for an indefinite period. Rather than working with the southern state governments organized under Johnson's policy, Radicals wanted to replace them with prolonged military occupation by federal troops and to treat those states as territories subject to government by direct congressional statute. Only direct federal control, they believed, could ensure that Confederates did not win the peace and provide adequate protection to freedmen. Radicals, in short, wanted to delay *restoration* of ex-Confederate states to full participation in national political life until Congress, by federal legislation, had *reconstructed* their internal social and political arrangements. To accomplish that transformation, Radicals wanted to prohibit Confederate military and civilian leaders, many of whom had come back to power under Johnson's governments, from holding office *and* from the ballot box. They also sought to enfranchise the freedmen, if not the North's blacks as well, by federal law. At a minimum, they would require by congressional decree that ex-Confederate states must enfranchise their adult black male residents in

The great New England Rivals: William Pitt Fessenden (left) and Charles Sumner (right)

order to win readmission to Congress. Freedmen could thus help elect what would be in effect territorial governments to replace the state and local officials chosen under Johnson's policy. Southern states, in Congressman George W. Julian's words, would undergo "a probationary training, looking to their restoration when they should prove their fitness for civil government as independent states."[9] In addition, some Radicals demanded federal guarantees for black education in the South; others, like Stevens, still wanted to confiscate planters' land and divide it among black families.

Moderates agreed with Radicals that ex-Confederate states did not yet merit readmission to Congress, that many men elected under Johnson's policies were objectionable, that the Confederate debt must be repudiated, and that greater protection for freedmen's rights was imperative. Except for confiscation, which they deemed an unconstitutional and immoral assault on property rights, Moderates did not question the justness of the Radicals' agenda. In 1866, however, they considered it far too extreme.

Unlike the party's purist ideologues, Moderate Republicans were pragmatic politicians who frequently identified themselves as "practical" men. They always placed top priority on the continued success of the Republican party as a whole. All would be lost, they argued, unless Republicans maintained control of northern state governments, Congress, and the White House. Accordingly, Republicans must shun any action that jeopardized their party's dominance in the North. Moderate Republicans, in sum, always cared more about their northern constituents' reactions to congressional programs for the South than about the benefits those programs might achieve within the South.[10] As one Radical described the difference between the two factions, "Policy is the rule of the one, Principle is the only guide for the other."[11]

Political prudence caused the Moderates to reject the Radicals' ambitious agenda in 1866. They wanted to distinguish themselves from the Democrats who lauded Johnson's program, but not on an extremist platform that could prove suicidal at the polls. "I have been a partisan long enough to know that extreme measures will not always promote the interests of a party," declared one moderate Republican congressman. "What will our people at home think of . . . rank and radical measures?"[12] Well aware of most white northerners' racist aversion to black suffrage, they fought any attempt to enact it or to make it a requirement for restoration that year. They were equally aware of Johnson's popularity in the North, to which both Union/Republican and Democratic state platforms in 1865 had attested, and they were therefore determined to avert a rupture with him. Hence they also rejected Radicals' calls for territorialization and sought to improve and discipline, but not abolish, the southern state governments elected under his program.

The question of readmission marked one separation between non-Radicals and Radicals. Moderates believed many northerners agreed with Johnson that the purpose of the Civil War would not be fully achieved until the Union was re-stored by the reintegration of the South into national political life. They knew that northern Democrats were demanding instant, unfettered restoration of the ex-Confederate states. Hence they feared that failure to restore those states to Congress in a timely fashion would guarantee defeat in northern elections. "The good of this country requires that these States should be admitted . . . just as soon as it can be done consistently with the safety of the people of this country," Maine's William Fessenden told the Senate in February 1866. Unnecessary delay would "demoralize" the nation.[13]

Most Moderates hoped to readmit at least some southern states before the 1866 congressional contests, and they feared catastrophe in 1868 if they had not restored the Union by then. Unlike the Radicals, who wanted to postpone restoration as long as possible, regardless of the political consequences, the Moderates always felt great pressure to find a formula that would return ex-Confederate states to Congress and would still protect the fruits of northern victory. In short, any provision in Reconstruction legislation that could hasten the return of southern states to Congress, no matter how rigorous the stipulations, would mark a triumph of the Moderates over the Radicals.

A second difference between the two Republican factions involved constitutional principle. Devotees of what historians have called state-centered federalism or "state-rights nationalism," Moderates recoiled from Radical demands directly to increase the power of the national government at the expense of the states.[14] It was not simply that the northern public's pleas for a reduction of federal income and excise taxes made increasing the size and assertiveness of the national government a political liability. Moderates believed that whatever increment of national power the Civil War had necessitated should be temporary. As in prewar days, state and local governments, not Washington, must enact most laws that shaped citizens' everyday lives. As Iowa's senator James W. Grimes said in May 1866 when calling for a surrender of the new wartime powers of the national government, "Let us go back to the original condition of things, and allow the States to take care of themselves."[15] Rather than expanding Washington's direct authority over citizens' lives, therefore, Moderates much preferred to enact federal restrictions on what state governments did with regard to their own residents. As the historian Herman Belz puts it, "Insisting on federal guarantees of state performance in fields such as civil rights, Republicans yet regarded the states as the vital engines of republican government" and continued to rely on "the federal principle of local control."[16]

Though Moderates generally exerted the greater influence over congressional policy, almost every piece of Republicans' Reconstruction legislation reflected the wishes of both wings. The Freedmen's Bureau and Civil Rights bills illustrate this pattern. Though drafted by the Moderate Lyman Trumbull, this legislation ostensibly embodied the Radicals' nationalistic approach. The Freedmen's Bureau bill extended the life and geographical reach of a federal agency explicitly designed to help former slaves; the Civil Rights Act made all blacks, North and South, United States citizens and provided federal judicial protection to blacks' civil rights throughout the nation. But the bills also represented a deliberate alternative to Radicals' demands for black enfranchisement, federal guarantees for blacks' education, and land redistribution to blacks.[17] As Radicals well knew, moreover, Moderates hoped that by providing some federal protection to black rights, Republicans might be more willing to recognize and readmit the existing Johnsonian state governments in the South, a concession Radicals regarded as anathema.

Most important, the protection offered by the Civil Rights Act of 1866 was intentionally limited to preserve state-centered federalism and *prevent* an increase in the direct responsibility of the national government for citizens' rights. For one thing, the federal judiciary was the least proactive branch of the national government. For courts to hear cases, blacks' rights had to have been previously violated. Moreover, the act restricted prosecutions of those who violated blacks' rights to state and local government officials while exempting private citizens. If, for example, a county sheriff saw three whites murder a black man and subsequently refused to arrest them, the United States government could bring charges against the sheriff, but not against the three murderers. Punishing crimes against black men and women by private individuals remained the responsibility of state, not national, officials.

Rather than directly expanding the national government's police powers and responsibility for enforcing them, in short, the Moderates' solution was to force southern legislators, judges, and law enforcement officials to provide blacks with the equal protection of *state* laws. By asserting concurrent jurisdiction with states over citizens' civil rights, the national government, to be sure, was assuming a new role as umpire or ombudsman to oversee and pressure southern officeholders into treating all citizens of a state equally. But the Moderates' assumption was that once those officeholders did so, there need be no national intervention in state affairs. As Trumbull himself said of his bill, "It will have no operation in any State where the laws are equal, where all persons have the same civil rights without regard to color or race."[18] The Moderates' goal was not to centralize power in Washington as Radicals wished, but to redefine the relationship between nation and state to protect the fruits of northern victory while still preserving federalism.[19] That goal would also be reflected in congressional Republicans' most important and enduring legislative achievement during 1866—the Fourteenth Amendment.

## THE FOURTEENTH AMENDMENT

As Congress was considering Trumbull's two measures protecting blacks' rights, the Joint Committee on Reconstruction was preparing a Constitutional amendment to govern the restoration of the southern states. Both Radicals and

Moderates believed that Congress must impose more stringent terms on ex-Confederate states than Johnson wanted. By the spring of 1866 most agreed that a constitutional amendment that southern states must ratify before returning to Congress, rather than a statute, could best accomplish this task.[20] Embedding their requirements in the Constitution would prevent Democrats from easily repealing them should they regain control of Congress. Radicals also saw an amendment as a chance to impose black suffrage on all the states, whereas Moderates viewed the process of ratification by freely elected southern state legislatures as meeting their essential test of self-government.

Republicans initially saw the amendment as an answer to three problems that Trumbull's bills did not address. It ensured that all Confederate debt was repudiated. It tried to stop ex-Confederate states from gaining votes in the House of Representatives and the Electoral College as a result of the sudden obsolescence of the Constitution's three-fifths clause, caused by emancipation. And it sought to guarantee that genuinely loyal men, not former Confederate leaders, would hold political office in the South. Johnson's vetoes of the Freedmen's Bureau and Civil Rights bills alerted Republicans to the advisability of incorporating a guarantee of blacks' civil rights in the amendment as well.

The framing of the amendment involved a complicated process of factional give-and-take.[21] Still it was a compromise that disappointed many Radicals because the Moderates rejected their demands for the explicit enfranchisement of blacks and the disfranchisement of white Confederates. Although Thaddeus Stevens eventually voted for the amendment, he privately called it a "shilly-shally bungling thing," while the abolitionist Wendell Phillips bluntly denounced it as "a fatal and total surrender" of the Radicals' agenda.[22]

The Fourteenth Amendment passed Congress in June 1866 and was finally ratified by the necessary three-fourths of the states two years later. Since its provisions, or at least its first section, have been absolutely central to the evolution of American constitutional law in the twentieth century, it merits close examination.

The first section incorporated the thrust of the Civil Rights Act in more general and intentionally ambiguous language. It declared "all persons born or naturalized in the United States" citizens of the nation "and of the State wherein they reside." It then stipulated: "No State shall make or enforce any law which shall abridge the privileges or immunities of citizens of the United States; nor shall any State deprive any person of life, liberty, or property, without due process of law; nor deny to any person within its jurisdiction the equal protection of the laws."

This cryptic language has engendered controversy among jurists, lawyers, historians, and constitutional scholars during the twentieth century. To the extent that they have tried to identify the Republicans' intentions, they have been hindered by the brief discussion of this clause during the congressional debates and subsequently during the 1866 campaign, compared with the other three, now largely ignored, sections of the amendment. Since Republicans in the 1860s sharply distinguished among civil, political, and social rights, however, it seems clear, as the eminent constitutional scholar Alexander M. Bickel has argued, that this section was "meant to apply neither to jury service, nor suffrage, nor antimiscegenation statutes, nor segregation," including segregation of schools.[23] By the "privileges and immunities" of U.S. citizens Republicans possibly meant only the specific rights to travel, marry, buy and sell property, make contracts, and so on, that they had already listed in the Civil Rights Act, as well as certain individual rights protected from federal abuse by the Bill of Rights.[24] It is noteworthy, however, that the ban on state discrimination here and elsewhere in the first section was *not* restricted to actions based on race, color, or previous condition of servitude, a fact of enormous subsequent significance. Courts would later rule that it also barred discrimination among persons based on class, ethnicity, gender, place of residence, and religion.

Both Moderates and Radicals found reason to applaud this clause. Moderates prevailed in the language that restricted official discriminatory state governmental action rather than directly empowering the national government with responsibility to protect citizens' rights from both private and public actions. Radicals took comfort from the guarantee of blacks' citizenship and equal rights before the law. Moreover, the amendment's little-discussed fifth section, which declared that "The Congress shall have the power to enforce, by appropriate legislation, the provisions of this article," appeared to open the door for subsequent direct national legislation that the Radicals sought.

The amendment's fourth section also occasioned little intraparty bickering. It sought to stop Democrats from reneging on payment of the nation's war debt or helping southerners receive compensation for their own losses. It guaranteed payment of the national debt in full, including promises of pensions and bounties to soldiers. It also declared all Confederate debts "illegal and void" and prohibited both the United States and any state government from paying "any obligation incurred" to aid the Confederate "insurrection" or "any claim for the loss or emancipation of any slave." Though slaveholders from loyal border states were denied any hope of compensation by this clause, it was aimed at former Confederates.

The second and third sections also targeted erstwhile rebels, but they provoked sharp disputes between Radicals and Moderates, disputes in which the Radicals suffered clear defeats. The third section encompassed political proscriptions against ex-Confederates, and especially the men who had returned to power in the South under Johnson's program. Radicals had a clear agenda here. They wanted the Johnsonian governments dissolved or declared provisional, and they wanted the wartime elite, if not all Confederates, banned from the right to vote and hold office. To their fury, the third section addressed only the last of these goals. It prohibited from the right to hold state and national executive, legislative, judicial, and military offices any Confederate supporter who, prior to 1861, had held a state or national office in which he had been required to swear an oath of allegiance to the United States Constitution.[25] And to stop Johnson or a future Democratic president from eviscerating this disqualification with executive pardons, it explicitly stipulated that "Congress may by a vote of two-thirds of each House, remove such disability," thereby lodging the power of pardon exclusively in the legislative branch.

Southern political leaders quickly recognized the menacing implications of this clause. It barred from office not only former congressmen, state legislators and judges, and United States military officers, but also prewar customs collectors, state militia members, local postmasters, and even lighthouse keepers working for the federal government. Radicals, however, complained that such men could still vote, that they would continue to hold local and state offices in the South until the amendment was ratified, and that no provision for pardon should have been allowed.

Even more disappointing to Radicals was the second section, which dealt with the basis of congressional representation once ex-Confederate states won readmission to Congress. No Republicans wanted their former enemies to enjoy a bonus of political power as a result of emancipation. The Radicals' solution was simple: mandate black enfranchisement in the amendment and count a state's entire population when apportioning House seats, a proposal that would have imposed black suffrage on the North as well. But Moderates would not consider black suffrage, especially in the North. Echoing several Union party state platforms in 1865, many Radicals called for basing each state's House delegation on the number of voters in each state, not the total population, as a fall-back position. That way, southern states that did not enfranchise blacks would lose, not gain, seats as a result of the obviation of the three-fifths clause. New England Republicans, however, instantly complained that this formula would cost their states seats. Women outnumbered men in most New England states, and the region also contained large numbers of unnaturalized alien immigrants. Neither group could be counted if apportionment were based on voters. That formula would also punish states such as Missouri, West Virginia, Maryland, and Tennessee, where Unionists clung to power by disfranchising ex-Confederates.

Thus the amendment's framers settled on a convoluted formula that enraged Radicals such as Charles Sumner, who called it "utterly reprehensible and unpardonable."[26] Reflecting the Moderates' insistence that state governments, not Washington, must determine suffrage qualifications, the second section effectively invited southern states *not* to enfranchise blacks, an offer that Radicals found unconscionable. Apportioning representatives among the states on the basis of their total populations, except Indians not taxed, it stipulated that any state that denied the right to vote for state and federal officials to any adult "male citizens" for any reason except "participation in rebellion or other crime" would have its representation "reduced in the proportion which the number of such male citizens shall bear to the whole number of male citizens twenty-one years of age in such State."

What this language implied is that if two-fifths of a state's potential voters were African Americans and if that state refused to enfranchise them, it would lose two-fifths of the members it would have been allotted in the House of Representatives and suffer a proportionate reduction in its electoral vote for president. During the congressional debates and later during the 1866 campaigns, most Moderates in fact insisted that ex-Confederate states would never enfranchise blacks. In 1866, that is, Moderates had no intention of building a southern wing of the Republican party based on black voters. Rather, they would protect the fruits of northern victory by reducing the South's potential power in national politics and preserve federalism to boot by stopping Radicals from nationalizing suffrage standards. "The political system of this Republic rests upon the right of the people to control their local concerns in their several states," Carl Schurz later asserted in defending the amendment. "This system was not to be changed in the work of reconstruction."[27]

Like the Fourteenth Amendment's first section, the second did not specify racial discrimination as the only reason that disfranchisement would trigger a penalty. Ostensibly, it included any hurdle that denied males of any color the vote. Theoretically, it would punish states for the arcane registration requirements, literacy tests, poll-tax requirements, grandfather clauses, and other devices adopted in the late nineteenth century to disfranchise blacks and poor whites. Yet this section of the Fourteenth Amendment has never been invoked. It has remained the deadest of dead letters in the Constitution.

The Moderates' adherence to states' rights, overt refusal to require black suffrage, and smug claims of triumph in the Fourteenth Amendment infuriated Radicals, who recognized all too well the essential validity of those claims. But Radical Republicans were not the only people appalled by the Fourteenth Amendment. Since it marked the first time that any provision of the Constitution explicitly identified the right to vote exclusively with males, the amendment incensed female proponents of women's suffrage. Having long cooperated with male abolitionists in the struggle for emancipation and black rights, suffragists had hoped to seize on the egalitarian zeal inspired during the Civil War to win the vote for women. Leaders of the movement such as Susan B. Anthony and Elizabeth Cady Stanton had even moved to Washington to lobby for that result. They were indignant that Republicans, however timidly, would put the political rights of black men ahead of white women's. As a result, writes the historian Eric Foner, "women's leaders now embarked on a course that severed their historic alliance with abolitionism and created an independent feminist movement."[28]

Three other ramifications of the Fourteenth Amendment's passage deserve emphasis. However much Radicals and Moderates disagreed about its content, they were even more divided over the issue of whether ratification of the amendment, by itself, should win ex-Confederate states readmission to Congress. The Moderates, who still sought to avert a break with Johnson, hoped so, and Congressman John Bingham, a member of the Joint Committee on Reconstruction, prepared a bill explicitly guaranteeing readmission after ratification. Radicals desperately fought that bill in committee, on the floor, and in the Republican caucus, and before Congress adjourned they prevented Republicans from passing any clear formulation of precisely what would be required for readmission. Nonetheless, when the Tennessee legislature quickly ratified the Fourteenth Amendment, Bingham pushed a measure instantly readmitting Tennessee to Congress that passed over die-hard Radical opposition on July 6. During the subsequent fall campaigns, moreover, Republican state platforms in Ohio, Michigan, and New York, like those of many individual congressional candidates elsewhere, explicitly pledged that ratification alone would assure immediate readmission. The official address of the party's national executive committee strongly implied the same guarantee.[29]

From the start of their deliberations, in fact, congressional Republicans intended the Fourteenth Amendment to serve as the party's platform in the 1866 congressional and state elections. Democrats' overwhelming vote against it reinforced their belief that it provided a distinctive Republican policy for Reconstruction. To neutralize any Democratic attempt at race baiting, many Republican candidates emphasized that the amendment did not impose black suffrage on the South, let alone the North. Some Republicans even defended their program on the openly racist grounds that protecting blacks' rights in the South would stop them from migrating to the North. The Fourteenth Amendment, argued the New York Moderate Roscoe Conkling, would "give them [blacks] liberty and rights at the South, [so] they will stay there and never come into a cold climate to die." To avert "the day when the southern freedmen shall swarm over the borders in quest of those rights which should be secured to them in their native states," even the Radical George Boutwell asserted, requires "a just policy on our part [that] leaves the black man in the South," for "an unjust policy in the South forces him from home and into" the North.[30]

If some Republicans shied from portraying their party as champions of blacks, reaffirming the antisouthern message that had brought Republicans to power in the 1850s and kept them there during the Civil War was quite another matter. Republican leaders knew that however much the Civil War had improved their constituents' attitudes toward blacks, it had clearly intensified their animosity toward the pro-Confederate majority of white Southerners. South bashing thus offered obvious political dividends to northern Republicans. Just as Democrats sought to draw the line between the parties on the issue of race, Republicans sought to distinguish themselves as the anti-Confederate party while labeling

Democrats as pro-Confederate sympathizers who would surrender the North's fruits of victory.

The parts of the Fourteenth Amendment that Republicans stressed during 1866—that is, its now forgotten last three sections—perfectly fitted this agenda. Although they could be presented as moderate in terms of preserving states' right to prescribe suffrage qualifications and not disfranchising most white Southerners, they could also be trumpeted for invalidating the Confederate debt and ensuring payment to northern bond holders and veterans, for proscribing most Confederate leaders from office, and for reducing ex-Confederate states' influence in Congress and the Electoral College. Simultaneously, Moderates promised, while their Reconstruction program was tougher on the South and juster to the North than Democrats' alternative, it could also bring about the quick restoration of the Union, because all it required for readmission was ratification of the amendment.

Despite the Republicans' avowals of the amendment's essential moderateness, both Andrew Johnson and southern state legislators outside of Tennessee found the requirement of ratification as the price of readmission intolerable. Unable to veto a constitutional amendment, Johnson publicly denounced the effrontery of Congress in passing it when the ex-Confederate states to which it would apply were still unrepresented, and he urged them not to ratify it. During the remainder of 1866 and early 1867 other southern legislatures rejected the amendment by overwhelming negative majorities. But they hardly needed Johnson's urging to do so. During the 1866 campaigns northern Democrats charged that southern states refused ratification because the amendment imposed black suffrage on them. In fact, the white southerners who controlled state governments under Johnson's policy objected primarily to the amendment's third section, because it would force most of them from public office and allow the die-hard anti-Confederate Unionists, who had been largely excluded from power except in Arkansas and Tennessee, to obtain it.

The amendment's disqualifying provisions, however, had no legal effect unless and until the amendment was ratified by three-fourths of the states. Counting the eleven ex-Confederate states—and in 1866 nearly everyone simply assumed they should be counted for purposes of ratification—there were thirty-seven states, with twenty-eight required for ratification. Thus, by refusing to ratify, the ten remaining Confederate states could keep the amendment from becoming part of the Constitution. The whites who had returned to power within the South could continue to control state and local governments. Those men regarded continued local control, especially with regard to black labor, to be far more important than renewed representation in Congress or the size of their congressional delegation.[31] Their stubbornness and Johnson's encouragement of it further guaranteed that the Fourteenth Amendment would be the central issue in the 1866 congressional elections.

## THE CONGRESSIONAL ELECTIONS OF 1866

Republicans had long since decided to chorus their party's traditional anti-southern refrain during the 1866 campaign. They expected to contrast the Four-teenth Amendment's defense of the fruits of northern victory with northern Democrats' willingness to sacrifice those achievements by urging the Confeder-ates' unconditional readmission to Congress. That case, Republicans believed, would trump Democrats' response that Republicans were subverting the objec-tive of the Civil War by insisting on a vindictive program that blocked reunion and favored blacks at the expense of whites. Yet Republicans had not planned on having to fight Andrew Johnson as well as Democrats. Throughout the spring of 1866, even after the vetoes of February and March, Moderates tried to shape a congressional Reconstruction policy they hoped Johnson could support. John-son's vehement attack on the amendment shattered these expectations. Two other actions by Johnson, however, fundamentally altered the calculus of the 1866 elections and made them a referendum on Johnson himself as well as on the Fourteenth Amendment.

First, Johnson's closest advisors seized on the passage of the amendment in June to break completely with most congressional Republicans by calling a Na-tional Union convention to meet in Philadelphia in August to rally support for Johnson. That call signaled unmistakably that the Union party that he claimed to lead was not the exclusively northern and intransigently antisouthern Republican party. The call also brought to a head a struggle among different groups that had supported Johnson's program since the spring of 1865. One group consisted of conservative Republicans, most of whom were such former Whigs as the Con-necticut senator James Dixon, the Pennsylvania senator Edgar Cowan, Illinois' Orville Browning (whom Johnson appointed Secretary of the Interior in July 1866), and, most significant, Secretary of State William H. Seward and his New York allies Thurlow Weed and Congressman Henry J. Raymond, editor of the *New York Times* and chairman of the Union-Republican party's national com-mittee. They hoped to reshape the Union party to enhance their influence within it by ostracizing Radicals while attracting more northern Democrats and espe-cially former southern Whigs to it.

Their plan did not work. Ex-Democrats in the Union party such as Navy Sec-retary Gideon Welles, Treasury Secretary Hugh McCulloch, Lincoln's postmas-ter general, Montgomery Blair, Indiana governor Oliver P. Morton, and Wisconsin's ultraconservative senator James Doolittle argued that no realign-ment beneficial to Johnson could occur if former Whigs like Seward attempted to revive the Whig party under the Union label. Simultaneously, Democratic leaders who had been trying to bring Johnson back to their party since he became president in 1865 refused to participate in any scheme dominated by Republi-cans, no matter how conservative. They hoped instead to convert the Union party into an appendage of the Democratic party.

Ultimately the latter two groups prevailed by broadening the call for delegates beyond supporters of the wartime Union coalition. Northern Democrats, including such notorious Copperheads as Clement Vallandigham and former New York Mayor Fernando Wood attended the convention, as did delegates from the South such as Alexander H. Stephens and South Carolina's Governor James Orr. Their participation drove almost all conservative Republicans away from Johnson and the Union party movement and back to the Republican party. Opened to cheers when the Massachusetts and South Carolina delegates ostentatiously marched into the hall arm in arm, the convention lavishly praised Johnson, called on northerners to elect congressmen who supported his Reconstruction program, and demanded the immediate restoration of Confederate states to Congress without ratification of the Fourteenth Amendment.[32]

Rather than breathing life into the Union party as a credible party of the center, the Philadelphia convention effectively killed the Union party movement, drove Johnson into the arms of the Democratic party, and caused Republicans to drop the Union label to avoid association with Johnson and the northern Democrats and southern ex-Confederates who now embraced him. By the fall of 1866, the widely predicted realignment of national politics had apparently fizzled. The campaign pitted Republicans against Democrats.

Second, Johnson plunged eagerly into the campaign against Republicans. Between early July and the end of December, he fired 1,644 Republican postmasters in the North and replaced them with his men. He also broke precedent by personally campaigning against Republican congressional candidates. During a disastrous "swing around the circle" (August 28 to September 15), Johnson spoke in Philadelphia, New York, Albany, Buffalo, Cleveland, Chicago, Indianapolis, Louisville, Cincinnati, and Pittsburgh, defending his policy and urging voters to elect men (that is, Democrats) who would support it. Hooted and heckled in a number of places, he lost his temper and lashed back in violent language considered beneath the dignity of the presidency. When one heckler shouted, "Hang Jeff Davis!" Johnson snapped, "Why not hang Thad Stevens and Wendell Phillips?"[33] Even his friends were mortified; Doolittle, for example, deplored the "fatal mistake of the President in making extemporaneous speeches."[34] Johnson's misguided tour disgusted the northern public and diminished his personal popularity. Rather than helping Democrats, it instead encouraged Republican congressional campaigners to label Johnson himself, and not—as Democrats charged—their own Reconstruction program, as the biggest obstacle to full reunion.

Two incidents in the South during the spring and summer reaffirmed the necessity of that program. Since the end of the war reports had filtered North about individual acts of violence against freedmen, but in 1866 came news of collective acts of mayhem. These were not so much "race riots" as white massacres of blacks that local white police forces aided and abetted. For three days in early May white mobs, composed primarily of Irish policemen and firemen, assaulted blacks

In this 1867 cartoon, Thomas Nast illustrates how Republicans attempted to lay blame for the Memphis and New Orleans massacres directly on Andrew Johnson's indifference to freedmen's safety and to his pro-Confederate policies. Standing directly behind Johnson is Secretary of State William Henry Seward, who had alienated many congressional Republicans by remaining in the Cabinet. Immediately below Seward's right shoulder, with his eyes averted from the arena, is Secretary of War Edwin M. Stanton. Below Stanton, in the garb of a Roman soldier, is Ulysses S. Grant, the commanding general of the army.

on the streets of Memphis and attacked black neighborhoods. At least forty-six blacks were killed, compared with only two whites, five black women were raped, and hundreds of black homes, churches, and schools were incinerated.[35]

Far worse was the affray in New Orleans two months later. Since 1864, when Unionists had elected Michael Hahn governor and adopted a free-state constitution, the Unionist cause in Louisiana had suffered a tailspin. Hahn resigned the governorship to accept a prospective seat in the U.S. Senate, making James Madison Wells the new governor. Wells sided with the conservative planters who had sought to avert emancipation; to gain additional support he allowed ex-Confederates to vote as soon as the war ended. By the summer of 1866, ex-Confederates controlled the legislature and most local governments, including that of New Orleans. Finally awakened to the damage he had wrought, Wells in the summer of 1866 lurched toward the radical Unionists who had sought black suffrage since 1863. They attempted to reconvene the 1864 constitutional convention to enfranchise blacks, prohibit ex-Confederates from voting, and launch a new state government.

General Philip Sheridan, commander of the military district that encompassed New Orleans, knew that the mayor and local police force were overtly hostile to this convention. When, in Sheridan's absence from the city, General Absalom Baird wired Washington for instructions, however, Secretary of War Edwin Stanton failed to give Johnson his telegram, and no instructions were sent. As a result, the army made no attempt to intervene to protect the delegates. As they marched toward the meeting hall on July 30, some twenty-five delegates and a procession of about two hundred black supporters were fired on by a white mob that included many policemen. When the radicals fled into the meeting hall to seek refuge from the fusillade, the mob surrounded it, firing through its windows at blacks inside and gunning down blacks when they attempted to escape the building. In what Sheridan later called "an absolute massacre," thirty-four blacks and three white radicals were killed and over one hundred people were injured. Johnson's lenient policy, complained General Joseph Holt two days later, had unleashed "the barbarism of the rebellion in its renaissance."[36]

The Memphis and New Orleans "riots" not only demonstrated the necessity of providing greater federal protection to southern blacks and of the need for the Fourteenth Amendment to disqualify many ex-Confederates from state and local office. They also encouraged Republican campaigners in 1866 to smear Democrats as Confederate sympathizers and to adopt a harsher antisouthern tone. Yet that tactic was also in part defensive, for during the summer and fall an organization of Union army veterans known as the Grand Army of the Republic, which differed in purpose and personnel from the wartime Union Leagues, emerged across the North. Within short order the G.A.R. would become a veritable wing of the Republican party that supplied reliable Republican votes in return for ever more generous pensions that Republican congressmen showered on veterans. But initially the G.A.R. was a nonpartisan group that posed a distinct threat to civilian Republican politicians, because one stimulus to its formation was precisely soldiers' grievances against those leaders. Angered that civilian politicians who had escaped the hard sacrifices demanded of soldiers during the war controlled most political offices, the veterans demanded that soldiers be given preference in appointments and party nominations. What was more, both the Democrats and Johnson astutely moved in 1865 to heed those demands for preferential treatment of veterans to deprive Republicans of the soldier votes that had proved so crucial in 1864. Many veterans' deep antipathy toward blacks, moreover, made those moves a distinct threat.[37]

Republican politicians therefore had to coopt the G.A.R. before it damaged their electoral chances among soldiers whose political inclinations tilted toward the Democrats. Purposely downplaying Republican efforts on behalf of blacks was a start, but only a start. The Illinois Republican party accordingly gave its at-large

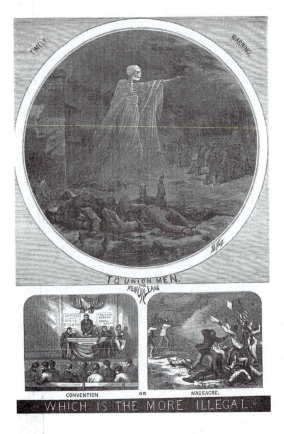

Thomas Nast illustrates how Republicans attempted to rouse voter support in the 1866 elections by exploiting northern anger at racial violence in the South.

congressional nomination in 1866 to General John A. Logan, a former Democrat and cofounder of the state's G.A.R. chapter, who despised the Republican senator Lyman Trumbull and vehemently opposed black suffrage.[38] Elsewhere, Republicans resorted to vitriolic antisouthern and anti-Democratic rhetoric, later to become famous as "waving the Bloody Shirt," to prove that Republicans meant to be tough on the South and to remind soldiers of the Democrats' pro-Confederate leanings.

In 1866, no Republican offered a more vivid example of this splenetic rhetoric than Indiana's Governor Morton, a one-time Democrat who served in the safety of the statehouse throughout the war. Until June 1866 he was one of Johnson's strongest supporters in the Union Republican party, and he hoped that the state legislature to be elected in 1866 would send him to the Senate. Fulminated Morton:

> Every unregenerate rebel, every deserter, every sneak who ran away from the draft calls himself a Democrat. . . . Every man who labored for the rebellion in the field, who murdered Union prisoners by cruelty and starvation . . . calls himself a Democrat. Every wolf in sheep's clothing who pretends to preach the gospel but proclaims the

righteousness of man-selling and slavery; every one who shoots down negroes in the streets, burns up negro school-houses and meeting-houses, and murders women and children by the light of their own flaming dwellings, calls himself a Democrat. . . . In short, the Democratic party may be described as a common sewer and loathsome receptacle into which is emptied every element of treason North and South, every element of inhumanity and barbarism which has dishonored the age.[39]

Armed with such rhetoric, bolstered by Johnson's slumping reputation, and determined, like most northerners, not to surrender in peace what they had won in the war, Republican candidates scored sweeping victories in the fall elections. Republicans retained two-thirds majorities in both houses of Congress and carried every non-Confederate state except Delaware, Kentucky, and Maryland. In many districts Republican incumbents had been replaced by new men, but there is no evidence that local organizations consciously displaced Moderates with Radicals. Rather, most of the new faces were the product of a traditional rotation of nominations from county to county in multicounty congressional districts.[40] But the contests had clearly shown that Republicans could stand up to Andrew Johnson and win. The question now was what they would do with their mandate.

| Congressional Reconstruction: The Second Phase, 1867–1869

I was a Conservative in the last session of this Congress," Thaddeus Stevens sarcastically announced on his return to the second session of the Thirty-ninth Congress in December 1866, "but I mean to be a Radical henceforth."[1] During the spring, the Moderates had frustrated the Radicals' goals and adopted a Reconstruction program primarily of their own design, but Stevens was correct in sensing that momentum had shifted in a radical direction. By December, even Moderate Republicans realized that they could not simply await ratification of the Fourteenth Amendment. Regardless of Andrew Johnson's objections, they believed, Congress must enact additional Reconstruction legislation to ensure protection of black rights in the South.

Two actions by congressional Republicans signalled their defiant self-confidence. The House and the Senate each expelled a prominent Democrat on flimsy pretexts, and in February Republicans passed a law calling the new Fortieth Congress into session in March 1867, immediately after the Thirty-ninth adjourned. Primarily, however, Republicans focused their efforts on formulating a new and sterner policy for the South. The results of their deliberations and those of Republicans in the new Fortieth Congress marked the second phase of Congressional Reconstruction.

Concern for blacks' safety was not all that spurred Republicans. Die-hard southern white Unionists, who had opposed the Confederacy throughout the war and who had been largely excluded from political office by pro-Johnson "Union" men, also implored Congress to dissolve the Johnson governments and start Reconstruction anew. The dividing line between these two groups of white Southerners had been highlighted by two gatherings in 1866. The pro-Johnson, ex-Whig, antisecessionist but pro-Confederate Unionists who dominated most southern state governments attended the Philadelphia National Union Convention in August and pledged their devotion to Johnson. A month later a Southern Loyalist Convention met in the same city, denounced ex-Confederates' control of most southern governments, endorsed the Fourteenth Amendment, and demanded that Congress, not Johnson, control Reconstruction.[2]

Yet the Southern Loyalist Convention also split along a fault line that prefigured the impending congressional debate and subsequent political developments in the South. Overwhelmingly outnumbered at home by pro-Confederate whites, delegates from unreconstructed Deep South states demanded that congressional Republicans enfranchise blacks to give them new political allies. Those from Tennessee, Arkansas, Missouri, Kentucky, West Virginia, Virginia, and Maryland, in contrast, spurned black suffrage as politically suicidal and asked Congress instead to disfranchise ex-Confederates as Missouri, Tennessee, and West Virginia had by state law. Congress would soon combine the two approaches.

Additional pressure for further legislation came from the publication in December 1866 of a Supreme Court decision entitled *ex parte Milligan*.[3] The court reversed the wartime conviction of an Indiana resident named Lambdin P. Milligan by a military tribunal on the grounds that no civilian could be tried by the army if civil courts were in operation, as they had been in Indiana at the time. Justice David Davis, author of the court's opinion, declared that it had nothing to do with the South, yet it appeared to question the legality of the Freedmen's Bureau courts and military commissions that during 1865 and 1866 had protected blacks, after Johnson had declared southern civilian courts legitimate.[4] Unless Congress did something to challenge the status of those civil courts and affirm military jurisdiction, Republicans agreed, a bulwark of black rights stood in jeopardy.

Although both Moderates and Radicals believed that the men who held southern office must be replaced because they failed to provide adequate protection to the freedmen, sharp differences continued to separate the two factions. For one thing, the Radicals now added to their agenda demands for Andrew Johnson's immediate impeachment and removal from office. The Moderates would successfully resist that effort until the spring of 1868. More important, Radicals and Moderates continued to disagree about the alternatives of a thoroughgoing, prolonged internal reconstruction of the South versus the timely readmission of ex-Confederate states to full political participation in the nation. If the Moderates now embraced the Radicals' earlier demands for the replacement of the Johnsonian state governments, they did so for quite different reasons than did Radicals.

Hoping to exploit northerners' outrage at the Memphis and New Orleans "riots," their frustration with southern states' refusal to ratify the Fourteenth Amendment, and their emphatic repudiation of Johnson at the polls, Radicals sought to enact their full agenda. Once Johnson's governments were abolished, they would territorialize the South and impose prolonged military rule on it, strip ex-Confederates of the right to vote, mandate black suffrage to elect provisional civil governments that would remain subordinate to Yankee generals, confiscate and redistribute rebels' property, and require equal education for both races. Still rejecting most of this agenda, Moderates continued to believe that the Republican party would be pummeled by northern voters in 1868 unless it had achieved political reunion with the South by the time of the presidential election. To the Radicals' dismay, therefore, the Moderates sought the replacement of the existing governments in order to speed up the process of state restoration to Congress. The upshot was that congressional Reconstruction policy in 1867 and 1868, like that of 1866, represented compromises between Radical and Moderate goals. As before, Moderates usually prevailed in the process.

## THE MILITARY RECONSTRUCTION ACTS

The non-Radical Republicans' preferred terms for the readmission of ex-Confederate states to Congress remained ratification of the Fourteenth Amendment. Because the existing southern state governments, aside from Tennessee's, refused to meet those terms, the Moderates were determined to force the election of new men who would. To help assure the choice of loyal men who heeded Congress's will, moreover, such Moderates as William Pitt Fessenden, Lyman Trumbull, and John Bingham were now prepared to include blacks in the electorate that chose them. Realizing that Johnson was sure to veto any such law, Moderates knew they must reach out to Radicals who sought instead to have the army govern the states into an undetermined future. Combining both goals, the Republicans united to pass four Military Reconstruction Acts over Johnson's vetoes in 1867 and 1868. These laws invalidated the Johnsonian governments in the South and reinaugurated the process of political Reconstruction on the basis of black suffrage and temporary, partial white disfranchisement.

The product of exceptionally bitter factional wrangling and frantic last-minute maneuvering, the first Military Reconstruction Act passed Congress over Johnson's veto on March 2, 1867, the last day of the session. To the Radicals' delight, it divided the ten ex-Confederate states that had refused to ratify the Fourteenth Amendment into five military districts—Virginia; North and South Carolina; Georgia, Alabama, and Florida; Mississippi and Arkansas; and Louisiana and Texas—and instructed the president to appoint a major general in command of each. Those generals were declared superior to civilian officials and empowered to deploy the army to protect lives and property, to make arrests and try civilians in military tribunals for private crimes, and to remove and replace any civilian officials who disobeyed or interfered with them. The law implied that some civilian officials must be removed, for it also declared immediately ineligible for office any individual disqualified from it by the as yet unratified Fourteenth Amendment. The existing Johnsonian state governments were declared "provisional" and subordinate to military authority, but, over Radicals' angry objections, the law did not require that those governments immediately be dispersed. Thus it did not guarantee that anti-Confederate loyalists could instantly replace pro-Johnson Unionists in state and local offices.

To the Radicals' dismay, moreover, the law made it clear that military rule would be temporary, not prolonged. It contained provisions sought by Moderates to bring about the states' restoration to Congress. It stipulated that a new registration of voters was to be held to identify men eligible to elect delegates to new state constitutional conventions. It mandated that blacks could vote in those elections and in the subsequent elections to ratify the new constitutions, and it required that the new constitutions guarantee blacks' right to vote in all future state and federal elections. What was more, it declared that all whites who were prohibited from holding office by the third section of the pending Fourteenth Amendment could not *vote* in the elections for convention delegates, serve as delegates, or participate in the subsequent ratification contests. And it required the new constitutions permanently to proscribe the same white Southerners from public office, while allowing the conventions to extend or end the temporary disfranchisement of those men at the delegates' discretion. Finally, it declared that once the new state constitution had been ratified by a majority of eligible voters, once the new state legislature elected under its provisions ratified the Fourteenth Amendment, and once that amendment became part of the federal Constitution, then troops would be removed, the new state government would be recognized, and the state "might be entitled to representation in Congress."[5]

The statute thus created a constitutional anomaly. After denying the legal validity of ten southern state governments, it then required them to ratify a constitutional amendment, something only fully equal and valid states could do. Hastily composed to reconcile conflicting demands while stopping Johnson from deploying a post adjournment pocket veto that could not be overridden, the law was also poorly written. Its confusing wording obscured rather than clarified what the precise relationship between military commanders and elected civilian officeholders was supposed to be. More important, its vague language left unclear precisely who—military commanders or elected governors—was to register voters, call a constitutional convention, and launch the process whereby the existing Johnsonian regimes could be displaced by new governments chosen by a reconstituted electorate. That ambiguity frustrated Republicans' intentions, for the white Southerners staffing the existing governments had no more interest in surrendering office by this process than they had by ratifying the Fourteenth Amendment in 1866.

The Republicans quickly recognized this fact. To rectify it, Republicans in the new Fortieth Congress, meeting in March rather than December as customary, passed a second Military Reconstruction Act over Johnson's veto on March 23, 1867. This act directed the federal military commanders to take the initiative in registering voters, calling conventions, and scheduling the elections of delegates, and in promoting the adoption of new state constitutions. The Radicals accepted this measure because it would hasten the destruction of the Johnsonian governments and thus open the opportunity for loyal men, both black and white, to come to power. Moderates, in turn, cheered the likelihood that the measure could hasten the restoration of ex-Confederate states to Congress.

Yet even this measure was not enough to produce the desired results because of obstructionism from white southerners and Andrew Johnson. Military commanders lacked sufficient troops to launch the process of registering voters and arranging elections. They required cooperation from civilian officials, but most of those officials refused to provide it. Long imbued with a tradition of deferring to civilian rule, most commanders refused to remove them and applied the ban on men disqualified by the Fourteenth Amendment only to newly elected men, not incumbents. The exception was General Philip Sheridan, commander of the Texas-Louisiana district. He removed a city judge, a city treasurer, and the mayor of New Orleans, and in June 1867 he replaced Governor James Madison Wells with Benjamin Flanders, a leader of the radicals who had sought black suffrage since 1864. In response, Johnson removed Sheridan and appointed General Winfield Scott Hancock, a Democrat who would be his party's presidential candidate in 1880. Armed with an opinion from Attorney General Henry Stanbery (June 20, 1867) that the laws did not allow military commanders to promulgate codes in defiance of states' civilian governments, Johnson also ordered his military commanders to defer to civilian authority.[6]

Properly fearful that Johnson meant to subvert the entire congressional program, Republicans called a special session of Congress in July 1867 to pass a third Military Reconstruction Act. This again represented a compromise, embodying the Radicals' assertion of direct national authority over the South while also promising to hasten the process of restoration that the Moderates sought. It flatly declared that existing state governments in the South were "not legal" and were fully subject to military commanders and the paramount authority of Congress. The commanding general of the army, Ulysses S. Grant, and the commanders of the military districts were directed to remove any state official who should "hinder, delay, prevent or obstruct the due and proper administration" of the reconstruction acts. Registration boards were ordered to purge voting lists of anyone suspected of falsely swearing he was not covered by the disqualifications of the Fourteenth Amendment. To further emphasize the supremacy of military power and to try to prevent Johnson from using his authority as commander in chief of the army to frustrate implementation of Congress's program, the act stipulated that no military commander, nor any officer acting under him, should be bound "by the opinion of any civil officer of the United States."

Three reconstruction acts had now been passed, two of them supplemental to the first. Some months elapsed; and then it became evident that the legislative machinery was not even yet accomplishing the Republicans' purpose—the election of new, more loyal southern state governments. The existing laws required that new state constitutions must be ratified by a majority of all registered voters, not merely a majority of votes cast. Seizing on this requirement to defeat the newly proposed constitution in Alabama, framed by delegates said to represent only freedmen and nonresidents, a conference of conservative ex-Confederates at Montgomery issued an appeal to whites to boycott the ratifying election. Through abstention, rather than negative votes, they might block the new constitution and force the Republican-dominated constitutional convention to change the rules to allow ratification by a majority of those who voted, not a majority of all registered voters. Any such opportunistic change in the procedural rules, crowed this Montgomery conference, would "exhibit . . . the fact that the constitution they impose is not the constitution of the people of Alabama, but . . . of a minority . . . and that, a negro minority."[7] The convention did not alter the rules. When the constitution was voted on (February 4, 1868), therefore, it was defeated because the affirmative vote of about seventy thousand was fewer than half of the approximately 167,000 registered voters.

This setback in Alabama caused congressional Republicans to pass a fourth reconstruction act on March 11, 1868 that did precisely what the Montgomery conference had predicted Alabama Republicans would do. It allowed ratification of new constitutions by a majority of those who voted, no matter how small the turnout was; the Republicans then used this retroactive law to certify the adoption of Alabama's constitution. With the presidential election that year, the Moderates were desperate to speed up restoration whereas the Radicals were equally determined to displace the Johnsonian state government with new men. Thus this act, like the other three, was a compromise between Republican factions.

## WHAT THE MILITARY RECONSTRUCTION ACTS SIGNIFIED

By March 1868, Congress had passed four laws that governed the reconstruction process in ten ex-Confederate states. But their terms, including the requirement of black enfranchisement, did not affect Tennessee, the border slave states that had remained loyal during the Civil War, or the North. Unlike the Civil Rights Act of 1866 and the Fourteenth Amendment, these laws did not apply to the entire nation. They were aimed exclusively at the defeated Confederates.

The Military Reconstruction Acts were once thought to epitomize Radical Reconstruction, and in many ways they *were* considerably more radical than Congress's first reconstruction program in 1866. They subordinated freely elected southern civil governments to temporary military rule. If they did not reduce states to formal territorial status, they lumped them into administrative districts that were subject to common military orders, not individual state laws. They explicitly sought to place in office new men who would heed Congress' will in the South. And they pursued that objective by forcing the ten states—and only those ten states—to grant blacks the vote, simultaneously disempowering white Southerners' traditional political elite.

Many Radicals, however, remained dissatisfied with these laws. Charles Sumner admitted that he voted for the second act "not because it is what I desire, but because it is all that Congress is disposed to enact at the present time." Wisconsin's Radical senator Timothy O. Howe called that bill a "monstrous blunder."[8] The laws, in fact, fell considerably short of the Radicals' wishes. As Michael Les Benedict has ably summarized, Congress' program "did not put Republicans in control of the restoration process as congressional and southern radicals pleaded." "It minimized disfranchisement," rather than incorporating the much broader and longer deprivation of Confederates' voting rights sought by Radicals. "It left officials of the Johnson state governments in office and in control of state patronage," rather than immediately dissolving those governments as Radicals insisted. And "it encouraged speedier restoration than radicals wanted," while ignoring Radical priorities like "education and land reform." Its "radicalism," Benedict concludes, "lay in one provision: black suffrage."[9]

Black suffrage had indeed been a source of conflict between Radicals and Moderates in early 1866. But the most zealous of Radical ideologues had wanted to impose it on the entire nation by statute or constitutional amendment, not just on ten southern states. By the spring of 1867, moreover, non-Radical Republicans viewed black suffrage as far preferable to the alternative they considered truly extreme: direct national governance of the defeated South through national law and prolonged military rule. Moderates still sought the fastest possible restoration of self-government in the South by the election of men who would protect black rights and merit readmission to Congress. They now saw black suffrage as an instrument to achieve those goals while still preserving state-centered federalism. They decided, in effect, that if the majority of pro-Confederate whites would not elect governments satisfactory to Congress, the Republicans would add blacks to, and remove influential whites from, the southern electorate in the hope that this new mix would choose acceptable governments.

Moderates, in sum, resorted to black suffrage in order to shun direct national responsibility for protecting blacks' rights. They would give blacks the vote and rely on blacks themselves to defend their rights in the arena of state politics. A new magazine, *The Nation*, recognized this fact. Negro suffrage, it argued as early as January 1866, "though brought forward as a radical remedy . . . is anything but radical." What *would* have been radical, Carl Schurz made clear in March 1867, was a shift of power within the federal system toward Washington. "Far from desiring centralization repulsive to the genius of this country," he wrote in defense of the first Military Reconstruction Act, "it is in the distinct interest of local self-government and legitimate State rights that we urge these propositions, and nothing can be more certain than that this is the only way in which a dangerous centralization of power in the hands of our general government can be prevented."[10]

Aside from averting centralization, the Moderates' support for black suffrage signaled a new strategy for dealing with the potential political power of restored southern states. Rather than reducing southern representation in Congress and the Electoral College, as they had intended the Fourteenth Amendment to do, they would now allow those states to gain the increased clout that resulted from emancipation and instead would compete for political control of southern state governments. In 1867, for the first time, they decided to build up a southern wing of the Republican party based on freedmen, anti-Confederate white loyalists, and any ex-Confederates who could be persuaded to cooperate with them. Indeed, to ensure that Republicans, rather than Johnson's Union supporters or Democrats, gained initial control of the new state governments created by the new state constitutions their program required, Republicans rigged the rules of the game. They not only enfranchised blacks; they disfranchised an unknown number of whites.

This strategy had profound implications. In effect, congressional Republicans were attempting to re-create a system of two-party competition in states from which it had disappeared in the 1850s or during the war. By relying on newly formed southern Republican coalitions and Republican state administrations, rather than national law, to secure the goals of congressional policy, they were entrusting the success of their program to the vagaries of electoral politics within the South. For that reason, what would demarcate and define the failure of Congressional Reconstruction was the defeat and overthrow of Republican state governments and Republican state parties in the South.

Yet the four reconstruction acts signaled something else as well. Since the national government lacked any civilian administrative bureaucracy to implement Congress's program, Republicans relied on the army to do the job. They could override Johnson's vetoes of their laws, but, as his removal of Sheridan demonstrated, Johnson's constitutional role as commander in chief gave him power over the men in the field whom Congress expected to carry out its measures. The clause in the third act forbidding district military commanders to heed orders from any civilian official in the federal government thus exposed a crucial subtheme of the Republicans' efforts to displace Presidential with Congressional Reconstruction. Johnson and congressional Republicans vied for control of the United States Army, which had remained the ultimate enforcer of federal authority in the South since the spring of 1865. The pivotal figures in that struggle were Secretary of War Edwin Stanton and especially the army's commanding general and the North's greatest war hero, Ulysses S. Grant.

## GRANT, THE ARMY, AND RECONSTRUCTION

On March 2, 1867, the day on which the first Military Reconstruction Act became law, congressional Republicans enacted three additional statutes that affected the ability of the army to carry it out. One, occasioned by the *ex parte Milligan* ruling, validated the decisions of all military trials held in the South since April 1865. A second, the Tenure of Office Act, sought to prevent Johnson from removing appointive federal officials from office without Senate approval. Johnson's sacking of northern postmasters during the last six months of 1866 in part provoked this legislation, but a provision relating to Cabinet members proved its most controversial and consequential feature. This stipulated that Cabinet officers should retain their posts "for and during the term of the President by whom they may have been appointed, and for one month thereafter, subject to the advice and consent of the Senate."[11] Republicans clearly intended this provision to stop Johnson from removing Stanton, the Cabinet member who most clearly sided with congressional Republicans and most vociferously protested Johnson's efforts to obstruct their program.

The third measure was an Army Appropriations Act, normally an annual piece of legislation; but the second section of the 1867 act was anything but conventional. As the historian James E. Sefton has summarized, it mandated "that the General-in-Chief's headquarters should be fixed at Washington, and that he could not be removed, suspended, or assigned to duty elsewhere except at his own request, unless the Senate gave prior approval. Moreover, all orders issued to the Army from the President and Secretary of War had to go through the General-in-Chief; orders not so routed were null and void, and to obey them could lead to imprisonment for two to twenty years."[12] Grant was the General-in-Chief, and congressional Republicans here sought to ensure that he, not Johnson, supervised the implementation of their program.

The immediate cause of the legislation was an attempt by Johnson in October 1866 to send Grant on a diplomatic mission to Mexico so that Johnson could replace him, if only temporarily, with the more conservative William T. Sherman as the army's commanding general. Grant and the congressional Republicans realized Johnson's motives, and Grant's refusal to leave Washington along with Sherman's refusal to be made a political catspaw aborted the scheme.[13] But it illustrated Johnson's determination to manipulate the army's most famous and popular commanders to forward his political goals. Of these men, none was so important to Johnson—and ultimately to congressional Republicans—as Grant.

Initially, Grant had seemed a likely ally for the president. He was committed to the principle of military subordination to civilian authority even while deeply distrustful of politicians. After Appomattox he favored the fastest possible reconciliation between southern and northern whites and quick restoration of southern representation in Congress, but he also remained determined not to allow politicians to sacrifice what the troops under his command had fought and died to win. Like most northern officers stationed in the South, Grant had far less interest in protecting freedmen's rights or enfranchising them than in restoring social order and getting blacks back to work on plantations. Even his disposition of troops reflected his desire to conciliate southern whites. Well aware of their particular animosity toward black troops, Grant wanted to use only white soldiers as occupation forces, but he recognized that pressure from northern civilians for the rapid demobilization of volunteers would leave him primarily dependent on blacks. Thus he urged the immediate dissolution of black volunteer regiments from the North and ordered that regiments composed of southern blacks be assigned to the West or to garrison duty along the Atlantic and Gulf coasts, rather than stationed in the interior of southern states where they might provoke white resentment. And after passage of an army reorganizing act in July 1866 allowed Grant to use regular army troops for occupation duty, he would urge that all black volunteers be mustered out.[14]

Recognizing Grant as a kindred spirit and eager to secure his immense prestige on behalf of his own program, Johnson sent Grant on a ten-day tour of the South Atlantic states in the late fall of 1865 to report on conditions there. Delighted that the general found that "the mass of thinking men of the south accept the present situation of affairs in good faith," Johnson forwarded the report to Congress in December 1865 to support his contention that Reconstruction was complete and that southern states deserved restoration. Radicals complained that Grant had become Johnson's puppet, but even in this report Grant recommended continued military occupation of the South and a prolongation of the Freedmen's Bureau. On receiving reports of violence against blacks elsewhere in the South, Grant ordered his commanders in the South to give military protection to blacks "charged with offenses for which white persons are not prosecuted or punished in the same manner and degree." This was in January 1866, before Congress passed any legislation. By directing the army in effect to overrule the Black Codes, Grant signaled in early 1866 that his priority was shifting from conciliating ex-Confederates to protecting black and white loyalists.[15]

Even after Johnson issued a proclamation in April 1866 declaring the insurrection over, Grant continued to insist that federal troops must offer military protection to blacks. Responding to the Memphis riots, in July 1866 he issued General Order No. 44, commanding officers in the South to arrest civilians for crimes whenever civilian authorities refused to do so, although in deference to Johnson he did not specify that such men would be tried by military commissions. And when Johnson proclaimed in August that "peace, order, tranquility, and civil authority existed throughout the nation," Grant, though disagreeing with his commander in chief, informed his subordinates that the proclamation had nullified his orders.[16] Having exploited Grant's deference to civilian authority to obstruct his efforts on behalf of freedmen, Johnson then dragged the unhappy general along with him during his swing around the circle to give the false impression that Grant endorsed his policies.

But Grant proved to be a skillful political infighter. Not only did he resist Johnson's efforts to dispatch him to Mexico later that fall; he also worked closely with congressional Republicans on the framing of the Military Reconstruction acts, especially the provisions sought by Moderates that attached a process for restoration to military rule. And once Congress had enacted the legislation, Grant, along with Edwin Stanton, instructed commanders in the South to ignore Attorney General Henry Stanbery's eviscerating interpretations of the Military Reconstruction Acts and to "enforce your own construction of the Military Bill until ordered [by Grant] to do otherwise."[17]

Grant's tough resistance to Johnson's efforts to delay enforcement of the Military Reconstruction Acts earned him plaudits from congressional Republicans. Then, in the summer of 1867, he allowed Johnson to manipulate him in a way that infuriated the Radicals and that became inextricably entangled in rancorous divisions between Moderates and Radicals over the issue of impeaching Johnson. Johnson had long chafed at Edwin Stanton's presence in his cabinet, and he had always questioned the applicability of the Tenure of Office Act to Stanton, since Stanton had been appointed during Lincoln's first term, not his second, during which Johnson replaced Lincoln. In any event, the law allowed interim removals when the Senate was not in session, and Stanton's active role in helping Republicans frame the Third Military Reconstruction Act in July 1867 triggered Johnson's attempt to replace him. As soon as Congress adjourned, the president demanded Stanton's resignation. When Stanton refused, Johnson offered the post to Grant on an interim basis in August, and Grant, believing that Stanton was doomed and that Johnson would appoint someone far less sympathetic to the congressional program than he if he declined, accepted the War Department portfolio, thereby incensing Radicals.

As both interim secretary of war and commanding general of the army, Grant still proved unable to prevent Johnson from replacing Sheridan and General Daniel Sickles with men more amenable to Johnson's attempt to frustrate congressional Reconstruction. Nonetheless, he pledged to Johnson that he would retain the post and keep Stanton out of it, and he kept that pledge until the Senate, now back in session, passed a resolution in January 1868 ordering Stanton's reinstatement. Despite Johnson's public cries of betrayal, Grant turned the office over to Stanton. In a calculated attempt to challenge the constitutionality of the Tenure of Office Act, Johnson then appointed General Lorenzo Thomas as a new interim secretary of war, directly attacking the Senate's action.

## THE IMPEACHMENT OF ANDREW JOHNSON

Because the appointment of an interim cabinet officer while Congress was in session directly violated the Tenure of Office Act's requirement of authorization from the Senate, on February 24, 1868, three days after Johnson named Thomas, the House of Representatives formally impeached him by a vote of 126 to 47. Every Republican present supported the resolution; all of the opposition came from Democrats. The equivalent of indictment by a grand jury, impeachment required Johnson to be tried before the Senate, acting as a jury, in proceedings over which the Chief Justice of the United States, Salmon Chase, would preside. Conviction and removal from office required a two-thirds majority vote by the senators.

Yet Thomas's appointment was the occasion for, not the fundamental cause of, the Republicans' attempt to remove Johnson from office. Equally important, the Radicals had begun the drive for impeachment in December 1866, three months before the Tenure of Office Act passed; Moderate Republicans who joined Radicals in supporting impeachment in February 1868 had steadfastly opposed it for the fourteen preceding months. In the second session of the Thirty-ninth Congress (December 1866–March 1867), Moderates used their control of the Republican caucus and committees to smother attempts to bring impeachment resolutions to a floor vote. They narrowly defined the purpose of the next Congress' special session in July 1867 explicitly to stop Radicals from renewing attempts at impeachment. And as recently as December 1867 most Moderate Republicans in the House joined Democrats in a roll-call vote to defeat a resolution of impeachment supported by their Radical colleagues.[18]

Just like Reconstruction policy itself, in sum, impeachment provoked serious divisions among congressional Republicans. From the start, the Radicals' case for ousting Johnson from office was straightforward and compelling. Citing Johnson's vetoes in 1866 and especially his efforts to deter southern states from ratifying the Fourteenth Amendment, the Radicals argued that the congressional Reconstruction program could never succeed so long as Johnson remained in office. In contrast, the Moderates regarded impeachment, just as they regarded confiscation of land or massive disfranchisement of former Confederates and prolonged military rule of the South, as too extreme for their northern constituents to stomach. Instead of removing Johnson, the Moderates tried to hem him in with a series of laws that restricted his presidential powers, laws that the Radicals constantly predicted could never work as long as Johnson remained the army's commander in chief and laws that, equally important, did damage to the office of the presidency itself while keeping a defiant obstructionist in it. Why not save the proper balance of constitutional power between that office and Congress, asked Radicals, by removing Johnson?

Because it was the Moderates, and not the Radicals, who were desperate to have southern states restored by the 1868 presidential election and because Johnson was manifestly subverting the South's compliance with congressional Republicans' terms for restoration, that question had particular force. Why did the Moderates fight so long to keep Johnson from being impeached, and why did they suddenly change their minds in February 1868?

At least four reasons can be offered for the Moderates' initial hesitation to impeach. All stemmed from partisan calculations and from an increasingly bitter battle between Radicals and Moderates for control of the Republican party and its 1868 presidential nomination. The Moderates' top priority remained retaining control of both the White House and Congress, and thus they blanched at any move that might threaten Republican success in the 1868 northern elections. Aware of Johnson's mass removal of Republican postmasters during 1866, the Moderates feared that inciting Johnson into an all-out slaughter of remaining Republican appointees would weaken the party's chances of winning in 1868. Furthermore, since men affiliated with the Moderate wing of the party who could help determine which Republicans became delegates to the national convention held many of those patronage posts, the Moderates, who feared the Radicals might control that gathering, sought to keep such vital allies in office.[19]

Second, the Moderates feared that supporting impeachment would identify the Republican party with the Radicals' entire agenda of confiscation and land redistribution, federally imposed requirements for free public schooling in the South, and black enfranchisement throughout the nation by federal statute. Such an identity, Moderates worried, would alienate enough northern voters to throw the 1868 congressional and presidential elections to the Democrats. The Radicals, complained Henry L. Dawes in July 1867 as the Moderates staved off yet another attempt at impeachment, "are determined to ruin the Republican party." Nonetheless, "The President . . . *does* continue to do the most provoking things. If he isn't impeached it wont [sic] be his fault."[20]

Johnson's removal of Sheridan and Sickles immediately after Congress adjourned that summer convinced even most Moderates that he must be impeached when Congress reassembled in late November. What saved him then were the results of the 1867 campaigns in the North for governors and state legislatures. Those returns reconvinced the Moderates that the stigma of radicalism would doom the party to defeat in 1868.[21]

According to Michael Les Benedict, the 1867 elections "marked the turning point in the battle between radical and nonradical Republicans."[22] In contrast to 1866, when Republicans had won sweeping victories by stressing the essential moderation of their Reconstruction program, in 1867 the Radicals publicly attacked their Moderate colleagues and insisted on making the elections a plebiscite on their entire agenda. Aside from immediate impeachment, enfranchisement of all the nation's adult African American males received the greatest emphasis in 1867. Radicals in Kansas, Minnesota, and Ohio scheduled referenda on enfranchising blacks through state constitutional amendments on the same day as the election; only last-minute second thoughts kept New York Radicals from following suit.[23] Everywhere black suffrage lost, and almost everywhere Republican turnout plummeted while the Democratic vote soared. Republicans maintained control of most northern state legislatures by reduced margins, but

Democrats carried the legislatures of Ohio and New York and the statewide offices in Pennsylvania. The North's three biggest states, which were absolutely essential to retaining the presidency, stood in jeopardy. Moderates blamed the disastrous outcome on the Radicals' mad insistence on pushing impeachment, confiscation, and black suffrage. As Professor Benedict summarizes the impact, "The Republican reverses of 1867 led to the defeat of radical hopes to impeach Andrew Johnson, stiffen the Reconstruction laws, and elect a radical president upon a radical platform in 1868."[24]

Proponents of women's suffrage were also disappointed by the 1867 results. The Kansas legislature had placed a referendum on enfranchising women along with that enfranchising blacks on the 1867 ballot. Elizabeth Cady Stanton and Susan B. Anthony had campaigned across the state for that measure, but it too went down to defeat. Many Republicans regarded woman suffrage as even more extreme than black enfranchisement, and Stanton and Anthony had in fact turned to Democrats for help during their speaking tour in Kansas. Yet some Radicals supported women's right to vote. The most important of these was Senator Ben Wade of Ohio. Wade was president *pro tem* of the Senate; there being no vice president, he would replace Johnson as president should the Republicans remove him. The prospect of Wade's elevation also deterred the Moderates from impeachment.[25]

The chastening 1867 results convinced almost all Moderates that the Republicans' only hope of carrying the 1868 presidential election was to run Grant, whose popularity among northern Republicans had been growing throughout 1867 despite his service in Johnson's cabinet. His platform, they further determined, must omit Radical goals. Concern about securing Grant's nomination was thus the third factor that caused them to shun Johnson's impeachment. Moderates feared that as acting president Wade could manipulate federal patronage to secure the party's presidential nomination for himself or some other Radical. To keep Wade out of the White House where, Moderates believed, he could destroy Republicans' chances of winning the 1868 election, Moderates had to oppose impeachment of Johnson. Thus when House Radicals finally pushed a motion to impeach Johnson to a vote in December 1867, 66 Moderate Republicans joined 42 Democrats to defeat the Radical motion, 57 to 108.[26]

Yet there was another reason why Moderates dreaded replacing Johnson with Wade, and this was the fourth reason that Radicals wanted and Moderates opposed impeachment. The relationship was not perfect, but those two blocs also divided over the issue of contracting the currency by reducing the amount of greenbacks in circulation in order to move the government and the nation back to a gold standard. In the spring of 1866 Congress had authorized Johnson's secretary of the treasury, Hugh McCulloch, to remove greenbacks from circulation; Moderates, especially Senator William Pitt Fessenden, applauded his vigorous efforts to do so. By the start of 1867, however, McCulloch's mild contraction had produced a recession by forcing prices down. Republicans who represented manufacturing districts or who favored extensive greenback circulation to ensure ample credit and low interest rates on private loans sought to change the law to stop McCulloch, and most of those Republicans were Radicals. Ben Wade, moreover, was perhaps the most vociferous opponent of currency contraction in Congress. Moderates, therefore, feared that Wade as president would sack McCulloch; to keep McCulloch in the treasury, they believed they had to keep Johnson in the White House. It was an additional reason they voted against impeachment in December 1867.[27]

House Moderates changed their minds between December 1867 and February 1868 primarily because Johnson, emboldened by the House vote against impeachment in December, went on a rampage that threatened to block the restoration of any of the remaining ten ex-Confederate states before the presidential election. Moderates had dreaded that prospect since December 1865 because they believed failure to secure political reunion would guarantee Republicans' defeat. Even before Johnson directly flouted the Senate in February by sacking Stanton and appointing Thomas to the War Department, Johnson removed General John Pope from his command in Georgia, General Wager Swayne from Alabama—thereby encouraging the white conservatives who sought to delay the adoption of a new state constitution there—and General Edward C. Ord, who commanded the Department of Mississippi and Arkansas. All were replaced with conservatives uncommitted to the congressional program. Simultaneously Johnson encouraged General John Schofield in Virginia to resist pleas from nascent Republicans there to remove pro-Johnson state officials who blocked the writing of a new state constitution for the Old Dominion. From across the South letters poured in to Republican congressmen warning that unless Johnson was removed and soldiers dedicated to the implementation of Congress' policies appointed in the South, political Reconstruction in accordance with Congress' terms would fail entirely.[28] Unless Johnson was "convicted and removed" wrote a Mississippi Republican in early 1868, "our efforts here will be defeated, and it will no longer be safe for a white man to advocate the principles of the Republican party in the State except under the immediate protection of federal bayonets."[29]

Aside from Johnson's flagrant violation of the Tenure of Office Act, fear that ex-Confederate states would not complete the steps Congress had mandated to secure readmission before Congress adjourned in the summer of 1868 explains why Moderate Republicans in the House shifted their stance on impeachment between December and February. That Republicans passed the Fourth Military Reconstruction Act, easing the requirements for Alabama's readmission, within two weeks of the House vote on impeachment suggests that panic motivated Moderates. So does the impeachment procedure in the House itself.

When Republicans voted on impeachment on February 24, no hearings on Johnson's supposed high crimes and misdemeanors had yet been held that session, nor had any formal charges been brought. Republicans voted to remove Johnson before they decided on the grounds for removal. Rather than invite the delay that a formal committee inquiry would ensure, Republicans on February 26 dispatched two members immediately to impeach Johnson before the bar of the Senate and to inform that body that in due time the House would produce formal articles of impeachment. Simultaneously, they voted to appoint a seven-man committee to prepare those articles. Six of those men were Republicans, and only Ohio's John Bingham and Iowa's James Wilson were Moderates who had previously opposed impeachment. Four were staunch Radicals: George Boutwell, Thaddeus Stevens, George W. Julian, and John A. Logan.

On March 2–3, House Republicans adopted eleven articles of impeachment. The first eight rang changes on the theme that Johnson had violated the law and the Constitution by removing Stanton after the Senate had reinstated him and by appointing Thomas on an *ad interim* basis with Congress in session. The ninth accused Johnson of attempting to inveigle a general into disobeying the terms of the March 1867 army act requiring all orders to go through Grant. The tenth, drawn up by the vindictive Ben Butler at Stevens's request, flayed Johnson for having delivered "inflammatory and scandalous harangues" against Congress in 1866 in an attempt to disgrace it. Thus Johnson was "guilty of a high misdemeanor in office" precisely because he had "brought the high office of the President of the United States into contempt, ridicule, and disgrace, to the great scandal of all good citizens," and *not* because he had violated any law. The eleventh article, the "omnibus" article, repeated the accusations about removing Stanton and added a charge that the president had publicly referred to the Thirty-ninth Congress as "a Congress of only part of the States, thereby denying, and intending to deny, that the legislation of said Congress was valid."[30] If nothing else could get Senate Republicans to convict Johnson, House impeachers seemed to believe, institutional pride and resentment might do the trick.

Having adopted formal resolutions of impeachment, none of which mentioned Republicans' chief grievance—Johnson's obstructionism of Reconstruction in the South—the House then named a committee of seven men to prosecute Johnson in the Senate. It included John Bingham, Wilson, George S. Boutwell, Thaddeus Stevens, and John A. Logan from the group that had drawn up the articles and two ardent Radicals, Thomas Williams of Pittsburgh and Ben Butler, who took the lead for the prosecution during the Senate trial.

No one expected that trial to be any less partisan than the proceedings in the House. Not a single House Democrat was among the House prosecutors, for no one in 1868 even pretended that impeachment of a president should be bipartisan. Everyone knew the Senate's Democrats would all vote for acquittal. Still, Senate Republicans possessed the two-thirds majority necessary to convict without a single Democratic vote. Thus Johnson's fate, and, many Republicans believed, the successful implementation of the congressional Republicans' Reconstruction program for the South, hinged on what Senate Republicans did.

## THE TRIUMPH OF THE MODERATES

After considerable wrangling over procedure in the Senate and a delay granted Johnson's defense team, Johnson's trial began on March 30. The decisive votes ending it were taken on May 16 and May 26. Johnson was not forced to appear in the Senate, and he was represented by able counsel, especially William M. Evarts, his lead attorney. Evarts argued that Johnson had committed no crime when he removed Stanton, because he believed the Tenure of Office Act to be unconstitutional and wanted to create a case to challenge the law in court. That argument was strengthened when General Sherman testified that establishing a test case was indeed Johnson's motive. Evarts also argued powerfully that removing Johnson would destroy the constitutional balance of power between the executive and legislative branches.[31] Johnson's defense was also aided by testimony from another officer that demolished the ninth article of impeachment.

It was aided even more by the essential flimsiness, not so much of House Republicans' reasons for ousting Johnson, but of the formal case they presented against him. The way House prosecutors presented that case testified to its weakness. Butler resorted to emotional cries that Johnson had repeatedly insulted Congress and that the "hopes of free institutions" required his conviction. The seriously ill Stevens angrily threatened that any Republican senator who voted for acquittal would "suffer . . . everlasting obloquy."[32] Passion persuaded most Senate Republicans, but not all. Some Moderates shared the Democrats' doubts

The impeachment trial of Andrew Johnson

that Johnson had broken the law, because the terms of the Tenure of Office Act did not encompass Stanton, who had been appointed during Lincoln's first term, not his second.

Whatever the merits of the prosecution's case, moreover, leading Moderates like Fessenden, Lyman Trumbull, and James Grimes continued to worry primarily about the disastrous impact Wade's elevation to the presidency might have on the nation and the Republican party. They not only feared McCulloch's ouster from the Treasury Department and his replacement by an anticontractionist, but they also worried that Wade's ascension would shift Republicans' attention from Reconstruction, on which they were reasonably united, to economic questions, which badly divided the party. And a divided party might lose the 1868 elections.[33]

On May 16, the Senate voted on the eleventh impeachment article, which Johnson's enemies had scheduled first since it seemed most likely to succeed. It did not because of Moderate opposition. Fessenden, Grimes, and Trumbull, joined by Joseph Fowler of Tennessee, John Henderson of Missouri, Edmund Ross of Kansas, and Henry Van Winkle of West Virginia, opposed conviction, thus denying the necessary two-thirds majority by precisely one vote, 35 to 19. Ten days later, votes on the second and third articles produced exactly the same alignment. Impeachment was dead, and Moderate Republicans, along with Democrats, had defeated it.[34]

Stopping Wade's ascension to the White House for the remainder of Johnson's term was not the Moderates' only success that spring. On May 19–20, 1868, between the two Senate votes, the Republican national convention met in Chicago. Though some delegates bitterly denounced the seven Moderate senators who had just voted to acquit Johnson, efforts to issue a formal resolution of censure against them failed utterly.[35] More important, the delegates unanimously nominated the Moderates' preferred presidential candidate, Ulysses S. Grant, on the first ballot. Nor would Moderates give Wade, whose days in the Senate were numbered once Democrats won the Ohio legislature in 1867, the solace of the vice presidential nomination. Instead, that post went to Indiana's Schuyler Colfax, who had been one of the centrist or Moderate leaders in the House.[36]

Yet it was the Republican platform that most decisively demonstrated the Moderates' control of the party. Aware of how much the Radicals' insistence on promoting black suffrage in the North had cost the party in 1867, Republicans adopted a two-faced plank on suffrage that left many Radicals sputtering about a retreat to expediency. "It is like most of the Republican platforms for the last six years," fumed an outraged Thaddeus Stevens, "tame and cowardly."[37] The controversial plank affirmed that "the guarantee by Congress of equal suffrage to all loyal men at the South was demanded by every consideration of public safety, of gratitude, and of justice, and must be maintained." Simultaneously, it asserted that "the question of suffrage in all the loyal States properly belongs to the peo-

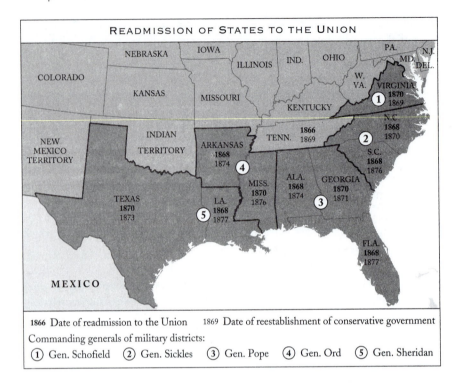

READMISSION OF STATES TO THE UNION

**1866** Date of readmission to the Union     **1869** Date of reestablishment of conservative government
Commanding generals of military districts:
① Gen. Schofield     ② Gen. Sickles     ③ Gen. Pope     ④ Gen. Ord     ⑤ Gen. Sheridan

ple of those States."[38] In other words, if majorities of white northerners wanted to deny African Americans the vote, Republicans would honor their wish, no matter how bigoted.

The platform's first plank also pointed to a third victory the Moderates had achieved by late May 1868. It "congratulate[d] the country on the assured success of the reconstruction policy of Congress, as evinced by the adoption, in a majority of the States lately in rebellion, of constitutions securing equal civil and political rights to all" and proclaimed that the national government had a "duty . . . to sustain those constitutions, and to prevent the people of such States from being remitted to a state of anarchy or military rule." Since prolonged "military rule" had been the Radicals' preferred reconstruction policy, this language openly repudiated the Radicals' agenda. More important, it reflected the fact that during the spring of 1868 political Reconstruction had been successfully implemented in most of the unreconstructed states.

The impeachment charges the House launched against Johnson had helped secure that result. Johnson understood the Moderates' eagerness to have restoration completed before the 1868 election, just as he knew that Moderates held the key to his fate in the Senate. Thus as soon as the House impeached him, Johnson pledged to Moderate senators that he would cease all opposition to implementation of Congress' policies for political Reconstruction. This time he kept his word. When the Senate voted in May, it was clear that all of the unrestored states except Virginia, Mississippi, and Texas would fulfill Congress' terms by the summer and be eligible for readmission.

That seven ex-Confederate states had complied with the terms of the Military Reconstruction Acts by June 1868 was not, of course, exclusively a Moderate triumph. Radicals and Moderates had joined to pass those laws, and the Radicals had always been as eager to replace the pro-Johnson governments as the Moderates were, if for different reasons. At the Radicals' insistence, moreover, Congress attached to the bills readmitting Alabama, Arkansas, Florida, Georgia, Louisiana, North Carolina, and South Carolina to Congress in June a stipulation that their state constitutions must never be modified to strip blacks of suffrage. Although a few Moderates protested that proviso as an unacceptable violation of state-centered federalism, the restoration of those seven states effectively buried the remainder of the Radicals' agenda. As Michael Les Benedict summarizes: "The opportunity for further nationally imposed social and political change in the South had ended. There would be no confiscation, no nationally enforced education policy, no long-term probation for southern states."[39]

That the Moderates now thoroughly dominated congressional Republican policy making became clear during the final session of the Fortieth Congress, held after the presidential election. Even with Grant heading the Republican ticket, that election had been far closer than many Republicans anticipated.[40] True, Grant resoundingly defeated his Democratic opponent, Horatio Seymour, New York's wartime governor, in the electoral vote, 214 to 80, and 3,012,000 to 2,703,000 in the popular vote. Nonetheless, Grant lost New York, New Jersey, and Oregon; in several other northern and western states, notably California, Connecticut, Indiana, Nevada, and Pennsylvania, his popular vote margins were dangerously slim. Grant also lost Delaware, Maryland, and Kentucky, where blacks had not been enfranchised, and, significantly, Georgia and Louisiana, where intimidation of black voters by the Ku Klux Klan dramatically reduced Republican turnout from the spring elections when new state constitutions had won ratification.

To protect black voters in the South, perhaps add black voters to the Republican column elsewhere in the nation, and fortify the commitment of the party's base in the North by reasserting their dedication to equal rights, the Republicans decided to do in the last session of the Fortieth Congress what the Radicals had sought since December 1865. They would enfranchise blacks throughout the nation by adding a Fifteenth Amendment to the United States Constitution.[41] Since states had traditionally defined for themselves who could vote and hold office within them, such an amendment raised once again concerns of federalism that had always divided Moderates from Radicals. The Radicals wanted a constitutional amendment that guaranteed the right to hold public office and to vote to all adult male citizens throughout the nation, without any exceptions save for participation in the rebellion. To Moderates, such a sweeping amendment constituted consolidation, a usurpation of states' right to shape their own political arrangements. Thus, Moderates insisted on a negatively phrased Fifteenth Amendment. It simply asserted, "The right of citizens of the United States to vote shall not be denied or abridged by the United States or by any State on account of race, color, or previous condition of servitude" and that "The Congress shall have power to enforce this article by appropriate legislation." As Radicals repeatedly warned, this amendment ducked the vital question of officeholding altogether. Moreover, it did not in fact guarantee African Americans the right to vote, since it practically invited states to use literacy or property-holding requirements to deny blacks and others the vote. Nonetheless, it was the Fifteenth Amendment that congressional Republicans passed in February 1869 and sent to the states for ratification.

Congressional Republicans would later require Virginia, Mississippi, and Texas to ratify the Fifteenth as well as the Fourteenth Amendment in order to gain readmission to Congress.[42] In 1870 and 1871, moreover, Congress would pass a series of Enforcement Acts that aimed in part at protecting the rights of southern African Americans to cast ballots. But those later laws, much like the Military Reconstruction Acts of 1867 and 1868, were direct responses to developments in the South. To understand what happened to the congressional program, therefore, it is necessary to shift focus from Washington back to the South itself.

## CHAPTER 30

# Reconstruction in the South

Starting in the summer and fall of 1867, qualified residents of the ten ex-Confederate states covered by the Military Reconstruction Acts[1] moved to elect delegates to new constitutional conventions, rewrite state charters, and install new state governments that ratified the Fourteenth Amendment as Congress demanded. Implementation of those acts was exclusively a Republican affair, and in most states it spurred the initial mobilization of Republican coalitions. Ex-Confederate Democrats fought the adoption of new constitutions at the polls, through calculated abstention aimed at delegitimizing the process, and, in some places, with extralegal violence and intimidation. Though initially unsuccessful and then briefly muted for tactical reasons, the Democrats' opposition to Republican governance and black political participation never ebbed. Within a decade they would defeat the Republicans in every southern state and reclaim political power for themselves, thereby ending the experiment congressional Republicans had launched.

The nature of that experiment was controversial at the time and has remained so ever since. During the first half of the twentieth century, the dominant and often overtly racist interpretation of this episode, employing labels like "Black Reconstruction" or "The Dreadful Decade," portrayed it as the worst calamity ever to befall the (white) South. According to this distorted stereotype, the southern Republican party was a pestiferous coalition of ignorant blacks, wholly unfit for citizenship, and their venal white allies. These included greedy Yankee carpetbaggers—men supposedly so destitute that they could carry all their possessions in small cloth satchels—who descended on the South with the sole hope of using political office to plunder white taxpayers, and the notorious scalawags, envious poor white southerners who betrayed their race and region. Empowered only because of Congress' draconian legislation, Republicans supposedly wrote biased and deeply flawed constitutions and then established black-dominated state governments that were extravagant, incompetent, and corrupt. They reportedly spent state funds in unprecedented amounts, and where those expenditures did not represent sheer waste, they went to politicos as graft or to Republican supporters as boodle.

In the process Republicans allegedly imposed unconscionably heavy burdens of bonded indebtedness on southern states. They then levied confiscatory taxes on real estate to pay the interest on that debt. Those taxes forced huge numbers of white planters and yeomen farmers to sell off their land and plunged many of the latter into the dependent status of sharecropper. Embarrassed and infuriated by this travesty, the good, honest, and intelligent majority of white southerners ultimately rose up to topple Republican regimes and "redeem" the South. With the return of white "home rule" under the auspices of the Democrats came retrenchment, lower taxes, and honest, competent government.

Almost every aspect of this hostile portrait of Reconstruction in the South has long since been rejected by historians. One of the purposes of this chapter is to summarize and assess their revisionist scholarship. It is important to remember, however, that politics did not monopolize the attention of either white or black Southerners. During the decade from 1867 to 1877, significant changes in the economic and social relationships between whites and blacks, the class relationships among whites, and even the relationships between men and women of both races also occurred. During this period, for example, blacks continued to develop their own churches and fraternal organizations and to flock to schools wherever they were available. Cash-starved planters and freedmen who desired more au-

"The First Vote," *Harper's Weekly*, November 16, 1867

"Political Meeting at the South," *Harper's Weekly*, November 16, 1867

tonomy worked out the arrangement that replaced plantation gang labor with sharecropping and the associated crop-lien system in the cotton- and tobacco-growing sectors of the South's economy.[2]

What was more, blacks who zealously embraced the right to vote in order to use government to improve their lot became more assertive in the social and economic sphere during 1867 and 1868. They organized strikes against white employers, refused to pay taxes to the existing white-controlled governments created during Presidential Reconstruction, and insisted that trolley cars in cities like Charleston and New Orleans be desegregated. More worrisome to whites, black men and women held rallies across the South in 1867 and 1868 to demand that the new constitutions or new Republican-controlled state governments mandate the confiscation of planters' land and its redistribution to the freedmen.[3]

In sum, political developments within the South cannot be isolated from their social and economic context if only because control of state and local governments potentially had enormous ramifications for blacks' and whites' daily lives. Those governments could set tax rates on property holders, determine the level of funding for schools, hospitals, and social services, provide jobs, administer the civil and criminal justice system, and influence the labor arrangements between whites and blacks. Government's importance was therefore a major reason that blacks invested so much hope in their newly granted right to participate in electoral politics. Blacks flocked to the polls in Alabama, wrote one northern observer, because they "hunger for the same chances as the white men."[4] Government's importance also explains why many white southerners regarded black suffrage and Republican rule with such dread and why the nature of political conflict and governance in the South during these years has generated such controversy among historians.

## THE REPUBLICAN COALITION AND THE MYTH OF BLACK RECONSTRUCTION

"Black Reconstruction" was not in fact that black, for in most states whites formed a majority of the electorate and held the majority of public offices. Though historians once spoke of massive white disfranchisement that allowed newly enfranchised African Americans, aided by Yankee military might, to impose Republican regimes on the South, the best estimates suggest that at most between a tenth and a fifth of any state's potential white electorate was temporarily disfranchised, and in most states the fraction was considerably smaller. That disability did not extend beyond the ratification elections in most states, and by 1871 only Arkansas continued to bar some Confederates from voting. In addition, some Confederate whites who were eligible to vote initially refused to do so, thereby reducing white participation still further. Nonetheless, blacks formed a majority of the potential electorate only in Louisiana, Mississippi, and South Carolina.[5]

Blacks did constitute the majority of Republican voters in every southern state. In 1867 and 1868, Republican organizers, some Freedmen's Bureau agents, and an emerging black political leadership operating through Union Leagues successfully urged blacks to go to the polls, often by reminding them that the Republicans' political foes were the masters who had inflicted slavery on them. Named after wartime northern patriotic clubs, the southern Union Leagues illustrate the inseparability of political activity from social and economic life. They educated and mobilized black voters, but they also raised money for black schools and churches, dispensed aid to the sick and poor, gave freedmen advice about contract disputes, and occasionally organized strikes against white employers. In part for this reason, declares historian Eric Foner, the Republican party "became an institution as central to the black community as the church and school."[6]

Yet nowhere in the South was that party solely a black organization. As northern Republicans who counseled caution on their new southern allies and even incipient black political leaders themselves realized, an exclusively African American party had no chance of achieving enduring political success in the South.[7] White support was crucial. From the start, therefore, black Republicans sought white allies even in states with black majorities. To attract white voter support, they were at first especially eager to elect whites rather than blacks to office. Georgia's blacks, reported one Republican, "went from door to door in the 'negro belt'" recruiting white Republican candidates.[8] As a result, black representation in Republican leadership positions almost always fell considerably below the proportion of black Republican voters.

The racial composition of the constitutional conventions that Republicans elected across the South in 1867 and 1868 exemplified this skew. When the ten states are considered as an aggregate, native white southerners formed the largest bloc of Republican delegates. Northern-born veterans of the Union army, who were usually elected from black-majority plantation regions, constituted about one-sixth of the delegates. Blacks were a majority only in the South Carolina and Louisiana conventions, and they composed about 40 percent of Florida's. Elsewhere blacks ranged between a fifth and a tenth of the delegates.[9]

Although African Americans would later push for a larger share of the elective and appointed offices controlled by Republicans, blacks never dominated southern Republican governments. Only two African Americans, Hiram Revels and Blanche K. Bruce, both from Mississippi, served in the United States Senate during Reconstruction; together, the eleven former states of the Confederacy elected only sixteen black Republicans to the House of Representatives during that ten-year period. No state ever elected a black as governor, although P. S.

Black political leaders:

Benjamin S. Turner

P. S. Pinchback

Blanche K. Bruce

Robert Smalls

Robert B. Elliott

Pinchback, Louisiana's lieutenant governor, briefly filled his state's governorship in 1872. In addition to Pinchback, five other blacks were elected as lieutenant governors in Louisiana, Mississippi, and South Carolina, and blacks served as state treasurers, state superintendents of education, and secretaries of state in those states, Florida, and Arkansas.[10] Only in South Carolina, however, was a black ever appointed to a state's supreme court.

Altogether over six hundred black men served as Republican state legislators during this decade, a revolutionary change from antebellum southern politics. Nonetheless, only in South Carolina did blacks dominate the lower house of the state legislature numerically and in terms of important committee chairman-ships.[11] Elsewhere blacks were underrepresented, especially in state senates. White domination of Republican legislative delegations was especially dispro-portionate in Texas, North Carolina, Georgia, and Florida.

In many ways, local officials—county commissioners, city councilors, tax as-sessors, justices of the peace, sheriffs, and municipal police forces—had a more direct impact on white and black southerners' everyday lives than even state offi-cials. In areas with black majorities, blacks enjoyed considerable success in win-ning local offices, although they never formed a majority of such officials elected in states as a whole. Fifteen black men in Mississippi and nineteen in Louisiana served as sheriff, for example, and blacks such as the Louisiana sheriff Henry Demas, the Little Rock judge Mifflin Gibbs, and the New Jersey–born Tunis G. Campbell, a justice of the peace in South Carolina, rendered valuable service to their black constituents. Though the record of these men in office was once the target of vitriolic denunciation by historians hostile to Reconstruction, revision-ists have demonstrated that they were generally as competent and as honest as their white counterparts, whether Republican or Democratic.[12]

Historians have also reassessed the identity, numbers, and motivations of the once-pilloried carpetbaggers and scalawags. Although the pejorative term "car-petbagger" was usually applied to white Republicans of northern birth, a surpris-ingly large proportion of blacks who assumed leadership roles during Reconstruction had been born or raised in the North. As the historian Eric Foner has shrewdly noted, "Reconstruction was one of the few times in Ameri-can history that the South offered black men of talent and ambition not only the prospect of serving their race, but greater possibilities for personal advancement than existed in the North."[13] Ministers, schoolteachers, veterans of the Union army, or the sons of prosperous southern free blacks who had been sent north for schooling, men such as the above-mentioned Mifflin Gibbs, who studied law at Oberlin College; the Ohio-born William Viney, who bought a rice plantation in South Carolina after the war and then became a Republican organizer; and Jonathan Gibbs, who attended Dartmouth College, often were the best-educated and most professionally accomplished black spokesmen in the party.

Northern-born whites did support the southern Republican party after 1867, but since they never composed so much as 2 percent of the potential electorate in

Scalawags and carpetbaggers:

James L. Alcorn

William G. Brownlow

Henry C. Warmoth

Albion W. Tourgee

Adelbert Ames

any southern state, they always played a more important role among the party's officeholders than as voters.[14] Some sixty such men eventually represented ex-Confederate states in Congress; so-called carpetbaggers also served as governors of Arkansas, Louisiana, Mississippi, South Carolina, Georgia, and Florida. Unlike the office-hungry vagabonds portrayed in the anti-Reconstruction legend, most of these northerners were middle-class lawyers, teachers, and businessmen, many of them Union army veterans, who came South after the war for economic or altruistic reasons. Many sank considerable capital into business enterprises and especially cotton plantations before they ever had a chance of winning electoral office.

Still, the failure of economic ventures often turned these northerners toward political careers as a way to earn a livelihood. And some carpetbaggers, such as James F. Casey and Stephen B. Packard, leaders of a corrupt Republican machine in New Orleans, or the South Carolina governor Robert K. Scott, were scoundrels. But such northerners as Adelbert Ames, Mississippi's last Republican governor, Governor Powell Clayton of Arkansas, and Daniel H. Chamberlain, South Carolina's last Republican governor, also provided Republicans with some of their most educated, talented, honest, and progressive leaders. Indeed, most carpetbaggers shared the faith of northern Republicans that an activist government was capable of achieving significant economic, social, and political reform that could modernize the South. Most also professed an egalitarian commitment to black rights that helps explain why African American voters tended to trust these northerners far more than the white southerners who joined the Republican coalition.[15]

The so-called scalawags were far more crucial than carpetbaggers to Republicans' electoral success. A diverse group in terms of political background, social status, and motivation, they shared a conviction that the emergence of a southern Republican party—and with it a renewal of two-party political competition in the South—allowed them to pursue economic aspirations and to channel political opposition to traditional regional and partisan foes. Hardly the poor white trash of legend, white Republican voters in Mississippi, Louisiana, and, to a lesser extent, Florida, were former Whigs from the black-belt plantation regions or businessmen from such cities as New Orleans, Natchez, and Jacksonville. They considered Republicans far more likely than Democrats to use state governments to sponsor economic development and recovery such as rebuilding levees and aiding railroad construction with state loans. Many of these one-time Whigs, who had belonged to the antebellum social and economic elite, could not abide the prospect of cooperating with the Democratic party, which they disparaged as the home of envious and ignorant poor whites.[16]

Though Whiggish black-belt planters and urban businessmen supplied Republican leaders in almost every ex-Confederate state, hill-country whites, most of whom had never owned slaves and many of whom had been prewar Democrats, composed the great majority of white Republican voters in Texas, Tennessee, Virginia, South Carolina, North Carolina, Georgia, Alabama, and Arkansas.[17] In the latter four states, Republicans attracted more than a fifth of the whites who voted for delegates to the new constitutional conventions.[18]

Such men had long resented the domination of their state governments by planters from the black-belt regions, but more immediate needs and grievances also propelled them toward the Republican party. By far the most important were wartime Unionism and a desire to avenge the persecution they had suffered at the hands of Confederates. Unlike ex-Whigs, these wartime loyalists had generally been excluded from political power by the Johnsonian Union regimes, and they saw in the Republican party the chance finally to exercise it. More than other Republicans, therefore, they demanded that ex-Confederates be permanently proscribed from both office and the ballot box and that state legislatures be reapportioned to reduce the black belt's power. Some even joined freedmen in demanding the confiscation of planters' land.

Other yeomen, who had faithfully fought for the Confederacy and who had long cherished their economic autonomy, returned from the army to find that their families had been forced into debt during the war. Threatened with foreclosures that could cost them their land, they responded to Republican promises, most notably in Georgia, that the party would include provisions for debt relief in new state constitutions. It was not simply planters, businessmen, and Yankee modernizers, therefore, who believed Republican rule could advance or protect whites' economic interests.[19]

As a general rule, scalawags lacked the altruistic, egalitarian commitment to black rights that characterized many carpetbaggers, a fact that most black Republicans quickly grasped. Elitist ex-Whig planters from areas with dense black populations, such as James Lusk Alcorn, Mississippi's preeminent scalawag who served both as governor and United States senator, simply assumed that their class should lead the Republican party and that blacks would defer to that leadership. Indeed, some of them became Republicans precisely to prevent blacks from controlling the party.[20] Hill-country loyalists and debt-ridden yeomen, who usually lived in areas with relatively small black populations, pragmatically accepted the necessity of protecting the civil and political rights of blacks so Republicans could obtain power statewide. Nonetheless, they often shared the same racist biases of other whites who opposed Reconstruction, and they blanched at anything that would promote blacks' social equality. Whatever their social class and economic interests, white southern Republicans might be alienated from the party should its black majority become too assertive or should interparty conflict with Democrats become defined exclusively along the color line.

The southern Republican party, in sum, was a heterogeneous coalition that contained many potential sources of internal factional tension. Carpetbaggers and scalawags not only competed with each other for elective and especially appointed offices, but the former were far more closely associated with the party's black majority than the latter. Over time, blacks did offend white Republicans by demanding more offices and more explicitly problack programs. The economic interests of different Republicans were also potentially at odds. Those who wanted economic development, for example, sought capital from the North to fund it, yet the governmental erasure of private debts and confiscation of planters' land demanded by some freedmen and poor white Republicans could inhibit necessary northern investment. Without northern funds, in turn, only tax increases could pay for the programs sought by development-minded Republicans or the school systems and aid to the poor demanded by freedmen. With slaves no longer available to tax, however, such levies would necessarily fall on land, some of which was owned by Republicans' white constituents. So irreconcilable did these competing interests seem that some historians have deemed the disintegration of the Republican party in the South inevitable.[21]

## REPUBLICAN GOVERNANCE: THE CONSTITUTIONAL CONVENTIONS

Whatever their disruptive potential, those internal divisions did not stop Republicans from seizing control of governments in every ex-Confederate state except Virginia. And they governed most of them for at least four years. Never as dismal as critics of Reconstruction once contended, the Republicans' record in office helps explain why they retained power as long as they did. Yet that record also contributed to their ultimate defeat.

Republican governance began with the new state constitutions that heavy Republican majorities drafted at conventions between 1867 and 1869. On the whole, they were progressive documents. They reformed states' judicial systems and, in many, the basis of legislative apportionment. Reflecting the Republicans' faith in activist government, these constitutions created state-funded systems of public education for the first time in the South's history. Many also mandated the erection of penitentiaries, orphanages, and hospitals for the insane and the indigent. Nine of the ten recognized married women's property rights, a major legal change from the antebellum period, and some modernized divorce law. For the first time, South Carolina's also ordered that presidential electors be chosen directly by the state's voters rather than by the legislature.

All the constitutions guaranteed blacks civil and political rights, although a provision stipulating blacks' right to hold office as well as to vote was defeated in Georgia. Several states, notably Georgia and Florida, also inhibited blacks' chances of gaining local office in black-majority areas. They granted governors and legislatures extensive powers to appoint local officials and rigged legislative apportionment to reduce black representation.[22]

On blacks' social equality, the constitutions were more ambiguous. Though black delegates and their carpetbagger allies defeated provisions requiring segregation in schools and other public accommodations, no constitution specifically demanded integration. Ultimately only the city of New Orleans experimented with interracial education. A few blacks protested that school segregation "makes the poor white children feel above the colored," thus "Bilding [sic] up the Wall of Separation Between the two races." Most freedmen, however, acquiesced in separate schools if they received adequate funding.[23]

Almost all of the conventions witnessed internal clashes among Republicans over mandatory school integration, debtor relief, confiscation, and continued political proscription of former Confederates. Ultimately, only Georgia's Republicans, in an overt bid for white yeomen votes, abrogated all private debts contracted before 1865. One reason for Republican opposition to debtor relief was its connection to the related confiscation question and blacks' hunger for land. Black delegates argued that relieving planters from debt would spare them from being forced to sell off land to pay those debts. To further the possibility that planters' land might exchange hands, most states called for general property taxes that would levy an unprecedented burden on real estate. Mississippi and Louisiana specifically provided that any land seized by the state for failure to pay taxes should be sold in relatively small lots that blacks might theoretically purchase. Everywhere, however, delegates heeded warnings from northern Republicans and moderates to shun state-mandated confiscation. As an alternative, South Carolina's constitution authorized the legislature to establish a state land commission that would purchase land with public funds and resell it to citizens on generous terms. Plagued by corruption and mismanagement until 1872, the

South Carolina land commission by 1876 had sold land to some fourteen thousand black families, one seventh of the black population.[24]

Provisions regarding ex-Confederates' political rights had the most direct implications for Republicans' continued control of state governments. In most states, the majority of Republican delegates, including blacks who protested the reduction of anyone's political rights, resisted demands from Unionist hill-country whites for prolonged disfranchisement. As a result, only Alabama and Arkansas, where white Unionists were especially influential in Republican delegations, perpetuated the disfranchisement of men disqualified by the Fourteenth Amendment's third section. Most other states allowed them to vote in the future.[25] The exceptions to this pattern were Mississippi and Virginia, where most black delegates demanded prolonged Confederate disfranchisement or disqualification from office. Opposition to those proscriptive clauses from white residents—and, significantly, from Yankee military officials in charge of implementing congressional policies—primarily explains why those two states, along with Texas, would not win readmission to Congress until 1870.[26]

When Virginia and Mississippi failed to ratify constitutions in 1868, Congress, at President Grant's urging, passed a law on April 10, 1869 allowing the constitutions and their proscriptive clauses to be submitted separately to the electorate. As the price for this concession, the same law required the new state legislatures in each to ratify both the Fourteenth and Fifteenth Amendments to obtain the readmission of their representatives and senators to Congress. In both, the constitution won ratification in 1869 but the proscriptive clauses were defeated. Virginia was readmitted to Congress in January 1870, and Mississippi followed it a month later.[27]

As in most other Confederate states, Republicans in Mississippi elected the governor and a heavy majority in the state legislature when they ratified the new constitution in 1869. In Virginia, however, Republicans did not. Nor did they ever control the Old Dominion between 1867 and 1877. The unique outcome there requires explanation.

An uneasy coalition of anti-Confederate white Unionists and newly enfranchised, radically oriented blacks, Virginia's Republican party was unusually militant in demanding black rights and the political proscription of ex-Confederates. Distrusting the wartime "Restored Governor" Francis Pierpont as too moderate, they persuaded the state's military commander, General John M. Schofield, to replace him with the Yankee general H. H. Wells, whom Republicans then nominated as their gubernatorial candidate in 1869. With ratification of the constitution assured once the proscriptive clause had been separated from it, Republicans seemed destined to capture the new state government.

At this point a key operator reshaped the course of Reconstruction in Virginia by splitting the Republican party. The Confederate general William Mahone, hero of the Battle of the Crater outside Petersburg, became a railroad executive after the war. He sought an act from the legislature to consolidate the Virginia and Tennessee Railroad that ran southwest from Lynchburg to Tennessee with two lines he controlled running from Lynchburg via Petersburg to Norfolk. Fearing that both Wells and the likely candidate of the Democratic-Conservatives favored rival railroad interests that also sought to merge with the Virginia and Tennessee, Mahone arranged a third ticket with Gilbert Walker, one of his business associates, as its gubernatorial candidate for the July 1869 elections. Democratic-Conservatives decided to support this so-called True Republican ticket for governor, and the two groups also ran fusion tickets for the legislature. The True Republican Walker won the governorship, and Conservatives and True Republicans also swept to heavy majorities in the legislature, guaranteeing that Mahone would get the railroad legislation he sought. Because True Republicans cooperated with Democrats more often than regular Republicans in the legislature and because Democratic-Conservatives on their own triumphed in 1871, Virginia effectively escaped Republican rule.[28]

## REPUBLICAN GOVERNANCE: EXPANSION OF THE PUBLIC SPHERE

The new state constitutions that Republicans drafted and Republicans' proclivity for governmental activism, along with emancipation and black enfranchisement themselves, had crucial implications for how Republicans across the South used the power they attained. Almost everywhere, Republican-controlled legislatures moved to provide greater protection for the rights and interests of their black constituents. They established state-supported school systems and other institutions that blacks could attend. They repealed the remnants of the discriminatory Black Codes, revised vagrancy laws, ameliorated harsh criminal codes that had allowed corporal punishment of blacks, and mandated parental approval for apprenticeships of their children. Rebuffing pressure from planters to provide state enforcement of their control over black employees, they instead rewrote crop lien and tenancy laws to ensure that sharecroppers, tenants, and other agricultural laborers received payment for their work.

In several states Republicans also attempted to pass state civil rights laws that required the integration of hotels, restaurants, theaters, streetcars, omnibuses, and especially railroad cars. The great majority of freedmen lacked the money to patronize such white establishments, with the exception of streetcars and omnibuses, and they remained primarily concerned with building an autonomous black community rather than mixing socially with whites. Yet all blacks viewed equal rights, just as they viewed suffrage, as a mark of equal citizenship with whites, and thus they vested great importance in the passage of civil rights laws. Many white Republicans, in contrast, opposed them, and the first such bills were buried in committees or vetoed by Republican governors such as Mississippi's James Lusk Alcorn and Florida's Harrison Reed. During the 1870s, however, Texas, Mississippi, Louisiana, Florida, and South Carolina all passed laws mandating equal treatment regardless of race in public accommodations, although such laws generally went unenforced once passed.[29]

Through the courts, if not statutes, Republicans also increased state regulation over what had hitherto been private domestic relationships to protect women and children from sexual assault, physical abuse, and economic neglect. Courts moved to transfer what had previously been the exclusive authority of white male heads of households over their dependents, including their slave dependents, to the state itself.[30] What was more, both white and black women often initiated the civil and criminal suits that triggered judges' decisions. Thus women, though still disenfranchised, actively participated in and redefined the public sphere by forcing the courts to adjudicate their grievances.

This change was an unintended consequence of attempts by the Johnsonian governments immediately after the war to formalize slave marriages and the legal obligations black men had toward their wives and children in those marriages. The point, at least originally, was to spare the state the cost of caring for black dependents by thrusting it on black heads of households. But those laws also now gave black men a claim on the law-enforcement resources of the state that white heads of households had always enjoyed to protect their dependent family members from depredations. The election of black Republican sheriffs and justices of the peace helped ensure that these new legal rights were exercised. Equally important, the formal legalization of relationships between husbands and wives and between parents and children allowed white and black women to go to court to enforce the obligations owed them, whether it be protection from rapists and abusive husbands or suits to force negligent fathers to provide adequate economic support. As the historian Laura F. Edwards shrewdly notes, whatever male policy makers and judges had intended, "the postwar years also opened new opportunities for African American and common white women, particularly poor white women, to secure public recognition of their legal rights as women—rights that had previously been denied them because of their race and class."[31]

Conservative elite white men, long accustomed to exclusive control over the public sphere, often greeted women's ability to enlarge government's agenda through lawsuits with dismay. Along with black women's vocal participation in Republican political rallies and the movement of some white women out of the home and into wage-paying jobs, it struck them as evidence of the undermining of traditional racial, class, and gender hierarchies by the congressional Republicans' Reconstruction program. To reassert those hierarchies, therefore, they often made explicit appeals to the "manhood" of white Southerners when calling on whites to unite in resistance to Reconstruction and defense of white supremacy. White unity, declared one North Carolina Democrat, was "a matter of self-defence, and appeals to the pride of race and manhood."[32]

Other aspects of Republican governance had more direct partisan salience for Republicans' ability to retain the power they initially won as a result of the Military Reconstruction Acts. State governments under Republican control *did* spend far more money annually than had their antebellum predecessors. Incidents of graft and extravagance undeniably occurred. Florida's Republicans, for example, spent more on state printing in 1869 than the entire state government had cost in 1860. In Arkansas a black supporter was paid nine thousand dollars by Republicans for repairing a bridge that had originally cost only five hundred dollars. South Carolina's Republican legislators voted one thousand dollars extra compensation for their speaker after he lost that amount on a horse race.[33] The list could be expanded almost indefinitely.

Yet the legal transformation of blacks from slaves to free citizens accounted for much of the increased expenditure. The requirement in the new state constitutions that legislatures establish tax-supported public school systems, hospitals, asylums for orphans and the insane, and penitentiaries would necessarily have forced an increase in public expenditure in any event. But now those institutions had to serve the states' black populations as well as their whites. Inevitably, annual expenditures under Republicans surpassed antebellum levels.

Increased public expenditures, moreover, *did* require heavier taxes on real estate, often when the market value of land was plummeting. Beyond that necessity, many African American supporters of the Republicans did hope to force planters to sell off land to escape the tax burden so that blacks might purchase it. Without question, this tax burden hurt some white planters. By 1875, for example, over six million acres in Mississippi, one-fifth of the land area of the state, had been forfeited to state and local governments for failure to meet tax payments on it. Because of blacks' poverty and whites' resistance, however, very little of this land ever came into the possession of freedmen. Instead, Republican taxes became a target for Democrats, especially when inability to pay them forced small white farmers, and not just planters, to lose their property.[34]

The obligation to pay the interest and principal on states' bonded indebtedness also required higher taxes. Public debt did mushroom after the war, but not nearly so high as the hostile stereotype of Reconstruction once posited. Nor were Republicans exclusively responsible for the increase. Almost everywhere, most of the new bonds were issued to subsidize the construction of railroad lines. The Johnsonian governments began to do so while they held power, and Republican regimes followed suit. Much of the supposed debt, moreover, took the form, not of state-issued bonds for which the state government was directly liable, but of state endorsements of railroad bonds. By such endorsements the state guaranteed the payments on bonds issued by railroad corporations should the companies default on those payments. In return for paying a railroad's obligations, state governments were to acquire ownership of its physical assets—the track, buildings, and rolling stock of the railroad company. Since many purchasers of railroad bonds preferred to take control of the railroads themselves in such a contingency or at least to keep ownership in private hands, they often worked out deals with state governments that significantly reduced the state's obligation. As the historian Horace Mann Bond calculated in the case of Alabama, for example, the state's debt at the end of Republican rule was only $12 million, not the $30 million that hostile historians had once charged. Of that $12 million, moreover, $9.5 million had been incurred before Republicans took office.[35]

Promotion of railroad construction and optimistic promises of the prosperity that such construction would bring to the South constituted the trademark feature of Republican governance between 1868 and 1873. When the Civil War ended, a veritable mania spread among white southerners that building railroads provided the key to economic recovery for the devastated region. Thus Republicans were responding to popular demand, and many enthusiastically trumpeted railroad promotion as the best way that the party could broaden its electoral base. Yet the program also entailed five significant negative consequences that ultimately damaged the party's fortunes.[36]

First, subsidies of railroads, especially in the form of direct loans of state bonds on which state governments owed annual interest payments, diverted scarce state funds from projects of more direct benefit to the party's black constituency such as schools or poor relief. Thus, railroad promotion became a source of blacks' grievance against the white Republican leaders who advocated the program.

Second, because so many new railroad companies sought charters of incorporation and governmental aid, rival firms bribed Republican legislators and governors to give their projects priority. Therefore, massive corruption *was* inherent in the program of railroad aid corruption that Democrats would later use to stigmatize Republicans as thieves.

Third, Republicans chartered far too many lines. Some lines could not sell enough bonds in northern money markets to complete construction, go into operation, and earn revenue to meet interest payments. Even so, too many completed roads were competing for the limited freight traffic that the slumping southern economy generated. They also failed to make enough money to meet interest payments. Both built and unbuilt lines thus defaulted on their obligations.

Fourth, once railroads defaulted on payments, then state governments had to honor their guarantees. To do so, they often had to raise tax rates. Hence Republicans handed Democrats the issue of high taxes as well as the issue of corruption with which to bludgeon them.

Fifth and perhaps most important, by promising repeatedly that railroad promotion would produce a new era of prosperity in the South, Republicans recklessly hitched their political fate to the vagaries of the southern economy itself.

They thereby opened themselves to partisan attack should economic conditions deteriorate, as they did with a vengeance after the financial panic in the fall of 1873.

Altogether, the central and most publicized component of Republicans' governance in the South—railroad promotion—was a political time bomb that eventually exploded in their faces. Along with other factors, that issue ultimately helped Democrats drive Republicans from office. Prior to their overthrow, however, southern Republican parties achieved a great deal. They constructed biracial coalitions in every state and won control of government everywhere save Virginia. They wrote estimable state constitutions that reformed southern governments and expanded the public services those governments provided their citizens. They wiped away the discriminatory Black Codes and enhanced blacks' rights. Most important, perhaps, by incorporating African Americans into the body politic, Republicans increased blacks' self-esteem and opportunity for public service on behalf of their community. In large part because of that achievement, however, most white Southerners reviled Republican governance, and they worked incessantly to bring it to an end.

| # The Failure of Reconstruction in the South

The vast majority of white southerners always regarded Congress's Reconstruction program and the Republican party it spawned in Dixie as alien abominations. Most never accepted the legitimacy of blacks' enfranchisement and political participation.[1] Such hostility, however, did not foreordain the failure of Reconstruction. Aside from Virginia, Republican regimes clung to power for varying lengths of time in all the other states subject to military reconstruction.[2] In Alabama and North Carolina, they were sufficiently resilient to survive losses in 1870 and bounce back to win the elections of 1872. Usually, however, defeat proved irreversible. They lost Georgia in 1871, Texas in 1873, Arkansas, Alabama, and North Carolina in 1874, Mississippi in 1875, and Florida, Louisiana, and South Carolina in the aftermath of the disputed elections of 1876. What requires explanation, therefore, is not so much the defeat of Republicans as why they were successful in most states for four to eight years and then toppled from power.

## THE PATTERN OF SOUTHERN POLITICS

White intolerance of Republican rule and violent persecution of freedmen and their white Republican allies were constants throughout the experiment of Reconstruction. So was debilitating factional division within the Republican party, particularly between carpetbaggers (who tended to control federal offices) and scalawags (who, initially at least, dominated state offices). Yet by themselves, none of these factors can account for the distinctive rhythm of southern politics between 1867 and 1877—the initial success and subsequent failure of the Republican party in the arena of electoral politics. Rather, so far as developments

within the South itself determined the fate of Reconstruction, the key to this
chronological pattern lies in the changing competitive strategies Republicans and
Democrats pursued against each other.

Across Dixie in 1868, the elections to ratify new constitutions in the spring
and summer and the subsequent presidential contest that fall witnessed a partisan battle between Republicans and Democrats over the implementation of
Congress's Reconstruction program. Republicans openly committed themselves
to black suffrage, the launching of new state governments with their men at the
helm, and ratification of the Fourteenth Amendment. Democrats virulently denounced black suffrage and opposed ratification of the new state constitutions.
Mississippi's Democrats, for example, pledged to defeat "the mongrel despotism
which the carpet-bag aliens and their African confederates are seeking to foist
on the people."[3] In North Carolina, a Democratic newspaper printed a poem
called "White Men Must Rule" in order to mobilize voters in defense of white
supremacy:[4]

"The Modern Samson"
In order to rouse Republicans to the polls, Thomas Nast cleverly links southern
Democrats' determination to strip blacks of the vote and thereby disempower them with
other enemies of the Republicans. Note that the statue of Johnson, clutching the veto as
his charter, is mounted on a pedestal listing the names of prominent Confederate
generals and politicians. The armed crowd celebrating the excision of suffrage rights from
blacks represents the Ku Klux Klan.

"This Is a White Man's Government" By portraying the Democratic party as a coalition of apelike Irishmen, unrepentant Confederate soldiers, and rich New York bondholders who raised the cry of white supremacy to grind black soldiers who had fought for the Union into the dust, Thomas Nast shows how Republicans in 1868 tried to motivate voters intent on implementing Reconstruction and protecting the fruits of northern victory.

Shall low-born scum and quondam slaves
 Give laws to those who own the soil?
No! by our grand-sires' bloody graves!
 No! by our homesteads bought with toil!
Our rights are rooted in our lands,
 Our law is written in the sky,
Fate flings the fiat from her hands—
 The WHITES shall rule the land or die.

When such calls failed to stop most state constitutions from winning ratification, Democrats redoubled their efforts in the fall presidential election of 1868 by promising that the election of Democrat Horatio Seymour and a Democratic Congress would produce repeal of the Republicans' heinous policies. If some white Democrats had refused to participate in the spring and summer elections, moreover, they turned out in droves in the presidential election. As a result, participation by potential voters, now including blacks as well as whites, approached the antebellum period's extraordinarily high rates.[5]

"We proclaim that we are opposed to negro suffrage under any circumstances, and stand ready to use all legitimate means to prevent its present and future exercise," one Democratic newspaper in Louisiana declared in 1868.[6] Yet Democrats, or at least some whites who shared their antipathy to Reconstruction, went beyond legitimate means to stop blacks from voting Republican. In Georgia and Louisiana, both of which Horatio Seymour carried in November over Ulysses S. Grant, Democratic sympathizers used terrorism to frighten blacks from the polls or to intimidate them into voting Democratic. In Louisiana, where almost one-fifth of the freedmen who dared vote in November cast (or were recorded as casting) Democratic ballots, the Republican vote plummeted from 64,901 in the spring to 33,262 in November, whereas the Democratic total soared from 38,046 to 80,325. In Georgia, Republicans lost and Democrats gained approximately 26,000 votes between the gubernatorial and presidential elections. Republicans lost thirty-eight counties they had carried in April, and their share of the total plummeted from 52 to 32 percent. Two months before this victory, moreover, Democrats in the new Georgia legislature, aided by some white Republicans, had expelled all its black members on the spurious pretext that the new state constitution did not allow blacks to hold public office. In 1868, partisan competition in the South was a bare-knuckled, no-holds-barred brawl over race and Reconstruction.[7]

Much, though never all, of the white violence against blacks during 1868 and later, as in the North Carolina and Alabama elections of 1870,[8] was a concerted effort by the secretly organized Ku Klux Klan and its counterparts (such as the Knights of the White Camelia in Louisiana) to aid the Democratic party by suppressing the black vote, smashing the newly organized Republican party, and restoring white supremacy. Started in Pulaski, Tennessee in the spring of 1866 as a secret social fraternity by a handful of young Confederate veterans, the Klan quickly changed into an organization designed, as one Mississippi Klansman later put it, to counteract "the threatened and rising arrogance of the negroes."[9]

In some ways a white counterpoint to the secretly organized and oath-bound Republican Union League, which fed whites' paranoia about an impending black uprising, the Klan operated primarily in counties with fairly even ratios between the races rather than in predominantly white or black areas. Notorious for nightriding raids by members disguised in cone-shaped hoods and flowing white gowns, it murdered, flogged, and beat blacks and their white friends. "Uppity" blacks, including many women, who offended whites by refusing to appear sufficiently deferential in public places or on the job, were often singled out as targets. As the historian George Rable puts it, "the organization was concerned with race control in the broadest meaning of the term and was especially sensitive to economic and social challenges to white hegemony."[10] During campaign seasons, however, the Klan and other terrorist organizations of its ilk focused on reducing the vote Republicans received from freedmen.

So effective was this terrorism in helping Democrats in a few states between 1868 and 1871 that some historians view the Klan as "a terrorist arm of the Democratic party, whether the party leaders as a whole liked it or not."[11] Indeed, despite their common objectives, the relationship between the Klan and the Democratic party is far from clear cut. For one thing, the Klan was so chaotically decentralized that even its county leaders, let alone Democratic politicians, often had no idea what local dens planned to do. Nor can Klan violence be credited with or blamed for driving Republicans from power, because its activity in most states peaked in the spring of 1868 and had virtually ceased everywhere by mid-1872, before most state Republican parties were toppled.[12] Moreover, whatever the synergy between the Democrats' anti-Reconstruction campaign and Klan violence in 1868, after that year, Klan terrorism most probably represented racist whites' frustration at, rather than their collusion with, Democratic politicos.

## THE POLITICS OF THE CENTER, 1869–1873

After the presidential election of 1868, both Republicans and Democrats abandoned that year's naked and often brutal confrontation over race and Reconstruction. Republican leaders knew that in every southern state except South Carolina they had needed white votes to win and that in Louisiana and Georgia black voters had not proved completely reliable. Thus they determined to reach out for additional white supporters by muting the party's problack image and instead pushing railroad promotion and economic development. Southern-born former Whigs among Republican leaders were especially eager to attract more ex-Whigs to the party in order to prevent blacks and carpetbaggers from dominating it.

After 1868, paradoxically, former Whigs also seized the leadership of the Democratic party in most southern states. They recognized that Democrats' great crusade against the Reconstruction laws had failed. Not only had Republicans carried most ex-Confederate states participating in the election, but Grant's triumph along with continued Republican control of Congress ensured that Reconstruction would not be rolled back in Washington. Equally important, inflammatory Democratic rhetoric like that used in 1868 could easily be blamed for inciting violence and justifying further federal intervention in the South. If Democrats needed evidence of this likelihood, Congress's reaction to events in Georgia provided it. In retaliation for the murder of a Republican judge and the ouster of blacks from the legislature, Republican congressmen in 1869 refused to seat Georgia's congressional delegation, reimposed military rule on the state, reinstated the blacks who had been expelled from the legislature, and required it to ratify the Fifteenth Amendment before removing troops and readmitting Georgia to Congress.[13]

The Democratic leaders who abandoned overt resistance to Reconstruction after 1868 also argued that the heterogeneous Republican coalition would disintegrate as soon as Democrats ceased fighting them and declared Reconstruction a *fait accompli*. "It is reconstruction and the issues growing out of it which preserve the unity of the Republican party," declared the state chairman of Georgia's Democratic party in 1869. "Strip them of the support which this question gives them and their dissolution will speedily follow." Democrats, echoed a North Carolina congressman in 1871, must insist that "every issue upon which [the Republicans] rode into power is settled and dead."[14]

Once the Republican party began to dissolve, Democratic strategists maintained, then Republican supporters could be attracted to the opposition. Some spoke of wooing blacks to the Democratic column by announcing Democrats' acceptance of black suffrage and other Reconstruction measures. But the main targets whom the ex-Whigs among Democratic leaders hoped to recruit were white scalawags, and especially the socially prominent former Whigs who had become Republicans. To attract ex-Whigs, these leaders insisted, the opposition must accept rather than fight Republican programs aimed at economic development that Whigs had always favored and lifelong Democrats had always opposed. It must jettison the Democratic label that Whigs found so offensive. And it must rename itself the Conservative party since most Whigs had always considered themselves social and political conservatives.

To a very large extent, therefore, southern politics from 1869 to 1873 revolved around two simultaneous battles.[15] The first was a bidding war between Republicans and Democratic-Conservatives for ex-Whigs. The other was a factional struggle within each party between Whig leaders and their increasingly restive non-Whig allies—carpetbaggers and blacks among Republicans, old-line Jacksonian Democrats among Democratic-Conservatives—who demanded policies and strategies that better reflected the interests and values of the majority wings of both parties.

With the reins of both parties in their hands, Whig leaders attempted to bring about a political realignment from which they and fellow Whigs might benefit. To do so, they scuttled the demands and interests of each party's mass base. Thus Republican leaders quashed explicitly problack measures and stifled blacks' growing demands for political office. Ex-Whig leaders of the Conservatives quashed their racist white supporters' calls for a crusade against expensive government and for white supremacy. Conservatives, indeed, often abdicated electoral opposition to Republicans altogether. To foster a realignment, they backed dissident Republican candidates for governor, rather than running their own man, in Mississippi and Virginia in 1869, in Arkansas, Louisiana, and South Carolina in 1872, and again in Mississippi in 1873.[16] Moderates at the center of the political spectrum, not ideologues on its extremes, thus dictated the terms of debate and competition—at least temporarily.

Republicans generally had the advantage in this situation. Grateful for the gains Republicans had already brought them and suspicious of Conservatives' protestations of a cease-fire, few black or white Republicans defected before 1872. Blacks in particular continued to vote faithfully for the Republicans. In contrast, die-hard, often virulently racist Jacksonians who had been pulled to the polls by the sharply polarized presidential campaign of 1868 now saw no reason to vote: their leaders had ceased opposition to black suffrage and to governmental economic programs they abominated. White bigots might vent their frustration through Klan violence. No matter how many blacks Klan members terrorized or how many individual Republican officeholders they killed, however, Democrats could never end the Republican party's control of government unless whites *voted* in large numbers for Democratic candidates so that Democrats won elections. And that they refused to do. Democratic turnout plunged across Dixie, and primarily as a result of the decreased *white* Democratic vote, Republicans were able to maintain power.

## THE POLITICS OF POLARIZATION, 1873–1877

Developments in 1872 and 1873 provided the pivotal turning point that ultimately doomed southern Republicans to defeat. The Democrats' alliance with Liberal Republicans in 1872 presented the crucial test of the Whiggish Conservatives' accommodationist strategy of winning over black and white Republican defectors.[17] It was a test they failed abjectly, thereby permanently discrediting their centrist strategy. Repelled by the Liberal Republican presidential candidate, Horace Greeley, as well as by many southern dissident Republican gubernatorial candidates whom Conservatives endorsed, traditional Democratic voters abstained in droves. Republicans swept the presidential and state elections across the South. Of former Confederate states, only Georgia, Tennessee, where Republicans had lost power three years earlier, and Texas went Democratic-Conservative.[18] This rout paved the way for regular Democrats to displace Whigs as leaders of the Conservative party. Fully aware that the Democratic-Conservatives' fundamental problem was apathy and abstention by potential white supporters,[19] the new Democratic leadership meant to stimulate white turnout by frontally attacking Republicans' record in office and by drawing the color line between the two parties as emphatically as possible.

Ironically, the flirtation with Liberal Republicans itself suggested their initial line of attack. For though northern Liberal Republicans demanded amnesty and an end to Reconstruction, they also pilloried the corruption of the Grant administration and of many Republican state machines in the North, and they called for retrenchment, tax relief, and civil service reform to restore honesty to government. Having chafed impatiently for four years against their leaders' acquiescence in Republicans' shady dealings with railroads, bond issues, and tax levies, southern Democrats welcomed this assault even if they gagged at Greeley. Thus attacks on Republicans' program of railroad promotion and the graft and heavy tax burdens that program entailed began to emerge in 1872.

Protected by traditional Democrats' marked aversion to Greeley, Republicans weathered these attacks in 1872. Even so, the Whig centrists' control of the party was weakened. Some, dismayed themselves by rising taxes and repulsed by the increasingly militant demands of their carpetbagger and black factional rivals, bolted to the reformist Liberal Republican–Conservative column that year.[20] Their defection opened opportunities for blacks and carpetbaggers to replace them in leadership positions.[21] More important, railroads whose bonds Republican state legislatures had endorsed began to fail in 1872 and early 1873. The financial crash in the fall of 1873 accelerated a trickle of defaults into a regionwide floodtide of bankruptcy. The economic disaster and massive forfeiture of railroad bond payments, which forced state governments to raise taxes or repudiate their obligations, permanently discredited Republican centrist leaders. Now the carpetbaggers and their black allies, who for years had demanded more public offices and problack policies, seized control of the Republican party.

Deeply embarrassed by the railroads' collapse, tarred as corruptionists, and skewered for tax-and-spend policies that proved ruinous to white landowners, the Republicans had little choice but to recant and retreat. By 1873 and 1874, they too advocated retrenchment, tax relief, and restoration of honest government, but this about-face could not protect them from the wrathful white taxpayers whom Democratic-Conservatives were now arousing against them.

Fully aware even before the outbreak of the panic that disillusioned whites would defect from the party, the Republicans' new carpetbagger and black leaders desperately tried to mobilize even more black voters by explicitly reemphasizing their party's commitment to black rights and interests. Starting in late 1872 and 1873, Republicans ostentatiously gave blacks more appointed and elective offices than previously. In the spring of 1873, Republican state legislators in Mississippi, Louisiana, Arkansas, and Florida enacted state civil rights laws and narrowly failed to pass one in Alabama. What was more, during 1874 southern Republican congressmen avidly pressed the House and Senate to pass a new federal civil rights law in order to reenforce the Republicans' problack image. Though this bill stalled in the House after passing the Senate, it became an issue in the 1874 elections, and it remained an issue after the House passed the bill in 1875.[22]

In one way, Republicans' shift of electoral tactics succeeded spectacularly. Black voters responded exactly as carpetbag and black Republican leaders hoped they would. Black turnout for Republican candidates burgeoned dramatically in Louisiana, Mississippi, South Carolina and elsewhere after 1872. Yet by consciously painting Republicans as the party of blacks, Republicans encouraged Democrats to run as the party of white supremacy. The old-line Democrats, or Bourbons as they were sometimes called, who gained control of the Conservative machinery and electoral strategy after 1873 undoubtedly would have race baited to mobilize previously apathetic whites in any event. But the Republicans aided them in drawing the color line between the parties by moving in that direction first. Since Republicans were now indisputably the champions of blacks, Democrats railed, all whites must vote Democratic-Conservative out of loyalty to their race. The route to victory, wrote one Democratic strategist in Alabama in 1874, was to appeal "to the interests, the pride and the prejudices of the white race" and to make "nigger or no nigger" the central issue of the campaign.[23] Any white traitors who still clung to the Republican party deserved social ostracism, economic isolation, and exile from the South—if not worse. "No white man," wrote one former Republican from Mississippi, "can live in the South in the future and act with any other than the Democratic party."[24]

The conservative white businessmen and planters who had led both parties continued to regard the reduction of partisan competition in the South to naked racial conflict as a calamity. Ex-Whig centrists, therefore, did not relinquish their control of the political arena to the more extreme elements of the Republican and Democratic parties without a struggle. In Mississippi's 1873 gubernatorial election, they followed the old formula of coalescing around a dissident Republican, the prominent scalawag and former United States senator and governor James Lusk Alcorn, who opposed the Republicans' leading carpetbagger, Adelbert Ames, in this contest. Alcorn took with him approximately half the whites who had supported him as a Republican in 1869; he reduced the Republican total by almost nine thousand votes since the 1872 presidential contest and raised the Democratic total from that debacle by five thousand votes. Nonetheless, because many white Democrats refused to vote for the former Whig and because blacks, a majority of Mississippi's electorate, voted enthusiastically for Ames, Ames easily crushed Alcorn by a margin of 58 to 42 percent.[25] After this rout, Mississippi's Democrats, like those in other states, resorted to new tactics.

Elsewhere in 1873 moderates turned to a variety of independent reform movements such as the Louisiana Unification Movement or Taxpayers Unions in Alabama, South Carolina, and other states. Often promoted by urban businessmen who blanched at the prospect of antistatist, laissez-faire Jacksonian Democrats returning to power by exploiting racist white-line tactics, these groups promised to respect blacks' civil and political rights. But they stressed the need to oust Republicans in order to retrench public expenditures, lower taxes, and restore honesty to government. Because "the necessity of checking corruption and procuring honest officials is paramount to all questions of party politics or affiliation," wrote South Carolina's leading proponent of an independent taxpayers' movement in 1874, "the only party needed in this state is the taxpayers' party, arrayed in solid opposition to the horde of nontaxpayers."[26]

By 1873 and 1874, however, such middle-of-the-road movements had little electoral appeal. Few blacks saw any reason to abandon the Republican party now that it was stressing a problack agenda. Nor did many whites find such organizations preferable to the Democratic-Conservative party. This party not only condemned Republicans' economic excesses itself, but it also now trumpeted the necessity of whites' solidifying behind the Democratic banner in order to drive blacks from power and restore white supremacy.

With the centrists' agenda eclipsed and partisan competition between Republicans and Democrats repolarized over race, the Republicans' days in office were numbered. They fell first in 1874 in states where whites constituted a majority of the electorate because of a surge in white turnout for Democrats. Both the movement of scalawags into the Democratic column and the mobilization of previous nonvoters by white-line tactics fed that surge. In Alabama, the Democratic vote soared by 31.6 percent between the gubernatorial elections of 1872 and 1874, and Democrats won even though the Republicans also gained some four thousand votes, presumably from grateful black constituents. In Arkansas, a badly fractured Republican party failed even to run a candidate against the Democrat A. H. Garland. Nonetheless, the Democratic vote doubled from 1872. North Carolina, where Congress' pending Civil Rights bill was an especially salient issue, held no gubernatorial contest that year, but Democrats swept the state legislative and congressional elections.[27]

After 1874, Republicans retained control of only Florida, which was spared a statewide election in 1874, and Louisiana, Mississippi, and South Carolina, where blacks formed a majority of the potential electorate. In these states, mobilizing more whites was not sufficient for Democrats to topple Republicans from power. Thus Democrats resorted once again to violence and intimidation to reduce the black vote on which the Republicans depended.

## CONSTANT WHITE TERRORISM AND FLUCTUATING FEDERAL INTERVENTION

Despite southern Democrats' professed acceptance of black suffrage and the finality of Reconstruction after 1868, white terrorism against Republican leaders and voters had never ceased. It required force to suppress the Ku Klux Klan by the end of 1872. Republican-controlled state militias did the job in Arkansas and Texas, but elsewhere federal prosecutors and troops brought the hooded riders to bay.[28]

Federal intervention was authorized by a new series of laws known as the Force or Enforcement Acts, which congressional Republicans passed over bitter Democratic opposition in 1870 and 1871, ostensibly in response to reports of Klan violence. Aimed at securing blacks' rights under the Fourteenth and Fifteenth Amendments, these laws significantly increased federal power by allowing the federal government to prosecute crimes committed by private individuals, not just public officials, in federal courts. The first Enforcement Act, passed on May 31, 1870, prohibited the use of force, bribery, or intimidation to stop blacks from voting. Its sixth section specifically made it a felony for groups of men to conspire, go in disguise, ride the public highways, or invade an individual's premises in order to deprive any citizen of "any right or privilege granted or secured to him by the Constitution or laws of the United States" or to punish him for having previously exercised such rights.[29] The fourth Enforcement Act, passed on April 20, 1871 explicitly at President Grant's urging, was called the Ku Klux Klan Act and outlawed the Klan and similar groups that interfered with citizens' civil or political rights. More important, it empowered the president to suspend habeas corpus, declare martial law, and insert federal troops into areas to quell Klan activity.

Outraged by the Klan's brutal terrorism and no doubt inspired as well by fear that Democratic victories in southern state and congressional elections of 1870 portended the rapid overthrow of southern Republican regimes, the Republican administration moved to quash the Klan. Led by Attorney General Amos T. Ackerman, the new Justice Department, which was created in July 1870, arrested suspected Klansmen and launched prosecutions against them across the South, but particularly in Mississippi, Tennessee, North Carolina, and South Carolina.[30] In the late fall of 1871, Grant declared martial law in nine piedmont South Carolina counties, and U.S. marshals and army troops made hundreds of arrests. In 1872 the conviction rate achieved by prosecutors in southern federal courts under the Enforcement Acts reached its peak.[31]

These actions effectively broke the back of the Klan and its secret counterparts elsewhere. But physical intimidation of and violence against Republican voters and officials never stopped, in large part because federal enforcement efforts began to decline markedly as early as the spring of 1873.[32] Now, indeed, white opponents of Republican rule brazenly organized in public as heavily armed paramilitary units known variously as White Leagues or Red Shirts. Determined to demonstrate the inability of Republican state administrations to preserve law and order, these groups paraded in broad daylight to intimidate black voters, disrupted Republican rallies, beat and shot blacks at polling places on election days to keep them from voting, and instigated antiblack riots that were little more than massacres.

On several occasions in Arkansas and especially in Louisiana white violence took the form of armed insurrections aimed at physically evicting Republican state officeholders from legislative chambers and other government buildings. At those times, federal troops were required to keep Republicans in power. But even when such putsches in state capitals failed, white gangs decimated Republican organizations and murdered Republican supporters in rural areas beyond the reach of troops. The massacre of over one hundred blacks in Colfax, Louisiana in April 1873 and the assassination of six white Republican leaders in that state's Red River Parish in 1874 were the most notorious of these shooting sprees. But vicious pogroms that left scores, if not hundreds, of blacks dead in Vicksburg, Mississippi in August 1874; Clinton, Mississippi in September 1875; and Hamburg, South Carolina in July 1876 also demonstrated whites' savage hostility to blacks and their ruthless determination to frighten blacks away from the polls no matter what the cost in black lives. Many courageous blacks continued to vote, but this terrorism proved decisive in weakening Republicans in their last strongholds.

The overt display of whites' solidarity against Republican rule by these armed clubs, along with more conventional methods of campaigning to bring out the white vote, undoubtedly contributed to the surging Democratic turnout in Deep South states between 1874 and 1876. The impact that white-on-black violence had in decreasing *statewide* rates of black turnout for Republicans is far more questionable. But statewide black turnout is not necessarily the best measure of the intimidation's impact. In the crucial 1875 elections in Mississippi, for example, Democrats frightened enough black voters away from the polls in certain key counties to reverse sharply heavy Republican majorities, capture five of six congressional districts, and, most important, secure strong majorities in the state legislature. As soon as the legislature met, it impeached the black lieutenant governor who had been elected two years earlier and forced Adelbert Ames to resign and leave the state rather than face impeachment himself.[33] Another state, this one with a black majority, had been "redeemed." And Democrats in the few remaining Republican bastions—Florida, Louisiana, and South Carolina—had learned a lesson for the impending (and as it turned out) decisive elections of 1876.

Mississippi's 1875 election is instructive for another reason, however. In answer to pleas from black voters across the state for protection, Governor Ames had telegraphed administration officials in Washington to send in federal troops as they had earlier that year in Louisiana to prop up the Republican regime. This time, however, the administration refused to intervene, just as it had earlier refused to help Republicans cling to power in Texas and Arkansas after Democrats had won elections in 1873 and 1874. And the refusal to help Ames in 1875 accurately portended the action of Washington authorities in Florida, Louisiana, and South Carolina in 1876.

Many developments within the South contributed to the defeat of southern Republican parties and with them of congressional Republicans' experiment in Reconstruction. The most important was the shift in Republican and Democratic electoral strategies after 1872 that resulted in a drawing of the color line between the parties, for increased white support for the Democrats was absolutely crucial in helping them win elections. Another was the taxpayers' backlash against Republicans' failed economic policies. Nonetheless, reductions of the black vote for Republicans and the decimation of Republicans' local leadership cadre by violence and intimidation were damaging, if not fatal, especially in preventing comebacks after initial defeats.

That violence occurred within the South, but it succeeded in large part because authorities in Washington stopped trying to prevent it. After launching the Reconstruction experiment in order to protect the fruits of northern victory in the Civil War and after initially supporting it with federal power, northern Republicans abandoned it after 1873. The question that cries for an answer is *why* they allowed that experiment to wither and die. To understand fully the failure of Reconstruction in the South, therefore, attention must be shifted back to northern Republicans and to their representatives in the nation's capital.

## CHAPTER 32

# The North, the Grant Administration, and Reconstruction

The North experienced some of the same developments as the South between 1868 and 1877, and they helped change northerners' attitudes toward the federal government's program of Reconstruction. Like white southerners, for example, northern taxpayers rebelled against expensive and dishonest government, and after 1872 they also pressed politicians to abandon the activist state that had characterized Republican governance since 1861. In the North, too, the onset of economic depression in the fall of 1873 brought widespread suffering and forced new issues to the top of government's agenda. Similarly, frenzied railroad construction and the corruption of public officials it often entailed also became political issues in the North and the burgeoning West. In the North, however, rate discrimination and unethical business practices by operating lines, rather than railroads' default on debt, generated public protest. By creating urgent needs at home that northerners wanted their elected officials to address, such developments fueled a growing impatience with Reconstruction in the South.

This insistence that government shift its focus from the South to the North eroded Republican policy makers' commitment to their Reconstruction program. Some northern Republican leaders never abandoned their devotion to blacks' rights and racial justice. But the majority of northern Republican politicians always cared more about retaining office in the North and Washington than about reforming the South. Hence they stood behind Reconstruction only so long as it seemed an electoral asset in the North.[1] They increasingly feared that northern Democrats, who had opposed federal Reconstruction policies from the outset, might topple them from power at home and thereby seize control of Congress and the presidency by exploiting northerners' growing disenchantment with federal intervention in the South. That fear ultimately caused Republicans to abandon Reconstruction.

To understand this change in federal policy, one must closely examine the two presidential terms of Ulysses S. Grant, the North's greatest war hero. As the historian William Gillette notes, "If ever reconstruction had a chance, it was during Grant's administration, when Republicans controlled—in fact, not just in form—both the presidency and Congress for the first time during the postwar period."[2]

## GRANT AS PRESIDENT

Few, if any, presidential administrations in American history have suffered such an ignominious reputation as Grant's. Citing the apparently pervasive political corruption that marred public life during the Grant years, William A. Dunning, writing in the first decade of the twentieth century, called his presidency "the nadir of national disgrace," and most subsequent historians have echoed that criticism.[3] Much of the era's peculation, however, was unconnected to Grant's administration. Nor were Republicans solely responsible for it. These were the years, after all, of the notorious Tweed Ring in New York City when the Democratic "Boss" William Marcy Tweed and his henchmen stole public funds on a scale that dwarfed graft in the South. On a single day, for example, the gang's auditors approved municipal expenditures of over $15 million, $14 million of which ended up in ring members' pockets.[4]

The stench of corruption spread far beyond New York. Republican machines in Philadelphia, Washington, D.C., and other cities poured millions of taxpayers' dollars into public construction so that they could rake off the boodle. State

Ulysses S. Grant as president

legislators in Pennsylvania sold divorces. The Kansas legislature was so polluted, as historian Mark Summers wryly remarks, that Kansas was "known as 'the Rotten Commonwealth,' or, worse, 'the Western Pennsylvania.'"[5] Only a few New England state legislatures emerged from the period relatively unscathed by graft, bribery, and influence peddling.

Grant had nothing to do with this sorry record. Nor was he responsible for all of the thievery associated with the federal government. One of the biggest scandals exposed during his presidency, for example, concerned the Crédit Mobilier. Epitomizing how insiders during this era pillaged public funds through intentional cost overruns, the Crédit Mobilier was a construction company composed of the corporate directors of the Union Pacific Railroad. In their capacity as the railroad's officials, they hired the Crédit Mobilier (that is, themselves) to build the road and readily paid its heavily padded bills with United States bonds that Congress had appropriated to subsidize construction. Then, through the agency of the Massachusetts Republican congressman Oakes Ames, the Crédit Mobilier supposedly bribed enough Republican congressmen by selling them its stock at prices substantially below market value to delay a congressional investigation of the company's raid on the Treasury. Yet most of the stock changed hands before Grant became president, and at least one historian has questioned whether the congressmen who received it were responsible for postponing exposure of this insider profiteering until the winter of 1872–1873.[6] Nonetheless, the scheme smelled of influence peddling, all of the implicated congressmen were Republicans, and Grant was tarnished with guilt by partisan association.

Other scandals came much closer to Grant, who, though personally honest, displayed abysmal judgment in picking advisors and indefensible laxity in overseeing their activities. His brother-in-law conspired with Jay Gould and Jim Fisk, two of the era's most piratical tycoons, to bamboozle Grant into helping them, at least temporarily, to corner the New York gold market so that they could sell gold at extortionate prices to businessmen who needed it.[7] Grant's second secretary of war, William W. Belknap, was forced to resign to escape congressional impeachment when it was discovered that his wife received payoffs from Indian traders to whom Belknap awarded lucrative trading licenses. His close friend and personal secretary Orville E. Babcock was accused of accepting bribes in return for using his influence to delay federal prosecution of the Whiskey Ring, in which internal revenue agents and whiskey distillers colluded to defraud the government of excise tax payments. Rather than immediately sacking Babcock, who was most likely guilty, Grant sprang to his defense and helped win his acquittal.[8] "As for President Grant," concludes the historian Mark Wahlgren Summers, "he compiled a record of gullibility and his intimates a record of graft that no whitewash could efface."[9]

Yet a stress on his administration's corruption does not explain its stance toward Reconstruction in the South, especially during Grant's first term from 1869 to 1873. To be sure, the northern public's growing anger about corruption at home jaundiced their attitude toward prodigal, and sometimes palpably dishonest, Republican governments in the South, while simultaneously increasing their empathy for southern taxpayers who insisted that only Republicans' expulsion from office could restore lean and clean government. But most of the exposures of Republican wrongdoing came only after Grant had won reelection and led other Republican candidates to triumph in 1872. The scandals involving Belknap and Babcock were aired in the winter of 1875–1876, after the federal government's retreat from enforcing Reconstruction had already degenerated into a rout.[10] To understand the northern Republicans' actions on Reconstruction after 1868, attention must be focused elsewhere.

The Republicans nominated Grant in 1868 because their setbacks in the 1867 elections convinced them they needed the popular military hero to retain the White House. Always scornful of career politicos, Grant reluctantly accepted the nomination, as he explained to Sherman, to avert a "contest for power for the next four years between mere trading politicians, the elevation of whom, no matter which party won, would lose to us, largely, the results of the costly war which we have gone through." Grant, moreover, hoped to bring the reunion that had been northerners' wartime objective to a successful conclusion by simultaneously conciliating white southerners and protecting blacks' civil and political rights.[11]

Personal ambition also explains his candidacy and his subsequent actions as president. After suffering embarrassing failures and humiliating obscurity before the war, he had won success and fame during it, and he dreaded losing his celebrity status once the war ended. He could have remained commanding general of the rapidly shrinking peacetime army, but the presidency offered a better chance of retaining popular adulation and the sudden social eminence it brought. As Grant's ablest biographer writes, "He and [his wife] Julia were determined to press on to higher ground, in order not to lose what they had gained."[12] Once in the White House, moreover, they determined to remain there as long as possible.

As in the cases of his predecessors Lincoln and Johnson, hope of winning reelection shaped Grant's actions as president. Unlike his two predecessors, however, Grant did not disagree with congressional Republicans about how to deal with Democratic opposition and the South. Instead, he quickly discerned that securing his own reelection and a just resolution of Reconstruction required cooperation with his party's congressional wing.

Grant never pleased all congressional Republicans. Senator Charles Sumner and a few others defeated a proposal he repeatedly urged on Congress during his first three years in office to annex Santo Domingo (the Dominican Republic) to the United States because the scheme reeked of corruption.[13] Other dissidents joined the Liberal Republican movement explicitly to deprive Grant of a second term. The great majority of congressional and northern Republican politicians, however, stood by Grant, at least until the middle of his second term, when their embarrassment at his administration's tarnished reputation helped dissuade him from seeking a third term.

This alliance between Grant and regular Republicans (or Stalwarts, as they came to be called) was of vital importance because Grant shared their determination to prevent Democrats from returning to power in the North. Yet Grant and the congressional Republicans also believed that they could win in the North by publicizing terrorist outrages against southern Republicans and thereby reigniting Northerners' antipathy toward Confederates. As Grant's attorney general put it in 1871, "All that is necessary to hold the majority of the northern voters to the Republican cause, is to show them how active and cruel the Confederate temper still is in the South."[14] The interaction of these views with Grant's sincere desire to secure blacks' rights best explains the federal government's actions regarding Reconstruction after 1868.

## THE POLITICAL CONTEXT OF GRANT'S PRESIDENCY

The Republicans had good reason to worry about the Democrats' threat to their hold on power. In 1868, Grant handily carried the electoral vote over New York's Horatio Seymour by a margin of 214 to 80, but his popular vote majority was only about 300,000 out of 5.7 million votes cast. The eight states Democrats won included Louisiana and Georgia, where the Republican vote had plummeted since the spring of 1868 and a minority of blacks clearly voted Democratic; Delaware, Maryland, and Kentucky, which by 1868 seemed permanently lost to the Republicans if the electorate remained exclusively white; and Oregon, New Jersey, and New York, the nation's biggest electoral prize. More ominous still for Republicans, the best estimates suggest that in 1868 the Democrats carried a majority of the white vote.[15] That tilt helped Democrats increase their seats in the House of Representatives from 47 to 69.[16]

The Democratic vote in the North seemed certain to increase over time because of the hundreds of thousands of European immigrants pouring into the country each year. Both Republican and Democratic politicians were acutely aware of this likelihood. By the spring of 1870 such Republican newspapers as the *Chicago Republican* printed tables of the numbers of Irish and German immigrants who had arrived since 1860, and on the House floor Republican congressmen explicitly warned about the dangers such immigrants posed to their party. Meanwhile, Democratic congressmen such as Wisconsin's Charles Eldridge openly boasted that Ireland was sending their party vessels full of her "robust and faithful sons."[17]

The 1868 returns therefore portended a Democratic comeback in the North. What seemed to stand between the Republicans and Democratic control of

Congress and the presidency were the new Republican parties in the South. Only the election of southern Republican congressmen that year had allowed Republicans to offset Democratic gains in the North and to retain their two-thirds majority in the House during the Forty-first Congress (1869–1871). Those southern Republican parties, moreover, were based largely, though not exclusively, on the loyalty of black voters. Approximately five hundred thousand southern blacks voted in the 1868 presidential election, and 450,000 (or 90 percent) of them supported Grant.[18] Blacks, in short, were far more reliable Republican voters than were whites. That fact helped determine Republicans' Reconstruction policies during Grant's first term.

## THE FIFTEENTH AMENDMENT

Republicans sought to counter or minimize impending Democratic gains in the North, but for most of Grant's first term they looked primarily to shoring up and expanding their party's southern base to offset those gains. In this endeavor, the partisan motives of some Republicans meshed with others' egalitarian commitment to the expansion and protection of blacks' rights. Republicans' first move after the 1868 election, for example, was to increase the black (and overwhelmingly Republican) electorate before the 1870 elections by passing the Fifteenth Amendment in February 1869. This not only provided a constitutional guarantee to blacks already granted the vote by the Military Reconstruction Acts, but Republican passage of the Amendment over united Democratic opposition in Congress might decrease black support for Democrats in the South. More important, it could also add black voters to the Republican column in such border states as Missouri, West Virginia, Kentucky, Maryland, and Delaware, helping to bolster slim Republican majorities in the first two of those states and to reverse Democratic majorities in the last two.[19]

The Fifteenth Amendment also granted blacks the vote in northern states where the margins between the two parties had often been close in 1868 and where new black voters might help offset some of the anticipated gain the Democrats would get from new immigrant voters. Republican proponents of the amendment certainly boasted of those potential Republican gains in the North to persuade reluctant colleagues to vote for the amendment. Thus Senator Charles Sumner, perhaps the foremost champion of black rights in the Republican party, declared during the Senate debates:

> You need votes in Connecticut, do you not? There are three thousand fellow citizens in that state ready at the call of Congress to take their place at the ballot box. You need them also in Pennsylvania, do you not? There are at least fifteen thousand in that great state waiting for your summons. Wherever you most need them, there they are; and be assured they will all vote for those who stand beside them in the assertion of Equal Rights.[20]

In fact, some northern Republican congressmen initially balked at the Fifteenth Amendment because northern state referenda on black suffrage since the end of the war had repeatedly been defeated. Thus Republicans appeared to be risking a white backlash at home that would help Democrats far more than new black voters could help their own party.[21] Republican leaders, however, clearly hoped to minimize this risk by rushing the amendment through in early 1869 and securing its ratification well before the next major set of northern congressional elections in the fall of 1870.[22]

To attain quick ratification, the popular Grant endorsed the amendment in his inaugural address and immediately pressed northern Republican governors to call their legislatures into session to ratify it. For the same reason, in April 1869 congressional Republicans, at Grant's urging, passed legislation concerning state constitutional referenda to hasten the readmission of Mississippi, Texas, and Virginia in time for the 1870 congressional elections. Those states might not only contribute more Republican congressmen, but because Congress required them to ratify the Fifteenth Amendment, they would hasten the amendment's adoption.[23] By the end of March, 1870, ratification was complete.

Many northerners at first misunderstood Grant's purposes. They assumed that his election, along with passage of the Fifteenth Amendment, signaled the end of the federal government's role in Reconstruction. "It is the general feeling,"

A John Kelly lithograph entitled "The Fifteenth Amendment, Celebrated May 19th 1870"

an Ohioan wrote to the Republican senator John Sherman in June 1870, "that we have done enough, gone far enough in governmental reconstruction, and that it is best for all that the southern communities should be left to manage themselves."[24] Many agreed with the Republican New York *Times* "that the work of the Republican party ... ends with the adoption of the Fifteenth Amendment,"[25] and that it was time for a major political reshuffling in which the Republican party would be displaced.

Grant, however, agreed with Republican politicians who wanted to fend off, not bring about, the widely bruited realignment. These Republicans insisted that the work of their party was in fact not yet done, that it was still needed to complete Reconstruction and fully secure blacks' rights because the Democrats, who had promised to repeal Reconstruction legislation during the 1868 campaign, could not be trusted to do the job. Indeed, as late as 1876 the Republicans were still declaring in their national platform that "the work of the Republican party is unfinished."[26]

A combination of motives thus accounted for northern Republicans' first steps regarding Reconstruction after Grant's election. Many still harbored a sincere commitment to the rights of African Americans. The Republicans also clearly wanted to increase their voting base, especially in the South, to counteract impending Democratic gains in the North. To quash talk about realignment, finally, they insisted that the Republican party must continue to protect what northerners had won in the war.

## THE ENFORCEMENT ACTS

All of these considerations shaped northern Republican leaders' reactions to Klan violence in the South between 1869 and 1872. They themselves were furious about the assaults on blacks and Republican organizers. But they also exploited their constituents' outrage at the Klan's atrocities by arguing that Confederates still might win the peace and that therefore Republican control of the national government remained necessary. At the same time they sought to bolster Republican strength in the South for the 1870 elections. On May 31, 1870, Congress passed the first Enforcement Act, outlawing bribery, fraud, intimidation, or violence to prevent blacks from voting and allowing federal prosecution of state election officials who refused to accept blacks' ballots. In June, Grant sent additional federal troops into North Carolina, although he refused to allow the Republican governor, William W. Holden, to call them out unless he first used his state militia to suppress the Klan.[27]

These efforts proved too little, too late. Not only did the Democrats win the 1870 state elections in Alabama and North Carolina, where the new Democratic legislature ousted Holden by impeachment. In the congressional elections of 1870 and 1871, the Democrats won a total of fifty-four House seats in the former Confederate states, compared with fifty-six for the Republicans. In border state congressional elections during those two years, moreover, Democrats captured thirty-four seats, compared with only two for the Republicans.[28]

Attributing the setbacks of 1870 to Klan terrorism, Grant called on Congress in March 1871 to pass tougher legislation to secure "life, liberty, and property and the enforcement of law in all parts of the United States." On the following day he issued a proclamation warning South Carolina's Klan that if it did not immediately disperse, he would send in troops. Congressional Republicans then facilitated his use of troops by passing the Ku Klux Klan Act on April 20, 1871. On November 10, 1871, after Democrats' growing success in southern congressional elections had become clear, Grant suspended the writ of habeas corpus in nine South Carolina counties and ordered troops and U.S. marshals to begin massive arrests of suspected terrorists.[29] Federal indictments of suspected Klansmen and especially their rates of convictions in federal trials surged in 1872 and 1873 in the former Confederate states, including Tennessee.[30]

During Grant's first term, in short, Republicans in Washington clearly tried to aid southern Republicans to counterbalance anticipated Democratic gains in the North. Yet even the Enforcement Acts of 1870–1871 reflected the northern Republicans' solicitude for their own electoral success at home. The first and fourth (Ku Klux Klan) acts and a much publicized congressional investigation of Klan violence in 1871 gave northern Republicans a valuable platform. It reawakened northerners' wartime animosities against Confederates by reattaching the Copperhead stigma to northern Democrats who stridently denounced federal enforcement. Congratulating Senator John Sherman on a tough speech against the Klan in early 1871, Ohio's governor, Rutherford B. Hayes, exulted, "Nothing unites and harmonises the Republican party like the conviction that Democratic victories [in 1870] strengthen the reactionary and brutal tendencies of the late rebel States."[31]

The second and third Enforcement Acts of July 14, 1870 and February 28, 1871 were aimed directly at reducing the Democratic vote in the North. Both applied only to cities with populations of twenty thousand or more people; of sixty-eight such cities in the nation, only five were in the former Confederate states. These acts allowed special deputy United States marshals to police congressional elections and arrest fraudulent voters. The 1871 law authorized federal judges, almost all of whom were Republicans, on request by a few citizens, to appoint two supervisors at every polling place who could challenge doubtful voters and count the votes. Here was the Republican response to the loss of New York and New Jersey in 1868 and 1870.

The great bulk of federal money spent on election enforcement during the 1870s and thereafter, in fact, was spent in the North, not the South.[32] Republican policy makers sought to prevent a Democratic comeback by preventing immigrants, especially illegally naturalized immigrants, from voting in New York,

Brooklyn, Baltimore, St. Louis, Chicago, Boston, and elsewhere. As the historian William Gillette concludes: "Congress, while framing the various acts, intensively investigated the electoral problems in northern cities, discussed the importance of northern elections, and then legislated a solution by regulating elections and registration there."[33]

Still other actions emphasize the Republicans' preoccupation with their party's fortunes in the North. For one thing, protecting southern blacks' right to vote was the only help northern Republicans offered their southern allies. When southern Republicans pressed their wealthier and more experienced northern colleagues to share campaign funds and send northern speakers to the South to stump for Republican candidates, for example, they received a cold shoulder. Northern Republicans insisted on retaining campaign resources exclusively for northern elections.[34] When Republicans from the South arrived in Congress, moreover, their northern colleagues treated them like orphans, not relatives. They repeatedly refused to share federal appropriations with the South, thereby depriving southern Republican congressional candidates of the ability to campaign on a record of bringing home federal funds to their money-starved districts.[35]

Northern Republicans' wariness about their own constituents' reactions to Reconstruction also explains much about the administration's seemingly erratic intervention in the South to protect black voters and prop up endangered Republican regimes. Although northern Republican voters fumed at Klan outrages and antiblack and anti-Republican violence, after 1869 the northern public grew increasingly impatient with any federal intervention in southern affairs. That reality influenced how Grant's administration deployed the two weapons at its disposal: Justice Department prosecution in federal courts of those who interfered with blacks' right to vote, whether they were election officials or armed thugs; and the injection of federal troops to guard the polls and Republican officeholders from Democratic challenges.

To minimize a northern backlash that Democrats could exploit, Grant's administration made almost no use of either weapon in states where it could not help Republicans win elections: untakable Democratic bastions such as Kentucky and states where Democrats quickly defeated Republicans as in Missouri, West Virginia, Virginia and Georgia. With the exception of Tennessee and North Carolina, where the government vigorously prosecuted suspected Klansmen in 1872 and 1873, moreover, it brought few if any cases in states where the black vote was not large enough by itself to bring Republicans victory.[36]

Massacres of blacks and armed insurrections against Republican state governments primarily determined when and where Grant sent in troops, but he usually did so only when the intervention could be brief and where it might directly benefit Republicans. Grant shrewdly timed these deployments as many months away as possible from the North's fall elections so that northern voters would have forgotten them when they went to the polls. In the winter of 1869–1870, for example, Grant sent troops back into Georgia to secure Republican control of the legislature and ratification of the Fifteenth Amendment and then quickly removed them. But when North Carolina's governor, William W. Holden, asked Grant to mobilize the federal troops in his state to guard the polls at its August elections, only months before northerners voted, Grant balked. Similarly, he would not allow the use of federal troops in Louisiana during 1872, an election year when Grant himself was a candidate and intervention might swell the Liberal Republican bolt. Yet in January 1873, after the 1872 elections were safely over and almost two years before the 1874 contests, he ordered the army in Louisiana to uphold the Republican state government in the face of a Democratic challenge and sent troops into Alabama to oust Democrats from the state legislature and thereby secure the election of a Republican United States senator.

Nothing underlines the administration's preoccupation with the northern ramifications of its southern policy so vividly as its refusal of Mississippi Governor Adelbert Ames's request for federal help in September 1875. By then the evidence and probable effectiveness of the White Leaguers' campaign of violence and intimidation to reduce the black vote on which Republican success depended was unmistakable. Yet Ames was not the only desperate Republican lobbying the administration. Ohio's Republicans warned that they would lose their own gubernatorial election in October if Grant sent troops to Mississippi and that defeat in 1875 meant the inevitable loss of Ohio in the 1876 presidential contest. Ohio trumped Mississippi in Republicans' political calculations. Troops were withheld. As Ames himself wrote after the election, "I was sacrificed last fall that Mr. [Rutherford B.] Hayes might be made Gov[ernor] of Ohio."[37]

## THE LIBERAL REPUBLICAN MOVEMENT AND THE BORDER STATES

Despite the administration's attempt to minimize a northern backlash against its Reconstruction policies, Republican efforts during Grant's first term were sufficiently vigorous to help ignite the Liberal Republican bolt against Grant. Liberal Republicanism originated in Missouri, Tennessee, and West Virginia. Numerous discontents merged to drive this revolt. Because Grant's most powerful appointee in Missouri headed the national Whiskey Ring, opposition to corruption, spoilsmen, and Grant's reelection became central components of the Missouri movement. In all three states, Liberal Republicans demanded an end to federal Reconstruction efforts, and especially repeal of the state laws proscribing Confederate sympathizers from the right to vote or hold office that their Republicans had used to cling to power since the end of the war.[38]

When regular Republican hard-liners refused to relent, Liberals bolted the party and forged coalitions with Democrats in 1869 and 1870 that captured state governments and restored Confederates' political rights. Some bolting Republicans, such as Tennessee's Dewitt Senter and Missouri's B. Gratz Brown and Carl Schurz, initially won governorships and Senate seats as a result of their deals with Democrats, but they had made a Faustian bargain. Reenfranchised whites outnumbered newly enfranchised blacks in all three states. By 1871 it was clear in Missouri and West Virginia, if not yet in Tennessee, that straight-line Democrats could carry state elections without any help from dissident Republicans.

The prominence of Liberal Republicanism in the border states may explain why Grant's administration made little effort to enforce blacks' voting rights in them, despite evidence that Democrats from Missouri to Delaware deployed violence, discriminatory election laws, and outright fraud to negate blacks' newly granted franchise.[39] If Grant was attempting to mollify Liberal Republicans by lax enforcement, however, he failed. In January 1872, Missouri's Brown and Schurz called for a national Liberal Republican convention in May. The previous September, Schurz defined the new party's goals: federal amnesty for Confederates and cessation of federal intervention in the South; civil service reform; rapid resumption of specie payments by the government; federal tax cuts; and tariff reduction.[40] This platform failed to bring Liberal Republicans victory in 1872 or to perpetuate the life of the new party beyond that election. The popular impulses the movement reflected and even many of the specific goals Schurz outlined, however, would shape much that happened in 1872 and especially during Grant's second term.

## CHAPTER 33

The Retreat from
Reconstruction

The Republicans' commitment to securing the black vote in the South
shaped federal Reconstruction policy for most of Grant's first term in office. Between 1872 and 1877, however, most northern Republican leaders became convinced that retaining power in Washington required the
abandonment of federal enforcement efforts in the South. Numerous factors
contributed to this shift in federal policy. Three were most important: the Liberal Republican challenge to Grant in 1872; a series of Supreme Court decisions
adverse to federal Reconstruction policies; and the reactions of the northern public to the economic depression following the Panic of 1873.

## LIBERAL REPUBLICANISM AND ITS CONSEQUENCES

With the notable exception of the Republican party itself, no third party in
American history has ever won the presidency or control of Congress. Nonetheless, because third parties usually vent popular demands that the existing major
parties have ignored or consciously dodged, they have often shifted the course of
public debate, enlarged the list of issues that government is obliged to address,
and forced one or both of the major parties to embrace their goals in order to
coopt whatever voting strength the new party has mobilized. The short-lived
Liberal Republican party illustrates this paradoxical fate.

From the start, its presidential campaign in 1872 was a fiasco. The Cincinnati
convention in May attracted a heterogeneous assemblage of Grant haters, reformers who demanded honest government and an end to the spoils system of political patronage, men who wanted to terminate Reconstruction, self-promoting

newspaper and magazine editors, proponents of hard money and free trade, office-hungry politicos, and just plain soreheads who could agree on little other than the need to replace Grant. A surprisingly large number of veteran Republican politicians including the Illinois senator Lyman Trumbull, Indiana's ex-congressman George W. Julian, Ohio's radical ex-congressman James Ashley, Pennsylvania's wartime governor Andrew Curtin, and ultimately even Charles Sumner, whose rift with Grant over the annexation of Santo Domingo proved unbridgeable, joined the Liberal Republican bolt. But the two favorites for the nomination at Cincinnati were Supreme Court Justice David Davis of Illinois, whom the small Labor Reform party had already nominated, and Charles Francis Adams, the wartime minister to England and the favorite of clean-government reformers and New England proponents of tariff reduction and sound money. Both men had drawbacks, however, and instead the convention nominated the long-time Whig and Republican New York editor Horace Greeley, with Missouri governor B. Gratz Brown as his running mate.

Greeley's selection was a calamity. He advocated amnesty, an end to Reconstruction, and clean government, but his lifelong dedication to high tariffs made him anathema to low tariff men. Over his long career, moreover, he had championed a lengthy list of social reforms ranging from prohibitionism to Fourierism (a kind of socialism) that made him seem a dizzy dreamer, if not downright dan-

"It Is Only a Truce to Regain Power ('Playing Possum')."
Grant and congressional Republicans attempted to stanch Republican defections to Liberal Republicanism by coopting some of Liberals' issues. Here Thomas Nast seeks the same end by portraying Horace Greeley and Charles Sumner attempting to persuade blacks to join hands with Ku Klux Klansmen who murdered them in the South and Irish Democrats who had done so in New York City during the 1863 draft riots.

gerous. His nomination drove thousands of Republicans back into the arms of the pro-Grant regulars.

Greeley's widely publicized denunciations of Democrats for over thirty years also complicated the consummation of a Liberal Republican–Democratic coalition. The Liberals may have been idealists, but they understood that they needed Democratic help to beat Grant. Even before the convention met, when an Adams-Trumbull ticket seemed likely, Carl Schurz secretly negotiated with Democratic leaders to arrange a coalition.[1] Tarred as corruptionists themselves after "Boss" William Tweed's conviction in 1871 and bereft of a candidate likely to defeat Grant, Democrats reluctantly endorsed Greeley and mobilized as many of their alienated supporters as they could for him.[2]

It was not enough. Grant carried every northern state and all but seven states in the South and border region. He swamped Greeley in the electoral vote, 286 to 42, and he won the popular vote 3,597,132 to 2,834,125, more than doubling his margin over Horatio Seymour in 1868. In all but five northern states, in fact, Greeley drew fewer votes, and often substantially fewer, than the straight Democrat Seymour had four years earlier. As a political party, Liberal Republicanism had fizzled.

The outcome of that election, however, is an inadequate measure of Liberal Republicanism's importance. It reshaped both major parties' strategies and focus in 1872 and thereafter. Ultimately, what made Liberal Republicanism significant was that the movement reflected many northerners' insistence that the sectional and racial issues that had dominated public life since 1860 must be buried and that politicians must address matters concerning governance and federal economic policy of far more significance to the northern public. The new party sought "the break-up of old parties," boasted E. L. Godkin, editor of *The Nation*, on the eve of the Cincinnati convention. "Reconstruction and slavery we have done with; for administrative and revenue reform we are eager."[3] Precisely because Democrats and Republicans recognized the resonance of this appeal in the North, both moved to embrace and thereby neutralize it.

Grant astutely addressed some of the Liberals' grievances even before Greeley's nomination in order to reduce the number of Republican bolters. He knew that many clean government reformers and growing numbers of outraged taxpayers blamed government corruption on the major parties' control of patronage. Only college-educated, nonpartisan, and disinterested gentlemen, the so-called best men, reformers insisted, should hold appointive governmental offices. The spoils system must be abolished, Liberal Republicans cried, and the way to do it was through civil service reform requiring all applicants for government jobs to pass written examinations and forbidding elected officials to remove them from office once appointed.[4]

Ever distrustful of politicos, Grant embraced this assault on the spoils system. He requested action from Congress in December 1870, and in March 1871 it authorized him to appoint a blue-ribbon commission to prepare a plan for civil service reform. Grant named genuine reformers to this body; George William Curtis, editor of *Harper's Weekly* and an ardent advocate of a professional civil service, chaired it. The commission wrote rules concerning the hiring, firing, and qualifications of federal employees. Grant endorsed those rules in December 1871 and kept his promise to adhere to them throughout 1872.[5]

In his December 1871 annual message, Grant also moved to preempt the Liberals' economic agenda and thereby neutralize another of their issues. He asked Congress to cut all federal excise taxes except those on liquor and tobacco, and Congress did so. He also requested tariff reduction, and in 1872 Congress, with regular Republicans in the lead, lowered duties by 10 percent. Finally, he asked Congress to arrange immediately for the federal government to resume specie payments.[6]

Resumption of specie payments remained a contentious issue until the 1876 election. Such a move required the immediate contraction of the amount of greenbacks in circulation so that the government could redeem them at their face value in gold. Because many inflation-minded Pennsylvania and midwestern Republicans opposed any reduction of the paper money in circulation, the Republicans did nothing in 1872 other than announcing in their national platform that they "confidently expect[ed] that our excellent national currency will be perfected by a speedy resumption of specie payment."[7]

The nationwide economic collapse following the panic of 1873 gave economic issues even greater salience than they had in 1872, but the demand for and enactment of federal excise tax cuts that year illuminated a fundamental change in public opinion that had an enduring impact. Since corruption was primarily associated with government expenditures underwritten by taxpayers, many property-holding voters began to equate honest government with inexpensive, do-nothing government. Consequently, they now defined "reform" solely as the election of honest men who would reduce taxes and cut expenditures, including federal expenditures on Reconstruction. Conversely, they opposed the enactment of programs that addressed social ills because such programs cost money. In its broadest and most enduring sense, that is, liberalism meant abandonment of activist government, and after 1872 both Republicans and Democrats deferred to that demand.[8] The triumph of liberalism, in short, meant that after 1872 neither major party dared compete for votes by advocating positive governmental programs. This conviction helped bring federal enforcement of Reconstruction to an end.

The Liberal Republicans' call for amnesty and cessation of federal intervention in the South reflected both their aversion to an activist state and their desire to bury sectional issues. Yet most Liberals did not equate the end of Reconstruction with an abandonment of blacks' rights. Such Republicans as Charles Sumner, James Ashley, George W. Julian, and Lyman Trumbull, who had helped frame the Republicans' original Reconstruction policies, could never have supported any party that did so. Rather they joined the movement for two reasons.

Most believed the repeated pledges from centrist Democrats in the South since 1869 that they would acquiesce in the Fourteenth and Fifteenth Amendments and the permanence of black suffrage. Hence they saw no danger to blacks in allowing such men to return to power within the South, because only that return seemed likely to destroy the corrupt Republican machines that supported Grant. Moderate Republicans such as Trumbull and Schurz, moreover, regarded expansion of federal police power that allowed federal prosecution of private citizens under the Enforcement Acts as a flatly unconstitutional subversion of state-centered federalism and an intolerable consolidation of power in Washington.[9]

Both concerns explain how the Democrats dealt with the Liberals in 1872. They endorsed a program known as the "New Departure," which pledged that, if restored to power in Washington, Democrats would not repeal any statute or constitutional amendment that Republicans had passed to expand blacks' rights. Hence, Democrats insisted, those measures were "no longer issues before the country."[10] The Democrats did not forsake race baiting or opposition to new Republican initiatives on Reconstruction, but they did declare old sectional issues dead, thereby ensuring that the Democrats would have to find different issues on which to seek votes after 1872.

Republicans hoping to coopt the Liberal Republican appeal could not repudiate Reconstruction itself in 1872, the year when federal enforcement efforts under Grant finally became serious. Indeed, the Republican national platform of 1872 explicitly defended the Enforcement Acts. Yet that same platform praised Republican congressmen for passing, at Grant's request, a sweeping amnesty act in May 1872 that restored the right to hold public office in the South to all but a handful of former Confederates. This bill, enacted only a year after passage of the Ku Klux Klan Act, inaugurated the northern Republicans' retreat from Reconstruction. The hope of winning back Liberal bolters after that election would hasten that retreat, but other developments also spurred it.

## THE SUPREME COURT AND RECONSTRUCTION

Prior to Grant's presidency, the Supreme Court had largely dodged any challenges to the congressional Republicans' Reconstruction program. In *Missouri v. Cummings* (1866), it declared unconstitutional a Missouri statute requiring all officeholders, attorneys, teachers, and priests to take an iron-clad oath that they had never sympathized with the Confederacy. But that was a state, not a federal, law. In 1868, when Congress passed a law denying that the Court had appellate jurisdiction to hear the appeal of a Mississippi editor protesting his trial by a military commission, the Supreme Court in *ex parte McCardle* refused to hear McCardle's appeal. Similarly, in two 1867 decisions, *Mississippi v. Johnson* and *Georgia v. Stanton*, the Court denied that it had the authority to issue injunctions to stop implementation of the Military Reconstruction Acts.

The Court's passivity toward Congress ended with Grant's presidency. The decision that signaled a change in the Court's mood had nothing directly to do with Reconstruction, but it indicated the justices' willingness to disallow congressional legislation. On February 7, 1870, by a 4–3 decision with Chief Justice Salmon P. Chase writing for the majority, the Court in *Hepburn v. Griswold* ruled that the Legal Tender Act of 1862 was unconstitutional because it impaired the obligation of contracts and was thus "inconsistent with the spirit of the Constitution."[11] On the same day, Grant nominated two new justices to fill vacancies on the Court; in 1871 they joined the three dissenters in *Hepburn* to reverse that decision and uphold the constitutionality of greenbacks. Nonetheless, a substantial minority of the Court clearly remained averse to an expansion of national authority, and during Grant's second term that minority became a majority with respect to Reconstruction.

In 1873, in the *Slaughterhouse Cases*, the Court narrowed the reach of the Fourteenth Amendment itself. The cases involved the challenge of butchers in New Orleans to the constitutionality of a monopoly that its municipal government had granted to a company of the city's slaughtering business. By depriving them of their right to earn a livelihood, the challengers maintained, this franchise violated the clause of the Fourteenth Amendment prohibiting state governments from depriving anyone of the privileges and immunities of national citizenship. The Court's majority rejected this suit on the grounds that the Fourteenth amendment was meant to apply only to blacks' rights. More important, it ruled that the privileges and immunities of national citizenship remained quite limited (and the examples it gave were almost irrelevant to blacks) and that Congress and federal courts under the Fourteenth Amendment could protect only those limited rights. Most civil and political rights, it further declared, remained under states' control, and with those rights the Fourteenth Amendment had "nothing to do."[12]

The Court's adherence to state-centered federalism and refusal to allow an expansion of national power proved even more damaging to federal enforcement in two cases that began to make their way through the federal court system in 1873. These retarded activity by the Justice Department in the South even before the Supreme Court announced its decisions in March 1876. *United States v. Cruikshank* involved one of the few white Louisianans successfully convicted in federal court for his participation in the bloody Colfax massacre of 1873. Effectively declaring the expansion of federal police power in the Enforcement Acts unconstitutional, the Court overruled Cruikshank's conviction on the grounds that the Fourteenth and Fifteenth Amendments prohibited only *state* violations of blacks' rights. Only local and state authorities, not the federal government, the Court insisted, could punish crimes by individuals.[13]

The companion case, *United States v. Reese*, reversed the conviction of a Kentucky election official who refused to allow a black to vote because he had failed to pay a required poll tax. Under the Fifteenth Amendment, declared the Court, the federal government could only bar state action that denied blacks the vote on the grounds of race or previous condition of servitude. It could not pass positive legislation, like certain sections of the first Enforcement Act, that guaranteed suffrage in all circumstances. State governments were free to impose any restrictions they wished on the right to vote as long as they were not ostensibly based on race. States, not the national government, controlled suffrage rights. Thus the door opened to a host of restrictive laws that southern states would pass after Reconstruction to limit, if not eradicate, blacks' right to vote.[14]

## THE PANIC OF 1873 AND THE SPECTER OF REALIGNMENT

Along with these actions by the nation's highest court, a sharp reversal in the party's electoral fortunes after 1872 hastened the Republicans' retreat from Reconstruction during Grant's second term. Public confidence in the Republican party began sinking in the winter of 1872–1873, when the Crédit Mobilier's bribery of congressmen was exposed and Republican congressmen voted themselves a retroactive pay raise that was widely denounced by furious taxpayers as the "Salary Grab."[15] Then, in the fall of 1873, the collapse of Jay Cooke's banking house ignited a financial panic, causing businesses to close their doors, workers to lose their jobs, and prices on farm products to plummet. The panic inaugurated the longest economic depression of the nineteenth century, one that lasted until the late 1870s in the North and far longer in the South.

Hard times sometimes diverted Northerners' attention from public life altogether as people scrambled to put food on their families' tables. But economic suffering also engendered still greater public anger with the incumbent Republicans, who had seemingly devoted far more attention to the South than to conditions in the North. Most sitting congressmen enjoyed a year's reprieve until they had to face voters in 1874, but Republican state parties were not so fortunate. In 1873 the Democrats increased their vote in Pennsylvania, carried the Minnesota and New York state legislatures, and elected governors as well as legislatures in Connecticut, Wisconsin, and Ohio.

Two aspects of these state elections merit emphasis. First, Republican officeholders in Washington could not shrug them off because state legislatures chose United States senators. Second, Democrats alone did not defeat Republicans. Especially in the Midwest, but almost everywhere, a host of splinter parties advocating different economic panaceas to combat hard times—Antimonopoly parties, Labor Reform parties seeking state laws to help workers, Greenbackers touting currency inflation to raise prices, and Granger parties demanding railroad regulation—cooperated with the Democrats to oust Republicans or siphoned off sufficient Republican votes to allow Democrats to win.

In 1874, as depression deepened, third-party movements, which customary Republican voters could support far more readily than the hated Democrats, spread to additional states. For example, in Indiana Antimonopolists and Grangers combined to run an independent legislative ticket pledged to lowering freight rates and destroying the railroads' political influence. Thus talk of realignment mushroomed again in the North, just as it did in the South at precisely the same time. In June 1874, the New York *Tribune* declared that major "party lines no longer certify anything but past prejudices"; a few months earlier the New York *Herald* had predicted that major party "disintegration . . . appears to be inevitable," even for the Republicans who had "no fixed policy—no principles of policy." As the historian Michael Perman notes, "New issues had to appear soon, it was believed, in order to breathe life into the political system."[16]

The 1873 results certainly demonstrated that northern voters would support parties that advanced new policies relevant to depressed economic conditions, rather than the old issue of Reconstruction, which Democrats and Liberal Republicans had already pronounced dead. After 1873, therefore, Grant and the congressional Republicans joined in a sprint away from enforcement. Congress slashed appropriations for the Justice Department, and the attorney general announced in the spring of 1874 that the government had achieved all its goals in the South.[17]

Desperate to woo back the Liberals, Grant appeared to repudiate Reconstruction even more emphatically. In January 1874 he issued a remarkable statement to reporters:

> I begin to think that it is time for the Republican party to unload. There has been too much dead weight carried by it. . . . I am tired of this nonsense. Let Louisiana take care of herself, as Texas will have to do. I don't want any quarrel about Mississippi State matters to be referred to me. This nursing of monstrosities has nearly exhausted the life of the party. I am done with them, and they will have to take care of themselves.

The New York *Herald* chorused in approval, "Reconstruction, the carpet-baggers, the usurpation of power supported by troops—all this is dead weight, a millstone, that if not speedily disengaged will carry republicanism to the bottom."[18]

None of this stilled northern voters' inclination in the spring elections of 1874 to punish the Republicans for hard times. Realizing that those defeats portended heavy losses in the North's fall congressional elections, Republicans lurched once again toward trying to save enough Republican House seats in the South to offset impending defeats in the North. By the fall, the same attorney general who had pronounced federal enforcement complete in the spring was urging his southern subordinates to "spare no effort or necessary expense" in prosecuting anyone who interfered with blacks' right to vote.[19] To mobilize black turnout in the South, moreover, Senate Republicans in May 1874 passed a Civil Rights bill that required the integration of railroads, steamships, streetcars, schools, theaters, hotels, and restaurants, although they could not persuade their House col-

In this "Bloody Shirt" attack on antiblack violence in the South, Thomas Nast reflects Republicans' desperate attempt to salvage the 1874 congressional elections by reminding northern voters of the Democrats' alliance with southern terrorists.

leagues to go along until early 1875, after the requirement for school integration was deleted.[20]

Though first introduced by Charles Sumner before his death in March 1874 and passed in part as a memorial to the Massachusetts senator's long championship of black rights, the Civil Rights Act of 1875 had little more than symbolic importance. The ability of a black who had been denied entry into an opera house or a first-class railroad car to hire a lawyer and sue the owner in federal court meant little to most black freedmen, who could not afford such luxuries. "Lacking any meaningful provisions for enforcement," concludes the historian Brooks D. Simpson, "the bill was an empty declaration of virtue, and not much of one at that."[21]

Far more meaningful to the tens of thousands of blacks who were subjected to intimidation by White Leaguers and Red Shirts in Alabama, Louisiana, Mississippi, and South Carolina would have been a renewed federal commitment to enforcement of their voting rights. Grant, for one, was willing to make it. In a blistering message to Congress in January 1875, he declared that so long as he was president, "Neither Kuklux [sic] Klans, White Leagues, nor any other asso-

ciations using arms and violence to execute their unlawful purposes can be permitted in that way to govern any part of this country." To put teeth into that declaration, he called on Congress for new legislation allowing him to suspend
habeas corpus and declare martial law to replace the Ku Klux Klan Act that had
expired at the end of 1872.[22]

By early 1875, however, congressional Republicans had had enough, and they
delayed any action on Grant's requested bill until it was too late to pass. Had
that bill "become a law," explained the Republican Speaker of the House, James
G. Blaine, "the defeat of the Republican party throughout the country would
have been a foregone conclusion." It could "not have saved the South," but if
passed it "would have lost us the North." "The truth is," one northern Republican wrote, "our people are tired out with this worn out cry of 'Southern outrages'!!! Hard times & heavy taxes make them wish the 'nigger,' 'everlasting
nigger,' were in _____ or Africa."[23]

## THE REPUBLICANS TURN NORTHWARD

By the winter of 1874–1875, northern voters were far more concerned with
their own economic suffering than with southern blacks' travails. Congressional
Republicans recognized even before the 1874 elections that they must do something about the slumping economy to save their necks from aggrieved northern
voters. With prices plummeting, businessmen faced bankruptcy, urban workers
suffered wage cuts and extensive unemployment, and farmers saw mortgages on
their land foreclosed or plunged deeper into debt to escape that calamity. The
Republicans' problem was to identify some remedy for hard times that did not
offend taxpayers and Liberal reformers who wanted retrenchment in government
expenditures.

Proposals abounded, but they usually divided Republicans against each other
and often fell within the jurisdiction of local and state governments, not Congress. Workers, whose previous public policy demands had focused primarily on
state legislation to shorten their workday and improve safety on the job, now
clamored for public relief, a demand that would only inflame taxpayers still further. In the Midwest, many farmers and the merchants who shipped their products to eastern markets attributed their economic woes to high and
discriminatory railroad rates that stole all their potential profits. Thus they
sought state laws that would regulate railroads and outlaw differentials in long-
and short-haul freight rates; they also sought to eradicate the railroad companies'
sway over public officials.

Contrary to popular myth, legislative battles over these so-called Granger
laws did not align farmers against representatives whom railroads had bought.
Instead, they pitted men who represented areas that already had railroad connections and wanted regulation against men from areas still without rail links who

feared that any state regulation would discourage railroads from building new lines to them. Thus, although third parties could organize around the antirailroad impulse, Republicans dared not take a unified party stance for or against these laws, lest they antagonize constituents in the areas whose interests they opposed.[24]

Nor could railroad regulation serve as the federal response to the depression, for which Republican congressmen searched in 1874. This fact became clear early that year when a Republican representative from Iowa moved that Congress establish a national railroad commission to set rates throughout the country. Most Democrats denounced this measure as more Republican consolidation, whereas Republicans themselves fractured along sectional lines. Westerners and southerners supported the proposal; New England and mid-Atlantic Republicans vehemently opposed it.[25]

If urban workers demanded public relief and farmers railroad regulation, manufacturers and mine owners—an important Republican constituency in many states—touted increased tariff protection as the key to recovery. The tariff clearly fell within the jurisdiction of Congress, and Republican congressmen were desperate to do something to stave off defeat in 1874. The tariff was a tax, but one that fell indirectly on consumers, unlike the hated excise and property taxes.[26] By promising that increased duties would protect American business and allow employers to rehire workers and raise wages, moreover, Republicans could offer tariff revision as an alternative to the public relief payments unemployed laborers demanded. At the risk of offending low-tariff men among Liberal Republicans, therefore, congressional Republicans in 1874 raised duties by the same 10 percent they had cut in 1872.

The Republicans knew, however, that even this move would not suffice to appease the electorate. By far the most loudly and widely supported remedy for the depression that northern voters urged on Congress in 1874 was to inflate the currency supply in order to raise prices. Farmers everywhere in the nation, industrial workers across the North, and Republican businessmen from central Pennsylvania west to Iowa all raised this cry; yet it posed a profound dilemma for both major parties. Reflecting the demands of banking and mercantile interests from Philadelphia north to Maine, both Democratic and Republican officeholders from northeastern states opposed any increase in the amount of paper money in circulation because it would inevitably delay the resumption of specie payments. To boot, hard-money men among the Liberal bolters whom Grant sought to bring back to the party were equally averse to it.

Even among the Pennsylvanians and westerners who wanted to increase the stock of paper money in circulation, partisan differences complicated monetary policy. The Republicans preferred what was called "free banking." This system would allow the unlimited chartering of new national banks that met the capitalization and other requirements stipulated by the government. It would also remove the hated cap on the total amount of national banknotes in circulation that had previously concentrated banknotes in the Northeast to the disadvantage of the South and West.[27] This proposal was anathema to farmers, labor leaders, and especially Democrats, who had long despised bankers. They sought to abolish the national banking system altogether and instead wanted to rely exclusively on government-printed greenbacks as the nation's currency. If the currency supply was expanded to raise prices, therefore, they insisted that more greenbacks, not more national banknotes, be issued.

In April 1874, western expansionists combined the two approaches and passed the so-called Inflation Act over the resistance of eastern hard-money men in both parties. This bill increased the amount of national banknotes in circulation by $46 million and greenback circulation by $18 million.[28] Aware that sound-money men among Liberals loathed this bill, Grant immediately vetoed it on April 22, 1874, even though a majority of Republicans in both houses of Congress favored it.[29] Subsequent legislation shifting banknotes from the East to the West failed to appease the inflationists. What mattered to furious voters, who saw inflation as a miracle drug to cure their economic ills, was that many Republicans had voted against—and Grant, the Republican president, had killed—the only federal measure that might offer them relief.

Grant's veto thus contributed to Republicans' rout in the 1874 congressional elections, one of the worst ever suffered by an incumbent party in American history. In the South, a racist white backlash against the pending civil rights bill and the White Leagues' intimidation of black voters helped Democrats. In the far more heavily populated North, however, hard times and the Republican party's failure to do anything meaningful about them caused normally Republican voters to abstain in droves or bolt to third parties and Democratic turnout to soar.[30] Republican candidates were slaughtered. The Democrats not only recaptured the House of Representatives, converting a 194–92 Republican margin in the Forty-third Congress (1873–1875) into a 181–107 Democratic majority in the Forty-fourth (1875–1877). Democrats also captured the governorships of California, Massachusetts, Missouri, New Jersey, and New York, and they reduced the Republicans' margin in the Senate from 63–11 in the Forty-first Congress (1869–1871) to 45–31 in the Forty-fourth.[31]

The long-feared postwar realignment against the Republicans appeared to be well under way by the end of 1874. A surge of discontented farmers and workers in the North and newly mobilized white Democrats in the South was cresting against them. The Republican party itself might escape replacement by a new organization, but it clearly seemed headed toward displacement from power in Washington. Avoiding that fate by rebuilding their electoral strength in the North, rather than salvaging Reconstruction in the South, thus became the Republicans' central objective.

## REALIGNMENT AVERTED

Between December 1874 and November 1876, the Republicans took a series of steps that slowed and partially reversed the surge against them in the North and positioned them to win the presidential election of 1876. The outcome of that election had profound implications for Republicans' fate in the party's three remaining southern bastions—Florida, Louisiana, and South Carolina—but after rejecting Grant's plea in early 1875 for new federal enforcement legislation, northern Republicans did little to help their southern counterparts. Instead, they focused on remedying weaknesses and dividing the forces arrayed against them in the North.

First, they moved adroitly to frame a credible monetary response to the nation's economic woes that could unify eastern and western Republicans and distinguish the Republican program from the greenback inflationism touted by the Democrats. Following Grant's recommendations in his December 1874 annual message, congressional Republicans passed the Specie Resumption Act in January 1875, and Grant signed it.[32] This legislation committed the government to resuming specie payments on January 1, 1879, thereby pleasing the eastern Republicans. It also incorporated the western Republicans' goal of free banking, that is, unlimited expansion of the national banking system. It further stipulated that for every one hundred dollars worth of new national banknotes issued, eighty dollars worth of greenbacks would be removed from circulation until the amount outstanding reached $300 million, where it would be permanently fixed. Thus the Republicans had contrived an ingenious formula that provided for specie resumption with moderate expansion, *not* contraction, of the total currency supply, even as it specifically rejected the Democrats' call for more greenbacks and abolition of the national banking system. The Republicans united for and the Democrats against this measure on the votes to pass it, giving the two parties sharply contrasting programs on monetary policy for the 1876 campaign.[33]

The Republicans also managed to neutralize the corruption issue and ensure that most, but never all, of the Liberal Republican bolters would be back in party ranks by the 1876 election. Ironically, Grant himself played a pivotal role in this achievement. Well before the fall elections in 1874 he had begun to appoint new Cabinet- and sub-Cabinet-level officials whom the Liberals admired. By far the most important was Benjamin H. Bristow as secretary of the treasury. Bristow was known for investigations that ended custom house fraud, reformed the Internal Revenue Service, and destroyed the Whiskey Ring. The Republicans appeared able and willing to clean their own house. Then, in June 1875, Grant announced that he would not seek a third term, freeing the Republicans from having to defend his record in 1876 and allowing them instead to run the scandal-free Ohio governor Rutherford B. Hayes as their presidential candidate. Democrats, too, ran a reformer, the Yale-educated New York governor Samuel J. Tilden, who in 1871 had helped bring down "Boss" Tweed.

"The Plank—Hitting the Nail on the Head"

Thomas Nast's cartoon vividly demonstrates that, as early as 1875, Republicans recognized and applauded Grant's attempt to make anti-Catholicism a central Republican issue in the 1876 presidential campaign.

The Specie Resumption Act and the neutralization of the clean-government issue helped reunite and reinvigorate northern Republican organizations. However, neither achievement meant much to the newly militant farmers, artisans, and industrial laborers who suffered most from the depression and who had helped to sweep Republicans from office in 1874. Such men far outnumbered the businessmen, bankers, professionals, propertied taxpayers, and intellectuals who applauded monetary and administrative reform. If they remained united against the Republicans, they would have the power to effect the same kind of depression-inspired, class-based realignment in the 1870s that would later rout the Republican party in the 1930s. Republicans sought to prevent that potentially lethal coalescence, which was based on shared economic grievances against the Republican establishment. To do so, they quite consciously (some might say cynically) reinstigated emotionally powerful residual animosities that redivided farmers and workers against each other along noneconomic lines and ultimately kept many, if not most, of them in the Republican ranks.

First, Republicans exploited latent divisions within the North itself by stirring up visceral Protestant animosities toward Catholics that had been largely, though never completely, submerged since the Know-Nothing outburst of the 1850s. Because the vast majority of Roman Catholic voters remained doggedly loyal to the Democratic party, the Republicans could profit from any increase of Protestant fear of Catholics. Republicans therefore mounted a crusade against a purported Catholic menace to the public school system that came from the demands of the Catholic clergy, supported by Democratic officeholders, that public tax revenue be used to fund Catholic parochial schools as well as public schools. Republicans, the party pledged, would thwart that threat, while Democrats would abet it. Thus Protestants must vote Republican.[34]

Then as today, primary and secondary public education fell within the jurisdiction of local and state governments, not Washington, yet Grant sought to nationalize the school issue and make it a centerpiece of the Republicans' 1876 presidential campaign. At a reunion of the Army of the Tennessee in September 1875, Grant announced that the Catholic threat to the public school system was now the greatest menace facing the United States and that "not one dollar" of its funds should "be appropriated to the support of any sectarian schools."[35] In his December 1875 annual message, he called on Congress to pass a constitutional amendment banning public aid to Catholic schools. When James G. Blaine in-

"The 'Bloody Shirt' Reformed."

Republicans again resort to the "Bloody Shirt" in 1876: In this cartoon (top left), Thomas Nast links the Democratic presidential candidate Samuel J. Tilden to the White Leaguers' massacre of blacks in Hamburg, South Carolina in the summer of 1876. Here (bottom right), Nast reminds northern voters what the result of a Democratic victory in the 1876 election will be.

" 'The Solid South'—Gaunt and Hungry"

troduced one, every Republican in the Senate voted for it, and Republicans endorsed it in their 1876 national platform.[36]

Republicans in 1876 relied even more heavily on waving the "Bloody Shirt" to restore their electoral majorities in the North. Though Republicans carefully refrained from promising additional legislation for the South, in their national and state platforms, newspaper editorials, and campaign speeches they constantly reminded northern civilians and especially Union army veterans that a Democratic victory would put the hated Confederates back in control of the national government. The Democrats, charged the Republican national platform, "sympathized with treason," applauded "the sentiments of unrepentant rebellion," and were "sending Union soldiers to the rear, and promoting Confederate soldiers to the front."

These scare tactics worked, but barely. The Democrats and Republicans could never agree on an official set of returns, but Democrats won a majority of slightly less than three hundred thousand in the nationwide popular vote.[37] It was the electoral vote that mattered, however. As the Republicans had feared, the Democrats won every border state and all but three former Confederate states. In contrast, because Republicans successfully lured their former supporters back into the party fold, Hayes carried all but three northern states—Connecticut, New Jersey, and Tilden's home state of New York. This harvest in the North gave Hayes 165 electoral votes. That total, significantly, included three electoral votes from the new state of Colorado, which Republicans had managed to have admitted in August 1876 precisely because they needed its electoral votes and two U.S. senators to bolster their strength.

Nonetheless, on election night in November 1876, Tilden seemed assured of victory since he led Hayes in the electoral vote count, 184 to 165. Had Colorado not participated in the election, Tilden would have won with 184 votes. But now, 185 constituted the necessary majority, and an additional twenty electoral votes were in dispute. One came from Oregon, which the Republicans had clearly if narrowly carried, but where they had foolishly named an elector who was ineligible because he held a federal job.[38] The other nineteen came from the three southern states where Republicans still clung to power—Florida, Louisiana, and South Carolina. Only Congress, which had the constitutional responsibility of counting the electoral votes, could determine who got these disputed votes and therefore became the next president. In maneuvering for a favorable outcome of that dispute, the Republicans would sacrifice what was left of their reconstruction experiment in the South.

CHAPTER 34 | # The End of Reconstruction

The presidential election of 1876 did not cause Reconstruction's failure; rather, it punctuated that collapse. By November 1876, Reconstruction as a political process was already finished in most ex-Confederate states. Republicans still held governorships, and federal troops still remained, in South Carolina, Florida, and Louisiana. Few northern Republicans, however, expected or were willing to help the Republicans win that year's gubernatorial contests in those states. Nor was Grant prepared to use federal force much longer to prop up tottering Republican regimes. When a new Democratic governor of Florida took office in January 1877, Grant withdrew federal troops from the state. In South Carolina and Louisiana, where the Democrats and Republicans each claimed to have won the state election and installed their own governors and legislatures, Grant stationed federal troops around the statehouses that Republicans occupied. But he refused to recognize the Republicans as winners, and unlike on previous occasions, he made no attempt to have soldiers disperse the rival Democratic governments, which almost all whites in those states recognized as legitimate. Everyone knew that Republicans' pretensions to power would evaporate as soon as the troops were ordered back to their barracks.[1]

But if northern Republicans were prepared to allow the Democrats to resume control of state governments in Louisiana, Florida, and South Carolina in 1877, they were not ready to do so until the electoral votes in each had been cast in December and sent to Washington. Exactly which candidate carried those states in November may never be known, although many historians believe that Tilden won Florida, whereas Hayes deserved the electoral votes of South Carolina and Louisiana.[2] Election day in all three had been unusually peaceful, but fraud and chicanery abounded. Local Democratic voting registrars refused to count black votes and submitted fictitious Democratic votes in their place. Their Republican counterparts stuffed ballot boxes with "votes" that African Americans might have cast had they not been frightened away from the polls by White Leaguer and Red Shirt intimidation prior to election day.

The Democrats claimed all three states, but the Republicans controlled the state canvassing boards that would determine the official winner in all three. In addition, to comply with federal election laws, the electoral results sent to Washington required the signature of the incumbent Republican governors, whose terms ran until January. To protect those Republican canvassing boards and governors from forcible ouster by Democrats, Grant posted federal troops around statehouses as soon as the polls closed.[3]

## THE DISPUTED RESULTS

By November 8, the day after the election, northern politicos recognized that Tilden's 184 electoral votes still left him one vote shy of the necessary majority, and that Republican canvassing boards in the three southern states could deter-

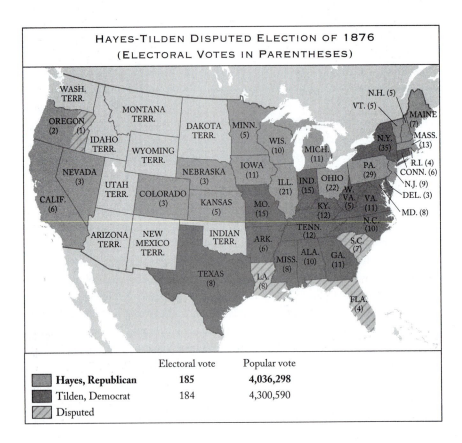

HAYES-TILDEN DISPUTED ELECTION OF 1876
(ELECTORAL VOTES IN PARENTHESES)

|  | Electoral vote | Popular vote |
|---|---|---|
| **Hayes, Republican** | **185** | **4,036,298** |
| Tilden, Democrat | 184 | 4,300,590 |
| Disputed | | |

mine the outcome. Both parties dispatched delegations of "visiting statesmen" to Louisiana and Florida to observe the official count. But weeks before a decision had been reached anywhere, Zachariah Chandler, the chairman of the Republican national campaign committee, announced to the press that Hayes had won the election, 185 to 184.[4]

The state canvassing boards in all three southern states worked to effect that result. Each inspected returns and interrogated registrars from individual counties or parishes. Hayes had clearly carried South Carolina, but its canvassing board refused to recognize equally valid results from the simultaneous state election indicating that the Democrat Wade Hampton had won the governorship. Instead, it threw out the returns from an entire county so that Republicans could control the next legislature, which, a state court ruled, had the exclusive power to decide who won the governorship. In Florida, where fraud and ballot-box stuffing by Republicans had been especially egregious, the canvassing board, over loud Democratic protests, converted a nominal forty-three-vote majority for Hayes into a nine hundred-vote margin. "It is terrible to see the extent to which all classes go in their determination to win," one of the northern Republican observers in Florida reported to his wife. "Money and intimidation can obtain the oath of white men as well as black to any required statement. A ton of affidavits could be carted into the state-house to-morrow, and not a word of truth in them. . . . If we win, our methods are subject to impeachment for possible fraud. If the enemy win, it is the same thing exactly—doubt, suspicion, irritation go with the consequence, whatever it may be."[5]

The brazenness of the Republican returning boards reached its extreme in Louisiana. In outright violation of state law, Republicans refused to add a Democrat to the four Republican members of the board. On at least two different occasions, its Republicans offered to count Tilden in if northern Democrats supplied bribes ranging from $250,000 to $1 million. Once this extortion was indignantly rejected, the board disallowed some fifteen thousand votes, thirteen thousand of which were for Tilden and the Democratic gubernatorial candidate, Francis Nicholls. Thus it converted Democratic majorities of six to eight thousand votes in the reported returns into Republican majorities of three to four thousand.[6]

In all three states, Democrats denounced these decisions, convened their own electoral colleges, and sent in slates of electoral votes in favor of Tilden. But the official returns—and the only ones bearing the required signatures from incumbent governors—all went to Hayes. If Congress counted those nineteen votes for Hayes, he, like Tilden, would have 184; the disputed vote from Oregon, which both Democrats and Republicans claimed, would decide the election.

Precisely who would tally those electoral votes, however, was unclear. According to the Twelfth Amendment of the Constitution, each state was to send its electoral votes, specifying how many popular votes each candidate for president and vice president received, under seal to the president of the Senate, in this case Michigan's Republican senator Thomas W. Ferry.[7] Then "the President of the Senate shall, in the presence of the Senate and the House of Representatives, open all the certificates and the votes shall then be counted." But counted by *whom*? Rarely has the imprecision of a passive verb proved so critical.

This vague language strongly suggested that the president of the Senate was to act essentially as a clerk who opened envelopes and read their contents aloud to the assembled lawmakers. Nonetheless, many Republicans asserted that he alone could decide which certificates to accept, and thus he alone could count Hayes in. The Democrats, who controlled the House by a huge majority, demanded that the House refuse to attend the required joint session with the Senate unless the Senate, which the Republicans controlled, agreed in advance that only members of the two chambers who attended that session could determine by a vote on the floor who got each state's vote. In that situation, Democrats would easily outvote Republicans since the House was so much larger than the Senate.[8] To that plan, Senate Republicans would never consent. Alternatively, militant Democrats demanded that if Ferry attempted to count the votes on his own, the House should reject his count as illegal, declare that no candidate had the necessary electoral majority, and then, as the Constitution stipulated, decide the outcome by a vote of the House of Representatives, which was also certain to elect Tilden.[9]

## THE ELECTORAL COMMISSION

The divided Congress therefore confronted a potential stalemate, with each chamber refusing to meet with the other to perform their joint constitutional obligation. Yet that standoff depended on the will of the respective parties' most militant wings prevailing in each chamber. Among House Democrats, southerners demanded resistance to a decision by Ferry, but northeastern Democrats, fearful of being labeled unlawful obstructionists who flouted the Constitution, opposed any course that prevented the inauguration of the new president on March 5. Thus Democratic unity crumbled.[10] Simultaneously, the northeastern Republicans, including the New York senator Roscoe Conkling, a Stalwart who had been expected to lead the hard-liners, responded to pressure from their conservative business constituents and abandoned the claim that Ferry alone could decide the election.[11]

With both parties internally divided over their initial strategies, Congress devised a compromise solution that was touted by Democrats and excoriated by most Republicans as a Democratic victory. On January 26, 1877 Congress created an electoral commission to examine the disputed returns from Oregon and the three southern states and report its findings to Congress. Of vast importance, the bill also required Congress to accept the commission's decisions as final unless the Senate and House, voting separately, both rejected them. Democrats gave this bill proportionately more support than Republicans in both chambers, although many southern Democrats in the House balked at even this concession.[12]

The commission consisted of fifteen members: three Republicans and two Democrats from the Senate; three Democrats and two Republicans from the House; and five Supreme Court justices. Those justices, whose names were known in advance of the vote on the bill, were the key to its passage. Two were Democrats and two were Republicans; they were expected to vote along party lines, as were the members from Congress. But the fifth justice, the man who would determine the outcome, was expected to be David Davis, an independent who had been mentioned as the Liberal Republicans' presidential nominee in 1872. Then, on January 25, Democrats in the Illinois legislature joined with Greenbackers to elect Davis to the United States Senate. Word of Davis's election reached Congress by telegraph before it voted on the 26th, but Democrats were now so committed to the bill as the only chance of electing Tilden in a way the nation could accept as legitimate that they voted overwhelmingly for the legislation. Although Davis was offered the post after the measure became law, he declined to serve on the grounds that he was now a senator, and the bill required five members from the Supreme Court.[13] Instead the fifth justice, who would cast the deciding vote on the commission, would be Joseph Bradley of New Jersey, a Republican whom Grant had appointed to the Court in 1870. In supporting the Electoral Commission bill, Democrats had ensured Hayes's election.

Starting on February 1, the president of the Senate began opening the states' electoral votes in alphabetical order before the joint session of Congress. When the conflicting returns from Florida were reached, they were turned over to the Electoral Commission while Congress recessed to await its decision. Democrats pressed the commission to go behind the electoral results and examine the disputed popular returns that Republican canvassing boards had counted out. Republicans countered that no such investigation could be completed by March 5 and that the only valid electoral results from the South were those with signatures of governors on them. These were the arguments the commission accepted. With Bradley casting the deciding vote, Republicans prevailed by an 8–7 margin and awarded Florida's votes to Hayes. The House and Senate voted separately on whether to accept this decision, and the Democratic House rejected it in a party-line vote. Without the concurrence of the Republican Senate, however, that protest was futile. So it went on the disputed votes from Louisiana, Oregon, and South Carolina. By an 8–7 party line vote, the Electoral Commission awarded them all to Hayes, giving him a margin of 185–184 over Tilden. This decision was announced on Friday, March 2. Three days later Hayes was inaugurated without incident.

## THE "COMPROMISE OF 1877"

As soon as the Electoral Commission announced on February 9 that it would not "go behind the returns" in the Florida case and was giving its votes to Hayes, the Democrats knew that Tilden had lost. Bitter House Democrats tried to delay the completion of the count so that no one would be officially elected by inauguration day, giving them an opportunity to declare that Tilden had won. They did so by repeatedly moving that the House recess rather than reconvene with the Senate to continue the count. According to one version of this episode, these die-hards were primarily Northerners and Westerners. In contrast, southern Democrats supposedly used a promise to oppose this threatened filibuster and allow Hayes's election as leverage to win specific commitments from Hayes and the Republican party about their future treatment of the South.

Briefly, these concessions included the withdrawal of federal troops guarding the statehouses in Louisiana and South Carolina; a public acknowledgment that Republicans renounced further intervention in the South; the appointment to Hayes's cabinet of a Southern Democrat who would appoint other Democrats to patronage posts in the South; and a commitment that the new administration would back congressional subsidies for internal-improvements projects in the South, particularly the rebuilding of collapsed levees along the Mississippi River in Louisiana and the construction of the Texas and Pacific Railroad from eastern Texas to San Diego. Though its terms were never written down, one eminent historian insists that this bargain between the Republican Hayes and southern Democrats had such important ramifications for future sectional relationships that it constituted the "Compromise of 1877," a sectional truce that was every bit as real and significant as the famous Compromise of 1850.[14]

Rutherford B. Hayes

Subsequent research by historians has challenged the factual accuracy of this interpretation. For example, in February while the electoral count was proceeding, most southern Democrats in the House promoted a filibuster, rather than resisting it. Northeastern Democrats, in contrast, led the fight against delay and forced Speaker Samuel J. Randall to announce to the House on February 24 that he would disallow all subsequent dilatory motions by Democratic bitter-enders. "The fact is," historian Michael Les Benedict concludes, "that Hayes owed his peaceful inauguration far more to the course taken by northern Democrats, particularly northeastern Democrats, than to that of the southerners."[15]

Whatever their impact in resolving the disputed election and allowing Hayes's inauguration, negotiations between southern Democrats and Hayes's closest Republican advisors did in fact occur between December and March. Hayes's friends bargained less to affect the short-term outcome of Congress's current deliberations than to attract long-term Democratic converts to the Republican party in the South so that Hayes could secure a reliable southern base and working majorities in Congress after he took office. The Republicans' strong comeback in the North in 1876, in fact, had allowed them to reduce the Democratic majority in the House of Representatives from over seventy seats in the current Congress to fewer than eighteen in its successor. Thus, one of the bargaining chips southern Democrats offered Hayes's friends during their negotiations was to produce the nine votes necessary to elect the Ohio Republican James A. Garfield as Speaker of the next House.

Hayes's top priority was to reshape the Republican party in the South by ousting carpetbaggers and their black allies from control and attracting to it instead what his Ohio ally Jacob Cox called "the best men representing the capital, the intelligence, the virtue and the revived patriotism of the old [that is, native-born white] population of the South." In short, like Lincoln, Johnson, and Grant before him, Hayes sought to effect a realignment in southern politics. He would do so by bringing back to the Republican party the ex-Whig, entrepreneurially oriented centrists who had once led both parties and who had been forced into the Democratic party after it drew the race line in the South.[16]

Although Hayes made clear from the moment of his nomination in 1876 that he sought reconciliation with white southerners, he also insisted from the start that blacks' rights must not be sacrificed. "What the South most needs is 'peace' and peace depends on the supremacy of the law," he announced when accepting his nomination. If white Southerners recognized "the constitutional rights" of blacks "without reserve or exception," Hayes declared, he could pursue "a civil policy which will wipe out forever the distinction between North and South in our common country" and foster "honest and capable local government" in the South.[17] That last statement was widely—and correctly—interpreted as indicating an abandonment of the remaining carpetbagger governments, but Hayes's solicitude for African Americans' rights never wavered. Indeed, during the post-election electoral dispute, he worried about Tilden's triumph primarily because it would consign "the poor colored men in the South" to a fate "worse than when [they were] in slavery."[18]

Enticing the South's educated and conservative white elite into the Republican party, in contrast, would benefit blacks by focusing partisan conflict, as Garfield put it, "on the great commercial and industrial questions rather than on questions of race and color."[19] It was the race line in southern politics caused by blacks' exclusive support for the Republican party that put them in jeopardy of white violence, chorused other Republicans. That solidarity behind Republicans was "no longer essential to their safety. On the contrary, it is now the cause of their greatest danger." Thus, Hayes should build "a conservative Republican party in the South that shall effectively destroy the color line & save the colored people." "With each party bidding against the other" for black votes, summarized a North Carolinian, "the negro's rights are assured. In a contest between the parties based on distinctions of race, the negro must eventually go down."[20]

In sum, Hayes sought a realignment in the South not just to reshape and broaden the Republican party there, but to shift the agenda of partisan conflict away from sectional and racial questions in both the North and the South. He had been nominated as a mutually acceptable compromise choice by mutually hostile Liberal Republican reformers, who had returned to the party by 1876, and Stalwart regulars who wanted to keep sectional antagonisms alive in the North by waving the "Bloody Shirt." He had worked carefully since his nomination not to antagonize either faction, but by February, when he decided to include Carl Schurz, the Stalwarts' greatest enemy, in his cabinet, he had shifted decisively toward the Liberals.[21] Like the Liberals, he welcomed the possibility of reconciliation with white southern Democrats to end Reconstruction once and for all, but only if he was convinced blacks' rights would be secure.

Though a few northern Republicans spoke of wooing former Whigs in the South by promising to support the economic programs that some southern Democrats demanded as a *quid pro quo* for allowing Hayes's inauguration, Hayes himself had little personal interest in those programs. In contrast, southern Democrats' insistence that Hayes appoint a southern Democrat to his Cabinet fitted perfectly with his hope to effect a realignment of southern politics. He named as his postmaster general Tennessee's David M. Key, a lame-duck senator whom Tennessee's Democrats had recently refused to reelect because of his cooperation with Republicans in the Senate, and Key filled one-third of the local postmasterships in the South with Democrats.[22]

Hayes was also ready to concede to the southern Democrats' top priority—the removal of federal troops from the state capitals of Louisiana and South Carolina and recognition of their Democratic state governments. So was Ulysses S. Grant, who believed that the two remaining Republican regimes merited no more federal help. The Fifteenth Amendment, he told his Cabinet, "had done the Negro no good, and had been a hindrance to the South, and by no means a political advantage to the North."[23] Nonetheless, Grant, like Hayes, demanded further assurances that the new Democratic governments would protect blacks' rights before he removed the troops.

This insistence, along with still further delays in Congress's count of electoral votes, led to a conference at the Wormley House hotel in Washington on the evening of February 26, 1877. Five Ohio Republicans, including Congressman Garfield and Senator John Sherman, represented Hayes. Three Louisiana Democrats and Henry Watterson, a Kentucky newspaperman who spoke for South Carolina Democrats, negotiated for the South. Grant had already told one of the Louisianans that he would remove the troops and allow the Democratic governor, Francis Nicholls, to assume power, so long as "violent excesses" against blacks were not committed. At the Wormley House the Ohioans indicated that Hayes agreed with Grant. The Louisianans pledged that Democrats would safeguard blacks' political and civil rights and offer equal educational opportunities to black and white children. Whatever the other components of the "Compromise of 1877," the Wormley House conference guaranteed Hayes' inauguration and the restoration of "home rule."[24]

On March 2, four days later, the count was completed and Hayes's election announced. That same day Grant directed the troops in Columbia and New Orleans to return to their barracks. Those orders, however, went astray. It fell to the new president to write the obituary for Reconstruction.

Repeating much of what he had previously said, Hayes in his inaugural address gave a qualified announcement that Reconstruction was over. "The National Government," he intoned, had "a moral obligation ... to employ its constitutional power and influence to establish the rights of the people it has emancipated, and to protect them in the enjoyment of those rights." Yet if southerners themselves honored those rights, he was "sincerely anxious to use every legitimate influence in favor of honest and efficient *self*-government" in the South. He went on to "assure [his] countrymen of the Southern States" of "his earnest desire" to adopt "a civil policy which will forever wipe out in our political affairs the color line and the distinction of North and South, to the end that we may have not merely a united North or a united South, but a united country."[25]

In this spirit, Hayes summoned both the Democrat Wade Hampton and the Republican Daniel Chamberlain to the White House in early April to discuss the South Carolina situation. Once again Hampton assured the president that he would protect the rights of blacks. Hayes issued orders for the troops guarding the statehouse in Columbia to leave the city. They did so on April 10. Chamberlain immediately left the state, and the Democrats took power officially. Hayes had made his decision on Louisiana even earlier, but the troops did not stand down until April 24. The Democrats now controlled every ex-Confederate state.

## CONSEQUENCES

"As a period when Republicans controlled Southern politics, blacks enjoyed extensive political power, and the federal government accepted responsibility for protecting the fundamental rights of black citizens," concludes the historian Eric Foner, "Reconstruction came to an irrevocable end with the inauguration of Hayes."[26] Certainly the *program* of Reconstruction that Republicans in Congress had launched a decade earlier, depending as it did on the Republican party's control of southern state governments to protect blacks' rights, had clearly failed by then—and years earlier in most ex-Confederate states. By the spring of 1877, not only the hope of more federal intervention was dead; so was any prospect that southern Republicans on their own could recapture southern state governments.

The Republicans' defeat in the South proved permanent, even in states such as Florida, Louisiana, and South Carolina, where the results had been remarkably close in 1876. In most southern states the so-called Redeemers, fearful of provoking the renewed federal intervention that Hayes had called a "moral obligation," did not disfranchise blacks by state law or constitutional revision until the late 1880s and 1890s. Black turnout on election days remained surprisingly high in the South until a decade or more after Reconstruction ended, and Republican candidates, some of them blacks, continued to be elected to state legislatures and even Congress.[27] But Democrats negated the impact of that black vote in various ways that ensured that Republicans would never again dominate most local and all state governments in the South. The Democrats' simplest expedient was taking over local voter registration boards as well as the state canvassing boards that decided who won statewide elections. They also reapportioned legislatures, declared previously elected offices appointive, and allowed Democratic legislatures and Democratic governors to name local officials in black-majority districts.[28]

If many blacks still voted in the South, moreover, they nonetheless suffered gravely from the Democrats' return to power. Incidents of white violence against blacks diminished if only because the threat of black voting had been negated, but the beating, lynching, and killing never stopped entirely. And now the freedmen had to depend on white Democratic sheriffs and judges for justice. The Democrats also revised state laws to reinforce the planters' control over their labor force, to change crop lien arrangements to blacks' disadvantage, to slash appropriations for the public schools that had been so important in educating blacks, and to increase penalties for petty crimes so as to force blacks into prison chain gangs. "Thus," the historian Eric Foner summarizes, "blacks in the Redeemers' New South found themselves enmeshed in a seamless web of oppression, whose interwoven economic, political, and social strands all reinforced one another."[29]

Hayes had hoped to prevent the Democratic rule in the South that produced these results by effecting a realignment that would mitigate racial antagonisms, but it too failed. When Hayes was elected, he publicly announced his desire to end Reconstruction, and he appointed a southern Democrat to his Cabinet. Otherwise, the purported "Compromise of 1877" collapsed. No southerners supported James Garfield for Speaker when the new House met in December 1877, and by the end of 1878 he was bitterly denouncing his fellow Ohio Republican Hayes for selling out southern Republicans.[30] During that session Congress did fund measures to rebuild levees in Louisiana,[31] but no appropriations materialized for the Texas and Pacific Railroad. Most important, no white movement toward the Republican party occurred. Except for mountainous areas where wartime anti-Confederate Unionist whites and their descendants steadfastly supported the Republican party out of sheer hatred of their Confederate antagonists, the once politically competitive South became a Democratic bastion, the "Solid South," as a result of the backlash against the Republicans' experiment in Reconstruction.

Nor had the Republicans' comeback in 1876 solved all their problems in the North. The Republicans had adopted anti-Catholic, pro–specie resumption, and antisouthern stances that year to unify their party and abort a realignment by groups with economic grievances against them that the 1873 and 1874 elections had portended. They achieved that goal, but they had not stopped the Democratic party from becoming closely competitive even in their formerly impregnable northern strongholds. Nor had they permanently unified their party, permanently satisfied farmers and industrial workers, or quashed all possibility of the dreaded anti-Republican realignment. By 1878, Republicans were once against sharply split along East/West regional lines over whether gold or silver should be the metal with which specie payments were resumed. Both a destructive strike by northern railroad workers in 1877 and the marked surge in the popular vote for Greenback-Labor candidates in the 1878 congressional and state elections, moreover, demonstrated that appeals to religious bigotry and sectional prejudice could not always divert the attention of discontented workers or hold them in Republican ranks.

What did seem the trend of the future after 1876 was the Republicans' and Democrats' mutual retreat from governmental activism, not just in dealing with the South but in addressing social and economic problems in the North. Northern states from New York to California joined Redeemers in the South in writing new state constitutions in the mid- and late 1870s that were lengthy and detailed compendiums of bans on governmental action, of things that state and local governments could *not* do. Next to the collapse of public support for blacks' rights and for social, economic, and political reform in the South, this widespread suspicion of government itself was one of biggest costs of the Reconstruction experiment, and it marked one of the sharpest reversals from the war and early postwar years.

Yet not all that had been achieved by the Civil War and Reconstruction was lost. Slavery had been ended forever, even if a caste system replaced it in the

South. The Thirteenth, Fourteenth, and Fifteenth Amendments had been added to the Constitution. And if courts in the nineteenth century narrowly interpreted them to reduce blacks' rights, both Congress and courts in the twentieth would use them to expand those rights. Whatever happened to the former slaves in the South after the end of Reconstruction, moreover, black men and women had gained a sense of independence and self-esteem during it that could never be wholly crushed. Black men and women had together created a rich institutional life for their communities, publicly protested for educational opportunities and equal civil and political rights for their race, and exploited those rights to the fullest extent that hostile whites would allow. Although only men could vote or hold public office, they and their descendants would remember with fierce pride the roles they had played as citizens, voters, and officeholders, and many of them were determined not to let whites forget that experience.

Most important, the Civil War and Reconstruction had restored the unity of the nation. Sectional resentments did not die. Northern Republicans waved the "Bloody Shirt" until the end of the century, and well into the next most white Southerners adhered to the Democratic party because of their hatred of what Republicans had done during the Civil War and Reconstruction. After that war, nonetheless, no one again ever seriously contemplated state secession from the Union. Internal disagreements never ended, but the nation itself was once again whole.

# Notes

## Chapter 1

1. Robert Johannsen, *To the Halls of Montezuma: The Mexican War in American Imagination* (New York, 1985), 247.

2. *United States Magazine and Democratic Review* 42 (1858): 343.

3. Kenneth Stampp, *1857: A Nation on the Brink* (New York, 1990), 217.

4. Paul Bourke and Donald DeBats, *Washington County: Politics and Community in Antebellum America* (Baltimore, 1995).

5. Charles McKay, *Life and Liberty in America* (New York, 1859), vi, 29.

6. Richard Brown, *Modernization: The Transformation of American Life 1600–1865* (New York, 1976); David Apter, *The Politics of Modernization* (Chicago, 1965); Walter Licht, *Industrializing America: The Nineteenth Century* (Baltimore, 1995).

7. Don Doyle, *The Social Order of a Frontier Community, Jacksonville, Illinois, 1825–1870* (Urbana, Ill., 1978), 261, 417.

8. J. C. G. Kennedy, *Preliminary Report on the Eighth Census*, 1860, 131; *The Statistical History of the United States* (New York, 1976), 27–30.

9. Warren Danderson, "Quantitative Aspects of Marriage, Fertility, and Family Limitation in Nineteenth-Century America," *Demography* 16 (August 1979): 339–58; Paul McClelland and Richard Zeckhauser, *Demographic Dimensions of the New Republic* (Cambridge, Mass., 1982), 10, 15; Robert Wells, *Revolution in American Lives: A Demographic Perspective* (Westport, Conn., 1982).

10. David Potter, *The Impending Crisis* (New York, 1976), 241; Robert Fogel, *Without Consent or Contract: The Rise and Fall of American Slavery* (New York, 1990), 308–10.

11. Dale Knobel, *Paddy and the Republic: Ethnicity and Nationality in Antebellum America* (Middletown, 1986), 156–70.

12. Steven Ross, *Workers on the Edge: Work, Leisure and Politics in Industrializing Cincinnati, 1788–1890* (New York, 1985); Fogel, 310–1; Jean H. Baker, *Ambivalent Americans: The Know-Nothing Party in Maryland* (Baltimore, 1977).

13. Patricia Limerick, *The Legacy of Conquest: The Unbroken Past of the American West* (New York, 1987), 280–7.

14. Jeremy Atack and Peter Passell, *A New Economic View of American History from Colonial Times to 1940* (New York, 1994).

15. Bureau of the Census, Population Schedules (Washington, D.C., 1866), 622, 670.

16. Otto Mayr and Robert Post, eds., *Yankee Enterprise: The Rise of the American System of Manufactures* (Washington, D.C., 1981), 53.

17. U.S. Congress, Senate Preliminary Report on the Eighth Census, 1860, 374.

18. Atack and Passell, 219.

19. Jeremy Atack and Fred Bateman, *To Their Own Soil: Agriculture in the Antebellum North* (Ames, Iowa, 1987).

20. John Mack Faragher, *Sugar Creek: Life on the Illinois Prairie* (New Haven, 1986), 266.

21. William Hutchinson, *Cyrus Hall McCormick: Seed-Time, 1809–1856* (New York, 1930), 1:468.

22. Robert Bruce, *The Launching of Modern American Science 1846–1876* (New York, 1987).

23. William Cronon, *Nature's Metropolis: Chicago and the Great West* (New York, 1991), 120.

24. Alfred Chandler, *The Railroads: The Nation's First Business* (New York, 1965), 49–50.

25. Atack and Passell, 160.

26. Quoted in Alan Dawley, *Class and Community: The Industrial Revolution in Lynn* (Cambridge, Mass., 1976), 78; Edward Stevens, *The Grammar of the Machine: Technical Literacy and Early Industrial Expansion in the United States* (New Haven, Conn., 1995).

27. Mayr and Post, 2–4, 25–43.

28. *Harpers Weekly,* October 31, 1856; Richard Bushman, *The Refinement of America: Persons, Houses, Cities* (New York, 1992), xiv–xix, 360.

29. Mayr and Post, 192.

30. Edward Pessen, "The Egalitarian Myth and American Social Reality: Wealth, Mobility, and Equality in the Era of the Common Man," *American Historical Review* 76 (October 1971): 989–1034.

31. Licht, 70.

32. Pessen, 989–1034; Ross, 337; Edward Pessen, *Riches, Class and Power: America before the Civil War* (New Brunswick, N.J., 1990), 86.

33. *America of the Fifties: Letters of Frederika Bremer* (New York, 1924), 79–80.

34. David Montgomery, *Workers' Control in America: Studies in the History of Work, Technology, and Labor Struggles* (Cambridge, 1979), 14.

35. Alice Kessler-Harris, *Out to Work: A History of Wage-Earning Women in the United States* (New York, 1982), 46.

36. Barbara Welter, "The Cult of True Womanhood, 1820–1860," *American Quarterly* 18 (1966): 151–74; Herbert Gutman, *Work, Culture and Society in Industrializing America: Essays in American Working-Class History and Social History* (New York, 1977), 51.

37. Sean Wilentz, *Chants Democratic: New York City and the Rise of the American Working Class* (New York, 1984), 242–9.

38. Allan Pred, *Urban Growth and City Systems in the United States* (Cambridge, Mass., 1980), 36.

39. John Duffy, *The Sanitarians: A History of Public Health* (Urbana, Ill., 1990).

40. James D. Richardson, ed., *A Compilation of the Messages of the Presidents* (Washington, D.C., 1908), 5:437.

41. Wilentz, 394; Christine Stansell, *City of Women: Sex and Class in New York, 1789–1860* (Urbana, Ill., 1987).

42. Lee Soltow and Edmund Stevens, *The Rise of Literacy and the Common School in the United States: A Socioeconomic Analysis to 1870* (Chicago, 1981), 119.

43. Frances Simkins, *A History of the South* (New York, 1953), 176.

44. Burton Bledstein, *The Culture of Professionalism: The Middle Class and the Development of Higher Education* (New York, 1976), 229.

45. W. R. Thayer, ed., *Life and Letters of John Hay* (New York, 1966), 1:35–39.

46. Barbara Solomon, *In the Company of Educated Women: A History of Women and Higher Education in America* (New Haven, Conn., 1985), 33.

47. Katherine Sklar, *Catharine Beecher: A Study in American Domesticity* (New Haven, Conn., 1973), 174.

48. *Complete Works of Ralph Waldo Emerson* (Boston, 1903), 10:329.

49. Johannsen, 282.

50. W. J. Rorabaugh, *The Alcoholic Republic: An American Tradition* (New York, 1979), 232–4.

51. William Freehling, *Road to Disunion, Secessionists at Bay, 1776–1854* (New York, 1990), 39–40, 292–4.

52. Lawrence Friedman, *Self and Community in American Abolitionism, 1830–1870* (New York, 1982), 195.

53. David Brion Davis, "Reflections on Abolitionism and Ideological Hegemony," *American Historical Review* 60 (October 1985): 805; Fogel, 356.

54. Ronald Walters, *The Anti-Slavery Appeal: American Abolitionists after 1830* (Baltimore, 1976), 10–12.

55. James B. Stewart, *Holy Warriors: Abolitionism and American Slavery* (New York, 1976), 78–80.

56. Howard H. Bell, *A Survey of the Negro Convention Movement, 1830–1861* (New York, 1969); Vincent Harding, *There Is a River: The Black Struggle for Freedom in America* (New York, 1981), 191.

57. Gerda Lerner, *The Grimké Sisters* (Boston, 1967).

58. Potter, 46–9.

59. Leon Litwack, *North of Slavery: The Negro in the Free States* (Chicago, 1961), 263.

60. Anne Rose, *Voices of the Marketplace: American Thought and Culture, 1830–1860* (New York, 1995), 60.

61. Charles Sellers, *The Market Revolution in Jacksonian America, 1815–1846* (New York, 1991), 370–1.

62. Philip Hone, *Diary of Philip Hone, 1828–1851* (New York, 1887), February 14, 1842.

63. Herman Melville, *Moby-Dick* (New York, 1976), 12–13.

64. David Reynolds, *Beneath the American Renaissance: The Subversive Imagination in the Age of Emerson and Melville* (New York, 1988), 495.

65. Reynolds, 7.

66. Joan Hedrick, *Harriet Beecher Stowe: A Life* (New York, 1994).

67. Nina Baym, *Women's Fiction: A Guide to Novels By and About Women, 1820–1870* (Ithaca, N.Y., 1978); Jane Tompkins, *Sensational Designs: The Cultural Work of American Fiction, 1790–1860* (New York, 1985).

68. Bremer, 92–4.

69. *Emerson* 6:31; Lewis Saum, *The Popular Mood of Pre–Civil War America* (Westport, Conn., 1980), 15–6.

70. Saum, 16, 17–26.

## Chapter 2

1. William Freehling, *The Road to Disunion* (New York, 1990) 16–18.

2. W. J. Cash, *The Mind of the South* (New York, 1971), 4.

3. Joan Cashin, *A Family Venture: Men and Women on the Southern Frontier* (New York, 1991), 33.

4. James Oakes, *The Ruling Race: A History of American Slaveholders* (New York, 1982), 69–95.

5. Carl Degler, *Place Over Time* (Baton Rouge, 1977), 48.

6. James Bonner, "Plantation Architecture of the Lower South on the Eve of The Civil War," *Journal of Southern History* 11 (August 1945): 371.

7. Oakes, 79.

8. Cash, 37.

9. J. Mills Thornton, *Politics and Power in a Slave Society: Alabama, 1800–1860* (Baton Rouge, 1978), 299.

10. Ralph Wooster, *The People in Power: Courthouse and Statehouse in the Lower South* (Knoxville, 1969), 54–55.

11. Cashin, 99–102. For a somewhat different conclusion, see Jane Turner Censer, "Southwest Migration Among North Carolina Families: The Disposition to Emigrate," *Journal of Southern History*, 57 (August 1991): 407–27.

12. James Buckingham, *The Slave States of America* (London, 1842) I: 46–55, 316, 369; 2:413–33.

13. David Goldfield, *Cotton Fields and Skyscrapers: Southern City and Region* (Baton Rouge, 1982), 32.

14. Goldfield, 28–29.

15. Michael Johnson, "Planters and Patriarchy: Charleston, 1800–1860," *Journal of Southern History* 46 (February 1980): 47–48.

16. Thomas Alexander et al., "The Antebellum North and South in Comparative Perspective," *American Historical Review* 85 (December 1980): 1152.

17. Robert Fogel and Stanley Engerman, *Time on The Cross: The Economics of American Negro Slavery* (Boston, 1974), 251; also Robert Fogel, *Without Consent or Contract: The Rise and Fall of American Slavery* (New York, 1989).

18. Fred Bateman et. al., "The Participation of Planters in Manufacturing in the Antebellum South," *Agricultural History*, 48 (April 1974): 285.

19. Alice Kessler Harris, *Out To Work: A History of Wage-Earning Women in the United States* (New York, 1982), 64.

20. George Fitzhugh, "Slavery Justified," in *Major Problems in the Civil War and Reconstruction*, ed. Michael Perman (Lexington, Mass., 1991), 43.

21. Peter Kolchin, *American Slavery, 1619–1877* (New York, 1993), 176.

22. Lee Soltow and Edmond Stevens, *The Rise of Literacy and the Common School: A Socioeconomic Analysis to 1870* (Chicago, 1981), 119.

23. Fred Bateman and Thomas Weiss, *A Deplorable Scarcity: Industrialism in the Slave Economy* (Chapel Hill, N.C., 1981), 162.

24. Fabian Linden, "Repercussions of Manufacturing in the Ante-Bellum South," *North Carolina Historical Review* 17 (October 1940), 321–2.

25. Eugene Genovese, *The Southern Tradition: The Achievements and Limitations of American Conservatism* (Cambridge, Mass., 1994), 68.

26. Kenneth Stampp, *The Peculiar Institution: Slavery in the Ante-bellum South* (New York, 1966), 34.

27. Quoted in Willie Lee Rose, ed., *A Documentary History of Slavery in North America* (New York, 1976), 176.

28. Daniel R. Hundley, *Social Relations in Our Southern States* (New York, 1860), 74.

29. Johnson, 46.

30. Stephanie McCurry, *Masters of Small Worlds: Yeoman Households and the Political Culture of the Antebellum Low Country* (New York, 1994), 88, 220.

31. Quoted in Carol Bleser, ed., *Secret and Sacred: The Diaries of James Henry Hammond* (New York, 1988), 9.

32. Jean Friedman, *The Enclosed Garden: Women and Community in the Evangelical South, 1830–1900* (Chapel Hill, N.C., 1985); Elizabeth Fox-Genovese, "Family and Female Identity in the Antebellum South: Sarah Gayle and Her Family," in *In Joy and Sorrow: Women, Family and Marriage in the Victorian South*, ed. Carol Bleser (New York, 1991), 19. For a description of some antebellum southern women that relies on court records, see Victoria Bynum, *Unruly Women: The Politics of Social and Sexual Control in the Old South* (Chapel Hill, N.C., 1992), 34–87.

33. Catharine Clinton, *Plantation Mistress* (New York, 1982), 232; Sally McMillen, *Motherhood in the Old South: Pregnancy, Childbirth and Infant Raising* (Baton Rouge, 1990), 32.

34. Peter Bardaglio, "Challenging Parental Custody Rights: The Legal Reconstruction of Parenthood in the Nineteenth-Century American South," *Continuity and Change* 4 (August 1989): 260; Peter Bardaglio, *Reconstructing the Household: Families, Sex and the Law in the Nineteenth Century South* (Chapel Hill, N.C., 1995), 5–36.

35. John Hope Franklin, *The Militant South, 1800–1861* (Cambridge, Mass., 1956), 19; David Grimsted, *American Mobbing: 1828–1861 Toward Civil War* (New York, 1998), xi, 85–113.

36. Lewis C. Gray, *History of Agriculture in the Southern United States 1860* (Washington, D.C., 1933), 2: 821, 757, 723, 748.

37. Kenneth Stampp, *The Imperiled Union: Essays on the Background of the Civil War* (New York, 1980), 455.

38. Bureau of the Census, *The Statistical History of the United States from Colonial Times to the Present* (New York, 1976), 518.

39. William Cooper, "The Cotton Crisis in the Antebellum South," *Agricultural History* 49 (April 1975): 384.

40. John Commons et. al. *Documentary History of American Industrial Society* (Cleveland, 1910), 1: 283–7.

41. Randolph Campbell and Richard Lowe, *Wealth and Power in Antebellum Texas* (College Station, Tex., 1977), 67.

42. Charles Bolton, *Poor Whites of the Antebellum South: Tenants and Laborers in Central North Carolina and Northeast Mississippi* (Durham, N.C., 1994), 6; William Harris, *Plain Folk and Gentry in a Slave Society: White Liberty and Black Slavery in Augusta's Hinterlands* (Middletown, Conn., 1985); for an important overview of the plain folk of the antebellum South see Randolph Campbell, "Planters and Plain Folks: The Social Structure of the Antebellum South," in *Interpreting Southern History*, ed. John Boles and Evelyn Nolen (Baton Rouge, 1987), 48–77.

43. Frank L. Owsley, *Plain Folk of the Old South* (Baton Rouge, 1949), 139; Gavin Wright, *The Political Economy of the Cotton South: Households, Markets, and Wealth in the Nineteenth Century* (New York, 1978), 166, 170–2.

44. Thornton, 87–91, 320–1, 447–8.

45. Steven Hahn, *The Roots of Southern Populism: Yeoman Farmers and the Transformation of the Georgia Upcountry, 1850–1890* (New York, 1983), 23.

46. For a rare diary of a yeoman, see Paul Escott, ed., *North Carolina Yeoman: The Diary of Basil Armstrong Thomasson, 1853–1862* (Athens, Ga., 1996), 154.

47. Hahn, 29.

48. Forest McDonald and Grady McWhiney, "The Antebellum Southern Herdsmen: A Reinterpretation," *Journal of Southern History* 41 (May 1975): 147.

49. Peter Wallenstein, *From Slave South to New South: Public Policy in the Nineteenth Century* (Chapel Hill, N.C. 1987); Thornton, 187–8, 303–6.

50. Hahn, 27.

51. *I'll Take My Stand: The South and the Agrarian Tradition* (New York, 1930), 71–2; also McCurry, 48–61.

52. James Oakes, *Slavery and Freedom: An Interpretation of the Old South* (New York, 1990), 105.

53. McCurry, 240; Eugene Genovese, "Yeomen Farmers in the Slaveholders' Democracy," *Agricultural History* 49 (April 1975): 337; George Fredrickson, *The Black Image in the White Mind: The Afro-American Character and Destiny, 1817–1914* (New York, 1971), 61, 93–94.

54. Robert R. Russel, "The Effects of Slavery Upon Nonslaveholders," *Agricultural History* 15 (April 1941): 112–27.

55. D. Harland Hagler, "The Ideal Woman in the Ante-Bellum South: Lady or Farmwife?" *Journal of Southern History* (August 1980): 404–14.

56. Morton Rothstein, "The Cotton Frontier of the Antebellum U.S. : A Methodological Battleground," *Agricultural History* 44 (Spring 1970): 160.

57. Gavin Wright, "'Economic Democracy' and the Concentration of Agricultural Wealth in the Cotton South, 1850–1860," *Agricultural History* 44 (January 1970): 63–93.

58. Lee Soltow, *Men and Wealth in the United States, 1850–1870* (New Haven, Conn., 1975), 122–3, 127–8, 145–6, 156–7, 166–73; William Dodd, *The Cotton Kingdom: A Chronicle of the Old South* (New Haven, Conn., 1919), 24.

59. William Parker, "Slavery and Southern Economic Development," *Agricultural History* 44 (January 1970): 119.

60. Wright, 63.

61. Cash, 60.

62. Oakes, *The Ruling Race*, 60.

63. Bolton, 109.

64. Elizabeth Fox-Genovese and Eugene Genovese, *Fruits of Merchant Capital: Slavery and Bourgeois Property in the Rise and Expansion of Capitalism* (New York, 1983), 5; see also Kolchin, 254.

65. Bolton, 109.

66. Quoted in Avery Craven, *The Coming of the Civil War* (New York, 1966), 424.

67. George Carey Eggleston, *A, Rebel's Recollections*, ed. David Donald (Baton Rouge, 1996), 1.

68. Theodore Rosengarten, *Tombee: Portrait of a Cotton Planter* (New York, 1986), 65, 34.

69. James Bonner, "Plantation Architecture of the Lower South on the Eve of the Civil War," *Journal of Southern History* 11 (August 1995): 372, 374.

70. Kenneth Greenberg, *Masters and Statesman: The Political Culture of American Slavery* (Baltimore, 1985), 18.

71. Donald G. Matthews, *Religion in the Old South* (Chicago, 1977), 136.

72. Eugene Genovese, *The World the Slaveholders Made: Essays in Interpretation* (Middletown, Conn., 1988).

73. Fogel and Engerman, *Time on the Cross*, 73; Oakes, *The Ruling Race*, 153; see also Robert Fogel, *Without Consent or Contract*, 64.

74. U. B. Phillips, *Life and Labor in the Old South* (Boston, 1929), 202–3.

75. Quoted in Ann Firor Scott, *The Southern Lady: From Pedestal to Politics, 1830–1930* (Chicago, 1970), 4.

76. C. Vann Woodward, ed., *Mary Chesnut's Civil War* (New Haven, Conn., 1981), 29; Catherine Clinton, "Southern Dishonor: Flesh, Blood, Race and Bondage," in *In Joy and Sorrow: Women, Family and Marriage in the Victorian South*, ed. Carol Bleser (New York, 1991), 52–68; Elizabeth Fox-Genovese, *Within the Plantation Household: Black and White Women of the Old South* (Chapel Hill, N.C., 1988); Marli Weiner, *Mistresses and Slaves: Plantation Women in South Carolina* (Urbana, Ill., 1998).

77. Franklin, *The Militant South*, 219, 221.

78. Greenberg, *Masters and Statesmen*, 130.

79. Charles Sellers, "Who Were the Southern Whigs?" *Journal of Southern History* 12 (February, 1946), 20–21. See also Michael Holt, *The Rise and Fall of the Whig Party* (New York, 1999), 32–35, 87–88, 236–8, 580–1.

80. John McCardell, *The Idea of a Southern Nation: Southern Nationalists and Southern Nationalism, 1830–1860* (New York, 1979), 336.

81. McCardell, 97, 22.

82. Oakes, 135.

83. William Cooper, *The South and the Politics of Slavery, 1828–1856* (Baton Rouge, 1978), 370.

84. Rollin Osterweis, *Romanticism and Nationalism in the Old South* (Gloucester, Mass., 1964), 3–5, 26.

85. Cash, viii.

86. Bertram Wyatt-Brown, *Southern Honor: Ethics and Behavior in the Old South* (New York, 1982), vii, xv, 34, 59–60.

87. David Donald, *Charles Sumner and the Coming of the Civil War* (New York, 1960), 349.

88. Larry Tise, *Proslavery: A History of the Defense of Slavery in America, 1701–1840* (Athens, Ga., 1987).

89. Donald, 348.

90. Quoted in Ronald T. Takaki, *A Pro-Slavery Crusade: The Agitation to Reopen the African Slave Trade* (New York, 1971), 67.

91. Quoted in Charles Sydnor, *The Development of Southern Sectionalism 1819–1848* (Baton Rouge, 1948), 338–9.

## Chapter 3

1. George Rawick, *The American Slave: A Composite Autobiography*, 19 vols. (Westport, Conn., 1972); Ira Berlin, *Remembering Slavery: African Americans Talk about Their Personal Experiences of Slavery and Emancipation* (New York, 1998).

2. Larry Tise, *Proslavery: A History of the Defense of Slavery in America* (Athens, Ga., 1987), 124, 347–62.

3. David Brion Davis, *The Problem of Slavery in Western Culture* (Ithaca, N.Y., 1966), 31; also Ira Berlin, *Many Thousand Gone: The First Two Centuries of Slavery in North America* (Cambridge, Mass., 1998), 8–14, 17–28.

4. David Brion Davis, "The Slave Trade and the Jews," *New York Review of Books* 41 (December 22, 1994): 14.

5. James Rawley, *The Transatlantic Slave Trade: A History* (New York, 1991), 164.

6. Quoted in Rawley, 428.

7. Robert Fogel and Stanley Engerman, *Time on the Cross: The Economics of American Negro Slavery* (Boston, 1974), 24.

8. Peter Kolchin, *American Slavery, 1619–1877* (New York, 1993), 38.

9. Philip Curtin, *The Atlantic Slave Trade: A Census* (Madison, Wisc., 1969), 280.

10. W. O. Blake, *History of Slavery and the Slave Trade* (1860), 284–90.

11. Rawley, 290.

12. Rawley, 319–20.

13. House Ex. Doc. No. 7, 36th Cong., 2d Sess., 1861, 15.

14. Winthrop Jordan, *White over Black: American Attitudes Toward the Negro 1550–1812* (Baltimore, 1968), 3–40.

15. Berlin, 29, 109–12, 118–20.

16. George Fredrickson, *White Supremacy: A Comparative Study in American and South African History* (New York, 1981), 70.

17. Fredrickson, 70.

18. Jordan, 44.

19. Kolchin, 240.

20. Kenneth Stampp, *The Peculiar Institution: Slavery in the Ante-Bellum South* (New York, 1956), 193, 207–9.

21. Eugene Genovese, *Roll, Jordan Roll: The World the Slaves Made* (New York, 1972), 27.

22. Berlin, 32, 360–1; Peter Bardaglio, *Reconstructing the Household: Families, Sex and the Law in the Nineteenth-Century South* (Chapel Hill, N.C., 1995), 28, 64.

23. Michael Stephen Hindus, *Prison and Plantation Crime: Justice and Authority in Massachusetts and South Carolina* (Chapel Hill, N.C., 1980).

24. Thomas D. Morris, *Southern Slavery and the Law, 1619–1860* (Chapel Hill, N.C., 1996).

25. Peter Kolchin, *Unfree Labor: American Slavery and Russian Serfdom* (Cambridge, Mass., 1987), 132.

26. William Harper, "Memoir on Slavery," in *The Ideology of Slavery: Proslavery Thought in the Antebellum South, 1830–1860*, ed. Drew Faust (Baton Rouge, 1981), 98–99.

27. Bardaglio, 28.

28. Genovese, 27, 28; on paternalism, Genovese, 5–6; Kolchin, *Unfree Labor*, 128–40.

29. Kolchin, *Unfree Labor*, 131.

30. William Freehling, *Slavery and Freedom* (New York, 1982), 18.

31. Genovese, 36.

32. Robert Fogel, *Without Consent or Contract: The Rise and Fall of American Slavery* (New York, 1989), 186–96.

33. Leon Litwack, *North of Slavery: The Negro in the Free States, 1790–1860* (Chicago, 1961), 83.

34. *Nashville* [Tenn.] *Republican Banner*, January 15, 1860, in Ira Berlin, *Slaves without Masters: The Free Negro in the Antebellum South* (New York, 1992), 46, 136, 217.

35. Helen T. Catterall, *Judicial Cases Concerning American Slavery and the Negro* (Washington, D.C., 1926) 1:431.

36. Berlin, *Slaves without Masters*, 9.

37. Gilbert Osofsky, *Puttin' on Ole Massa: The Slave Narratives of Henry Bibb, William Wells Brown and Solomon Northrup* (New York, 1947), 232–405.

38. Berlin, *Slaves without Masters*, 265.

39. John Hope Franklin, *From Slavery to Freedom: A History of Negro Americans* (New York, 1947), 221.

40. Suzanne Lebsock, *The Free Women of Petersburg: Status and Culture in a Southern Town, 1784–1860* (New York, 1985), 97–99.

41. Michael Johnson and James Roark, *Black Masters: A Free Family of Color in the Old South* (New York, 1984), 85–91.

42. James Oakes, *The Ruling Race: A History of American Slaveholders* (New York, 1982), 38; Kolchin, *American Slavery*, 101.

43. Oakes, 38–39; Kolchin, 243.

44. William Scarborough, *The Overseer: Plantation Management in the Old South* (Athens, Ga., 1966) 5; Kolchin, *American Slavery*, 102–5.

45. Genovese, 366.

46. William Van Deburg, *The Slave Drivers: Black Agricultural Labor Supervisors in the Antebellum South* (New York, 1988), 1–30.

47. Robert Starobin, ed., *Blacks in Bondage: Letters of American Slaves* (New York, 1974), 21.

48. John Blassingame, *The Slave Community: Plantation Life in the Ante-Bellum South* (New York, 1972), 250; Wilma King, *Stolen Childhood: Slave Youth in Nineteenth-Century America* (Bloomington, Ind., 1995).

49. Frederick Douglass, *The Life and Times of Frederick Douglass, Written by Himself* (New York, 1962), 124.

50. Kolchin, *Unfree Labor*, 54.

51. Genovese, 332.

52. Elizabeth Fox-Genovese, *Within the Plantation Household: Black and White Women in the Old South* (Chapel Hill, N.C., 1988), 172–3.

53. Fox-Genovese, 172–3.

54. Harriet Jacobs, *Incidents in the Life of A Slave Girl, Written by Herself* (Cambridge, Mass., 1987), 27.

55. Herbert Gutman and Richard Sutch, "Victorians All? The Sexual Mores and Conduct of Slaves and Their Masters," *Reckoning with Slavery: A Critical Study in the Quantitative History of American Negro Slavery*, ed. Paul David (New York, 1976), 152.

56. Melton McLaurin, *Celia, a Slave* (Athens, Ga., 1991).

57. Roger Ransom and Richard Sutch, *One Kind of Freedom: The Economic Consequences of Emancipation* (New York, 1977), 3–4.

58. Carl Degler, *The Other South: Southern Dissenters* (New York, 1974), 42–45.

59. Fogel and Engerman, 109–17; Fogel, *Without Consent or Contract*, 147–51.

60. Richard Sutch, "The Care and Feeding of Slaves," in *Reckoning with Slavery: A Critical Study in the Quantitative History of American Negro Slavery* (New York, 1976), 230–301.

61. John Boles, *Black Southerners, 1619–1869* (Lexington, Ky., 1983), 67.

62. Lawrence W. Levine, *Black Culture and Black Consciousness: Afro-American Folk Thought from Slavery to Freedom* (New York, 1978).

63. Herbert Gutman, *The Black Family in Slavery and Freedom* (New York, 1977), 8–15; Brenda Stevenson, *Life in Black and White: Family and Community in the Slave South* (New York, 1996).

64. Jacobs, 78–85, 98–105; Osofsky, 179.

65. Kolchin, *American Slavery*, 97.

66. Boles, 179; David Robertson, *Denmark Vesey* (New York, 1999).

67. Norman Yetman, *Life Under the Peculiar Institution: Selections From the Slave Narrative Collection* (New York, 1970), 12.

68. Michael Johnson, "Runaway Slaves and the Slave Communities in South Carolina, 1799 to 1830," *William and Mary Quarterly* 38 (July 1981): 418.

69. Charles S. Snydor, "Pursuing Fugitive Slaves," *South Atlantic Quarterly* 28 (April 1929): 152–64; Eugene Genovese, *From Rebellion to Revolution: Afro-American Slave Revolts in the Making of the New World* (New York, 1981), 1–50.

70. Larry Gara, *The Liberty Line: The Legend of the Underground Railroad* (Lexington, Ky., 1961), 67.

71. Fogel and Engerman, 248.

72. Betty Mitchell, *Edmund Ruffin: A Biography* (Bloomington, 1981), 12, 35–36.

73. Ransom and Sutch, *One Kind of Freedom: The Economic Consequences of Emancipation* (New York, 1977), 3.

74. Alfred Conrad and John Meyer, "The Economics of Slavery in the Ante-Bellum South," *Journal of Political Economy* 66 (April 1958): 97, 121.

75. Frederic Bancroft, *Slave-Trading in the Old South* (Baltimore, 1931), 60, 117, 355, 393, 395.

76. Fogel and Engerman, 98.

77. Fogel and Engerman, 96–98.

78. Kolchin, *American Slavery*, 174.

79. Ransom and Sutch, 4.

80. Frederick Law Olmsted, *The Cotton Kingdom: A Traveller's Observation on Cotton and Slavery in the American Slave States* (New York, 1953), 2:299–300.

81. Peter Kolchin, "Historians and Antebellum Slavery," in *A Master's Due: Essays in Honor of David Herbert Donald*, ed. William Cooper, Michael Holt, and John McCardell (Baton Rouge, 1985), 99.

82. Claudia Dale Goldin, *Urban Slavery in the American South 1820–1860: A Quantitative Study* (Chicago, 1976), 35; Richard Morris, "The Measure of Bondage in the Slave States," *Mississippi Valley Historical Review* 41 (September 1954): 230–9.

83. Elizabeth Fox-Genovese and Eugene D. Genovese, *Fruits of Merchant Capital: Slavery and Bourgeois Property in the Rise and Expansion of Capitalism* (New York, 1983), 55.

## Chapter 4

1. Thomas P. Kettell, *Southern Wealth and Northern Profits . . .* (New York, 1860).

2. *Niles Weekly Register*, quoted in John McCardell, *The Idea of a Southern Nation: Southern Nationalists and Southern Nationalism* (New York, 1979), 97; for evidence of similar views, see *De Bow's Review*, esp. 20: 483ff; 21:308ff; 22:265ff, 657ff; 25:220ff.

3. Charles A. Beard and Mary R. Beard, *The Rise of American Civilization* (New York, 1930), 1:664–5; 2:29.

4. Joel Silbey, *The Shrine of Party: Congressional Voting Behavior 1841–1852* (Pittsburgh, 1967). For a quantitative study of voting patterns in the House of Representatives that demonstrates the influence of party discipline on voting behavior, see Thomas B. Alexander, *Sectional Stress and Party Strength: A Study of Roll Call Voting Patterns in the U.S. House of Representatives, 1836–1860* (Nashville, 1967).

5. Michael Holt, *The Political Crisis of the 1850s* (New York, 1978), 134. Also Michael Morrison, *Slavery and the American West: The Eclipse of Manifest Destiny and the Coming of the Civil War* (Chapel Hill, N.C., 1997).

6. Quoted in William Gienapp, "The Crisis of American Democracy," in *Why the Civil War Came*, ed. Gabor Boritt (New York, 1996), 85.

7. David Potter, *The Impending Crisis, 1848–1861* (New York, 1976), 43.

8. William Gienapp, "Nebraska, Nativism and Rum," *Pennsylvania Magazine of History and Biography* 109 (October 1985): 471; Eric Foner, "The Wilmot Proviso Revisited," *Journal of American History* 56 (September 1969): 276–9; Holt, 58.

9. Thelma Jennings, *The Nashville Convention: The Southern Movement for Unity 1848–1851* (Memphis, 1980).

10. The northern states added after 1812 were Indiana (1816), Illinois (1818), Maine (1820), Michigan (1837), Iowa (1846), and Wisconsin (1848). Those of the South were Mississippi (1817), Alabama (1819), Missouri (1820), Arkansas (1836), Texas (1845), and Florida (1845).

11. *Congressional Globe*, 31st Cong., 1st Sess., 1849, 1: 27–29.

12. Holt, 84.

13. At the same time Webster and his backers did have a secondary motive. As the Boston *Advertiser* explained: "It is thought that the passage of the Fugitive Slave Bill should place the South in a humor to favor some modification of the tariff, for the benefit of those Northern men who have jeopardized their political standing for conciliation." David D. Van Tassel, "Gentlemen of Property and Standing," *New England Quarterly* 23 (September 1950): 319.

14. Robert F. Dalzell, *Daniel Webster and the Trials of American Nationalism, 1843–1852* (Boston, 1975), 191, 194, 215.

15. Holman Hamilton, "Democratic Senate Leadership and the Compromise of 1850," *Mississippi Valley Historical Review* 41 (December 1954): 415.

16. Holman Hamilton, "Texas Bonds and Northern Profits," *Mississippi Valley Historical Society* 43 (March 1957): 579–94.

17. Mark Stegmaier, *Texas, New Mexico and the Compromise of 1850* (Kent, Ohio, 1996).

18. The territorial legislatures of New Mexico and Utah "might legislate on the subject of slavery either to prohibit it, or to establish it, or to regulate it subject to a possible veto by the governor or a

possible disallowance by Congress." Robert Russel, "What Was the Compromise of 1850?" *Journal of Southern History* 23 (August 1956): 296, 304.

19. *U.S. Statutes at Large* 9 (1850): 462–5; James G. Randall, *Constitutional Problems under Lincoln* (Urbana, Ill., 1964), 421.

20. Potter, 113–4.

21. Stegmaier, 291.

22. William Freehling, *The Road to Disunion* (New York, 1990), 509–10.

23. Holt, 98.

24. Amos Ettinger, *The Mission to Spain of Pierre Soulé* (New Haven, 1932), 361–4.

25. McCardell, 259. Robert E. May, *The Southern Dream of a Caribbean Empire* (Baton Rouge, 1973).

26. *Senate Reports*, No. 15, 33rd Cong., 1st sess., 1854, 3.

27. In 1818–1820 the problem of slavery in Missouri and related questions had produced serious controversy. The House twice passed the Tallmadge amendment prohibiting further introduction of slavery into the state and freeing slave-born children at the age of twenty-five; but the Senate disagreed. After a compromise Missouri was admitted as a slave state; Maine was admitted as a free state and in all national territory north of 36° 30′ "slavery and involuntary servitude, otherwise than in the punishment of crimes . . . shall be . . . forever prohibited." *Annals of Congress*, 16th Cong., 1st sess., 427–30 (February 18, 1820).

28. George F. Milton, *Eve of Conflict: Stephen A. Douglas and the Needless War* (Boston, 1934), 34–35; Robert Johannsen, *Stephen A. Douglas* (New York, 1973), 211.

29. Because the Kansas-Nebraska Act had such dramatic effects on the parties, Douglas's motivations have long been a matter of dispute among historians. See Roy Nichols, "The Kansas-Nebraska Act: A Century of Historiography," *Mississippi Valley Historical Review* 43 (September 1956): 187–212; Holt, 147; Johannsen, 408; Freehling, 551–8.

30. Allan Nevins, *Ordeal of the Union* (New York, 1947), 2: 102.

31. James C. Malin, "The Motives of Stephen A. Douglas in the Organization of the Nebraska Territory: A Letter Dated December 17, 1853," *Kansas Historical Quarterly* 19 (November 1951): 351–2.

32. Malin, 353.

33. Potter, 160. Some historians believe that northern Whigs originated the repeal in order to help southern Whigs appear as the most faithful defenders of slavery. William Gienapp, *The Origins of the Republican Party 1852–1856* (New York, 1987), 70. Others explicitly reject the importance of northern scheming; Freehling, 555. See also Michael F. Holt, *The Rise and Fall of the American Whig Party: Jacksonian Politics and the Onset of the Civil War* (New York, 1999), 806–21.

34. *Congressional Globe*, 33rd Cong., 1st sess., 1854, 281–2. Some southerners, including Alexander H. Stephens, approved the bill, though southern extremists later assailed Douglas. Eric Foner, *Free Soil, Free Labor, Free Men: The Ideology of the Republican Party before the Civil War* (New York, 1970), 83.

35. Avery Craven, *The Growth of Southern Nationalism, 1848–1861* (Baton Rouge, 1953), 204; Johannsen, 401.

36. Gienapp, 76.

37. Holt, 51.

38. Gienapp, 273; Tyler Anbinder, *Nativism and Slavery: The Northern Know-Nothings and the Politics of the 1850s* (New York, 1992).

39. Samuel Johnson, "The Emigrant Aid Company in the Kansas Conflict," *Kansas Historical Quarterly* 6 (February 1937): 21.

40. Paul W. Gates, *Fifty Million Acres: Conflicts over Kansas Land Policy* (Ithaca, N.Y., 1954), 21.

41. Gates, 2–3.

42. Samuel A. Johnson, "The Genesis of the New England Emigrant Aid Company," *New England Quarterly* 3 (January, 1930): 118.

43. Johnson, 118–9.

44. Gienapp, 170.

45. James C. Malin, *John Brown and the Legend of '56* (Philadelphia, 1942), 509.

46. Oswald Garrison Villard, *John Brown, 1800–1859* (Boston, 1910), 148 ff.

47. Malin, 754–8.

48. Stephen Oates, "John Brown and His Judges: A Critique of the Historical Literature," *Civil War History* 17 (March 1971): 5–24.

49. After an unsuccessful effort by the House of Representatives to expel him, Brooks defiantly resigned. He was then reelected by his district. The civil courts of the District of Columbia fined Brooks three hundred dollars for assault, but never imprisoned him.

50. Gienapp, 303; on Sumner, David Donald, *Charles Sumner and the Coming of the Civil War* (New York, 1960).

51. James Buchanan, *Works*, ed. John B. Moore (Philadelphia, 1908), 10:92, 96.

52. Kirk Porter and Donald Johnson, *National Party Platforms, 1840–1964* (Urbana, Ill., 1966), 31–33.

## Chapter 5

1. William Cooper, *The South and the Politics of Slavery 1828–1856* (Baton Rouge, 1978), 362.

2. *De Bows Review*, 9 (1850): 120–4.

3. George Fitzhugh, *Cannibals All! or Slaves without Masters* (Cambridge, Mass., 1960), 11, 15, 16, 223.

4. Allan Nevins, *The Emergence of Lincoln* (New York, 1950), I: 405–9.

5. John McCardell, *The Idea of a Southern Nation: Southern Nationalists and Southern Nationalism* (New York, 1979), 206.

6. Joshua Giddings, *Speeches in Congress* (New York, 1968), 451, 461; also James Brewer Stewart, *Joshua Giddings and the Tactics of Radical Politics* (Cleveland, 1970).

7. Don Fehrenbacher, *Slavery, Law and Politics: The Dred Scott Case in Historical Perspective* (New York, 1981), 129.

8. Vincent Hopkins, *Dred Scott's Case* (New York, 1967), 182; Fehrenbacher, 137.

9. Misspelled "Sandford" in *Howard's Reports*.

10. Fehrenbacher, 164–9.

11. Roy Nichols, *The Disruption of American Democracy* (New York, 1967), 66.

12. *Dred Scott v. Sanford*, 19 Howard 60, 407–8 (U.S. 1857).

13. Fehrenbacher, 193.

14. For quoted passages, see 19 Howard 405, 406, 427, 430, 400.

15. It has often been claimed that Taney was going outside his province in declaring the Compromise void after holding that the circuit court had no jurisdiction; and his announcement on this phase of the case has usually been regarded as an *obiter dictum*. Even so, it was a solemn announcement of judicial doctrine by the Supreme Court of the United States. Some historians maintain that Taney's denial of the power of Congress to exclude slavery from the territories was not an *obiter dictum* at all, because a court is obliged to explore every pertinent phase of the case before it in order not to overlook any essential right that may be involved. One legal historian concludes, however, that in supporting his opinion Taney used irrelevant arguments, incorrectly invoked the principle of "vested rights," and misapplied the "due process of law" doctrine. See Edward Corwin, "The Dred Scott Decision . . ." *American Historical Review* 18 (October 1911): 52–70. Fehrenbacher agrees that the charge of *obiter dictum* was misleading if by that is meant the court dealt with extraneous issues not under its purview; see Fehrenbacher, 180.

16. Fehrenbacher, 231, 235, 229.

17. Thomas Morris, *Free Men All: The Personal Liberty Laws of the North* (Baltimore, 1974).

18. James D. Richardson, ed., *A Compilation of the Messages and Papers of the Presidents, 1778–1897* (Washington, D.C., 1896), 5:404–7.

19. David Meerse, "Presidential Leadership, Suffrage Qualifications, and Kansas," *Civil War History* 24 (December 1979): 293–312.

20. Nichols, 125.

21. James Buchanan, *Works*, ed. J. B. Moore (Philadelphia, 1908), 10:183, 190, 192.

22. *Congressional Globe*, 35th Cong., 1st sess. (April 29, 1858).

23. Roy P. Basler et al., eds., *The Collected Works of Abraham Lincoln* (New Brunswick, N.J., 1953) 2: 461. Hereafter cited as Lincoln, *Collected Works*.

24. David Herbert Donald, *Lincoln* (New York, 1995), 22.

25. Donald, 170.

26. Lincoln, *Collected Works*, 3:211–2.

27. Robert Johannsen, *Stephen A. Douglas* (New York, 1973), 666.

28. Lincoln, *Collected Works*, 3:179.

29. Lincoln, *Collected Works*, 3:265–6, 92–93.

30. Harold Holzer, ed., *The Lincoln-Douglas Debates* (New York, 1993), 96.

31. Holzer, 106.

32. Stephen Oates, *To Purge This Land With Blood: A Biography of John Brown* (New York, 1970), 290–8.

33. Wendell Phillips, *Speeches, Lectures, and Letters* (Boston, 1864), 272.

34. Oswald Garrison Villard, *John Brown, 1800–1859* (Boston, 1910), 237–83, 498–9, 554.

35. *Congressional Globe*, 36th Cong., 1st Sess., 1859, 553.

36. Joel Silbey, "The Surge of Republican Power," ed. William Gienapp, et. al. in *Essays on American Antebellum Politics, 1840–1860* (College Station, Tex., 1982), 229.

37. William Gienapp, "The Crisis of American Democracy," in *Why The Civil War Came*, ed. Gabor Boritt (New York, 1996), 108.

38. Steven Channing, *A Crisis of Fear: Secession in South Carolina* (New York, 1970), 208.

39. *Congressional Globe*, 36th Cong., 1st Sess., 658, 2321–2. The vote on this resolution was 35 to 21, the opposition being made up of twenty Republicans and the Douglas Democrat Pugh of Ohio. Douglas was absent at the time of the vote.

40. John Taylor, *William Henry Seward* (New York, 1991).

41. Lincoln, *Collected Works*, 3:547.

42. Lincoln, *Collected Works*, 3:368.

43. Eric Foner, *Free Soil, Free Labor, Free Men: The Ideology of the Republican Party before the Civil War* (New York, 1970), 11–39. For the Republican platform, see Kirk Porter and Donald Johnson, *National Party Platforms* (Urbana, Ill., 1966), 31–33.

44. *New York Times*, September 7, 1860.

45. *New York Times*, September 7, 1860.

46. Foner, 11.

47. Lincoln, *Collected Works*, 4:135.

48. Emerson D. Fite, *The Presidential Campaign of 1860* (New York, 1911), 333.

49. New Jersey gave four of its seven electoral votes to Lincoln and three to Douglas.

50. William Gienapp, "Who Voted For Lincoln?" in *Abraham Lincoln and the American Political Tradition*, ed. John L. Thomas (Amherst, Mass., 1986), 50–98.

51. William Freehling, "The Divided South, Democracy's Limitations, and the Causes of the Peculiarly North American Civil War," in *Why the Civil War Came*, ed. Gabor Boritt (New York, 1996), 148.

52. William Barney, *The Secessionist Impulse: Alabama and Mississippi in 1860* (Princeton, N.J., 1974), 90.

53. Isabella Martin and Myrta Lockett Avary, eds., *A Diary from Dixie as Written by Mary Boykin Chesnut* (New York, 1905), 1.

## Chapter 6

1. Steven Channing, *A Crisis of Fear: Secession in South Carolina* (New York, 1970), 265.

2. David Donald, "The Proslavery Argument Revisited," *Journal of Southern History* 37 (February 1971): 3–18.

3. Channing, 282–5.

4. Kenneth Greenberg, *Masters and Statesmen: The Political Culture of American Slavery* (Baltimore, 1985), 134.

5. William Freehling and Craig Simpson, eds., *Secession Debated: Georgia's Showdown in 1860* (New York, 1992).

6. "From the Autobiography of Herschel V. Johnson, 1856–1867," *American Historical Review* 30 (January 1925): 324; also Freehling and Simpson, xiv–xxi.

7. "Autobiography," 323.

8. Ulrich Phillips, *Georgia and States Rights* (Washington, D.C., 1902), 200–4.

9. Michael Johnson, *Toward a Patriarchal Republic: The Secession of Georgia* (Baton Rouge, 1977).

10. J. Mills Thornton, *Politics and Power in a Slave Society: Alabama, 1800–1860* (Baton Rouge, 1978), 424–30.

11. "Autobiography," 327–8.

12. James Oakes, *The Ruling Race: A History of American Slaveholders* (New York, 1982), 239.

13. Ralph Wooster, "An Analysis of the Membership of Secession Conventions in the Lower South," *Journal of Southern History* 24 (August 1958): 360–8; Ralph Wooster, "The Secession of the Lower South: An Examination of Changing Interpretations," *Civil War History* 7 (June 1965): 117–28; Peyton McCrary, et al., "Class and Party in the Secession Crisis: Voting Behavior in the Deep South, 1856–1861," *Journal of Interdisciplinary History* 8 (Winter 1978): 429–55.

14. Roy P. Basler, et al., eds., *The Collected Works of Abraham Lincoln* (New Brunswick, N.J., 1953), 4:264. Hereafter cited as Lincoln, *Collected Works.* Also Kenneth Stampp, "The Concept of a Perpetual Union," *Journal of American History* 65 (June 1978): 5–33; Gienapp, "The Crisis of American Democracy," in *Why the Civil War Came*, ed. Gabor Boritt (New York, 1996), 85–86.

15. Barney, *The Secessionist Impulse: Alabama and Mississippi in 1860* (Princeton, N.J., 1974), 296.

16. James McPherson, *Battle Cry of Freedom: The Civil War Era* (New York, 1988), 253–4.

17. Philip Auchampaugh, *James Buchanan and His Cabinet on the Eve of Secession* (Lancaster, Pa., 1926), 63–64.

18. Mark Summers, *The Plundering Generation: Corruption and the Crisis of the Union, 1849–1861* (New York, 1987), 259; Michael Holt, *The Political Crisis of the 1850s* (New York, 1978), 214; Michael Birkner, ed., *James Buchanan and the Political Crisis of the 1850s* (Cranbury, N.J., 1996).

19. Roy Nichols, *The Disruption of American Democracy* (New York, 1948), 378.

20. James D. Richardson, ed., *A Compilation of the Messages and Papers of the Presidents, 1787–1897* (Washington, D. C., 1892), 5:626–37.

21. David Potter, *The Impending Crisis, 1848–1861* (New York, 1976), 520.

22. Potter, 523.

23. Edward McPherson, *The Political History of the United States during the Great Rebellion* (Washington, 1865), 37; also William Barney, *The Road to Secession: A New Perspective on the Old South* (Princeton, 1974), 196–7.

24. *Congressional Globe*, 35th Cong., 2d Sess., 1284–5, 1403. The amendment was adopted by the House on February 28, 1861 (133 to 65) and by the Senate on March 2 (24 to 12). Some House Republicans voted for the proposition, but the negative votes were all Republican.

25. *Congressional Globe*, 35th Cong., 2d Sess., 114.

26. Lincoln, *Collected Works*, 4:150, 154.

27. *Appleton's American Annual Cyclopaedia* (New York, 1861–1865), 700.

28. *Congressional Globe*, 36th Cong., 2d Sess., 1254–5, 1402.

29. Lucius Chittenden, *A Report of the Debates and Proceedings in the Secret Session of the Conference Convention* (New York, 1864), 9, 14, 135–6, 151.

30. Robert Gunderson, *Old Gentlemen's Convention: The Washington Peace Conference of 1861* (Madison, Wisc., 1961), 100.

31. Chittenden, 468–9.

32. Barney, 198.

33. Summers, 292; David Meerse, "Buchanan, Corruption and the Election of 1860," *Civil War History* 12 (June 1966): 119.

34. John Nicolay and John Hay, *Abraham Lincoln: A History* (New York, 1890), 2:398–9.

35. Auchampaugh, 72–73.

36. Richardson, 8:3186–9.

37. At Fort Pickens off the coast of Pensacola, Florida, the power of federal forces forestalled an attack. When Jefferson Davis as president of the Confederacy encouraged attack, Bragg, the commanding officer, resisted, arguing the forces were too strong. Grady McWhiney, "The Confederacy's First Shot," *Civil War History* 14 (March 1968):5–14.

38. On the day the *Star of the West* sailed, an order to recall the ship was issued by the War Department with the president's approval, because Anderson had suggested that reinforcements be sent later at the government's convenience. But the order came too late to prevent the ship's departure. The countermanding order has occasioned additional criticism of Buchanan, although it signified no weakening of the administration's general determination to hold Sumter.

39. Dunbar Rowland, *Jefferson Davis, Constitutionalist: His Letters, Papers and Speeches* (Jackson, Miss., 1923), 5:205.

40. C. Vann Woodward, ed., *Mary Chesnut's Civil War* (New Haven, Conn., 1981), 3.

41. Alexander Stephens, *A Constitutional View of the Late War Between the States* (Philadelphia, 1868).

42. Marshall de Rosa, *The Confederate Constitution of 1861: An Inquiry into American Constitutionalism* (Columbia, S.C., 1981).

43. De Rosa, 121–2.

44. James Randall, *Constitutional Problems under Lincoln* (Urbana, Ill., 1951), 13ff.

45. Jefferson Davis, *Rise and Fall of the Confederate Government* (New York, 1881), 1:52; William Davis, *Jefferson Davis: The Man and His Hour* (New York, 1991), 283.

46. *Journal of the Congress of the Confederate States of America* (Washington, D.C., 1907), Senate Doc. 234, 58, 1:52–53, 103–5, 124.

## Chapter 7

1. Daniel Crofts, *Reluctant Confederates: Upper South Unionists in the Secession Crisis* (Chapel Hill, N.C., 1989), 215.

2. Roy P. Basler, et al., eds., *The Collected Works of Abraham Lincoln* (New Brunswick, N.J., 1953), 4:149–53. Hereafter cited as Lincoln, *Collected Works*.

3. Daniel Crofts, "A Reluctant Unionist: John A. Gilmer and Lincoln's Cabinet," *Civil War History*, 24 (September 1978): 225–49.

4. Lincoln, *Collected Works*, 4:262–71.

5. David Potter, *Lincoln and His Party in the Secession Crisis* (New Haven, Conn., 1942), 329. For the opposing view that Lincoln's inaugural meant a "rejection of compromise," which "might very well lead to conflict," and that the president "accepted that risk, and for that reason . . . took . . . enormous pains to absolve himself from the charge of aggression," see Kenneth Stampp, *And the War Came: The North and the Secession Crisis* (Baton Rouge, 1950), 209.

6. Arthur Cole, "Lincoln's Election: An Immediate Menace to Slavery in the States?" *American Historical Review* 36 (July 1931): 744; Crofts, *Reluctant Confederates*, 262, 268–9.

7. Crofts, *Reluctant Confederates*, 262.

8. *Congressional Globe*, 36th Cong., 2d Sess., 309; For a similar statement by Alexander Stephens on Democratic control of both House and Senate, see his *Constitutional View of the War between the States* (Chicago, 1868), 2: 282ff.

9. Henry Shanks, *The Secession Movement in Virginia, 1847–1861* (Richmond, 1934), 155–6.

10. John Letcher to J. D. Davidson, March 9, 1861, Davidson Papers, McCormick Library, Wheaton, Ill.

11. *Richmond Enquirer*, March 7, 1861.

12. David Y. Thomas, *Arkansas in War and Reconstruction, 1861–1874* (Little Rock, 1926), 62.

13. James Fertig, *The Secession and Reconstruction of Tennessee* (Chicago, 1898).

14. Mark Kruman, *Politics and Parties in North Carolina, 1836–1865* (Baton Rouge, 1983), 181.

15. Kruman, 212.

16. Joseph Sitterson, *The Secession Movement in North Carolina* (Chapel Hill, N.C., 1939), 196–7, 238–40.

17. Frank Moore, ed., *Rebellion Record* (New York, 1868), I: 18; see also Robert Underwood Johnson and Clarence Buel, eds., *Battles and Leaders of the Civil War* (New York, 1888), 1:33–39; on Twiggs, Jeanne Heidler, "Embarrassing Situation: David Twiggs and the Surrender of Union Forces in Texas, 1861," in *Lone Star Blue and Gray: Essays on Texas in the Civil War*, ed. Ralph Wooster (Austin, 1995), 93.

18. Crofts, *Reluctant Confederates*, 257–8.

19. Kenneth Stampp, *And the War Came: The North and the Secession Crisis, 1860–1861* (Baton Rouge, 1950), 205, 223, 226, 241, 245–6, 251, 156–7.

20. Joel Silbey, *A Respectable Minority: The Democratic Party in the Civil War Era, 1860–1868* (New York, 1977), 39–40, Robert Johannsen, *Stephen A. Douglas* (New York, 1973), 855; Philip Paludan, *"A People's Contest": The Union and the Civil War, 1861–1865* (New York, 1942), xviii–xxi; Howard Perkins, *Northern Editorials on Secession* (New York, 1942), 652.

21. Potter, 353; James G. Randall, *Lincoln, The President: Springfield to Gettysburg* (New York, 1945), 1:320; for the views of the Cabinet, Lincoln, *Collected Works*, 6:192–220.

22. *Annual Report, American Historical Association*, 1915, 211. See also testimony of John B. Baldwin, 39th Cong., 1st Sess., February 10, 1866, 102ff, 115ff, House Report No. 30, pt. 2; William Harris, "The Southern Unionist Critique of the Civil War," *Civil War History*, 31 (March 1985): 50–51. In *The Lincoln Nobody Knows* (New York, 1958, 121–2), Richard Current finds the story of Lincoln's negotiations with Virginia "questionable" and "casts doubt on the Lincoln version" of his willingness to surrender Sumter if he could keep Pickens. A new version of this incident appears in Crofts, *Reluctant Confederates*, 301–4.

23. Lincoln, *Collected Works*, 4:424–5. Not until April 6 did Lincoln learn that his order to reinforce Pickens had, through a misunderstanding of the local commander, not been executed. After new orders from the president, Pickens was reinforced on April 12 and remained in Union hands throughout the war.

24. Potter, 360.

25. Lincoln, *Collected Works*, 4:317.

26. Lincoln, *Collected Works*, 4:323. The execution of the Sumter plan was bungled. Orders issued through Secretary Welles of the Navy Department assigned a powerful warship, the *Powhatan*, to the Sumter expedition; but Seward put through an order, which the president signed without reading, transferring the *Powhatan* to another fleet intended for Pickens. When Lincoln overruled Seward, directing him to restore the ship to the Sumter expedition, Seward sent the new order in his own name. The commander of the *Powhatan* refused to obey it. Thus, the *Powhatan* did not sail with the Sumter expedition, and without it the expedition could not be successful.

27. Lincoln, *Collected Works*, 4:351.

28. Theodore Pease and James Randall, eds., *The Diary of Orville Browning* (Springfield, Ill., 1925), I: 476.

29. Charles Ramsdell, "Lincoln and Fort Sumter," *Journal of Southern History* 3 (August 1937): 259–88.

30. Grady McWhiney, "The Confederacy's First Shot," *Civil War History* 14 (March 1968): 14.

31. Richard Current, *Lincoln and the First Shot* (Philadelphia, 1963), 133–4; Current, "The Confederates and the First Shot," *Civil War History* 7 (December 1961): 356; Allan Nevins, *War for the Union* (New York, 1959), 1: 68.

32. Johnson and Buel, I: 75.

33. Johnson and Buel, I: 75.

34. Samuel Crawford, *History of the Fall of Fort Sumter* (New York, 1896), 425.

35. Current, *Lincoln and the First Shot*, 200.

36. Crofts, *Reluctant Confederates*, 164–94, 362–3.

37. James Woods, *Rebellion and Realignment: Arkansas' Road to Secession* (Fayetteville, 1987), 124–5.

38. Quoted in James Patton, *Unionism and Reconstruction in Tennessee, 1860–1869* (Chapel Hill, N.C., 1934), 14.

39. Fertig, 26–27.

40. Quoted in Joseph Sitterson, *The Secession Movement in North Carolina* (Chapel Hill, N.C., 1939), 196–7, 238–40.

41. Joseph Hamilton, ed., *Correspondence of Jonathan Worth* (Raleigh, N.C., 1909), 1:150–1.

42. *New York Times*, August 29, 1860.

43. Johannsen, 177.

44. Nevins, 1:35.

45. *Congressional Globe*, 36th Cong., 2d Sess., 1391. See also *ibid.*, 1460, 1503–5.

46. John Nicolay and John Hay, *Abraham Lincoln: A History* (New York, 1890), 4:80; Johannsen, 859.

47. Perkins, 729, 730.

## Chapter 8

1. Edward Conrad Smith, *The Borderland in the Civil War* (New York, 1927), 3n.

2. E. Merton Coulter, *The Civil War and Readjustment in Kentucky* (Gloucester, Mass., 1966), 7–8, 17.

3. Lowell Harrison, *The Civil War in Kentucky* (Lexington, Ky., 1975), 5.

4. Coulter, 41.

5. Harrison, 8, 9.

6. Coulter, 91.

7. C. N. Feamster, *Calendar of the Papers of John Jordan Crittenden* (Washington, 1913), 258.

8. Coulter, 54, 99–100.

9. Daniel Crofts, *Reluctant Confederates: Upper South Unionists in the Secession Crisis* (Chapel Hill, N.C., 1989), 355.

10. Crofts, 355.

11. Harry Volz, "Party, State and Nation: Kentucky and the Coming of the Civil War" (Ph.D. diss., University of Virginia, 1982), 439–68.

12. *War of the Rebellion . . . Official Records of the Union and Confederate Armies* (Washington, D.C., 1880–1901), 3rd ser., 4:1269; for Confederate figures, *ibid.*, 4th ser., 1:962.

13. Coulter, 139.

14. Coulter, 187.

15. John Pendleton Kennedy, *The Border States: Their Power and Duty in the Present Disordered Condition of the Country* (n.p., 1860).

16. Jean Baker, *The Politics of Continuity: Maryland Political Parties, 1858–1870* (Baltimore, 1973), 55–58.

17. William Evitts, *A Matter of Allegiances: Maryland from 1850 to 1861* (Baltimore, 1974), 176–82.

18. Frank Towers, "Secession in an Urban Context: Class and Politics in Baltimore, April 1861," *Maryland Historical Magazine* (forthcoming).

19. Baker, 58–62.

20. Baker, 70, 72.

21. Harold Hancock, "Civil War Comes to Delaware," *Civil War History* 2 (December 1956): 29–46.

22. Hancock, 40.

23. Hancock, 40.

24. Frank Moore, ed., *Rebellion Record* (New York, 1868), 1:155.

25. For a complete review of these complex events, see William Parrish, *Turbulent Partnership: Missouri and the Union, 1861–1865* (Columbia, Mo., 1963).

26. Michael Fellman, *Inside War: The Guerrilla Conflict in Missouri during the American Civil War* (New York, 1989), 23.

27. Richard S. Brownlee, *Gray Ghosts of the Confederacy: Guerrilla Warfare in the West, 1861–1865* (Baton Rouge, 1958), 10.

28. Albert Castel, *A Frontier State at War: Kansas, 1861–1865* (Ithaca, N.Y., 1958), 53.

29. Brownlee, 48; Fellman, 95.

30. Castel, 63, 131, 136.

31. Brownlee, 126.

32. Moore, 7:406.

33. For underlying causes see Charles Ambler, *Sectionalism in Virginia from 1776 to 1861* (New York, 1964); Richard Curry, *A House Divided: A Study of Statehood Politics and the Copperhead Movement in West Virginia* (Pittsburgh, 1964); also James G. Randall, *Constitutional Problems under Lincoln* (Urbana, Ill., 1964), 433–76.

34. Robert Underwood Johnson and Clarence Buel, *Battles and Leaders of the Civil War* (New York, 1868) 1:137.

35. *Congressional Globe*, 37th Cong., 3rd sess., 50–51.

36. Senator Willey wrote to Pierpoint on December 17, 1862: "We have great fears that the President will veto the new State bill." Pierpoint Papers, Virginia State Archives. Also Theodore Pease and James Randall, eds., *The Diary of Orville Browning* (Springfield, Ill., 1925), I: 596.

## Chapter 9

1. Joseph Glatthaar, *Partners in Command: The Relationships between Leaders in the Civil War* (New York, 1994), viii–ix.

2. For an analysis of this surprisingly high number, Dee Alexander Brown, *The Galvanized Yankees* (Urbana, Ill., 1963); Richard Current, *Lincoln's Loyalists: Union Soldiers from the Confederacy* (Boston, 1992).

3. Herman Hattaway, "The Civil War Armies: Creation, Mobilization and Development," in *On the Road to Total War: The American Civil War and the German Wars of Unification, 1861–1871,* eds. Stig Forster and Jorg Nagler (New York, 1997), 174.

4. Herman Hattaway and Archer Jones, *How the North Won: A Military History of the Civil War* (Urbana, Ill., 1980), 17.

5. Robert Underwood Johnson and Clarence Buel, *Battles and Leaders of the Civil War* (New York, 1888), I:222.

6. Thomas Livermore, *Numbers and Losses in the Civil War in America, 1861–1865* (Boston, 1901), 3.

7. Beauregard attributed the defeat of the South to the narrow military policy of the Confederate government, and its failure to attempt decisive strokes. Johnson and Buel, I: 22. For modern opinions on the subject, see David Donald, ed., *Why the North Won the Civil War* (New York, 1960); also Richard Beringer, et. al., *Why the South Lost the Civil War* (Athens, Ga., 1986), 440–2; Gabor Boritt, ed., *Why the Confederacy Lost* (New York, 1992).

8. Philip Paludan, *"A People's Contest": The Union and Civil War, 1861–1865* (New York, 1988), 18.

9. Richard Moe, *The Last Full Measure: The Life and Death of the First Minnesota Volunteers* (New York, 1993); James Robertson, *Soldiers Blue and Gray* (Columbia, S.C., 1988), 12.

10. Johnson and Buel, I:87.

11. Moe, 9.

12. Hattaway, "The Civil War Armies," 175. Johnson and Buel, I:7n; William Tecumseh Sherman, *Memoirs of General W. T. Sherman* (New York, 1892), 2:383. George Ness, *The Regular Army on the Eve of the Civil War* (Baltimore, 1990). The United States Army permitted its officers to resign with honorable discharges and enter Confederate service, which was a large factor in the military effectiveness of the South. The number of officers of the rank of brigadier general or higher who were furnished to the Confederacy from the army of the United States was 182. Emory Upton, *Military Policy of the United States* (Washington, D.C., 1917), 241.

13. Johnson and Buel, I:94.

14. Upton, 216–8.

15. Robertson, 19.

16. Edward Hagerman, *The American Civil War and the Origins of Modern Warfare* (Bloomington, Ind., 1988), x, xii.

17. Hagerman, xii.

18. Stephen Sears, *George B. McClellan: The Young Napoleon* (New York, 1988), 85.

19. *Wars of the Rebellion . . . Official Records of the Union and Confederate Armies* (Washington, D.C., 1880–1901), 1st Ser., 2:236. Hereafter cited as *Offic. Rec.*

20. Samuel S. Cox, *Three Decades of Federal Legislation, 1855–1885* (Providence, 1885), 158.

21. George McClellan, *McClellan's Own Story* (New York, 1887), 67–68.

22. Johnson and Buel, I:252.

23. Steven Woodworth, *Davis and Lee at War* (Lawrence, Kans., 1995), 2, 25–27.

24. Hudson Strode, *Jefferson Davis, Confederate President* (New York, 1959), 123–4. For the controversy on this subject, see *Offic. Rec.*, 1st Ser., 2:504ff.; Johnson and Buel, I:198ff.; Douglas Freeman, *Lee's Lieutenants: A Study in Command* (New York, 1944), 1:76–78; T. Harry Williams, *P.G.T. Beauregard: Napoleon in Gray* (Baton Rouge, 1956), 96–99; Gilbert Govan and James Livingood, *A Different Valor: The Story of Joseph Johnston* (Indianapolis, 1956), 59–60, 407; Craig Symonds, *Joseph E. Johnston: A Civil War Biography* (New York, 1992).

25. Hattaway and Jones, 68.

26. Johnson and Buel, 1:427; Ulysses S. Grant, *Personal Memoirs Of U.S. Grant* (New York, 1885), 1:311–2.

27. *New York Times*, February 17, 1862.

28. *Offic. Rec.*, 1st ser., 7:426–37.

29. Johnson and Buel, 1:485.

30. Hattaway and Jones, 169; Hagerman, 166–9.

31. Johnson and Buel, 1:487.

32. Grant, 1:342.

33. John C. Ropes, *The Story of the Civil War* (New York, 1933) 2:76; J. F. C. Fuller, *The Generalship of Ulysses S. Grant* (New York, 1981), 114.

34. William McFeely, *Grant: A Biography* (New York, 1981), 114.

35. Hattaway and Jones, 169–70.

36. Hattaway and Jones, 77.

37. *Offic. Rec.*, 1st Ser., 10: Pt. 1, 744–62.

## Chapter 10

1. "All Quiet along the Potomac" was a popular poem by Mrs. Ethelind Eliot Beers published in *Harpers* in November 1861.

2. Stephen Sears, "Lincoln and McClellan," in *Lincoln's Generals* ed. Gabor Boritt (New York, 1994), 19; T. Harry Williams, *Lincoln and His Generals* (New York, 1952), 25.

3. Joseph Glatthaar, *Partners in Command: The Relationships between Leaders in the Civil War* (New York, 1994).

4. Glatthaar, 53; Kenneth P. Williams, *Lincoln Finds a General* (Bloomington, 1949), 2:479.

5. Stephen Sears, *George B. McClellan: The Young Napoleon* (New York, 1988), xi.

6. Sears, *McClellan*, xi, 99.

7. Lord Charnwood, *Abraham Lincoln* (New York, 1916), 277.

8. Warren W. Hassler, *General George B. McClellan: Shield of the Union* (Westport, Conn., 1974), 115.

9. W. R. Thayer, *The Life and Letters of John Hay* (Boston, 1915), I:124.

10. Sears, *McClellan*, 104.

11. *War of the Rebellion . . . Official Records of the Union and Confederate Armies* (Washington, D.C., 1880–1901), 1st Ser., II: Pt. 3, 130. Hereafter cited as *Offic. Rec.* Sears, *McClellan*, 168.

12. Yorktown itself had strong defenses, but the Confederate fortified line from Yorktown across the peninsula to the James River had weak points. Sears, *McClellan*, 180.

13. Stephen Sears, *To The Gates of Richmond: The Peninsula Campaign* (New York, 1992), 279–89; 352–5; Williams, 1:231.

14. James Randall, *Lincoln the President* (New York, 1945), 2:97. After the war, Lee declared that McClellan could not have entered Richmond at this time because he [Lee] "had taken every precaution to prevent it . . . that it [Richmond] could not have been taken unless his own men had acted much worse than he had any reason to expect they would . . . and that he was much stronger then than when Grant was before Richmond, as then he had only 45,000 men." Theodore Pease and James Randall, eds., *The Diary of Orville Hickman Browning* (Springfield, Ill., 1925), 2:216-217. Also Emory Upton, *Military Policy of the U.S.* (Washington D.C., 1917), 312n.; Edward Hagerman, *The American Civil War and the Origins of Modern Warfare* (Bloomington, Ind., 1988), 49; Herman Hattaway and Archer Jones, *How the North Won: A Military History of the Civil War* (Urbana, Ill., 1983), 73.

15. Hagerman, 50; Byron Farwell, *Stonewall: A Biography of General Thomas J. Jackson* (New York, 1992). Over this decision to withhold McDowell's corps rages one of the great controversies of the Civil War. For opposing views see Hassler, 78–81; K. P. Williams, 1:159–60.

16. Hattaway and Jones, 187–8.

17. Robert Underwood Johnson and Clarence Buell, *Battles and Leaders of the Civil War* (New York, 1888), 2:220.

18. Douglas Freeman, *R. E. Lee* (New York, 1937), 1:414–5, 422–3, 439.

19. Alan Nolan, *Lee Considered: General Robert E. Lee and Civil War History* (Chapel Hill, N. C., 1991), 32–39.

20. Hagerman, 123; Thomas Connelly, *The Marble Man: Robert E. Lee and His Image in Contemporary Society* (New York, 1978); Hagerman, "Looking for the American Civil War: War, Myth, and Culture," *Armed Forces and Society,* 9 (Winter 1983): 341–7; Emory Thomas, *Robert E. Lee* (New York, 1995); Gary Gallagher, ed., *Lee The Soldier* (Lincoln, Neb., 1996); Joseph Harsh, *Confederate Tide Rising: Robert E. Lee and the Making of Southern Strategy, 1861–1862* (Kent, Ohio, 1998). Harsh argues that the aggressive offensive strategy was the Confederacy's only hope for victory and that victories on the battlefield would demoralize the North. See also Albert Castel, "The Historian and the General: Thomas Connelly and Robert E. Lee," in *Lee the Soldier,* ed. Gary Gallagher (Lincoln, Neb., 1996), 209–23.

21. Robert Krick, *Conquering the Valley: Stonewall Jackson at Port Republic* (New York, 1996), 493–6.

22. Steven Woodworth, *Davis and Lee at War* (Lawrence, Kans., 1995), 170.

23. Sears, *McClellan,* 218.

24. McClellan, 487; William Starr Myers, *General George Brinton McClellan* (New York, 1934), 306ff. The Harrison's Landing letter was for Lincoln's "private consideration" (Myers, 307). McClellan's letter has been bitterly attacked in K. P. Williams, 1: 249–50 and warmly defended in Randall, 2:101–4; Hassler, 177–8; Sears, "Lincoln and McClellan," 38.

25. Glatthaar, 81.

26. Most historians have been hostile to Halleck, quoting Lincoln's remark that the general proved to be little more than "a first-rate clerk." T. Harry Williams, *Lincoln and His Generals* (New York, 1952), 139. K. P. Williams, on the other hand, argues that Halleck was a leader who "was a devoted student of military art and science and of the laws of war; who had an exalted sense of duty; who straightened out great confusion in Missouri . . . who for many months held a position in Washington harder than any other General in Chief or Chief of Staff has had; and whose telegrams had an enviable clarity." K. P. Williams, 5: 282. Halleck found it difficult to survive in the political environment of Washington and declared that he wanted "to go back to private life as soon as possible and never again to put my foot in Washington." Hattaway and Jones, 240.

27. McClellan, 497.

28. David Donald, ed., *Inside Lincoln's Cabinet: The Civil War Diaries of Salmon P. Chase* (New York, 1934), 97.

29. Robert Krick, *Stonewall Jackson at Cedar Mountain* (Dayton, Ohio, 1991); Frank Vandiver, *Mighty Stonewall* (New York, 1957), 344; K. P. Williams, 1:301: Douglas Freeman, *Lee's Lieutenants* (New York, 1942), 2:43–46.

30. John Hennessy, *Return to Bull Run: The Campaign and Battle of Second Manassas* (New York, 1993), 458; also David Martin, *The Second Bull Run Campaign, July–August 1862* (New York, 1996).

31. The responsibility for McClellan's failure to support Pope is heatedly argued. On the one hand, it has been suggested that Pope, taking credit for himself, wanted to win the battle without McClellan's cooperation. On the other, it can be said that McClellan moved with even more than his customary slowness, that he spoke loftily of leaving Pope "to get out of his scrape" (*Offic. Rec.,* 1st ser., 12: 98), and that Lincoln thought McClellan "acted badly toward Pope" and "wanted him to fail." Tyler Dennett, ed., *Lincoln and the Civil War in the Diaries and Letters of John Hay* (Westport, Conn., 1972), 47.

32. Hattaway and Jones, 230.

33. Freeman, *Lee,* 2:343.

34. Johnson and Buell, 2:549–52.

35. Freeman, *Lee*, 2:357; Frank Moore, ed., *Rebellion Record* (New York, 1868), 5:75.

36. Hassler, 238.

37. Stephen Sears, *Landscape Turned Red: The Battle of Antietam* (New Haven, Conn., 1983), 127.

38. James Robertson, *General A. P. Hill: The Story of a Confederate Warrior* (New York, 1987), 136–8.

39. Robertson, 141.

40. Robertson, 327; for a higher Confederate estimate of 13,724 casualties, Herman Hattaway, *Shades of Blue and Gray* (New York, 1977).

41. Sears, *Landscape*, 342; Gary Gallagher, *Antietam: Essays on the 1862 Campaign* (Kent, Ohio, 1989), 56.

42. Hattaway and Jones, 244.

43. Frederick Maurice, *Robert E. Lee, the Soldier* (Boston, 1925), 115. See also Freeman, *Lee* 2:97ff.; *Johnson and Buell*, 2:271 ff.

44. Hagerman, 146.

45. Roy P. Basher et al., eds., *The Collected Works of Abraham Lincoln* (New Brunswick, N.J., 1953), 5:474. Hereafter cited as Lincoln, *Collected Works*.

46. McClellan, 648.

47. Glatthaar, 53.

48. Glatthaar, 89–90.

49. William Marvel, "The Making of a Myth: Ambrose Burnside and the Union High Command at Fredericksburg," in *The Fredericksburg Campaign*, ed. Gary Gallagher (Chapel Hill, 1995), 4–5.

50. Johnson and Buell, 3:78; Freeman, *Lee* 2:458. Referring to the impossibility of carrying the Fredericksburg position by direct assault, General Hooker, revisiting the scene after the war, said, "I never think of this ground but with a shudder." Johnson and Buell, 3:78, 215.

51. Richard Moe, *The Last Full Measure: The Life and Death of the First Minnesota Volunteers* (New York, 1993), 213.

52. Hattaway, 106–11.

53. Thomas Livermore, *Numbers and Losses in the Civil War in America, 1861–1865* (Boston, 1901) 96. These numbers probably refer to army aggregates before the battle. As to Lee, it has been estimated that his effective strength at Fredericksburg was about 58,500, and that fewer than 20,000 were "actively engaged." Johnson and Buell, 3:147.

54. Glatthaar, 31.

55. Lincoln, *Collected Works* 6: 31.

56. A. Wilson Greene, "Morale, Maneuver and Mud: The Army of the Potomac, December 16, 1862–January 26, 1863," in *The Fredericksburg Campaign*, ed. Gary Gallagher (Chapel Hill, N.C., 1995), 201.

57. Lincoln, *Collected Works*, 6: 78–79.

## Chapter 11

1. Fred Shannon, *The Organization and Administration of the Union Army* (Cleveland, 1928); Theodore Pease and James Randall, eds., *The Diary of Orville Hickman Browning* 1:487; Stephen Ambrose, *Halleck: Lincoln's Chief of Staff* (Baton Rouge, 1962), 102.

2. Philip Paludan, *"A People's Contest": The Union and Civil War, 1861–1865* (New York, 1988), 19.

3. James McPherson, *For Cause and Comrades: Why Men Fought in the Civil War* (New York, 1997), viii, 46, 114; McPherson, *What They Fought For, 1861–1865* (New York, 1995), 28.

4. James Geary, *We Need Men: The Union Draft in the Civil War* (DeKalb, Ill., 1991), 29.

5. Emory Upton, *The Military Policy of the United States* (Washington, D.C., 1917), 434, 436.

6. The regulations issued by the War Department under the president's authority for executing the Militia Act of 1862 prescribed the quotas of the states and called on the governors to fill them. If no state system of conscription existed, the regulations prescribed that designated state officials appointed by the governor, chiefly sheriffs and commissioners, were to make the enrollment, consider exemptions, and conduct the draft. Provost marshals in the states, appointed by the War Department acting on nominations by the governors, were to deal with disorder, enforce attendance, keep the men in service, and perform similar duties in this halfway stage on the way to conscription. *War of the Rebellion . . . Official Records of the Union and Confederate Armies* (Washington, D.C., 1880–1901), 3rd Ser., 2:291, 333–5. Hereafter cited as *Offic. Rec.* Richard Bensel, *Yankee Leviathan: The Origins of Central State Authority in America, 1859–1877* (New York, 1990), 122; James Randall, *Constitutional Problems under Lincoln* (Urbana, Ill., 1950), 252ff.

7. Robert Chamberlain, "The Northern State Militia," *Civil War History* 4 (June 1958): 197.

8. *Congressional Globe*, 37th Cong., 3rd sess., 976; Roy P. Basler, et al., eds. *The Collected Works of Abraham Lincoln* (New Brunswick, N.J., 1953), 6:370. Hereafter cited as Lincoln, *Collected Works*.

9. Edward Wright, *Conscientious Objectors in the Civil War* (Philadelphia, 1931), 165; Shannon, 2:255–6; Rufus Jones, ed., *The Record of a Quaker Conscience: Cyrus Pringle's Diary* (New York, 1918); Peter Brock, *Pacifism in the United States from the Colonial Era to the First World War* (Princeton, N.J., 1968), 751; Geary, 59–64.

10. Shannon, 2:106; *Offic. Rec.*, 3rd Ser., 5:613; Eugene Murdock, *One Million Men: The Civil War Draft in the North* (Westport, Conn., 1980), 8–11, 208–10.

11. Geary, 83.

12. Murdock, *One Million Men*, 160–3, 255, 357; Eugene Murdock, *Patriotism Limited, 1862–1865* (Kent, Ohio, 1967), 107.

13. James Barrett, "The Bounty Jumpers of Indiana," *Civil War History* 4 (December 1958): 431; Thomas R. Kemp, "Community and War: The Civil War Experience of Two New Hampshire Towns," *Toward a Social History of the Civil War,* ed. Maris Vinovskis (New York, 1990), 39; J. Matthew Gallman, *Mastering Wartime: A Social History of Philadelphia during the Civil War* (New York, 1990), 17–18.

14. Murdock, *One Million Men*, 340–1; *Offic. Rec.*. 3rd Ser., 5:720–30, *Second Report of the Provost Marshal General* (Washington, D.C., 1919), 376–7; Gallman, 17–18.

15. *Offic. Rec.*, 1st Ser., 23:Pt. 1, 395–7; 1st ser., 39:Pt. 2, 35; 43:Pt. 1, 973; Shannon, 2:175–243; William Hesseltine, *Lincoln and the War Governors* (New York, 1948), 280.

16. Lawrence Lader, "New York's Bloodiest Week," *American Heritage* 10 (June 1959): 44–49, 95–98; Robert Ernst, *Immigrant Life in New York City, 1825–1863* (Port Washington, N.Y., 1965), 291.

17. Stewart Mitchell, *Horatio Seymour of New York* (Cambridge, Mass., 1938), 330–4.

18. Iver Bernstein, *The New York City Draft Riots: Their Significance for American Society and Politics in the Age of the Civil War* (New York, 1990), 8.

19. James Geary, "Civil War Conscription in the North," *Civil War History* 32 (September 1986): 221; Kemp, 50.

20. Grace Palladino, *Another Civil War: Labor, Capital, and the State in the Anthracite Regions of Pennsylvania, 1840–1868* (Urbana, Ill., 1990), 8.

21. Geary, "Civil War Conscription in the North," 208–20; Murdock, *One Million Men*, 344; Vinovskis, 11. Any judgment on desertion necessarily involves the point of comparison. Ella Lonn describes a desertion rate of one in seven for the North and one in nine for the South—in all 200,000 for the North, 104,000 for the South. Ella Lonn, *Desertion during the Civil War* (Lawrence, Kans., 1998), 226.

22. A. Howard Meneely, *The War Department, 1861* (New York, 1928), 141.

23. David Tod to Edwin Stanton, January 28, 1862, Edwin Stanton Papers, Library of Congress, Washington, D.C.

24. Oliver Morton Correspondence, Indiana State Library, Indianapolis; Randall, 410 n.; Meneely, 150.

25. Randall, 426–7; 46th Cong., 2d sess., 1880, 6, 199, Sen. Ex. Doc. No. 74; *U.S. Statutes at Large* 12 (1861): 261, 276.

26. Meneely, 269–71.

27. Allan Nevins, *Frémont: Pathmaker of the West* (New York, 1955), 647.

28. Meneely, 263–5, 274, 275–6; Shannon, 1:64, 69, 120.

29. Herman Hattaway and Archer Jones, *How the North Won: A Military History of the Civil War* (Urbana, Ill., 1983), 90.

30. *Congressional Globe*, 37th Cong., 2d sess., 1888.

31. Geary, 7–8.

32. Benjamin P. Thomas and Harold Hyman, *Stanton: The Life and Times of Lincoln's Secretary of War* (Westport, Conn., 1962), 143.

33. Russell Weigley, *Quartermaster of the Army: Montgomery Meigs* (New York, 1977).

34. Bell Wiley, *Life of Billy Yank: The Common Soldier of the Civil War* (New York, 1971), 224, 238, 240; Reid Mitchell, *Civil War Soldiers: Their Expectations and Their Experiences* (New York, 1988), 142, 144.

35. *Shoddy* was the term used for a type of inexpensive wool steamed and pressed together. Gary Bunker and John Appel, "Shoddy, Anti-Semitism and the Civil War," *American Jewish History* 8 (1994): 43–71.

36. *Harper's Monthly Magazine* 29 (June 1864), 227–8.

37. Wiley, 60–61.

38. Robert Bruce, *Lincoln and the Tools of War* (Indianapolis, 1956), 99–100.

39. Robert Bruce, *The Launching of Modern American Science, 1846–1876* (New York, 1987), 307.

40. Shannon, 1:128–42.

41. James Robertson, *Soldiers Blue and Gray* (Columbia, S.C., 1988), 79.

42. *Offic. Rec.*, 3rd Ser., 5:109, 757–8. See also Shannon, 2:179 n., and, for a general treatment of the subject, Ella Lonn, *Desertion during the Civil War* (New York, 1928).

43. Thomas Livermore, *Number and Losses in the Civil War in America, 1861–1865* (Boston, 1901), 8, 47–48; Gary Gallagher, *The Confederate War* (Cambridge, Mass, 1997), 29; Frank Freeman, *Gangrene and Glory: Medical Care during the Civil War* (Madison, N.J., 1999).

44. Robertson, 135. This point of accelerating desertions is contested by Gary Gallagher, in *The Confederate War*, 30–32. Gallagher argues that the problem was not a linear one of increasing gravity, but rather was episodic. All observers can agree about the difficulty of counting it.

45. Randall Jimerson, *The Private Civil War: Popular Thought during the Sectional Conflict* (Baton Rouge , 1988), 232; Vinovskis, 10.

46. Lonn, 151; *New York Times*, December 2, 1862.

47. Lonn, 234.

48. Reid Mitchell, 182; Joseph Glatthaar, *The March to the Sea and Beyond: Sherman's Troops in the Savannah and Carolinas Campaigns* (New York, 1985), 190–3.

49. Hattaway and Jones, 43, 104–6.

50. Edward Hagerman, *The American Civil War and the Origins of Modern Warfare* (Bloomington Ind., 1988); xv–xvi.

51. John Eisenhower, *Agent of Destiny: The Life and Times of General Winfield Scott* (New York, 1997); Charles Elliott, *Winfield Scott: The Soldier and the Man* (New York, 1957), 735–6; George McClellan to Ellen McClellan, July 27, 1861, George McClellan Papers, Library of Congress, Washington, D.C.

52. Lincoln, *Collected Works* 5:155.

53. W. A. Croffut, ed., *Fifty Years in Camp and Field: The Diary of Major-General Ethan Allen Hitchcock* (New York, 1909), 437–43; James Randall, *Lincoln the President* (New York, 1945), 2: 84–85.

54. Upton, 289–93; Nathaniel Stephenson, *Abraham Lincoln and the Union* (New York, 1918), 233–4; Hattaway and Jones, 99, 101–5.

55. Lincoln, *Collected Works,* 5: 312–3.

56. T. Harry Williams, *Lincoln and His Generals* (New York, 1962), 301; Ambrose, 59–62.

57. Ambrose, 102–3.

58. K. P. Williams, *Lincoln Finds a General,* 5: 277; Hattaway and Jones, 119–24.

59. Lincoln, *Collected Works,* 7: 239.

60. Hattaway and Jones, 335.

61. William Hesseltine, *Civil War Prisons: A Study in War Psychology* (New York, 1964).

62. Hesseltine, 32–33.

63. Hesseltine, 76ff. A parole was a promise not to serve again until properly exchanged. A soldier wrote a pledge dictated to him and made two copies, one for himself to carry and one for the opposing officer. His name was entered on a parole list and a copy was sent to each side.

64. James McPherson, *Battle Cry of Freedom: The Civil War Era* (New York, 1988), 792; *Offic. Rec.* 2d, Ser., 5: 128.

65. Albert Castel, "The Fort Pillow Massacre," *Civil War History,* 4 (1958): 47–49; John Cimprich and Robert Mainfort, "Fort Pillow Revisited: New Evidence about an Old Controversy," *Civil War History* 28 (1982), 293–306.

66. *Offic. Rec.,* 2nd Ser., 7:52–63.

67. Reid Mitchell, "Our Prison System: Supposing We Had Any: The Confederate and Union Prison Systems," *On the Road to Total War: The American Civil War and the German Wars of Unification,* ed. Stig Forster and Jorg Nagler (New York, 1997), 565–85.

68. "Report of the Committee of Confederate Congress," in Edward A. Pollard, *The Lost Cause* (New York, 1866), 636–7.

69. Robert Eberly, "Prison Town," *Civil War Times Illustrated* 38 (March 1999): 30–4.

70. Bruce Catton, "Prison Camps of the Civil War," *American Heritage* 10 (August 1959): 8, 96.

71. T. Harry Williams, *Lincoln and the Radicals* (Madison, Wisc., 1941), 344–5; Pollard, 625.

## Chapter 12

1. E. Merton Coulter, *The Confederate States of America: 1861–1865* (Baton Rouge, 1950), 309.

2. *Journal of the Congress of the Confederate States of America* (Washington, D.C., 1909), 1:163–5, 168–9.

3. Randall Jimmerson, *The Private Civil War: Popular Thought during the Sectional Conflict* (Baton Rouge, 1988), 16.

4. Bell I. Wiley and Hirst Milhollen, *They Who Fought Here* (New York, 1959), 22–23.

5. Gary Gallagher, *The Confederate War* (Cambridge, Mass., 1997), 28–29.

6. Bell Wiley, *The Life of Johnny Reb: The Common Soldier of the Confederacy* (Indianapolis, 1943), 20.

7. Drew Faust, *Mothers of Invention: Women of the Slaveholding South in the American Civil War* (Chapel Hill, N.C., 1996), 15.

8. Faust, 13–14.

9. Gallagher, 63–101.

10. James Robertson, *Soldiers Blue and Gray* (Columbia, S.C., 1988), 10.

11. David Donald, "The Confederate as a Fighting Man," *Journal of Southern History* 25 (May 1959): 180.

12. *Appleton's American Annual Cyclopaedia* (New York, 1862), 243.

13. Coulter, 314–5.

14. Clement Eaton, *A History of the Southern Confederacy* (New York, 1954), 86.

15. Reid Mitchell, *Civil War Soldiers: Their Expectations and Experiences* (New York, 1988), 160.

16. Albert Moore, *Conscription and Conflict in the Confederacy* (New York, 1934), 356–7; for number of substitutes, Robertson, 38.

17. Robertson, 37–38.

18. Emory Thomas, *The Confederacy as a Revolutionary Experience* (Columbia, S.C., 1991).

19. John Robbins, "The Confederacy and the Writ of Habeas Corpus," *Georgia Historical Quarterly* 55 (Spring, 1971): 93–94.

20. Coulter, 200, 206.

21. Coulter, 207.

22. Eaton, 135.

23. Richard Beringer et. al., *Why The South Lost the Civil War* (Athens, Ga., 1986), 214.

24. Louise Hill, *State Socialism in the Confederate States of America* (Charlottesville, Va., 1936); Thomas, *The Confederacy as a Revolutionary Experience*; Raimondo Luraghi, *The Rise and Fall of the Plantation South* (New York, 1978).

25. Charles Ramsdell, "General Robert E. Lee's Horse Supply, 1862–1865," *American Historical Review* 35 (July 1930): 763, 775; Blake Magner, *Traveller and Company: Horses of Gettysburg* (Gettysburg, 1995).

26. Douglas Ball, *Financial Failure and Confederate Defeat* (Urbana, Ill., 1991), 20.

27. George Eggleston, *A Rebel's Recollections*, ed. David Donald, (Bloomington, 1959), 158–9.

28. Beringer et al., 9.

29. Charles Ramsdell, "The Confederate Government and the Railroads," *American Historical Review* 22 (July 1917): 795.

30. Robert C. Black, *The Railroads of the Confederacy* (Chapel Hill, N.C., 1952), 137.

31. Black, 63, 164.

32. Eugene Lerner, "The Monetary and Fiscal Programs of the Confederate Government, 1861–1865," *Journal of Political Economy* 62 (December 1954): 509.

33. Ball, 9, 239–41.

34. For precise statements of amounts raised by the Confederacy through taxes, loans, and paper money, see Richard C. Todd, *Confederate Finance* (Athens, Ga., 1954); John Schwab, *The Confederate States of America, 1861–1865* (New York, 1901), 287. For the Confederate budget, see Ball, 286.

35. For a careful summary of these and other provisions of this complicated legislation, see Todd, 140–1; James L. Nichols, "The Tax-in-Kind in the Department of the Trans-Mississippi," *Civil War History* 5 (December 1959): 388–9.

36. Edward Younger, ed., *Inside the Confederate Government: The Diary of Robert Garlick Hill Kean* (Baton Rouge, 1985), 41.

37. Coulter, 182.

38. Lerner, 520.

39. Rembert Patrick, *Jefferson Davis and His Cabinet* (Baton Rouge, 1994), 219–20.

40. Ball, 27–29; Judith Fenner Gentry, "A Confederate Success in Europe: The Erlanger Loan," *Journal of Southern History* 36 (May 1970): 155–9.

41. Schwab, 36.

42. Todd, 84; Lerner, 507.

43. Patrick, 224.

44. Coulter, 154.

45. Todd, 120; Schwab, 172.

46. Ralph L. Andreano, "A Theory of Confederate Finance," *Civil War History* 11 (December 1965): 27; Patrick, 243.

47. Eugene Lerner, "Money, Prices, and Wages in the Confederacy, 1861–65," *Journal of Political Economy* 63 (February 1955): 23–24; Lerner, 522.

48. Gordon Wright, "Economic Conditions in the Confederacy as Seen by the French Consuls," *Journal of Southern History* 7 (May 1941): 211.

49. Younger, 108.

50. John B. Jones, *A Rebel War Clerk's Diary* (Philadelphia, 1866), 2: 212.

51. Albert Kirwan, *The Confederacy* (New York, 1970), 138.

52. Faust, 88.

53. Lerner, 33.

54. Georgia Tatum, *Disloyalty in the Confederacy* (New York, 1970), 94.

55. Charles Ramsdell, *Behind the Confederate Lines* (New York, 1969), 62–68; Paul Escott, "The Cry of the Sufferers: The Problem of Welfare in the Confederacy," *Civil War History* (September 1977): 228–40.

56. Paul Escott, *After Secession: Jefferson Davis and the Failure of Confederate Nationalism* (Baton Rouge, 1978), 160; Escott, "The Cry of the Sufferers," 228–40.

57. Ramsdell, 46.

58. Faust, 32. For the opposing position, Gallagher, 162–3.

59. Joan Cashin, "Into the Trackless Wilderness: The Refugee Experience in the Civil War," in *A Woman's War: Southern Women, Civil War, and The Confederate Legacy,* eds. Edward Campbell and Kim Rice (Richmond, 1996), 29–53.

60. Drew Faust, "Confederate Women and the Narratives of War," *Journal of American History* (March 1990): 1206, 1224; George Rable, *Civil Wars: Women and the Crisis of Southern Nationalism* (Urbana, Ill., 1989), 84; Faust, *Mothers of Invention*, 243–8.

61. Stephen Ash, *When the Invaders Came: Conflict and Chaos in the Occupied South, 1861–1865* (Chapel Hill, N.C., 1996), 42.

62. Hugh Bailey, "Disloyalty in Early Confederate Alabama," *Journal of Southern History* 23 (November 1957): 525.

63. Claude Elliott, "Union Sentiment in Texas, 1861–1865," *Southwestern Historical Quarterly* 50 (April 1947): 450.

64. Tatum, 89.

65. Mark Kruman, "Dissent in the Confederacy: The North Carolina Experience," *Civil War History* 17 (December 1981): 297–99.

66. Albert B. Moore, *Conscription and Conflict in the Confederacy* (New York, 1924), 20–21.

67. Henry Shanks, "Disloyalty to the Confederacy in Southwestern Virginia, 1861–1865," *North Carolina Historical Review* 21 (April 1944): 123.

68. Thomas Bryan, *Confederate Georgia* (Athens, Ga., 1953), 155.

69. Tatum, 124.

70. Ted Worley, "The Arkansas Peace Society of 1861: A Study in Mountain Unionism," *Journal of Southern History* 24 (November 1958): 454; Frank Owsley, "Defeatism in the Confederacy," *North Carolina Historical Review* 3 (April 1926): 445–6.

71. Horace Raper, "William W. Holden and the Peace Movement in North Carolina," *North Carolina Historical Review* 31 (October 1954): 507; Edgar Folk, *W. W. Holden: A Political Biography* (Winston-Salem, N.C., 1982).

72. Frank Klingberg, *The Southern Claims Commission* (Berkeley, 1955), 17–19.

73. Beringer et. al, 203–53.

74. A. D. Candler, ed. *Confederate Records of the State of Georgia* (Atlanta, 1966), 2: 19–21, 24ff., 107, 114.

75. Beringer, 286–7.

76. Louise Hill, "Governor Brown and the Confederacy," *Georgia Historical Quarterly* 21 (December 1937): 346–7; Candler, 3:245; Bryan, 87; Louise Hill, *Joseph E. Brown and the Confederacy* (Westport, Conn., 1972), 96.

77. Raper, 508.

78. Richard Yates, "Zebulon B. Vance as War Governor of North Carolina, 1862–1865," *Journal of Southern History* 3 (February 1937): 59; Coulter, 389 n.

79. Beringer et. al., 28, 231–3.

80. Candler, 2:305–6; Mark Neely, *Southern Rights and the Myth of Southern Constitutionalism* (Charlottesville,Va., 1999).

81. Frank Owsley, *State Rights in the Confederacy* (Gloucester, Mass., 1925), 180–1, 190–1.

82. Beringer et al., 286.

83. Coulter, 374–5; James Z. Rabun, "Alexander H. Stephens and Jefferson Davis," *American Historical Review* 58 (January, 1953), 307; Rosser H. Taylor, ed., "Boyce-Hammond Correspondence," *Journal of Southern History* 3 (August 1937): 354.

84. Younger, 100.

85. Joseph Durkin, *Confederate Navy Chief: Stephen R. Mallory* (Columbia, S.C., 1987), 176.

86. Frank Vandiver, *Rebel Brass: The Confederate Command System* (Baton Rouge, 1956), 26–27.

87. Drew Faust, *The Creation of Southern Nationalism: Ideology and Identity in the Civil War South* (Baton Rouge, 1988), 17.

88. Durkin, 179.

89. Bell Wiley, *The Road to Appomattox* (New York, 1956), 28.

90. Escott, *After Secession,* 269–72.

91. Patrick, 178.

92. William C. Davis, *Jefferson Davis* (New York, 1991), 482–6; Hudson Strode, *Jefferson Davis: Confederate President,* 350.

93. Frank Vandiver, "Jefferson Davis and Confederate Strategy," in Avery Craven, *The American Tragedy: The Civil War in Retrospect* (Hampden-Sydney, Va., 1959), 20.

94. Wiley, 10.

## Chapter 13

1. Michael Holt, "Abraham Lincoln and the Politics of Union," in *Political Parties and American Political Development*, ed. Michael Holt (New York, 1992), 323–53.

2. James Randall, *Constitutional Problems under Lincoln* (Bloomington, Ind., 1950), 49–50.

3. Roy P. Basler et al., eds., *The Collected Works of Abraham Lincoln* (New Brunswick, N.J., 1953), 4:429. Hereafter referred to as Lincoln, *Collected Works.*

4. Lincoln, *Collected Works,* 5:242.

5. Charles Warren, *The Supreme Court in United States History* (Boston, 1937), 2:382.

6. Prize Cases, 67 U.S. 635; Stuart Bernath, *Squall across the Atlantic: The American Civil War Prize Cases and Diplomacy* (Berkeley, 1970).

7. Allan Bogue, *The Earnest Men: Republicans of the Civil War Senate* (Ithaca, N.Y., 1981), 39; Allan Bogue, "The Radical Voting Dimension in the U.S. Senate During the Civil War," *Journal of Interdisciplinary History* 3 (Winter 1973): 449–74; Glenn Linden, "Radicals and Economic Policies, The Senate, 1861–1873," *Journal of Southern History* 32 (May 1966): 189–99.

8. Frank Heck, "John C. Breckinridge in the Crisis of 1860–1861," *Journal of Southern History* 21 (August 1955): 316–46.

9. William C. Davis, *Breckinridge: Statesman, Soldier, Symbol* (Baton Rouge, 1992).

10. Hans Trefousse, *Andrew Johnson: A Biography* (New York, 1989), 1, 51–2, 109–25.

11. Lincoln, *Collected Works*, 4:438–439, 426.

12. *U.S. Statutes at Large* 12 (1861): 326.

13. *U.S. Statutes at Large* 12 (1861): 255.

14. *Congressional Globe*, 37th Cong., 1st Sess., 222–3. (A similar resolution also passed the Senate on July 25.)

15. C. Vann Woodward, "Equality: America's Deferred Commitment," *American Scholar* 27 (Winter 1958): 460.

16. Hans L. Trefousse, "The Joint Committee on the Conduct of the War: A Reassessment," *Civil War History* 10 (March 1964): 5–19; Bruce Tap, *Over Lincoln's Shoulder: The Committee on the Conduct of the War* (Lawrence, 1998).

17. William Pierson, "The Committee on the Conduct of the Civil War," *American Historical Review* 23 (April 1918): 575–76.

18. Trefousse, "The Joint Committee," 8.

19. T. Harry Williams, "Investigation: 1862," *American Heritage* 6 (December 1954): 17–21.

20. Leonard Curry, *Blueprint for America: Nonmilitary Legislation of the First Civil War Congress* (Nashville, 1968) 244; on economic legislation, Heather Cox Richardson, *The Greatest Nation on Earth: Republican Economic Policies During the Civil War* (Cambridge, Mass., 1997).

21. *Congressional Globe*, 37th Cong., 1st Sess. (1861), 415.

22. Lincoln, *Collected Works*, 6: 328–31.

23. Lincoln, *Collected Works*, 4: 438.

24. Reinhard H. Luthin, "Abraham Lincoln and the Tariff," *American Historical Review* 49 (July 1944): 622.

25. *House Report No. 78*, 42nd Cong., 3rd Sess., Pt. I, 1.

26. Philip Paludan, *"A People's Contest": The Union and the Civil War, 1861–1865* (New York, 1988), 137.

27. *Nebraska City People's Press*, September 20, 1860.

28. Richardson, 208.

29. Paul Gates, *History of Public Land Law Development* (Washington D.C., 1968), 393–9; Paludan, 134–5.

30. Paludan, 132.

31. Stanley Engerman and J. Matthew Gallman, "The Civil War Economy: A Modern View," in *Toward A Total War*, eds. Stig Forster and Jorg Nagler (New York, 1997), 220.

32. James McPherson, *Battle Cry of Freedom* (New York, 1988), 450.

33. Report of the Secretary of the Interior, House Ex. Doc., 39th Cong., 1st Sess., 1865, xii, 1; McPherson, 450.

34. Frank Klement, "Middle Western Copperheadism and the Genesis of the Granger Movement," *Mississippi Valley Historical Review* 37 (March 1952): 679–94.

35. Frank Klement, *The Copperheads in the Middle West* (Chicago, 1960), 202, 205. But see also David Long, "I Say We Can Control That Election: Confederate Policy Toward the 1864 Election," *Lincoln Herald* (Fall 1997): 111–27.

36. Mark Neely, *The Fate Of Liberty: Abraham Lincoln and Civil Liberties* (New York, 1991), 128, 131, 233.

37. Randall, 176ff.

38. James Vallandigham, *Life of Clement L. Vallandigham* (Baltimore, 1872), 277ff.

39. Jean Baker, *Affairs of Party: The Political Culture of Northern Democrats in the Mid-Nineteenth Century* (New York, 1997), 158–65.

40. Lincoln, *Collected Works*, 6: 237.

41. Joseph George, "Military Trials of Civilians under the Habeas Corpus Act of 1863," *Lincoln Herald* 98 (Winter 1996): 126–39.

42. *Ex parte Vallandigham*, 1 Wall. 243 (1864).

43. *Ex parte Milligan*, 4 Wall. 2 (1866).

44. Neely, 184; Warren, 2:427.

45. Lincoln, *Collected Works*, 6:260–9, 300–6.

46. Randall, 120–7.

47. *U. S. Statutes at Large* 12 (1863): 755.

48. John A. Marshall, *American Bastile: A History of the Illegal Arrests and Imprisonments during the Late Civil War* (Philadelphia, 1869).

49. Richard Franklin Bensel, *Yankee Leviathan: The Origins of Central State Authority* (New York, 1990), x.

50. Lincoln, *Collected Works*, 6:492.

## Chapter 14

1. Stanley Engerman and J. Matthew Gallman, "The Civil War Economy: A Modern View," in *On the Road to Total War*, ed. Stig Forster and Jorg Nagler (New York, 1997), 220. The question of whether the Civil War retarded or advanced the American economy will be addressed in the chapters on Reconstruction.

2. Robert Stanley, *Dimensions of Law in the Service of Order: The Origins of the Federal Income Tax, 1861–1913* (New York, 1993), 23, 273 n. 27.

3. Paul Studenski and Herman E. Krooss, *Financial History of the United States: Fiscal, Monetary, Banking and Tariff* (New York, 1952), 137.

4. Richard Bensel, *Yankee Leviathan: The Origins of Central State Authority in America, 1859–1877* (New York, 1990), 241.

5. Davis R. Dewey, *Financial History of the United States* (New York, 1936), 299.

6. The rate of 7.3 percent was adopted for convenience. On a one-hundred-dollar note the interest was two cents a day.

7. On July 1, 1861, the public debt of the United States stood at $90 million. Report of the Secretary of the Treasury, 39th Cong., 1st Sess., 1865, 253 House Ex. Doc. 3; Dewey, 299.

8. Robert T. Patterson, "Government Finance on the Eve of the Civil War," *Journal of Economic History* 12 (Winter 1952): 43–44.

9. Heather Cox Richardson, *The Greatest Nation of the Earth: Republican Economic Policies During the Civil War* (Cambridge, Mass., 1997), 66.

10. Bray Hammond, *Sovereignty and an Empty Purse: Banks and Politics in the Civil War* (Princeton, N.J., 1970), 60–63; John Niven, *Salmon Chase* (New York, 1995), 264–6.

11. Frederick Blue, *Salmon P. Chase: A Life in Politics* (Columbus, 1957), 154, 155.

12. Hammond, 61.

13. There was a six-hundred-dollar exemption, the amount of the excess above six hundred dollars being taxed at 3 percent. *U.S. Statutes at Large*, 12 (1861): 309; Stanley, 17–22.

14. *U.S. Statutes at Large*, 13 (1864): 223, 281; Leonard Curry, *Blueprint for Modern America: Nonmilitary Legislation of the First Civil War Congress* (Nashville, 1968), 157–8; Richardson, *The Greatest Nation*, 129.

15. James D. Richardson, ed., *A Compilation of the Messages and Papers of the Presidents, 1787–1897* (Washington, D.C., 1896), 10:415.

16. Bensel, 169.

17. Curry, 179.

18. Report of the Secretary of the Treasury, 39th Cong., 1st Sess., 1865, 18, House Ex. Doc. 3.

19. While the legal tender bill was pending in Congress, Chase was consulting with bankers, and a "plan" was worked out involving some of the features of the later national banking system but avoiding the necessity of making the United States notes legal tender. Chase's conferences with the

bankers are of interest as showing that he may have been seeking to avert the Legal Tender Act, whereas the slight attention of the lawmakers to the treasury's efforts is illustrative of that poor coordination between the legislative and executive branches that has often characterized the American system of government.

20. Niven, 332.

21. Bensel, 152.

22. Engerman and Gallman, 217–29.

23. Horace White, *Money and Banking*, 5th ed. (Boston, 1911), 126–7.

24. *U.S. Statutes at Large*, 13 (1864): 132–3.

25. Dewey, 296–7.

26. Richardson, *The Greatest Nation*, 96–7.

27. Report of the Secretary of the Treasury, 38th Cong., 2d Sess., 1864, 52–53, House Exec. Doc. 3.

28. George Opdyke to Salmon Chase, December 14, 1862, Salmon P. Chase Papers, Library of Congress, Washington, D.C.

29. Richardson, *The Greatest Nation*, 87.

30. Robert Sharkey, *Money, Class, and Party: An Economic Study of Civil War and Reconstruction* (Baltimore, 1975), 226–7; Bensel, 263. National banknotes were redeemable in greenbacks, which were legal tender save for import duties and bond interest. Because they could redeem banknotes (but not vice versa) greenbacks could satisfy the legal reserve requirements of the national banks.

31. Act of March 3, 1865, to become effective July 1, 1866, *U.S. Statutes at Large*, 13 (1865): 484.

32. Sharkey, 229–31.

33. Bensel, 272.

34. George LaVerne Anderson, "The National Banking System, 1865–1875: A Sectional Institution" (Ph D. dissertation, University of Illinois, 1933), 3–35; Anderson, "Western Attitudes toward National Banks, 1873–1874," *Mississippi Valley Historical Review* 23 (September 1936): 205–16.

35. For a critical evaluation of Chase, see Hammond, 348–51. On insider information, Niven, 353–8.

36. Sidney Ratner, *American Taxation: Its History as a Social Force in Democracy* (New York, 1942), 68.

37. Curry, 162; Broadus Mitchell, *A History of the Greenbacks* (Chicago, 1963), 419.

38. David Donald, *Inside Lincoln's Cabinet: The Civil War Diaries of Salmon Chase* (New York, 1954), 35–36; Bensel, 277–9.

39. Niven, 449.

40. Engerman and Gallman, 241–2.

41. Marshall A. Robinson, "Federal Debt Management: Civil War, World War I, and World War II," *American Economic Review* 45 (May 1955): 389; for the costs of the war, Claudia Goldin and Frank Lewis, "The Economic Costs of the American Civil War: Estimates and Implications," *Journal of Economic History* 35 (June 1975): 299–327.

42. Milton Friedman, "Price, Income, and Monetary Changes in Three Wartime Periods," *American Economic Review* 42 (May 1952): 614.

43. Douglas Ball, *Financial Failure and Confederate Defeat* (Urbana, Ill., 1991), 261–8.

44. Richardson, *The Greatest Nation*, 90.

## Chapter 15

1. Howard Jones, *The Union in Peril; The Crisis over British Intervention in the Civil War* (Chapel Hill, 1992).

2. *The History of the [London] Times* (London, 1984), 2:359.

3. John Mason, Marquis of Lothian, to Earl Russell, July 21, 1862, *Official Records of the Union and Confederate Navy in the War of the Rebellion* (Washington D.C., 1894), 2d ser., 3:500. Hereafter cited as *Official Records (Navy)*.

4. Belle B. Sideman and Lillian Friedman, *Europe Looks at the Civil War* (New York, 1960), 22.

5. Worthington C. Ford, ed., *A Cycle of Adams Letters, 1861–1865* (Boston, 1920), 1:220.

6. James Randall, *Lincoln the Liberal Statesman* (New York, 1947), 237 n. 1.

7. J. R. Pole, *Abraham Lincoln and the Working Classes of Britain* (London, 1959), 15.

8. Mary Ellison, *Support for Secession: Lancashire and the American Civil War* (Chicago, 1972), 11.

9. Duke of Argyll to William Ewart Gladstone, August 23, 1861, Gladstone Papers, British Museum.

10. James Randall, *Lincoln the President* (New York, 1945), 2:32.

11. Thurlow Weed to Archbishop John Hughes, December 22, 1861, Seward Papers, University of Rochester Library.

12. Eugene Berwanger, *The British Foreign Service and the American Civil War* (Lexington, Ky., 1994).

13. *Official Records (Navy)*, 2d ser., 3:191–5. Treaties then in force between the United States and Great Britain were to be assumed as also existing between the Confederacy and Britain, with one exception. The Confederacy, though prohibiting the African slave trade, would not assist other countries in promoting that object, as was provided by the Webster-Ashburton treaty.

14. Ford, *Adams*, 1:ix; Charles Francis Adams, *Charles Francis Adams* (Boston, 1900), 126, 145.

15. Ephraim D. Adams, *Great Britain and the American Civil War* (New York, 1925), 1:126; Frederic Bancroft, *The Life of William H. Seward* (Gloucester, Mass., 1967), 2:169ff.

16. C. F. Adams, 197–8.

17. Frank Owsley, *King Cotton Diplomacy: Foreign Relations of the Confederate States of America* (Chicago, 1931), 52.

18. *Official Records (Navy)*, 2d Ser., 3, 296, 484; Gordon Warren, *Fountain of Discontent: The Trent Affair and the Freedom of the Seas* (Boston, 1981), 10.

19. John B. Moore, *The Principles of American Diplomacy* (New York, 1918), 114–5.

20. E. D. Adams, 1:212.

21. Sideman and Friedman, 101.

22. Allan Nevins, *The War for the Union* (New York, 1959), 1:388.

23. Gordon Warren, "Imperial Dreamer: William Henry Seward and American Destiny," *Makers of American Diplomacy*, eds. Frank Merli and Theodore Wilson (New York, 1974), 104.

24. Ford, I:76, 81, 83.

25. Warren, 219. Warren disputes the importance of two weeks of delayed communication.

26. Howard Beale, ed., *The Diary of Edward Bates, 1859–1866* (New York, 1971), 216.

27. Bancroft, *Seward*, 2:241–424; Alfred Chandler, "Du Pont, Dahlgren, and the Civil War Nitre Shortage," *Military Analysis of the Civil War* (New York, 1977), 201–2.

28. E. D. Adams, 1:234.

29. Ford, 1:93, 99.

30. Norman Ferris, *The Trent Affair: A Diplomatic Crisis* (Knoxville, 1977), 203.

31. Jones, 98.

32. Eli Evans, *Judah P. Benjamin: The Jewish Confederate* (New York, 1991), 116.

33. Robert Browning, *From Cape Charles to Cape Fear: The North Atlantic Blockading Squadron during the Civil War* (Tuscaloosa, Ala., 1995), 251.

34. Frank and Harriet Owsley, *King Cotton Diplomacy: Foreign Relations of the Confederate States of America* (Chicago, 1959), 137, 142, 145.

35. Daniel Crook, *Diplomacy during the American Civil War* (New York, 1975), 72–77.

36. Crook, 147.

37. L. B. Schmidt, "The Influence of Wheat and Cotton on Anglo-American Relations during the Civil War," *Iowa Journal of History and Politics* 16 (July 1918), 400, 431, 435, 439.

38. Sideman and Friedman, 175.

39. E. D. Adams, 2:38.

40. C. F. Adams, 280.

41. E. D. Adams, 2:73, 54–55.

42. *Official Records* (*Navy*), 2d Ser., 3:587.

43. Jones, 228.

44. *Official Records* (*Navy*), 1st Ser., 1:754.

45. C. F. Adams, 316, 321.

46. Papers relating to foreign affairs, 38th Cong., 1st Sess., 1863, pt. 1, 243–4, House Exec. Doc. 1.

47. E. D. Adams, 2:136–7.

48. Papers relating to foreign affairs, 38th Cong., 1st Sess., 1863, pt.1, 418, House Exec. Doc. 1.

49. Brian Jenkins, *Britain and the War for Union* (Montreal, 1970), 2:313.

50. Norman Graebner, "Northern Diplomacy and European Neutrality," in *Why the North Won the Civil War*, ed. David Donald (Baton Rouge, 1960), 55–78.

51. Lynn Case and Warren F. Spencer, *The United States and France: Civil War Diplomacy* (Philadelphia, 1970), 59; Norman Ferris, *Desperate Diplomacy: William H. Seward's Foreign Policy, 1861* (Knoxville, 1976), 11.

52. Lynne Case, ed., *French Opinion on the United States and Mexico: Extracts from the Reports of the Proceureurs Generaux* (New York, 1936), 257–8, 498–9.

53. Sideman and Friedman, 211.

54. House Executive Document 1; Papers relating to foreign affairs, 38th Congress, 1st session, 1863, 781–3; Case and Spencer, 427–80.

## Chapter 16

1. Roy P. Basler et al., eds., *The Collected Works of Abraham Lincoln* (New Brunswick, N.J., 1953), 4:250. Hereafter cited as Lincoln, *Collected Works*.

2. William McFeely, *Frederick Douglass* (New York, 1991), 212; *Douglass Monthly*, July 1861.

3. Ira Berlin, "The Destruction of Slavery," in *Freedom: A Documentary History of Emancipation*, ed. Ira Berlin et al. (New York, 1985), Ser. 1, 1:2.

4. The term *contraband*, as applied to slaves captured by Union military forces and as a slang word to African Americans generally, has been traced to Butler, who had declared that " 'contraband' [referring to illicit goods] was the ground upon which I refuse to release the slaves." In correspondence at the time, however, the word *contraband* did not occur. Benjamin F. Butler, *Autobiography and Personal Memoirs of Major-General Benjamin F. Butler: Butler's Book* (Boston, 1892), Ch. vi; John Nicolay and John Hay, *Abraham Lincoln: A History* (New York, 1890), 4: 387–9; Chester Hearn, *When the Devil Came to Dixie: Ben Butler in New Orleans* (Baton Rouge, 1997); Berlin, "The Destruction of Slavery," 15–16, 72.

5. Michael Fellman, *Inside War: The Guerrilla Conflict in Missouri during the American Civil War* (New York, 1989), 67; James McPherson, *For Cause and Comrade: Why Men Fought in the Civil War* (New York, 1997), 126.

6. Lincoln, *Collected Works*, 6:532.

7. Lincoln, *Collected Works*, 5:222; Edward Miller, *Lincoln's Abolitionist General: The Biography of David Hunter* (Columbia, S.C., 1997).

8. In the Confiscation Act of 1862 no procedure was specified by which emancipation was to be accomplished, the confiscating sections of the act (providing for the "sale of property") being obviously inapplicable to slaves who were to be freed. James Randall, *Constitutional Problems under Lin-*

*coln* (Urbana, Ill., 1951), 357–64; Herman Belz, *Emancipation and Equal Rights: Politics and Constitutionalism in the Civil War Era* (New York, 1978), 36; Herman Belz, *A New Birth of Freedom: The Republican Party and Freedmen's Rights, 1861–1866*, (Westport, Conn., 1976).

9. Belz, *Emancipation*, 26, 28.

10. House Report No. 262, 43nd Cong., 1st Sess., 6ff.

11. Lincoln, *Collected Works*, 5:371–2.

12. Richard Current, *The Lincoln Nobody Knows* (New York, 1963), 221–2.

13. In the heated partisanship of the time, some thought that proponents of the emancipation measure had plotted "to 'put one over' on the people of Delaware." H. Clay Reed, "Lincoln's Compensated Emancipation Plan and Its Relation to Delaware," *Delaware Notes*, seventh series (Newark, Del., 1931), 44; William Williams, *Slavery and Freedom in Delaware, 1839–1865* (Wilmington, 1996); Patience Essah, *A House Divided: Slavery and Emancipation in Delaware, 1638–1865* (Charlottesville, Va., 1996).

14. Lincoln, *Collected Works*, 5:160.

15. Lincoln, *Collected Works*, 5:145, 160.

16. Nicolay and Hay, 5:213.

17. David Herbert Donald, *Lincoln* (New York, 1995), 396.

18. Lincoln, *Collected Works*, 5:420.

19. Lincoln, *Collected Works*, 5: 48–49, 388–9.

20. Current, 225–6.

21. John Nicolay and John Hay, eds., *Abraham Lincoln: Complete Works* (New York, 1890), 2: 479; Lincoln, *Collected Works*, 5:148–56.

22. New York *World*, January 7, 1863.

23. Frederic Bancroft, *Seward* (Gloucester, Mass., 1967), 2:339.

24. Earl Russell to Lord Lyons, January 17, 1863, in Henry Wheaton, *Elements of International Law*, ed. William Lawrence (London: 1863), suppl., 37.

25. Lynn M. Case, *French Opinion on the United States and Mexico, 1860–1867* (New York, 1936); George Blackburn, *French Newspaper Opinion in the Civil War* (Westport, Conn., 1997).

26. Quincy *Whig*, November 10, 1862; Jean H. Baker, *Affairs Of Party: The Political Culture of Northern Democrats in the Mid-Nineteenth Century* (Ithaca, N.Y. 1983), 181–93; Joel Silbey, *A Respectable Minority: The Democratic Party in the Civil War Era, 1860–1868* (New York, 1977), 101–2.

27. Ira Berlin, "The Destruction of Slavery," 300–1; Richard Sewell, *A House Divided: Sectionalism and the Civil War, 1848–1865* (Baltimore, 1988), 169; James McPherson, *The Negro's Civil War: How American Blacks Felt and Acted during the War for the Union* (Urbana, Ill., 1982), 50, 61; Vincent Harding, *There Is a River* (New York, 1981), 236; McFeely, 215–6.

28. Lincoln, *Collected Works*, 6:408, 428–9, 7:281; Donald, 377.

29. James McPherson, *Abraham Lincoln and the Second American Revolution* (New York, 1990), 34.

30. Lincoln, *Collected Works*, 8:333.

31. *Congressional Globe*, 38th Cong., 1st Sess, 20, 3460; *Congressional Globe*, 37th Cong., 3rd Sess., 77, 92; Berlin, "The Destruction of Slavery," 36.

32. Ira Berlin, et al., *Slaves No More* (New York, 1992), 46.

33. Ira Berlin, "The Destruction of Slavery," 300–1.

34. Barbara Fields, *Slavery and Freedom on the Middle Ground: Maryland during the Nineteenth Century* (New Haven, Conn., 1988), 119.

35. Berlin, "The Destruction of Slavery," 314–5.

36. Bell Wiley, *Southern Negroes, 1861–1865* (Baton Rouge, 1953), 73–75, 77, 82–83; Elizabeth Fox-Genovese, *Within the Plantation Household: Black and White Women of the Old South* (Chapel Hill, N.C., 1988), 219.

37. Randolph Campbell, *An Empire For Slavery: The Peculiar Institution in Texas, 1821–1865* (Baton Rouge, 1989), 231–51.

38. Herbert Aptheker, *Negro Slave Revolts in the United States* (New York, 1939), 95; Irwin Jordan, *Black Confederates and Afro-Yankees in Civil War Virginia* (Charlottesville, Va., 1995), 177, 180, 254.

39. Harding, 236; McFeely, 215–6.

40. Senate Documents No. 1, 38th Cong., 1st Sess., 1864, 2; Louis S. Gerteis, *From Contraband to Freedman: Federal Policy toward Southern Blacks, 1861–1865* (Westport, Conn., 1973), 74; Berlin, *Slaves No More*, 39–40.

41. Wiley, 227; *War of the Rebellion . . . Official Records of the Union and Confederate Armies* (Washington, D.C., 1880–1901), 3rd Ser., 3:1139–44. Hereafter cited as *Offic. Rec.*

42. Robert Underwood Johnson and Clarence Buel, eds., *Battles and Leaders of the Civil War* (New York, 1887), 4: 688–9.

43. Susie King Taylor, *A Black Woman's Memoirs: Reminiscences of My Life in Camp With the 33rd U.S. Colored Troops* (New York, 1988); Catherine Clinton, "Susie King Taylor," in *Forgotten Heroes*, ed. Susan Ware (New York, 1997), 96–102.

44. Frank Moore, *Rebellion Record*, (New York, 1868), 5: 89.

45. Moore, 6: 32.

46. Moore, 6: 381.

47. David Donald, ed., *Inside Lincoln's Cabinet: The Civil War Diaries of Salmon Chase* (New York, 1954), 99–100; Philip Paludan, *"A People's Contest": The Union and the Civil War, 1861–1865* (New York, 1988), 209.

48. James Henry Gooding, *On the Altar of Freedom: A Black Soldier's Civil War Letters from the Front* (New York, 1992), 4.

49. Berlin, "The Destruction of Slavery," 35; McFeely, 225; Philip Foner, *The Life and Writings of Frederick Douglass* (New York, 1950), 3:94.

50. Dudley Cornish, *The Sable Arm: Negro Troops in the Union Army, 1861–1865* (New York, 1956), 59, 66, 78; Ira Berlin, "The Black Military Experience," in *Freedom: A Documentary History of Emancipation, 1861–1867*, ed. Ira Berlin et al. (New York, 1982), Ser. 2, 9, 12, 230, 44–45; Joseph T. Glatthaar, *Forged in Battle: The Civil War Alliance of Black Soldiers and White Officers* (New York, 1990), 7–9.

51. Joseph T. Glatthaar, "Black Glory: The African-American Role in Union Victory," in *Why the Confederacy Lost*, ed. Gabor Boritt (New York, 1992), 158–9; Glatthaar, *Forged in Battle*, 265–8.

52 Lincoln, *Collected Works*, 7:282.

53. Lincoln, *Collected Works*, 6:154, 158, 440, 409; Nicolay and Hay, *Abraham Lincoln*, 2:562, 6:452–5, 468.

54. Cornish, 214; Glatthaar, *Forged in Battle*, 279–80.

55. Thomas Higginson, *Army Life in a Black Regiment* (New York, 1962), 29.

56. Gooding, 38.

57. Glatthaar, *Forged in Battle*, 141.

58. James Robertson, *Soldiers Blue and Gray* (New York, 1991), 36; Glatthaar, *Forged in Battle*, xiii.

59. Randall Jimerson, *The Private Civil War: Popular Thought during the Sectional Conflict* (Baton Rouge, 1988), 99.

60. Higginson, app.

61. Gooding, 119–20; Glatthaar, *Forged in Battle*, 183.

62. Cornish, 184, 192, 195.

63. *Offic. Rec.*, 2d Ser., 5: 797; *Journal of the Confederate Congress*, 1863, 3:386–7; Moore, 5:62; James Hollandsworth, "The Execution of White Officers from Black Units by Confederate Forces During the Civil War," *Louisiana History* 35 (Fall 1994): 475–89.

64. Senate Reports, No. 63, 38th Congress, 1st Sess., passim; House Reports No. 65, 38th Cong., 1st Sess., 3–86; Moore, 7:1; John Cimprich and Robert Mainfort, "Fort Pillow Revisited: New Evidence about an Old Controversy," *Civil War History* 28 (1982): 293–306.

65. Lincoln, *Collected Works*, 7: 302–3.

66. Glatthaar, *Forged in Battle*, 156–7.

67. William Harris, *With Charity for All: Lincoln and the Restoration of the Union* (Lexington, Ky., 1997), 170–96.

68. Berlin, "The Black Military Experience," 588–9.

69. *Congressional Globe*, 38th Cong., 1st sess., 1490, 2995; *Congressional Globe*, 38th Cong., 2d Sess., 531; Lawanda Cox, "Lincoln and Black Freedom," in *The Historian's Lincoln: Pseudohistory, Psychohistory and History*, ed. Gabor Boritt (Urbana, Ill., 1988), 181.

70. Earl Maltz, *Civil Rights, the Constitution, and Congress, 1863–1869* (Lawrence, Kans., 1990) 26.

71. Foner, 3:386.

72. Lincoln, *Collected Works*, 6: 408–9.

## Chapter 17

1. *War of the Rebellion . . . Official Records of the Union and Confederate Armies* (Washington, D.C., 1880–1901), 1st series, 6:432. Hereafter cited as *Official Records*.

2. Thomas Connelly and Archer Jones, *Politics of Command: Faction and Ideas in Confederate Strategy* (Baton Rouge, 1967); Thomas Connelly, "Robert E. Lee and the Western Confederacy: A Criticism of Lee's Strategic Ability," *Civil War History* 15 (June 1969): 132. For a rebuttal, Albert Castel, *Winning and Losing in the Civil War: Essays and Stories* (Columbia, S.C., 1996), 68–74.

3. Mark Grimsley, *The Hard Hand of War: Union Military Policy toward Southern Civilians, 1861–1865* (New York, 1995), 143.

4. Edward Pollard, *The Lost Cause: A New Southern History of the Confederates* (New York, 1866), 345.

5. Herman Hattaway and Archer Jones, *How the North Won: A Military History of the Civil War* (Urbana, Ill., 1983), 308.

6. *Official Records*, 1st ser., 18:267–341; Robert Underwood Johnson and Clarence Buel, *Battles and Leaders of the Civil War* (New York, 1887), 3:244, 4:533 n.

7. Ernest Furgurson, *Chancellorsville, 1863: Souls of the Brave* (New York, 1992): Johnson and Buel, 3:237–238.

8. Furgurson, 88; Johnson and Buel, 3:157, also 152, 172.

9. Hattaway and Jones, 380.

10. Furgurson, 172–3; also Stephen Sears, *Chancellorsville* (Boston, 1996).

11. John A. Carpenter, "O. O. Howard: General at Chancellorsville," *Civil War History* 3 (March 1957): 59.

12. Douglas Freeman, *R. E. Lee: A Biography* (New York, 1924), 543, 544, 560–3; Gerald Linderman, *Embattled Courage: The Experience of Combat in the American Civil War* (New York, 1987); on Jackson's death, James Robertson, *Stonewall Jackson: The Man, The Soldier, The Legend* (New York, 1997), 744–50, 920, n. 35.

13. Charles Royster, *The Destructive War: William Tecumseh Sherman, Stonewall Jackson, and the Americans* (New York, 1991), 35; on Jackson's plans for invading the North, Bevin Alexander, *Lost Victories: The Military Genius of Stonewall Jackson* (New York, 1992), 35.

14. Richard McMurry, *Two Great Rebel Armies* (Chapel Hill, N.C., 1989).

15. Roy P. Basler et al., ed., *The Collected Works of Abraham Lincoln* (New Brunswick, N.J., 1953), 6:249, 257. Hereafter cited as Lincoln, *Collected Works*.

16. Lincoln, *Collected Works*, 6:11.

17. For an analysis of the continuing controversy over the Confederate battle plans and the responsibility of Longstreet and Lee for the defeat, see William Piston, "Cross Purposes: Longstreet, Lee, and the Confederate Attack Plans for July 3 at Gettysburg," in *The Third Day at Gettysburg and Beyond*, ed. Gary Gallagher (Chapel Hill, N.C., 1994), 31–56. The most comprehensive study of the battle is Edwin Coddington, *Gettysburg Campaign: A Study in Command* (Norwalk, Conn., 1968); also Harry Pfanz, *Gettysburg: The Second Day* (Chapel Hill, N.C., 1987), 153–5.

18. Johnson and Buel, 3:406–19.

19. William Piston, *Lee's Tarnished Lieutenant: James Longstreet and His Place in Southern History* (Athens, Ga., 1987), 49–50; Arthur Fremantle, *Three Months in the Confederate States, April–June 1863* (New York, 1864), 237–46, 247.

20. Freeman, 3:43–48, 86–95; Lee's report in *Official Records*, 1st ser., *27*, 2:320, 321; Donald Sanger and Thomas Hay, *James Longstreet* (Gloucester, Mass., 1952), 176; for a defense of Stuart, see John W. Thomason, Jr., *Jeb Stuart* (New York, 1934), 423–7. For an analysis of Stuart's behavior that emphasizes his complexity and goes beyond his traditional image as a southern cavalier, Emory Thomas, *Bold Dragoon: The Life of J. E. B. Stuart* (New York, 1986).

21. Freeman, 3:119.

22. Johnson and Buel, 3:364.

23. Hattaway and Jones, 408. On the double-loaded muskets, see James Robertson, *Soldiers Blue and Gray* (New York, 1991), 221.

24. Hattaway and Jones, 408; Gabor Boritt, ed., *The Gettysburg Nobody Knows* (New York, 1997); for an analysis of Pickett's charge in the American mind, Carol Reardon, *Pickett's Charge in History and Meaning* (Chapel Hill, N.C., 1997).

25. Robert Bee, "Fredericksburg on the Other Leg, Sergeant Ben Hirst's Narrative of Important Events, Gettysburg, July 3, 1863," in *The Third Day at Gettysburg and Beyond*, ed. Gary Gallagher (Chapel Hill, N.C., 1994), 137.

26. *Lee's Dispatches: The Unpublished Letters of Robert E. Lee*, ed. Douglas Freeman (New York, 1915), 110: Jeffry Wert, *General James Longstreet: The Confederacy's Most Controversial Soldier: A Biography* (New York, 1993), 286–97.

27. Thomas Nelson Page, *Robert E. Lee: Man and Soldier* (New York, 1911), 349.

28. Lincoln, *Collected Works*, 6:318.

29. Pollard, 1:326–7.

30. Archer Jones, *Confederate Strategy from Shiloh to Vicksburg* (Baton Rouge, 1961), 5–8.

31. Benjamin Cooling, *Fort Donelson's Legacy: War and Society in Kentucky and Tennessee, 1862–1863* (Knoxville, 1997).

32. Steven Woodworth, *Jefferson Davis and His Generals* (Lawrence, Kans., 1990), 123–4, 198; Stephen Ash, *Middle Tennessee Society Transformed: War and Peace in the Upper South, 1860–1870* (Baton Rouge, 1988), 84–105.

33. For these raids see Johnson and Buel, 3:3, 28, 37, 451, 484; *Official Records*, 1st ser., 16, 1:731–84, 815–9, 871–82; Edward Longacre, *Mounted Raids of the Civil War* (Lincoln, 1994), 175–201; James Ramage, *Rebel Raider: The Life of General John Hunt Morgan* (Lexington, Ky., 1974); Jack Hurst, *Nathan Bedford Forrest: A Biography* (New York, 1994). For an instance when raids by Forrest and Morgan resulted in depriving Bragg of more than half of his cavalry, Hattaway and Jones, 318.

34. James McDonough, *Shiloh, In Hell before Night* (Knoxville, 1977).

35. D. Warren Lambert, *When the Ripe Pears Fell: The Battle of Richmond, Kentucky* (Richmond, Ky., 1997).

36. Only eleven states seceded, although both Missouri and Kentucky had dissident minority Confederate governments. To acknowledge them, the Confederate flag had thirteen stars.

37. James McDonough, *War in Kentucky* (Knoxville, 1994).

38. Peter Cozzens, *The Darkest Days of the War: The Battles of Iuka and Corinth* (Chapel Hill, N.C., 1997).

39. Johnson and Buel, 3:604, 474; Thomas Livermore, *Numbers and Losses in the Civil War* (Bloomington, Ind., 1957), 97.

40. Herman Hattaway. *Shades of Blue and Gray* (Columbia, Mo., 1997), 131–2.

41. William Tecumseh Sherman, *Memoirs of W. T. Sherman* (New York, 1887), 1: 294.

42. *Official Records*, Ser. 1, 24, 3: 268–9.

43. Robertson, *Soldiers Blue and Gray*, 143.

44. James Arnold, *Grant Wins at Vicksburg: Decision at Vicksburg* (New York, 1997), 294–301; *Official Records*, 1st ser., 24, 1:57.

45. Johnson and Buel, 3:644.

46. Johnson and Buel, 3: 644; on the feckless Bragg, Judith Lee Hallock, *Braxton Bragg and Confederate Defeat* (Tuscaloosa, 1991) 2: 13, 17–22; Grady McWhiney and Perry Jamieson, *Attack and Die: Civil War Military Tactics and the Southern Heritage* (Tuscaloosa, 1982), 18, 72–73.

47. Sidney Lanier, *Tiger Lilies,* ed. Garland Greever (Baltimore, 1945), 134.

48. Peter Cozzens, *This Terrible Sound: The Battle of Chickamauga* (Urbana, Ill., 1992), 403–4; Steven Woodworth, *Six Armies in Tennessee: Great Campaigns of the Civil War* (Lincoln, 1998).

49. Livermore, 105–6. Also Johnson and Buel, 3:673–5.

50. Ulysses S. Grant, *Personal Memoirs of U.S. Grant* (New York, 1917), 2:48.

51. James McDonough, *Chattanooga: Death Grip on the Confederacy* (Knoxville, 1984).

52. C. Vann Woodward, ed., *Mary Chesnut's Civil War* (New Haven, Conn., 1981), 469.

53. Donald Sanger and Thomas Hay, *James Longstreet* (Gloucester, Mass., 1968), 1:212.

54. Sanger and Hay, 223; Piston, 76–78.

55. Among other documents revealing confusion and disorder, the Bragg papers contain the penciled draft of a letter to Jefferson Davis, from Dalton, Georgia, December 1, 1863, in which Bragg comments on his "shameful discomfiture" in the Chattanooga campaign. "The disaster [he writes] admits of no palliation, and is justly disparaging to me as a commander. . . . I fear we both erred in the conclusion for me to retain command here after the clamor raised against me." Bragg Papers, Western Reserve Historical Society, Cleveland, Ohio; also John Hoffman, *The Confederate Collapse and the Battle of Missionary Ridge: The Reports of James Patton Anderson and His Brigade Commanders* (Dayton, 1985); Hallock, 2: 139–41.

56. Johnson and Buel, 3: 726 n.

57. Woodward, 501.

## Chapter 18

1. Joseph Glatthaar, *Partners in Command: The Relationships Between Leaders in the Civil War* (New York, 1994), 153–4, 199–206, 217–8; Brooks Simpson, *Let Us Have Peace: Ulysses S. Grant and the Politics of War and Reconstruction* (Chapel Hill, N.C., 1991), 54–56.

2. Herman Hattaway and Archer Jones, *How the North Won: A Military History of the Civil War* (Urbana, Ill., 1983), 511–3.

3. Gerald Linderman, *Embattled Courage: The Experience of Combat in the American Civil War* (New York, 1987), 20, 34–60; Richard Beringer, et al., *How the South Lost the Civil War* (Athens, Ga., 1986), 310–4, 432–5; Glatthaar, 153–4.

4. Anita Palladino, ed., *Diary of a Yankee Engineer* (New York, 1997), 51, 75, 81.

5. Reid Mitchell, *Civil War Soldiers* (New York, 1987), 61.

6. Linderman, 118.

7. Thomas Connelly and Barbara Bellows, *God and General Longstreet: The Lost Cause and the Southern Mind* (Baton Rouge, 1982), 14; Drew Faust, "Christian Soldiers: The Meaning of Revival-

ism in the Confederate Army," in *Southern Stories: Slaveholders in Peace and War* (Columbia, S.C., 1992).

8. James Robertson, *Soldiers Blue and Gray* (New York, 1991), 119.

9. Robertson, 119.

10. Thomas Lowry, *The Story the Soldiers Wouldn't Tell: Sex in the Civil War* (Mechanicsburg, Pa., 1994), 123. Court-martial records are in the Records of the Judge Advocate's Office, Record Group 153, National Archives. Martha Hodes, *White Women, Black Men: Illicit Sex in the Nineteenth-Century South* (New Haven, Conn., 1997). Preliminary samples of military courts-martial reveal that black women were usually the victims of sexual assaults, that black soldiers were disproportionately charged with rape, and that many rapes went unreported. Professor Charles Ritter, personal communication.

11. Charles Harvey Brewster, *When This Cruel War Is Over: The Civil War Letters of Charles Harvey Brewster* (Amherst, Mass., 1992), 285.

12. Robertson, 215.

13. James McPherson, *For Cause and Comrade: Why Men Fought in the Civil War* (New York, 1997), 114–5; Joseph Allan Frank, *With Ballot and Bayonet: The Political Socialization of American Civil War Soldiers* (Athens, Ga., 1998).

14. Robertson, 211.

15. Judith Hallock, *Braxton Bragg and Confederate Defeat* (Tuscaloosa, 1991), 2:139.

16. Earl Hess, "Refusing to Fight: The Breakdown of Combat Morale in the Civil War," unpublished paper.

17. Randall Jimmerson, *The Private Civil War: Popular Thought during the Sectional Conflict* (Baton Rouge, 1988), 30.

18. Earl Hess, *The Union Soldier in Battle: Enduring the Ordeal of Combat* (Lawrence, Kans., 1997).

19. James McPherson, *What They Fought For, 1861–1865* (Baton Rouge, 1994), 28.

20. Elizabeth Leonard, *All the Daring of the Soldier: Women of the Civil War Armies* (New York 1999).

21. Mitchell, 127.

22. Brooks Simpson, "Great Expectations: The Northern Press and The Opening of the Wilderness Campaign," in *The Wilderness Campaign*, ed. Gary Gallagher (Chapel Hill, N.C., 1997), 1–35.

23. Robert Underwood Johnson and Clarence Buel, *Battles and Leaders of the Civil War* (New York, 1887), 4: 152–3, 182–4, 187, 196n, 198n.

24. Johnson and Buel, 4: 248.

25. Johnson and Buel, 4: 230.

26. Gordon Rhea, *The Battle of the Wilderness, May 7–12* (Baton Rouge, 1994); Gordon Rhea, *The Battle for Spotsylvania Court House and the Road to Yellow Tavern, May 7–12* (Baton Rouge, 1997); Thomas Livermore, *Numbers and Losses in the Civil War in America, 1861–1865* (Bloomington, Ind., 1957), 113–4.

27. Ulysses S. Grant, *Personal Memoirs of U.S. Grant* (New York, 1917), 276.

28. Edward Hagerman, *The American Civil War and the Origins of Modern Warfare: Ideas, Organization and Field Command* (Bloomington, Ind., 1988), 262.

29. Hagerman, 253–5.

30. George Cary Eggleston, "Notes on Cold Harbor," in *Battles and Leaders of the Civil War*, ed. Robert Underwood Johnson and Clarence Buel (New York, 1888), 4: 231.

31. Grant, 2: 291.

32. William C. Davis, *The Battle of New Market* (Baton Rouge, 1975).

33. Johnson and Buel, 4: 451.

34. Hattaway and Jones, 591.

35. Johnson and Buel, 4: 147.

36. Edward Longacre, *Army of Amateurs: Ben Butler's Campaign on the James* (Mechanicsburg, Pa., 1997), 71–85, 87–100. For a reassessment of the Bermuda Hundred campaign in April–June 1864 that argues that blame for Butler's failure rests with the Union corps commanders William F. Smith and James R. Gilmore as well as with Grant, see William Robertson, *Back Door to Richmond: The Bermuda Hundred Campaign* (Newark, Del., 1987).

37. Edwin Redkey, ed., *A Grand Army of Black Men: Letters From African-American Soldiers in the Union Army* (New York, 1992), 111.

38. Joseph Glatthaar, *Forged in Battle: The Civil War Alliance of Black Soldiers and White Officers* (New York, 1990), 150; Hattaway and Jones, 615; Laurence Hauptman, *Between Two Fires: American Indians in the Civil War* (New York, 1995). Indians served in both the Union and Confederate armies, even as U.S. soldiers waged war intermittently against the Santee in Minnesota, the Cheyenne in Colorado, and the Navaho in Arizona and New Mexico.

39. Redkey, 112.

40. Grant, 2: 315.

41. *War of the Rebellion . . . Official Records of the Union and Confederate Armies* (Washington, D.C., 1880–1901), 1st ser., 36, 1:789–92; hereafter cited as *Official Records*. Stephen Starr, *The Union Cavalry in the Civil War* (Baton Rouge, 1985), 2:506–8.

42. Roy Morris, *Sheridan: The Life and Wars of General Phil Sheridan* (New York, 1992), 168–9; Paul Hutton, *Phil Sheridan and His Army* (Lincoln, 1985).

43. Gordon Rhea, "The Union Cavalry in the Wilderness: The Education of Philip Sheridan and James Wilson," in *The Wilderness Campaign*, ed. Gary Gallagher (Chapel Hill, N.C., 1997), 106–35.

44. Johnson and Buel, 4:233ff; Morris, 175–7.

45. Morris, 179.

46. Mark Grimsley, *The Hard Hand of War: Union Military Strategy toward Southern Civilians, 1861–1864* (New York, 1995), 213.

47. William McFeely, *Grant: A Biography* (New York, 1981), 186.

48. For a classic account of this battle by a beardless cadet with a zest for life and a flair for writing, see John S. Wise, "The Most Glorious Day of My Life" in *The End of an Era*, ed. John S. Wise (Boston, 1902), 285–309; also Davis, 49–50, 93–96; 179–81.

49. Everard Smith, "Chambersburg: Anatomy of a Confederate Reprisal," *American Historical Review* 96 (April 1991): 432–55.

50. Johnson and Buel, 4:497–8.

51. Roy P. Basler et al., eds., *The Collected Works of Abraham Lincoln* (New Brunswick, N.J., 1953), 7:438. Hereafter cited as Lincoln, *Collected Works*.

52. A. Wilson Greene, "Union Generalship in the 1864 Valley Campaign," in *Struggle for the Shenandoah: Essays in the 1864 Valley Campaign*, ed. Gary Gallagher (Kent, Ohio, 1991), 60.

53. Johnson and Buel, 4:513.

54. Morris, 202; also *Official Records,* 1st Ser., 43, 1:25.

55. For the controversy surrounding the replacement of Johnston by Hood, see Albert Castel, *Decision in the West: The Atlanta Campaign of 1864* (Lawrence, Kans., 1992); Craig Symonds, *Joseph E. Johnston,* (New York, 1992) and Richard McMurry, *John Bell Hood* (Lexington, Ky., 1981). For Grant and Sherman's strategy, see Castel, 90.

56. Grant, 2:272; Glatthaar, 137–9.

57. Johnson and Buel, 4:250.

58. Joseph Glatthaar, *The March to the Sea and Beyond: Sherman's Troops in the Savannah and Carolinas Campaigns* (New York, 1985), 40; figures on reenlistment in Sherman's army, Glatthaar, 39.

59. William Cooper, "Jefferson Davis as a War Leader," *Journal of Southern History* 36 (May 1970): 194–8; Richard McMurry, *Two Great Rebel Armies* (Chapel Hill, N.C., 1989), 128–31;

Richard McMurry, *John Bell Hood and the Fight for Southern Independence* (Lawrence, Kans., 1982), 116–9.

60. Hattaway and Jones, 607; Beringer, 266, 327, 333–4; David Coffey, *John Bell Hood and the Struggle for Atlanta* (Abilene, 1998).

61. Hattaway and Jones, 625; Grimsley, 186–90.

62. *Official Records*, Ser. 1, 39, 2:480, 503; Hattaway and Jones, 638.

63. Glatthaar, *Partners*, 158–9.

64. Had Sherman joined Grant, Hood expected to march through the Cumberland Gap to reinforce Lee. Johnson and Buel, 4:427.

65. Grant to Sherman, November 1, 1864, in William T. Sherman, *Memoirs of General William T. Sherman* (New York, 1990), 2:164.

66. Sherman, 2:165.

67. Hattaway and Jones, 655; making Georgia "howl," Sherman, 2:152; Grimsley, 169, 190–9.

68. Richmond *Enquirer*, November 21, 1864 (copies in *New York Times*, November 25, 1864). Quotation from Augusta *Constitutionalist* in Charles Royster, *The Destructive War: William Tecumseh Sherman, Stonewall Jackson, and the Americans* (New York, 1991), 189.

69. Sherman, 2:171–2, 175.

70. Glatthaar, *March to the Sea*, 72.

71. *Battles and Leaders*, 4: 672.

72. *Official Records*, 1st Ser., 42, 1:804; *Official Records*, 1st Ser., 42, 3:116; Johnson and Buel, 4:686; Grimsley, 193–5. On the postwar uses of Sherman's campaign, Gaines Foster, *The Ghosts of the Confederacy: Defeat, The Lost Cause, and the Emergence of the New South, 1865–1913*, (New York, 1987).

73. Glatthaar, 134.

74. Royster, 328.

75. Sherman, 2:231; on the behavior of Sherman's troops in Savannah, which counters the stereotype of his bummers, John Barrett, *Sherman's March through the Carolinas* (Chapel Hill, N.C., 1956); 27.

76. Glatthaar, *March to the Sea*, 54.

77. Sherman, 2:254.

78. Report of the Committee on Conduct of the War, 38th Cong., 2d Sess., 1864, 1:287, Report of General Sherman, supplement to Senate Report 142.

79. Sherman to Henry Halleck, December 24, 1864, *Official Records*, Ser. 1, 44:799.

80. James Davidson, "Who Burned Columbia?" *Southern Historical Society Papers* (Richmond, 1874), 7:190.

81. Sherman, 2:287; Royster, 18–33; Barrett, 62–94.

## Chapter 19

1. Joseph Durkin, *Stephen R. Mallory: Confederate Navy Chief* (Columbia, S.C., 1987), 150.

2. William Fowler, *Under Two Flags: The American Navy in the Civil War* (New York, 1990), 42; Philip Stern, *The Confederate Navy: A Pictorial History* (New York, 1992).

3. Durkin, 64–65, 133, 168–9.

4. Philip Melvin, "Stephen Russell Mallory, Southern Naval Statesman," *Journal of Southern History* 10 (May 1944): 156.

5. Milton Perry, *Infernal Machines: The Story of Confederate Submarine and Mine Warfare* (Baton Rouge, 1965). For a favorable assessment of the Confederate Navy, see Raimondo Luraghi, *A History of the Confederate Navy* (Annapolis, 1996).

6. Charles Boynton, *History of the Navy during the Rebellion* (New York, 1867), 1:100; Report of the Navy Department, 37th Cong., 3rd Sess., 1861, 3:24, House Exec. Doc. 1. The report of the Navy Department, July 4, 1861 (37th Cong., 1st Sess., 1861, 86, House Exec. Doc. 1) erroneously

reports the number in commission on March 4, 1861, as twenty-four. On naval strategy, Howard Nash, *A Naval History of the Civil War* (South Brunswick, Me., 1975), 16.

7. For a summary of naval administration during the Civil War, see Charles Paullin, "A Half-Century of Naval Administration in America. . ." *U.S. Naval Institute Proceedings*, 1913, 38: 1309–36 and 1913, 39: 165–95; also Charles Paullin, *History of Naval Administration* (Annapolis, 1985); John Niven, *Gideon Welles: Lincoln's Secretary of the Navy* (New York, 1973).

8. Boynton, 1: 139; Paullin, 38: 1310.

9. Ivan Musicant, *Divided Waters: The Naval History of the Civil War* (New York, 1995), 3.

10. Paullin, "Naval Administration," 38: 1328.

11. Stephen Wise, *Lifeline of the Confederacy: Blockade Running during the Civil War* (Columbia, S.C., 1988), 221.

12. Report of the Secretary of the Navy, 37th Cong., 3rd sess., December 1, 1862, 3: 3, House Exec. Doc. 1.

13. Musicant, 134.

14. Musicant, 156.

15. William Chapman White and Ruth White, *Tin Can on a Shingle* (New York, 1987); Robert S. McCordock, *The Yankee Cheese Box* (Philadelphia, 1938).

16. William C. Davis, *The Fight Between the Ironclads* (Mechanicsburg, Pa., 1994).

17. Musicant, 43–44.

18. Elliot Ashkenazi, ed., *The Civil War Diary of Clara Solomon* (Baton Rouge, 1995), 350–351.

19. Mary Ryan, *Women in Public: Between Banners and Ballots* (Baltimore, 1990), 137–47.

20. *Journal of the Congress of the Confederate States of America* (Washington, D.C., 1904), 6:13. Hereafter cited as *Journal*, Confed. Cong.

21. *Journal*, Confed. Cong., 1:181.

22. Report on proceedings in U.S. Circuit Court, Philadelphia, November 4, 1861, in J. H. Ashton to Edward Bates, November 4, 1861, Edward Bates Papers, Library of Congress. Also William Robinson, *Confederate Privateers* (Columbia, S.C., 1928), 151; James Randall, *Constitutional Problems Under Lincoln* (Urbana, Ill., 1951), 38–95, 215.

23. Colyer Meriweather, *Raphael Semmes* (Philadelphia, 1913), 110; John M. Taylor, *Confederate Raider* (Washington, D.C., 1994).

24. Warren Spencer, *Raphael Semmes: The Philosophical Mariner* (Tuscaloosa, 1997).

25. Statement of John McIntosh Kell, in Robert Underwood Johnson and Clarence Buel, *Battles and Leaders of the Civil War* (New York, 1887) 4:603n.

26. Meriwether, 285.

27. Musicant, 325–6.

28. Fowler, 299.

29. Johnson and Buel, 4:362.

30. Johnson and Buel, 4:642.

31. Wise, 3, 226.

32. Nash, 301–2.

## Chapter 20

1. Jean H. Baker, "In Eclipse: Democratic Culture and the Crucible of Civil War," in *Democrats and the American Idea*, ed. Peter Kovler (Washington, D.C., 1992), 104.

2. Josiah Benton, *Voting in the Field* (Boston, 1915).

3. Orville H. Browning, *Diary of O. H. Browning* (Springfield, Ill., 1925), I: 499, 503.

4. Michael Holt, "Abraham Lincoln and the Politics of Union," in *The American Political Tradition*, ed. John L. Thomas (Amherst, Mass., 1986), 111–37.

5. James Ford Rhodes, *History of the United States from the Compromise of 1850* (New York, 1904), 3:473n.

6. William Harris, *With Charity for All: Lincoln and the Restoration of the Union* (Lexington, Ky., 1997), 107–11, 129–31.

7. Joel Silbey, *A Respectable Minority: The Democratic Party in the Civil War Era* (New York, 1977), 42.

8. Browning, 1:585, 587–8.

9. William Salter, *The Life of James W. Grimes* (New York, 1876), 156; Winfred A. Harbison, "The Opposition to President Lincoln within the Republican Party" (Ph.D. dissertation, University of Illinois, 1930), 77.

10. Harbison, 77; *Journal of Illinois Historical Society*, 2 (1907): 48–49.

11. Henry Pearson, *The Life of John Andrew* (Boston, 1904), 2:3; Harbison, 78.

12. By applying the name of a poisonous snake to Democrats, Republicans linked the latter to treasonous, antiwar ideas and practices and suggested that all Democrats supported the extremist ideas of a few party members.

13. Philip Paludan, *"A People's Contest": The Union and the Civil War* (New York, 1988), 97.

14. Paul Kleppner, *The Third Electoral System, 1853–1892: Parties, Voters and Political Cultures* (Chapel Hill, N.C., 1979), 77.

15. *Illinois State Register*, September 9, 1862; also Harry E. Pratt, "The Repudiation of Lincoln's War Policy in 1862: The Stuart-Swett Campaign," *Journal of the Illinois State Historical Society* 24: 129–40.

16. Browning, 1: 582.

17. On the possibility of such a caucus, Browning, 1:596–7; Francis Fessenden, *Life and Public Services of William Pitt Fessenden* (Boston, 1907), 1:231–6.

18. Fessenden, 1:239.

19. Browning, 1:600–1.

20. Fessenden, 1:239.

21. Howard Beale, ed., *The Diary of Edward Bates* (New York, 1971), 269–70.

22. Browning, 1:603; Beale, 270.

23. John Nicolay and John Hay, *Abraham Lincoln: A History* (New York, 1890), 6:271.

24. David Herbert Donald, *Lincoln* (New York, 1995), 400–4.

25. Silbey, 73.

26. Horace Greeley to Edwin M. Stanton, June 1, 1863, Stanton Papers, Library of Congress.

27. Paludan, 97.

28. Jean H. Baker, *Affairs of Party: The Political Culture of Northern Democrats in Mid-Nineteenth-Century America* (New York, 1998), 143–75.

29. Silbey, 82.

30. Silbey, 147.

31. Chase to ex-Governor William Sprague, November 26, 1863, Chase Papers, Library of Congress.

32. Horace M. Dudley, "The Election of 1864," *Mississippi Valley Historical Review* 18 (March 1932): 501; John Niven, *Salmon P. Chase: A Biography* (New York, 1995).

33. As early as December 9, 1863, the day after Lincoln's announcement of his policy concerning the restoration of the South, a meeting was held in Washington to launch Chase's name as candidate for the presidency. Memorandum bearing the endorsement "Organization to make S. P. Chase President, December 9, 1863," Chase Papers, Library of Congress.

34. For Lincoln's response, Roy P. Basler et al., eds., *The Collected Works of Abraham Lincoln* (New Brunswick, N.J., 1953), 8:52. Hereafter cited as Lincoln, *Collected Works*.

35. Lincoln, *Collected Works*, 8:101.

36. David Long, *Jewel of Liberty: Abraham Lincoln's Re-Election and the End of Slavery* (Mechanicsburg, Pa., 1994), 37–39; John Waugh, *Reelecting Lincoln: The Battle for the 1864 Presidency* (New York, 1997).

37. Lincoln, *Collected Works*, 7:374.

38. Lincoln's role in the nomination of Andrew Johnson was later disputed. For a summary of the conflicting evidence on this point, stressing the president's support of Johnson, see James G. Randall and Richard N. Current, *Lincoln the President* (New York, 1945), 4:130–4. For the opposing view, see James Glonek, "Lincoln, Johnson and the Baltimore Ticket," *Abraham Lincoln Quarterly* 6 (March 1951): 255–71.

39. Details of this disagreement between Lincoln and congressional Republicans will be discussed in Chapter 24. See also Herman Belz, *Reconstructing the Union: Theory and Policy during the Civil War* (Ithaca, N.Y., 1969), 168–73; Michael Les Benedict, *A Compromise of Principle: Congressional Republicans and Reconstruction, 1863–1869* (New York, 1974); Harris, 186–190.

40. Lincoln, *Collected Works*, 7:419.

41. Larry Nelson, *Bullets, Ballots and Rhetoric: Confederate Policy for the United States Presidential Contest of 1864* (University, Ala., 1980), 9.

42. Frank Klement, *Dark Lanterns: Secret Political Societies, Conspiracies, and Treason in the Civil War* (Baton Rouge, 1984), 91–135.

43. Harriet Owsley, "Peace and the Presidential Election of 1864," *Tennessee Historical Quarterly* 18 (March 1959): 3–19.

44. W. C. Jewett to Horace Greeley, July 5, 1864, Greeley Papers, Library of Congress.

45. Edward C. Kirkland, *Peacemakers of 1864* (New York, 1927), 76.

46. Lincoln, *Collected Works*, 7: 435.

47. Kirkland, 73; for a discussion of the efforts of the Confederate secret service to launch clandestine operations against the North from Canada, see William Tidwell, *April '65: Confederate Covert Action in the American Civil War* (Kent, Ohio, 1995), 105–59.

48. William C. Davis, *Jefferson Davis: The Man and His Hour* (New York, 1991), 589–96; Hudson Strode, *Jefferson Davis: Tragic Hero* (New York, 1964), 77; Kirkland, 94–95.

49. Lincoln, *Collected Works*, 8:151.

50. New York *Sun*, June 30, 1889. In this issue the *Sun* published a collection of documents illustrating the "secret movement to supersede Abraham Lincoln in '64."

51. New York *Sun*, June 30, 1889.

52. New York *Sun*, June 30, 1889; Silbey, 42.

53. Nicolay and Hay, 9: 251n.

54. Silbey, 106–9.

55. Long, 60–62.

56. Charles R. Wilson, "McClellan's Changing Views on the Peace Platform of 1864," *American Historical Review* 38 (April 1933): 498–505. A more recent appraisal of McClellan's reaction appears in Stephen Sears, "McClellan and the Peace Plank: A Reappraisal," *Civil War History* 36 (March 1990): 57–75.

57. Pearson, 2:162; Gideon Welles, *Diary of Gideon Welles* (New York, 1960), 2:135.

58. Klement, 1–6.

59. New York *Sun*, June 30, 1889.

60. Mark Dunkelman, "Hurray for Old Abe! Fenton! And Dr. Van Aernam! The 1864 Election, as Perceived by the 154th New York Volunteers," *Lincoln Herald* (Spring 1966): 18.

61. Long, 234.

62. William F. Zornow, *Lincoln and the Party Divided* (Norman, Okla., 1954), 214–5; on sailors, Mark Neely, *The Last Best Hope of Earth: Abraham Lincoln and the Promise of America* (Cambridge, Mass., 1993), 177–8.

63. John D. Caton to George McClellan, December 18, 1864, John Caton Papers, Library of Congress.

64. Silbey, 149.


## Chapter 21

1. These figures are for enlistments, and some reenlistments are included. For the effect of such mobilizations on local communities see Maris Vinovskis, "Have Social Historians Lost the Civil War?" in *Toward a Social History of the Civil War: Exploratory Essays*, ed. Maris Vinovskis (New York, 1990), 1–30; also Thomas Kemp, "Community and War: The Civil War Experience of Two New Hampshire Towns," in *Toward a Social History of the Civil War*, 31–77. Especially for the South, the figures are based on estimates. James McPherson calculates that there were 2,100,000 Union soldiers and sailors and 882,000 Confederates. James McPherson, *Battle Cry of Freedom: The Civil War Era* (New York, 1988); 306–41.

2. Herman Hattaway and Archer Jones, *How the North Won: A Military History of the Civil War* (Urbana, Ill., 1983), 721.

3. Joseph K. Barnes, ed., *The Medical and Surgical History of the War of the Rebellion* (Washington, D.C., 1870).

4. Philip Paludan, *"A People's Contest": The Union and Civil War, 1861–1865* (New York, 1988), 327–8.

5. Quoted in Jane Schultz, "'Souls and Body In the Work': Female Hospital Workers and the Politics of Care," unpublished paper.

6. Kristie Ross, "Arranging a Doll's House: Refined Women as Union Nurses," in *Divided Houses: Gender and the Civil War*, eds. Catherine Clinton and Nina Silber (New York, 1992), 97–113.

7. Ednay Cheney, ed., *Louisa May Alcott, Her Life, Letters, and Journals* (Boston, 1923), 140–1.

8. Cheney, 105; Louisa May Alcott, *Hospital Sketches* (Cambridge, Mass., 1960).

9. Schultz, 6.

10. Jane Ellen Schultz, "Women at the Front" (Ph.D. dissertation, University of Michigan, 1977), 272–3; Lauren Cook Burgess, *An Uncommon Soldier: The Civil War Letters of Sarah Rossetta Wakeman* (Pasadena, Md., 1994); for the story of Amy Frank, *The Sibyl*, June 1863; also Ann Russo and Cheris Kramarae, *The Radical Women's Press* (New York, 1991), 140–1; Elizabeth Leonard, *All the Daring of the Soldier: Women of the Civil War Armies* (New York, 1999).

11. Jane Schultz, *Women at the Front* (Chapel Hill, 1999).

12. Elizabeth Leonard, *Yankee Women: Gender Battles in the Civil War* (New York, 1994); F. L. Sarmiento, *Life of Pauline Cushman: The Celebrated Union Spy and Scout* (Philadelphia, 1865).

13. Paludan, 158.

14. J. Matthew Gallman, *The North Fights the War: The Home Front* (Chicago, 1994), 88–107; Jeanie Attie, *Patriotic Toil: Northern Women and the American Civil War* (Ithaca, N.Y., 1998), 25–27, 198–219.

15. James Marten, ed., *Lessons of War: The Civil War in Children's Magazines* (Wilmington, 1998).

16. Walt Whitman, "Long, Too Long O Land," *Drum Taps* (Philadelphia, 1900), 263.

17. The figures of R. G. Dun and Company do not include the border states. *Appleton's Annual American Cyclopaedia* (New York, 1861–1865), 1861, 312; New York *Herald*, January 1, 1863; Emerson Fite, *Social and Industrial Conditions in the North during the Civil War* (New York, 1930), 105–6; Glenn Porter and Harold Livesay, *Merchants and Manufacturers* (Baltimore, 1971), 116–30; Margaret Myers, *The New York Money Market* (New York, 1971), 264.

18. Myers, 260–4.

19. *New York Times*, July 2, 1863.

20. Paludan, 145.

21. Richard Beringer, personal communication.

22. Paludan, 158.

23. Report of the Commissioner of Agriculture for the Year 1865, 10.

24. *Appleton's Annual American Cyclopaedia*, 1862, 5.

25. Stephen De Canio and Joel Mokyr, "Inflation and Wage Lag During the Civil War, *Explorations in Economic History* 14 (October 1977): 315–24.

26. New York *Herald*, March 24, 1864; Myers, 26.

27. *New York Times*, March 19, 1864.

28. New York *Herald*, March 1, 1864.

29. *New International Encyclopedia* (New York, 1905), 12:9.

30. Charlotte Erickson, *American Industry and the European Immigrant, 1860–1885* (Cambridge, Mass., 1957), vii, 7, 63; David Montgomery, *Beyond Equality: Labor and the Radical Republicans*, (Urbana, Ill., 1981), 35.

31. *Appleton's Annual American Cyclopaedia*, 1863, 413.

32. Paludan, 183.

33. *Fincher's Trades' Union Review*, May 14, 1864.

34. Montgomery, 35; *Fincher's*, February 26, 1865.

35. Norman J. Ware, *The Labor Movement in the United States, 1860–1895: A Study in Democracy* (New York, 1929), 1–2.

36. Montgomery, 93.

37. Montgomery, 93; Joseph Rayback, *A History of American Labor* (New York, 1959), 111–2; John Commons et al., *History of Labor in the United States* (New York, 1935), 2:33–37.

38. Grace Palladino, *Another Civil War: Labor, Capital and the State in the Anthracite Regions of Pennsylvania, 1840–1868* (Urbana, Ill. 1990), 142–4.

39. Fite, 184–7; Rayback, 110–3; Montgomery, 99.

40. Philip Kunhardt et al., *P. T. Barnum: America's Greatest Showman* (New York, 1995), 154–5.

41. Gallman, 88.

42. Jean Baker, *Mary Todd Lincoln: A Biography* (New York, 1987).

43. New York *Herald*, January 25, 1864; Gallman, 84–86.

44. Gallman, 88.

45. Chester Hearn, *When the Devil Came Down to Dixie: Ben Butler in New Orleans* (Baton Rouge, 1997), 195; James Marshall, ed., *Private and Official Correspondence of General Benjamin F. Butler* (Norwood, Mass., 1917), 2:424–6, 518–9.

46. New York *Herald*, June 21, 1864.

47. *Official Records*, Ser. 1., 22, 1:230.

48. John Simon, ed., *The Papers of Ulysses S. Grant* (Carbondale, Ill., 1967), 7: 50–56.

49. *Papers of Grant*, 8:37–40; Brooks Simpson, *Let Us Have Peace: Ulysses S. Grant and the Politics of War and Reconstruction* (Chapel Hill, N.C., 1991).

50. *Appleton's Annual American Cyclopaedia*, 1863, 199.

51. Edward Moore, *The Rebellion Record* (New York, 1865), 5:41. But see New York *Herald*, July 20, 1862.

52. New York *Herald*, January 5, February 27, 1864; Eric Monkken, *Police in Urban America, 1860–1920* (New York, 1981), 78–82; also Fite, 305.

53. For an analysis of the implications of this legislation, Theda Skocpol, *Protecting Soldiers and Mothers: The Political Origins of Social Policy in the United States* (Cambridge, Mass., 1991), 106.

54. Amy Holmes, "'Such Is the Price We Pay': American Widows and the Civil War Pension System," *Toward a Social History of the Civil War: Exploratory Essays*, ed. Maris Vinovskis (New York, 1990), 172.

55. Skocpol, 149; Holmes, 171–95.

56. J. Matthew Gallman, "Voluntarism in Wartime: Philadelphia's Great Central Fair," in *Toward A Social History of the Civil War: Exploratory Essays*, ed. Maris Vinovskis (New York, 1990), 93–116.

57. George Frederickson, *The Inner Civil War: Northern Intellectuals and the Crisis of the Union* (New York, 1956), 102; Attie, 87–121.

58. Frederickson, 98–112; J. Matthew Gallman, *Mastering Wartime: A Social History of Philadelphia during the Civil War* (New York, 1990), 146–65, esp. 164; Stephen Oates, *Woman of Valor: Clara Barton* (New York, 1994).

59. Ida Husted Harper, *The Life and Work of Susan B. Anthony* (North Stratford, N.H., 1998), 2: 225–40).

60. Frederic Bancroft, *The Life of William Seward* (Gloucester, Mass., 1967), 2: 220.

61. Gallman, 95–96.

62. Frank Friedel, "The Loyal Publication Society: A Pro-Union Propaganda Agency," *Mississippi Valley Historical Review* 26 (December 1939): 364.

63. Abraham Lincoln, *Collected Works*, 7:23. For other drafts of the Gettysburg address, *ibid.*, 7: 17–22. There is no foundation for the often-repeated myth that the speech was unappreciated by contemporaries. For the Gettysburg address as an ideological statement of a new America, Gary Wills, *Lincoln at Gettysburg: The Words that Remade America* (New York, 1992).

64. Ian Beckett, *War Correspondents and the American Civil War* (New Haven, 1994).

65. John Marszalek, *Sherman's Other War: The General and the Civil War Press* (Memphis, 1981), 164–7.

66. Mark Neely, *The Fate of Liberty: Abraham Lincoln and Civil Liberties* (New York, 1991), 58–60.

67. New York *World*, February 7, 1863.

68. Douglas S. Freeman and Grady McWhiney, eds., *Lee's Dispatches* (New York, 1957), 23, 265, 329.

69. Timothy Sweet, *Traces of War: Poetry, Photography and the Crisis of the Union* (Baltimore, 1990), 86.

70. *Brother against Brother: The Time-Life Books History of the Civil War* (New York, 1990), 152.

71. Paludan, 339, 342, 348; James Moorhead, *American Apocalypse: Yankee Protestants and the Civil War, 1860–1869* (New Haven, Conn., 1978).

72. Lincoln, *Collected Works*, 8:333. Also Glen Thurow, "Lincoln and American Political Religion," in *The Historian's Lincoln: Pseudohistory, Psychohistory and History*, ed. Gabor Boritt (Urbana, Ill., 1988), 125–43.

## Chapter 22

1. Daniel Sutherland, *Seasons of War: The Ordeal of a Confederate Community* (New York, 1995).

2. George Rable, *Civil Wars: Women and the Crisis of Southern Nationalism* (Urbana, Ill., 1989), 182.

3. Gary Gallagher, *The Confederate War* (Cambridge, Mass., 1997), 157.

4. Gallagher, 157.

5. Richard Beringer, "Confederate Identity and the Will to Fight," in *On the Road to Total War*, ed. Stig Forster and Jorg Nagler (New York, 1997), 75.

6. J. Tracy Power, *Lee's Miserables: Life in The Army of Northern Virginia from the Wilderness to Appomattox* (Chapel Hill, N.C., 1998), 9, 287, 297–98.

7. James Randall, *Constitutional Problems under Lincoln* (Urbana, Ill., 1951), 221ff.

8. Chester Hearn, *When the Devil Came to Dixie: Ben Butler's Occupation of New Orleans* (Baton Rouge, 1977); James Parton, *General Butler in New Orleans* (New York, 1864); Benjamin

Butler, *Autobiography and Personal Reminiscences of Major-General Benjamin F. Butler* (Boston, 1892), 1:490.

9. *National Intelligencer*, October 29, 1862.

10. Charles Royster, *The Destructive War: William Tecumseh Sherman, Stonewall Jackson and the Americans* (New York, 1991), 364.

11. Richard Beringer et al., *Why the South Lost the Civil War* (Athens, Ga., 1986), 251.

12. Catherine Clinton, *Tara Revisited: Women, War and the Plantation Legend* (New York, 1995), 132.

13. Stephen Ash, *Middle Tennessee Society Transformed, 1860–1870: War and Peace in the Upper South* (Baton Rouge, 1988).

14. Ella Lonn, *Desertion during the Civil War* (New York, 1928); James Robertson, *Soldiers Blue and Gray* (Columbia, S.C., 1988), 135.

15. Robertson, 79.

16. Bessie Martin, *Desertion of Alabama Troops from the Confederacy* (New York, 1932), 148.

17. Randall Jimmerson, *The Private War: Popular Thought during the Sectional Conflict* (Baton Rouge, 1998), 233.

18. Beringer "Confederate Identity," 93; Power, 307.

19. *War of the Rebellion . . . Official Records of the Union and Confederate Armies* (Washington, D.C., 1880–1901), 1st Ser., 17, 2: 791–2. Hereafter cited as *Official Records*.

20. J. William Harris, *Plain Folk and Gentry in a Slave Society: White Liberty and Black Slavery in Augusta's Hinterlands* (Middletown, Conn., 1986). Harris compiled a sample from three Georgia counties. See also Peter Wallenstein, "Rich Man's War, Rich Man's Fight: Civil War and the Transformation of Public Finance in Georgia," *Journal of Southern History* 50 (February 1984): 15–42. On class division, Paul Escott and Jeffrey Crow, "The Social Order and Violent Disorder: An Analysis of North Carolina in the Revolution and Civil War," *Journal of Southern History* 52 (August 1986): 373–402; Wayne Durrill, *War of a Different Kind: A Southern Community in the Great Rebellion* (New York, 1990).

21. Drew Faust, *The Creation of Confederate Nationalism: Ideology and Identity in the Civil War South* (Baton Rouge, 1988), 43–45.

22. Paul Escott, *After Secession: Jefferson Davis and the Failure of Southern Nationalism* (New York, 1976), 94.

23. Robertson, 136.

24. Rable, 108.

25. Herman Hattaway and Archer Jones, *How the North Won: A Military History of the Civil War* (Urbana, Ill., 1983), 671.

26. Lonn, 62–69, 74.

27. Beringer et al., *Why the South Lost*, 266.

28. Drew Faust, "Confederate Women and the Narratives of War," in *Divided Houses: Gender and the Civil War,* ed. Catherine Clinton and Nina Silber (New York, 1992), 183.

29. Drew Faust, *Mothers of Invention: Women of the Slaveholding South in the American Civil War* (Chapel Hill, N.C., 1996), 56.

30. C. Vann Woodward, ed., *Mary Chesnut's Civil War* (New Haven, Conn., 1981), 377.

31. *Chesnut*, 702.

32. Faust, "Narratives," 179.

33. Joan Cashin, "'Since the War Broke Out': The Marriage of Kate and William McLure" in *Divided Houses: Gender and the Civil War*, ed. Catherine Clinton and Nina Silber (New York, 1992), 200–12.

34. Faust, *Mothers of Invention*, 247.

35. Faust, *Mothers of Invention*, 191, 195.

36. Clinton, 66–75.

37. Mary Massey, *Ersatz in the Confederacy* (Columbia, S.C.), 57, 61–62.

38. Edward Moore, *The Rebellion Record* (New York, 1865), 7:48; also Rable, 109–10.

39. E. Merton Coulter, *The Confederate States of America* (Baton Rouge, 1950), 422–4.

40. Massey, 72–73.

41. *Chesnut*, 422; Eugene Lerner, "Money, Prices and Wages in the Confederacy, 1861–1865" in *The Economic Impact of the Civil War*, ed. Ralph Andreano (Cambridge, Mass., 1962), 11–72.

42. John B. Jones, *A Rebel War Clerk's Diary at the Confederate States Capital* (Philadelphia, 1866), 2:89–90.

43. Jones, 1:196, 221.

44. *Chesnut*, 323.

45. Message of Governor Vance to the North Carolina General Assembly, Nov. 17, 1862, *Official Records*, Ser. 4, 2:181; Paul Escott, "Poverty and Governmental Aid for the Poor in North Carolina," *North Carolina Historical Review* 61 (October 1984): 484; Escott, *After Secession*, 142.

46. Ella Lonn, *Salt as a Factor in the Confederacy* (New York, 1933).

47. Beringer, *Why the South Lost*, 218–21; Marion Smith, "The Saute Cave Confederate Niter Works," *Civil War History* 29 (December 1983): 293–315.

48. Richard Bensel, *Yankee Leviathan: The Origins of Central State Authority, 1859–1897* (New York, 1990), 183, also 146–8.

49. Beringer, *Why the South Lost*, 219.

50. George Rable, *The Confederate Republic: A Revolution against Politics* (Chapel Hill, N.C., 1994).

51. David Scarboro, "North Carolina and the Confederacy: The Weakness of States' Rights During the Civil War," *North Carolina Historical Review* 56 (April 1979): 133–49; Marc Kruman, "Dissent in the Confederacy: The North Carolina Experience," *Civil War History* 27 (December 1981): 293–313.

52. A. Sellew Roberts, "The Peace Movement in North Carolina," *Mississippi Valley Historical Review* 11 (June 1924): 190–9. There is a tradition that Jones County "seceded" from Mississippi and formed the "Republic of Jones," but in fact no such secession occurred. "The county was certainly in the hands of outlaws, who might well have . . . seceded," writes John K. Bettersworth. "Actually, they did agree not to pay taxes. . . . Anarchy rather than government prevailed in this 'free state' during the war; and one must look in vain for anything like an organized movement of the counter-secession, even though the fact that the majority of the people were in one way or another disloyal to the Confederacy is fairly well established." John Bettersworth, *Confederate Mississippi: The People and Policies of a Cotton State during Wartime* (Baton Rouge, 1943), 227–67.

53. Paul Escott, *After Secession*, 155; Thomas Alexander and Richard Beringer, *The Anatomy of the Confederate Congress: A Study of the Influence of Membership Characteristics on Legislative Voting Behavior* (Nashville, 1972), 330.

54. *Journal of the Congress of the Confederate States of America* (Washington D.C., 1904), 7:266–7. Hereafter cited as *Journal, Confed. Cong.*

55. Mark Neely, "Confederate Bastille: Jefferson Davis and Civil Liberties," Frank Klement Lectures, Marquette University, 1993.

56. *Official Records*, Ser. 4, 3: 646–8; Ludwell Johnson, "Trading with the Enemy: The Evolution of Confederate Policy," *Virginia Magazine of History and Biography* 78 (July 1970): 310–4.

57. James Rabun, "Alexander H. Stephens and Jefferson Davis," *American Historical Review* 58 (January 1953), 308; E. Merton Coulter, *The Confederate States of America* (Baton Rouge, 1950), 540.

58. Rabun, 290–311; Coulter, 540.

59. *Journal of the Confederate Congress*, 7:255, 611–12; Bensel, 153–5. Two earlier exceptions to the South's all-white army were the organization of an Alabama regiment of blacks and the enlistment of Creoles for the defense of Mobile.

60. *Official Records*, Ser. 4, 3:1012–13, also Ser. 1, 46, 3:1356–7; Ser. 1, 1:682, 723–5; Ira Berlin, *Freedom: The Destruction of Slavery* (New York, 1985).

61. Robert Durden, *The Gray and the Black: The Confederate Debate on Emancipation* (Baton Rouge, 1972), 135–42.

62. Beringer, *Why the South Lost*, 92–93, 350–4. On southern guilt about slavery, there is some controversy. See Kenneth Stampp, "The Southern Road to Appomattox," in *The Imperiled Union: Essays on the Background of the Civil War*, ed. Kenneth Stamp (New York, 1980), 246–69. Also James Oakes, *The Ruling Race: A History of the Meaning of American Slaveholding* (New York, 1982).

63. Drew Faust, "Christian Soldiers: Revivalism in the Confederate Army," *Journal of Southern History* 53 (February 1987): 63–90. Quote from Robertson, 174.

64. Reid Mitchell, *Civil War Soldiers* (New York, 1988), 173.

65. Beringer, *Why the South Lost*, 367.

## Chapter 23

1. Kenneth Stampp, *The Imperiled Union: Essays on the Background of the Civil War* (New York, 1980), 266.

2. Joseph Glatthaar, *The March to the Sea and Beyond: Sherman's Troops in the Savannah and Carolinas Campaign* (New York, 1985), 155, 162.

3. Richard Beringer, "Confederate Identity and the Will to Fight," in *On the Road to Total War*, ed. Stig Forster and Jorg Nagler (New York, 1997), 83.

4. Steven Tripp, *Yankee Town, Southern City: Class and Race in Civil War Lynchburg* (New York, 1997).

5. Richard Beringer et al., *The Elements of Confederate Defeat: Nationalism, War Aims, and Religion* (Baton Rouge, 1988), 153.

6. Roy P. Basler et al., *The Collected Works of Abraham Lincoln* (New Brunswick, N.J., 1953), 8:275–6. Hereafter cited as Lincoln, *Collected Works*.

7. Lincoln, *Collected Works*, 8:279, 285.

8. Rowland Dunbar, ed., *Jefferson Davis, Constitutionalist: His Letters, Papers, and Speeches* (Jackson, Miss., 1923), 6:466.

9. C. Vann Woodward, ed., *Mary Chestnut's Civil War* (New Haven, Conn., 1981), 780.

10. Ernest Furgurson, *Ashes of Glory: Richmond at War* (New York, 1996), 336, 345.

11. Brooks Simpson, *Let Us Have Peace: Ulysses S. Grant and the Politics of War and Reconstruction* (Chapel Hill, N.C., 1991), 82–85; on Lee's first response, 81–82, 78.

12. Ulysses S. Grant, *Personal Memoirs of Ulysses S. Grant* (New York, 1952), 2: 500. Grant states that in addition to the twenty-eight thousand paroled at Appomattox, the Federals had captured over nineteen thousand Confederates between March 29 and the date of surrender, "to say nothing of Lee's other losses." According to Lee's statement, confirmed by his staff, he had on April 2 a total of thirty-three thousand men from the Chickahominy River to Dinwiddie Courthouse. Meade stated that at this time his army numbered over fifty thousand south of the James River. Douglas S. Freeman, *R. E. Lee: A Biography* (New York, 1934), 4: 153.

13. Robert Underwood Johnson and Clarence Buel, *Battles and Leaders of the Civil War* (New York, 1887), 4: 738; Grant, 2: 294; Freeman, 4: 142n; J. Tracy Power, *Lee's Miserables: Life in the Army of the Potomac from the Wilderness to Appomattox* (Chapel Hill, N.C., 1998), 282.

14. Richard Beringer et al., *Why the South Lost the Civil War* (Athens, Ga., 1986), 297.

15. Beringer, *Why the South Lost*, 342.

16. Freeman, 4: 84.

17. George Fredrickson, "Why the Confederacy Did Not Fight a Guerrilla War," Fortenbaugh Lecture, Gettysburg College, 1996, 28.

18. Mary Stanard, *Richmond: Its People and Its Story* (Philadelphia, 1923), 209.

19. Lincoln, *Collected Works*, 8: 332–3.

20. Lincoln, *Collected Works*, 8: 399–404.

21. Dunbar, 6: 530.

22. Dunbar, 6: 530, 541, 544.

23. Raoul Naroll, "Lincoln and the Sherman Peace Fiasco—Another Fable?" *Journal of Southern History* 20 (November 1954): 483.

24. John F. Marszalek, *Sherman: A Soldier's Passion for Order* (New York, 1994), 345–6.

25. For one international comparison see Beringer, *Why the South Lost*, 440–1.

26. Thomas Livermore, *Numbers and Losses in the Civil War in America, 1861–1865* (Bloomington, Ind., 1957), 1–10.

27. Reid Mitchell, *Civil War Soldiers* (New York, 1987), 204.

## Chapter 24

1. An important exception to this traditional chronology is Eric Foner, *Reconstruction: America's Unfinished Revolution, 1863–1877* (New York, 1988). Foner begins in 1863 because he sees the freeing of slaves and the experience of blacks as central to the story of Reconstruction. Other scholars extend the story to 1879, when many southern states wrote new constitutions after the toppling of their Reconstruction governments. See, for example, Michael Perman, *The Road to Redemption: Southern Politics, 1869–1879* (Chapel Hill, N.C., 1984).

2. William Gillette, *Retreat from Reconstruction, 1869–1879* (Baton Rouge, 1979), xiii.

3. For succinct summaries of this often rancorous historiographical controversy, see Bernard A. Weisberger, "The Dark and Bloody Ground of Reconstruction Historiography," *Journal of Southern History* 25 (November 1959): 427–47; Eric Foner, "Reconstruction Revisited," *Reviews in American History* 10 (December 1982): 82–100; and Eric Foner, *Reconstruction: America's Unfinished Revolution*, xix–xxvii.

4. Foner, *Reconstruction: America's Unfinished Revolution*, xxvi.

5. The best succinct discussion of these divergent northern attitudes at the end of the war remains Eric McKitrick, *Andrew Johnson and Reconstruction* (Chicago, 1960), 15–84.

6. Clemenceau quoted in Kenneth M. Stampp, *The Era of Reconstruction* (New York, 1966), 109.

7. The quotations are taken from Harold Hyman, *A More Perfect Union: The Impact of the Civil War and Reconstruction on the Constitution* (Boston, 1975), 299, 305, 310; on pp. 282–368, he offers numerous examples of the remarkably varied and pervasive governmental activism after the war. The surge of governmental activity at all levels of the federal system, of which Reconstruction was only one example, and Democratic resistance to it, is also a central theme of Morton Keller, *Affairs of State: Public Life in Late-Nineteenth-Century America* (Cambridge, Mass., 1977), 35–237.

8. James M. McPherson, *The Negro's Civil War: How American Blacks Felt and Acted during the War for the Union* (New York, 1965), 245–70; Foner, *Reconstruction: America's Unfinished Revolution*, 28.

9. Foner, *Reconstruction: America's Unfinished Revolution*, pp. 110–7.

10. William Gillette, *The Right to Vote: Politics and the Passage of the Fifteenth Amendment*, rev. ed. (Baltimore, 1969), 26–28; LaWanda and John H. Cox, "Negro Suffrage and Republican Politics: The Problem of Motivation in Reconstruction Historiography," *Journal of Southern History* 33 (1967): 303–30.

11. Herman Belz, *A New Birth of Freedom: The Republican Party and Freedmen's Rights, 1861–1866* (Westport, Conn., 1976), 158; Michael Les Benedict, *The Impeachment and Trial of Andrew Johnson* (New York, 1973), 10.

12. The two best studies of northern Democrats during the Civil War are Joel H. Silbey, *A Respectable Minority: The Democratic Party in the Civil War Era, 1860–1868* (New York, 1977); and Jean H. Baker, *Affairs of Party: The Political Culture of Northern Democrats in Mid-Nineteenth Century America* (Ithaca, N.Y., 1983).

13. The debt and tax burden imposed on the North's civilian population by the national government has been described above, pp. (297–303), but it is essential to remember that local and state governments also issued bonds and raised taxes to unheard-of levels to raise troops and supplies, to pay commutation fees and bounties for substitutes so that local residents could escape the draft, and to aid the families of absent soldiers. See, for example, Thomas R. Kemp, "Community and War: The Civil War Experience of Two New Hampshire Towns," in *Toward a Social History of the American Civil War*, ed. Maris A. Vinovskis (New York and Cambridge, 1990), 31–77; and Iver Bernstein, *The New York City Draft Riots: Their Significance for American Society and Politics in the Age of the Civil War* (New York and Oxford, 1990), 200–2.

14. Foner, *Reconstruction: America's Unfinished Revolution*, 148.

15. Bureau of the Census, *Historical Statistics of the United States from Colonial Times to 1970* (Washington, D.C., 1975), 106.

16. The information in this paragraph is based on Maris A. Vinovskis, "Have Social Historians Lost the Civil War? Some Preliminary Demographic Speculations," and Amy E. Holmes, " 'Such Is the Price We Pay': American Widows and the Civil War Pension System," both in *Toward a Social History of the American Civil War*, ed. Maris A. Vinovskis (New York and Cambridge, 1990), 21–25, 171–95; and Theda Skocpol, *Protecting Soldiers and Mothers: The Political Origins of Social Policy in the United States* (Cambridge, Mass., 1992), 102–51, esp. pp. 106–7.

17. Holmes, "American Widows and the Civil War Pension System," p. 173.

18. David Montgomery, *Beyond Equality: Labor and the Radical Republicans, 1862–1872* (New York, 1967), 33.

19. Susan Previant Lee and Peter Passell, *A New Economic View of American History* (New York, 1979), 228. The impact of the Civil War on the North's economy is a hotly debated topic, and much of that controversy is ably summarized and analyzed in Lee and Passell, 223–39. But see also Thomas Cochran, "Did the Civil War Retard Industrialization?" *Mississippi Valley Historical Review* 48 (September 1961): 197–210; Jeffrey Williamson, "Watersheds and Turning Points: Conjectures on the Long-Term Impact of Civil War Financing," *Journal of Economic History* 34 (September 1974): 636–61; Claudia Goldin and Frank Lewis, "The Economic Cost of the American Civil War: Estimates and Implications," *Journal of Economic History* 35 (June 1975): 299–326; and Saul Engbourg, "The Impact of the Civil War on Manufacturing Enterprise," *Business History* 21 (1979): 148–62.

20. Rendigs Fels, *American Business Cycles, 1865–1897* (New York, 1959), 92.

21. *Historical Statistics of the United States*, 731; Montgomery, 11.

22. Fred A. Shannon, *The Farmer's Last Frontier: Agriculture, 1860–1897* (New York, 1945), 417.

23. Shannon, 47, 49, 55, 162; Foner, *Reconstruction: America's Unfinished Revolution*, 463.

24. William Cronon, *Nature's Metropolis: Chicago and the Great West* (New York, 1991), 213–24.

25. On Chicago, see Cronon's dazzling *Nature's Metropolis*.

26. Keller, 165.

27. The political ramifications of railroad construction and regulation will be discussed more fully in later chapters, but for the 1850s precedents for regulation, see Frederick Merk; "Eastern Antecedents of the Grangers," *Agricultural History* 23 (1949): 1–8; Lee Benson, *Merchants, Farmers, and Railroads: Railroad Regulation and New York Politics, 1850–1887* (Ithaca, N.Y., 1955). On the later Granger laws in the Midwest, see George H. Miller, *Railroads and the Granger Laws* (Madison, Wisc., 1971). For the centrality of railroad building to Reconstruction in the South, see Mark W. Summers, *Railroads, Reconstruction, and the Gospel of Prosperity: Aid Under the Radical Republicans* (Princeton, N.J., 1984).

28. Cronon, 207–49; Alfred D. Chandler, Jr., *The Visible Hand: The Managerial Revolution in American Business* (Cambridge, Mass., 1977), 299–301.

29. The best study of the iron and steel industry in the nineteenth century remains Peter Temin, *Iron and Steel in 19th Century America: An Economic Inquiry* (Cambridge, Mass., 1964), but for the

symbiotic relationship between Carnegie's railroading past and steel-making future, as well as the technological proficiency of the J. Edgar Thomson Works, see Chandler, 259–69.

30. This paragraph is based on Chandler, 90, 259; Williamson; and especially Montgomery, 5–44.

31. Montgomery, 29–30; Stuart Blumin, "Hypothesis of Middle-Class Formation in Nineteenth-Century America: A Critique and Some Proposals," *American Historical Review* 90 (1985): 299–338; Cindy Sondik Aron, *Ladies and Gentlemen of the Civil Service: Middle-Class Workers in Victorian America* (New York, 1987); Olivier Zunz, *Making America Corporate, 1870–1920* (Chicago, 1990).

32. Montgomery, 90–113; Grace Palladino, *Another Civil War: Labor, Capital, and the State in the Anthracite Regions of Pennsylvania, 1840–1868* (Urbana, Ill., 1990). For a summary and assessment of the literature positing that the wage gap was key to manufacturing prosperity during the war, see Lee and Passell, 229–33.

33. Keller, 169; Montgomery, 42–44, 126–34, 140, and *passim*.

34. Quoted *ibid*, pp. 90–91.

35. See above, pp. 298, 300.

36. The literature on the complicated money question after the Civil War is extensive. The account here is primarily based upon Robert Sharkey, *Money, Class, and Party: An Economic Study of the Civil War and Reconstruction* (Baltimore, 1959); Irwin Unger, *The Greenback Era: A Social and Political History of American Finance, 1865–1879* (Princeton, N.J., 1964); Walter T. K. Nugent, *The Money Question During Reconstruction* (New York, 1967); Richard F. Bensel, *Yankee Leviathan: The Origins of Central State Authority in America, 1859–1877* (New York and Cambridge, 1990), 238–365.

37. The divisions among various economic interest groups over these and other economic questions in the postwar period are ably presented in Stanley Coben, "Northeastern Business and Radical Reconstruction: A Reexamination," *Mississippi Valley Historical Review* 46 (1959): 67–90; Irwin Unger, "Business Men and Specie Resumption," *Political Science Quarterly* 74 (1959): 46–70; and especially Unger, 41–162.

38. Nugent, 27–28.

39. Sharkey, 102–4, 135–40.

40. Sharkey, 186–206; Montgomery, 340–55, 425–47.

41. Gerald D. Jaynes, *Branches Without Roots: Genesis of the Black Working Class in the American South, 1862–1882* (New York, 1986), 8–9 and *passim*.

42. Lee and Passell, 235; Williamson.

## Chapter 25

1. Dan T. Carter, *When the War Was Over: The Failure of Self-Reconstruction in the South, 1865–1867* (Baton Rouge, 1985), 103–4.

2. Carter, 6–23, quotations 10–11.

3. Robert Driver, *Lexington and Rockbridge County in the Civil War* (Lynchburg, Va., 1989), 99; Lexington *Gazette*, April 20, May 4, 1865.

4. Mary N. Stanard, *Richmond: Its People and Its Story* (Philadelphia, 1923), 212; Michael Chesson, *Richmond After the War: 1865–1890* (Richmond, 1981), 72, 93; Leslie Winton Smith, "Richmond during Presidential Reconstruction" (Ph.D. dissertation, University of Virginia, 1974), 328–9.

5. John Richard Dennett, *The South as It Is: 1865–1866* (reprint: New York, 1965), 8.

6. Whitlaw Reid, *After the War* (New York, 1866), 206–7, quoted in Gerald D. Jaynes, *Branches Without Roots: Genesis of the Black Working Class in the American South, 1862–1882* (New York, 1986), 37; Dennett, 8–9, 44–45; Lexington, Virginia *Gazette*, May 4, 1865.

7. Carl Schurz, *Reminiscences of Carl Schurz* (New York, 1907–1908), 3: 167.

8. Theodore Salutos, "Southern Agriculture and the Problems of Readjustment, 1865–1877," *Agricultural History* 30 (April 1956): 61.

9. Lawrence N. Powell, *New Masters: Northern Planters during the Civil War and Reconstruction* (New Haven, Conn., 1980), quotation, xii; Richard N. Current, *Those Terrible Carpetbaggers: A Reinterpretation* (New York, 1988).

10. Jaynes, 37, n. 20; Terry Seip, *The South Returns to Congress: Men, Economic Measures, and Intersectional Relationships, 1869–1879* (Baton Rouge, 1983).

11. Jaynes, 35–36. Jaynes's brilliant book provides the most extended analysis of how inadequate credit contributed to the postwar impoverishment of the South.

12. Roger Ransom and Richard Sutch, *One Kind of Freedom: The Economic Consequences of Emancipation* (New York and Cambridge, 1977), 41–42.

13. Eugene M. Lerner, "Southern Output and Agricultural Income, 1860–1880" *Agricultural History* 33 (July 1959): 133; Carter Goodrich, "Public Aid to the Railroads in the Reconstruction South," *Political Science Quarterly* 71 (September 1956): 438.

14. Ransom and Sutch, 152; Gavin Wright, *The Political Economy of the Cotton South: Households, Markets, and Wealth in the Nineteenth Century* (New York, 1978), 164.

15. Eric Foner, *Reconstruction: America's Unfinished Revolution, 1863–1877* (New York, 1988), 170–3, 399, 402–3.

16. Ransom and Sutch, 9.

17. Claudia Goldin and Frank Lewis, "The Economic Cost of the American Civil War: Estimates and Implications," *Journal of Economic History* 35 (June 1975): 299–326.

18. Robert Fogel, *Without Consent of Contract: The Rise and Fall of American Slavery* (New York, 1989), 89.

19. Gavin Wright and Howard Kunreuther, "Cotton, Corn, and Risk in the Nineteenth Century," *Journal of Economic History* 35 (September 1975): 526–551.

20. Robert Gallman and Ralph V. Anderson, "Slaves as Fixed Capital: Slave Labor and Southern Economic Development," *Journal of American History* 64 (June 1977): 41–45.

21. Ransom and Sutch, 9. 44–47, 106–70.

22. Fogel, 98–102.

23. Jaynes, 15, 35, and *passim*.

24. Wright and Kunreuther; Armstead L. Robinson, "Beyond the Realm of Social Consensus: New Meanings of Reconstruction for American History," *Journal of American History* 68 (September 1981): 280–4; Foner, 393–94.

25. Ransom and Sutch, *One Kind of Freedom*, pp. 52–53.

26. Compare Ransom and Sutch, 52, with Jaynes, 30–53 and *passim*. The discussion that follows depends heavily on Jaynes's analysis.

27. Jaynes, 26.

28. Foner, 77–126; quotation, 78. The fullest study of the range of reactions to emancipation during and immediately after the war is Leon Litwack, *Been in the Storm So Long: The Aftermath of Slavery* (New York, 1979), but the excellent literature on this important subject is too vast to cite fully here.

29. Ira Berlin, Barbara J. Fields, Stephen F. Miller, Joseph P. Reidy, and Leslie S. Rowland, *Slaves No More: Three Essays on Emancipation and the Civil War* (Cambridge and New York, 1992), 135.

30. Louis S. Gerteis, *From Contraband to Freedman: Federal Policy Toward Southern Blacks, 1861–1865* (Westport, Conn., 1973), 7.

31. McPherson, *The Negro's Civil War: How American Blacks Felt and Acted during the War for the Union* (New York, 1965), 128, 130.

32. Foner, 77–123.

33. McPherson, 299–300; George M. Fredrickson, *The Black Image in the White Mind: The Debate on Afro-American Character and Destiny, 1817–1914* (New York, 1971), 175–7.

34. Foner, 69.

35. Herman Belz, *A New Birth of Freedom: The Republican Party and Freedmen's Rights, 1861–1868* (Westport, Conn., 1976), pp. 75–96; Herman Belz, "The Freedmen's Bureau Act and the Principle of No Discrimination According to Color," *Civil War History* 21 (September 1975): 197–217.

36. Gerteis, 39–50; William S. McFeely, *Yankee Stepfather: General O. O. Howard and the Freedmen* (New Haven, 1968), 149–65.

37. Michael Perman, *Reunion Without Compromise: The South and Reconstruction, 1865–1868* (Cambridge and New York, 1973), 47–48.

38. Ransom and Sutch, 4, 9, 44–47, and *passim*.

## Chapter 26

1. William C. Harris, *With Charity For All: Lincoln and the Restoration of the Union* (Lexington, Ky., 1997), 10. My account of Virginia is taken from pp. 19–23 of Harris' book, the most recent, fullest, and best account of Lincoln's reconstruction efforts during the war. The best study of Congress' wartime deliberations over Reconstruction remains Herman Belz, *Reconstructing the Union: Theory and Policy during the Civil War* (Ithaca, N.Y., 1969).

2. Roy P. Basler et al., *The Collected Works of Abraham Lincoln* (New Brunswick, N.J., 1953), 4: 428. Hereafter cited as Lincoln, *Collected Works*. Lane quoted in Harris, 23.

3. Harris, 10.

4. *Ibid*, 34; Belz, 40–99.

5. Harris, 32.

6. Lincoln, *Collected Works*, 6: 469.

7. Lincoln, *Collected Works*, 5: 302–3.

8. On Louisiana and Tennessee, see Harris, 40–56, 73–77. Harris also demonstrates that the Democrat Johnson stalled reorganization because he feared that his former Whig political enemies who dominated Unionists in occupied Middle and West Tennessee would control the new state government if he allowed an election.

9. Recognizing his total dependence on federal support, Virginia's Pierpont shifted gears and endorsed Lincoln's Emancipation Proclamation as early as December 1862. Tennessee's Johnson, in part to curry Lincoln's backing against anti-emancipation Whig Unionists, did so during 1863.

10. Harris, 56.

11. In Tennessee, Johnson, with Lincoln's backing, refused to validate a gubernatorial and state legislative election called for August 1863 by proslavery Whig Unionists from western and middle Tennessee on the grounds that East Tennesseans could not participate, whereas miscommunication among Lincoln and federal agents in Louisiana also delayed action there. Harris, 105–20. Arkansas, in contrast, took steps toward creating a loyal government that met Lincoln's specifications. Unionists there in late October 1863 called for a new state constitutional convention that would establish a new free-state government to meet in January 1864. See Harris, 126–8.

12. Lincoln's Proclamation can be found in Lincoln, *Collected Works*, 7:53–56. In his annual message of the same day, Lincoln elaborated on the rationale of his proclamations; the relevant sections of the annual message can be found *ibid.*, 50–53.

13. By December 1863, in fact, only a few of the most radical congressional Republicans still insisted that seceded states had reverted to a territorial stage. Most instead now cited the Constitutional clause guaranteeing states a republican form of government as the basis for congressional, not executive, control over Reconstruction. See Belz, 129–39.

14. The pertinent clause of Lincoln's amnesty proclamation announced "that any provision which may be adopted by such State government in relation to the freed people of such State, which shall recognize and declare their permanent freedom, provide for their education, and which may yet be consistent, as a temporary arrangement, with their present condition as a laboring, landless, and homeless class, will not be objected to by the national Executive." Lincoln, *Collected Works*, 7:55. For Banks's contract system in Louisiana, see Chapter 25.

15. Shortly after the war, however, the disfranchising provisions were significantly moderated.

16. Harris, 197–211.

17. Congress later refused to count the electoral votes for Lincoln from Tennessee or those cast by Louisiana's Unionist legislature in 1864.

18. For Tennessee, see Harris, 212–28. The new free-state constitution won ratification by a vote of 25,293 to 48. Though smaller than the November turnout, that vote still met Lincoln's 10 percent test, since approximately 145,000 Tennesseans had voted in the 1860 presidential election.

19. The literature on the wartime reconstruction of Louisiana is now substantial. We have relied heavily on the lucid and succinct analysis in Harris, 171–96, but see also the somewhat contradictory accounts in Peyton McCrary, *Abraham Lincoln and Reconstrruction: The Louisiana Experiment* (Princeton, N.J., 1978); LaWanda Cox, *Lincoln and Black Freedom: A Study in Presidential Leadership* (Columbia, S.C., 1981); Ted Tunnel, *Crucible of Reconstruction: War, Radicalism and Race in Louisiana, 1862–1867* (Baton Rouge, 1984).

20. Lincoln, *Collected Works*, 89–90.

21. The Louisiana convention did not complete the new state constitution until almost three weeks after Congress adjourned on July 4, 1864, and it was not ratified until September. Thus, when congressional Republicans voted on the Wade-Davis bill, it was still not certain that Louisianans would abolish slavery on their own.

22. Though I have generally followed the excellent account of the Wade-Davis bill in Belz, 168–243, this stress on placing reconstruction on a statutory basis as the bill's primary aim is taken from Michael Les Benedict, *A Compromise of Principle: Congressional Republicans and Reconstruction, 1863–1869* (New York, 1974), 70–83. Unlike Belz, Cox, and McCrary, indeed, Benedict downplays events in Louisiana as catalysts for the bill.

23. A copy of the Wade-Davis bill can be found in James D. Richardson, ed., *A Compilation of Messages and Papers of the Presidents, 1787–1897* (Washington, D.C., 1896), 6: 223–6. Intriguingly, unlike the Thirteenth Amendment, which banned both slavery and involuntary servitude, the Wade-Davis bill mentioned only the latter, but there is no explicit evidence that in doing so congressional Republicans meant to prohibit the kind of apprenticeship programs Lincoln had condoned.

24. This proscription, of course, would also prevent such men from voting for congressmen and presidential electors.

25. Richardson, 6:222–3.

26. Belz, 229–43.

27. Lincoln, *Collected Works*, 7:243.

28. Harris, 182–96.

29. Lincoln, *Collected Works*, 8:399–405.

30. David Donald, ed., *Inside Lincoln's Cabinet*, 268; Lincoln is quoted in David Herbert Donald, *Lincoln* (New York, 1995), 591.

31. Richardson, 6:356.

32. Richardson, 6:355.

33. For the central role that winning white southern support played in Johnson's political calculations, see David Donald, *The Politics of Reconstruction, 1863–1867* (Baton Rouge, 1965), 17–25.

34. Eric Foner, *Reconstruction: America's Unfinished Revolution, 1863–1877* (New York, 1988), 219; Michael Perman, *Reunion Without Compromise: The South and Reconstruction, 1865–1868* (Cambridge and New York, 1973), 197.

35. *Appleton's American Annual Cyclopaedia* (New York 1865), 801; Kenneth Stampp, *The Era of Reconstruction, 1865–1877* (New York, 1965), 51–52.

36. Hans L. Trefousse, *Andrew Johnson: A Biography* (New York, 1989), 210; Richardson, 6:337–8.

37. In addition to the Pierpont government in Virginia, Johnson also recognized the legitimacy of the wartime Union governments established in Arkansas, Louisiana, and Tennessee. Thus his proclamations concerning the requirements for restoration applied only to the seven remaining Confederate states.

38. Richardson, 6:310–4.

39. Richardson, 6:311–2.

40. The North Carolina proclamation, the language of which, except for the names of states and provisional governors, was repeated in subsequent proclamations, can be found in Richardson, 6:312–4.

41. Perman, 71–72. Perman's book contains the fullest treatment of Johnson's interactions with his provisional governors and of his attempts to get them to secure the protection of black rights short of suffrage.

42. For Johnson's southern political strategy, see David Donald, *The Politics of Reconstruction* (Baton Rouge, 1965), 17–22; and Perman, quotation, p. 97. On the resurgence of southern Whigs to office during Presidential Reconstruction, see Thomas B. Alexander, "Persistent Whiggery in the Confederate South, 1860–1877," *Journal of Southern History* 27 (1961): 305–29.

43. Perman, 65 and *passim*.

44. Pride of place in first recognizing that Johnson and such advisors as Secretary of State William H. Seward hoped to make the wartime Union party permanent by adding more Democrats and southern ex-Confederates to it belongs to LaWanda Cox and John H. Cox, *Politics, Principle, and Prejudice, 1865–1866: Dilemma of Reconstruction America* (Glencoe, Ill., 1963).

45. Robert M. T. Hunter to Andrew Johnson, September 27, 1865, quoted in Perman, 195.

## Chapter 27

1. Aside from Michael Perman's *Reunion without Compromise: The South and Reconstruction, 1865–1868* (Cambridge, 1973), the best study of southern behavior and the motives for it between 1865 and 1867 is Dan T. Carter, *When the War Was Over: The Failure of Self-Reconstruction in the South, 1865–1867* (Baton Rouge, 1985).

2. Eric Foner, *Reconstruction: America's Unfinished Revolution, 1863–1877* (New York, 1988), 191.

3. William S. McFeely, *Yankee Stepfather: General O. O. Howard and the Freedmen* (New Haven, Conn., 1968), 112–4, 130–48; Foner, 159–63.

4. James D. Richardson, ed., *A Compilation of Messages and Papers of the Presidents 1787–1897* (Washington, D.C. 1896), 6:357.

5. The books by Perman and Carter provide the fullest assessment of this mood.

6. *Appleton's American Annual Cyclopaedia* (New York, 1865), 809.

7. Jack B. Scroggs, "Southern Reconstruction: A Radical View," *Journal of Southern History* 24 (November 1958): 408.

8. Perman, 11.

9. Foner, 224.

10. Foner 225, 197.

11. Foner, 224.

12. Foner, 199–203.

13. Perman, 79.

14. Foner, 224.

15. The Union/Republican state platforms of 1865 can be found in *Appleton's American Annual Cyclopaedia* for 1865 under each northern state's entry.

16. The pathbreaking study of Democratic courtship of Johnson in 1865 and 1866 is LaWanda Cox and John H. Cox, *Politics, Principle, and Prejudice, 1865–1866: The Dilemma of Reconstruction America* (Glencoe, Ill., 1963); but see also Edward L. Gambill, *Conservative Ordeal: Northern Democrats and Reconstruction, 1865–1868* (Ames, Iowa, 1981).

17. Herman Belz, *Emancipation and Equal Rights: Politics and Constitutionalism in the Civil War Era* (New York, 1978), 73–74, 109–14; Foner, 226, 231.

18. Foner, 239; Eric L. McKitrick, *Andrew Johnson and Reconstruction* (Chicago, 1960), 253–73.

19. The literature on the operation of the Freedmen's Bureau in the South is now immense. For older accounts, see George R. Bentley, *A History of the Freedmen's Bureau* (Philadelphia, 1955) and McFeely. For a superb recent monograph on a single state, see Paul A. Cimbala, *Under the Guardianship of the Nation: The Freedmen's Bureau and the Reconstruction of Georgia, 1865–1870* (Athens, Ga., 1997).

20. Bentley, 104–5.

21. Belz, 114.

22. Bentley, 116–7.

23. William M. Wiecek, "The Reconstruction of Federal Judicial Power, 1863–1875," *American Journal of Legal History* 13 (October 1969): 333–59; Stanley I. Kutler, *Judicial Power and Reconstruction Politics* (Chicago, 1968).

24. Belz, 110.

25. Foner, 251. On the final votes on the Civil Rights bill, all Senate Republicans supported passage, and in the House all but six Republicans did. Michael Les Benedict, *A Compromise of Principle: Congressional Republicans and Reconstruction, 1863–1869* (New York, 1974), 162.

26. Belz, 116–7; Richardson, 405–13. Additional implications of the Civil Rights Law of 1866 will be discussed in the following chapter.

27. Richardson, 6: 398–405.

28. Richardson, 6:405–13.

29. Hans L. Trefousse, *Andrew Johnson: A Biography* (New York, 1989), 244. The quotations from his speech are from the same page.

30. *Ibid.*

31. Foner, 248–9.

32. Cox and Cox, 173.

33. In July congressional Republicans would pass a slightly modified bill extending the life of the Freedmen's Bureau over Johnson's veto.


## Chapter 28

1. A word about terminology is in order here. Although at least two generations of historians have documented the existence of Republican factions and numerous statistical studies of roll-call voting patterns in Congress have found Republicans ranged along a spectrum from ultra conservative to ultraradical, historians disagree about what to call the Radicals' opponents. For example, in his *Compromise of Principle: Congressional Republicans and Reconstruction, 1863–1869* (New York, 1974), the best study of congressional policy making, Michael Les Benedict divides Republicans into Conservatives, Centrists, and Radicals and lumps the first two groups as non-Radicals when distinguishing them from Radicals. Nonetheless, following the practice of earlier historians, we label the non-Radicals Moderates, even though that group encompasses a broad spectrum of opinion and behavior, as, indeed, does the Radical category itself.

2. Here we follow Benedict, *A Compromise of Principle*; Michael Les Benedict, "Preserving the Constitution: The Conservative Basis of Radical Reconstruction," *Journal of American History* 61 (June 1974): 65–90; and Herman Belz, *Emancipation and Equal Rights: Politics and Constitutionalism in the Civil War Era* (New York, 1978).

3. Benedict, *A Compromise of Principle*, 22.

4. See, for example, Eric L. McKitrick, *Andrew Johnson and Reconstruction* (Chicago, 1960); William R. Brock, *An American Crisis: Congress and Reconstruction, 1865–1867* (New York, 1963); David Donald, *The Politics of Reconstruction* (Baton Rouge, 1965); and Edward L. Gambill, "Who Were the Senate Radicals?" *Civil War History* 11 (June 1965): 237–43.

5. The most famous example of this interpretation is Howard K. Beale, *The Critical Year: A Study of Andrew Johnson and Reconstruction* (New York, 1930). Among the most important studies that have demolished it are Robert P. Sharkey, *Money, Class, and Party: An Economic Study of Civil War and Reconstruction* (Baltimore, 1959); Stanley Coben, "Northeastern Business and Radical Reconstruction: A Re-examination," *Mississippi Valley Historical Review* 46 (June 1959): 67–90; Irwin Unger, *The Greenback Era: A Social and Political History of American Finance* (Princeton, N.J., 1964); and Glenn M. Linden, "'Radicals' and Economic Policies: The House of Representatives, 1861–1873," *Civil War History* 13 (March 1967): 51–65.

6. Benedict, *A Compromise of Principle*, 59–69.

7. Eric Foner, *Reconstruction: American's Unfinished Revolution, 1863–1877* (New York, 1988), 233–4.

8. Benedict, *A Compromise of Principle*, 58.

9. Benedict, *A Compromise of Principle*, 137.

10. Benedict, *A Compromise of Principle*, 57; the most forceful exposition of congressional Republicans' northern orientation throughout the process of Reconstruction is William Gillette, *Retreat from Reconstruction, 1869–1879* (Baton Rouge, 1979).

11. Benedict, *A Compromise of Principle*, 58.

12. Benedict, *A Compromise of Principle*, 57.

13. Benedict, *A Compromise of Principle*, 135.

14. Benedict, "Preserving the Constitution"; Belz, 117–50.

15. Benedict, "Preserving the Constitution," 68–69.

16. Belz, 142.

17. The Freedmen's Bureau bill did authorize the government to lease or sell southern land it possessed to freedmen in forty-acre plots, but Radicals like Thaddeus Stevens bitterly complained that the poverty-stricken freedmen could never pay the purchase price or annual rent. His attempt to amend the bill in the House to restrict rents to two cents per acre per year was crushed by the Moderates. Benedict, *A Compromise of Principle*, 149–50.

18. Benedict, *A Compromise of Principle*, 149.

19. For a vigorous, if not totally compelling, dissent from the interpretation of Belz and Benedict incorporated here, one that argues that Republicans expected the national government directly to protect blacks from both private and public acts of discrimination and abuse and intended their program to force a "revolutionary change" in American federalism, see Robert J. Kaczorowski, "To Begin the Nation Anew: Congress, Citizenship, and Civil Rights after the Civil War," *American Historical Review* 92 (February 1987): 45–68.

20. A raft of possible amendments were submitted to the committee, but ultimately it combined the most important provisions from them in a single, omnibus amendment.

21. Detailed analyses of this process can be found in Joseph B. James, *The Framing of the Fourteenth Amendment* (Urbana, Ill, 1956); and William E. Nelson, *The Fourteenth Amendment: From Political Principle to Judicial Doctrine* (Cambridge, Mass., 1988).

22. Kenneth M. Stampp, *The Era of Reconstruction, 1865–1877* (New York, 1965), 141–2.

23. Alexander M. Bickel, "The Original Understanding and the Segregation Decision," *Harvard Law Review* 49 (November 1955): 1, 58.

24. Belz, 122.

25. Because counties and incorporated towns and muncipalities were considered creations of state governments, the amendment's disqualification would apply to most local public officials as well.

26. Benedict, *A Compromise of Principle*, 153.

27. Quoted in Benedict, "Preserving the Constitution," 77.

28. Foner, 255; Ellen Carol DuBois, "Outgrowing the Compact of the Fathers: Equal Rights, Woman Suffrage, and the United States Constitution, 1820–1878," *Journal of American History* 74 (December 1987): 844–52; and Ellen Carol DuBois, *Feminism and Suffrage: The Emergence of an Independent Women's Movement in America* (Ithaca, N.Y., 1978).

29. Benedict, *A Compromise of Principle*, 186–91, 196–7, 211.

30. C. Vann Woodward, *American Counterpoint: Slavery and Racism in the North-South Dialogue* (Boston, 1971), 170.

31. Foner, 259.

32. For this jockeying and results, see Benedict, *A Compromise of Principle*, 191–6; Foner, *Reconstruction*, 260–1, 264; and LaWanda Cox and John H. Cox, *Politics, Principle, and Prejudice, 1865–1868: The Dilemma of Reconstruction America* (Glencoe, Ill., 1963).

33. Foner, p. 265.

34. Doolittle to O. H. Browning, October 7, 1866, quoted in Theodore Pease and James Randall, eds., *The Diary of Orville Browning* (Springfield, Ill., 1925), 2:93n.

35. Foner, 262.

36. Quoted in Foner, 263.

37. Mary R. Dearing, *Veterans in Politics: The Story of the G.A.R.* (Baton Rouge, 1954), 50–112; Gary Lee Cardwell, "The Rise of the Stalwarts and the Transformation of Illinois Republican Politics, 1860–1880" (Ph.D. dissertation, University of Virginia, 1976), 92–120.

38. Illinois had been granted an additional congressional seat in 1862, but political strife had stopped reapportionment of the state's districts. Thus the legislature created an at-large, statewide district. That Republicans nominated the former Democratic political leader Logan for this seat attests to their fear of the G.A.R. and their desperation to appease ex-Democrats among veterans.

39. Stampp, 117.

40. Lawrence N. Powell, "Rejected Republican Incumbents in the 1866 Congressional Nominating Conventions: A Study in Reconstruction Politics," *Civil War History* 19 (September 1973): 218–37.

## Chapter 29

1. Ellis P. Oberholtzer, *A History of the United States since the Civil War* (1926), 1:422; Hans L. Trefousse, *Thaddeus Stevens: Nineteenth-Century Egalitarian* (Chapel Hill, N.C., 1997), 200–3.

2. For the Southern Loyalist Convention, see Michael Les Benedict, *A Compromise of Principle: Congressional Republicans and Reconstruction, 1863–1869* (New York, 1974), 200–2, 210–1; and Eric Foner, *Reconstruction: America's Unfinished Revolution* (New York, 1988), 270.

3. The case itself had first been decided in April 1866, but the full opinion was not released until December.

4. Although Johnson had vetoed the Freedmen's Bureau bill in February 1866, Congress passed another measure prolonging the bureau's life over his veto in July.

5. The act merely outlined a method. It left for the future the declaration whether that method had been complied with in particular states. Readmission of any state to the Union still required a special act of Congress as to that state. *U.S. Statutes at Large*, 14 (1867): 428–9.

6. Johnson's obstruction of the acts will be examined at greater length later in this chapter. The impact of the Military Reconstruction Acts in the South will be discussed in the next chapter.

7. *Appleton's American Annual Cyclopaedia* (New York, 1868), 15–16.

8. Benedict, 242.

9. Benedict, 243.

10. Michael Les Benedict, "Preserving the Constitution: The Conservative Basis of Radical Reconstruction," *Journal of American History* 61 (June 1974): 84.

11. *U.S. Statutes at Large*, 14 (1867): 430, quoted in James E. Sefton, *The United States Army and Reconstruction, 1865–1877* (Baton Rouge, 1967), 112. Sefton discusses the three measures described here on pp. 111–3.

12. Sefton, 111.

13. For an able discussion of this episode and its relationship to contemporaneous political developments in Maryland, whose Democratic governor Johnson sought to aid, see Brooks D. Simpson, *"Let Us Have Peace": Ulysses S. Grant and the Politics of War and Reconstruction, 1861–1868* (Chapel Hill, N.C., 1991), 154–9.

14. Simpson, 101–24; Brooks D. Simpson, "Quandaries of Command: Ulysses S. Grant and Black Soldiers," in *Union and Emancipation: Essays on Politics and Race in the Civil War Era*, ed. David W. Blight and Brooks D. Simpson (Kent, Ohio, 1997), 123–49. Throughout 1865 and 1866 blacks outnumbered whites among federal troops in the South by at least a three-to-one ratio, and in Mississippi, Louisiana, and Texas the ratio was considerably higher. Sefton, 52.

15. Simpson, *"Let Us Have Peace,"* 123–9.

16. Simpson, *"Let Us Have Peace,"* 143–6; Sefton, 80.

17. Simpson, *"Let Us Have Peace,"* 185.

18. The discussion in this and the following paragraphs depends heavily on Benedict, *Compromise of Principle*, 244–314; and Michael Les Benedict, *The Impeachment and Trial of Andrew Johnson* (New York, 1973).

19. While serving briefly as Lincoln's secretary of the treasury after the ouster of Salmon Chase, for example, William Pitt Fessenden, the Senate's most important Moderate, had appointed a number of allies whom he was determined to protect.

20. Benedict, *A Compromise of Principle*, 253.

21. In 1867, only spring elections in Connecticut, New Hampshire, and Rhode Island featured contests for the House of Representatives. All other northern elections were for state offices, although the new state legislatures chosen in some states could fill seats in the Senate. But even where no federal offices were at stake, Republicans viewed the results as a poll of public attitudes toward Republican actions in Washington.

22. Benedict, *A Compromise of Principle*, 257.

23. On New York, see James C. Mohr, "New York: The De-Politicization of Reform," in *Radical Republicans in the North: State Politics During Reconstruction*, ed. James C. Mohr (Baltimore, 1976), 68–69.

24. Benedict, *A Compromise of Principle*, 257.

25. On Kansas, see Foner, 313, 315.

26. Benedict, *Impeachment and Trial of Andrew Johnson*, 81.

27. Benedict, *Impeachment and Trial of Andrew Johnson*, 83, Chart 2. McCulloch withdrew about $44 million worth of greenbacks, reducing the total amount in circulation from $400 to $356 million. In early 1868 Congress rescinded the 1866 law that had allowed McCulloch to engage in such contraction.

28. Foner, 334; Benedict, *A Compromise of Principle*, 289–90.

29. Hans L. Trefousse, *The Radical Republicans: Lincoln's Vanguard for Racial Justice* (New York, 1969), 390.

30. Kenneth Stampp, *The Era of Reconstruction, 1865–1877* (New York, 1965), 150–1.

31. *Congressional Globe*, 40th Cong., 2d Sess., 1868, suppl.: 349.

32. *Ibid.*, 29–51, 322–3.

33. Benedict, *Impeachment and Trial of Andrew Johnson*, 132–6.

34. By early May, before the Senate cast any votes, it was well known that even more Republicans would vote against conviction on the remaining articles, so after the votes on May 26 no attempt was made to hold roll calls on them.

35. Benedict, *A Compromise of Principle*, 314.

36. On Colfax's factional affiliation, see Benedict, *A Compromise of Principle*, 177.

37. Benedict, *A Compromise of Principle*, 326.

38. *Appleton's American Annual Cyclopaedia*, 1868, 744–5.

39. Benedict, *A Compromise of Principle*, 324. Benedict ably discusses the disputes between Radicals and non-Radicals over the 1868 restoration on 315–24.

40. The 1868 presidential campaign will be examined more closely in subsequent chapters.

41. Republican motivations for passing the Fifteenth Amendment after the presidential election have been the source of considerable historiographical controversy. In *The Right to Vote: Politics and the Passage of the Fifteenth Amendment* (Baltimore, 1965), William Gillette argues that since blacks had already been enfranchised in most southern states by the Military Reconstruction Acts, Republicans aimed primarily at adding potential black votes to their ranks in Tennessee, the border states, and the North. Arguing that Republicans knew that promoting black suffrage would cost them more votes from outraged whites than they could possibly gain from blacks, others insist that an altruistic commitment to equal rights motivated Republicans. See especially LaWanda and John H. Cox, "Negro Suffrage and Republican Politics: The Problem of Motivation in Reconstruction Historiography," *Journal of Southern History* 33 (August 1967): 303–30; and Glenn M. Linden, "A Note on Negro Suffrage and Republican Politics," *Journal of Southern History* 36 (August 1970): 411–20.

42. Georgia, which was expelled from Congress for reasons to be explained in the next chapter, was also required to ratify the Fifteenth Amendment in order to gain readmission to Congress in 1870.

## Chapter 30

1. It will be recalled that Tennessee was exempted from the terms of these laws because it had been readmitted to Congress after ratifying the Fourteenth Amendment in the summer of 1866.

2. In places where and times when tobacco growing was especially profitable, however, black workers often preferred cash wages or rental of land to cash. See Laura F. Edwards, *Gendered Strife and Confusion: The Political Culture of Reconstruction* (Urbana and Chicago, 1997), 80–91. For the change to the sharecropping system, see above, Chapter 25.

3. Eric Foner, *Reconstruction: America's Unfinished Revolution, 1863–1877* (New York, 1988), 281–90.

4. Foner, 291.

5. Because of white abstention, blacks also formed a temporary majority of the electorate in Alabama and Florida in 1867. Foner, 294.

6. Foner, 281–91, 293, quotation 291.

7. The fullest analysis of northern Republicans' relationship with the southern wing of their party is Richard H. Abbott, *The Republican Party and the South, 1855–1877: The First Southern Strategy* (Chapel Hill, N.C., 1986).

8. Foner, 351.

9. Foner, 317–8.

10. Foner, 353.

11. On South Carolina, see especially Thomas Holt, *Black over White: Political Leadership in South Carolina during Reconstruction* (Urbana, 1977).

12. Much of this revisionist literature is summarized in Foner's magisterial *Reconstruction*, but pride of place in reassessing the proportions and performance of black officeholders belongs to Vernon Lane Wharton, *The Negro in Mississippi, 1865–1880* (Chapel Hill, N.C., 1947). The nature and achievements of Republican governance in the South will be analyzed below.

13. Foner, 286.

14. Foner, 296–7.

15. By far the fullest and most imaginatively written modern revisionist assessment of the carpetbaggers is Richard N. Current, *Those Terrible Carpetbaggers: A Reinterpretation* (New York, 1988); but for the economic necessity that turned failed Yankee planters toward political careers, see Lawrence N. Powell, "The Politics of Livelihood: Carpetbaggers in the Deep South," in *Region, Race, and Reconstruction: Essays in Honor of C. Vann Woodward*, ed. J. Morgan Kousser and James M. McPherson (New York, 1982), 317–21.

16. The pathbreaking study that identified scalawags as antebellum Whig planters is David Donald, "The Scalawag in Mississippi Reconstruction," *Journal of Southern History* 10 (1944): 447–60; for an important downward correction of Donald's estimates of how many Mississippi whites voted Republican, however, see Warren Ellem, "Who Were the Mississippi Scalawags?" *Journal of Southern History* 38 (1972): 217–40. Canter Brown, Jr., *Ossian Bingley Hart: Florida's Loyalist Reconstruction Governor* (Baton Rouge, 1997) is a biography of an important Whig scalawag from Florida.

17. Allen W. Trelease, "Who Were the Scalawags?" *Journal of Southern History* 29 (1963): 445–68.

18. Foner, 314.

19. On the importance of debt relief in explaining the initial support of hill whites for Georgia's Republican party, see Armstead L. Robinson, "Beyond the Realm of Social Consensus: New Meanings of Reconstruction for American History," *Journal of American History* 68 (1981): 276–97. Robinson's article, in turn, derives heavily from Elizabeth Studley Nathans, *Losing the Peace: Georgia Republicans and Reconstruction, 1865–1871* (Baton Rouge, 1968).

20. Michael Perman, *The Road to Redemption: Southern Politics, 1869–1879* (Chapel Hill, N.C., 1984), 47.

21. Robinson, "Beyond the Realm of Social Consensus," argues that the Republican party foundered on the rock of class conflict among both whites and blacks. Foner, 348–9, stresses that "debilitating factionalism" was a luxury that the Republican party "could scarcely afford."

22. For the complicated maneuvers in Florida that produced this result—maneuvers that involved the drafting of rival radical and moderate constitutions by separate conventions and the intervention of army officials and Republican congressmen on behalf of the moderate version that intentionally disempowered blacks—see Jerrell H. Shofner, "Florida: A Failure of Moderate Republicanism," in *Reconstruction and Redemption in the South*, ed. Otto H. Olsen (Baton Rouge, 1980), 13–26.

23. Karen L. Zipf, "'The WHITES shall rule the land or die': Gender, Race, and Class in North Carolina Politics," *Journal of Southern History* 65 (August 1999): 521; Foner, 367.

24. Foner, 375.

25. The Georgia, Florida, Texas, South Carolina, and North Carolina constitutions eschewed disfranchisement. Louisiana's barred anyone who had voted for the secession ordinance or been a pro-Confederate newspaper editor from voting, but it exempted from that ban anyone who took an oath pledging acceptance of Congress's Reconstruction program. Foner, 324.

26. Mississippi's constitution was defeated in a referendum in the spring of 1868 because whites objected to a clause that continued the disfranchisement of some twenty-five hundred white Missis-

sippians. In Virginia, the military commander, General John M. Schofield, refused to allow elections in 1868 because he objected to the constitution's clauses proscribing some ex-Confederates from voting or holding office.

27. For developments in Mississippi, see William C. Harris, *The Day of the Carpetbagger: Republican Reconstruction in Mississippi* (Baton Rouge, 1979), 115–257; for Virginia, see Jack P. Maddex, Jr., "Virginia: The Persistence of Centrist Hegemony," in *Reconstruction and Redemption in the South*, ed. Otto H. Olsen (Baton Rouge, 1980), 113–55.

28. In addition to Maddex, see Perman, *Road to Redemption*, 11–12, and Louis Moore, "The Elusive Center: Virginia Politics and the General Assembly, 1869–1871," *Virginia Magazine of History and Biography* 103 (April 1995): 207–36.

29. Foner, 369–73.

30. The pathbreaking study of this process is Peter W. Bardaglio, *Reconstructing the Household: Families, Sex, and the Law in the Nineteenth-Century South* (Chapel Hill, N.C., 1995).

31. Edwards, 196, 199, and *passim*.

32. Zipf, 515. Zipf's article is filled with examples of such gendered calls on the manhood of whites to defend themselves, but see also Edwards.

33. E. Merton Coulter, *The South during Reconstruction, 1865–1877* (Baton Rouge, 1947), 148–9.

34. William C. Harris, "Mississippi: Republican Factionalism and Mismanagement," in *Reconstruction and Redemption in the South*, ed. Otto H. Olsen (Baton Rouge, 1980), 95–96; Foner, 375–6; J. Mills Thornton III, "Fiscal Policy and the Failure of Reconstruction in the Lower South," in *Race, Region, and Reconstruction: Essays in Honor of C. Vann Woodward*, ed. J. Morgan Kousser and James M. McPherson (New York, 1982), 349–94.

35. Horace Mann Bond, "Social and Economic Forces in Alabama Reconstruction," *Journal of Negro History* 23 (July 1938): 336–43.

36. Mark W. Summers, *Railroads, Reconstruction, and the Gospel of Prosperity: Aid Under the Radical Republicans, 1865–1877* (Princeton, N.J., 1984).

## Chapter 31

1. For examples of historians who argue that Reconstruction and the Republicans failed because southern whites never accepted their legitimacy, see William R. Brock, "Reconstruction and the American Party System," and Otto H. Olsen, "Southern Reconstruction and the Question of Self-Determination," both in *A Nation Divided: Problems and Issues of the Civil War and Reconstruction*, ed. George M. Fredrickson (Minneapolis, 1975), 81–141.

2. Republicans also held power in Tennessee and the border states of Missouri and West Virginia until 1870, but in those states they depended on draconian disfranchisement of former Confederates by state law, not black enfranchisement as in the former Confederate states. The border states are discussed in the next chapter in connection with the Liberal Republican movement.

3. Jackson *Clarion*, May 19, 1868, quoted in William C. Harris, *The Day of the Carpetbagger: Republican Reconstruction in Mississippi* (Baton Rouge, 1979), 159.

4. Raleigh *North Carolinian*, February 15, 1868, quoted in Karen L. Zipf, "'The WHITES shall rule the land or die: Gender, Race, and Class in North Carolina Politics," *Journal of Southern History* 65 (August 1999): 525.

5. There was no popular vote for president in South Carolina prior to the Civil War, but in 1868 79.6 percent of the potential electorate turned out. In Alabama the figure was 77.9 percent, whereas it had been 78.7 percent in 1860; in Georgia, 73.2 percent, as opposed to 85.1 percent in 1860; in Louisiana, 75.9 percent, almost twenty points higher than the rate in any antebellum presidential election; and in North Carolina, 91.2 percent, compared to 95.5 percent in 1860. In contrast, Arkansas, where ex-Confederates were still disfranchised, saw a turnout rate of only 49 percent.

Florida Republicans chose electoral votes in the state legislature. Mississippi, Virginia, and Texas did not participate in the election.

6. Quoted in Allen W. Trelease, *White Terror: The Ku Klux Klan Conspiracy and Southern Reconstruction* (New York, 1971), xl.

7. For the role of violence in Louisiana, Georgia, and elsewhere in 1868, see George C. Rable, *But There Was No Peace: The Role of Violence in the Politics of Reconstruction* (Athens, Ga., 1984), 74–79. On the expulsion of blacks from the Georgia legislature in September 1868 and the voting shifts between April and November, see Elizabeth Studley Nathans, *Losing the Peace: Georgia Republicans and Reconstruction, 1865–1871* (Baton Rouge, 1968), 121–4, 144. Regression estimates of black and white voting behavior in Louisiana in November 1868 suggest that 14 percent of blacks voted Democratic, 58 percent voted Republican, and 28 percent abstained. Conversely, three-fourths of potential white voters went Democratic while almost all the others abstained. These estimates are taken from Stuart Delery, "One Supreme and Final Effort: Redemption in Louisiana, 1868–1877" (senior thesis, University of Virginia, 1990).

8. For the reduction of the Republican vote by the Klan that helped produce Democratic victories in Alabama and North Carolina in 1870, see Sarah Woolfolk Wiggins, "Alabama: Democratic Bulldozing and Republican Folly," and Otto H. Olsen, "North Carolina: An Incongruous Presence," both in *Reconstruction and Redemption in the South*, ed. Otto H. Olsen (Baton Rouge, 1980), 57, 183.

9. Trelease, xliii. Trelease's book is now the standard source on the Ku Klux Klan, but on the broader question of white violence against blacks and Republicans during Reconstruction, see also Rable.

10. Rable, 92.

11. Trelease, xlvii.

12. Trelease, 63; Rable, 101. Armed intervention by federal troops and criminal prosecution of Klan members in federal courts, both authorized by a series of Force Acts that congressional Republicans enacted in 1870 and 1871, were largely responsible for the suppression of the Klan. Those federal efforts will be discussed later in this chapter as well as in the following chapter.

13. Trelease, 78; Nathans, 147–66.

14. Michael Perman, *The Road to Redemption: Southern Politics, 1869–1879* (Chapel Hill, N.C., 1984), 18–19.

15. The analysis here rests heavily on Perman, 3–131.

16. John D. McEnery, the Conservatives' gubernatorial candidate in Louisiana in 1872, was a Democrat, but his running mate for lieutenant governor was a Liberal Republican. Equally important, the incumbent centrist Republican governor, Henry Clay Warmouth, very publicly advocated and aided this coalition, actions that resulted in his impeachment by regular Republican members of the state legislature after the election was over.

17. We discuss the Liberal Republican movement at greater length in the following chapter.

18. Disputed returns from Arkansas and Louisiana caused Congress not to count the electoral vote from either state.

19. Because Texas, Virginia, Florida, and Mississippi recorded no popular votes in 1868, changes in turnout there cannot be measured. Voter turnout increased in Arkansas, Alabama, and Tennessee because of the return of voting rights to ex-Confederates between 1868 and 1872. But in Georgia, turnout rates plunged from 73 percent in 1868 to 55 percent in 1872. In North Carolina, they declined from 91.7 to 80.5 percent, and in South Carolina they dropped from 79.6 to 60.4 percent. U.S. Census Bureau, *Historical Statistics of the United States from Colonial Times to 1970* (Washington, D.C., 1975), 1072. Statistical estimates of whites' voting patterns in Louisiana suggest that whereas three-fourths of white males voted for Horatio Seymour in 1868, only three-fifths of them turned out for Greeley in 1872. These figures are taken from Delery.

20. The defection by Louisiana's incumbent Republican governor Henry C. Warmouth is the most famous example of an exodus from the Republican party, but the exodus took place in Arkansas, South Carolina, and elsewhere as well. As Michael Perman suggests (*Road to Redemption*, 115), the power of the regular carpetbagger-black wing of the party in those three states probably best explains the readiness of centrists to leave the party.

21. For example, in Mississippi, where over a fifth of potential white voters went Republican in 1869, only about 15 percent did in 1872. See Warren A. Ellem, "Who Were the Mississippi Scalawags?" *Journal of Southern History* 38 (May 1972): 222.

22. Perman, 136–40; the details of the Civil Rights Act of 1875 will be discussed in the next chapter.

23. Eric Foner, *Reconstruction: America's Unfinished Revolution, 1863–1877* (New York, 1988), 552.

24. Quoted in John R. Lynch, *The Facts of Reconstruction* (New York, 1913), 122.

25. Ellem, 222, 235; see also David Donald, "The Scalawag in Mississippi Reconstruction," *Journal of Southern History* (1944): 447–60; and Harris, 459–80.

26. Perman, 154–5, quotation p. 166. Perman provides the fullest account of these movements and of the internal strife within both parties over which electoral tactics to pursue, but for more on the Louisiana Unification Movement, see T. Harry Williams, "The Louisiana Unification Movement of 1873," *Journal of Southern History*, 11 (August 1945): 349–69.

27. Gubernatorial returns can be found in Congressional Quarterly, *Guide to U.S. Elections* (Washington, D.C., 1975) 1–3; for North Carolina, see Perman, 141.

28. Rable, 104–6.

29. William Gillette, *Retreat from Reconstruction, 1869–1879* (Baton Rouge, 1979), 25; Lou Falkner Williams, *The Great South Carolina Ku Klux Klan Trials, 1871–1872* (Athens, Ga., 1996), 41.

30. For data on prosecutions and dismissals under the Enforcement Acts, see Everett Swinney, "Enforcing the Fifteenth Amendment, 1870–1871," *Journal of Southern History* 28 (May 1962): 202–18; and Gillette, 43–44.

31. Swinney op. cit.; Gillette, op. cit.; Lou Falkner Williams, *The Great South Carolina Ku Klux Klan Trials 1871–1872* (Athens, Ga., 1996) is an exemplary recent study of events in South Carolina.

32. Gillette, 36.

33. Foner, 558–63. The estimated white vote for Republicans plunged from a high of over ten thousand in 1869 to less than a thousand in 1875. Ellem, 222.

## Chapter 32

1. Northern Republican policy makers' predominant concern with the North, not the South, is the central theme of William Gillette, *Retreat from Reconstruction, 1869–1879* (Baton Rouge, 1979).

2. Gillette, xii.

3. William A. Dunning, *Reconstruction, Political and Economic, 1865–1877* (New York, 1907), Chapter 18.

4. Allan Nevins, *The Emergence of Modern America, 1865–1878* (New York, 1927), 186.

5. Mark Wahlgren Summers, *The Era of Good Stealings* (New York, 1993), 5. Summers's witty and insightful book is by far the most perceptive analysis of corruption and of the partisan uses to which the corruption *issue* was put after the Civil War.

6. Summers, 50–54.

7. For this scheme to succeed, the federal government had to be stopped from selling some of its own gold deposits on the New York Gold Exchange. Indeed, the scheme collapsed on September 24, 1869 (Black Friday) when the Treasury Department, at Grant's instruction, released gold, causing

prices to plunge. Many speculators were ruined, but not Gould and Fisk, who received prior warning from Grant's brother-in-law that a release was coming and who managed secretly to sell off most of their holdings before the crash.

8. For a careful appraisal of the various charges of malfeasance leveled at members of Grant's administration, see William S. McFeely, "Ulysses S. Grant, 1869–1877," in *Responses of the Presidents to Charges of Misconduct*, ed. C. Vann Woodward (New York, 1974), 115–40.

9. Summers, 5.

10. As will be shown below, when the Forty-fourth Congress opened in December 1875, the Democrats had regained control of the House of Representatives, and Democrats pushed the investigations of Grant's men to embarrass the Republicans.

11. Brooks D. Simpson, *The Reconstruction Presidents* (Lawrence, Kans., 1998), 133–5, quotation p. 133. The discussion below draws heavily on Simpson's insightful analysis of Grant's southern Reconstruction policies, pp. 133–96. For a quite different assessment of Grant and especially of his commitment or lack thereof to black rights, see William S. McFeely, *Grant: A Biography* (New York, 1981).

12. McFeely, 277 and *passim*.

13. Simpson, 145–48; David Donald, *Charles Sumner and the Rights of Man* (New York, 1970), 435–80. Grant's administration first negotiated a treaty of annexation, which the Senate refused to ratify; then Grant proposed annexation by a joint resolution of the two houses of Congress. By the end of 1871, he abandoned the effort.

14. Simpson, 156.

15. Charles Coleman, *The Election of 1868: The Democratic Effort to Regain Control* (New York, 1933), 369.

16. Congressional election returns can be found in Michael J. Dubin, *United States Congressional Elections, 1788–1997: The Official Results* (Jefferson, N.C., 1998).

17. *Chicago Republican*, May 27, 1870; *Congressional Globe*, 41st Congress, 2d Sess., June 9, 1870, 4274.

18. William Gillette, *The Right to Vote: Politics and the Passage of the Fifteenth Amendment* (Baltimore, 1965), 40–41.

19. The Military Reconstruction Acts' requirement of black enfranchisement did not apply to the border states or to Tennessee, but in 1868 Republicans, who still controlled that state, had revised Tennessee's constitution to enfranchise the state's adult black males. For an estimate of the potential black vote in the border states that compares it to the partisan margins in the 1868 presidential election, see William Gillette, "Anatomy of a Failure: Federal Enforcement of the Right to Vote in the Border States during Reconstruction," in *Radicalism, Racism, and Party Realignment: The Border States during Reconstruction*, ed. Richard O. Curry (Baltimore, 1969), 266, n. 2. Even with new black supporters, Republicans could not overcome Democrats' statewide majority in Kentucky, but black enfranchisement might help yield some Republican congressmen from that state.

20. Gillette, *The Right to Vote*, 48.

21. That Republicans would lose more than they gained in the North by passing the Fifteenth Amendment and that egalitarian altruism rather than political opportunism therefore motivated Republicans is the central argument of LaWanda and John H. Cox, "Negro Suffrage and Republican Politics: The Problem of Motivation in Reconstruction Historiography," *Journal of Southern History* 33 (August 1967): 303–30.

22. New Hampshire, Connecticut, and Rhode Island, however, held congressional elections in March and April 1869, immediately after passage of the amendment. Nor did early ratification and new black voters help Republicans in the North's 1870 and 1871 congressional elections. Republicans lost 21 and Democrats gained 18 seats in those elections, with Independents capturing the others. Together with Republican losses in the South, the Republican majority of 100 seats over

Democrats in the Forty-first Congress (1869–1871) fell to 28 seats in the Forty-second Congress (1871–1873).

23. See above, Chapter 30. When Congress reimposed military rule on Georgia in 1869, it also required that Georgia ratify the Fifteenth Amendment before being readmitted to Congress.

24. Quoted in Simpson, 144; the following paragraphs draw heavily on Simpson's insightful discussion of Grant's southern strategy, 133–96.

25. Simpson, 148.

26. Arthur M. Schlesinger, Jr., ed., *History of U.S. Political Parties* (New York, 1973), 2: 1371.

27. Simpson, 151.

28. In these calculations, Tennessee is counted with the border states. Prior to 1876, when a recently passed congressional statute required all congressional elections throughout the nation to be held on the same day in November of even-numbered years, states scheduled congressional elections whenever they wished. Thus such elections were held in different months in both odd- and even-numbered years.

29. For Grant's various messages and proclamations, see James D. Richardson, ed., *A Compilation of the Messages and Papers of the Presidents, 1787–1897* (Washington, D.C., 1896), 7:127–8, 135–6, and 139–41. Grant issued additional warnings that he would suspend habeas corpus in South Carolina on October 17 and November 3, 1871; Richardson, 137–9.

30. Gillette, *Retreat from Reconstruction*, 43–44; Gillette, "Anatomy of a Failure," 298.

31. Gillette, *Retreat from Reconstruction*, 46–47.

32. Gillette, *Retreat from Reconstruction*, 49.

33. Gillette, *Retreat from Reconstruction*, 49.

34. Richard H. Abbott, *The Republican Party and the South, 1855–1877* (Chapel Hill, N.C., 1967).

35. For the record of southern Republicans in Congress, see Terry L. Seip, *The South Returns to Congress: Men, Economic Measures, and Sectional Interrelationships, 1868–1879* (Baton Rouge, 1983).

36. Gillette, *Retreat from Reconstruction*, 43–44.

37. Gillette, *Retreat from Reconstruction*, 150–60, quotation 159.

38. For the origins of the Liberal Republican movement in the border states, see Jacqueline Balk and Ari Hoogenboom, "The Origins of Border State Liberal Republicanism," in Richard O. Curry (ed.), *Radicalism, Racism, and Party Realignment* (Baltimore, 1969), pp. 220–44, as well as the essays on individual states in that volume.

39. For the physical and political mistreatment blacks suffered in the border states and the administration's failure to do much about it, see Gillette, "Anatomy of a Failure," and the other essays in Curry. Klan violence against blacks was so egregious in Tennessee that Grant insisted the federal government intervene there to protect blacks' rights. Those efforts in fact substantially increased the Republican vote between 1869, when the Liberal Republican–Democratic coalition first won control of the state, and 1872.

40. Eric Foner, *Reconstruction: America's Unfinished Revolution, 1863–1877* (New York, 1988), 500. For able discussions of Liberal Republicanism as a national movement, see Foner, 488–511; and Summers, 166–79, 215–28.

## Chapter 33

1. Eric Foner, *Reconstruction: America's Unfinished Revolution, 1863–1877* (New York, 1988), 502.

2. Furious at the endorsement of Greeley, a few Democratic dissidents ran Charles O'Conor on a Democratic and Labor Reform ticket. In an election that drew 6.4 million men to the polls, O'Conor amassed a total of 29,489 votes.

3. Quoted in Foner, 500.

4. For the civil service movement, see Ari Hoogenboom, *Outlawing the Spoils: A History of the Civil Service Reform Movement, 1865–1883* (Urbana, Ill., 1961); and John G. Sproat, *"The Best Men": Liberal Reformers in the Gilded Age* (New York, 1968).

5. Mark Wahlgren Summers, *The Era of Good Stealings* (New York, 1993), 100–1.

6. James D. Richardson, ed., *A Compilation of the Messages and Papers of the Presidents, 1787–1897* (Washington, D.C., 1896), 7: 148.

7. The 1872 national Republican platform can be found in Arthur M. Schlesinger, Jr., ed., *History of U.S. Political Parties* (New York, 1973), 2: 1355–7.

8. For excellent discussions of Liberalism, see Foner, 488–99; David Montgomery, *Beyond Equality: Labor and the Radical Republicans, 1862–1872* (New York, 1967), 379–86.

9. Michael Les Benedict, "Preserving the Constitution: The Conservative Basis of Radical Reconstruction," *Journal of American History* 61 (June 1974): 88–90.

10. Schlesinger, 2:936.

11. 8 Wall. 603 (1870).

12. Foner, 531.

13. Foner, 530–1.

14. William Gillette, *Retreat from Reconstruction, 1869–1879* (Baton Rouge, 1979), 295–7.

15. Summers, 231–43.

16. Michael Perman, *The Road to Redemption: Southern Politics, 1869– 1879* (Chapel Hill, N.C., 1984) 152–3.

17. Gillette, 31, 36.

18. Gillette, 182.

19. Gillette, 37.

20. For the framing of this bill, see Gillette, 190–210.

21. Brooks D. Simpson, *The Reconstruction Presidents* (Lawrence, Kans., 1998), 181.

22. Simpson, 178–81.

23. Simpson, 176, 181.

24. For the political fault lines over the Granger laws in the Midwest, see George H. Miller, *Railroads and the Granger Laws* (Madison, Wisc., 1971).

25. Foner, 521.

26. In 1872, when congressional Republicans abolished most excise taxes, they also ended the wartime federal income tax.

27. See Chapter 24.

28. In the Senate, 41 percent of the Democrats favored and 59 percent opposed this measure. Among Republican senators, 57 percent voted in favor and 43 percent against it. In the House, Democrats split 48 percent in favor and 52 percent against. Republicans divided 62 percent in favor and 38 percent against. In both chambers, in short, Republicans provided the winning margin. See Irwin Unger, *The Greenback Era: A Social and Political History of American Finance, 1865–1879* (Princeton, N.J., 1964), 410.

29. Unger, 411.

30. For the drop-off in Republican turnout between 1872 and 1874 in the North, see Paul Kleppner, *The Third Electoral System, 1853–1892: Parties, Voters, and Political Cultures* (Chapel Hill, N.C., 1979), 126–8.

31. Thirteen of the new Democratic seats in the Senate came from the South, but seven, including two Anti-Monopoly–Democratic coalition men from California, came from the North. Republicans actually lost twenty seats in this period, but Colorado's admission as a state in 1876 provided them with two more senators.

32. For Grant's recommendations and his unusual message to Congress on January 14, 1875 proudly announcing that he had signed the law, see Richardson, 7: 285–7, 314–6.

33. In the House of Representatives, for example, 97 percent of the Democrats voted against final passage of the bill in January 1875, whereas 86 percent of Republicans voted in favor. After the Democrats took control of the House in the next Congress, they tried to repeal the Specie Resumption Act in August 1876. On the vote, 80 percent of the Democrats supported repeal, and 87 percent of the Republicans opposed it. For the first time since the end of the war, the parties had taken consistent and contrasting positions on the vexing money question. Unger, 255–63, 413.

34. On the Republicans' use of the school issue in Ohio and other midwestern states, see Kleppner, 214–35; for New Jersey, see Samuel T. McSeveney, "Religious Conflict, Party Politics, and Public Policy in New Jersey," *New Jersey History* 110 (Spring–Summer 1992): 18–44. Public tax support for Catholic schools was a viable and extraordinarily contentious partisan issue in the nineteenth century in part because the Supreme Court had ruled in 1833 that the first eight amendments of the Constitution applied only to the national government, not to the states. Thus aid to Catholic schools by state and local governments was not automatically deemed an unconstitutional violation of the First Amendment's separation of church and state clause.

35. Kleppner, 242.

36. Richardson, 7:334–5; Kleppner, 233. For the Republicans' 1876 national platform, see Schlesinger, 2:1371–3.

37. According to the Republicans, the count was Tilden, 4,285,992, and Hayes, 4,033,768. Democrats gave it as Tilden, 4,300,590, and Hayes, 4,036,298. Schlesinger, 2:1406. These are the tallies recorded by Congress after the election when it sought to determine who had won the electoral vote.

38. Article II, Section 1 of the Constitution clearly states: "no Senator or Representative, or person holding an office of trust or profit under the United States, shall be appointed an elector."

## Chapter 34

1. Brooks D. Simpson, *The Reconstruction Presidents* (Lawrence, Kans., 1998), 192–3; Keith Ian Polakoff, *The Politics of Inertia: The Election of 1876 and the End of Reconstruction* (Baton Rouge, 1973), 210–31.

2. C. Vann Woodward, *Reunion and Reaction: The Compromise of 1877 and the End of Reconstruction* (Boston, 1951), 19. On the basis of the popular votes originally reported, some of which were undoubtedly fictitious, one could argue that Hayes won South Carolina and Florida, whereas Tilden won Louisiana.

3. In South Carolina and Florida, the incumbent Republican governors Daniel H. Chamberlain and Marcellus L. Stearns ran for reelection in 1876, but in Louisiana, where William Pitt Kellogg was the incumbent Republican, Stephen Packard had been the Republican candidate in 1876. Their Democratic competitors were Wade Hampton in South Carolina, George F. Drew in Florida, and Francis T. Nicholls in Louisiana.

4. Here Chandler counted all three of Oregon's electoral votes in Hayes's column. It was only later that Democratic leaders in the East would instruct Oregon's Democratic governor to disqualify the technically ineligible Republican elector from that state and to send to Washington electoral votes cast by two Republicans and one Democrat who had been substituted for the disqualified Republican. Polakoff, 225–8.

5. Polakoff, 216.

6. Polakoff, 210–4. State law stipulated that the board have five members, at least one of whom must represent the "out" party, in this case the Democrats.

7. The vice president was normally president of the Senate, but the Republican vice president, Henry Wilson, had died, making Ferry, the president *pro tempore* of the Senate, its acting president.

8. The Democrats had a majority of seventy-four over Republicans in the House, not counting three Independents who were likely to vote with the Democrats, whereas the Republican edge in the Senate was only fourteen seats.

9. This was true even though the Constitution stipulated that in any such vote in the House the vote would be cast by states with each state having only one vote, for Democratic representatives controlled a large majority of the state delegations.

10. On the militance of southern Democrats, see Polakoff, 241; and Michael Les Benedict, "Southern Democrats in the Crisis of 1876–1877: A Reconsideration of *Reunion and Reaction,*" *Journal of Southern History* 64 (November 1980): 489–524.

11. In 1877, March 4, the traditional date of inaugurations, fell on a Sunday. Polakoff, 232–314, provides a detailed analysis of divisions in both parties during this congressional session.

12. In the Senate, Republicans voted 24–16 in favor of the measure; Democrats supported it 23–1. In the House, Republicans opposed the bill 33–68; Democrats supported it, 154–18. Thirteen of the eighteen Democratic dissenters were southerners, and altogether southern Democrats divided 25–13 on the measure. Polakoff, 279; Benedict, "Southern Democrats in the Crisis of 1876–1877," 510–1. Polakoff reports the favorable Democratic vote in the House as 158, but we have used Benedict's figures.

13. Polakoff, 283, suggests that Davis opposed the whole idea of an electoral commission and might have declined to serve on it in any event, but he cited his election to the Senate, when the law required five members from the Supreme Court, as an excuse not to do so. Davis resigned from the Court on March 5, 1877.

14. C. Vann Woodward, *Reunion and Reaction: The Compromise of 1877 and the End of Reconstruction* (Boston, 1951); C. Vann Woodward, "Yes, There Was a Compromise of 1877," *Journal of American History* 60 (June 1973): 215–23.

15. Benedict, "Southern Democrats in the Crisis of 1876–1877," 497. In addition to Benedict's article, the main challenges to Professor Woodward's interpretation are Polakoff, *The Politics of Inertia,* and Allan Peskin, "Was There a Compromise of 1877?" *Journal of American History* 60 (June 1973): 63–75.

16. Simpson, 199–217, quotation p. 205.

17. Polakoff, 105; Simpson, 202.

18. Simpson, 203.

19. Peskin, 70.

20. Polakoff, 250; Simpson, 205.

21. Benedict, "Southern Democrats in the Crisis of 1876–1877," 518–9. Both Benedict and Polakoff, *The Politics of Inertia,* stress how central these rivalries between Stalwarts and Liberal Republicans were in shaping events from the summer of 1876 until the resolution of the electoral crisis.

22. Key had been appointed to fill the seat of none other than Andrew Johnson, whom Tennessee's Democrats had sent back to the Senate in early 1875 but who had died in the summer of that year. Democrats in the Tennessee legislature refused to reelect Key because he had cooperated too much with Republicans. Thus he seemed a perfect candidate for realignment. Polakoff, 296–7.

23. Eric Foner, *Reconstruction: America's Unfinished Revolution, 1863–1877* (New York, 1988), 577.

24. Polakoff, 310–1.

25. James D. Richardson, ed., *A Compilation of the Messages and Papers of the Presidents, 1787–1897* (Washington, D.C., 1896), 7:458–60.

26. Foner, 587.

27. J. Morgan Kousser, *The Shaping of Southern Politics: Suffrage Restriction and the Establishment of the One-Party South, 1880–1910* (New Haven, Conn., 1974).

28. For the Democrats' actions in the South after regaining power, see Michael Perman, *The Road to Redemption: Southern Politics, 1869–1879* (Chapel Hill, N.C., 1984), 178–220; and Foner, 587–601.

29. Foner, 598.

30. Simpson, 216.

31. Woodward, "Yes, There Was a Compromise of 1877," 219.

# Suggested Readings*

## CHAPTER 1

Jeremy Atack and Fred Bateman, *To Their Own Soil: Agriculture in the Antebellum North* (Ames, Iowa, 1987); Richard Brown, *Modernization: The Transformation of American Life 1600–1865* (New York, 1976); Walter Licht, *Industrializing America: The Nineteenth Century* (Baltimore, 1995); Patricia Limerick, *The Legacy of Conquest: The Unbroken Past of the American West* (New York, 1987); Allan Pred, *Urban Growth and City Systems in the United States* (Cambridge, Mass., 1980); Lewis Saum, *The Popular Mood of Pre–Civil War America* (Westport, Conn., 1980); James B. Stewart, *Holy Warriors: Abolitionism and American Slavery* (New York, 1976).

## CHAPTER 2

Victoria Bynum, *Unruly Women: The Politics of Social and Sexual Control in the Old South* (Chapel Hill, N.C., 1992); Joan Cashin, *A Family Venture: Men and Women on the Southern Frontier* (New York, 1991); Catherine Clinton, *Plantation Mistress* (New York, 1982); Elizabeth Fox-Genovese, *Within the Plantation Household: Black and White Women of the Old South* (Chapel Hill, N.C., 1988); David Goldfield, *Cotton Fields and Skyscrapers: Southern City and Region* (Baton Rouge, 1982); John McCardell, *The Idea of a Southern Nation: Southern Nationalists and Southern Nationalism 1830–1860* (New York, 1979); Stephanie McCurry, *Masters of Small Worlds: Yeoman Households and the Political Culture of the Antebellum Low Country* (New York, 1994); James Oakes, *The Ruling Race: A History of American Slaveholders* (New York, 1982); Bertram Wyatt-Brown, *Southern Honor: Ethics and Behavior in the Old South* (New York, 1982).

*After their first mention, although they may be appropriate reading for other chapters, references are not repeated.

## CHAPTER 3

Ira Berlin, *Many Thousands Gone: The First Two Centuries of Slavery in North America* (Cambridge, Mass., 1998); John Blassingame, *The Slave Community: Plantation Life in the Antebellum South* (New York, 1972); Robert Fogel, *Without Consent or Contract: The Rise and Fall of American Slavery* (New York, 1989); Robert Fogel and Stanley Engerman, *Time on the Cross: The Economics of American Negro Slavery* (Boston, 1974); Eugene Genovese, *Roll, Jordan Roll: The World the Slaves Made* (New York, 1972); Peter Kolchin, *American Slavery, 1619–1877* (New York, 1993); Lawrence Levine, *Black Culture and Black Consciousness: Afro-American Folk Thought from Slavery to Freedom* (New York, 1978); James Rawley, *The Transatlantic Slave Trade: A History* (New York, 1991); Brenda Stevenson, *Life in Black and White: Family and Community in the Slave South* (New York, 1996).

## CHAPTER 4

Tyler Anbinder, *Nativism and Slavery: The Northern Know-Nothings and the Politics of the 1850s* (New York, 1992); Gabor Boritt (ed.), *Why the Civil War Came* (New York, 1996); David Donald, *Charles Sumner and the Coming of the Civil War* (New York, 1960); Eric Foner, *Free Soil, Free Labor, Free Men: The Ideology of the Republican Party before the Civil War* (New York, 1970); William Freehling, *The Road to Disunion: Sectionalism at Bay, 1776–1854* (New York, 1987); William Gienapp, *The Origins of the Republican Party 1852–1856* (New York, 1987); Michael Holt, *The Political Crisis of the 1850s* (New York, 1978); Michael Holt, *The Rise and Fall of the American Whig Party: Jacksonian Politics and the Onset of the Civil War* (New York, 1999); Michael Morrison, *Slavery and the American West: The Eclipse of Manifest Destiny and the Coming of the Civil War* (Chapel Hill, N.C., 1997); Mark Stegmaier, *Texas, New Mexico and the Compromise of 1850* (Kent, Ohio, 1996).

## CHAPTER 5

William Cooper, *The South and the Politics of Slavery, 1828–1852* (Baton Rouge, 1978); David Herbert Donald, *Lincoln* (New York, 1995); Don Fehrenbacher, *Slavery, Law and Politics: The Dred Scott Case in Historical Perspective* (New York, 1981); Harold Holzer (ed.), *The Lincoln-Douglas Debates* (New York, 1993); Thomas Morris, *Free Men All: The Personal Liberty Laws of the North* (Baltimore, 1974); Stephen Oates, *To Purge This Land With Blood: A Biography of John Brown* (New York, 1970); James Rawley, *Race and Politics: Bleeding Kansas and the Coming of the Civil War* (Philadelphia, 1960); Gerald Wolff, *The Kansas-Nebraska Bill: Party, Section and the Coming of the Civil War* (New York, 1980).

## CHAPTER 6

William Barney, *The Road to Secession: A New Perspective on the Old South* (New York, 1972); William Barney, *The Secessionist Impulse: Alabama and Mississippi in 1860* (Princeton, N.J., 1974); Steven Channing, *A Crisis of Fear: Secession in South Carolina* (New York, 1970); William Davis, *Jefferson Davis: The Man and His Hour* (New York, 1991); William Freehling and Craig Simpson (eds.), *Secession Debated: Georgia's Showdown in 1860* (New York, 1992); Michael Johnson, *Toward a Patriarchal Republic: The Secession of Georgia* (Baton Rouge, 1977); Mark Summers, *The Plundering Generation: Corruption and the Crisis of the Union, 1849–1861* (New York, 1987); Ralph Wooster, *The Secession Conventions of the South* (Princeton, N.J., 1962).

## CHAPTER 7

Daniel Crofts, *Reluctant Confederates: Upper South Unionists in the Secession Crisis* (Chapel Hill, N.C., 1989); Richard Current, *Lincoln and the First Shot* (Philadelphia, 1963); Mark Kruman, *Politics and Parties in North Carolina, 1836–1865* (Baton Rouge, 1983); Mark Neely, *The Last Best Hope of Earth: Abraham Lincoln and the Promise of America* (Cambridge, Mass., 1993); David Potter, *Lincoln and His Party in the Secession Crisis* (New Haven, Conn., 1942); Kenneth Stampp, *And the War Came: The North and the Secession Crisis, 1860–1861* (Baton Rouge, 1950).

## CHAPTER 8

Jean Baker, *The Politics of Continuity: Maryland Political Parties, 1858–1870* (Baltimore, 1973); Albert Castel, *A Frontier State at War: Kansas, 1861–1865* (Ithaca, N.Y., 1958); Richard Curry, *A House Divided: A Study of Statehood Politics and the Copperhead Movement in West Virginia* (Pittsburgh, 1964); Michael Fellman, *Inside War: The Guerrilla Conflict in Missouri during the American Civil War* (New York, 1989); William Parrish, *Turbulent Partnership: Missouri and the Union, 1861–1865* (Columbia, Mo., 1963); James G. Randall, *Constitutional Problems under Lincoln* (Urbana, Ill., 1950).

## CHAPTER 9

Richard Beringer et al., *Why the South Lost the Civil War* (Athens, Ga., 1986); Gabor Boritt (ed.), *Why the Confederacy Lost* (New York, 1992); Edward Hagerman, *The American Civil War and the Origins of Modern Warfare* (Bloomington, Ind., 1988); Herman Hattaway and Archer Jones, *How the North Won: A Military History of the Civil War* (Urbana, Ill., 1980); Philip Paludan, *"A People's Contest": The Union and the Civil War, 1861–1865* (New York, 1988); Stephen Sears, *George B. McClellan: The Young Napoleon* (New York, 1988).

## CHAPTER 10

Gabor Boritt, (ed.), *Lincoln's Generals* (New York, 1994); Douglas Freeman, *R.E. Lee* (New York, 1937); John Hennessy, *Return to Bull Run: The Campaign and Battle of Second Manassas* (New York, 1993); Alan Nolan, *Lee Considered: General Robert E. Lee and Civil War History* (Chapel Hill, N.C., 1991); Stephen Sears, *Landscape Turned Red: The Battle of Antietam* (New Haven, Conn., 1983); T. Harry Williams, *Lincoln and His Generals* (New York, 1952); Steven Woodworth, *Davis and Lee at War* (Lawrence, Kans., 1995).

## CHAPTER 11

Iver Bernstein, *The New York City Draft Riots: Their Significance for American Society and Politics in the Age of the Civil War* (New York, 1990); Robert Bruce, *The Launching of Modern American Science, 1846–1876* (New York, 1987); James Geary, *We Need Men: The Union Draft in the Civil War* (DeKalb, Ill., 1991); Reid Mitchell, *Civil War Soldiers: Their Expectations and Experiences* (New York, 1988); Eugene Murdock, *Patriotism Limited, 1862–1865* (Kent, Ohio, 1967); Eugene Murdock, *One Million Men: The Civil War Draft in the North* (Westport, Conn., 1980); Fred Shannon, *The Organization and Administration of the Union Army, 1861–1865* (Cleveland, 1928).

# CHAPTER 12

Stephen Ash, *When the Invaders Came: Conflict and Chaos in the Occupied South, 1861–1865* (Chapel Hill, N.C., 1996); Douglas Ball, *Financial Failure and Confederate Defeat* (Urbana, Ill., 1991); E. Merton Coulter, *The Confederate States of America: 1861–1865* (Baton Rouge, 1950); Paul Escott, *After Secession: Jefferson Davis and the Failure of Confederate Nationalism* (Baton Rouge, 1978); Drew Faust, *The Creation of Southern Nationalism: Ideology and Identity in the Civil War South* (Baton Rouge, 1988); Gary Gallagher, *The Confederate War* (Cambridge, Mass., 1997); James Robertson, *Soldiers Blue and Gray* (Columbia, S.C., 1988); Emory Thomas, *The Confederacy as a Revolutionary Experience* (Columbia, S.C., 1991).

# CHAPTER 13

Richard Franklin Bensel, *Yankee Leviathan: The Origins of Central State Authority in America, 1859–1877* (New York, 1990); Allan Bogue, *The Earnest Men: Republicans of the Civil War Senate* (Ithaca, N.Y., 1981); Leonard Curry, *Blueprint for America: Nonmilitary Legislation of the First Civil War Congress* (Nashville, 1968); Mark Neely, *The Fate of Liberty: Abraham Lincoln and Civil Liberties* (New York, 1991); Heather Cox Richardson, *The Greatest Nation on Earth: Republican Economic Policies during the Civil War* (Cambridge, Mass., 1997).

# CHAPTER 14

Ralph Andreano, (ed.), *Economic Change in the Civil War Era* (Greenville, Del., 1965), Bray Hammond, *Sovereignty and an Empty Purse: Banks and Politics in the Civil War* (Princeton, N.J., 1970); John Niven, *Salmon P. Chase: A Biography* (New York, 1995); Robert Sharkey, *Money, Class and Party: An Economic Study of Civil War and Reconstruction* (Baltimore, 1975); Robert Stanley, *Dimensions of Law in the Service of Order: The Origins of the Federal Income Tax, 1861–1913* (New York, 1993).

# CHAPTER 15

Mary Ellison, *Support for Secession: Lancashire and the American Civil War* (Chicago, 1972); Brian Jenkins, *Britain and the War for the Union* (Montreal, 1974); Howard Jones, *The Union in Peril: The Crisis over British Intervention in the Civil War* (Chapel Hill, N.C., 1992); Gordon Warren, *Fountain of Discontent: The* Trent *Affair and the Freedom of the Seas* (Boston, 1981).

# CHAPTER 16

Herman Belz, *A New Birth of Freedom: The Republican Party and Freedmen's Rights, 1861–1866* (Westport, Conn., 1976); Herman Belz, *Emancipation and Equal Rights: Politics and Constitutionalism in the Civil War Era* (New York, 1978); Ira Berlin, "The Destruction of Slavery," in *Freedom: A Documentary of Emancipation*, ed. Ira Berlin et al. (New York, 1985) Ser. 1, 1:2; Lawanda Cox, *Lincoln and Black Freedom: A Study in Presidential Leadership* (Columbia, S.C., 1981); Louis S. Gerteis, *From Contraband to Freedman: Federal Policy toward Southern Blacks, 1861–1865* (Westport, Conn., 1973); William McFeely, *Frederick Douglass* (New York, 1991).

## CHAPTER 17

Ernest Furgurson, *Chancellorsville, 1863: Souls of the Brave* (New York, 1993); Gary Gallagher, (ed.), *The Third Day at Gettysburg and Beyond* (Chapel Hill, N.C., 1994); Mark Grimsley, *The Hard Hand of War: Union Military Policy toward Southern Civilians, 1861–1865* (New York, 1995); Judith Lee Hallock, *Braxton Bragg and Confederate Defeat* (Tuscaloosa, 1991); Archer Jones, *Confederate Strategy from Shiloh to Vicksburg* (Baton Rouge, 1961); Richard McMurry, *Two Great Rebel Armies* (Chapel Hill, N.C., 1989); Charles Royster, *The Destructive War: William Tecumseh Sherman, Stonewall Jackson, and the Americans* (New York, 1991).


## CHAPTER 18

Joseph Allan Frank, *With Ballot and Bayonet: The Political Socialization of American Civil War Soldiers* (Athens, Ga., 1998); Gary Gallagher (ed.), *The Wilderness Campaign* (Chapel Hill, N.C., 1997); Gary Gallagher (ed.), *Struggle for the Shenandoah: Essays in the 1864 Valley Campaign* (Kent, Ohio, 1991); Joseph Glatthaar, *The March to the Sea and Beyond: Sherman's Troops in the Savannah and Carolina Campaigns* (New York, 1985); Earl Hess, *The Union Soldier in Battle: Enduring the Ordeal of Combat* (Lawrence, Kans., 1997); Randall Jimmerson, *The Private War: Popular Thought during the Sectional Conflict* (Baton Rouge, 1988); Gerald Linderman, *Embattled Courage: The Experience of Combat in the American Civil War* (New York, 1987); James McPherson, *For Cause and Comrades: Why Men Fought in the Civil War* (New York, 1997); Craig Symonds, *Joseph E. Johnston* (New York, 1992).


## CHAPTER 19

Joseph Durkin, *Stephen R. Mallory: Confederate Navy Chief* (Columbia, S.C., 1987); Raimondo Luraghi, *History of the Confederate Navy* (Annapolis, 1996); Ivan Musicant, *Divided Waters: The Naval History of the Civil War* (New York, 1995); Howard Nash, *A Naval History of the Civil War* (South Brunswick, Me., 1975); Stephen Wise, *Lifeline of the Confederacy: Blockade Running during the Civil War* (Columbia, S.C., 1988).


## CHAPTER 20

Jean H. Baker, *Affairs of Party: The Political Culture of Northern Democrats in Mid-Nineteenth-Century America* (New York, 1998); Herman Belz, *Reconstructing the Union: Theory and Practice during the Civil War* (Ithaca, N.Y., 1969); William Harris, *With Charity for all: Lincoln and the Restoration of the Union* (Lexington, Ky., 1997); Frank Klement, *Dark Lanterns, Secret Political Societies, Conspiracies, and Treason in the Civil War* (Baton Rouge, 1984); David Long, *Jewel of Liberty: Abraham Lincoln's Reelection and the End of Slavery* (Mechanicsburg, Pa., 1994); Joel Silbey, *A Respectable Minority: The Democratic Party in the Civil War Era* (New York, 1977).


## CHAPTER 21

Jeanie Atie, *Patriotic Toil: Northern Women and the American Civil War* (Ithaca, N.Y., 1998); Catherine Clinton and Nina Silber (eds.), *Divided Houses: Gender and the Civil War* (New York, 1992); J. Matthew Gallman, *The North Fights the War: The Home Front* (Chicago, 1994); Elizabeth Leonard, *All the Daring of the Soldier: Women of the Civil War Armies* (New York, 1999); James Moorhead, *American Apocalypse: Yankee Protestants and the Civil War, 1860–1869*

(New Haven, 1978); David Montgomery, *Beyond Equality: Labor and the Radical Republicans* (Urbana, Ill., 1981).

## CHAPTER 22

Catherine Clinton, *Tara Revisited: Women, War and the Plantation Legend* (New York, 1995); Drew Faust, *Mothers of Invention: Women of the Slaveholding South in the American Civil War* (Chapel Hill, N.C., 1996); Malcolm McMillan, *The Disintegration of a Confederate State: Three Governors and Alabama's Home Front, 1861–1865* (Macon, Ga., 1986); Mark Neely, *Southern Rights: Political Prisoners and the Myth of Confederate Constitutionalism* (Charlottesville, 1999); George Rable, *Civil Wars: Women and the Crisis of Southern Nationalism* (Urbana, Ill., 1989); George Rable, *The Confederate Republic: A Revolution against Politics* (Chapel Hill, N.C., 1994).

## CHAPTER 23

Richard Beringer et al., *The Elements of Confederate Defeat: Nationalism, War Aims, and Religion* (Baton Rouge, 1988); Ernest Furgurson, *Ashes of Glory: Richmond at War* (New York, 1996); John Marszalek, *Sherman: A Soldier's Passion for Order* (New York, 1994); J. Tracy Power, *Lee's Miserables: Life in the Army of Northern Virginia from the Wilderness to Appomattox* (Chapel Hill, N.C., 1998).

For further reading, consult the following bibliographies: David Eicher, *The Civil War in Books: An Analytical Bibliography* (Urbana, Ill., 1997); Eugene Murdock, *The Civil War in the North: A Selected Bibliography* (New York, 1987); Steven Woodworth (ed.), *The American Civil War: A Handbook of Literature and Research* (Westport, Conn., 1996).

## CHAPTER 24

Eric Foner, *Reconstruction: America's Unfinished Revolution, 1863–1877* (New York, 1988); Harold M. Hyman, *A More Perfect Union: The Impact of the Civil War and Reconstruction on the Constitution* (Boston, 1975); Morton Keller, *Affairs of State: Public Life in Late-Nineteenth-Century America* (Cambridge, Mass., 1977); Walter T. K. Nugent, *The Money Question during Reconstruction* (New York, 1967); Grace Palladino, *Another Civil War: Labor, Capital, and the State in the Anthracite Regions of Pennsylvania, 1840–1868* (Urbana, Ill., 1990); Irwin Unger, *The Greenback Era: A Social and Political History of American Finance, 1865–1879* (Princeton, N.J., 1964); Maris A. Vinovskis, (ed.), *Toward a Social History of the Civil War* (New York and Cambridge, 1990).

## CHAPTER 25

Ira Berlin, Barbara J. Fields, Stephen F. Miller, Joseph P. Reidy, and Leslie S. Rowland, *Slaves No More: Three Essays on Emancipation and the Civil War* (Cambridge and New York, 1992); Dan T. Carter, *When the War Was Over: The Failure of Self-Reconstruction in the South, 1865–1867* (Baton Rouge, 1985); Gerald D. Jaynes, *Branches without Roots: Genesis of the Black Working Class in the American South, 1862–1882* (New York, 1986); Leon Litwack, *Been in the Storm So Long: The Aftermath of Slavery* (New York, 1979); Michael Perman, *Reunion without Compromise: The South and Reconstruction, 1865–1868* (Cambridge and New York, 1973); Lawrence N. Powell, *New Masters: Northern Planters during the Civil War and Reconstruction* (New Haven, Conn., 1980); Roger Ransom and Richard Sutch, *One Kind of Freedom: The Economic Consequences of Emancipation* (New

York and Cambridge, 1977); James L. Roark, *Masters Without Slaves: Southern Planters in the Civil War and Reconstruction* (New York, 1977); Gavin Wright, *The Political Economy of the Cotton South: Households, Markets, and Wealth in the Nineteenth Century* (New York, 1978).


## CHAPTER 26

Michael Les Benedict, *A Compromise of Principle: Congressional Republicans and Reconstruction, 1863–1869* (New York, 1974); LaWanda Cox and John H. Cox, *Politics, Principle, and Prejudice, 1865–1866: Dilemma of Reconstruction America* (Glencoe, Ill., 1963); David Donald, *The Politics of Reconstruction, 1863–1867* (Baton Rouge, 1965); Peyton McCrary, *Abraham Lincoln and Reconstruction: The Louisiana Experiment* (Princeton, N.J., 1978); Eric McKitrick, *Andrew Johnson and Reconstruction* (Chicago, 1960); Kenneth M. Stampp, *The Era of Reconstruction* (New York, 1966); Hans L. Trefousse, *Andrew Johnson: A Biography* (New York, 1989).


## CHAPTER 27

George R. Bentley, *A History of the Freedmen's Bureau* (Philadelphia, 1955); Edward L. Gambill, *Conservative Ordeal: Northern Democrats and Reconstruction, 1865–1868* (Ames, Iowa, 1981); Stanley I. Kutler, *Judicial Power and Reconstruction Politics* (Chicago, 1968); William S. McFeely, *Yankee Stepfather: General O. O. Howard and the Freedmen* (New Haven, Conn., 1968).


## CHAPTER 28

William R. Brock, *An American Crisis: Congress and Reconstruction, 1865–1867* (New York, 1963); Ellen Carol DuBois, *Feminism and Suffrage: The Emergence of an Independent Women's Movement in America* (Ithaca, N.Y., 1978); Joseph B. James, *The Framing of the Fourteenth Amendment* (Urbana, Ill., 1956); William E. Nelson, *The Fourteenth Amendment: From Political Principle to Judicial Doctrine* (Cambridge, Mass., 1988); Xi Wang, *The Trial of Democracy: Black Suffrage and Northern Republicans, 1860–1910* (Athens, Ga., 1997).


## CHAPTER 29

Michael Les Benedict, *The Impeachment and Trial of Andrew Johnson* (New York, 1973); William Gillette, *The Right to Vote: Politics and the Passage of the Fifteenth Amendment* (Baltimore, 1965); James C. Mohr (ed.), *Radical Republicans in the North: State Politics during Reconstruction* (Baltimore, 1976); James E. Sefton, *The United States Army and Reconstruction, 1865–1877* (Baton Rouge, 1967); Brooks D. Simpson, *"Let Us Have Peace": Ulysses S. Grant and the Politics of War and Reconstruction, 1861–1868* (Chapel Hill, N.C., 1991); Hans L. Trefousse, *Thaddeus Stevens: Nineteenth-Century Egalitarian* (Chapel Hill, N.C., 1997).


## CHAPTER 30

We make no attempt here or in the suggested readings for the next chapter to list the several generations of studies of Reconstruction in all the individual southern states. For information on those, students should consult the bibliographies in the revised second edition of this volume, James G. Randall and David Donald, *The Civil War and Reconstruction* (Lexington, Mass., 1969), and Eric Foner, *Reconstruction: America's Unfinished Revolution, 1863–1877* (New York, 1988).

Richard H. Abbott, *The Republican Party and the South, 1855–1877: The First Southern Strategy* (Chapel Hill, N.C., 1986); Peter W. Bardaglio, *Reconstructing the Household: Families, Sex, and the Law in the Nineteenth-Century South* (Chapel Hill, N.C., 1995); Richard N. Current, *Those Terrible Carpetbaggers: A Reinterpretation* (New York, 1988); Laura F. Edwards, *Gendered Strife and Confusion: The Political Culture of Reconstruction* (Urbana, Ill., 1997); William C. Harris, *The Day of the Carpetbagger: Republican Reconstruction in Mississippi* (Baton Rouge, 1979); Thomas Holt, *Black over White: Political Leadership in South Carolina during Reconstruction* (Urbana, Ill., 1977); J. Morgan Kousser and James M. McPherson (eds.), *Region, Race, and Reconstruction: Essays in Honor of C. Vann Woodward* (New York, 1982); Elizabeth Studley Nathans, *Losing the Peace: Georgia Republicans and Reconstruction, 1865–1871* (Baton Rouge, 1968); Otto H. Olsen (ed.), *Reconstruction and Redemption in the South* (Baton Rouge, 1980); Michael Perman, *The Road to Redemption: Southern Politics, 1869–1879* (Chapel Hill, N.C., 1984); Mark W. Summers, *Railroads, Reconstruction, and the Gospel of Prosperity: Aid Under the Radical Republicans, 1865–1877* (Princeton, N.J., 1984).

## CHAPTER 31

George M. Fredrickson (ed.), *A Nation Divided: Problems and Issues of the Civil War and Reconstruction* (Minneapolis, 1975); William Gillette, *Retreat from Reconstruction, 1869–1879* (Baton Rouge, 1979); George C. Rable, *But There Was No Peace: The Role of Violence in the Politics of Reconstruction* (Athens, Ga., 1984); Allen W. Trelease, *White Terror: The Ku Klux Klan Conspiracy and Southern Reconstruction* (New York, 1971); Lou Falkner Williams, *The Great South Carolina Ku Klux Klan Trials, 1871–1872* (Athens, Ga., 1996).

## CHAPTER 32

Richard O. Curry (ed.), *Radicalism, Racism, and Party Realignment: The Border States during Reconstruction* (Baltimore, 1969); William S. McFeely, *Grant: A Biography* (New York, 1981); Terry L. Seip, *The South Returns to Congress: Men, Economic Measures, and Sectional Relationships, 1868–1879* (Baton Rouge, 1983); Brooks D. Simpson, *The Reconstruction Presidents* (Lawrence, Kans., 1998); Mark Wahlgren Summers, *The Era of Good Stealings* (New York, 1993).

## CHAPTER 33

Ari Hoogenboom, *Outlawing the Spoils: A History of the Civil Service Reform Movement, 1865–1883* (Urbana, Ill., 1961); Paul Kleppner, *The Third Electoral System, 1853–1892: Parties, Voters, and the Political Cultures* (Chapel Hill, N.C., 1979); George H. Miller, *Railroads and the Granger Laws* (Madison, Wisc., 1971); John G. Sproat, *"The Best Men": Liberal Reformers in the Gilded Age* (New York, 1968).

## CHAPTER 34

Keith Ian Polakoff, *The Politics of Inertia: The Election of 1876 and the End of Reconstruction* (Baton Rouge, 1973); C. Vann Woodward, *Reunion and Reaction: The Compromise of 1877 and the End of Reconstruction* (Boston, 1951).

# Credits

**Chapter 1: p. 8,** National Archives 115-JD-315; **p. 10,** © Collection of the New-York Historical Society #52091; **p. 11,** Library of Congress; **p. 15,** U.S. Army Military History Institute; **p. 19,** The Warder Collection; **p. 20,** Sophia Smith Collection, Smith College. Photograph by Broadbent and Taylor, 914 Chestnut Street, Philadelphia; **p. 21,** © Bettmann/CORBIS.

**Chapter 2: p. 32,** Courtesy of South Caroliniana Library, University of South Carolina, Columbia; **p. 34,** The Museum of the Confederacy, Richmond, Virginia; **p. 36,** © Collection of the New-York Historical Society #47843; **p. 38,** From *The American South: A History,* 2d edition, by William J. Cooper, Jr., and Thomas E. Terrill (New York: McGraw Hill, 1991) by permission of William J. Cooper, Jr.; **p. 43,** Library of Congress LC-D4-70120.

**Chapter 3: p. 64,** New Hampshire Historical Society; **p. 66,** © Collection of the New-York Historical Society #50473; **p. 68,** From the Penn School Collection. Permission granted by Penn Center, Inc., St. Helena Island, SC.; **p. 69,** Library of Congress LC-USZ62-90345; **p. 70,** Sophia Smith Collection, Smith College.

**Chapter 4: p. 80,** Library of Congress LC-USZ62-92043; **p. 83,** Library of Congress LC-USZ62-689; **p. 86,** National Portrait Gallery, Smithsonian Institution; **p. 92,** Library of Congress; **p. 95,** Kansas State Historical Society.

**Chapter 5: p. 104,** Library of Congress; **p. 111,** Courtesy of the Illinois State Historical Library; **p. 115,** The Western Reserve Historical Society, Cleveland, Ohio; **p. 120,** Library of Congress LC-USZ62-8878; **p. 121,** Library of Congress.

**Chapter 6: p. 127,** Library of Congress; **p. 133,** Chicago Historical Society 00034; **p. 142,** National Archives 111-B-4141; **p. 145,** National Archives 111-B-4146; **p. 147,** The Museum of the Confederacy, Richmond, Virginia.

**Chapter 7: p. 150,** Library of Congress; **p. 151,** Library of Congress LC-USZ62-48089; **p. 162,** Provided courtesy of HarpWeek.com; **p. 163,** National Archives 121-BA-914A.

**Chapter 8: p. 173,** American Heritage Picture Collection; **p. 177,** Used by permission, State Historical Society of Missouri, Columbia, all rights reserved; **p. 178,** Kansas State Historical Society; **p. 180,** Frank & Marie-Therese Wood Print Collections, Alexandria, Va.

**Chapter 9: p. 186,** Library of Congress LC-USZ62-64430; **p. 186,** Library of Congress LCUSZ62-33407; **p. 195,** National Archives 111-B-4624; **p. 197,** From *The Civil War Through the Camera* by Henry W. Elson (New York: McKinlay, Stone & Mackenzie, 1912; reprint Arno Press, 1979); **p. 198,** Chicago Historical Society P&S-1920.1645, Paul Phillipateaux; **p. 199,** American Heritage Picture Collection.

**Chapter 10: p. 204,** Library of Congress; **p. 205,** West Point Museum Collection, United States Military Academy; **p. 209,** Collection of the Mercer Museum of the Bucks County Historical Society; **p. 211,** National Archives 111-B-1564; **p. 220,** Courtesy Antietam National Battlefield; **p. 223,** John Henry Kurtz.

**Chapter 11: p. 228,** Provided courtesy of HarpWeek.com; **p. 229,** Chicago Historical Society ICHi-00791; **p. 230,** Provided courtesy of HarpWeek.com; **p. 231,** Provided courtesy of HarpWeek.com; **p. 233,** Library of Congress; **p. 237,** National Archives 111-B-4559; **p. 244,** U.S. Army Military History Institute.

**Chapter 12: p. 248,** Library of Congress; **p. 249,** Library of Congress; **p. 255,** Library of Congress; **p. 262,** Laing Communications, Inc.; **p. 263,** From *The Book of Anecdotes and Incidents of the War of the Rebellion* by Frazar Kirkland (Hartford, Conn.: Hartford Publishing Co., 1866).

**Chapter 13: p. 273,** National Archives 111-B-4218; **p. 275,** National Archives 111-BA-1215; **p. 279,** Library of Congress LC-USZ62-99838; **p. 290,** Library of Congress.

**Chapter 14: p. 298,** Library of Congress; **p. 299,** Department of the Treasury.

**Chapter 15: p. 312,** From the Collections of the South Carolina Historical Society; **p. 317,** William Gladstone Civil War Collection; **p. 318,** Frank & Marie-Therese Wood Print Collections, Alexandria, Va.

**Chapter 16: p. 326,** The Granger Collection, New York; **p. 327,** Provided courtesy of HarpWeek.com; **p. 333,** Courtesy of the Lincoln Museum, Fort Wayne, IN (#151); **p. 336,** From *Frank Leslie's Illustrated Newspaper,* January 24, 1863; **p. 337,** Provided courtesy of HarpWeek.com; **p. 340,** National Archives; **p. 341,** Library of Congress.

**Chapter 17: p. 348,** National Archives 111-B-2775; **p. 353,** Library of Congress LC-B8171-0277; **p. 355,** National Park Service; **p. 363,** Louisiana State University, Department of Archives and Manuscripts, Baton Rouge; **p. 364,** The Old Courthouse Museum, Vicksburg, MS; **p. 369,** Library of Congress.

**Chapter 18: p. 372,** The Western Reserve Historical Society, Cleveland, Ohio; **p. 373,** Library of Congress LC-BH8255-80; **p. 373,** National Archives; **p. 374,** Library of Congress LC-B8161-7722A; **p. 375,** Archive Photos; **p. 377,** *The Civil War Through the Camera* by Henry W. Elson (New York: McKinlay, Stone & Mackenzie, 1912; reprint Arno Press, 1979); **p. 381,** Library of Congress; **p. 384,** Library of Congress LC-USZ62-2350; **p. 387,** Library of Congress; **p. 389,** Library of Congress; **p. 391,** Library of Congress.

**Chapter 19: p. 395,** From the Collections of The New Jersey Historical Society, Newark, New Jersey; **p. 396,** National Archives 111-B-4583; **p. 397,** Library of Congress LC-B812-1375; **p. 400,** The Abraham Lincoln Foundation of the Union League of Philadelphia; **p. 402,** The Historic New Orleans Collection, accession no. 1974.80.

**Chapter 20: p. 411,** Used by permission, State Historical Society of Missouri, Columbia, all rights reserved; **p. 412,** Courtesy, Museum of Fine Arts, Boston. Reproduced with permission. ©1999 Museum of Fine Arts, Boston. All Rights Reserved; **p. 424,** Courtesy of the Smithsonian Institution; **p. 426,** *Illustrated London News,* December 3, 1864.

**Chapter 21: p. 429,** The Newark Museum/Art Resource, NY; **p. 430,** U.S. Army Military History Institute; **p. 434,** Courtesy George Eastman House; **p. 435,** Leib Archives, East Berlin, PA; **p. 440,** © Collection of the New-York Historical Society #64352; **p. 441,** Chicago Historical Society ICHi-22142, Baker & Company; **p. 442,** Chicago Historical Society ICHi-22103; **p. 445,** Library of Congress; **p. 446,** Library of Congress.

**Chapter 22: p. 451,** The Western Reserve Historical Society, Cleveland, Ohio; **p. 452,** Provided courtesy of HarpWeek.com; **p. 453,** The Old Courthouse Museum, Vicksburg, MS; **p. 456,** Virginia Military Institute Archives; **p. 458,** The Museum of the Confederacy, Richmond, Virginia; **p. 459,** Library of Congress; **p. 460,** U.S. Army Military History Institute.

**Chapter 23: p. 469,** Library of Congress LC-B8171-7169; **p. 470,** West Point Museum Collection, United States Military Academy; **p. 472,** Library of Congress; **p. 474,** The Civil War Library and Museum, Philadelphia, PA; **p. 475,** Library of Congress LC-B8171-7926.

**Chapter 24: p. 481,** Private Collection; **p. 485,** Montana Historical Society; **p. 486,** Union Pacific Historical Collection; **p. 487,** Carnegie Library of Pittsburgh.

**Chapter 25: p. 496,** Library of Congress LC-USZ62-117574; **p. 501,** © Collection of the New-York Historical Society #50819; **p. 501,** © Collection of the New-York Historical Society #37628.

**Chapter 26: p. 517,** National Archives; **p. 518,** National Archives.

**Chapter 27: p. 530,** Provided courtesy of HarpWeek.com; **p. 531,** Provided courtesy of HarpWeek.com; **p. 531,** Library of Congress; **p. 534,** Provided courtesy of HarpWeek.com.

**Chapter 28: p. 538,** National Archives; **p. 538,** National Archives; **p. 539,** National Archives; **p. 540,** National Archives; **p. 552,** Provided courtesy of HarpWeek.com; **p. 554,** Provided courtesy of HarpWeek.com.

**Chapter 29: p. 572,** Library of Congress.

**Chapter 30: p. 578,** Provided courtesy of HarpWeek.com; **p. 579,** Provided courtesy of HarpWeek.com; **p. 581,** Library of Congress; **p. 583,** Library of Congress.

**Chapter 31: p. 595,** Provided courtesy of HarpWeek.com; **p. 594,** Provided courtesy of HarpWeek.com.

**Chapter 32: p. 606,** Library of Congress; **p. 611,** Library of Congress.

**Chapter 33: p. 618,** Provided courtesy of HarpWeek.com; **p. 625,** Provided courtesy of HarpWeek.com; **p. 630,** Provided courtesy of HarpWeek.com; **p. 631,** Provided courtesy of HarpWeek.com; **p. 631,** Provided courtesy of HarpWeek.com.

**Chapter 34: p. 638,** Library of Congress.

*Every effort has been made to contact the copyright holders of each of the illustrations. Rights holders of any illustrations not credited should contact W. W. Norton & Company, Inc., 500 Fifth Avenue, New York, NY 10110, in order for a correction to be made in the next reprinting of our work.*

# Index